Essentials of Money, Banking, and Financial Markets

The Addison-Wesley Series in Economics

Abel/Bernanke
Macroeconomics

Allen
Managerial Economics

Berndt
The Practice of Econometrics

Bierman/Fernandez
Game Theory

Binger/Hoffman
Microeconomics with Calculus

Bowles/Edwards
Understanding Capitalism

Branson
Macroeconomic Theory and
Policy

Brown/Hogendorn
International Economics

Browning/Zupan
Microeconomic Theory and
Applications

Burgess
The Economics of Regulation

Byrns/Stone
Economics

Canterbery
The Literate Economist: A Brief
History of Economics

Carlton/Perloff
Modern Industrial Organization

Caves/Frankel/Jones
World Trade and Payments

Cooter/Ulen
Law and Economics

Ehrenberg/Smith
Modern Labor Economics

Ekelund/Tollison
Economics

Ekelund/Tollison
Economics: Private Markets

Filer/Hamermesh/Rees
The Economics of Work
and Pay

Fusfeld
The Age of the Economist

Gordon
Macroeconomics

Gregory
Essentials of Economics

Gregory/Ruffin
Economics

Gregory/Stuart
Soviet Economic Structure and
Performance

Griffiths/Walls
Intermediate Microeconomics

Gros/Steinherr
Winds of Change: Economic
Transition in Central and Eastern
Europe

Hartwick/Olewiler
The Economics of Natural
Resource Use

Hogendorn
Economic Development

**Hoy/Livernois/McKenna/Rees/
Stengos**
Mathematics for Economics

Hubbard
Money, the Financial System, and
the Economy

Hughes/Cain
American Economic History

Hunt
History of Economic Thought

Hunt
Property and Prophets

Husted/Melvin
International Economics

Krugman/Obstfeld
International Economics: Theory
and Policy

Kwoka/White
The Antitrust Revolution

Lipsey/Courant
Economics

McCarty
Dollars and Sense

Melvin
International Money and Finance

Miller
Economics Today

Miller/Benjamin/North
The Economics of Public Issues

Miller/Fishe
Microeconomics: Price Theory in
Practice

Miller/Van Hoose
Essentials of Money, Banking, and
Financial Markets

Mills/Hamilton
Urban Economics

Mishkin
The Economics of Money,
Banking, and Financial Markets

Parkin
Economics

Petersen
Business and Government

Phelps
Health Economics

Riddell/Shackelford/Stamos
Economics

Ritter/Silber
Principles of Money, Banking,
and Financial Markets

Rohlf
Introduction to Economic
Reasoning

Ruffin/Gregory
Principles of Economics

Salvatore
Microeconomics

Sargent
Rational Expectations and
Inflation

Scherer
Industry Structure, Strategy,
and Public Policy

Schotter
Microeconomics: A Modern
Approach

Sherman/Kolk
Business Cycles and
Forecasting

Smith
Case Studies in Economic
Development

Studenmund
Using Econometrics

Su
Economic Fluctuations and
Forecasting

Tietenberg
Environmental and Natural
Resource Economics

Tietenberg
Environmental Economics and
Policy

Todaro
Economic Development

Zerbe/Dively
Benefit-Cost Analysis

Essentials of Money, Banking, and Financial Markets

ROGER LeROY MILLER
Institute for University Studies, Arlington, Texas

DAVID D. VAN HOOSE
University of Alabama

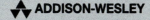 **ADDISON-WESLEY**

An imprint of Addison Wesley Longman, Inc.

Reading, Massachusetts • Menlo Park, California • New York • Harlow, England
Don Mills, Ontario • Sydney • Mexico City • Madrid • Amsterdam

Executive Editor: John Greenman
Supplements Editor: Julie Zasloff
Project Editorial Manager: Melonie Salvati
Design Manager: John Callahan
Text Designer: Sarah Johnson
Cover Designer: Scott Russo
Cover Photo: © The Stock Market
Art Studio: Electra Graphics, Inc.
Electronic Production Manager: Su Levine
Desktop Administrator: Laura Leever
Senior Manufacturing Manager: Willie Lane
Electronic Page Makeup: Interactive Composition Corporation
Printer and Binder: R. R. Donnelley and Sons, Company
Cover Printer: The Lehigh Press, Inc.

Library of Congress Cataloging-in-Publication Data
Miller, Roger LeRoy.
    Essentials of money, banking, and financial markets / Roger Miller,
David VanHoose.
        p.   cm.
    Includes index.
    ISBN 0-673-98126-6
    1. Money. 2. Monetary policy. 3. Banks and banking. 4. Financial
institutions. I. VanHoose, David D. II. Title.
HG221.M6459   1996
332.1—dc20   96-13104
                                                         CIP

ISBN 0-673-98126-6

12345678910—DOC—99989796

Pour Marie-Christine,
Le prochain chapitre va être le meilleur. Merci pour tout.

R.L.M.

To Alfred C. VanHoose,
Who taught me the value of hard work

D.D.V.

Brief Contents

Detailed Contents

Preface

The world of money, banking, and financial institutions is currently undergoing some of the most dramatic changes that have occurred in the last several decades. The advent of E-cash (digital money), the merger of some of the world's greatest banks, and the relentless blurring of the distinction among different types of financial institutions are but a few of these many changes. Students in business, economics, and general studies need to be aware of these important changes not only for their professional lives, but also for their day-to-day lives. Perhaps just as important, today's business and economic students must have a thorough grasp of the essentials of money, banking, and financial institutions in order to understand the full range of their other courses.

So, this first edition of *Essentials of Money, Banking, and Financial Markets* has twin goals: to teach the basics of money and banking and to introduce students to the new, changing world of money and banking.

LEARNING THE ESSENTIALS

In spite of the shortness of this text, all of the essentials of money, banking, and financial markets are thoroughly discussed. We make sure that the reader ends up with a complete understanding of:

- Money, liquidity, and payment systems
- Financial instruments of the money and capital markets
- The risk and term structures of interest rates
- Derivative securities and their uses
- Depository and nondepository financial institutions
- Depository institution management and performance
- Regulation of depository institutions
- Depository institutions and the money supply process
- The central banking functions of the Federal Reserve
- How the Federal Reserve conducts monetary policy
- Time lags and credibility problems in monetary policy
- International dimensions of financial markets and monetary policy

EMPHASIS ON THE EXCITEMENT OF TODAY'S CHANGES

Interspersed throughout all chapters students will find important, learning-motivating features, of which there are three general categories:

Policy Notebooks

Because policy is in the news so much, we felt it appropriate that there be a special feature concerned just with policy issues. These features are appropriately placed and cover a variety of topics, including:

- How to Save $400 Million a Year—Get Rid of the Dollar Bill (and the Penny, Too)
- Should Bond and Stock Market Funds Be in M2?
- Digital Banking Is on the Rise
- The Fed and the Federal Funds Rate
- Is the Commercial Banking Industry in Decline?
- The Difficulty in Targeting Real Interest Rates

Management Notebooks

The world of money, banking, and financial institutions is, at the heart, centered around profit-making institutions. Managers run these institutions and are faced with management issues all the time. We therefore added a special feature that discusses management issues. These include:

- Why There Are so Few Agricultural-Based Futures
- The Rise in On-Line Banking
- Does it Pay to Open More Branches?
- Bank Managers Opt for More Mutual Fund Sales
- Cutthroat Competition in Mutual Funds
- Using Computer Models for Small-Business Lending

Global Notebooks

Money and banking can no longer be considered simply a domestic issue. Not only are major banks forming alliances with banks around the world, but rapid change in telecommunications have made banking a global activity. Knowledge and understanding of some of the global issues in this subject are not only exciting to read about, but also important. We have included among others the following:

- Bartering or Simply New Currencies?
- Immigrants Bring Money Pools to the United States

- Reducing Default Risk by Banking on Italian Cheese
- Islamic Banking—How to Lend Without Charging Interest
- Will the Japanese Bail Out Their Banks?
- Megamergers Around the World

Critical Thinking Exercises

Critical thinking is an important aspect of every college student's education. We make sure that students are introduced to critical-thinking activities by ending each "Policy," "Management," and "Global Notebook" with critical-thinking questions called "For Critical Analysis." The suggested answers to these critical-thinking questions are included in the *Instructor's Manual*.

PEDAGOGY, PEDAGOGY, PEDAGOGY

Learning cannot occur in a vacuum. We have made sure that readers of this text have at their disposal an ample number of pedagogical devices that will help them master the material.

Key Questions and Answers
Within the Text of Each Chapter

A unique pedagogical feature of *Essentials of Money, Banking, and Financial Markets* is the simultaneous inclusion of four to seven key questions at the beginning of each chapter with indications of where the key questions can be answered within the text. The student immediately sees the relationship between the text materials while reading the chapter text and the key questions.

The Stress Is on Vocabulary

Because vocabulary is often a stumbling block, we have boldfaced all important vocabulary terms within the text. Immediately in the margin these boldfaced terms are defined. They are further defined in the end-of-text glossary.

Summing Up

The chapter summary is in a numbered point-by-point format and corresponds to the chapter-opening learning objectives, further reinforcing the full circular nature of the learning process for each chapter.

Questions and Problems

Each chapter ends with a set of five to eight questions and problems. They are of increasing difficulty. Suggested answers are provided in the *Instructor's Manual*.

THE SUPPLEMENTS

Even though *Essentials of Money, Banking, and Financial Markets* is a short, relatively inexpensive paperback, we have not stinted on additional supplements for this text. They are described below.

Study Guide

The *Study Guide* is designed to facilitate active learning by students. It provides summaries of chapter contents, along with lists of the key terms for students to look for and define in their own words as they read the text. To assist students in testing their understanding of the material, the *Study Guide* also includes 20 multiple-choice and 10 short-answer questions per chapter.

Instructor's Manual

The *Instructor's Manual* is intended to simplify the teaching tasks that instructors face. For each chapter it offers an overview of key concepts and objectives and a detailed outline built upon chapter headings in the text. Also included are further discussion questions, answers to chapter questions and problems, suggested answers to the critical thinking questions in the "Policy," "Management," and "Global Notebooks."

Test Bank   One of the most challenging aspects of teaching is evaluation of student performance. To assist instructors in this endeavor, a *Test Bank* that includes 40 multiple-choice and 10 short-answer questions per chapter, along with correct answers, is available to all adoptors of *Essentials of Money, Banking, and Financial Markets*.

ACKNOWLEDGMENTS

We benefited from an extremely active and conscientious group of reviewers of the manuscript for this first edition of *Essentials of Money, Banking, and Financial Markets*. At times they were harsh and without pity, but the rewrites of the manuscript improved accordingly. To the following reviewers, we extend our sincere appreciation for the critical nature of your comments that we think helped make this a much better text.

> Mary Acker, Iona College
> Elias C. Grivoyannis, Seton Hall University
> Gregory Hamilton, Marist College
> Margaret Landman, Bridgewater State College
> Les Manns, Doane College
> Michael L. Marlow, California Polytechnic State University, San Luis Obispo
> Golan Mohammed, Texas A&M University, Galveston
> Jayen B. Patel, University of Alabama, Huntsville
> Debra Snyder, York College, Nebraska
> Robert Stauffer, Roanoke College
> Ramona Wolf, American Institute of Banking, Reading, Pennsylvania
> Ali H. M. Zadeh, Susquehanna University

Many other individuals were involved in this project. We of course must thank our long-standing editor, John Greenman, who encouraged us at all phases of the project and made sure that we took the reviewers comments to heart. Our production team was second to none. The copy editor, Cynthia Hausdorff, masterfully rearranged our prose to make the book read more smoothly. Our project editor, Melonie Salvati, cracked the whip at every stage to make sure the project was on time. Sue Jasin of K&M Consulting helped immensely with the manuscript preparation and formatting and for that we extend our sincere thanks.

We anticipate revising this text for years to come and therefore welcome all comments and criticism from both students and professors alike.

R.L.M.
D.D.V.

Essentials of Money, Banking, and Financial Markets

PART 0

Introduction

1

Money–An Introduction

KEY QUESTIONS

1. What are the functions of money?

2. What distinguishes commodity monies, commodity standards, and fiat monies?

3. What is liquidity?

4. What are monetary aggregates, and how are they constructed?

5. Do changes in payments technologies affect our definitions of money?

All major network cameras were focused on one person—the chair of the Board of Governors of the Federal Reserve System of the United States. Commentators pointed out that he had been placed next to the First Lady. The financial press the next day was buzzing. Did this mean that the new Democratic president had already made peace with the Republican-appointed head of this nation's central bank? Or was it simply a ploy to assure the financial markets that no changes were in store? That so much TV time and newsprint could be spent speculating about the relationship between the president and the chair of the Fed (as the Federal Reserve System is typically called) tells you something. It tells you that whoever runs this nation's central bank is important—indeed, some say that the chair of the Fed is the most powerful individual in the United States, behind the president. Why? Because, according to some, the chair of the Fed and colleagues on the Board of Governors of the Federal Reserve System enact policies that affect every aspect of the United States economy. Even those who have doubts about this importance argue that the policies that the Fed chair and the Board adopt have considerable effects on inflation. All want Congress to keep closer tabs on what that person does.

Why is the Federal Reserve System such an important institution and why should you be concerned about it? The reason is that it influences the total amount of money that circulates in our economy. The Fed also regulates the nation's banking system. Finally, it is the government's bank.

OBJECTIVES OF THIS BOOK AND HOW THEY RELATE TO YOU

Not surprisingly, a key objective of this text is to help you understand the roles that the Federal Reserve System plays in the U.S. economy. But before we can accomplish this task, you must learn a considerable amount about money and financial markets. As you will learn, these two topics are closely related. The reason is that banking institutions issue checking-deposit liabilities that are part of the stock of money circulating in the economy. This chapter explains the concept of money and discusses how money is measured in today's economy. Chapter 2 presents an overview of financial markets, financial instruments, and financial institutions. Together, these two chapters introduce essential concepts that you will need to understand as you proceed through this text. By the time you have completed this book, you should have a clear understanding about why the Federal Reserve System is such a closely watched institution.

To be sure, if you continue your studies in the field of economics, knowledge of money, banking, and financial institutions is critical to understanding macroeconomics and international trade and finance, as well as economic growth and development. If you chose a career in finance, the connection between this course and the rest of your courses is perhaps even more obvious. Indeed, one might say that the basis of the field of finance is a beginning course in money, banking, and financial institutions. If you are going on to study business and management in general, you will be faced with a variety of problems, dilemmas, and issues throughout your studies and your business career, all of which will relate in some way to what you are going to learn in this text. After all, every day businesspeople have to decide about where to keep excess cash and in what type of financial instruments, how to pay for inventory, whether or not a potential investment can be undertaken, and so on.

Finally, even students who go into other fields can benefit from a course in money, banking, and financial institutions. Virtually everyone in this economy at one time borrows money, uses a checking-type account, saves, invests, borrows for a car or house, and so on. Money and banking affect us all.

MONEY AND ITS FUNCTIONS

In general, any item that people are willing to accept in exchange for goods and services is **money.** Many of us think of money mainly as coins or dollar bills. But money is much more than that. For instance, most of what constitutes today's money is held in accounts in financial institutions such as banks, savings and loan associations, and credit unions.

money   Anything that functions as a medium of exchange, store of value, unit of account, and standard of deferred payment.

Money's Functions

Money performs four important functions. It is a medium of exchange, a store of value, a unit of account, and a standard of deferred payment.

medium of exchange   An attribute of money that permits it to be used as a means of payment.

barter   The direct exchange of one good for another without the use of money.

store of value   An attribute of money that allows it to be held for future use without loss of value in the meantime.

Medium of Exchange   The primary role of money is as a **medium of exchange.** This means that people who trade goods, services, or financial assets such as stocks and bonds are willing to take money in exchange for these items. Using money in this way saves people from having to exchange goods, services, and financial assets directly. Such direct exchange is called **barter.** Barter requires finding others willing to exchange items directly. Hence, barter is very costly. This is why money exists.

Store of Value   But money has other important uses. Among these is its use as a **store of value.** People can set aside money with an intent to purchase other items later. In the meantime, money retains value that may be applied to those future purchases. For instance, funds held in a checking account are available to spend on goods or services today or a week or a month from today.

Unit of Account   A third function of money is its role as a **unit of account.** This means that people keep their financial accounts by valuing goods, services, and financial assets in terms of money. In addition, households and businesses quote prices of goods, services, and financial assets in money terms. For example, any price of a good sold in an American grocery store is in dollar terms.

unit of account   An attribute of money that permits it to be used as a measure of the value of goods, services, and financial assets.

Standard of Deferred Payment   Finally, money also is a **standard of deferred payment.** Loan contracts specify future dollar repayments in terms of money. Such a contract is a right to defer repayment of a loan until a later date. Parties to the contract typically agree to meet financial terms specified in units of money.

standard of deferred payment   An attribute of money that permits it to be used as a means of valuing future receipts in loan contracts.

1

What are the functions of money?   Money is a medium by which payments are made. As such, it functions as a medium of exchange. In addition, money is a store of value, a unit of account, and a standard of deferred payment.

Barter and the Development of Money

The earliest economies relied on barter. A person who wished to exchange a good or service that he or she owned or had produced would have to find a second individual willing to purchase that good or service. Yet that second person would have to possess or be willing to produce a good or service that the first person desired. There would have to be a "double coincidence" of wants: Two individuals coincidentally would have to be willing and able to make a trade.

One way that sellers found to get around the double coincidence problem of barter was to establish centralized locations for trade. They set up street markets and trading posts. Interested buyers would know that at these locations they could obtain certain goods. At first buyers would take goods to such marketplaces in order to barter in exchange for goods offered for sale at those locations. Eventually, however, sellers in street markets and trading posts began to accept *intermediate goods* as media of exchange. Purchasers brought with them items that were easy to carry, that were durable, that were easy to recognize, and that were easy to divide into small units for the purpose of "making change." These goods ultimately became money.

GLOBAL NOTEBOOK
Bartering or Simply New Currencies?

One of the reasons there has been growth in commerce and, indeed, increased material well being, has been the move away from bartering. After all, bartering requires a double coincidence of wants. It involves much higher transaction costs than does using some type of money. Nonetheless, a form of moneyless trading called a Local exchange trading system (Lets) has developed in Britain and elsewhere. Rather than being an actual barter system, Lets is probably closer to a system of development of local currencies—currencies used only by people involved with the Lets system. Participating in a Lets requires payment of an initial one-time registration fee using *normal* currency and a small annual administration fee using the local currency. You are given an account in local currency as part of the registration fee, a checkbook, and a local directory that lists the goods and services available. A small levy is charged on each transaction. There are no restrictions on credit and no interest charges.

In all there are more than 200 such systems in Britain involving at least 20,000 people. In Spain the system is called Trueque (which means "to barter" in Spanish). That system was started by an American, Dan Wagman,

who had been living in Spain for 16 years. Another similar system was started in Magdeburg in the eastern part of Germany. There are similar systems in the Netherlands, and by now probably in the Canary Islands and Denmark.

Even though all of the organizers of such systems claim that they are a return to barter, there is no physical exchange of goods for goods or goods for services. That is the nature of true barter. Local exchange trading systems are not really a form of moneyless trading either. They are simply a way of using an alternative money. There is one major reason why some people would prefer to use such "local" money as opposed to, say, checks and regular money—to avoid paying taxes. So far, there are no official records that have to be submitted to any governments listing exchanges made using these local monies. Consequently, individuals who receive unemployment compensation but who continue to work do not have to worry about there being any record if they are paid as part of a Local exchange trading system.

For Critical Analysis: *What might prevent Americans in small cities from establishing Local exchange trading systems?*

COMMODITY MONIES, COMMODITY STANDARDS, AND FIAT MONIES

Historically, there have been three types of money. Goods with practical day-to-day uses that also serve as money are *commodity monies*. Monies that have little inherent value of their own but which are "backed" by the value of another commodity are *commodity standards*.

Finally, monies that have value only because they serve as money are *fiat monies.*

Commodity Monies

Commodity money is a physical good that people use as a medium of exchange. A commodity money, such as tobacco, porpoise teeth, sheep, or a metal, typically has value in alternative uses. Because metals are especially easy to divide into smaller units, they ultimately emerged as the most common type of commodity money.

commodity money   A good with a nonmonetary value that also is used as money.

Precious Metals   Among metals, gold and silver eventually emerged as the main forms of commodity money. These metals were portable, durable, very recognizable, and, most important, were valued highly by nearly everyone because of their relative scarcity and intrinsic usefulness.

The Purchasing Power of Money   The **purchasing power of money** refers to the value of money measured by what a person can buy with that money. In nations in which gold and silver have been used as money, the value of money has been the amount of goods and services that gold and silver could be used to purchase. The going market price for gold or for silver, therefore, was a direct measure of the value of money.

purchasing power of money The value of money in terms of the amount of real goods and services it buys.

Commodity Standards

There are two key drawbacks to using gold or silver as money. One is that two lumps of a metal such as gold or silver may have different market values because the purity of the metal in the lumps can differ. Another is that even if they have the same purity, one may be more densely packed than another. For this reason, before sellers accepted gold or silver in exchange, they typically had to verify the purity and weight of the gold or silver that the buyer had offered. This could be a costly and time-consuming process.

commodity standard   A money unit whose value is fully or partially backed by the value of some other physical good such as gold or silver.

Standardization   To avoid this, people began to use **commodity standards,** monetary units whose values were backed by gold or silver. A monetary system in which the value of the medium of exchange depends on the value of gold is a **gold standard.** In the case in which silver served as the underlying commodity for the system, a *silver standard* was in force. Some nations have used both gold and silver as the basis for their monetary systems. Such a system, in which the value of money depends on the values of two precious metals, is a **bimetallic standard.**

gold standard   A monetary system in which the value of money is linked to value of gold.

bimetallic standard   A commodity standard in which the value of money depends on the values of two precious metals, such as gold and silver.

Under the earliest gold, silver, or bimetallic standards, people would take gold or silver dust or nuggets to a goldsmith, who would craft the dust or nuggets into tokens of equal purity and weight. The goldsmith typically would stamp the token to verify that this had been done. These tokens often were formed into flat, thin disk shapes to make them more portable and recognizable. They came to be called *coins*.

Ultimately, coins became the main form of money. There were two reasons for this. One was that after a while many shopkeepers would only accept coins validated by the stamp of recognized goldsmiths. The other, however, was that governments got involved. In the eighth century, King Pepin the Short of France (the father of Charlemagne) introduced the first government-regulated system of coinage. He decreed that a pound of silver would be divided into 240 "pennies." Twelve of these were equal to one-twentieth of a pound of silver, which in turn was exchangeable for a "solidus" of gold, as defined by the Byzantine empire during the third and fourth centuries. In England, a solidus was known as a "shilling," and so twelve of the French silver coins were known as a shilling in Britain.

Seigniorage   From the eighth century until our own time, commodity standards were the predominant type of monetary system. Governments either regulated or operated mints that produced the coins that citizens used in exchange. The rationale for government regulation of the minting process was to ensure public confidence in a nation's money. Many governments, however, got into the business of producing money for a more basic reason: They could profit from it. Mints owned and operated by kings, queens, or their agents would purchase gold or silver in the form of dust or nuggets. Then they would produce coins that would be issued at a face value that typically exceeded the value of the gold or silver content of the coins. The king's or queen's treasury would keep the difference, which was known as **seigniorage.** Seigniorage essentially amounted to a tax, because it was a transfer from citizens to the government.

seigniorage The difference between the market value of money and the cost of its production, which accrues to the government that produces and issues money.

Over time, kings and queens learned that they could increase their seigniorage by reducing the weight of the coins they issued. Or they could reduce the true gold or silver content of coins by mixing in other metals such as brass or aluminum, which was called *debasement* of the coins. Sometimes they even issued decrees saying that henceforth a coin that they had issued would be worth more than it had been previously.

Paper Money   For centuries governments implemented commodity standards almost solely through coinage. The idea was that the metal content of the coins gave them inherent value. But once governments mastered the tricks of changing weights, debasing, or issuing decrees, they effectively broke the link between the value of the money unit (the coin) and the value of the commodity standard (the gold or silver in the coin). Once governments did this, it was easy for them to think of alternatives to coinage.

One of these was paper money. While some European nations experimented with paper money from time to time, American colonists were the first to accept the idea of paper-based commodity standards. Because gold and silver were particularly scarce in the first colonies, the colonial governments issued paper money that initially was backed by the value of European (typically British or Spanish) coins. This colonial paper money, then, was backed by European coins that, in turn, were backed by gold or silver.

Colonial governments quickly became frustrated with using such an approach. Despite efforts by the British parliament in 1751 and 1764 to stop them, colonial governments began issuing paper monies that were not linked to the value of any other commodity. Instead, the monies amounted to *bills of credit* that the governments promised to redeem at a future date. The colonial governments would use these bills of credit to purchase items or construct public works projects. Those who obtained the bills of credit in exchange then could use them as media of exchange for other goods. As long as people were confident that the governments could raise sufficient tax revenues to redeem the paper bills as promised, the bills circulated as money.

These bills were the first American paper monies. They also were the first step toward today's **fiat money** system. The reason was that the values of the monies that the colonial governments issued were no longer related to any commodity. Instead, the value of money depended on people's confidence in the taxing authority of the government. This was true as well of the "Continentals" issued by the union of colonies during and after the American War of Independence. Unfortunately for this paper money, however, people lost confidence in the taxing power of the confederation of colonies. The value of the Continental money plummeted, hence the phrase "not worth a Continental" became popular for years afterward.

fiat money   A token that has value only because it is accepted as money.

Fiat Money

Throughout much of its history, the U.S. government sought to maintain a gold standard. Yet, from time to time there were experiments with paper bills of credit. The nation's banking system also grew dramatically, and banknotes and checking accounts became more widespread. Nevertheless, until 1971 the U.S. dollar was tied to gold in some fashion.

In 1971 the United States renounced its commitment to the gold standard that was in place at the time. Under the gold standard, the American government had formally tied the value of the dollar to a fixed amount of gold, and other nations, in turn, linked their currencies to the dollar. In 1971 the United States broke the dollar's ties to gold. And in 1973 most other developed nations agreed to allow their own currencies to "float" in value relative to the dollar. Effectively, the United States and other developed nations decided to experiment with a fiat-money system. At present we are in the third decade of this "experiment."

In a fiat-money system, money has value *only* because it is acceptable as a medium of exchange. In the past, fiat money was issued by governments as paper currency or cheap metal coins. But the only paper money of the American federal government (the U.S. Treasury) today consists of U.S. notes, called greenbacks, that were used to finance the Civil War and that are still in circulation. Most paper money in circulation today is issued by central banks. For instance, look at the paper currency that you use. It is composed of Federal Reserve Notes issued by the Federal Reserve System—an independent government agency that functions as the central bank of the United States.

Many private financial institutions legally issue fiat money in the form of checkable deposits that we think of as checking accounts. Banks, savings and loan associations, and credit unions are examples of such institutions.

2

What distinguishes commodity monies, commodity standards, and fiat monies?
Commodity monies are goods that are used as monies but which also have other intrinsic uses. Commodity-standard monies are money tokens whose values are related to those of other commodities. Fiat monies are monies that have value only because they are accepted as media of exchange.

DEFINING AND MEASURING MONEY AND LIQUIDITY

Students often are surprised to learn that economists have trouble agreeing about how to define and measure the amount of money in circulation. Yet economists do have trouble reaching agreement on this fundamental issue. Some economists believe that whatever we call "money" should be whatever functions solely as an immediately available means of payment. *Cash* (paper currency and coins) would fit this definition of money, as would checking accounts and traveler's checks.

Other economists, however, believe that this approach is too narrow. They argue that money is also a store of value, and so they argue that other items ought to be included. Among these would be readily accessible savings deposits and other easily redeemable assets. Such financial assets, this second group of economists contends, can be so easily converted into the medium of exchange that we ought to count them as money.

This dispute revolves around the notion of **liquidity,** or the ease with which a person can sell or redeem an asset for a known amount of cash at short notice and at low risk of loss of its nominal value. To those who emphasize the medium-of-exchange approach to measuring money, cash, traveler's checks, and checking accounts are appropriate measures of money because they are the most obviously liquid of assets. After all, they *already* are cash; there is no "redeeming" that must be done! But those who emphasize money's function as a store of value point out that there are many assets in today's world that are extremely liquid. Although they technically are not media of exchange, it would be easy for their owners to convert them for such use.

There is no simple solution to this dispute. Good arguments can be made by reasonable people on both sides. As we shall see, the Federal Reserve System—our central bank—has sought to satisfy both groups by defining and measuring money in more than one way.

> **liquidity**   The ease with which buyer can sell or redeem an asset for a known amount of cash at short notice and at low risk of loss of nominal value.

3

What is liquidity?   Liquidity refers to the ease and speed with which a person can sell an asset for a given amount of money at low cost.

CURRENT MEASURES OF THE AMOUNT OF MONEY IN CIRCULATION

The Federal Reserve System (commonly called the Fed) defines several measures of the stock of money, and these appear on a weekly basis in the *Wall Street Journal*'s "Federal Reserve Data" column. Figure 1.1 on page 12 displays a sample of this column. The measures of money that the Fed reports are sums of various groupings of financial assets. For this reason, the Fed calls them **monetary aggregates.** Each of these monetary aggregates differs according to the liquidity of the assets that are included or excluded.

> **monetary aggregate**   A grouping of assets that are sufficiently liquid to be defined as a measure of money.

The Monetary Base

The **monetary base,** which economists sometimes call "high-powered money," is the narrowest measure of money. It is the amount of money produced directly by actions of the government and/or a central bank

> **monetary base**   The sum of currency in circulation plus reserves of depository institutions.

FIGURE 1.1 *The* Wall Street Journal's "Federal Reserve Data" Column

This column appears each Friday and includes the latest information about monetary aggregates. *Source:* Reprinted by permission of The Wall Street Journal, © 1996 Dow Jones & Company, Inc. All Rights Reserved Worldwide.

FEDERAL RESERVE DATA

MONETARY AGGREGATES
(daily average in billions)

	One week ended:	
	Apr. 1	Mar. 25
Money supply (M1) sa	1127.0	1126.3
Money supply (M1) nsa	1121.4	1103.3
Money supply (M2) sa	3725.5	3721.6
Money supply (M2) nsa	3725.3	3702.8
Money supply (M3) sa	4675.7	4676.4
Money supply (M3) nsa	4669.8	4657.6
	Four weeks ended:	
	Apr. 1	Mar. 4
Money supply (M1) sa	1126.8	1127.5
Money supply (M1) nsa	1115.1	1115.0
Money supply (M2) sa	3724.4	3722.7
Money supply (M2) nsa	3717.1	3712.5
Money supply (M3) sa	4678.7	4678.4
Money supply (M3) nsa	4668.9	4666.2
	Month	
	Mar.	Feb.
Money supply (M1) sa	1126.2	1117.0
Money supply (M2) sa	3722.7	3690.3
Money supply (M3) sa	4677.6	4639.6

nsa-Not seasonally adjusted. sa-Seasonally adjusted.

KEY ASSETS AND LIABILITIES
OF THE 8 LEADING NEW YORK BANKS
(in millions of dollars)

	Apr. 3, 1996	Change from Mar. 27, 1996	
ASSETS:			
Total loans, leases and investments, adjusted	229,314	+	964
Commercial and industrial loans	41,568	+	328
Loans to depository and financial institutions	25,847	+	1,472
Loans to individuals	25,891	+	547
Real estate loans	59,050	−	644
U.S. government securities	50,027	−	671
Other securities including municipal issues	9,574	−	27
Municipal securities	4,037	−	8
LIABILITIES:			
Demand deposits	48,042	+	2,913
Other transaction deposits including NOW accounts	7,291	+	144
Savings and other nontransaction deposits	103,363	+	5,010
Includes large time deposits of $100,000 or more	20,899	+	2,649

COMMERCIAL PAPER OUTSTANDING
(in millions of dollars)

All issuers	703,652	+	6,363
Financial companies	510,479	+	6,765
Nonfinancial companies	193,173	−	402

MEMBER BANK RESERVE CHANGES

Changes in weekly averages of reserves and related items during the week and year ended April 10, 1996 were as follows (in millions of dollars)

		Chg fm	wk end
	Apr. 10, 1996	Apr. 3, 1996	Apr. 12, 1995
Reserve bank credit:			
U.S. Gov't securities:			
Bought outright	377,055	− 421	+ 8,403
Held under repurch agreemt	6,337	+ 2,836	+ 4,574
Federal agency issues:			
Bought outright	2,521	− 5	− 887
Held under repurch agreemt	57	− 943	− 136
Acceptances			
Borrowings from Fed:			
Adjustment credit	34	+ 7	+ 25
Seasonal borrowings	19	+ 6	− 42
Extended credit	....	....	....
Float	831	+ 759	+ 508
Other Federal Reserve Assets	31,372	+ 154	− 3,590
Total Reserve Bank Credit	418,226	+ 2,392	+ 8,856
Gold Stock	11,053	.... −	1
SDR certificates	10,168	.... +	2,150
Treasury currency outstanding	24,207	+ 14	+ 956
Total	463,654	+ 2,406	+ 11,961
Currency in circulation	419,041	+ 1,886	+ 14,270
Treasury cash holdings	318	+ 3	− 49
Treasury dpts with F.R. Bnks	5,986	− 30	+ 1,008
Foreign dpts with F.R. Bnks	212	+ 32	+ 37
Other dpts with F.R. Bnks	372	− 32	+ 3
Service related balances, adj	5,869	− 61	+ 1,851
Other F. R. liabilities			

that acts on its behalf. In the United States, the monetary base is the sum of currency *outside* the federal government, the Fed, and depository institutions, plus reserves of depository institutions.

Currency   In the United States, **currency** has two main components. One is the dollar value of coins (mainly pennies, nickels, dimes, quarters) minted by the U.S. Treasury and held *outside* the Treasury, the Federal Reserve banks, and depository institutions. The other is the dollar value of Federal Reserve Notes issued by Federal Reserve banks. As stated earlier, some currency notes issued in the past by the U.S. Treasury remain in circulation, but this is a very small part of total currency.

currency   Coins and paper money.

POLICY NOTEBOOK

How to Save $400 Million a Year—Get Rid of the Dollar Bill (and the Penny, Too)

A dollar isn't what it used to be, that is for sure. A one-dollar bill today buys a fraction of what it bought in, say, 1870. It is not surprising, then, that people today find coins almost a nuisance because they are worth so little. A quarter is the highest valued coin in general use (although there are some half-dollars and a few silver dollars floating around out there). But a quarter will not even buy most newspapers today. That means that one-dollar bills get used a lot, much more than they did when they could really buy something. The Bureau of Engraving and Printing prints over 4 billion one-dollar bills each year, each costing four cents to make. Those dollar bills last about 17 months.

If, instead, one-dollar coins were made, they would each cost about eight cents but last 30 years. On a per-year basis, that means that if we eliminated one-dollar bills and used one-dollar coins, we would be spending only one-tenth as much per year to keep this particular unit of our currency in circulation. The General Accounting office and the Federal Reserve estimate that about $400 million a year would be saved.

Everybody is doing it. Most industrialized nations have phased in high-denomination coins while eliminating their paper-currency equivalent. Britain, for example, no longer has one-pound notes, but instead has one-pound coins (valued at about $1.60). Japan eliminated the 500 yen note in 1990 and replaced it with a coin that has a value of about $6. Spain, Norway, New Zealand, France, Canada, and Australia have acted similarly.

While we are at it, we could probably eliminate the penny. When it first appeared in 1793, it could buy a sandwich. Handling pennies costs countless hours in labor for counting, rolling, and banking them. Basically, there is no place for the penny anymore. Nonetheless, the U.S. Mint makes over 13 billion pennies a year.

For Critical Analysis: *Who would stand to benefit from the replacement of dollar bills with dollar coins? Who would be the gainers and who would be the losers if the penny were completely eliminated?*

Depository Financial Institution Reserves

Commercial banks, savings banks, savings and loan association, and credit unions are **depository financial institutions** or, more simply, *depository institutions*. Such institutions issue checking and savings deposits. As discussed below, such deposits are key components of broader measures of money. Depository institutions also must hold funds on deposit with Federal Reserve banks. These funds and the cash that the institutions hold in their vaults constitute the **reserves** of such institutions. The source of these funds ultimately is the Fed itself, as we shall discuss in greater detail in Chapter 10.

Figure 1.2 displays the relative sizes of these two components of the monetary base in 1996. The percentages here are typical figures that we would observe at any time. Currency normally is the bulk of the monetary base.

M1: A Basic Definition of "Cash"

A broader definition of money, a monetary aggregate called **M1,** is also shown in Figure 1.2. This measure of the quantity of money—which the *Wall Street Journal* and other publications often call "the money supply," has three components: currency, traveler's checks issued by institutions other than depository financial institutions, and transactions deposits held at depository institutions.

Currency and Traveler's Checks

The currency component of M1 is the same as that used to compute the monetary base. Only traveler's checks issued by nondepository institutions such as American Express,

depository financial institutions Financial institutions that offer checking and savings deposits and that legally must hold reserves on deposit with Federal Reserve banks or in their vaults.

reserves Cash held by depository institutions in their vaults or on deposit with the Federal Reserve System.

M1 Currency plus transactions deposits.

FIGURE 1.2   Components of the Monetary Base and M1

($ billions). *Source:* Board of Governors of the Federal Reserve System, H.6(508) *Statistical Release,* March 1996.

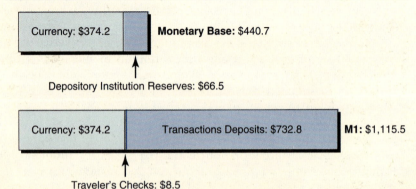

Currency: $374.2 | Monetary Base: $440.7

Depository Institution Reserves: $66.5

Currency: $374.2 | Transactions Deposits: $732.8 | M1: $1,115.5

Traveler's Checks: $8.5

Citibank, Thomas Cook, and other such firms are included as part of M1. The reason is that depository institutions place the funds that they use to redeem traveler's checks in special transactions deposit accounts already counted among transactions deposits.

Transactions Deposits   Deposits at financial institutions from which holders may write checks for purchasing goods, services, or financial assets are **transactions deposits.** There are three types of transactions deposits. One is **demand deposits.** Demand deposits are noninterest-bearing checking deposits. Holders may convert funds in such deposits to currency "on demand," or may write a check on these deposits to third parties, who in turn may access funds from the deposits "on demand." Another type of transactions deposit is **negotiable-order-of-withdrawal,** or **NOW, accounts.** NOW accounts are interest-bearing deposits that also offer checking privileges. The third type of transactions deposit is **automatic-transfer-system,** or **ATS, accounts.** ATS accounts are combinations of interest-bearing savings accounts and noninterest-bearing demand deposits. Typically, holders of ATS accounts maintain small demand-deposit balances. Yet they may write sizable checks payable from their demand-deposit accounts, because funds are transferred automatically from their savings accounts to cover any shortfalls.

As Figure 1.2 indicates, transactions deposits together constitute the bulk of the M1 measure of money. The amount of currency amounts to less than a third of M1, and traveler's checks are a relatively insignificant component.

transactions deposits
Checking accounts.

demand deposits   Non-interest-bearing checking accounts.

negotiable-order-of-withdrawal (NOW) accounts
Interest-bearing checking deposits.

automated-transfer-system (ATS) accounts   Combined interest-bearing savings accounts and noninterest-bearing checking accounts in which the former is drawn upon automatically when the latter is over-drawn.

M2: Cash Plus Other Liquid Assets

The monetary base and M1 are alternative definitions of "cash money." The monetary base measures funds made available directly by the U.S. Treasury and Federal Reserve System, while M1 measures funds more broadly available to the public at large. Both definitions of money include only assets that are spendable at a moment's notice.

Yet there are other financial assets that may be converted very quickly into cash. **M2** is a broadened definition of money that includes such assets. The monetary aggregate M2 is equal to M1 *plus* the following:

1. Savings deposits and money market deposit accounts at depository institutions.
2. Small-denomination time deposits at depository institutions.
3. Funds held by individuals, brokers, and dealers in money market mutual funds.

M2   M1, plus savings and small-denomination time deposits, and balances in individuals' and broker-dealers' money market mutual funds.

TABLE 1.1 The Components of M2

M1	$1,115.5
Small-denomination time deposits	929.4
Savings deposits and money market deposits	1,178.4
Individual and broker–dealer money market mutual funds	492.1
M2	$3,715.4

Source: Board of Governors of the Federal Reserve System, H.6(508) *Statistical Release,* March 1996, $ billions.

Table 1.1 lists the dollar amounts of the components of M2 in 1996.

savings deposits   Interest-bearing savings accounts without set maturities.

money market deposit accounts   Savings accounts with limited checking privileges.

small-denomination time deposits   Deposits with set maturities and denominations of less than $100,000.

money market mutual funds   Pools of funds from savers that managing firms use to purchase short-term financial assets such as Treasury bills and commercial paper.

Savings Deposits and Money Market Deposit Accounts   **Savings deposits** are interest-bearing deposits without set maturities. **Money market deposit accounts** are savings accounts that permit limited checking privileges.

Small-Denomination Time Deposits   Time deposits have set maturities, meaning that the holder must keep the funds on deposit for a fixed length of time to be guaranteed a negotiated interest return. **Small-denomination time deposits** have denominations of less than $100,000. There are a variety of small-denomination time deposits, including 6-month money market certificates of deposit and 2- to 4-year-maturity certificates of deposit.

Money Market Mutual Funds   Many financial companies today offer **money market mutual funds,** which are pools of funds from savers that managing firms use to purchase short-term financial assets. Among these are such assets as Treasury bills and large certificates of deposits issued by depository financial institutions such as banks. Individuals, brokers, dealers, and larger institutions hold balances at money market mutual funds. The Fed has determined, however, that institutional balances at money market mutual funds typically are not very liquid. Therefore, the Fed includes only individual and broker-dealer holdings in M2. Institutional balances are included in a broader measure of money.

Figure 1.3 compares the monetary base, M1, and M2. In 1996, M2 was over ten times larger than the monetary base and was about three and one-half times larger than M1. Indeed, savings and money market accounts together were larger than M1. The total amount of small-denomination time deposits also exceeded M1. These comparisons are typical of those we would observe at any time we might choose to measure these definitions of money.

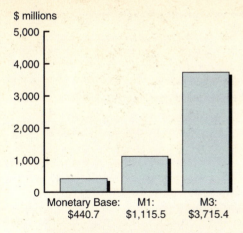

$ millions

| Monetary Base: | M1: | M3: |
| $440.7 | $1,115.5 | $3,715.4 |

FIGURE 1.3   Comparing the Monetary Base, M1, and M2

($ billions). *Source:* Board of Governors of the Federal Reserve System, H.6(508) *Statistical Release*, March 1996.

M3: The Broadest Monetary Aggregate

The Fed makes greatest use of the monetary base and M1 and M2 measures of money. Nevertheless, it does have a very broad money definition that it calls **M3.** This measure of money adds to M2 the following items:

1. Large-denomination time deposits at depository institutions.
2. Term repurchase agreements and term Eurodollars.
3. Institution-only money market mutual fund balances.
4. Repurchase agreements at depository institutions and Eurodollar deposits held by American residents (other than depository institutions) at foreign branches of American depository institutions.

Table 1.2 (page 18) lists the amount of the components of M3 in 1996.

Large-denomination time deposits are time deposits issued by depository institutions in amounts of $100,000 or more. A **repurchase agreement** is a contract to sell financial assets, such as U.S. Treasury bonds, with a promise to repurchase them at a later time, typically at a slightly higher price. This means that the original holder of financial assets who initiates the repurchase agreement effectively borrows funds

M3   M2, plus large-denomination time deposits, term Eurodollars and repurchase agreements, and institution-only money market mutual funds.

large-denomination time deposits   Deposits with set maturities and denominations greater than or equal to $100,000.

repurchase agreement   A contract to sell financial assets with a promise to repurchase them at a later time.

TABLE 1.2   The Components of M3

M2	$3,715.4
Large-denomination time deposits	427.3
Repurchase agreements and Eurodollar deposits	276.1
Institution-only money market mutual funds	248.7
M3	$4,667.5

Source: Board of Governors of the Federal Reserve System, H.6(508) *Statistical Release,* March 1996, $ billions.

Eurodollars   Dollar-denominated deposits located outside the United States.

for a time. **Eurodollar** deposits are dollar-denominated deposits in foreign depository institutions and in foreign branches of American depository institutions. Despite the name Eurodollar, such deposits might, for instance, be in Japanese or Australian branches of American banks. Finally, *institution-only money market mutual funds balances* include all balances at mutual funds that are not held by individuals, brokers, and dealers.

What each of these financial assets share in common is that they are fairly liquid, yet experience has indicated that they are not as liquid as those included in M2. And so the Fed includes them in its M3 definition instead.

Figure 1.4 compares the magnitudes of all four measures of money: the monetary base, M1, M2, and M3. Although M3 is not too much larger than M2, the additional assets it includes—large-denomination time deposits and so on—tend to be much less liquid than those that constitute M2. As a result, the Fed has tended to place less weight on M3 as a reliable measure of money. It also deemphasizes the monetary base, because checking deposits are such an important means by which households and firms purchase goods, services, and financial assets. Therefore, most of the Fed's attention is devoted to the M1 and M2 monetary aggregates.

Figure 1.5 shows annual percentage growth rates in M1 and M2 since 1970. As the figure shows, these two monetary aggregates have grown at different rates. Sometimes the growth of one has declined while the other has grown more quickly. This has complicated the Fed's efforts to decide which of these aggregates is the more useful measure of money.

4

What are monetary aggregates and how are they constructed?   Monetary aggregates are groupings of financial assets that are combined, based on their degrees of liquidity, into overall measures of money. The monetary base, M1, M2, and M3 are today's basic monetary aggregates. Of these M1 and M2 are the two that are most important to the Federal Reserve System.

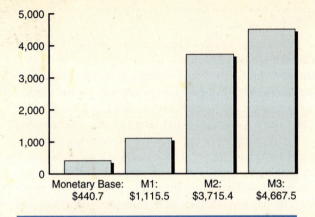

FIGURE 1.4   Comparing All Four Measures of Money

($ billions). *Source:* Board of Governors of the Federal Reserve System, H.6(508) *Statistical Release,* March 1996.

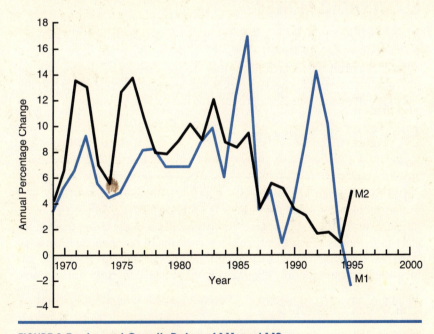

FIGURE 1.5   Annual Growth Rates of M1 and M2

The Federal Reserve's two key monetary aggregates often grow at different rates. *Source: 1996 Economic Report of the President.*

Other Aggregates

L   M3 plus all other liquid assets.

The Fed also tabulates two other types of aggregates. One of these is an even broader measure of liquidity than M3, which the Fed calls **L.** It is equal to M3 plus other, somewhat less-liquid financial assets, including banker's acceptances, commercial paper, and several Treasury securities. In 1996 this liquidity aggregate amounted to $5,783.3 billion.

Some economists have questioned the usefulness of aggregates such as M1, M2, M3, and L, which are constructed by simply summing together dollar values of various assets. These economists have developed monetary aggregates, known as **divisia aggregates** that weight individual assets according to how frequently they are used to make purchases. Essentially, this approach tries to account for differences in liquidity by assigning different liquidity weights to assets.

divisia aggregates   Measures of money that weight individual assets according to the frequency with which they are used to make purchases.

The Fed tabulates both L and divisia aggregates. In recent years it has tried to evaluate the extent to which divisia aggregates might be better guides for its policies. But at present the Fed does not make too much direct use either of L or divisia aggregates when it makes policy decisions.

MONEY IN A CHANGING WORLD—ELECTRONIC MONEY

History has taught us that money is not immune to technological change. For instance, private banknotes once were the most common form of money. Yet even when such notes were legal currency, technological improvements that made checks simpler and less costly to process gradually led to greater use of checking accounts as a means of payment.

Nonelectronic Payments

As we prepare to cross into a new century, currency, checks, and traveler's checks constitute the media of exchange that are most widely used. Other paper-based means of payment include credit card transactions and money orders. As panel (a) of Figure 1.6 shows, about 98 percent of all transactions in the United States for 1999 will be made using these nonelectronic means of payment. Electronic means of payment such as **wire transfers**—payments made via telephone lines or through fiber optic cables—will account for only about 2 percent of total American transactions.

wire transfers   Payments made via telephone lines or through fiber optic cables.

Electronic Payments

We presently live in a period in which improvements in information-processing technology have the potential to alter conceptions of what constitutes a means of payment. Panel (b) of Figure 1.6 shows why this is the case. Although nonelectronic means of payment will continue to account for the lion's share of the total number of *exchanges* in the

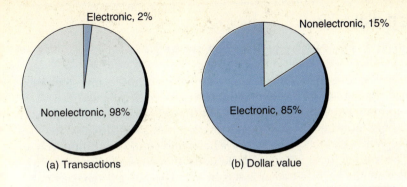

FIGURE 1.6   Electronic vs. Nonelectronic Payments
As panel (a) indicates, nonelectronic transactions account for nearly all payments in the United States. Nevertheless, panel (b) shows that the bulk of the dollar value of exchanges is accomplished through electronic means of payment. *Source:* Author's estimates.

United States, by 1999 about 85 percent of the *dollar value* of such exchanges will be made with *electronic* means of payment. Only about 15 percent of the dollar value of 1999 transactions will be made with checks, currency, or other physical means of payment.

Direct transfers between parties of exchanges account for the bulk of electronic payments. **Automated clearing houses** also process payments on behalf of parties to transactions. **Point-of-sale (POS) transfers** also are becoming more common, even though the technology for POS transfers has been available since the 1960s. A POS transfer is an automatic transfer of funds from a deposit account to a retailer accomplished electronically on demand at the location at which an exchange takes place. For instance, a typical department store POS cash register essentially is a minicomputer that can communicate with other computers. Once appropriate arrangements have been made with a depository institution, an individual could use a plastic card with magnetically encoded account information to permit the department store POS cash register to transfer funds directly from the individual's deposit account to the account of the department store.

Another electronic means of payment is through **automated bill payment.** This is a payments technology in which individuals arrange for depository institutions to pay some of their bills. The depository institutions automatically deduct funds from their accounts and transfer them electronically to designated receivers of the funds.

automated clearing houses
Institutions that process payments electronically on behalf of senders and receivers of those payments.

point-of-sale (POS) transfer
Electronic transfer of funds at the time a sale is made from a buyer's account to the account of a firm from which a good or service has been purchased.

automated bill payment
Direct payment of bills by depository institutions on behalf of their customers.

Computer Shopping

A number of firms are selling goods, services, and financial assets over the electronic information system known as the *Internet*. The Internet is a system that links mainframe and personal computers around the

Should Bond and Stock Market Funds Be in M2?

Liquidity is not the only factor the Fed assesses to determine which monetary aggregate it should emphasize. Another important issue is the variability and predictability of a monetary aggregate. In the late 1980s the Fed began to pay closest attention to M2 because it was more predictable than M1. But in the early 1990s, M2 suddenly became much less stable.

One reason for this, as documented by John Duca of the Federal Reserve Bank of Dallas, was the explosive growth (see the figure below) in *bond and equity mutual funds.* These funds are similar to money market mutual funds except that their assets consist of holdings of bonds and stocks (equities) instead of the shorter-term, lower-risk holdings of money market funds. Bond and eq-

uity funds provide liquidity to investors by giving them access to credit lines and permitting them to shift assets among bond, equity, and money market funds at little cost.

Because bond and equity funds offer considerable liquidity, they share similarities with other assets in M2. This has led some economists in the Federal Reserve System to propose including these funds in M2. These economists have been monitoring *M2+*, which is M2 plus bond and equity fund balances. In recent years M2+ has been more stable than the traditional M2, which may eventually lead the Fed to replace M2 with the new M2+.

For Critical Analysis: *Why should the Fed care which definition of the money supply it publishes each month?*

Growth of Bond and Equity Mutual Funds

After an initial leveling off in the late 1980s, the assets of bond and equity mutual funds grew considerably in the 1990s. *Sources:* John V. Duca, "Would the Addition of Bond or Equity Funds Make M2 a Better Indicator of Nominal GDP?" Federal Reserve Bank of Dallas *Economic Review,* 1994; more recent data from Federal Reserve Bank of Dallas.

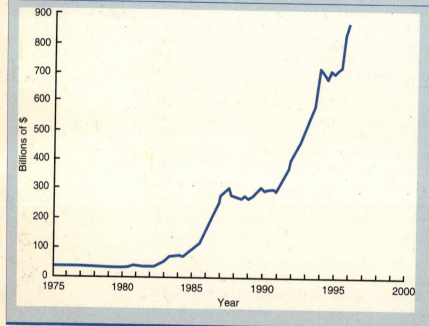

United States and the rest of the world. Individuals most commonly use the Internet to send electronic mail or to access information from remote locations. The potential exists, however, for ever-increasing numbers of people and firms to be able to arrange and execute financial transactions over the Internet. Indeed, some companies already have set up systems for such exchanges. These and other innovations in electronic payments technology promise to revolutionize the manner in which payments will be made in the coming century.

Will they also revolutionize the meaning of money? The answer to this question remains unresolved at present. If what matters for measuring money are the means that people use to make the most transactions, then clearly checks and currency remain the key components of any measure of money. Yet it is undeniable that new information-processing technology broadens the liquidity of a number of financial assets by making them more readily convertible to cash. This indicates that, in the future, monetary aggregates likely may need to include even more items than they do at present.

5

Do changes in payments technologies affect our definitions of money?   Most likely, the answer is yes. As the ability to transfer funds electronically becomes more widespread, it makes more assets convertible to money and thereby increases their liquidity. This may require including more assets in monetary aggregates.

SUMMARY

1. **The Functions of Money:** Money has four functions. It is a medium of exchange, a store of value, a unit of account, and a standard of deferred payment.

2. **Commodity Monies, Commodity Standards, and Fiat Monies:** A commodity money is a good with its own intrinsic value that has uses other than as money. A commodity standard is some type of token money unit whose value is linked in some way to that of a commodity such as gold or silver. Fiat money is a good that has value only because it is acceptable in an exchange for goods and services.

3. **Liquidity:** Liquidity is the ease with which assets may be converted into money that may be spent directly on goods, services, or financial assets. The most liquid assets are those typically defined as money.

4. **Monetary Aggregates:** Monetary aggregates are combinations or groups of highly liquid assets. Common measures of money are monetary aggregates such as the monetary base, M1, M2, and M3. A measure of overall liquidity in the economy is the aggregate L. Divisia aggregates are measures of money in which assets are weighted

by the frequency of their use in payments before being summed to form an aggregate measure of money.

5. **Payments Technologies and Definitions of Money:** Technological change in the processes by which payments are made can affect how we define money. While nonelectronic payments continue to predominate in typical transactions, the bulk of dollars in transactions are transferred electronically. As such electronic transfers become more common, overall asset liquidity may increase, and new assets may gain sufficient liquidity to be classified as money.

QUESTIONS AND PROBLEMS

1. If a money is a medium of exchange, must it be a store of value? Can you think of any real-world examples in which the two functions might be separated, with one type of money acting as the exchange medium but the other taking on the role of a store of value?

2. What are some advantages and disadvantages of the alternative forms of money: commodity monies, commodity standards, and fiat monies? Is fiat money necessarily preferable to the other two forms of money? Why or why not?

3. Consider the following data ($ billions), and calculate the monetary base, M1, and M2.

Currency	$ 450
Savings deposits and money market deposit accounts	1,400
Small-denomination time deposits	1,000
Traveler's checks	10
Reserves of depository financial institutions	80
Overnight repurchase agreements	100
Total money market mutual funds	500
Institution-only money market mutual funds	200
Overnight Eurodollars	50
Demand deposits	450
Other checkable deposits	490

4. Suppose that M1 is equal to $1,350 billion. The monetary base is equal to $500 billion, and transactions deposits and traveler's checks combined amount to $925 billion. What is the amount of reserves at depository financial institutions?

5. Explain in your own words why the growth in electronic means of payment might complicate the task of defining and measuring money.

2

Financial Markets, Instruments, and Institutions

KEY QUESTIONS

1. What is the main economic function of financial markets?

2. What are primary and secondary markets for financial instruments?

3. What distinguishes money markets from capital markets?

4. What are the main types of financial instruments?

5. Why do financial intermediaries exist?

6. What are the main types of financial institutions?

Technology has done wonders for most aspects of business, including money, banking, and financial institutions. Optical character readers now sort and transfer the relevant information on billions of checks a year—a job that used to be done by hand. But technology has also caused problems for banks and other financial institutions. Consider the Family Farm Preservation group based in Tigerton, Wisconsin. Believing that paper money is worthless because the Federal Reserve System is illegal, they used technology to launch a campaign to circulate counterfeit money orders. The money orders were duplicated on sophisticated, high-tech photocopying machines. They looked so real that one California financial institution lost more than $30,000 when it released legal title to two cars before it realized that the money orders were fraudulent.

Today's high-tech copy machines, computers, and laser printers are able to spew out almost perfect copies of bank checks, traveler's checks, money orders, letters of credit, and stock and bond certificates. According to the Secret Service's financial crimes division, losses to our nation's banks for such fraud is increasing dramatically, up to several billion dollars a year at a minimum. Relative novices, using today's color copiers, can reproduce currency so well that it fools almost everybody. Much of this high-tech counterfeiting with currency, checks, and money orders involves nationwide operations. One group working out of Southern California counterfeited corporate checks on color laser printers, then recruited individuals in at least five states to cash them. One large California bank lost $2 million.

Such high-tech counterfeiting clearly has an effect on our financial institutions and markets. In this chapter you will learn more about them.

SAVING AND INVESTMENT

As we discuss below, *financial markets* help direct financial resources from the owners of these resources to those who use them to finance productive activities. The owners of financial resources are individuals who accumulate resources rather than expending them each year. These individuals are *savers* of financial resources. When other individuals or businesses make use of financial resources to finance productive endeavors, they are *investing* these resources. Financial markets bring the two groups—those who save and those who invest—together.

Saving   The key economic function of financial markets is to channel saving to investment. **Saving** is forgone consumption. And so when individuals do not spend all their after-tax income received within a given year, those individuals have saved some of their money income.

saving   Forgone consumption.

Investment   But savers do not want all their savings to sit idly in money balances if there are alternatives that yield returns. Typically such alternatives exist. The reason is that other individuals or firms usually are undertaking **investment,** or additions to the stock of capital goods. **Capital goods,** in turn, are goods that may be used to produce other goods or services in the future.

investment   Additions to the stock of capital goods.

capital goods   Goods that may be used to produce other goods or services in the future.

Investment in capital goods can require significant financial resources, and so individuals and firms that invest often must borrow funds to make such investment possible. They borrow these funds from savers, promising to return the funds. The borrowers also promise **interest,** or payments for the use of the savers' funds. The borrowers finance the interest payments using revenues from the production that their new capital goods makes possible.

interest   Payments for the use of the funds of savers.

Savers are the ultimate *lenders* in our economy. Many of the *borrowers* are firms or individuals who wish to undertake investment. Some individuals, of course, borrow to finance current consumption. But the main reasons for lending and borrowing are that savers desire future interest income on the savings they hold today, while most borrowers desire to finance investment projects that they expect will yield returns in the future.

1

What is the main economic function of financial markets?   The main economic role for financial markets is to direct saving to those who wish to make capital investments.

FINANCIAL MARKETS

Financial markets facilitate the lending of funds from saving to those who wish to undertake investments. Companies that wish to borrow to finance investment projects sell IOUs to savers, as Figure 2.1 on page 28 illustrates. Financial markets are markets for these IOUs. The various forms of IOUs are known collectively as **financial instruments.** Such instruments, which also are called **securities,** are claims that those who lend their savings have on the future incomes of the borrowers who use those funds for investment.

financial instruments   Claims that those who lend their savings have on the future incomes of the borrowers who use those funds for investment.

securities   Financial instruments.

FIGURE 2.1   The Function of Financial Markets
Financial markets facilitate the transfer of funds from savers to those who wish to invest in capital goods. Individuals or companies offer financial instruments to savers in exchange for funds they use to finance investment projects.

When most of us think of "instruments," we think of tools, such as those that surgeons use to repair damaged heart or muscle tissue. We refer to financial claims as instruments because they are also tools. In contrast to the finely fashioned metal instruments that surgeons use, financial instruments are paper documents. Yet just as a surgeon uses instruments as tools to perform delicate tasks, individuals and firms can use financial instruments to undertake crucial exchanges of financial resources. They also can use financial instruments to help reduce the risks of financial loss.

There are two basic ways to categorize financial markets. One, which distinguishes between primary or secondary markets, separates types of financial markets depending upon whether or not they are markets for newly issued instruments. The other, which distinguishes between capital and money markets, defines financial markets on the basis of the instruments' maturities. The **maturity** of an instrument is the time ranging from the date of issue until final principal and interest payments are due to the holders of the instruments. Maturities of less than a year are **short-term maturities,** while maturities in excess of ten years are **long-term maturities.** Maturities ranging from one to ten years are **intermediate-term** maturities.

Primary and Secondary Financial Markets

There are many financial markets. For this reason it is helpful to classify such markets into categories. One way to do this is to distinguish between primary and secondary financial markets.

Primary Markets   A **primary market** is a financial market in which a newly issued financial instrument is purchased and sold. For instance, consider a newly formed business that offers to sell shares of ownership (commonly called stocks). It sells these shares in a primary financial market. Likewise, when the United States Treasury issues new Treasury securities to fund some of the public debt (which increases when the

maturity   Time until final principal and interest payments are due to the holders of a financial instrument.

short-term maturity   Maturity less than one year.

long-term maturity   Maturity more than ten years.

intermediate-term maturity   Maturity between one year and ten years.

primary market   Market for newly issued financial instruments.

federal government spends more than it has received in revenues), these are sold in a primary market.

The first attempt by a business to issue ownership shares to the public in the primary market is called an *initial public offering (IPO)*. While businesses could attempt to manage an IPO on their own, many rely on the assistance of **investment banks.** These are institutions that specialize in marketing initial ownership shares offered by new businesses. Investment banks typically *underwrite* such issues, meaning that they guarantee the businesses fixed share prices. Essentially, the investment banks temporarily purchase the shares of the businesses. Then they attempt to resell them in the primary market at a slightly higher price. They keep the difference between the purchase price and the resale price (often 10 percent) as a profit.

investment banks Institutions that specialize in marketing and underwriting sales of ownership shares in firms.

Secondary Markets   Most financial instruments that are sold in primary markets have maturities that range from several months to many years. Shares of ownership in firms (stocks) have no set maturities. Firms, in principle, last forever; they are "going concerns." Bonds issued by the United States Treasury have fixed maturities in excess of ten years. Yet a time may be reached at some point following the initial purchase of such ownership shares or bonds, but before their maturity dates, when the original purchaser no longer wishes to hold them. Then that original owner may sell them in a **secondary market.** This is simply a market for financial instruments that were issued at some point in the past.

secondary market Market for financial instruments issued at some time in the past.

The presence of secondary markets contributes to the efficient functioning of primary markets. The reason is that the ability to purchase or sell previously issued financial instruments makes such instruments much more liquid than they otherwise would be. For instance, persons contemplating purchasing shares of ownership in a fledgling company are much more likely to buy such shares if they know that there is a readily available market in which they can sell them if they later wish to access their funds or become dissatisfied with the performance of the company.

There are many active secondary markets for financial instruments. Included among these are secondary markets for United States Treasury securities, for shares of ownership in corporations, and for state and local municipal bonds. Now there also are secondary markets for many consumer credit obligations and for business, mortgage, and consumer loans of financial institutions. For instance, each year banks package billions of dollars of their credit card loans into separate securities that they sell in secondary markets.

Much as investment bankers facilitate the functioning of primary markets, **brokers** assist in matching borrowers and lenders in secondary markets. Typically, brokers specialize in a secondary market in which they have developed the greatest knowledge of the factors that

brokers Institutions that specialize in matching buyers and sellers of financial instruments in secondary markets.

influence risks, costs, and returns relating to instruments exchanged in that market. Brokers receive fees for the services they provide to secondary market buyers and sellers. For instance, brokers at a firm such as Merrill Lynch earn fee income for attempting to help their clients earn the highest possible returns from shares of ownership in corporations.

2

What are primary and secondary markets for financial instruments? Primary markets are markets in which newly issued financial instruments are purchased. Secondary markets are markets in which previously issued financial instruments are traded.

Money Markets and Capital Markets

As discussed in more detail below, financial instruments come in a variety of maturities. For instance, there are 3-month Treasury bills and 20-year Treasury bonds. Banks and other depository financial institutions issue 6-month certificates of deposit and 2½-year time deposits. Banks make overnight loans to each other every day.

Firms, banks, and individuals trade these and other instruments in many different financial markets. Economists and traders have adopted the convention of classifying markets into two broad groups based on the maturities of the financial instruments exchanged in those markets. As we shall discuss in the next chapter, maturities of financial instruments influence the interest yields of those instruments. Thus, separating financial markets by maturity is a way of grouping together sets of markets whose interest rates tend to be closely linked.

money market Market for a financial instrument with a maturity of less than one year.

Money Markets The term **money markets** refers to markets for financial instruments with short-term maturities of less than one year. The money markets include markets for short-maturity Treasury securities such as 3- and 6-month Treasury bills. They also include markets for bank 6-month certificates of deposit, which is the category that includes most of the large certificates of deposit included in the M3 measure of money discussed in Chapter 1.

The market for repurchase agreements also is a money market. Nearly all repurchase agreements have relatively short maturities. Indeed, as we noted in Chapter 1, many repurchase agreements have 1-day maturities.

federal funds market Money market in which banks borrow from and lend to each other deposits that they hold at Federal Reserve banks.

Banks do a significant amount of money market trading in the market for repurchase agreements. In addition, they lend to each other directly in a money market known as the **federal funds market.** In this private market, banks borrow from and lend to each other deposits that they hold at Federal Reserve banks. This is why it is called a market for "federal" funds, even though the funds actually belong to the lending banks themselves. Federal funds are discussed in more detail in Chapter 4.

Money market trading typically is very active, with many buyers and sellers entering the market with offers each day. As a result, money market instruments tend to be liquid. Because there are so many potential buyers, a seller of an instrument in this market usually can find someone who is willing to buy that instrument at a mutually agreeable price.

Capital Markets   Markets for financial instruments with maturities of one year or more are **capital markets.** The reason for this name is that instruments with such long maturities are most likely to be associated directly with funding capital investment projects.

There are several capital markets. Among these are markets for stock shares of ownership in businesses and bonds issued by corporations. Also included are markets for longer term securities issued by the U.S. Treasury and agencies of the U.S. government, state and local municipal securities, home mortgages, and bank commercial and consumer loans.

Trading in capital markets certainly can be very active. But generally there are relatively fewer buyers and sellers interacting in these markets within a given day. As a consequence, capital market instruments are less liquid as compared with money market instruments.

capital market Market for a financial instrument with a maturity of one year or more.

3

What distinguishes money markets from capital markets?   Money markets are markets in which financial instruments with maturities of less than one year are traded. Instruments with maturities equal to or more than one year are traded in capital markets.

FINANCIAL INSTRUMENTS

There are many financial instruments. Each has its own special set of characteristics. It is most straightforward, however, to categorize instruments based on their maturities.

Money Market Instruments

Money market instruments have maturities shorter than one year. Because they are so widely traded, money market instruments typically are more liquid than capital market instruments. Most also are less risky because of their shorter terms to maturity. Fewer "bad" things can happen within, say, three months as compared with what might happen during a span of twenty years. And so market traders usually have fewer risk concerns about a corporation's 3-month commercial paper as compared with a 20-year corporate bond.

Because of their high liquidity and relatively low risk, money market instruments are widely held and traded by banks and other depository institutions. Large corporations and individuals hold and exchange these instruments as well. Figure 2.2 displays the relative magnitudes of holdings of these instruments.

U.S. Treasury bills Short-term debt obligations of the federal government, issued in maturities of 3, 6, or 12 months.

Treasury Bills   Most money market traders regard **U.S. Treasury bills** as the most liquid money market instrument. Treasury bills are short-term debt obligations of the federal government. The government issues them in maturities of 3, 6, or 12 months.

Traders also view Treasury bills as very safe assets. After all, if the government really feels that it needs to pay them off, it can always raise

---

FIGURE 2.2   Holdings of Money Market Instruments

Treasury bills, commercial paper, and certificates of deposit are the predominant instruments of the money markets. *Source:* Board of Governors of the Federal Reserve System, *Federal Reserve Bulletin* and HG(301) Statistical Release, 1996.

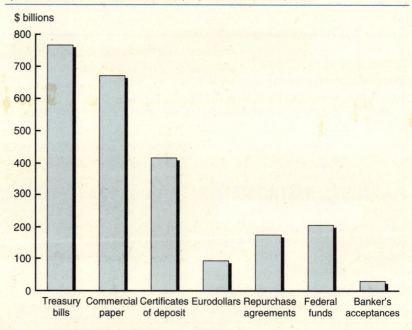

taxes. It is this taxing authority of the government that makes most individuals regard Treasury bills as having extremely little risk.

Commercial Paper

Commercial Paper Banks, corporations, and finance companies often need to obtain short-term funding. One way to obtain such funds is to issue **commercial paper,** which is a short-term debt instrument. For businesses, commercial paper has become an important substitute for borrowing directly from banks.

commercial paper A short-term debt instrument issued by businesses in lieu of borrowing from banks.

Certificates of Deposit

Certificates of Deposit Banks also raise short-term funds by issuing **certificates of deposit (CDs).** Most CDs are short-term time deposits with maturities of six months, although banks also issue CDs with longer maturities. At one time, certificates of deposit were *nonnegotiable,* meaning that the original purchaser could not sell them without incurring interest penalties. Since 1961, however, banks have issued *negotiable CDs.* They now are traded actively in a secondary money market.

certificates of deposit (CDs) Time deposits issued by banks and other depository institutions, many of which are negotiable instruments traded in secondary markets.

Eurodollars

Eurodollars As you learned in Chapter 1, dollar-denominated deposits in banks located outside the United States are Eurodollar deposits. These deposits may be in foreign banks or in foreign branches of American banks. Many of these deposits are negotiable. In effect, a Eurodollar deposit amounts to a type of CD that is held outside the United States.

Repurchase Agreements

Repurchase Agreements As defined in Chapter 1, a repurchase agreement is a contract to sell a financial asset with the understanding that the seller will buy back the asset at a later date and, typically, at a higher price. This means that effectively the seller of the asset *borrows* from the buyer. And so a repurchase agreement amounts to a very short-term loan. Most repurchase agreements have maturities ranging between one and fourteen days. Banks and large corporations are active traders in the market for repurchase agreements.

Federal Funds

Federal Funds When banks borrow from or lend to one another, the funds they trade are federal funds. These are privately owned funds but are held on deposit at Federal Reserve banks. Many federal funds loans have maturities of one day, though maturities of a week or two are not uncommon. The interest rate at which federal funds are exchanged is the *federal funds rate.* As you will learn in Chapter 13, the federal funds rate is a closely watched indicator of Federal Reserve monetary policy.

Banker's Acceptances

Banker's Acceptances A **banker's acceptance** is a bank loan that typically is used by a company to finance storage of or shipment of goods. These instruments commonly arise from international trade arrangements. They are traded in secondary money markets.

banker's acceptance A bank loan typically used by a company to finance storage or shipment of goods.

Capital Market Instruments

The maturities of capital market instruments exceed one year. Financial instruments with both intermediate-term (1–10 year) maturities and long-term (more than 10 year) maturities are included in this category.

As compared with money market instruments, capital market instruments are regarded as being somewhat more risky. They are also less liquid than money market instruments. Figure 2.3 shows the relative amounts of holdings of capital market instruments.

equities Shares of ownership, such as corporate stock, issued by business firms.

dividends Periodic payments to holders of firms' equities.

Equities   Business **equities** are shares of ownership, such as common stock, that corporations issue. Owners of equities are *residual claimants* on the income and net worth of a corporation. This means that all holders of the corporation's debt must be paid before the equity owners. The key advantage of equity ownership, however, is that the rate of return on equities varies with the profitability of the firm. Equities typically offer **dividends,** which are periodic payments to holders that are related to the corporation's profits.

FIGURE 2.3   Holdings of Capital Market Instruments

Mortgage instruments and Treasury notes and bonds are key capital market instruments. *Source:* Board of Governors of the Federal Reserve System, *Federal Reserve Bulletin*, 1996.

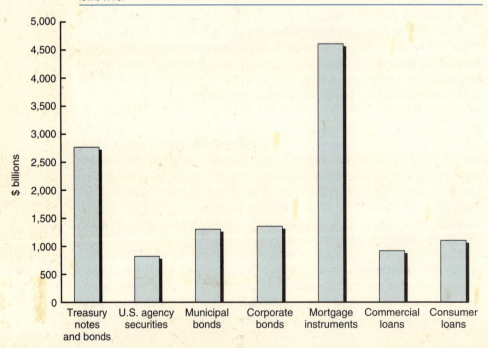

Because corporations are ongoing concerns as long as they remain profitable, equities that they issues have no stated maturities. Hence, they are long-term financial instruments and are classified among capital market instruments.

Corporate Bonds

Corporate Bonds   Corporations may wish to fund capital expansions by borrowing instead of by issuing stock. One way to borrow is by issuing **corporate bonds,** which are long-term debt instruments. A typical corporate bond pays a fixed amount of interest twice each year until maturity. Some corporate bonds are *convertible*, meaning that the holder has the right to convert them into a certain number of equity shares prior to maturity. Corporations that offer such a convertibility feature usually do so to make the bonds more attractive to potential buyers.

corporate bonds Long-term debt instruments of corporations.

Another feature that can make corporate bonds attractive to potential holders is the degree of liquidity that they offer, as compared with equities. Corporate bonds typically are liquid instruments because they are traded in secondary markets. Most corporations that issue these bonds must have a high credit rating to encourage secondary market trading.

U.S. Treasury Notes and Bonds

U.S. Treasury Notes and Bonds   These are long-term debt instruments issued by the U.S. Treasury. Treasury notes have maturities that range from 1 to 10 years, and Treasury bonds have maturities in excess of 10 years. Because these financial instruments have low risk they are traded widely in secondary markets. This makes them the most liquid capital market instrument.

Securities of U.S. Government Agencies

Securities of U.S. Government Agencies   These are long-term debt instruments issued by a variety of federal agencies. For instance, one agency called the Government National Mortgage Association (GNMA, or Ginnie Mae) issues securities backed by the value of household mortgages that it holds.

Municipal Bonds

Municipal Bonds   Long-term securities issued by either state or local governments are called **municipal bonds.** An attractive feature of these bonds for many holders is that the interest payments typically are free of federal income tax. Consequently, the stated interest rates on such bonds are lower than the rates on corporate bonds.

municipal bonds Long-term debt instruments issued by state and local governments.

Mortgage Loans and Mortgage-Backed Securities

Mortgage Loans and Mortgage-Backed Securities   Long-term loans to individual homeowners or to businesses for purchases of land and buildings are **mortgage loans.** Most mortgage loans are made initially by savings banks, savings and loan associations, and commercial banks.

mortgage loans Long-term loans to individual homeowners or to businesses for purchases of land and buildings.

These depository institutions sell many of the mortgage loans they initiate to other institutions. The purchasing institutions, which include GNMA and other governmental or quasi-governmental agencies, fund

mortgage-backed security
Financial instruments whose return is based on underlying returns on mortgage loans.

their mortgage purchases by issuing **mortgage-backed securities.** These are financial instruments whose returns are derived from the underlying returns on the mortgage loans held by the issuer, such as GNMA. The existence of secondary markets for mortgage-backed securities makes mortgage loans more liquid instruments because depository financial institutions that initiate such loans can then sell them to other institutions, such as GNMA.

Commercial and Consumer Loans   Long-term loans made by banks to businesses are **commercial loans.** Long-term loans that banks and other institutions, such as finance companies, make to individuals are **consumer loans.** Until recently there were not many secondary markets for these loans, and so they traditionally have been the most illiquid capital market instruments. As we shall discuss in Chapter 9, however, banks have worked in recent years to increase the liquidity of the loans that they make.

commercial loans   Long-term loans made by banks to businesses.

consumer loans   Loans that banks and other institutions make to individuals.

4

What are the main types of financial instruments? Key money market instruments include U.S. Treasury bills, commercial paper, bank certificates of deposit, Eurodollar deposits, and federal funds loans. The most important capital market instruments include business equities, corporate bonds, U.S. Treasury securities and other securities issued by federal government agencies, municipal bonds, mortgage loans, and consumer and business loans.

The money market and capital market instruments above are among the most important of financial instruments. There are many others, however, as you will learn. For the moment, we shall turn our attention to institutions that specialize in trading, holding, or even creating such instruments.

FINANCIAL INTERMEDIATION

When individual savers allocate some of their saving to a business by purchasing a corporate bond, they effectively make a direct loan to the business. That is, they assist in the *direct finance* of the capital investment that the business desires to undertake.

But the process of financing such endeavors is not always so direct. Consider, for instance, what may happen if the saver also purchases a long-term time deposit issued by a banking firm. The bank, in turn, may use these funds, together with those of other deposit holders, to buy corporate bonds issued by the same business. In this instance, the saver has *indirectly financed* business capital investment. The bank, in turn, has *intermediated* the financing of the investment.

Figure 2.4 illustrates the difference between direct and indirect finance. In the case of direct finance, a financial intermediary such as a bank plays no role. A saver lends directly to parties who undertake investment. Under indirect finance, however, some other institution channels the funds of savers to those who wish to make capital investments.

This latter process of indirect finance, which is the most common way in which funds are channeled from saving to investment, is **financial intermediation.** Institutions that serve as the middlemen in this process are *financial intermediaries.* These intermediaries exist solely to take the funds of savers and redistribute those funds to the ultimate borrowers.

Asymmetric Information

Why should savers wish to channel their funds through some other institution instead of lending them directly? Most economists agree that one key reason is the presence of *asymmetric information* in financial markets.

financial intermediation   Indirect finance through the services of an institutional middleman who channels funds from savers to those who ultimately make capital investments.

FIGURE 2.4   Indirect Finance Through Financial Intermediaries

Savers who provide funds directly in exchange for financial instruments of companies undertake *direct finance* of the capital investments of those companies. Financial intermediaries make *indirect finance* possible by issuing their own financial instruments, using the funds they obtain from savers to finance capital investments of businesses.

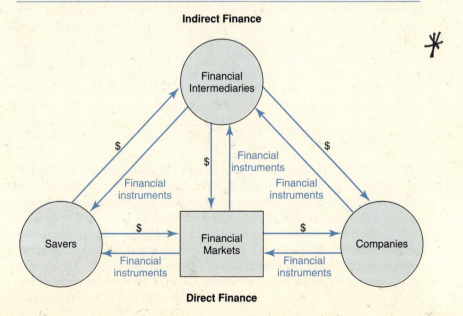

Suppose that you have an opportunity to purchase a high-yield municipal bond issued by a city that is 800 miles from where you live. As we shall discuss later, one reason that such a bond may have a high yield is that the city is undertaking a risky investment project. For instance, the town may be planning to use the funds to develop a trash-recycling and trash-incineration program that has uncertain financial prospects. Unless you happen to be an expert on the economics of trash recycling and incineration, it would be very difficult for you to evaluate the true riskiness of the municipal bond. This would make it difficult for you to compare the yield on this bond with yields on alternative financial instruments.

In contrast, the city that issues the municipal bond likely has much more information about the prospects of its program for dealing with its trash. It may be that the prospects are very good for long-term economic success. Or it may be that the program has been launched primarily for short-term political gains that the city's mayor and town council expect to reap from efforts to please environmentally conscious voters. Either way, the city that issues the municipal bond has information about its risk that you do not possess. Any time one party in a financial transaction has information not possessed by the other party, **asymmetric information** exists.

asymmetric information
Possession of information by one party in a financial transaction but not by the other party.

Adverse Selection
In the situation discussed above, the city has information that you do not have as you contemplate whether or not to purchase its municipal bond. Suppose the city's leaders know at the outset that the long-term prospects for the city's recycling/incineration program are not good. Yet they also wish to make an investment in such a program because they think voters would like it. The city's leaders would know that their bond may have *adverse,* or bad, consequences for those, such as you, who purchase their bonds. This problem of asymmetric information is **adverse selection.** This is the tendency for those who desire funds for unworthy projects to be the most likely to want to borrow or to issue debt instruments. The existence of such poor-quality instruments can make people less willing to lend to or hold debt instruments issued by those seeking to finance high-quality projects.

adverse selection   The likelihood that those who desire to issue financial instruments have in mind using the funds they receive for unworthy, high-risk projects.

Moral Hazard
Suppose, however, that the leadership of the city issuing the municipal bond has a good-faith intention to operate the city's recycling and incineration program in a profitable manner. Yet after the city sells the bonds, an election produces a new set of leaders who permit the program to become inefficient and unprofitable. This would raise your risk of not receiving promised yields on the city's municipal bond. The possibility that a borrower might engage in behavior that increases risk after a loan has been made or a debt instrument has been purchased is **moral hazard.** That is, after the financial market

moral hazard   The possibility that a borrower might engage in more-risky behavior after a loan has been made.

transaction has been made, the borrower might increase the riskiness of the instrument the lender holds, thereby acting "immorally" from the perspective of the lender.

Certainly, one way for you to deal with this problem would be to make several 800-mile trips to initially assess and then to continue to monitor the situation. By acquiring as much direct information as you could, you would reduce the asymmetry of information about the municipal bond's prospects. This would reduce the extent of both the adverse selection and the moral hazard problems that you face as a potential purchaser of the city's municipal bond.

But doing this could be very costly to you. First, you would have to pay direct costs to make the trips. In addition, you would incur opportunity costs because you could better use your time in other ways.

Benefits of Financial Intermediation

Financial intermediaries exist to save you and other potential holders of financial instruments from incurring such costs. These institutions cannot eliminate the adverse selection and moral hazard problems that stem from asymmetric information. What they can do, however, is specialize in collecting information about the prospects of financial instruments and in monitoring the performance of those who issue such instruments.

For instance, intermediaries could specialize in checking up on the prospects of municipal bonds that cities issue for trash disposal and recycling programs. This would reduce the extent of potential adverse selection problems in the market for municipal bonds. They also could keep tabs on the performances of such programs in various cities. Cities that did not manage their programs well would have a difficult time issuing municipal bonds in the future because intermediaries would be less likely to purchase them. The potential for moral hazard problems thereby would be reduced. Investment banks involved in assisting municipalities with new bond issues try to perform such a function.

In secondary markets, brokers perform similar functions. They provide their clients with updated information that they are able to glean from their daily presence in these markets. This enables their clients to overcome somewhat the asymmetric information problems they otherwise would face.

Economies of Scale

Another important reason why financial intermediaries exist is **economies of scale.** Some intermediaries make it possible for many people to pool their funds together. This increases the size, or *scale*, of the amounts of funds that are saved. It also enables intermediaries to simultaneously manage the larger pool of funds for all individuals. This can reduce the average fund management costs below those that

economies of scale The reduction that can be achieved in the average cost of managing funds by pooling savings together and spreading the management costs across many savers.

individuals would incur if they all were to manage their savings alone. When intermediaries manage funds for many people at a lower average cost than people would face individually, then financial economies of scale exist. Several financial institutions, such as pension funds and mutual funds, largely owe their existence to their ability to provide such cost savings to individual savers.

5

Why do financial intermediaries exist?   One reason that they exist is to address problems arising from asymmetric information, which can cause adverse selection and moral hazard problems. Another reason is financial economies of scale, or the ability to spread costs of managing funds across large numbers of savers.

POLICY NOTEBOOK
Digital Banking Is on the Rise

In 1990 there were 80,000 automatic teller machines (ATMs) in the United States. Today there are closer to 120,000. ATMs may not be the cornerstone of digital banking, however. Banks and other financial institutions are gearing up to offer personal-computer-based home banking and banking that uses telephones with screens and keyboards attached.

Policymakers are finding that digital banking is less available in low-income areas at the same time that the traditional branch bank is disappearing from such neighborhoods. One study in New York City found that in the South Bronx there was one ATM per 120,000 residents. In contrast, in middle- and high-income parts of Manhattan, there is one ATM for about every 8,000 residents. Obviously, as home banking with personal computers increases, there will be fewer lower-income consumers using such services. Why?

Because such consumers rarely own personal computers. Essentially they may be shut out of such services.

As ATMs become more sophisticated—some allow customers to open accounts and apply for loans—the lack of them in low-income areas limits such residents' access to the banking world.

Some policy solutions to this problem involve placing personal computers in facilities such as public libraries and schools. Additionally, financial institutions that are worried about crime around ATMs have started to install them in drug stores, supermarkets, and next to police stations.

For Critical Analysis: *What type of regulations might be made to ensure that electronic banking services are available in low-income neighborhoods?*

FINANCIAL INSTITUTIONS

Financial circumstances for various firms and individuals vary widely. This is why there are so many different kinds of financial instruments and markets. Likewise, there are many ways for asymmetric information to exist in financial markets. In large measure, this helps to explain why there are many different types of firms that serve as financial intermediaries. These firms typically are called *financial institutions*.

Insurance Companies

Many people worry that they might have an automobile accident someday. As a result, they seek to insure themselves against the risk of financial losses arising from property damages or personal injuries. But the likelihood of experiencing an automobile accident depends on a number of factors. One is where a person lives. If you live in a city that experiences many accidents, then the likelihood of an accident is higher than if you live in a small rural community.

    Another factor, naturally, is how safely you drive, on average. Your own behavior determines how safely you drive. This leads to an asymmetric information problem. You know if you are generally a safe driver, but whoever might offer you insurance does not. Hence, there is an adverse selection problem for those who would provide you and others with insurance policies. In addition, once you are covered by insurance you might feel "safer" and drive a little less safely as a result. And so there also is a moral hazard problem in insurance.

Why Insurance Companies Exist

Insurance companies specialize in trying to limit adverse selection and moral hazard problems unique to efforts to insure against possible future risks of loss. They issue *policies*, which are promises to reimburse the holder for damages suffered in the event of a "bad" event, such as an auto accident. Certainly, individual households could insure other households. But such direct interaction in insurance usually is limited to informal agreements. For instance, parents often stand ready to lend financial assistance to their young-adult children who experience "bad" events. So in a sense they offer insurance. But parents also have a lot of information about their children's behavior that others do not have. Most of us, therefore, ultimately must turn to insurance companies that specialize in dealing with the asymmetric information problems associated with insuring risks.

Types of Insurance Companies

There are two basic kinds of insurance companies. *Life insurance companies* charge premiums for policies that insure people against the financial consequences associated

insurance companies Financial institutions that specialize in trying to limit adverse selection and moral hazard problems by insuring against future risks of loss.

with death. They also offer specialized policies, called **annuities,** which are financial instruments that guarantee the holder fixed or variable payments at some future date.

　　Property and casualty insurers insure against risks relating to property damage and liabilities arising from injuries or deaths caused by accidents or adverse natural events. Property and casualty insurance companies offer policies that insure individuals and businesses against possible property damages or other financial losses resulting from injuries or deaths sustained as a result of accidents, adverse weather, earthquakes, and so on.

Pension Funds

Pension funds are institutions that specialize in managing funds that individuals have put away to serve as a nest egg when they retire from their jobs and careers. Part of what many workers get paid is in the form of contributions that their employers make to such funds.

　　The key specialty of pension funds is creating financial instruments called *pension annuities.* These are similar to the annuities offered by life insurance companies. But life insurance annuities usually are intended as supplements to a person's income at some fixed point in the future, whether or not a person is working at the time. In contrast, pension annuities apply only to the future event of retirement. Most people regard pension annuities as their main source of future income after retirement.

　　Why do people use the services of pension funds instead of saving funds on their own? One reason certainly is asymmetric information, because those who operate pension funds may be better informed about financial instruments and markets than those who save for retirement. But there is another reason that probably is more important. This is the existence of economies of scale. Many people would find it very costly to monitor the instruments they hold on a day-by-day basis throughout their lives. Pension funds do this for many people at the same time, thereby spreading the costs across large numbers of individuals.

　　Pension funds hold about $750 billion in financial instruments. While they do hold some money market instruments, they are major holders of capital market instruments such as corporate equities and corporate bonds. Consequently, as members of the baby-boom generation (those born within the decade or so after World War II) have contributed more funds to their pension funds, these funds have taken a larger role in the capital markets.

　　Pension funds exist to protect future pensioners from losses on their retirement savings. Hence, they specialize in monitoring capital market instruments for risks that might arise from adverse selection and moral hazard problems experienced by issuers. They also develop special packages of pension plans. For instance, the main pension fund for college teachers, TIAA-CREF, offers a plan that is based on holdings of financial instruments issued by environmentally friendly companies.

Mutual Funds

A **mutual fund** is a mix of redeemable instruments, called "shares," in the fund. These shares are claims on the returns on financial instruments held by the fund, which typically include equities, bonds, government securities, and mortgage-backed securities.

Mutual funds usually are operated by investment companies, which charge shareholders fees to manage the funds. The popularity of mutual funds increased considerably during the 1970s and 1980s. During those two decades, the assets held in these funds grew by a factor of over 60 times the initial level. Indeed, by 1996 there were over 7,000 mutual funds in operation.

One reason for the growth of mutual funds is that many shareholders believe that investment company managers know best how to balance risks and returns on their behalf. This makes shareholders willing to pay fees for the managers' knowledge and skills.

There is a more important reason, however, for the growth of mutual funds. Like pension funds, mutual funds take advantage of financial economies of scale. Mutual fund shareholders typically pay lower fees to investment companies than they might have to pay brokers to handle their funds on a personal basis. The reason is that mutual fund managers can spread the costs of managing shareholders' funds across all the shareholders.

mutual fund   A mix of financial instruments managed on behalf of shareholders by investment companies that charge fees for their services.

Depository Financial Institutions

Another type of financial institution that is able to deal with asymmetric information is a *depository financial institution* or, for short, *a depository institution*. As we discussed in Chapter 1, one key characteristic of a depository institution is that its liabilities include various deposits, such as time, savings, or checking accounts. But most depository institutions also specialize in asymmetric information problems specific to loan markets.

Commercial Banks   Many different kinds of businesses would like to borrow to finance capital investments. While some investment projects have excellent potential payoffs, others are much riskier.

As noted previously, typically only the most creditworthy businesses can borrow by issuing corporate bonds or commercial paper. This is because the bonds or paper they issue are perceived to have a low risk of loss. Other companies may be as creditworthy, but they are smaller and less well known to potential purchasers. In addition, these good credit risks may not be easy to distinguish from other firms of similar size that are not as well managed.

MANAGEMENT NOTEBOOK
Cutthroat Competition in Mutual Funds

Investment companies market mutual funds primarily through brokers. But many investment companies also use the services of salespeople who convince brokers to market specific mutual funds to potential shareholders. These people are called mutual fund wholesalers. Much as many insurance companies maintain sales forces to pitch their particular insurance products, a number of mutual funds have depended on wholesalers to convince brokers to pitch their funds.

The 1990s have been tough on wholesalers. As the number of mutual funds grew in the 1980s, the number of wholesalers grew as well. Stock and bond prices also rose considerably in the early 1990s, which helped spur further growth in mutual funds. Beginning in 1994, however, bond and stock prices fell off. Suddenly the 7,400 mutual funds in existence by 1995 found themselves competing for each other's business rather than adding new business stemming from growth. Indeed, some mutual funds began to run losses. They were unable to raise their fees because they would lose business to other competitors.

Who gained from this situation? Brokers did. Indeed, some mutual funds began handing over some of their management fees directly to brokers simply to induce them to continue steering business their way. Who lost? Besides mutual fund managers who surrendered part of their fee incomes to brokers, mutual fund wholesalers were the big losers. They found themselves working harder to sell to brokers at the same time that mutual funds were seeking to cut their commissions.

By 1996 the ranks of wholesalers were thinning. One reason for this was that many left wholesaling work. The other was that mutual funds that did not depend on wholesalers gained at the expense of those who had built their businesses using such sales forces. While 63 percent of mutual funds used the services of wholesalers in 1993, by 1996 only about 50 percent did so. Mutual fund wholesaling may be a dying profession.

For Critical Analysis: *Why were mutual funds that had never used wholesalers at a competitive advantage relative to those that had used wholesalers as a sales force?*

This exposes potential lenders to possible risks arising from adverse selection. It can be hard to tell which firms are safe to lend to as compared to those that may misdirect loans into projects likely to fail. Likewise, after a loan is granted, there is always a chance of a change in management or, even more, lax management by existing directors of a firm. And so there also is a moral hazard problem associated with loans to business.

This is one key reason why commercial banks play an important role in financial markets. **Commercial banks** are depository financial institutions that specialize in sizing up the risk characteristics of loan applicants. They collect information about the creditworthiness of individuals and businesses seeking loans and try to limit the institutions'

commercial banks Depository financial institutions that offer checking deposits and which specialize in making commercial loans.

exposure to adverse selection difficulties. In addition, commercial banks keep tabs on the customers to whom they lend money. This limits the risks arising from moral hazard.

Savings Banks and Savings and Loan Associations   A large chunk of capital investment in the United States is residential housing. **Savings banks** and **savings and loan associations** are depository institutions that traditionally have specialized in extending mortgage loans to individuals who wish to purchase homes. Just as there is asymmetric information in business loan deals, a person who wants a mortgage loan may or may not be a good risk. That person also may or may not become a bad risk after receiving the loan. And so there are adverse selection and moral hazard problems specific to mortgage lending.

savings bank   Another type of depository institution that has specialized in mortgage lending.

savings and loan associations   A type of depository institution that traditionally has specialized in making mortgage loans.

GLOBAL NOTEBOOK

Immigrants Bring Money Pools to the United States

All the financial institutions we have discussed in this chapter and elsewhere are ones that you can look up in the Yellow Pages or the White Pages of the cities and towns where they are located. There is another financial institution, which comes from "the old country," whose phone number you will never be able to look up. It is a money pool—a method of raising cash for weddings, homes, businesses, and college tuition. It can also be called a rotating savings and credit association. The way it works is easy—a group of individuals pool a specified amount of money every week (or month). After a specified time, the members of the pool who have contributed are assigned a number. Each number is written on an individual piece of paper which is put into a hat. A number is pulled from the hat. The lucky winner goes home with tax-free, interest-free money to use as a down payment on a house or to buy a car or to send a child to college.

Money pools are called *ekub* by Ethiopians, *pasanaqu* by Bolivians, *tong-tine* by Cambodians, and *keh* by Koreans.

In some pools the money is apportioned not by lottery but by need. In all pools, it is the members of the group who decide how much and how often to pay into the pool and how the money will be apportioned. Each member collects the kitty only once, then the saving cycle begins again.

Some of the reasons why newly arrived immigrants turn to money pools is because they do not want to pay interest on a bank loan or, as is often the case, they have no credit history and therefore do not qualify for such a loan.

For Critical Analysis: *The benefit to someone who collects the money pool early on is obvious. Those who collect later, in contrast, apparently receive no advantage over putting such saving into a savings account where it would earn interest. Why do you think people are nonetheless willing to become part of money pools?*

credit union   A type of depository institution that accepts deposits from and makes loans only to a closed group of individuals who are eligible for membership.

Credit Unions
A **credit union** is a depository institution that accepts deposits from and makes loans only to a closed group of individuals. To be a member of a credit union and eligible for its services, a person usually must be employed by a business with which the credit union is affiliated. Most credit unions specialize in making consumer loans, although some have branched into the mortgage loan business.

Finance Companies

finance company   A financial institution that specializes primarily in making loans to relatively high-risk individuals and businesses.

A **finance company** also specializes in making loans to individuals and businesses. Finance companies, however, do not offer deposits. Instead, they use the funds invested by their owners or raised through issuing other instruments to make loans to households and small businesses. Many finance companies specialize in making loans to people and firms that depository institutions regard as high risks.

GOVERNMENT-SPONSORED FINANCIAL INSTITUTIONS

In 1996 the United States government spent over $125 billion more than it received in revenues. To fund this deficit in its accounts, the federal government borrowed heavily in the money and capital markets. In recent years Congress and the executive branch have made efforts to reduce deficit spending. Nevertheless, the government likely will remain the single largest borrower in the United States for some years to come.

The federal government also operates or subsidizes some of the largest financial institutions in the United States. Among these are the Federal Financing Bank (FFB), which coordinates federal and federally assisted borrowing. The FFB intermediates loans issued by government agencies, using funds made available by the U.S. Treasury from tax receipts. For instance, tax dollars involved in loans by government agencies to private companies or municipalities. They are used to make loans to certain small businesses or for bailouts of large companies, such as Chrysler Corporation, or of cities, including Washington, D.C. Nevertheless, FFB transactions typically do not show up on the official government budget. Hence, they do not appear in official deficit figures.

Several other financial institutions operate outside the formal budgetary structure of the government yet are very much governmental institutions. Some of these specialize in agricultural lending. Among these, the most important are the Banks for Cooperatives, Federal Intermediate Credit Banks, and Federal Land Banks. All three organizations are supervised directly or indirectly by the Farm Credit Administration.

The government also sponsors four institutions that support the housing market. These are the Federal National Mortgage Association (FNMA, or Fannie Mae), the Government National Mortgage Association (GNMA, or Ginnie Mae), the Federal Home Loan Bank system (FHLBs), and the Federal Home Loan Mortgage Corporation (FHLMC, or Freddie Mac). These agencies make mortgage markets more liquid by buying mortgages with funds that they raise by selling mortgage-backed securities.

We shall have more to say about this latter group of government-sponsored financial institutions in later chapters. Indeed, Chapters 4 and 5 are devoted to developing a significantly greater understanding of financial instruments and institutions. The first step in this process, however, will be to learn much more about interest rates and the calculation of interest yields on various types of instruments.

6

What are the main types of financial institutions? These include depository institutions, such as commercial banks, savings banks, savings and loan associations, and credit unions. Other important financial institutions include insurance companies, pension funds, mutual funds, and finance companies. Brokers, investment banks, and various government-sponsored institutions round out the main groupings of financial institutions.

SUMMARY

1. **The Main Economic Function of Financial Markets:** Financial markets channel funds of savers to individuals and businesses who wish to make capital investments.

2. **Primary and Secondary Markets for Financial Instruments:** Primary markets are financial markets in which newly issued financial instruments are bought and sold. Secondary markets are markets in which individuals and firms exchange previously issued financial instruments.

3. **Money Markets Versus Capital Markets:** Money markets are financial markets in which individuals and firms exchange financial instruments with maturities of less than one year. Capital markets are markets for instruments with maturities equal to or greater than one year.

4. **The Main Types of Financial Instruments:** The most important money market instruments are U.S. Treasury bills, commercial paper, bank certificates of deposit, Eurodollar deposits, and federal funds loans. Key capital market instruments include business

equities, corporate bonds, U.S. Treasury securities and other securities issued by federal government agencies, municipal bonds, mortgage loans, and consumer and business loans.

5. **Financial Intermediaries:** Financial intermediaries help to reduce problems stemming from the existence of asymmetric information in financial transactions. Asymmetric information can lead to adverse selection and moral hazard problems. Financial intermediaries also may permit savers to benefit from economies of scale, which is the ability to reduce average costs of managing funds by pooling funds and spreading costs across many savers.

6. **The Main Types of Financial Institutions:** One main group is depository institutions, which include commercial banks, savings banks and savings and loan associations, and credit unions. In addition, there are insurance companies, pension funds, mutual funds, finance companies, brokers, investment banks, and government-sponsored institutions such as the Federal Financing Bank, agricultural credit institutions, and mortgage financing institutions.

QUESTIONS AND PROBLEMS

1. Recently, a Florida county commissioner and her husband, a Washington lobbyist, were indicted for securities laws violations. Allegedly they sought to improve the terms under which the county could issue new municipal bonds. Suppose this information had not come to light and had made the municipal bonds more risky than they otherwise might have seemed to potential buyers. Would this have been an example of adverse selection or of moral hazard? Explain your reasoning.

2. Commercial banks make various types of loans, such as loans to businesses, but they also offer a variety of deposit options, such as checking accounts. Do you believe that, in the absence of asymmetric information problems in lending, commercial banks might cease to exist? Or would there still be a place for commercial banks? Explain your reasoning.

3. Both life insurance companies and pension plans issue annuities. Can you explain how it is that they, nonetheless, are generally regarded as fundamentally different types of financial intermediaries?

4. During the early years following the formation of the United States, its first Treasury secretary, Alexander Hamilton, worked hard to develop conditions in which secondary financial markets could emerge and grow. Based on this chapter's discussion, can you rationalize Hamilton's actions?

5. Commercial banks and savings banks issue loans and hold other financial instruments that yield returns in the form of interest income. These banks pass on some of this interest income to their depositors through the interest rates they pay on deposits they maintain. Bank deposits also are federally insured. Mutual fund shares, in contrast, are not federally insured. Would you expect that mutual fund shares would pay higher or lower returns to shareholders, as compared with rates of return on bank deposits? Explain your reasoning.

P A R T 00

The Financial System

3

Interest Rates

KEY QUESTIONS

1. Why must we compute different interest yields?

2. How does risk cause market interest rates to differ?

3. Why do market interest rates vary with differences in terms to maturity of financial instruments?

4. What is the real interest rate?

5. How are the interest yields on bonds issued in different countries related?

6. What interest rates are the key indicators of financial market conditions?

O
n February 2, 1995, television network news reports showed frantic activity in the bond market. On that day, the Fed announced that it would raise its target for a key interest rate, known as the federal funds rate, by one-half percent, to 6 percent. That seemingly small increase in one particular interest rate in the economy sent shock waves to the bond markets, not only in America but around the world. Traders everywhere were shouting orders to sell their bonds because bond prices were falling.

On Thursday, July 7, 1995, just the opposite situation occurred. Television network financial news reports showed similar frantic activity in the bond markets. But this time traders were shouting out orders to buy bonds with rising prices. Interest rates rise and interest rates fall. So do bond prices. In the late 1970s interest rates rose by several percentage points, whereas in the early 1990s they fell by several percentage points. The interesting questions are: (1) Why do traders behave as they do in the above examples? and (2) How are interest rates and bond prices related?

These are the two key questions that will be answered in this chapter. Along the way you will see how inflation affects interest rates. You will also discover that interest rates in other countries are affected by and affect interest rates in the United States. The first order of business, though, is to understand what interest rates are and how you can calculate interest yields.

CALCULATING INTEREST YIELDS

By holding financial instruments such as loans or bonds, savers and financial institutions extend credit to the individuals or firms that have issued the instruments. The amount of credit extended is the **principal** amount of the loan or the bond. Those who hold financial instruments do so because they earn income from the issuers in the form of *interest*. The percentage return earned is the **interest rate.** For a simple interest, 1-year loan, for instance, the interest rate is equal to the ratio of total interest during the year to the principal of the loan. That is, the interest rate is equal to the amount of interest divided by the loan principal.

The interest return from holding a financial instrument is its yield to the owner. Therefore, this interest return often is called the *interest yield*.

principal   The amount of credit extended when one makes a loan or purchases a bond.

interest rate   The percentage return, or percentage yield, earned by a financial instrument.

Different Concepts of Interest Yields

There are different ways to think about the interest yields on financial instruments. The most important of these are nominal yield, current yield, and yield to maturity.

Nominal Yield   Suppose that a bond is issued in an amount of $10,000, with an agreement to pay $700 in interest every year. The annual payment of $700 is the bond's annual **coupon return.** This is simply the fixed amount of interest that the bond yields each year. It is called a coupon return because many bonds used to have coupons that actually represented titles to interest yields.

The **nominal yield** on a bond is equal to

$$i_N = C/F$$

where i_N is the nominal yield, C is the coupon return, and F is the face amount of the bond. The annual nominal yield of a $10,000 bond with a $700 coupon return is equal to $700/$10,000 = 0.07, or 7 percent.

Current Yield   The current price of a bond in the secondary market typically is not the face value of the bond. Bonds often sell at prices that differ from their face values. For this reason, anyone contemplating a bond purchase often is interested in the **current yield** of a bond. This is equal to

$$i_C = C/P.$$

where i_C denotes current yield, C is the coupon return, and P is the current market price of the bond.

For instance, the current market price of a bond with a face value of $10,000 might be $9,000. If the coupon return on the bond is $700 per year, then the annual current yield on this bond is equal to $700/$9,000 = 0.078, or 7.8 percent.

Yield to Maturity   A bond's yield to maturity is the rate of return that would be earned if the bond were held until maturity. Calculating this yield can be complicated. The reason is that the bond's market price and its face value normally differ.

Typically, bonds are sold at a *discount,* meaning that a bond's selling price is below its face value. Hence, there is an automatic capital gain if the bond is held to maturity. A **capital gain** is simply a rise in the value of a financial asset when it is redeemed or sold as compared to its market value when it was purchased. At the same time, the bond pays a coupon return. The yield to maturity must account for both the capital gain and the coupon returns that a bond yields to its owner.

Calculating Discounted Present Value

To understand the interplay between coupon returns and capital gains in calculating bond yields, consider a specific example—a bond whose maturity is three years. The bond's face value is $10,000. Its annual coupon return is $700. Hence, its nominal yield per year is $700/$10,000 = 0.07, or 7 percent.

Discounted Present Value   To compute the yield to maturity on this bond, we need to determine its market price. Note the bond's owner receives three payments: $700 after the first year, $700 after the second year, and $10,700 (the principal plus the third year's interest) after the third year. Therefore, the amount that the buyer is willing to pay for this bond must equal the value of these payments, from the buyer's perspective, at the time she purchases the bond.

Today's value of payments to be received at future dates is the **discounted present value** of those payments. Discounted present value is a key financial concept because it enables us to determine how much a future sum is worth from the perspective of today, given current market interest rates. As shown in Table 3.1, the future value of a

discounted present value
The value today of a payment to be received at a future date.

TABLE 3.1   Present Values of a Future Dollar

This table shows how much one dollar received a given number of years in the future would be worth today at different rates of interest. For instance, at an interest rate of 8 percent, one dollar to be received 20 years from now would have a value of less than 25 cents, and one dollar to be received 40 years from now is worth less than 5 cents.

	COMPOUNDED ANNUAL INTEREST RATE				
Year	**3%**	**5%**	**8%**	**10%**	**20%**
1	.971	.952	.926	.909	.833
2	.943	.907	.857	.826	.694
3	.915	.864	.794	.751	.578
4	.889	.823	.735	.683	.482
5	.863	.784	.681	.620	.402
6	.838	.746	.630	.564	.335
7	.813	.711	.583	.513	.279
8	.789	.677	.540	.466	.233
9	.766	.645	.500	.424	.194
10	.744	.614	.463	.385	.162
15	.642	.481	.315	.239	.0649
20	.554	.377	.215	.148	.0261
25	.478	.295	.146	.0923	.0105
30	.412	.231	.0994	.0573	.00421
40	.307	.142	.0460	.0221	.000680
50	.228	.087	.0213	.00852	.000109

How does this work?

dollar falls more quickly at higher interest rates. This means that the present value of the payments a bond owner will receive also declines as interest rates increase, thereby reducing the amount that a buyer would be willing to pay for the bond. Consequently, you must understand how to calculate the discounted present value of a future payment before you can understand how to compute bond prices.

In the case of the specific bond in our example, with a face value of $10,000 and three annual payments of $700 each, suppose that the prevailing market interest rate is $i = 0.08$, or 8 percent. Consider the first year's return on the bond, which is $700. Note that saving $648.15 for one year at an interest rate of 8 percent would yield an amount of $648.15 (the initial amount) plus 0.08 times $648.15 (the interest), or $648.15 times the factor 1.08. But this works out to be $700. This means that from today's perspective, a $700 payment one year from now at a market interest rate of 8 percent is worth $648.15. Consequently, $648.15 is the discounted present value of $700 one year from now at an interest rate of 8 percent. This amount is equal to the future payment of $700 divided by the sum of $1 + 0.08$, or $700/(1.08)$ = $648.15. This implies that a formula for calculating the discounted present value of a payment to be received a year from now is

$$\text{Discounted present value} = \frac{\text{Payment one year from now}}{(1 + i)}$$

But the bond also pays another $700 two years after the time of purchase. Note that at a market interest rate of 8 percent, holding $600.14 for two years would yield $700. The reason is that if one begins with $600.14 and saves it for one year, the accumulated saving would be equal to $600.14 times 1.08, or $648.15. If we then save $648.15 for another year, we end up with $648.15 times 1.08, or $700. This tells us that the discounted present value of $700 to be received two years from now is equal to $700/[(1.08)(1.08)] = $700/(1.08)^2 = $600.14.

From the logic of this calculation, we can see that a general formula for computing the discounted present value of a payment to be received n years in the future is

$$\text{Discounted present value} = \frac{\text{Payment } n \text{ years from now}}{(1 + i)^n}$$

In our 2-year example, $n = 2$, $i = 0.08$, and the payment two years from now is $700.

At the end of the third year, the buyer of the 3-year bond receives the principal of $10,000 and a final $700 interest payment. We can calculate the discounted present value of this amount using the formula above:

Discounted present
value of $10,700
three years hence $= \dfrac{\$10,700}{(1.08)^3}$

$$= \$8,494.00$$

That is, today's value of the $10,700 that the bondholder will receive when the 3-year bond matures is $8,494.00.

The Market Price of a Bond We now can calculate the market value, or price, of this 3-year bond. It is how much the buyer would perceive it to be worth at the purchase date, given a market interest rate of 8 percent. This is the sum of the discounted present values of the payments received in each of the three years. Using the calculations that we have done above, this is

[handwritten: X.926   X.857.   X.794]

Price of 3-year bond $= \dfrac{\$700}{(1.08)} + \dfrac{\$700}{(1.08)^2} + \dfrac{\$10,700}{(1.08)^3}$

$$= \$648.15 + \$600.14 + \$8,494.00$$

$$= \$9,742.29$$

And so $9,742.29 is the market value of the 3-year bond with a face value of $10,000 when the market interest rate is 8 percent.

Calculating the Yield to Maturity   *[handwritten: NO!]*

So what is the yield to maturity on this bond? To figure this out, we could write our formula in a different way:

$$\$9,742.29 = \dfrac{\$700}{(1 + i_m)} + \dfrac{\$700}{(1 + i_m)^2} + \dfrac{\$10,700}{(1 + i_m)^3}$$

where i_m represents the yield to maturity for the bond. We already know that the value for i_m that fits this expression is 0.08. Hence, the yield to maturity for this bond is 8 percent (the market interest rate).

It is easy for us to see that 8 percent is the yield to maturity because we constructed the problem with simple numbers. But note that if the market price on the left-hand side of the equation were to rise from $9,742.29 to some larger number, the value for i_m would have to fall. Calculating i_m then would require solving a cubic equation! For this reason, traders typically use programmed calculators or bond yield tables when evaluating yields to maturity on long-term bonds.

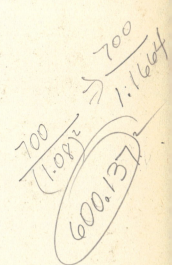

[handwritten margin notes: 700, 1.1664, 700/(1.08)², 600.137]

Yields on Nonmaturing Bonds
Some financial instruments never mature. For instance, one instrument issued by the British government, a *consol*, pays a fixed coupon return forever. When the bearer dies, she can pass this instrument on to heirs, who receive the coupon return each year during their lifetimes.

perpetuity A bond with an infinite term to maturity.

Such a financial instrument is a perpetual bond, or **perpetuity**. This is simply a bond that never matures. It turns out that the discounted present value of the coupon returns on a perpetuity is easy to calculate. It is equal to the coupon return divided by the market interest rate. For instance, if the annual coupon return is equal to an amount, C, and the annual interest rate is i, then the price of a perpetuity is

$$\text{Perpetuity price} = C/i$$

We let you prove this in problem 1 at the end of the chapter.

This simple formula illustrates an important fact:

Existing bond prices are inversely related to interest rates.

Suppose that the fixed coupon return is $500 per year. If the market interest rate is 5 percent, then the price of the perpetuity is equal to $500/(0.05) = $10,000. But if the market interest rate rises to 7 percent, then the perpetuity's price is equal to $500/(0.07) = $7,142.86. A rise in the interest rate causes the bond's price to decline.

This makes sense. When the market interest rate rises, the discounted present value of each year's coupon return declines. But the bond's price is the sum of the discounted present values of the coupon returns for all the years. Hence, the bond's price must fall.

Consols are not especially commonplace today. But recall that corporate equities also have no maturity date. Equities, therefore, are a type of perpetuity. Indeed, we might think of the annual dividend on a share of stock as the "coupon return," and the annual rate of return derived from the share as the "interest rate." Then to get a rough approximation of the share price, the dividend is divided by the stock's annual rate of return. The reasons why this is only an approximation is that stock dividends typically are not constant over time and that rates of return on shares also vary from year to year.

Yields on Treasury Bills
The Wall Street Journal and other newspapers publish data on money market interest rates each day. Figure 3.1 displays a sample "Money Rates" column from the *The Wall Street Journal*. Listed in the column are interest rates on various money market instruments, such as federal funds, commercial paper, bank certificates of deposit, and Treasury bills.

The published Treasury bill rates are based on a fictitious 360-day year. They are calculated from the equation,

MONEY RATES

Thursday, April 11, 1996

The key U.S. and foreign annual interest rates below are a guide to general levels but don't always represent actual transactions.

PRIME RATE: 8.25%. The base rate on corporate loans posted by at least 75% of the nation's 30 largest banks.

DISCOUNT RATE: 5%. The charge on loans to depository institutions by the Federal Reserve Banks.

FEDERAL FUNDS: 5 1/2% high, 5 1/4% low, 5 1/4% near closing bid, 5 3/8% offered. Reserves traded among commercial banks for overnight use in amounts of $1 million or more. Source: Prebon Yamane (U.S.A.) Inc.

CALL MONEY: 7%. The charge on loans to brokers on stock exchange collateral. Source: Dow Jones Telerate Inc.

COMMERCIAL PAPER placed directly by General Electric Capital Corp.: 5.32% 30 to 44 days; 5.31% 45 to 76 days; 5.29% 77 to 89 days; 5.30% 90 to 119 days; 5.31% 120 to 270 days.

COMMERCIAL PAPER: High-grade unsecured notes sold through dealers by major corporations: 5.42% 30 days; 5.41% 60 days; 5.41% 90 days.

CERTIFICATES OF DEPOSIT: 4.73% one month; 4.77% two months; 4.85% three months; 5.03% six months; 5.27% one year. Average of top rates paid by major New York banks on primary new issues of negotiable C.D.s, usually on amounts of $1 million and more. The minimum unit is $100,000. Typical rates in the secondary market: 5.40% one month; 5.45% three months; 5.59% six months.

BANKERS ACCEPTANCES: 5.28% 30 days; 5.26% 60 days; 5.27% 90 days; 5.28% 120 days; 5.29% 150 days; 5.29% 180 days. Offered rates of negotiable, bank-backed business credit instruments typically financing an import order.

LONDON LATE EURODOLLARS: 5 1/2% - 5 3/8% one month; 5 1/2% - 5 3/8% two months; 5 17/32% - 5 13/32% three months; 5 9/16% - 5 7/16% four months; 5 9/16% - 5 7/16% five months; 5 5/8% - 5 1/2% six months.

LONDON INTERBANK OFFERED RATES (LIBOR): 5 1/2% one month; 5 9/16% three months; 5 21/32% six months; 5 15/16% one year. The average of interbank offered rates for dollar deposits in the London market based on quotations at five major banks. Effective rate for contracts entered into two days from date appearing at top of this column.

FOREIGN PRIME RATES: Canada 6.75%; Germany 3.35%; Japan 1.625%; Switzerland 3.875%; Britain 6.25%. These rate indications aren't directly comparable; lending practices vary widely by location.

TREASURY BILLS: Results of the Monday, April 8, 1996, auction of short-term U.S. government bills, sold at a discount from face value in units of $10,000 to $1 million: 5.03% 13 weeks; 5.19% 26 weeks.

OVERNIGHT REPURCHASE RATE: 5.33%. Dealer financing rate for overnight sale and repurchase of Treasury securities. Source: Dow Jones Telerate Inc.

FEDERAL HOME LOAN MORTGAGE CORP. (Freddie Mac): Posted yields on 30-year mortgage commitments. Delivery within 30 days 8.14%, 60 days 8.19%, standard conventional fixed-rate mortgages; 5.125%, 2% rate capped one-year adjustable rate mortgages. Source: Dow Jones Telerate Inc.

FEDERAL NATIONAL MORTGAGE ASSOCIATION (Fannie Mae): Posted yields on 30 year mortgage commitments (priced at par) for delivery within 30 days 8.19%, 60 days 8.24%, standard conventional fixed rate-mortgages; 6.75%, 6/2 rate capped one-year adjustable rate mortgages. Source: Dow Jones Telerate Inc.

MERRILL LYNCH READY ASSETS TRUST: 4.78%. Annualized average rate of return after expenses for the past 30 days; not a forecast of future returns.

FIGURE 3.1 Money Rates

Each day *The Wall Street Journal* reports data on money market interest rates. *Source:* Reprinted by permission of *The Wall Street Journal*, © 1996 Dow Jones & Company, Inc. All Rights Reserved Worldwide.

$$i_T = \frac{F - P}{F} \times \frac{360}{n}$$

where i_T is the T-bill rate, F is the face value, P is the price paid, and n is the number of days to maturity.

Consider the 13-week (3-month, or 91-day) T-bill rate of 5.03 percent. The face value of a T-bill is $10,000, and so F in the equation is equal to $10,000. The number of days to maturity, n, is equal to 91. The average price at which T-bills sold on this date was $9,872.98. Using the formula then gives us

$$i_T = \frac{F - P}{F} \times \frac{360}{n}$$

$$= \frac{\$10,000 - \$9,872.98}{\$10,000} \times \frac{360}{91}$$

$$= \frac{\$127.02}{\$10,000} \times 3.96$$

$$= 0.0503$$

And so the published T-bill yield was 5.03 percent.

Of course, a year really lasts 365 days. A T-bill yield based on the true 365-day year is called the **coupon yield equivalent** (also known as the *bond equivalent yield*). This is an annualized T-bill rate that can be compared with annual yields on other financial instruments. To calculate the coupon yield equivalent, we use the formula,

coupon yield equivalent   An annualized T-bill rate that can be compared with annual yields on other financial instruments.

$$i_E = \frac{F - P}{F} \times \frac{365}{n}$$

where i_E is the coupon yield equivalent for the T-bill. Hence, the coupon yield equivalent corresponding to the published yield of 5.76 percent in Figure 3.1 would have been

$$i_E = \frac{\$10,000 - \$9,872.98}{\$10,000} \times \frac{365}{91}$$

$$= \frac{\$127.02}{\$10,000} \times 4.01$$

$$= 0.0509$$

The coupon yield equivalent for this T-bill is 5.09 percent. It is higher than the published yield of 5.03 percent because it takes into account the actual number of days in the year.

Traders have a practical use for the formula for the coupon yield equivalent. They use it to determine the yields associated with quoted prices on T-bills being traded in the secondary T-bill market. For instance, suppose that an individual holds a 13-week T-bill for 30 days but then offers to sell it at a price of $9,920. To figure out the yield over the remaining 61 days to maturity, a potential buyer would use the coupon yield equivalent formula. P would be set equal to $9,920 and n equal to 61:

$$
\begin{aligned}
i_E &= \frac{F - P}{F} \times \frac{365}{n} \\[2mm]
&= \frac{\$10,000 - \$9,920}{\$10,000} \times \frac{365}{61} \\[2mm]
&= \frac{\$80}{\$10,000} \times 5.98 \\[2mm]
&= 0.0478
\end{aligned}
$$

This means that the approximate annual yield on this T-bill at the quoted price would be 4.78 percent. The purchaser could compare this yield with those on other available instruments. Then he could decide if he wished to pay a price of $9,920.

1

Why must we compute different interest yields?   The reason is that interest yields differ depending on the basis of comparison used to evaluate the yield and on the period of time the financial instrument will be held. This leads to different concepts of interest yields and several ways to calculate yield.

THE RISK STRUCTURE OF INTEREST RATES

Examining the "Money Rates" column in Figure 3.1 reveals that market interest rates differ across financial instruments. Two key factors account for the differences in rates. One is the term to maturity. The other is risk. Following standard practice, we consider each separately. In reality, however, it is the two factors together that cause market interest rates to differ.

The **risk structure of interest rates** refers to the relationship among yields on financial instruments that have the *same maturity* but differ on the basis of default risk, liquidity, and tax considerations.

risk structure of interest rates   The relationship among yields on financial instruments that have the same maturity but differ because of variations in default risk, liquidity, and tax rates.

Default Risk

default risk The chance that an individual or a firm that issues a financial instrument may be unable to honor its obligations to re-pay the principal and/or to make interest payments.

There is always the possibility that an individual or a firm that issues a financial instrument may be unable to honor obligations to pay off the principal and/or interest. This means that any bond is subject to some degree of **default risk.**

The United States government has the power to raise taxes to pay off its bonds. If needed, it could even print money to do so. For U.S. Treasury securities, therefore, default risk is very small. The chance of default on a newly issued 20-year Treasury bond, for instance, is meager.

But consider a 20-year corporate bond. Even if the company that issues it today has a very solid credit rating, there is always a chance that its fortunes could change within a few years. Ten or fifteen years from now the company could be near bankruptcy. And so the perceived default risk for the corporate bond is greater than for the 20-year Treasury bond. As a result, individuals and firms will hold corporate bonds as well as Treasury bonds only if the corporate bond pays a sufficiently higher return to compensate for the greater risk of default.

The Risk Premium The amount by which the corporate bond rate exceeds the Treasury bond rate because of greater default risk is the

GLOBAL NOTEBOOK

Reducing Default Risk by Banking on Italian Cheese

It takes about 1,500 pounds (700 kilos) of milk to make one drum of Grana Padana cheese, which is produced on the outskirts of Cremona in northern Italy. Each drum of cheese has to age for 12 to 18 months before it is ready to be sold. Northern Italian farmers in this small community rarely feel financially able to tie up their capital for that long. And banks in the area aren't too keen about taking unsecured promissory notes (financial instruments) in exchange for lending the cheese farmers money. One enterprising bank, Cassa di Risparmio delle Province Lombarde, otherwise known in the region as Cariplo, has figured out how to

help these dairy farmers. The Cariplo takes the maturing cheese as collateral for loans to farmers and puts the cheese in a unique type of bank vault. The bank has over 30 billion Italian lira worth of cheese as a security for about 18 billion lira worth of loans. These cheese banks started over 40 years ago. Farmers depositing their cheese at the bank receive about 70 percent of the wholesale value of the cheese as a loan.

For Critical Analysis: *What might stop other banks from agreeing to accept cheese as collateral to reduce the risk of default on loans?*

corporate bond's **risk premium.** Suppose that just before the company issues 20-year bonds, word spreads that prospects for one of its products have worsened. Those who were contemplating purchasing its bonds now are unwilling to do so unless the company offers an even higher interest rate relative to the 20-year Treasury bond rate. The risk premium on the bond will rise because the chance that the company may default is greater than it was before the news.

Rating Securities   Default risk clearly is an important consideration in bond purchases. Two predominant institutions that rate the risks of bonds are the Standard and Poor's Corporation and Moody's Investors Services. Just as professors assign grades to students for relative performance, Standard and Poor's and Moody's rate the relative default risks of bonds issued by corporations.

These institutions assign several grades to differentiate low, medium, and high risks. Yet both use two broad risk categories. **Investment-grade securities** are those judged to have a fairly low risk of default.

So-called **junk bonds** have significantly greater default risk. Naturally, the risk premiums for junk bonds are larger than those for investment grade securities. One person's junk, of course, is another's treasure. To an individual who very much dislikes risk, junk bonds truly are "junk," hence the name. But to one who appreciates high yields and is willing to take on risk, junk bonds are worth holding.

Liquidity

Another reason why corporate bond rates exceed interest rates on U.S. Treasury bonds of identical maturities is that corporate bonds are less liquid financial instruments. Recall that the secondary market for Treasury securities is well developed and typically has much trading activity. This means that the holder of a Treasury bond knows that the Treasury bond will be easy to sell if the need arises.

The secondary market for corporate bonds, however, is not always as active. Sometimes holders who wish to sell corporate bonds enter the secondary market only to find that few stand ready to buy. Hence, a corporate bond may be more difficult to "unload" for cash at a later date. For this reason a corporate bond is less liquid than a U.S. Treasury bond.

This means that (all other factors held constant) bondholders typically will require a higher interest rate on corporate bonds relative to the rate on a Treasury bond of the same maturity. The higher corporate bond rate compensates the bondholders for the chance that they might have more trouble selling the corporate bonds at a future date.

The Liquidity Premium   A difference in default risk is not the only reason why bond rates may diverge. There also is a *liquidity premium*

risk premium   The amount by which one instrument's yield exceeds another's because the latter is riskier and less liquid.

investment-grade securities Bonds with relatively low default risk.

junk bonds Bonds with relatively high default risk.

that accounts, in part, for the difference in interest rates on two bonds with identical maturities.

Distinguishing between risk and liquidity premiums is a difficult proposition, however. For instance, junk bonds are less liquid than investment-grade securities because the secondary market for the latter typically is more active. But a key reason for there having less secondary market trading of junk bonds is that fewer individuals are willing to incur the risk holding them.

Liquidity and Risk   Clearly, there is an interaction between default risk and liquidity in determining bond interest rate differences. Hence, the term risk premium typically is used broadly to characterize interest rate differences resulting from *both* default risk and liquidity considerations. When people refer to a risk premium on one bond relative to another, they really are talking about a difference that arises because one bond has higher risk of default *and* because it is less liquid.

Figure 3.2 charts average annual yields on long-term U.S. Treasury bonds, the highest-rated, long-term investment-grade securities (Moody's Aaa), and medium-rated investment grade securities

---

FIGURE 3.2   Long-Term Bond Yields

Treasury bonds have greater liquidity and lower default risk compared with corporate bonds, and so they consistently have lower yields. In addition, the highest-rated corporate bonds (Moody's Aaa) have lower default risk compared with the lowest-rated corporate bonds (Moody's Baa), and so the highest-rated corporate bonds also have lower yields. *Source:* Board of Governors of the Federal Reserve System, *Federal Reserve Bulletin*, various issues.

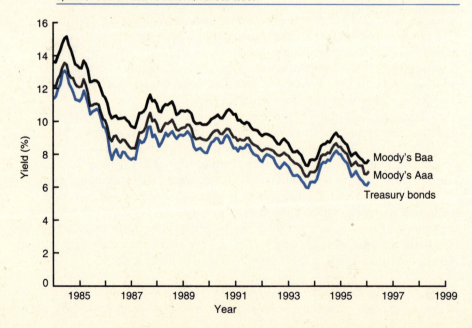

(Moody's Baa). All three are plotted on a monthly basis for the period 1984 to 1996. The interest yields on both classes of corporate bonds always are greater than the yield on Treasury bonds. The reason is that Treasury bonds have much lower default risk and are very liquid. Likewise, the presence of a risk premium is apparent in a comparison of the rates on medium- versus highly rated corporate bonds.

Tax Considerations

A final reason why bonds with identical maturities may have different interest yields is that tax laws treat some bonds differently than others. Individuals typically are not required to pay either federal or state taxes on interest earnings from municipal bonds. This means that the pretax and after-tax yields on municipal bonds are identical. But interest earnings on Treasury bonds are subject to federal taxation, which depresses their after-tax yields.

For this reason, higher pretax interest rates are required to induce individuals to hold both Treasury bonds and municipal bonds simultaneously. As a result, pretax (market) Treasury bond yields tend to exceed yields on municipal bonds, as shown in Figure 3.3.

FIGURE 3.3   Municipal and Treasury Bond Yields

Interest earnings from municipal bond are exempt from federal taxation, but interest earnings on Treasury bonds are subject to federal taxation. Consequently, Treasury bond yields exceed the yields on municipal bonds. *Source:* Board of Governors of the Federal Reserve System, *Federal Reserve Bulletin,* various issues.

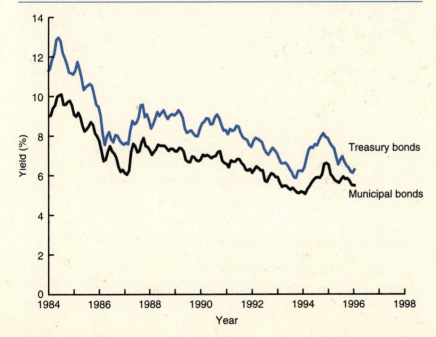

2

How does risk cause market interest rates to differ? Differences in degrees of default risk and liquidity result in risk premiums that affect the yields on financial instruments. Risk premiums differ across instruments, which is one key reason why yields differ. Some instruments also are taxed at different rates, which causes their market rates to diverge.

THE TERM STRUCTURE OF INTEREST RATES

term structure of interest rates The relationship among yields on financial instruments with identical risk, liquidity, and tax characteristics, but differing terms to maturity.

The **term structure of interest rates** refers to the relationship among yields on financial instruments that possess the *same risk, liquidity, and tax characteristics*, but have differing terms to maturity. Even if bonds with different maturities are identical in every other respect, their yields typically diverge.

The Yield Curve

yield curve A chart depicting yields on bonds with the same risk characteristics but differings yields to maturity.

This divergence of interest yields across different terms to maturity is easily seen by plotting a **yield curve.** This is a chart that depicts the relationship among yields on similar bonds with different terms to maturity. Figure 3.4 shows a typical yield curve for Treasury securities. *The Wall Street Journal* plots the Treasury security yield curve in each day's issue.

The yield curve in Figure 3.4 slopes upward. This is the normal shape of a yield curve. Interest yields usually are greater as the term to maturity increases. But sometimes yield curves are downward-sloping. This happened, for instance, in the late 1970s. When the yield curve slopes downward, it is said to be an **inverted yield curve.** In such a situation, interest yields decline as the term to maturity rises.

inverted yield curve A yield curve that slopes downward.

Why isn't the yield curve simply horizontal? That is, why do interest yields vary with the term to maturity? Economists have offered three basic theories that seek to address this question. These are the segmented-markets theory, the expectations theory, and the preferred-habitat theory.

Segmented-Markets Theory

segmented-markets theory A theory of the term structure of interest rates that views bonds with differing maturities as nonsubstitutable, so that their yields differ because they are determined by separate markets.

According to the **segmented-markets theory** of the term structure of interest rates, bonds with differing terms to maturity are not perfectly substitutable. As a result, they are traded in separate markets. Each market determines its own unique yield.

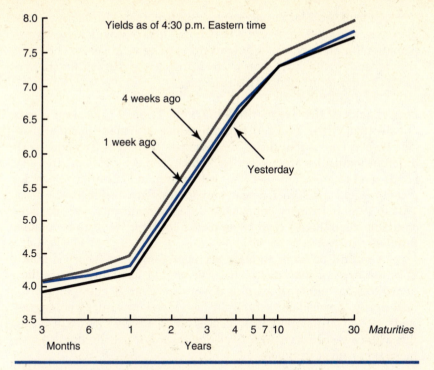

FIGURE 3.4 The Yield Curve

This is a typical, upward-sloping yield curve for U.S. Treasury securities. *Source:* Federal Reserve and U.S. Commerce Department.

Matching Maturities For instance, depository institutions such as commercial banks offer time deposits with relatively short terms to maturity of one to three years. They often wish to "match" these with assets such as Treasury bonds with similar 1- to 3-year maturities, and so they buy such Treasuries. Pension funds, in contrast, have pension liabilities with much longer terms to maturity. Consequently, it is natural that they should wish to hold Treasury bonds with 10- to 20-year maturities. According to the segmented markets theory, bond yields will reflect such differences in trading patterns.

Suppose that initially the yields across Treasury bonds with differing maturities are the same. If banks decide to hold more 1- to 3-year-maturity Treasury bonds, however, the demand for such bonds will rise, causing an increase in their market price. As a result, the market yield on the bonds will fall. If all other factors are unchanged, the yields on Treasury bonds with 1- to 3-year maturities will be lower than those on Treasury bonds with 10- to 20-year maturities. That is, market yields will differ across terms to maturity, just as we see when we plot yield curves. Indeed, in this example the yield curve slopes upward.

A nice feature of the segmented markets theory is that it can explain why the yield curve is not horizontal. It also provides a ready explanation for an upward- or downward-sloping yield curve: The slope will depend on the differences in conditions in the markets for shorter- versus longer-term financial instruments.

Drawbacks of the Segmented-Markets Theory   But simplicity is not always a virtue. There are two difficulties with the segmented-markets theory. One is that the theory assumes that Treasury bonds with different maturities are not perfect substitutes, yet yields on Treasury bonds tend to move together. This can be seen in Figure 3.5, which depicts the yields on 1-year, 5-year, and 30-year Treasury securities from 1984 to 1996. If Treasury bonds with different maturities were not substitutable, then there would be no reason for their yields to be related. But they clearly are.

A second problem with the segmented-markets theory is that it does not explain why the yield curve should have any natural tendency to slope either upward or downward over its entire range. Yet historically, the yield curve typically has sloped upward. Over long periods, downward-sloping yield curves are relatively rare occurrences. But when a yield curve does slope downward, it usually does so over most, if not all, of its range.

FIGURE 3.5   Treasury Security Yields

The yields on Treasury securities tend to be higher for longer maturities. Nevertheless, the yields on Treasury securities with different maturities tend to move together over time. *Source:* Board of Governors of the Federal Reserve System, *Federal Reserve Bulletin,* various issues.

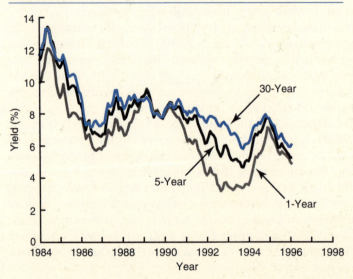

Expectations Theory

The **expectations theory** addresses the first difficulty with the seg-mented-markets hypothesis. It explains how expectations about future yields can cause yields on instruments with different maturities to move together. In addition, it can provide insight into why the yield curve may systematically slope upward or downward.

expectations theory A the-ory of the term structure of interest rates that views bonds with differing matu-rities as perfect substitutes, so that their yields differ only because short-term in-terest rates are expected to rise or fall.

Choosing Between Bonds with Differing Maturities   The essen-tial elements of the expectations theory can be understood by consider-ing a situation in which an individual saver faces a 2-year planning horizon. The saver has two alternatives. One is to place funds in a 2-year bond for the two years. This bond yields an annual interest rate of I. The other alternative is for the saver to hold 1-year bonds for each of the two years. Under this alternative, the saver would place funds in a 1-year bond for the first year at an interest rate of i_1. The saver then would place the principal plus the interest accumulated during the first year in another 1-year bond during the second year. At the beginning of the two periods, when the saver must make her decision, she expects that the in-terest rate on the 1-year bond during the second year will be i_2^e.

This individual is willing to hold *either* 1-year or 2-year bonds only if she anticipates that her rate of return across the two years is the same. This is true if

$$I = (i_1 + i_2^e)/2$$

That is, the annual interest rate on the 2-year bond (I) must equal the av-erage expected annual interest rate from holding 1-year bonds ($i_1 + i_2^e$). If the 2-year bond rate falls below the expected average of 1-year rates, then the saver would hold only 1-year bonds. But if the 2-year bond rate were above the expected average of 1-year rates, then the saver would hold only 2-year bonds. Consequently, the above condition must be met in the bond markets to induce this saver and others to hold bonds of both maturities.

Suppose that the 1-year bond pays $i_1 = 0.06$ during the first year and is expected to yield $i_2^e = 0.08$ during the second year. In this case the 2-year bond rate (I) will be the average of 0.06 and 0.08, which is $(0.06 + 0.08)/2 = 0.07$. Panel (a) of Figure 3.6 on page 70 shows the yield curve for this example. The *actual* interest yield for the 1-year bond is $i_1 = 0.06$, or 6 percent. For the 2-year bond the interest yield is higher, at $I = 0.07$, or 7 percent. Therefore, the yield curve relating bonds with 1- and 2-year maturities slopes upward.

Now suppose that for some reason savers anticipate that 1-year bond rates will fall sharply. Specifically, suppose that the expectation of the 1-year bond rate during the second period falls to $i_2^e = 0.04$, or 4 percent. If the 1-year bond rate is still $i_1 = 0.06$, then the 2-year bond rate must change to induce savers to be willing to hold either 1- or 2-year bonds. The new 2-year bond rate will have to be

$$I = (i_1 + i_2^e)/2 = (0.06 + 0.04)/2 = 0.05$$

The 2-year bond now will yield 5 percent per year. Panel (b) of Figure 3.6 shows the new yield curve for 1- and 2-year bonds. It slopes downward.

What has changed to cause the yield curve to be downward-sloping, or inverted? Before the 1-year bond rate was expected to *rise* from 6 percent to 8 percent. This caused the yield curve in panel (a) of Figure 3.6 to slope upward. But now the 1-year bond rate is expected to *fall* from 6 percent to 4 percent. This causes the yield curve's slope to be inverted, as is seen in panel (b). The yield curve now slopes downward.

Strengths and Weaknesses of the Expectations Theory   Clearly, the expectations theory is not as simple as the segmented-markets theory. But it has a very important virtue: It potentially can explain why yield curves slope upward or downward. An upward-sloping yield curve indicates a general expectation by savers that short-term interest rates will rise. A downward-sloping yield curve indicates a general expectation that short-term interest rates will decline.

FIGURE 3.6   Sample Yield Curves for the Expectations Theory

Panel (a) shows the upward-sloping yield curve that arises under the expectations theory of the term structure of interest rates. If the 1-year bond rate is expected to rise from 6 to 8 percent, then the 2-year bond rate is the average of the current and expected 1-year bond rates, or 7 percent. Panel (b) displays the downward-sloping yield curve that results if the 1-year bond rate is expected to fall from 6 to 4 percent. In this case the 2-year bond rate is the average of the current and expected 1-year bond rates, or 5 percent.

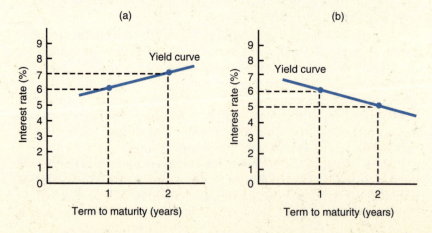

There is a problem with the expectations theory, however. Yield curves usually slope upward. According to the expectations theory, this would imply that savers almost *always* expect short-term interest rates to rise. But over long periods interest rates typically are as likely to fall as they are to rise. This means that the expectations theory cannot be a complete theory of the term structure of interest rates.

The Preferred-Habitat Theory

The **preferred-habitat theory** combines elements of the segmented-markets theory and the expectations theory. According to the segmented-markets theory, bonds whose maturities differ are not at all substitutable. The expectations theory, in contrast, assumes that bonds with different maturities are *perfect* substitutes. This is why savers would hold both 1- and 2-year bonds only if their expected returns were equal.

According to the preferred-habitat theory, bonds with different maturities are substitutable, but only imperfectly. Under this theory, savers generally have a slight preference to hold bonds with shorter maturities. Recall from Chapter 2 that money market trading is broader and more active than trading in capital markets. Consequently, money market instruments—bonds with shorter maturities—are more liquid. This greater liquidity of short-term bonds can make them somewhat more attractive to savers than longer-term bonds. And so savers can "prefer the habitat" of money markets just as animals prefer their own special habitat or location in the wild.

preferred-habitat theory A theory of the term structure of interest rates that views bonds as imperfectly substitutable, so that yields on longer-term bonds must be greater than those on shorter-term bonds, even if short-term interest rates are not expected to rise or fall.

The Term Premium   To induce savers to hold longer-term bonds, the returns on those bonds actually must slightly exceed the returns on shorter-term bonds. That is, savers would need to earn a **term premium** on longer-term bonds. This would compensate savers for holding long-term bonds as well as short-term bonds.

Consequently, the preferred-habitat theory modifies the expectations hypothesis by adding a term premium. Using our 2-year example, the rate on the 2-year bond now would be

$$I = TP + \frac{i_1 + i_2^e}{2}$$

where TP is the term premium for the 2-year bond.

For instance, suppose that $i_1 = i_2^e = 0.06$, so that savers expect the 1-year bond rate to remain at 6 percent for both years. Suppose also that savers have a strong preference to hold 1-year bonds and that the term premium is $TP = 0.01$, or 1 percent. This 1 percent premium in the long-term yield is what would be needed to induce savers to hold 2-year bonds as well as 1-year bonds. The 2-year bond rate would be

term premium   An amount by which the yield on a long-term bond must exceed the yield on a short-term bond to make individuals willing to hold either bond if they expect short-term bond yields to remain unchanged.

$$I = TP + \frac{i_1 + i_2^e}{2}$$

$$= 0.01 + \frac{0.06 + 0.06}{2}$$

$$= 0.01 + 0.06 = 0.07$$

Under these conditions the 2-year bond rate is equal to 7 percent even though the 1-year bond rate is expected to remain at 6 percent over both years. This implies that the yield curve relating the yields on 1- and 2-year bonds slopes upward, as shown in panel (a) of Figure 3.7. The yield curve slopes upward even though the 1-year bond rate is not expected to rise. Hence, over a long period in which interest rates are equally likely to rise or fall, the yield curve typically will have a positive slope.

Explaining Changes in the Slope of the Yield Curve   Now suppose that all the numbers in our example stay the same except for the expectation of the 1-year bond rate for the second year. Let's suppose that savers expect the 1-year bond rate to fall from 6 percent in the first year to 4 percent in the second. Then the preferred-habitat theory

---

FIGURE 3.7   Sample Yield Curves for the Preferred-Habitat Theory

Panel (a) shows the upward-sloping yield curve that arises under the preferred-habitat theory of the term structure of interest rates. If there is a 1 percent term premium and if the 1-year bond rate is expected to remain unchanged at its current level of 6 percent, then the 2-year bond rate is the sum of the term premium and the average of the current and expected 1-year bond rates, or 1 percent + 6 percent = 7 percent. Panel (b) displays the horizontal yield curve that results if the 1-year bond rate is expected to fall from 6 to 4 percent. In this case the 2-year bond rate is the sum of the term premium and the average of the current and expected 1-year bond rates, or 1 percent + 5 percent = 6 percent.

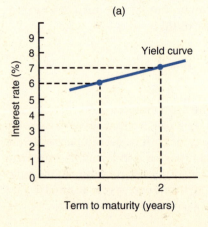

(a)

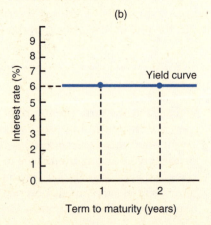

(b)

would predict that the 2-year bond rate would be

$$I = TP + \frac{i_1 + i_2^e}{2}$$

$$= 0.01 + \frac{0.06 + 0.04}{2}$$

$$= 0.01 + 0.05 = 0.06$$

Hence, the 1- and 2-year bond rates would be equal. The yield curve would be horizontal, as in panel (b) of Figure 3.7.

Using our example, this means that the only way that the yield curve could slope downward would be if the 1-year bond rate were expected to fall from 6 percent to *below* 4 percent. In contrast, if the 1-year bond rate were expected to fall only a little, say from 6 percent to 5.5 percent, the yield curve still would slope upward.

The preferred-habitat theory predicts that the yield curve typically will slope upward. This squares with the real-world facts. It also predicts that the yield curve will slope downward only in situations in which short-term interest rates are expected to decline sharply. Such situations can arise from time to time over long periods, but they nevertheless will be relatively rare. And so inverted yield curves should be observed infrequently. This is what we observe.

One feature of the preferred-habitat theory is that it enables us to infer general interest rate expectations simply by looking at a yield curve. On the one hand, if we see that a yield curve for Treasury securities is nearly horizontal or inverted, then we can surmise that most savers believe that rates on T-bills are likely to decline. On the other hand, if we observe a very steeply sloped yield curve for Treasury securities, then we can expect that most savers believe that T-bill rates are likely to rise. In the intermediate situation in which most savers do not expect short-term interest rates to change, then in contrast to the expectations theory's prediction of a horizontal yield curve, the preferred-habitat theory indicates that the Treasury security yield curve will have a fairly shallow, upward slope. In fact, this is typically what we see.

3

Why do market interest rates vary with differences in the terms to maturity of financial instruments   Yields across maturities will not be equal for two reasons. One is the expectation that short-term rates may rise or fall. Another is that short-term financial instruments generally are more liquid and less risky than longer-term instruments. Hence, a term premium is needed to induce individuals to be indifferent between holding either long-term or short-term instruments.

NOMINAL VERSUS REAL INTEREST RATES

To this point, we have only discussed interest rates in *current-dollar* terms. There is a problem with this, however. Inflation can erode the value of interest received as a financial instrument matures. Any individual must take this into account when evaluating how much to save.

nominal interest rate   A rate of return in current dollar terms that does not reflect anticipated inflation.

For instance, suppose that a saver can earn a stated current-dollar or **nominal interest rate** of $i = 0.04$ (4 percent) on each dollar that he allocates to a 1-year bond. Suppose also that the saver expects that prices of goods and services will rise by a factor of $p^e = 0.03$ (3 percent) during the coming year, where p^e is the expected rate of inflation. This is the rate of inflation that he anticipates facing. Such a rate of inflation will reduce the amount of goods and services that his interest return will permit him to purchase.

That is, though he earns positive interest on the bond, the saver anticipates that inflation will eat away at that interest at the rate p^e. Hence, the **real interest rate,** or the expected inflation-adjusted interest rate, that the saver anticipates is approximately equal to

real interest rate   The anticipated rate of return from holding a financial instrument, after taking into account the extent to which inflation is expected to reduce the amount of goods and services this return could be used to buy.

$$r = i - p^e$$

$$= 0.04 - 0.03 = 0.01$$

where r denotes the real interest rate. In terms of what his savings can buy, this saver actually can anticipate earning only 1 percent on the 1-year bond!

The real interest rate is crucial for determining *how much* individuals save. The reason is that saving is forgone consumption. This individual is likely to give up more consumption now if the real rate of return on saving is higher. This means that the real interest rate is a crucial determinant of how much a nation saves. Countries with high nominal interest rates often experience very low saving rates because expected inflation is so high. Indeed, U.S. interest rates reached double-digit levels in the 1970s, and expected inflation also was in double digits. During some intervals in that decade, real interest rates were *negative*, which strongly discouraged saving.

In deciding how to allocate saving among alternative financial instruments, however, an individual saver is safe in comparing current-dollar, or nominal, yields. After calculating the real yield on each instrument, the saver can subtract the same expected inflation rate, p^e, from each instrument's annual nominal yield. If the nominal yield on one instrument exceeds the nominal yield on the other, then so too will its real yield.

4

What is the real interest Rate?   This is the anticipated inflation-adjusted yield on a financial instrument. The real interest rate is approximately equal to the current-dollar yield less the expected rate of inflation.

INTEREST RATES IN AN INTERDEPENDENT WORLD *NO!*

Americans do not hold financial instruments issued only by local, state, or federal governments or by American corporations. Many U.S. citizens, businesses, and financial institutions also hold bonds issued by foreign governments and foreign businesses. Such bonds are not denominated in U.S. dollars. Instead, they are denominated in the currency of the nation of origin.

For instance, suppose that an American bank is considering holding either U.S. Treasury bonds or bonds issued by the government of Japan. The bonds have the same maturity. In addition, the bank views both bonds as possessing equally low risk. And so, holding other factors constant, it might view the bonds as perfect substitutes. Yet the U.S. Treasury bond has an annual interest yield of i_{US} that applies to the *dollar* denomination of the bond. In contrast, the Japanese bond has a *lower* annual interest yield of i_J that applies to the *yen* denomination of the bond.

The Exchange Rate, Depreciation, and Appreciation

How would the bank evaluate this situation? First, it must account for the different currency denominations of the bond. To do this, the bank must take into account the dollar-yen **exchange rate.** This is the dollar price of the yen, measured in dollars per yen.

Suppose that the current dollar-yen exchange rate is $0.01 per yen, or $S = \$0.01/\text{yen}$, where S denotes the current exchange rate. (Hence, $1 = 100 yen.) Note that if S were to increase, say to a value of $0.015, this would mean that it would take more dollars to obtain one yen. This would mean that the dollar would lose some of its value relative to the yen. When the dollar loses value relative to the currency of another country, such as the Japanese yen, then the dollar **depreciates.** Hence, a rise in the value of S implies a *depreciation* of the value of the dollar relative to the yen. But if the dollar depreciates relative to the yen, then the yen has **appreciated** relative to the dollar. The yen's dollar value increases with a rise in the exchange rate, S.

Suppose that the dollar depreciates relative to the yen at a rate s over time. Here, a positive value of s indicates a positive *rate of*

exchange rate   The value of one currency in terms of another.

depreciation   A decline in the value of one currency relative to another.

appreciation   A rise in the value of one currency relative to another.

depreciation of the dollar versus the yen. This would imply a fall in the value of the dollar relative to the yen. Indeed, between 1987 and 1996 the dollar depreciated relative to the yen at an average rate of 4 percent per year.

International Interest Parity

Now let's think about the decision faced by our hypothetical bank. If it holds the dollar-denominated U.S. Treasury bond, then its total return is simply the interest return i_{US} But if it holds the Japanese government bond, then it earns interest at the rate i_J. In addition, however, it anticipates that the dollar value of the yen-denominated bond will rise at an expected rate of s^e.

This bank—as well as others making a similar decision—will be willing to hold either American or Japanese government bonds only if the anticipated returns on the two are equal. This will be true when

$$i_{US} = i_J + s^e$$

To induce holdings of *both* the American and Japanese bonds, the U.S. Treasury bond rate must equal the Japanese government bond rate plus the rate at which the dollar is expected to depreciate relative to the yen.

This condition is very common-sensical. If the yen is appreciating relative to the dollar, then the dollar is depreciating relative to the yen. This means that for a dollar-denominated U.S. Treasury bond to yield a return comparable to the return on a Japanese bond, the U.S. bond's yield must be higher to compensate for any expected depreciation in the dollar relative to the yen. If s^e is positive, then potential holders of the bonds anticipate that the yen will appreciate and the dollar will depreciate. The U.S. Treasury bond's interest yield must be greater than the yield on the Japanese government bond to make up for this expected depreciation of the dollar. The amount by which the U.S. Treasury bond yield will exceed the Japanese government bond yield is equal to the rate at which the dollar is expected to depreciate relative to the yen, or s^e.

The technical name for this condition is **uncovered interest parity.** This condition applies to interest yields on bonds with identical risks and terms to maturity, but denominated in different national currencies. According to the uncovered interest parity condition, the interest rate for the bond denominated in the currency that is expected to depreciate must be the greater of the two interest rates. Or, to say it in another way, the yield of the bond denominated in the currency that is expected to depreciate must exceed the other bond's yield by the rate at which the currency is expected to depreciate.

uncovered interest parity
A condition that applies to bonds denominated in different national currencies but possessing identical risks and maturities, in which the yield on one bond is equal to the yield on the other bond plus the expected rate of depreciation of the currency in which the other bond is denominated.

5

How are interest yields on bonds issued in different countries related?   As long as the bonds share other common characteristics, uncovered interest parity will hold. This means that the yield on the bond denominated in a currency that holders anticipate will depreciate must pay a yield that exceeds the other bond's yield by the expected rate of currency depreciation.

SOME IMPORTANT INTEREST RATES

know.

There are many financial markets. Hence, there are many interest rates. Yet there are three that are especially important as barometers of conditions in financial markets.

The Federal Funds Rate

One of these key interest rates is at the shortest end of the maturity spectrum. It is the **federal funds rate.** This is the market rate on interbank loans. As you learned in Chapter 2, the term federal funds is used only because banks make the loans by transferring reserves that they hold at Federal Reserve banks. Most of these loans have maturities of one or two days, and so these are very short-term loans. Indeed, some federal funds loans have effective maturities of only a few hours.

    Because the federal funds rate is a ready measure of the price that banks must pay to raise funds, the Federal Reserve often uses it as a yardstick by which it measures the effects of its policies. Consequently, the federal funds rate is a closely watched indicator of the Federal Reserve's intentions.

    The federal funds rate reported daily in *The Wall Street Journal* (see Figure 3.1 on page 59) is really an average of rates across banks. Some banks pay lower interest rates than others to borrow federal funds because they are better credit risks. In addition, some very large banks both borrow and lend federal funds, even during the same day. These banks act as *dealers* in the federal funds market. They profit from lending federal funds at rates that slightly exceed the rates at which they borrow federal funds. Brokers also are active in the federal funds market. They match banks that need to borrow federal funds with other depository institutions that are willing to lend.

federal funds rate   A short-term (usually overnight) interest rate on interbank loans in the United States.

The Prime Rate

The **prime rate** is the rate that banks charge on the loans they make to the most creditworthy business borrowers. These are the borrowers

prime rate   The interest rate that American banks charge on loans to the most creditworthy business borrowers.

with the lowest perceived risk of default. Many other lending rates are based on the prime rate, and so it is a key indicator of conditions in loan markets.

Figure 3.8 displays the behavior of the prime rate since 1929. Note that until the 1970s the prime rate showed little variation. Since then, however, the prime rate has been less rigid. There are two likely explanations for this. One is that interest rates generally have been more volatile since the beginning of the 1970s. Another is that nationwide competition among banks has increased since that time. As a result, banks have adjusted the prime rate more quickly to variations in other market interest rates.

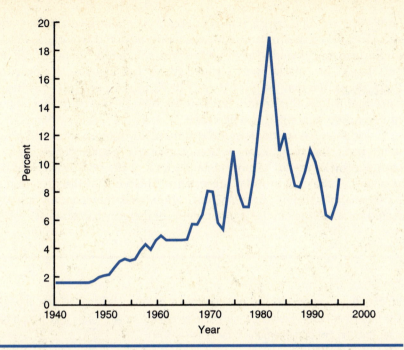

FIGURE 3.8   The Prime Rate
The prime rate has been much more variable since the 1970s. *Source: 1996 Economic Report of the President.*

The London Interbank Offer Rate (LIBOR)

In international financial markets, bonds and deposits are denominated in different currencies and pay interest yields that apply to these various currency denominations. It can become complicated for those who trade such instruments to compare interest yields for such instruments. This is particularly true in **Eurocurrency markets.** These are markets for bonds, loans, and deposits denominated in currencies of given nations, yet held and traded outside those nations' borders. The market for Eurodollar deposits is an example of a Eurocurrency market.

To assist in comparing interest rates in Eurocurrency markets, traders have adopted the convention of quoting rates on such bonds, loans, and deposits using a single interest rate as a benchmark. This benchmark rate is the **London Interbank Offer Rate,** or **LIBOR.** LIBOR is the interest rate at which six large London banks stand willing to lend to or to borrow from each other when market trading opens on a given day.

In a sense, LIBOR is the international equivalent of the American federal funds rate. It is a rough measure of the cost of funds to London

Eurocurrency markets
Markets for bonds, loans, and deposits denominated in currencies of given nations, yet held and traded outside those nations' borders.

London Interbank Offer Rate (LIBOR)   The interest rate on interbank loans traded among six large London banks.

banks that are especially active in international financial markets. Consequently, it is a useful barometer of conditions in those markets. Rates on Eurocurrency bonds, loans, and deposits therefore are measured as "markups" or "markdowns" from LIBOR. For instance, a Eurocurrency bond rate may be quoted as "LIBOR plus 1 percent." This indicates that if LIBOR currently is 5 percent, then the Eurocurrency bond rate in question is equal to 6 percent.

We shall have more to say about these key interest rates and how to interpret their movements in later chapters. In the next chapter, however, we shall provide a more detailed look at the wide variety of financial instruments in today's economy. This will set the stage for a fuller analysis of how financial institutions and the economy are affected by variations in the interest yields of these instruments.

6

What interest rates are the key indicators of financial market conditions? The three most widely watched interest rates are the federal funds rate, the prime rate, and the London Interbank Offer Rate (LIBOR).

SUMMARY

1. **Computing Different Interest Yields:** Any interest yield must have a basis of comparison, such as the principal of a loan, face value of a bond, or market price of either a loan or a bond. Additionally, the effective yield on any financial instrument depends on the remaining number of days, weeks, or months until it matures. All these factors affect the calculation of alternative yields on financial instruments. Hence, different yields must be considered.

2. **Risk and Market Interest Rates:** Risky and fairly illiquid financial instruments will be held when other less risky and more liquid instruments are available only if risk premiums are included in their yields. Therefore, yields on riskier and fairly illiquid instruments typically are higher than the yields on other instruments.

3. **Market Interest Rates and Different Terms to Maturity:** There are two reasons why interest yields differ based on term to maturity. One is that yields on longer-term financial instruments depend on expectations about yields on shorter-term instruments. Another is that longer-term instruments typically are less liquid and more risky. Consequently, longer-term financial instruments are more likely to be held if they have a somewhat higher yield than shorter-term instruments.

4. **The Real Interest Rate:** This is the nominal interest rate minus the expected rate of inflation. It provides a measure of the extent to which it is anticipated that inflation will reduce the purchasing power of interest earned on financial instruments.

5. **Relating Interest Yields on Bonds Issued in Different Countries:** For bonds that are identical in all respects other than the fact that they are denominated in different nations' currencies, yields are related through the uncovered interest parity condition. This says that a bond denominated in a currency whose value is expected to depreciate must offer a yield that is higher than the yield on other bonds. The difference in yields will equal the expected rate of currency depreciation.

6. **Key Interest Rate Indicators of Financial Market Conditions:** The federal funds rate is a measure of the immediate cost of funds for American banks and is an important indicator of Federal Reserve monetary policy. The prime rate is a barometer of aggregate loan market conditions and is a base for other lending rates. The London Interbank Offer Rate (LIBOR) is the basis for interest rate quotes on many internationally traded financial instruments.

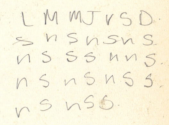

QUESTIONS AND PROBLEMS

1. The formula for the price of a consol with an annual coupon return of C is C/r. Note that the discounted present value of C dollars received every year forever is equal to the infinite sum,

$$P = C/(1 + r) + C/(1 + r)^2 + C/(1 + r)^3 + C/(1 + r)^4 + \cdots$$

The amount P is the price that a buyer would be willing to pay to hold this consol. And so P should equal C/r. Prove that this is true. [*Hint:* Try multiplying the equation above by the factor $1/(1 + r)$. Subtract the resulting equation from the equation above. Then solve for P.]

2. Suppose that an individual holds a 26-week (182-day) T-bill for 80 days but then offers to sell it to you at a price of $9,850. The face value of the T-bill is $10,000. What is the T-bill's yield over the remaining 102 days before it will mature?

3. Suppose that an individual holds a 13-week (91-day) T-bill for a number of days but then offers to sell it to you at a price of $9,920. The coupon equivalent yield for the T-bill, which has a face value of $10,000, is 5.84 percent. How many days remain before this bill matures?

4. Suppose that a U.S. Treasury bill has an annualized yield of 6.5 percent. A German government bill with the same maturity and equal risk characteristics has an annualized yield of 5.5 percent. Which country's currency is expected to *depreciate?* What is the expected rate of depreciation of this nation's currency?

5. The real interest rate on a Treasury bond is 3 percent. The anticipated inflation rate is 4.5 percent. What is the Treasury bond's nominal yield?

Financial Instruments

KEY QUESTIONS

1. What are the key financial instruments of the money and capital markets?

2. What is interest rate risk, and what are its determinants?

3. What are derivative securities?

4. Which derivative securities are most commonly traded?

5. What are some commonly used foreign exchange instruments?

In the year 1717 Johann Baring migrated from northern Germany to Britain and became a wool merchant. In 1762 two of his sons, John and Francis, formed Barings Bank. In 1803 Barings Bank helped the United States nearly double its size by financing the nation's purchase of the Louisiana Territory from France. The bank also was instrumental in providing credit to the British government during the Napoleonic wars (1803–1815). A grateful British government bestowed lordly titles on the Baring family. In 1970 the bank's ownership passed to a charitable foundation. Baring family members continued to manage the bank, but some of its profits were used to finance a number of British charities.

In 1995 this venerable bank collapsed. Financial bets by a poorly supervised, 27-year-old manager in Singapore turned sour. As a result, the bank lost billions of dollars. The remnants of Barings Bank were bought by its former competitors. The collapse of Barings Bank revolved around a single fact: The bank's top managers lost a sense of the need to keep a watchful eye on the pool of financial instruments that mid-level managers had purchased. In addition to standard money and capital market instruments, Barings Bank accumulated a portfolio of more complex and more risky instruments. Poor risk management brought down the bank.

In this chapter we discuss many of the financial instruments that were involved in the collapse of Barings Bank. We begin with some standard instruments of the money and capital markets. Then we turn our attention to what are called *derivative securities*. These were the instruments that caused Barings to collapse. Yet you will learn that they are also instruments banks use to *reduce* their risks of loss.

KEY INSTRUMENTS OF THE MONEY AND CAPITAL MARKETS

In Chapter 2 we briefly surveyed instruments of the money and capital markets. A few of these are extremely important. And so we begin our discussion of financial instruments by providing an in-depth look at these key securities.

Treasury Securities

Treasury securities are U.S. government obligations that are exchanged in both the money markets and the capital markets. As previously defined, Treasury bills are instruments with maturities of less than one year. Treasury notes and bonds have maturities of one year or more.

Treasury Bills   The federal government issues Treasury bills (T-bills) with minimum denominations of $10,000. Each successive T-bill denomination is in $5,000 increments. T-bills have terms to maturity of 91 days (3 months), 182 days (6 months), and 52 weeks (12 months). The government sells T-bills at a discount from the face value denomination. T-bills are negotiable instruments, which means that the bearer of a T-bill can sell the bill in the secondary market.

Treasury Auctions   The U.S. Treasury sells T-bills with 91-day and 182-day maturities in auctions each week. It sells 52-week T-bills every four weeks. These Treasury auctions, as well as sales of other, longer-term Treasury bonds, are **Dutch auctions.** In a Dutch auction, parties interested in purchasing new T-bills submit bids at varying prices. The Treasury then starts with the bid at the lowest yield—which is the highest-price bid and the one most favorable to the Treasury—and sells (allocates) securities to one bidder after another until it funds its new debts. The low-yield (high-price) bidders who successfully purchase the T-bills all receive the *highest* accepted yield, which is the yield offered in the last accepted bid.

Dutch auction   An auction in which the winning bidders all receive a return consistent with the last accepted bid.

For instance, imagine that there are only five bids for T-bills in a given week. The five bidders in essence offer yields of 6.81, 6.82, 6.84, 6.85, and 6.87 percent. The Treasury accepts the three lowest-yield bids and funds its debt for the week by issuing T-bills to these three bidders. Even though the two lowest bidders offered yields of 6.81 and 6.82 percent, all three receive the yield of 6.84 percent offered in the third and last bid accepted.

Before the early 1990s the Treasury sold T-bills in regular auctions, in which low bidders received exactly the bids they made. For instance, in the simple example above, the three winning bidders would have received yields of the 6.81, 6.82, and 6.84 percent that they bid. This meant that the "winning" bidder at 6.81 percent actually ended up receiving a *lower* yield than others who successfully bought T-bills. This was known as the **winner's curse** of a regular auction: The winning bidder got a lower yield than others whose bids were less favorable to the Treasury (which would have to pay a higher price).

winner's curse   Situation in which a winning bidder in an auction receives a lower return than at least one participant who submitted a weaker bid.

Two potential problems stemmed from the winner's curse. One was that it reduced the incentive to be the lowest bidder. This tended to push up the average yields offered for T-bills. Another was that one way to avoid the winner's curse was resort to *collusion,* by conspiring with other bidders to make sure that winning bids were all nearly the same. In August of 1991, in fact, the bond trading firm Salomon Brothers admitted that it had engaged in such activities. This helped spur the Treasury to switch to a Dutch auction technique.

Competitive and Noncompetitive Bids   Any Treasury auction has two parts: competitive bidding and noncompetitive bidding. The Dutch auction applies to *competitive bids* such as those discussed above, in which high-yield, losing bids fail to purchase T-bills. The Treasury also accepts *noncompetitive bids*. These are offers to buy T-bills at the same yield as accepted competitive bids. Those who make noncompetitive bids do so to avoid being shut out of the auction. They want to be sure that they purchase T-bills at the prevailing market yield.

Treasury notes   Treasury securities with maturities ranging from 1 to 10 years.

Treasury bonds   Treasury securities with maturities of 10 years or more.

Treasury Notes and Bonds   The U.S. Treasury issues two categories of financial instruments with maturities of more than one year. These are Treasury notes and Treasury bonds. **Treasury notes** have maturities ranging from one to ten years. **Treasury bonds** have maturities of ten years or more. Both notes and bonds have minimum denominations of $1,000.

The Treasury sells most notes and bonds at auctions. It sells some, however, by *cash subscription*. Under this arrangement, the Treasury exchanges new securities for other outstanding or maturing Treasury securities rather than making cash payments for these obligations.

Corporate Equities

Shares of equity ownership in a corporation entitle the owner to claims on the corporation's earnings and assets. Shares are most commonly issued in two forms: common stock and preferred stock.

common stock   Shares of corporate ownership that entitle the owner to vote on management issues but which offer no guarantees of dividends or of residual value in the event of corporate bankruptcy.

Common Stock   Ownership of **common stock** entitles the shareholder to have some direct say about how a company conducts its business. This is because common stock ownership permits the shareholder to participate in meetings with other shareholders. At such meetings the shareholder can cast votes for a company's board of directors and may have some input concerning other matters such as management strategy.

Owners of common stock are the *residual claimants* of a company. This means that if the company were to go bankrupt, common stockholders are the last in line for any remaining assets of the firm. These residual assets could very well have less value than the stated value of the company's stock. Hence, compared with creditors of the company, owners of common stock take on the greatest default risk. For this reason they are granted the greatest say in management.

The potential liability of a stockholder, however, is limited to the value of the individual's shareholdings. Hence, if a company goes bankrupt, the most that a stockholder can lose is the amount of funds that he or she has allocated to shares in that company.

POLICY NOTEBOOK

We're Finally Letting U.S. Treasuries Keep Pace with Inflation

In 1996, the U.S. Treasury Department announced the possibility of selling so-called index bonds. An index bond is one for which the principal and the coupon are adjusted upward every month by the rate of inflation. This policy change is an important step to ensure for those who buy such instruments that the value will not fall with unexpected inflation. This is exactly what happened during the 1970s, when the rate of inflation was much greater than anticipated. Consequently, U.S. Treasury bondholders saw the real value of their principal and yields fall.

Bond indexing is not a new idea. During the American Revolution the government of Massachusetts issued indexed bonds. Canada,

Australia, Britain, Israel, and Sweden have already sold substantial quantities of indexed debt. The Union Bank of Switzerland—a private entity—offered inflation-adjusted certificates of deposits a few years ago.

The benefit to any purchaser of such bonds is obvious—a guarantee against inflationary erosion of real values. If the price level rises 5 percent next year, the owner of an indexed U.S. Treasury bond would see the principal value of such a $1,000 bond increase to $1,050. The coupon payment would also be 5 percent higher.

For Critical Analysis: *How will the new indexed bonds work if the rate of inflation becomes negative, i.e., the general level of all prices fell?*

Preferred Stock   Those who hold **preferred stock** have no voting rights. They sacrifice the power to influence the company's management in exchange for a guarantee that they will receive any dividends paid to stockholders. And if the company is forced into bankruptcy, preferred stockholders have first crack (seniority) at claiming any residual value of the firm after other creditors have been paid.

Stock Exchanges   Corporate equity shares are traded in **stock exchanges,** which are organized physical locations that function as marketplaces for stocks. Members of stock exchanges function both as brokers and as dealers. As brokers these stock exchange members trade on behalf of others, and as dealers they trade on their own accounts.

There are several stock exchanges in the United States. The oldest and largest is the New York Stock Exchange. This exchange began in 1792. Roughly half of the stock trading in the United States is done in the New York Stock Exchange. Shares of many of the largest American corporations are traded there. There are a fixed number of membership positions in the New York Stock Exchange, which are called seats; there are 1,300 seats in the Exchange. Over 500 of these are owned by securities firms. About a third of these firms are Exchange *specialists*. These specialist firms

preferred stock   Shares of corporate ownership that entail no voting rights but that entitle the owner to dividends, if any are paid by the corporation, and to any residual value of the corporation after all other creditors have been paid.

stock exchanges   Organized marketplaces for corporate equities and bonds.

are responsible for laying out and honoring basic ground rules for orderly trading activity in the Exchange. Figure 4.1 explains how to read New York Stock Exchange data published in *The Wall Street Journal.*

Another important exchange is the American Stock Exchange, which is also in New York City. Shares of mainly small and medium-sized companies are traded on the "Amex," although some oil and gas company stocks are listed here as well. Many foreign stocks also are traded there.

There also are regional stock exchanges in such cities as Chicago, San Francisco, and Boston. These exchanges mainly handle trading in stocks of regionally based companies. They also list some of the stocks traded on the New York and American Stock Exchanges. More than half of the companies listed in the New York Stock Exchange also list their stocks regionally. This broadens the secondary

FIGURE 4.1 Reading Stock Quotes

Each day *The Wall Street Journal* reports New York Stock Exchange and American Stock Exchange stock prices using the format shown above. To understand how to read published stock quotes, consider the information for each column in the quote for the common stock of Citicorp, which is the holding company that owns Citibank. *Source:* Reprinted by permission of *The Wall Street Journal,* © 1996 Dow Jones & Company, Inc. All Rights Reserved Worldwide.

52 Weeks Hi	Lo	Stock	Sym	Div	Yld %	PE	Vol 100s	Hi	Lo	Close	Net Chg
3⅜	½	Chyron	CHY		...	41	1752	3¼	3⅛	3¼	+ ⅛
45⅛	34	Cilcorp Inc	CER	2.46	5.8	15	266	43⅛	42½	42⅝	– ¼
53	22¾	CincBell	CSN	.80	1.7	dd	1440	47⅞	47¼	47¼	– ⅜
n 26⅝	24⅞	CincGE deb	JRL	2.07	8.2	...	61	25¼	25⅛	25¼	+ ⅛
73⅜	57	CincGE pfB		4.75	7.5	...	2	64	63½	63½	–1
33⅝	20¾	CincMilacron	CMZ	.36	1.4	8	516	25⅞	25⅛	25½	+ ⅜

52 Weeks Hi: Highest dollar price of a share of Citicorp common stock during the past 52 weeks. In this case that price is $82.

52 Weeks Lo: Lowest dollar price of a share of Citicorp common stock during the past 52 weeks. In this case that price is $44 5/8.

Stock: Corporate name of Citicorp.

Sym: Exchange symbol that identifies Citicorp, CCI.

Div: Annual dollar dividend per share, or $1.80 per share.

Yld %: Stock yield measured as the annual dividend as a percentage of the closing price for the day, or $1.80 divided by 76 3/8 times 100, or approximately 2.4 %.

PE: Ratio of stock price to the annual earnings per share. This is equal to 9 for Citicorp.

Vol 100s: Hundreds of Citicorp shares traded this day, or 31,370,000 shares.

Hi: Highest price at which Citicorp shares traded that day, or $77 5/8 per share.

Lo: Lowest price at which Citicorp shares traded that day, or $74 1/2 per share.

Close: Price of Citicorp shares at day's end, or $76 3/8 per share.

Net Chg: Dollar change in closing price of Citicorp shares relative to previous day's closing price, which was a decline of $0.50.

market for their stocks, making them more liquid and, consequently, more marketable.

Over-the-Counter Stocks   In recent years a number of corporations have chosen not to be listed on the organized exchanges. Shares in these corporations are **over-the-counter (OTC) stocks** that are traded in decentralized markets. OTC trading volumes have increased in recent years as more and more stocks are traded on electronic networks that link traders around the world. Indeed, in 1995, OTC trading volumes surpassed trading volumes on the American Stock Exchange.

> **over-the-counter (OTC) stocks**   Equity shares offered by companies that do not meet listing requirements for major stock exchanges but are traded instead in decentralized markets.

Corporate Debt Instruments

Both nonfinancial and financial corporations issue money market and capital market debt obligations. The most important type of short-term debt instrument issued by corporations is commercial paper. Corporate bonds are capital market instruments.

Commercial Paper   Banks and corporations issue commercial paper ranging in maturity from 2 to 270 days. Most issuers sell commercial paper at a discount, as the Treasury does for T-bills. Some commercial paper instruments offer coupon returns, however.

Typically only the most creditworthy banks and corporations are able to sell commercial paper to finance short-term debts. Nevertheless, Moody's & Standard and Poor's assign credit ratings to different issuers. Consequently, the commercial paper issues of some companies may have higher yields than others because of differences in risk perceptions.

Corporate Bonds   Although corporate bonds can be as varied as the corporations that issue them, they have a few characteristics in common. For one thing, all corporate bond yields are subject to both state and federal taxation. In addition, when a corporation issues a bond it often establishes a **sinking fund,** which is an account the corporation draws upon to make coupon payments or to redeem the bonds at maturity.

> **sinking fund**   An account from which a corporation draws funds to make bond interest payments or to redeem bonds upon maturity.

Most corporate bonds are issued in denominations of $1,000. Bonds issued by major corporations are traded along with equity shares on the New York and American Stock Exchanges.

1

What are the key financial instruments of the money and capital markets? The most important money and capital market instruments are U.S. Treasury securities (bills, notes, and bonds), corporate equities (common and preferred stock), and corporate debt instruments (commercial paper and corporate bonds).

INTEREST RATE RISK AND FINANCIAL INSTRUMENT DURATION

In Chapter 3 we explained how to compute interest yields and discussed how interest rates and the market prices of financial instruments are related. As Figure 4.2 indicates, interest rates can be volatile over time. This means that the market values of financial instruments also can vary considerably. As a result, there is an inherent risk in holding financial instruments such as those discussed above.

Interest Rate Risk

A key issue that anyone who holds financial instruments must face is that such instruments are risky. One source of risk, of course, is the risk of default. Another, however, is the fact that the market value of an instrument varies with interest rates changes. This type of risk is called **interest rate risk.**

> **interest rate risk**   The possibility that the market value of a financial instrument will change as interest rates vary.

You learned in Chapter 3 that bond prices and interest yields are interdependent. Furthermore, you learned that the effective yield on an instrument such as a Treasury bill depends upon the time remaining until the instrument matures. For this reason, it should not be surprising

---

FIGURE 4.2   Selected Interest Rates

Interest rates can vary considerably over time. This exposes owners of financial instruments to the risk of capital losses. *Source: 1996 Ecomonic Report of the President.*

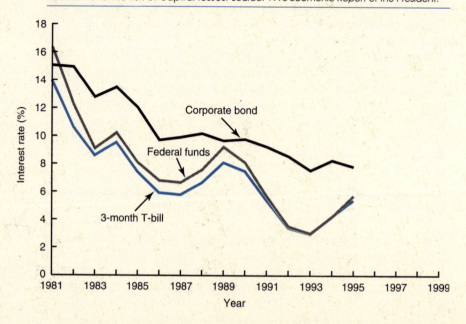

to learn that the variation in bond prices in response to interest rate changes depends on how much time remains until the bond matures.

The price of a bond is its market value. The extent to which a bond's value varies as interest rates change depends on the time to maturity. Thus, interest rate risk is related to the bond's maturity date.

Term to Maturity and Interest Rate Risk   To better understand why time to maturity matters for interest rate risk, consider an example of two very simple bonds. One pays $10,000 after a single year. The other pays $10,000 after the passage of two years. Such bonds are known as **zero-coupon bonds,** because they pay lump-sum amounts at maturity.

Table 4.1 calculates the prices of the two bonds for market interest rates of 7 and 8 percent. A rise in the market interest rate from 7 percent to 8 percent causes the price of each bond to decline. And so holders of the bonds would incur **capital losses,** meaning that the values of the bonds as part of their financial wealth holdings would fall.

The calculations in Table 4.1 show that the percentage capital loss on the 2-year bond is 1.9 percent. This is more than twice as large as the 0.9 percent capital loss on the 1-year bond. The reason is that the rise in market interest rate from 7 to 8 percent applies across two years for the 2-year bond. But the same rise in the interest rate affects the price of the 1-year bond for only the 1-year lifetime of the bond.

This simple example illustrates that the *lifetime* of a bond plays a key role in determining the proportionate capital loss that bondholders must incur when market interest rates rise. Bonds with longer terms to maturity are susceptible to greater risk of capital loss. This means that bonds with longer lifetimes have greater exposure to interest rate risk.

Frequency of Coupon Returns and Interest Rate Risk   Another key factor affecting the extent of interest rate risk is how often bonds pay coupon returns. For instance, think about a zero-coupon bond that pays $10,000 to the bearer after two years, as compared with a bond that pays a stream of $10,000 at quarterly intervals ($1,250 per quarter for 8 quarters) over two years. The holder of the

zero-coupon bonds   Bonds that pay lump-sum amounts at maturity.

capital loss   A loss in financial wealth resulting from a decline in the market value of a financial instrument.

TABLE 4.1 Effect of an Interest Rate Increase on the Market Price of Two Zero-Coupon Bonds

This example illustrates that following an expected rise in the market interest rate, the fall in price of a long-maturity bond is proportionately greater than that for a short-maturity bond.

	1-Year $10,000 Zero-Coupon Bond	2-Year $10,000 Zero-Coupon Bond
Bond price at 8% rate	$10,000/1.08 = \$9,259.26	$10,000/1.08^2 = \$8,573.39
Bond price at 7% rate	$10,000/1.07 = \$9,345.79	$10,000/1.07^2 = \$8,734.39
Dollar price change	−$86.53	−$161.00
Percentage price change	($86.53/$9,345.79) × 100 = −0.9%	($161.00/$8,573.39) × 100 = −1.9%

latter bond receives returns on the bond much more quickly. Hence, if market interest rates rise, the effective capital loss on the bond that pays out quarterly coupon returns will be lower, even though both bonds have the same, 2-year maturity.

Therefore, *two* factors influence interest rate risk. One is term to maturity, or a bond's lifetime. The other is how often a bond pays returns to the holder. To assess interest rate risk, bond traders need to be able to measure these factors together. They do this using a concept called **duration.** This is a measure of the average time required to receive all payments of principal and interest. From a technical standpoint, bond traders calculate duration as a weighted average of the present values of payments over the full maturity of a financial instrument. They use computer spreadsheet programs or financial calculators to do such calculations. Then they use the duration measures for alternative bonds to decide on how to allocate bond holdings in an effort to reduce overall exposure to interest rate risk.

duration   A measure of the average time spanning all payments of principal and interest on a financial instrument.

2

What is interest rate risk, and what are its determinants?   Interest rate risk is the chance that the price of a financial instrument may vary because of unexpected changes in market interest rates. The two key determinants of interest rate risk are the maturity and frequency of returns on financial instruments. Instruments of longer maturities and with less-frequent returns possess greater interest rate risk.

Reducing Interest Rate Risk   How can an individual, a company, or a financial institution reduce interest rate risks? One answer would be to hold bonds with shorter durations, avoid zero-coupon bonds, and seek bond holdings that yield frequent coupon returns.

Another approach would be to hold financial instruments with short maturities, such as money market securities like Treasury bills or commercial paper. Short-maturity instruments have a lower risk of capital losses in the face of interest rate increases than instruments of longer maturity.

There are three problems with this second strategy, however. One is that if the yield curve slopes upward, it is much more likely that long-duration instruments will yield greater returns. This is true because, holding all other factors constant, duration increases with the term to maturity. In turn, the longer the term to maturity is the greater the interest rate is, if the yield curve has its typical upward slope. Hence, holding only short-duration instruments is a low-return strategy.

Second, there are costs entailed in continually rolling over short-term instruments. For one thing, doing so takes some time and effort. Also more brokerage fees may have to be paid. In addition, keeping funds in short-maturity instruments with short durations also leads to greater exposure to **reinvestment risk.** This refers to the chance that market yields may be lower when a short-term instrument matures. Should this be the case one might have been better off placing available funds into holdings of longer-term instruments.

Finally, holding only short-maturity instruments ignores the potential risk reduction that can be gained from **portfolio diversification,** or spreading risk by holding instruments with different characteristics. For instance, when money market (short-term) yields fall, capital market (long-term) yields may be rising. If one has allocated all available funds to a portfolio, or set, of short-duration, money market instruments, then the total return on the portfolio will decline. But if part of the portfolio of financial instruments consists of longer-duration capital market instruments, then a rise in yields on these instruments could help offset the effect on the total portfolio return of a decline in money market yields.

Hedging

Certainly, allocating most funds to holdings of short-duration instruments is a possible strategy for dealing with interest rate risk. There is another strategy, however. This is to **hedge** interest rate risk using other financial instruments, called derivatives. A hedge is a financial strategy that reduces the risk of capital losses. A *perfect hedge* is a strategy that completely eliminates such risk.

Two key requirements are necessary for hedging against interest rate risk. One is *flexibility*. The extent of interest rate risk faced by various individuals, businesses, and financial institutions differs. One corporation, for instance, may hold primarily securities with short durations but rather high risk of default. Another may hold securities with longer durations but lower default risk. The ability of both companies to hedge the interest rate risks they face requires the existence of a financial contract that is sufficiently flexible to satisfy the companies' different situations.

Another key requirement for successful hedging is the ability to conduct *speedy* financial transactions. Market interest conditions may change quickly. Consequently, those who wish to hedge against interest rate risk must be able to respond with dispatch to swings in financial market conditions.

DERIVATIVE SECURITIES AND HEDGING

During the past two decades, many individuals, firms, and financial institutions have achieved the flexibility and speed needed for hedging by using what are now called *derivative securities*, or derivatives. Examples

reinvestment risk The possibility that available yields on short-term financial instruments may decline, making holdings of longer-term instruments preferable.

portfolio diversification Holding financial instruments with different characteristics so as to spread risk across the entire set of instruments.

hedge A financial strategy that reduces the risk of capital losses arising from interest rate risk.

of derivative securities are *forward contracts,* such as interest rate or exchange rate forward contracts, and *financial options,* such as stock options. Before we discuss the various kinds of derivatives, let's first try to understand what derivatives are and how they can be used to hedge against interest rate risk.

Any financial instruments whose returns are linked to, or derived from, the returns of other financial instruments are **derivative securities.** There are many types of derivative securities. But let's begin by thinking about the concept of derivatives with a simple, real-world example.

It is often the case that a home buyer takes possession of the house at a date a few weeks after a loan contract is arranged with a lender. For instance, a couple buying an existing home may arrange a mortgage loan a few weeks before the family living in the home departs. Yet the mortgage loan contract must specify an interest rate that will apply when the loan amount actually is transferred from the mortgage lender to the couple on the exact date of purchase and possession.

Consider the following example. A couple has arranged to purchase a house on May 1. They have to arrange mortgage financing for the house. They finalize a mortgage loan on April 15, or 15 days before the actual date of purchase. They and the mortgage lender both know the prevailing mortgage interest rate as of April 15 when the loan contract is finalized. But neither party knows what the mortgage rate will be on May 1, when the couple actually will get the loan.

Typically when such a loan contract is negotiated, the borrower is given options concerning the interest rate. One option would be to borrow on May 1 at whatever the prevailing market mortgage rate turns out to be on that date. But normally a mortgage lender also will offer to let the home buyer "tie down" a current market mortgage rate. For instance, in our example the mortgage lender may point out that the mortgage rate on April 15 is, say, 8 percent. The couple then may be given the option either of "locking in" that interest rate for the loan that will begin on May 1 or of accepting whatever the interest rate is when May 1 arrives.

This contract for the terms of a mortgage loan is an illustration of a simple derivative instrument. Suppose that the couple chooses to accept the market interest rate that will prevail as of May 1 that would tie the value of the loan to the market interest rate on other mortgage loans as of that date. That is, the value of the mortgage would be derived from the interest rate on other mortgages on this date.

In contrast, suppose the couple chooses to lock in the mortgage rate as of April 15. For the mortgage lender, the profitability of this loan will depend on what the market-clearing mortgage rate turns out to be on May 1. If the May 1 rate turns out to be below the April 15 rate, then the mortgage lender will earn a greater profit. If the May 1 rate ends up above the April 15 rate, then the mortgage lender's profit will be lower than it would have been otherwise. Consequently, the value of the

derivative securities
Financial instruments whose returns depend on the returns of other financial instruments.

mortgage to the lender also will be derived from the mortgage rate that prevails on May 1.

And so this simple arrangement for the terms of a mortgage loan is a type of derivative instrument. The mortgage loan is negotiated on April 15. But the value of the mortgage loan to both the borrower and the lender ultimately depends on the market mortgage rate that will prevail on May 1.

Derivatives as Hedging Instruments

The above example illustrates the idea of how a return on a financial instrument may be *derived* from the return on another instrument. It also is an example of an **interest-rate forward contract.** Such a contract guarantees the future sale of a financial instrument at a specified interest rate as of a specific date. In our example, on April 15 the mortgage lender and borrower agree to enter into terms of the mortgage loan at a future date, May 1. On April 15 they agree on the amount of the mortgage loan on May 1. And they agree that the interest rate applicable to the mortgage will be determined on that date. Hence, the parties in the loan agreement agree on an interest rate that will apply at a *forward* date.

To see how an interest-rate forward contract can be a *perfect* hedge for two parties to such a contract, consider a different example. In this example, a commercial bank feels certain that next year it will receive $8 million in interest and principal payments from very creditworthy customers who have borrowed from the bank. The bank's managers have decided that next year they will reduce the bank's lending somewhat and that they will place $4 million into default-risk-free 5-year Treasury notes. The commercial bank would like to be certain, however, that in one year's time it will receive the *current* market interest yield of, say, 7 percent on 5-year Treasury notes.

At the same time, suppose that a savings bank holds over $4 million in 5-year Treasury notes that are several years from maturity. The savings bank's managers are concerned that market interest rates may rise above 7 percent at some point beyond next year. Such an interest rate increase would yield a capital loss on these bond holdings because their prices would fall.

In this situation both parties could hedge against the risks they face by entering into an interest-rate forward contract. The commercial bank could agree today to buy $4 million worth of 5-year Treasury notes from the savings bank *one year from now* at a price that would reflect the 7 percent interest yield currently in effect for those bonds. This would ensure that the commercial bank would earn today's 7 percent market rate beginning one year from now. For the savings bank, the risk of capital loss within the next year on $4 million of its current Treasury note holdings is eliminated. The savings bank's managers know

interest-rate forward contract   A financial contract that entails the sale of a financial instrument at a certain interest rate on a specific future date.

that they will be assured next year of receiving a price consistent with a 7 percent yield one year from now.

Derivatives as Speculative Instruments

Derivative securities can be used to hedge against risks. Yet they also can be used for risky speculation. To see this, let's slightly expand on the story in the last example.

Derivatives Speculation   Suppose now that the managers of the commercial bank currently believe that the cost of raising funds, which now averages 5 percent, is likely to fall. This view, however, runs counter to prevailing wisdom, which is that average funding costs for commercial banks are likely to increase significantly during the coming year. Yet the commercial bank managers are so certain of their own views that they are willing to enter into the interest-rate forward contract with the savings bank.

This contract commits the bank to buying the $4 million in 5-year Treasury notes from the savings bank next year at a price consistent with *today's* market yield of 7 percent. If the prevailing view that the commercial bank's interest funding costs will rise significantly by next year turns out to be correct, the net interest profit that the bank will earn next year on the Treasury notes will be much lower than the bank's managers currently *speculate* it will be. Indeed, if average funding costs rise to 7 percent or more, net profit could be zero or even negative. Hence, if funding costs really are likely to rise, the commercial bank in this example has entered into a highly speculative, and potentially very risky, contract.

Losses from Derivatives   This shows that while one may use derivative securities to hedge against risks, one may also use them to speculate. During the 1980s derivative trading boomed as financial managers recognized the ways in which derivative securities could be used to hedge against risks. But many managers also found that they could earn significant short-run profits by speculating with derivatives. But some made speculations that turned out to be wrong, incurring large losses rather than earning profits.

Dramatic examples of how derivative securities can lead to speculative losses occurred with increasing frequency in the mid-1990s. Table 4.2 highlights some of these losses. The most dramatic were the 1994 loss of over $1.5 billion by Orange County, California, and the 1995 loss of over $2 billion by Barings Bank of Britain. The Orange County loss led to layoffs for county employees and tax increases for citizens of the county. As noted in the opening to this chapter, Barings Bank's long history was cut short by its significant derivatives losses.

TABLE 4.2 Major Derivatives Losses in the Mid-1990s

A number of companies and municipalities experienced multimillion dollar losses from derivatives trading in the 1990s.

Estimate of Loss	Company or Municipality	Primary Derivative
$50 million	First Boston	Options
$260 million	Volkswagen	Currency futures
$100 million	Cargill Fund	Mortgage derivatives
$157 million	Procter and Gamble	Currency futures
$100 million	Florida State Treasury	Mortgage derivatives
$20 million	Gibson Greeting Cards	Swaps
$35 million	Dell Computer	Swaps and options
$20 million	Paramount Communications	Swaps
$150 million	Glaxo, Inc.	Mortgage derivatives
$1,500 million	Orange County, California	Mortgage derivatives
$50 million	Capital Corp. Credit Union	Mortgage derivatives
$195 million	Wisconsin Investment Funds	Swaps
$25 million	Escambia County, Florida	Mortgage derivatives
$2,000 million	Barings Bank, UK	Stock index futures

Where did all this "lost" money go? Certainly, it did not disappear. What happened was that it was transferred from the companies and government agencies that made "bad bets" in their speculative strategies to those who made "good bets." Consider our example of the fictitious commercial bank and savings bank. If the commercial bank's managers are wrong in their guess that average bank funding costs will fall within one year, then they could lose on the interest-rate forward contract. But the savings bank, by selling Treasury notes next year, would gain.

For each loser in derivatives speculation, there also must be a winner on the other side of the transaction.

3

What are derivative securities? Derivative securities are financial instruments whose returns are based on the returns of other financial instruments.

NO!

THE MOST COMMONLY USED DERIVATIVES

There are several types of derivative securities. What they all have in common is that their returns are based on the returns of other instruments. An individual, company, or financial institution may use any

*) Bets with someone elses funds.
You borrow high payoff low.
Diff → gain.

derivative security to hedge against risk. But any derivative also may be used for risky speculation.

Forward Contracts

long position   An obligation to purchase a financial instrument at a given price and at a specific time.

short position   An obligation to sell a financial instrument at a given price and at a specific time.

In our example of an interest-rate forward contract between a fictitious commercial bank and a savings bank, the commercial bank agreed to buy Treasury notes in one year at a price consistent with the current market yield. Hence, it took a **long position.** This means that the commercial bank went out on a limb by locking into a fixed yield on the Treasury bonds. The savings bank selling the notes took a **short position.** By entering into the contract, its managers were able to get the Treasury notes off their books more quickly and thereby avoid any potential capital loss from possible increases in market yields.

Interest-rate forward contracts are an important means of hedging or speculating for a number of financial market participants. But there are a couple of factors that limit the size of the market for these derivative securities. One is that it can be difficult sometimes for two parties to agree on the terms of an interest-rate forward contract. Our example assumed that both the commercial bank and the savings bank had mutually compatible desires concerning 5-year Treasury notes. In fact, however, hammering out a mutually agreeable interest-rate forward contract can be a complicated undertaking.

A second problem is default risk. In the example of the interest-rate forward contract between a commercial bank and a savings bank, the commercial bank could find itself in a losing position if its funding costs rise dramatically within a year's time. It could be better off defaulting on the contract. This means that before agreeing to the contract, the savings bank must worry about the potential for an adverse selection problem. The savings bank also must be concerned about moral hazard at the commercial bank during the year before the Treasury note sale is to take place. Such problems of asymmetric information have deterred the use of interest-rate forward contracts, because they can make these contracts somewhat illiquid instruments.

Futures

futures contract   An agreement to deliver to another a specific amount of a standardized commodity or financial instrument at a designated future date.

interest rate future   Contract to buy or sell a financial instrument at a specified price at a certain date in the future.

A **futures contract** is an agreement by one party to deliver to another a standardized amount of a commodity or financial instrument at a specific future date. There are two key futures contracts: *interest rate futures* and *stock index futures.*

Interest Rate Futures   Like interest-rate forward contracts, **interest rate futures** are contracts to buy or sell financial instruments at specified prices at certain dates in the future. In contrast to interest-rate forward contracts, however, interest rate futures contracts require delivery of *standard quantities* of a given instrument. In addition, holders of interest rate futures experience profits or losses on the contracts during the entire period before the contract expires, whereas such profits or losses occur only at the expiration date of an interest-rate forward contract.

Consider, for instance, a futures contract on a 5-year U.S. Treasury note. This is an agreement to buy or sell 5-year U.S. Treasury notes in standard denominations of $100,000 in a trade conducted under the auspices of the Chicago Board of Trade (CBOT), a futures exchange that started in 1865. To conduct an interest-rate futures exchange, the 5-year Treasury note futures contract must meet requirements that CBOT establishes. Other interest rate futures traded on the CBOT include interest rate futures on Treasury bonds, on federal funds, and on an index of municipal bond rates. Interest rate futures related to these and other financial instruments are traded also on the Chicago Mercantile Exchange and on other regional exchanges.

Now consider for the last time the example involving the commercial bank and the savings bank. Let us suppose that they may wish to agree today to trade 5-year Treasury notes next year. Because the futures contract is standardized, there is no need to iron out specific details concerning the contract. Both parties either take it or leave it. Furthermore, because futures exchanges are such organized markets, futures contracts are very liquid instruments. A holder of a futures contract can easily sell it to another party. It is mostly for this reason that interest rate futures have become more predominant, while the use of interest-rate forward contracts has tended to languish.

Stock Index Futures   Agreements to deliver on a given date a portfolio of stocks represented by a stock price index are **stock index futures.** In the case of the Standard & Poor's (S&P) 500 index futures traded on the Chicago Mercantile Exchange, the stock portfolio is representative of the 500 companies listed in the S&P index of the market values of 500 firms.

stock index future   Promises of future delivery of a portfolio of stocks represented by a stock price index.

To calculate the value of an S&P 500 index futures contract, one multiplies the prevailing futures price times $500. For instance, if the S&P 500 futures price is 300, then the value of the contract is equal to $150,000. And so if you were to agree to *sell*, or take a *short position*, with an S&P 500 futures contract, you would guarantee to deliver a cash amount of $500 times whatever the futures price turns out to be at the date in the contract. The buyer, on the other hand, takes a *long position* and agrees to pay 300 times $500 for this contract today. Suppose that when the date arrives the market price of the futures contract turns out to be equal to 200, giving it a dollar value of $100,000. Then the buyer would lose $50,000, because the buyer will have paid $150,000 for the $100,000 cash payment that the seller is obligated to make. The seller, in turn, would gain the $50,000.

In the Barings Bank failure in early 1995, a manager of a Barings Singapore office took extensive long positions in Japanese Nikkei 225 stock

MANAGEMENT NOTEBOOK
Why Are There so Few Agricultural-Based Futures?

The futures market has its origins in farming, when in 1865 the first futures were launched on the Chicago Board of Trade. The Chicago Mercantile Exchange was originally founded as the Butter and Egg Board. Today, 60 million futures contracts on food products change hands each year, but that is only one-fourth of the total futures trading in America—the rest being taken up by financial futures.

Financial futures were started in 1972. How did they get to be so important relative to food-product futures? Of course, the underlying financial markets are much bigger—the American government alone has outstanding debt of over $4 trillion. But rational managers in the agricultural sector are another reason. They have not had to cover themselves against risk because government has done it for them. Until 1996 the U.S. government spent between $8 and $12 billion a year guaranteeing farmers a minimum price for certain crops and insuring them against crop failure. In the European Union (15 European countries), a similar program costs

about $50 billion a year. Not surprisingly, the agricultural futures market in Europe is even weaker than in the United States.

Another reason has to do with the difficult nature of designing futures for many food products. Some of the markets are too small or have too few companies for there to be active trading. For example, the cranberry market only has two major companies.

The reason that Europeans do not use contracts from the Chicago Board of Trade or the Chicago Mercantile Exchange is that such contracts are often based on a different variety of the same agricultural product.

There is also another problem and it has to do with the seasonality of many agricultural goods. It is harder to develop year-round interest in an agricultural-futures contract if people eat the underlying food product only once a year.

For Critical Analysis: *What do you predict will happen to agricultural-futures markets now that the federal government has cut back on farm subsidies?*

index futures. These are stock index futures based on an index of 225 firms whose stocks are traded in Japan. The Barings manager speculated that the Nikkei 225 stock price index would rise. Unfortunately for Barings Bank, the index fell. As in our S&P 500 example above, Barings Bank found itself obligated to come up with cash. Unlike our example, the cash amounted to over $2 billion, not the rather insignificant $50,000 in our example.

option   A financial contract giving the owner the right to buy or sell an underlying financial instrument at a certain price within a specific period of time.

Options

An **option** is a financial contract that gives the buyer the right to buy or sell an underlying financial instrument at a certain price within a given period of time. This right does not oblige the buyer of the option to buy or sell. It gives the buyer the *option,* hence the name of this derivative security. The specific price at which the buyer of the option can exercise the right to buy or sell a financial instrument is the **exercise price,** also called the *strike price.*

Types of Options   One type of option gives the buyer the right to exercise the right of purchase or sale at any time before or including the date on which the contract expires. This option is called an **American option.** In contrast, a **European option** permits the buyer to exercise the right of purchase or sale *only* on the date that the contract expires.

Options that permit the buyer to *purchase* a financial instrument at the exercise price are **call options.** Options that allow the buyer to *sell* a financial instrument at the exercise price are **put options.**

Stock Options and Futures Options   Typically firms use options to hedge against the risk of stock price changes or of interest rate movements. The most common types of options, therefore, are **stock options,** which are options to buy or sell corporation equity shares, and **futures options,** which are options to buy or sell stock index futures or interest rate futures.

As the stock index futures market has become more liquid in recent years, trading in the futures options market has grown relative to trading of stock options.

> **More options relating to stock *derivatives* are traded than options based on actual stocks. Futures options are derivatives of derivatives!**

Interest-Rate Swaps

Financial contracts that oblige an individual or firm to trade a set of interest payments to which they are entitled for a different set of interest payments owed to another individual or firm are **interest rate swaps.** There are several types of interest rate swaps. One is the *forward swap,* in which the start date for the swap is delayed anywhere from a few days to a few years. Another is the *swap option* (or *swaption*), which gives the owner the right to enter into a swap when the swap's market price reaches an exercise or strike price. There also are "amortizing swaps," "appreciating swaps," "roller coaster swaps," and so on.

The most important type of interest rate swap, however, is the *plain vanilla swap* (or *bullet swap*). Under this contract, the two parties to the contract simply agree to trade streams of interest payments to which each is entitled. For instance, a life insurance company might exchange a stream of fixed interest payments to a commercial bank for the commercial bank's stream of future interest payments derived

exercise price   The price at which the holder of an option has the right to buy or sell a financial instrument; also known as the strike price.

American option   An option in which the holder has the right to exercise the right to buy or sell a security any time before and/or including the date on which the contract expires.

European option   An option in which the holder has the right to exercise the right to buy or sell only on the day that the contract expires.

call option   An option contract giving the holder the right to purchase a financial instrument at a specific price.

put option   An option contract giving the owner the right to sell a financial instrument at a specific price.

stock options   Options to buy or sell firm equity shares.

futures options   Options to buy or sell futures contracts.

interest rate swaps   A contractual exchange of one set of interest payments for another.

from a portfolio of 10-year Treasury notes. The life insurance company thereby would receive interest payments that would vary with market conditions, while the commercial bank would receive fixed interest payments. This arrangement might help both companies hedge against interest rate risks that they face. Of course, there is nothing to keep one or both companies from speculating rather than hedging.

Mortgage Derivatives

The earliest securities whose returns were derived from mortgage instruments were mortgage-backed securities. As noted in Chapter 2, the most basic of these simply pass through to the owners the interest earnings from pools of mortgages.

collateralized mortgage obligations (CMOs) Mortgage-backed derivatives that split regular principal and interest payments from pools of mortgages into separate payment streams that are paid to CMO holders at varying intervals.

More complex forms of mortgage-backed derivative instruments are **collateralized mortgage obligations (CMOs).** These are mortgage-backed derivatives in which the regular principal and interest payments made on mortgage pools are separated into different payment streams, which are paid to CMO holders at varying rates. Typical CMOs pay bondholders on schedules that are different from the payment schedules of the underlying mortgage pools. For instance, there are fast-pay bonds, whose maturities are shorter than the mortgage pools from which the interest returns are derived. There also are CMOs whose returns are related to some interest rate index, such as the London Interbank Offer Rate (LIBOR) discussed in Chapter 3, even though the underlying mortgage pool may contain only fixed-rate mortgages.

Because CMOs (and other derivative securities) can be so complicated and so varied in structure, there are people who specialize in determining how to price these instruments. This task now is known as *financial engineering*. Despite the best efforts of financial engineering specialists, however, many of the large derivatives losses by companies and municipalities in the 1990s stemmed from CMOs and other mortgage derivatives. Following some of these large losses, CMO trading activity declined sharply in 1995 and 1996. It remains to be seen if the popularity of CMOs will recover in the remaining years of the decade.

4

Which derivative securities are most commonly traded?   The most commonly held and traded derivatives are interest-rate forward contracts, interest rate and stock index futures, financial option contracts, and interest rate swaps.

FOREIGN EXCHANGE MARKET DERIVATIVES

Today many American individuals and businesses hold financial instruments issued in other nations and denominated in currencies other than the U.S. dollar. As a result, they must try to protect themselves from risks beyond those related to interest rate movements. Specifically, they must concern themselves with risks arising from variations in exchange rates between national currencies.

Foreign Exchange Risks

The possibility that the market value of financial instruments denominated in foreign currencies may be affected by changes in exchange rates is **foreign exchange risk.** Foreign exchange risk arises in three basic ways.

Accounting Risk When exchange rates change, the market value of foreign-currency-denominated financial instruments changes even if the underlying interest returns on those instruments are unaffected. The risk of such variations in the market value of these financial instruments is called **accounting risk.**

> To see how accounting risk can arise, consider an example in which an American bank has issued a certificate of deposit (CD) to a German company, denominated in deutsche marks (abbreviated DM) and equal to 10,000 DM. Suppose that 1 DM was equal to $0.75 when the bank first issued the CD. At this point the dollar value of the bank's deposit liability to the German firm is $7,500. But if the dollar's value falls in the foreign exchange market, so that 1 DM rises in value to $0.80, then the dollar value of the CD liability of the bank increases to $8,000. Purely as a matter of accounting, therefore, the bank's dollar liabilities have increased because of the exchange rate change.

Transaction Risk Another important type of foreign exchange risk is **transaction risk.** This is the chance that the value of a financial instrument issued to fund a transaction denominated in another currency could change as a result of an exchange rate movement affecting the underlying value of the transaction.

> Consider, for instance, a banker's acceptance. As noted in Chapter 2, this is a bank loan that often is used to finance the international shipment of an export or import good. Suppose that a small American computer manufacturer purchases a large number of microchips from a Japanese firm. The American firm pays for shipment from Japan and finances the shipment using a banker's acceptance. It agrees to pay the Japanese importer in yen, the Japanese currency, upon receipt of the microchips. The shipment takes several weeks, but in the

foreign exchange risk The possibility that changes in exchange rates may affect the market value of financial instruments.

accounting risk The possibility that the market value of a foreign-currency-denominated financial instrument may change as a result of variations in exchange rate, even if the interest return on the instrument remains the same.

transaction risk The possibility that the market value of a financial instrument used to find an international transaction may vary because an exchange rate change alters the value of the transaction.

meantime the dollar's value relative to the yen declines. This means that the American computer manufacturer must come up with more dollars to pay for the microchips. If the American firm is operating on a thin profit margin, this could cause the firm to default on its obligation, leaving the bank as the responsible party. Hence, the exchange rate change would increase the bank's risk from issuing the banker's acceptance to this American company.

Currency Risk   Recall from Chapter 3 that for bonds of two nations with identical maturities and risk characteristics, the difference between their interest yields is equal to the expected rate of depreciation of the currency of one of the nations relative to the currency of the other. This means that exchange rate volatility can also cause expectations of currency depreciation to vary. As a result, interest rates on financial instruments issued in different nations can converge or diverge in unpredictable ways. The fact that changes in exchange rates can affect the underlying returns on financial instruments denominated in other currencies is **currency risk.**

currency risk   The possibility that exchange rate movements may affect the underlying returns on financial instruments.

Just as individuals, firms, and financial institutions may desire to hedge or to speculate in light of interest rate risk, they also may wish to use hedging or speculative strategies in the face of foreign exchange risks. They commonly use **foreign exchange derivatives** to deal with such risks. These are derivative securities whose returns stem from financial instruments returns that are sensitive to exchange rate fluctuations.

Foreign exchange derivatives parallel other types of derivative securities. There are foreign exchange forward contracts, and foreign exchange futures, options, and swaps.

Forward Currency Contracts

forward currency contract   A contract that requires delivery of a foreign-currency-denominated financial instrument at a given price on a specific date.

As in a forward interest rate contract, a **forward currency contract** calls for delivery of a financial instrument at a predetermined price on a specific date. But in the case of a forward currency contract, the financial instrument is a given sum of foreign currency. Furthermore, the price of the sum of currency is expressed in terms of a given exchange rate.

forward exchange rate   The exchange rate at which a forward currency contract is traded.

The Forward Exchange Rate   The exchange rate at which a forward currency contract is traded is the **forward exchange rate.** This forward exchange rate typically differs from the **spot exchange rate,** which is the rate of exchange that applies to *immediate* delivery of a currency offered in exchange for another.

spot exchange rate   The rate of exchange of two currencies to be traded immediately.

Figure 4.3 shows exchange rate quotes as they appear in *The Wall Street Journal.* Both spot and forward exchange rates appear for those nations whose currencies trade most actively in the forward exchange markets.

CURRENCY TRADING

Thursday, April 11, 1996

EXCHANGE RATES

The New York foreign exchange selling rates below apply to trading among banks in amounts of $1 million and more, as quoted at 3 p.m. Eastern time by Dow Jones Telerate Inc. and other sources. Retail transactions provide fewer units of foreign currency per dollar.

Country	U.S. $ equiv. Thu	U.S. $ equiv. Wed	Currency per U.S. $ Thu	Currency per U.S. $ Wed
Argentina (Peso)	1.0012	1.0012	.9988	.9988
Australia (Dollar)	.7898	.7877	1.2661	1.2695
Austria (Schilling)	.09487	.09485	10.541	10.543
Bahrain (Dinar)	2.6525	2.6525	.3770	.3770
Belgium (Franc)	.03241	.03244	30.850	30.830
Brazil (Real)	1.0152	1.0147	.9850	.9855
Britain (Pound)	1.5122	1.5146	.6613	.6602
30-Day Forward	1.5116	1.5120	.6616	.6614
90-Day Forward	1.5089	1.5127	.6627	.6611
180-Day Forward	1.5090	1.5112	.6627	.6617
Canada (Dollar)	.7371	.7368	1.3567	1.3573
30-Day Forward	.7374	.7370	1.3562	1.3569
90-Day Forward	.7377	.7374	1.3556	1.3562
180-Day Forward	.7450	.7442	1.3422	1.3438
Chile (Peso)	.002452	.002440	407.75	409.85
China (Renminbi)	.1197	.1197	8.3524	8.3518
Colombia (Peso)	.0009639	.0009639	1037.50	1037.50
Czech. Rep. (Koruna)	....	....	....	....
Commercial rate	.03640	.03641	27.473	27.462
Denmark (Krone)	.1724	.1727	5.8000	5.7915
Ecuador (Sucre)	....	....	....	....
Floating rate	.0003283	.0003287	3046.00	3042.00
Finland (Markka)	.2129	.2136	4.6973	4.6821
France (Franc)	.1960	.1979	5.1025	5.0526
30-Day Forward	.1962	.1982	5.0962	5.0461
90-Day Forward	.1967	.1987	5.0838	5.0338
180-Day Forward	.1974	.1994	5.0657	5.0151
Germany (Mark)	.6656	.6678	1.5025	1.4975
30-Day Forward	.6668	.6689	1.4998	1.4949
90-Day Forward	.6690	.6714	1.4947	1.4894
180-Day Forward	.6772	.6755	1.4767	1.4804
Greece (Drachma)	.004130	.004137	242.15	241.73
Hong Kong (Dollar)	.1293	.1293	7.7325	7.7329
Hungary (Forint)	.006731	.006747	148.56	148.21
India (Rupee)	.02923	.02926	34.215	34.180
Indonesia (Rupiah)	.0004287	.0004289	2332.50	2331.63
Ireland (Punt)	1.5625	1.5608	.6400	.6407
Israel (Shekel)	.3174	.3183	3.1505	3.1415
Italy (Lira)	.0006371	.0006365	1569.50	1571.00
Japan (Yen)	.009221	.009222	108.45	108.44
30-Day Forward	.009259	.009260	108.00	107.99
90-Day Forward	.009338	.009339	107.10	107.08
180-Day Forward	.009453	.009454	105.79	105.78
Jordan (Dinar)	1.4124	1.4124	.7080	.7080
Kuwait (Dinar)	3.3333	3.3333	.3000	.3000
Lebanon (Pound)	.0006323	.0006321	1581.50	1582.00
Malaysia (Ringgit)	.3979	.3963	2.5135	2.5235
Malta (Lira)	2.7548	2.7586	.3630	.3625
Mexico (Peso)	....	....	....	....
Floating rate	.1331	.1336	7.5125	7.4825
Netherland (Guilder)	.5959	.5972	1.6782	1.6745
New Zealand (Dollar)	.6769	.6816	1.4773	1.4671
Norway (Krone)	.1542	.1543	6.4862	6.4797
Pakistan (Rupee)	.02921	.02921	34.230	34.230
Peru (new Sol)	.4253	.4269	2.3512	2.3422
Philippines (Peso)	.03817	.03817	26.200	26.200
Poland (Zloty)	.3819	.3857	2.6185	2.5930
Portugal (Escudo)	.006475	.006475	154.45	154.44
Russia (Ruble) (a)	.0002036	.0002044	4912.00	4892.00
Saudi Arabia (Riyal)	.2666	.2666	3.7505	3.7505
Singapore (Dollar)	.7101	.7096	1.4083	1.4092
Slovak Rep. (Koruna)	.03376	.03320	29.619	30.119
South Africa (Rand)	.2408	.2389	4.1525	4.1850
South Korea (Won)	.001279	.001279	782.05	782.05
Spain (Peseta)	.007952	.007985	125.76	125.23
Sweden (Krona)	.1492	.1490	6.7027	6.7093
Switzerland (Franc)	.8191	.8262	1.2209	1.2104
30-Day Forward	.8215	.8278	1.2173	1.2080
90-Day Forward	.8265	.8336	1.2099	1.1996
180-Day Forward	.8344	.8418	1.1984	1.1880
Taiwan (Dollar)	.03681	.03681	27.167	27.169
Thailand (Baht)	.03948	.03950	25.328	25.317
Turkey (Lira)	.00001379	.00001384	72536.00	72254.00
United Arab (Dirham)	.2722	.2722	3.6732	3.6732
Uruguay (New Peso)	....	....	....	....
Financial	.1325	.1325	7.5500	7.5500
Venezuela (Bolivar)	.003448	.003448	290.00	290.00
Brady Rate	.002169	.002169	461.00	461.00
SDR	1.4461	1.4499	.6915	.6897
ECU	1.2449	1.2470	....	....

Special Drawing Rights (SDR) are based on exchange rates for the U.S., German, British, French, and Japanese currencies. Source: International Monetary Fund.

European Currency Unit (ECU) is based on a basket of community currencies.

a-fixing, Moscow Interbank Currency Exchange

FIGURE 4.3   Exchange Rates

Each day *The Wall Street Journal* reports data on exchange rates for the currencies of over 50 nations. *Source:* Reprinted by permission of *The Wall Street Journal,* © 1996 Dow Jones & Company, Inc. All Rights Reserved Worldwide.

Covered Interest Parity

The existence of forward exchange instruments means that interest rates on bonds of different nations will be related. To see this, suppose that an American has two alternatives. One is to purchase a 1-period, dollar-denominated bond with an interest yield of i_{US}. After one year's time, the person will have accumulated $1 + i_{US}$ dollars for each dollar saved.

The other savings alternative is to use each dollar to buy British pounds at the spot exchange rate of S dollars per pound, thereby obtaining $1/S$ pounds for each dollar. Then the person could use the $1/S$ pounds to buy a 1-year British bond that pays at the rate of i_{UK}. After one year's time, the person would have accumulated $(1/S)(1 + i_{UK})$ *pounds.* When the person buys the British bond, however, the individual simultaneously sells this quantity of pounds in the forward market at the forward rate of F dollars per pound. This "covers" the individual against risk of exchange rate changes by ensuring that the effective return on the British bond will be $(F/S)(1 + i_{UK})$.

The returns on the two bonds will be equal if $1 + i_{US} = (F/S) \times (1 + i_{UK})$. As you will show in a problem at the end of the chapter, this means that both bonds will be held only if i_{US} is approximately equal to i_{UK}, plus the quantity $(F - S)/S$, or

$$i_{US} = i_{UK} + \frac{(F - S)}{S}$$

covered interest parity   If no barriers exist to international financial transactions and a forward exchange market exists, then the interest rate on an American bond should be equal to the interest rate on a foreign bond, plus a forward discount.

This condition is **covered interest parity.** The quantity $(F - S)/S$ is called the *forward discount*, and so the condition of covered interest parity says that the interest rate on an American bond should approximately equal the interest rate on the foreign (British) bond plus the forward discount.

Note that if $(F - S)/S$ is positive, then the forward exchange rate, F, exceeds the spot exchange rate, S. This means that the dollar has a lower value in terms of pounds—it takes more dollars to buy pounds—in the forward exchange market as compared with the spot exchange market; that is, the dollar trades at a discount in the forward market. As a result, covered interest parity indicates that the interest rate on the American dollar-denominated bond should be higher than the rate on the British pound-denominated bond.

Currency Futures, Options, and Swaps

Derivative securities in the foreign exchange markets parallel derivatives in domestic markets. *Currency futures* are contracts specifying *standard* volumes of particular currencies to be exchanged on a specific date. Most currency futures are traded on the Chicago Mercantile Exchange.

Currency options are contracts that give the owner the right to buy or sell a fixed amount of a given currency at a specified exchange rate at a certain time. Currency call options give the owner the right to buy a currency, while currency put options give the owner the right to sell a currency.

Recall that interest rate swaps are exchanges of flows of interest payments. In contrast, *currency swaps* are exchanges of payment flows denominated in different currencies. Figure 4.4 illustrates how a currency swap works. Ford Motor Company earns a flow of deutsche mark revenues from selling cars in Germany, while Mercedes-Benz earns dollar revenues from selling cars in the United States. But Ford pays dollar dividends and interest to holders of its stocks and bonds, and Mercedes-Benz pays deutsche mark dividends and interest to holders of its stocks and bonds. Hence, Ford and Mercedes-Benz can

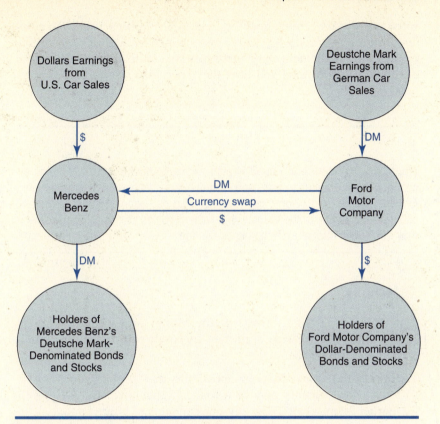

FIGURE 4.4   The Mechanics of a Currency Swap

Ford Motor Company receives deutsche mark earnings from selling cars in Germany, and Mercedes-Benz receives dollar earnings from selling cars in the United States. The two companies could use a currency swap contract to trade deutsche mark and dollar earnings to make payments to holders of their bonds and stocks.

use a swap contract to exchange their deutsche mark and dollar earnings to simplify the task of making payments to their stockholders and bondholders.

Just as interest rate futures, options, and swaps may be used to hedge against interest rate risk, currency futures, options, and swaps may be used to hedge against foreign exchange risk. These foreign exchange derivatives also may be used for speculative trading intended to profit from anticipated changes in market exchange rates. Such trading can yield either profits or losses to those who speculate.

There are inherent risks in holding and trading traditional money and capital market instruments, and derivative securities such as interest rate and currency futures, options, and swaps. Derivative securities can be used to hedge against such risks or to try to profit from them. As we discussed in Chapter 2, financial institutions exist to intermediate risks. A key management goal for financial institutions is to balance interest rate and foreign exchange risks while maintaining maximum profitability. In the next chapter we turn to a more detailed discussion of financial institutions and how they specialize in efforts to achieve this goal.

5

What are some commonly used foreign exchange instruments?   Foreign exchange forward contracts and foreign currency derivatives, including currency futures, options, and swaps, typically are used as hedges against foreign exchange risk, which is the chance that market values of financial instruments may vary when market exchange rates change.

SUMMARY

1. **Key Financial Instruments of the Money and Capital Markets:** These are U.S. Treasury securities, corporate equities, and corporate debt instruments.

2. **Interest Rate Risk:** This is the possibility that the market prices of financial instruments may be affected by unanticipated changes in market interest rates. The key determinants of interest rate risk are the instrument's term to maturity and the frequency with which it yields returns. Interest rate risk increases as the term to maturity lengthens and as the frequency of returns declines.

3. **Duration:** The duration of a financial instrument is a measure of the average time necessary before the owner receives all payments of principal and interest. Duration is calculated as a weighted average of the present values of payments over the full maturity of a financial instrument.

4. **Derivative Securities:** These are financial instruments whose returns depend on the returns of other financial instruments.

5. **The Most Commonly Traded Derivative Securities:** These include interest-rate forward contracts, interest rate and stock index futures, options, and interest rate swaps.

6. **Foreign Exchange Instruments:** Foreign exchange instruments offer the potential for hedging against foreign exchange risks, which are the chances that market prices of financial assets may vary because of movements in currency exchange rates. Commonly used foreign exchange instruments include foreign exchange forward contracts and foreign exchange futures, options, and swaps.

QUESTIONS AND PROBLEMS

1. Explain in your own words the nature of the "winner's curse" that existed before the U.S. Treasury switched to Dutch auctions for U.S. Treasury securities. Also, explain how using Dutch auctions deals with this problem.

2. In your own words explain the meaning of the term *interest rate risk.*

3. Explain in your own words why it makes sense that both the differences in bond lifetimes and the frequency of bond coupon returns influence the degree of interest rate risk on bonds.

4. What is the difference between a futures contract and a futures option contract? Explain briefly.

5. In recent years many observers have questioned the extent to which derivatives really hedge risk even when they are used with that intention. These observers argue that any hedging strategy is based on assumptions about future interest rate movements, thus making hedging and risky speculative behavior difficult to distinguish. Evaluate this argument.

6. As discussed in the chapter, an American who can cover risks of exchange rate movements with a forward exchange contract will be indifferent between holding American or British bonds if the return on each dollar held in the American bond, $1 + i_{US}$, is equal to the return on the British bond, $(F/S)(1 + i_{UK})$. Note that F/S can be written as $[S + (F - S)]/S = 1 + (F - S)/S$, and use this fact to derive the covered interest parity condition. (*Hint:* Note that if $(F - S)/S$ is a small fraction and if i_{UK} is a small fraction, then the product of i_{UK} and $(F - S)/S$ is very close to zero.)

5

Financial Institutions

KEY QUESTIONS

1. What do securities market institutions do, and how does the government regulate these institutions?

2. What do insurance companies do, and who regulates them?

3. How are pension funds structured, and why have they grown?

4. What is the special role of finance companies?

5. How do mutual funds differ?

6. In what ways are financial institutions becoming more alike?

*I*n *the 1950s television watchers saw commercials featuring Speedy, the then-famous Alka Seltzer "spokesperson." In the mid-1990s television viewers were again treated to a black-and-white commercial featuring a talking house reminiscent of Speedy. The house wasn't selling Alka Seltzer this time, but rather the services offered by Home Savings. The 30-second commercial included an elaborate production number with ice-skating bank tellers. Home Savings' ad agency, Chiat/Day, wanted to make people remember the good old days when they believed in banks and actually got good service.*

Competition in the banking industry, with more than 25,000 different banks, S&Ls, and credit unions vying for customers' deposits, has forced these financial institutions to seek new ways to get more business and to have a competitive edge. Banks are trying to set themselves apart from the crowd by using creative advertising just as consumer product firms have been doing for years. Banks are actually trying to establish distinct brand images.

Banks are just one part of a much bigger picture called financial institutions in America.

INTRODUCTION

Because of the inherent problems of adverse selection and asymmetric information in many financial dealings, financial intermediaries comprise a crucial component of the extensive financial system of the United States. Yet only two and a half centuries ago there were just a handful of banks, insurance companies, securities firms, and other financial institutions in America. The unparalleled growth of the financial intermediation industry in the United States is one of the nation's successes.

Until the 1930s many institutions performed a broad array of financial intermediation services. Commercial banks, for instance, acted as investment banks and securities brokers, as well as providing commercial lending and checking account services. Insurance companies sometimes made commercial loans, as did investment banks and securities brokers. Indeed, many of these institutions provided such a variety of services that it was difficult to group institutions by category.

Following the Great Depression in the 1930s, a number of legal restrictions separated financial institutions into readily identifiable groups. These classifications, which are a legacy of that period, remain with us today. In recent years Congress has contemplated several proposals for revisions of government-engendered categories of financial institutions.

As we approach the twenty-first century, some in Congress champion a return to the less-regulated days of the nineteenth and early twentieth centuries.

Recognizing the differences and similarities among the services provided by various financial institutions is a requirement for understanding the crucial roles these institutions play in our financial system. Appreciating their differences and similarities also is necessary background for evaluating recent proposals for restructuring financial institutions in the United States.

This chapter discusses two broad categories of financial institutions. One is *depository institutions*, which include commercial banks, savings banks and savings and loan associations, and credit unions. These institutions issue checking and savings deposits as debt instruments. The other category is *nondepository institutions*, which do not issue deposit liabilities. The chapter also examines how the functions of these institutions have begun to overlap, which in turn has led to calls for removal of artificial barriers between their activities.

Because we shall devote considerable space to depository institutions in later chapters, much of the emphasis in the current chapter is on nondepository institutions. The various types of nondepository financial institutions in the United States provide a broad array of financial services. Some, called *securities market institutions*, specialize in intermediating risks in securities markets; others, known as *insurance companies*, insure individuals and firms against risks of future losses. Other financial institutions called *pension funds* offer pension plans that provide retirement security income to workers. Financial institutions called *finance companies* make loans to individuals and firms that commercial banks, savings banks, and credit unions might deem uncreditworthy, while others known as *mutual funds* provide specialized portfolio management skills.

SECURITIES MARKET INSTITUTIONS

When business firms issue new shares of stock or offer to sell new bonds, both the firms and those who contemplate buying their securities face two asymmetric information problems. One stems from adverse selection. Some of the firms that issue new securities may have an incentive to do so because they are strapped for cash and teetering on the edge of financial disaster. Those considering buying new stock or bond offerings recognize this possibility and need to be able to identify creditworthy firms. The firms themselves recognize this and need a way to signal their creditworthiness to potential purchasers of their securities. Securities market institutions, such as investment banks and securities brokers and dealers, help provide this signal by intermediating between the firms and the purchasers of their securities.

Securities market institutions also help minimize moral hazard problems that arise when firms that have been successful in raising funds via security issues misuse those funds. By monitoring the performance of issuing firms, these institutions assure stock- and bondholders that the firms have maintained their creditworthiness. This insures that the shares of stock or the bonds of issuing firms remain liquid instruments retaining risk the characteristics they possessed when first issued.

Investment Banks

As discussed in Chapter 2, investment banks are financial institutions that serve as intermediaries between businesses that issue stocks and bonds and purchasers of those securities. Typically, investment banks specialize in **securities underwriting,** which means that they guarantee that the issuing firm will receive a specified minimum price per share of stock or per bond.

Under **firm-commitment underwriting,** an investment bank actually purchases the new securities offered by a business and then distributes them to dealers and other buyers. The investment bank seeks to profit from a spread between the price it pays the issuing firm and the actual price that others pay for the securities. In contrast, under **standby-commitment underwriting** an investment bank earns commissions for helping the issuing firm sell its securities and agrees only to purchase any securities that remain after the initial sale. It then seeks to find buyers for those remaining securities.

Another possible arrangement is for the investment bank to act solely as an *agent* for the firm. The firm then pays the investment bank a commission for its marketing services. Under such an arrangement, which is called a **best-efforts deal,** the investment bank usually has an option to buy a portion of the issuing firm's securities, but it is not obligated to exercise that option. Best-efforts deals were more common in the nineteenth and early twentieth centuries than they have been in recent decades. Nowadays, these arrangements tend to arise when the securities of the issuing firms are regarded as highly risky.

Securities Brokers and Dealers

While some financial firms are either brokers or dealers, in many cases a firm that acts as a broker also is a dealer. As discussed in Chapter 2, a *broker* specializes in matching buyers and sellers in secondary financial markets. Brokers receive commissions and fees as payment for their services. A **dealer,** in contrast, sells securities from its own portfolio and seeks to profit by buying low and selling high. *Broker-dealers* engage in both types of business. Most major Wall Street brokerage firms are broker-dealers, trading both on behalf of customers and on their own account.

securities underwriting   A guarantee by an investment bank that a firm that issues a new stock or bond will receive a specified minimum price per share of stock or per bond.

firm-commitment underwriting   An investment banking arrangement in which the investment bank purchases and then resells to dealers and other purchasers all securities offered by a business.

standby-commitment underwriting   An investment banking arrangement in which the investment bank earns commissions for helping an issuing firm sell its securities, but with a guarantee that the investment bank will purchase for resale any unsold securities.

best-efforts deal   An investment banking arrangement in which the investment bank has an option to buy a portion of the issuing firm's securities but is not required to do so.

dealer   A financial intermediary that buys and sells stocks and bonds from its own portfolio in pursuit of trading profit.

Types of Brokers

full-service broker A broker that offers a range of trading and consulting services.

discount broker A broker that specializes only in trading on clients' behalf.

over-the-counter (OTC) broker-dealer A broker-dealer who trades shares of stock that are not listed in organized stock exchanges.

National Association of Securities Dealers (NASD) A self-regulating group of OTC broker-dealers that determines trading rules for its members.

NASD automated quotation system (NASDAQ) A national market system of computer and telephone links between over-the-counter broker-dealers.

specialists Stock exchange members who are charged with trading on their own accounts to prevent dramatic movements in stock prices.

limit orders Instructions from other stock exchange members to specialists to execute stock trades at specific prices.

Types of Brokers   When a broker makes a securities trade on a customer's behalf, it acts as the customer's *agent* in the stock or bond market. This means that the broker makes the trade in place of the customer but must act as the customer wishes. A **full-service broker** offers a range of other financial services, including consultations about what financial instruments to buy or sell and other financial planning advice. The only service that a **discount broker** offers is making securities trades for clients.

One type of discount broker is a **share broker,** which bases its commission charges on the number of shares it trades on a customer's behalf. In contrast, a **value broker** determines its commission charges based on a percentage of the dollar value of each transaction. For those who wish to trade sizable volumes of securities, a share broker's services entail lower cost. Those who typically trade small numbers of shares gain from using the services of a value broker.

Over-the-Counter (OTC) Broker-Dealers   Another type of broker is an **over-the-counter (OTC) broker-dealer,** which specializes in trading shares of stock that are not listed in organized stock exchanges. Such over-the-counter stocks are traded in decentralized markets linking OTC broker-dealers. As noted earlier, OTC stocks typically are those of smaller companies that do not meet listing requirements for the New York or American Stock Exchanges.

Although OTC stock trading falls outside the rules of these centralized exchanges, listed stocks still must meet standards set by the **National Association of Securities Dealers (NASD),** which is a self-regulating group of OTC broker-dealers. This group also operates the **NASD automated quotation system (NASDAQ),** a national market system of computer and telephone links between OTC broker-dealers.

Specialists   Some broker-dealers perform special roles in the securities markets. These are **specialists,** members of stock exchanges who are responsible for preventing wide swings in stock prices. They do this by adding to or reducing their own holdings of a given stock to counteract significant changes in demand or supply conditions.

Specialists are also responsible for executing specific trades called **limit orders.** A limit order is an instruction from another stock exchange member to execute a trade when a stock's price reaches a certain level. For instance, a specialist might receive a limit order when a stock's share price is $25 to sell a given amount of shares on the ordering broker's behalf if the price slips to $23. Only if the share price reaches $23 would the specialist make the trade. But if the share price does hit $23, the specialist is bound by the rules of the exchange to do so. In return for this service the specialist receives a commission from the ordering broker.

As brokers place limit orders, specialists list them in ledgers called *specialist's books*. For a given specialist, the ledger details the specialist's own holdings of securities and the sequence of limit orders received from other brokers. If the specialist's book contains an unexecuted limit order, then the specialist cannot trade securities on its own account at the limit order price *until* it first executes the limit order. From time to time this restriction can entail a sacrifice of earnings for the specialist. The limit order commissions that the specialist receives compensates the specialist for this sacrifice.

Regulation of Securities Market Institutions

All securities markets institutions must meet regulations established by the **Securities and Exchange Commission (SEC).** Congress created the SEC in the *Securities Exchange Act of 1934*. The SEC is composed of five commissioners appointed by the president of the United States on a rotating basis to 5-year terms. The president names one of these individuals as chair of the SEC.

Securities and Exchange Commission (SEC)   A group of five presidentially appointed members whose mandate is to enforce rules governing securities trading.

The SEC's mandate is to enforce both the 1934 Act as well as the *Securities Act of 1933*. The 1933 Act requires that all securities for sale be registered and that detailed information about each security be disclosed in a **prospectus,** or formal written offer to sell securities. The 1934 Act requires securities market institutions to refrain from fraudulent activities or from efforts to manipulate stock and bond prices. In light of these requirements, the SEC lists and enforces a number of rules that govern securities trading. It also oversees and approves rules established by groups such as the NASD.

prospectus   A formal written offer to sell securities.

1

What do securities market institutions do, and how does the government regulate these institutions?   Investment banks underwrite and market new stock and bonds that corporations issue. Brokers trade securities on behalf of clients, and dealers trade on their own accounts. The Securities and Exchange Commission regulates the activities of these firms.

INSURANCE INSTITUTIONS

As we discussed in our brief survey of financial institutions in Chapter 2, insurance companies are financial institutions that specialize in trying to limit adverse selection and moral hazard problems by insuring against unpredictable future losses. The policies they issue are promises to repay the policyholder if such a loss occurs. In return, insurance companies receive premiums from the owners of the policies, who are called policy holders. The companies set aside most of these premiums as *reserves*, from which payments are made to policyholders who experience losses. The remaining portion of premiums are the companies' revenues. Reserves are composed of securities and cash.

Dealing with Asymmetric Information Problems in Insurance

There are a number of features common to most insurance policies. Companies design these features to reduce the extent of problems faced in light of asymmetric information. After all, those who apply for insurance know much more about their own risks of loss than do the insurance companies, and those who receive insurance can do the most to limit the risks of such losses.

Limiting Adverse Selection

One way that insurance companies reduce the adverse selection problem is by restricting the availability of insurance. Insurance companies will not sell every available policy to every individual. For instance, suppose that an individual has a spouse and four children but no life insurance. This person then learns of impending death from an illness for which there is no cure. If the individual cares about the spouse and children, then the person has every incentive after learning of the illness to purchase a life insurance policy. If the insurer would permit a person in such a situation to buy such a policy, then the insurer would be taking on a 100 percent probability of a claim that would amount to more than the premiums it would collect from that individual. No insurance company could stay in business for very long if it made its policies available to all who might want to buy them.

Insurers also deal with the adverse selection problem by limiting how much insurance any one individual or firm can buy. To reduce their companies' exposure to losses from policies taken out by applicants who may know that they have life-shortening conditions, insurers typically place a limit on the dollar amount of coverage an individual may purchase. In addition, insurance companies typically require policyholders who purchase large life insurance policies or who decide to signficantly increase their current policy coverage to undergo blood tests or other physical examinations.

Limiting Moral Hazard in Insurance

Another feature of insurance policies is that they contain provisions that restrict the behavior of policyholders. These provisions are intended to reduce the extent of the moral hazard problem that insurers also face.

As noted above, limiting the amount of insurance can counter the adverse selection problem. It also can reduce the extent of some moral hazard problems. For example, if a company that operates agricultural grain elevators could insure the elevators for more than they are worth, then there would be little incentive for the company to operate them safely by keeping flammable liquids or spark-producing equipment away from them. This would increase the risks of explosions and thereby raise the insurer's chances of having to make payments on losses. Hence, insurers typically limit policy coverages to the maximum possible losses that policyholders could incur.

One key weapon against moral hazard problems is an insurance company's ability to cancel insurance because of "bad behavior" by a policyholder. A feature common to most insurance policies is a threat of cancellation if the policyholder develops a record of reckless behavior after the policy has been issued.

Insurance companies also combat the moral hazard problem by offering policies with *deductible* and *coinsurance* features. A **deductible** is a fixed amount of a loss that a policyholder must pay before the insurance company must provide promised payments. For example, if a homeowner's child throws a rock through a $400 picture window in the insured house and the homeowner's policy has a $200 deductible against such a loss, then the homeowner must pay $200 of the cost of replacing the window. The insurance company pays the remaining $200. The presence of the deductible feature gives the homeowner an incentive to lecture the child about throwing rocks, thereby reducing the risk that the homeowner and the insurer would incur such a loss. This feature of the policy also gives the homeowner a reason to monitor the child's behavior.

Coinsurance is an insurance policy feature in which the policyholder pays a fixed percentage of any loss above the specified deductible. In the example of the broken picture window, a policy with a coinsurance feature might require that the policyholder pay 10 percent of the loss over the $200 deductible. If the homeowner's policy has this feature, then the total loss to the homeowner is $220—the $200 deductible plus 10 percent of the additional $200 loss ($20). This coinsurance feature would give the homeowner an added incentive to keep rocks from flying from the child's hands.

Determining Policy Premiums   The essential principle of insurance is the pooling of risks of loss that might be incurred by individual members of a large group. Even though all the members of the group might experience a loss, only a small number actually will incur a loss. For example, over any 1-year period, on average two of every 1,000 retail businesses might experience a major fire. For the two businesses that incur such a loss, the destruction caused by the fire would be sufficient to destroy the business. But what if the risk of fire damage were distributed across all 1,000 businesses? Each one can pay yearly one-thousandth of the expected loss to the two of their number who would incur a fire loss. Then, when the actual losses occur, there would be sufficient funds on hand to reimburse the two businesses that, on average, experience fires.

deductible   A fixed amount of an insured loss that a policyholder must pay before the insurer is obliged to make payments.

coinsurance   An insurance policy feature in which a policyholder pays a fixed percentage of a loss above a deductible.

actuary   An individual who specializes in using mathematical and statistical principles to calculate insurance premiums and to estimate an insurance company's net worth.

Insurance companies use this type of statistical approach to compute appropriate policy premiums. They use the services of **actuaries,** who specialize in using mathematical and statistical principles to calculate premiums that will cover expected losses to policyholders. Premiums that are just sufficient to cover expected insured losses are called *actuarially fair* insurance premiums. Actuaries also assist in estimating the value of the insurance company itself, which is never known for certain because the company's losses—and consequently its liabilities—are subject to risk.

Premiums on insurance policies actually are somewhat higher than the actuarially fair premiums, because such premiums effectively are the prices of various insurance policies. As with any market price, the premium for an insurance policy also reflects revenue and cost conditions faced by insurers. For instance, when interest rates are low, insurance premiums tend to rise. The reason is that the loss reserves held by the insurance companies earn interest, and if interest rates are low the companies must bolster reserves and maintain their profitability by raising premiums.

Life Insurance

There are about 400 million life insurance policies in effect in the United States in any given year. Life insurance companies typically classify policies into separate categories. *Ordinary* life policies in amounts of $1,000 or more and *industrial* life policies in amounts of less than $1,000 cover individuals. *Group* life policies cover a number of people under terms specified by a master contract that applies to all who are covered. Finally, *credit* life policies insure a borrower against loan foreclosure in the event of death before full payment of the loan. Figure 5.1 shows the current distribution of such policies.

whole life policy   A life insurance policy whose benefits are payable to a beneficiary on an insured person's death and which also accumulates a cash value that maybe redeemed by the policyholder prior to death.

Most policies issued by life insurance companies guarantee payments to a designated beneficiary, such as a spouse or child, when the insured individual dies. Actuaries determine the actuarially fair premiums for life insurance policies using historical experience on probabilities of death at various ages. Because life expectancies across many policyholders are predictable, life insurance companies have a good idea how much in benefits they will need to pay out in future years. Consequently, the companies typically feel secure holding relatively illiquid, long-term corporate bonds and stocks as sizable components of their portfolio of financial instruments.

level-premium policy   A whole life insurance policy under which an insurance company charges fixed premium payments throughout the life of the insured individual.

Whole Versus Term Life Insurance   There are two basic types of life insurance policies. One is a **whole life policy,** in which insurance is payable at the death of the insured and in which the policy has an accumulated cash value that the policyholder may draw upon before death. Whole life policies come in two forms. One is the **level-premium policy,** in which the insurance company charges fixed premium

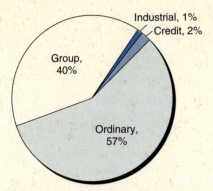

FIGURE 5.1   The Distribution of Life Insurance Policies

Ordinary and group insurance policies account for the bulk of life insurance policies in the United States. (Percentages rounded to nearest whole number.) *Source: American Council of Life Insurance, Life Insurance Fact Book, 1996.*

payments throughout the life of the insured individual. The other form of whole life policy is the **limited-payment policy,** in which the insured individual pays premiums only for a fixed number of years and is insured during and after the payment period. Both kinds of whole life policies typically have a *cash surrender value,* meaning that the insured individual can exchange the policy for a lump-sum payment after a specified date. Consequently, some people use whole life policies as a type of saving instrument.

The other basic type of life insurance policy is a **term life policy.** Under this kind of policy an individual is insured only during the limited period in which the policy is in effect. Premiums for term life policies depend on the age of the insured person, and typically they increase each time they are renewed. The reason is that as an individual ages, the chance of death during the term of the next policy increases. Nevertheless, term life policies typically have lower premiums over an average lifespan compared with whole life policies. The reason is that a term life policy has no cash surrender value, and so has no additional savings component. The premium, therefore, reflects only the risks that the insurer takes on by providing the policy.

Annuities   Payments that life insurers guarantee to beneficiaries may be in the form of a lump sum or an annuity, which is a stream of payments over a stated period or perhaps until the death of the beneficiary. There are two types of annuities. A **fixed annuity** makes payments to the holder in regular installments of constant dollar amounts

limited-payment policy   A whole life insurance policy under which an insured individual pays premiums only for a fixed number of years but is insured during and after the payment period.

term life policy   A life insurance policy under which an individual is insured only for the limited period during which the policy is in effect.

fixed annuity   A financial instrument, typically issued by an insurance company, that pays regular, constant installments to the owner beginning at a specific future date.

variable annuity   A financial
instrument, typically issued
by an insurance company, beginning on a specific future
date, that pays the owner a
stream of returns that depends on the value of an underlying portfolio of assets.

beginning at a specific future time. In a **variable annuity,** the payouts
that a holder receives depend on the value of the underlying portfolio
of assets that the insurance company uses to fund the payouts.

Property-Casualty Insurance

Insurance against property and casualty losses covers a variety of
contingencies. Property-casualty companies issue policies covering
losses stemming from accidental or fire damage to automobiles,
buildings, boats, ships, crops, factory equipment, furnaces, and so on.
Policies also cover losses resulting from injuries or deaths due to accidents. Businesses cover employees through policies offered in the
form of worker's compensation insurance. Finally, property-casualty
companies also offer policies covering liabilities stemming from automobile accidents, poorly designed or produced products, or medical
malpractice. Figure 5.2 shows the present distribution of premiums
by line of business for all property-casualty insurance companies.

Because property-casualty companies insure against such a variety of losses, actuaries for these companies treat each line of business
separately for purposes of premium calculation. Furthermore, the varied nature of these lines of business makes it more difficult for property-casualty insurers to be certain of the likely payouts to insured individuals and firms. For this reason, property-casualty insurance
companies usually hold much more diversified portfolios of financial
instruments as compared with life insurance companies.

**FIGURE 5.2   The Distribution of Property-Casualty
                    Premiums by Line of Business**

Premiums for policies covering autos account for nearly
half of the total premium volumes of property-casualty
insurers. (Percentages rounded to nearest whole number.) *Source:* Insurance Information Institute, *Fact Book,* 1996.

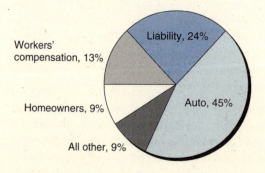

Regulation of Insurance Companies

Although insurance companies must meet the terms of a number of federal laws and regulations, the primary supervisory authorities for life insurance companies are in each of the fifty states. Insurance companies must meet not only the standards established by the state in which they are incorporated but also standards set in the states in which they sell policies. This means that if companies do business in all states, they must meet the minimum standards specified by the toughest state regulatory body.

2

What do insurance companies do, and who regulates their activities?   Insurance companies offer policies that guarantee to cover losses of life and property. They use a variety of techniques to minimize the adverse selection and moral hazard problems inherent in insurance. Individual states regulate insurance companies. Because companies do business in many or all states the toughest state regulators can affect nationwide industry standards.

PENSION FUNDS

As Figure 5.3 on page 122 indicates, growth in the share of financial institution assets held in pension funds has increased steadily since the 1950s. There are two likely reasons for the growth of pension funds. One is the gradual aging of the baby-boom generation. Most baby boomers began working in the 1960s and 1970s. As they have aged, their incomes and consequently their contributions to pension funds have risen. Another reason is that pension funds have become more popular savings vehicles for many people. This has happened both because pension funds have made pension arrangements more flexible over time and because most pension income is tax-deferred, meaning that contributions and earnings are not taxable until individuals begin drawing on accumulated pension savings.

Types of Pensions

Any pension is an arrangement in which an employer agrees to provide benefits to retired employees. Usually such benefits are annuities. Pensions may be **contributory pensions,** meaning that both the employer and the employee contribute to the pension fund. In contrast, **noncontributory pensions** entail contributions only by employers.

contributory pensions   Pensions funded by both employer and employee contributions.

noncontributory pensions   Pensions funded solely by employers.

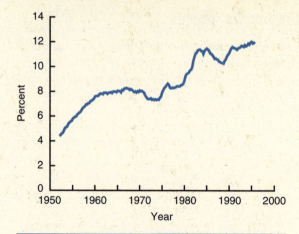

FIGURE 5.3   Pension Funds' Share of Financial Institution Assets

The share of total assets of all privately owned financial institutions held by pension funds has increased steadily since the 1950s. *Source:* Board of Governors of the Federal Reserve System, *Flow-of-Funds Accounts,* various issues.

terminally funded pensions
Pensions that must be fully funded by the date an employee retires.

Terminally funded pensions call for full funding of and payment of benefits to an employee beginning at the retirement date of the employee. An employee covered by such a pension is said to be *vested* when the employee has earned enough service time to be eligible to receive retirement benefits even if he or she leaves the employer prior to actually retiring. For instance, a public school teacher who is vested in the pension fund of a state teachers' retirement fund will receive benefits upon retirement even if the teacher leaves the public school before retirement age to teach at a private school.

pay-as-you-go pensions
Pensions that are not fully funded when employees retire.

Some employers offer **pay-as-you-go pensions,** in which pensions are not fully funded when employees retire. Instead, the employer funds pension benefits for current retirees out of current earnings produced by current (nonretired) workers. Some employers operate pension plans that combine terminal funding with pay-as-you-go funding provisions.

single-employer pensions
Pensions established by an employer only for its own employees, and nontransferable to other employers.

Single-employer pensions are those that an employer establishes only for its own employees. Funding and benefits for such pensions are nontransferable. In contrast, under **multi-employer pensions** employees may transfer accumulated funds and benefit rights when they change jobs. (This is called pension *portability.*) Multi-employer pensions typically apply to a specific industry. For instance, many colleges and professors contribute to TIAA-CREF, which is a multi-employer pension fund

multi-employer pensions
Pensions whose accumulations and benefit rights may be transferred from one employer to another.

for colleges and universities. But accumulations and benefit rights from that plan generally are not transferable if a professor leaves a college to enter private industry or government service. (But all accumulations up to that point are fully vested and available as annuities.)

Pension Fund Insurance and Regulation

Many pension funds have insurance to cover the contingency that they will be unable to honor obligations to make future payments to retirees. Such funds operate under legal contracts that are mutually binding on both the pension fund and the insurer. Pension funds that are not insured typically fund their benefits under a *trust* agreement, in which a neutral party, called the *trustee*, administers the distribution of benefits to retirees.

In 1974 concerns about the solvency of some pension funds led Congress to pass the *Employment Retirement Income Security Act* (*ERISA*). This Act and subsequent amendments set out federal rules for disclosure of pension information, funding arrangements, and vesting provisions. It also created the **Pension Benefit Guaranty Corporation (PBGC),** which provides federal insurance for all pensions with tax-deferred benefits. These are the bulk of pensions in the United States.

The PBGC suffers from significant adverse selection and moral hazard problems. Because its insurance is available to all pension funds that offer federal tax benefits, it cannot deny insurance to any pension fund that meets that criterion. Furthermore, it has limited powers to impose restrictions on underfunded pension funds. As a result of these problems, by 1987 the PBGC had $1.5 billion more in liabilities than assets; its net worth was negative. By 1996 this negative net worth had mushroomed to over ten times this amount! Because the PBGC is a federally guaranteed financial institution, taxpayers currently owe this amount to pensioners insured by the PBGC.

Pension Benefit Guaranty Corporation (PBGC)   An agency of the federal government that provides federal insurance for all pensions with tax-deferred benefits.

3

How are pension funds structured, and why have they grown?   Noncontributory pension funds accumulate via funding provided solely by employers, whereas contributory pension funds are also funded by employees. Some pensions have terminal funding, which requires that they be fully funded at the time an employee retires. Pay-as-you-go pensions are funded out of the firm's current earnings. Pension funds have grown significantly because of the aging of the baby boom generation, the growing flexibility of the funds, and the tax deferments permitted by law.

GOVERNMENT CREDIT AGENCIES

The PBGC is one example of several agencies of the federal government that provide financial services. As discussed in Chapter 2, most government credit agencies, such as the Government National Mortgage Association (GNMA), the Federal National Mortgage Association (FNMA), and the Federal Home Loan Mortgage Company (FHLMC) are responsible for making mortgage markets more liquid by selling mortgage-backed securities and purchasing mortgages. The Federal Housing Administration (FHA), Department of Housing and Urban Development (HUD), and the Veterans Administration (VA) also assist eligible individuals to purchase homes by making mortgage loans directly to those individuals or by subsidizing and guaranteeing loans they receive from private lenders.

The federal government also operates the Farm Credit System, which makes loans to farmers. Such loans are guaranteed by the Farmer's Home Administration. The Student Loan Marketing Association is a government-assisted agency that purchases student loans guaranteed by the Department of Education.

Figure 5.4 displays the share of financial instruments held by government credit agencies, which grew steadily until the 1980s. The

---

FIGURE 5.4   **Share of Ownership of Financial Instruments Held by Government-Sponsored Institutions**

The share of dollars in financial instruments held by government-sponsored agencies increased rapidly from the mid-1950s, to a high in 1980, and then fell. In recent years this share has nearly returned to its earlier high. *Source:* Board of Governors of the Federal Reserve System, *Flow-of-Funds Accounts*, various issues.

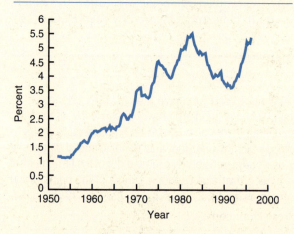

portion of financial instruments held by these government-sponsored agencies declined during the 1980s, but has risen rapidly in recent years. Nevertheless, the share held by these agencies has never exceeded 6 percent.

In recent years key members of Congress have discussed curtailing many of the loan guarantees relating to programs for farmers, students, and veterans. But the greatest potential threat to taxpayers probably lies in the underfunded pensions insured by the Pension Benefit Guaranty Corporation. As members of the baby-boom generation gradually reach retirement age early in the 21st century, pension fund payouts will escalate. Absent efforts to offset the multibillion dollar negative net worth of the PBGC, taxpayers almost certainly will find themselves bailing out a number of underfunded private pension plans.

FINANCE COMPANIES

Finance companies traditionally have specialized in lending to businesses and individuals of insufficient size and/or creditworthiness to issue financial instruments in the money or capital markets or to borrow from other lenders such as commercial banks. **Business finance companies** typically make loans to small businesses. In many instances they extend credit by saving the small businesses the trouble of collecting unpaid bills. A business finance company often purchases bills owed to a small firm at a discount from the face value of the bills. For example, a small business might have $51,000 in unpaid bills. Of these, the business might reasonably expect to collect $50,000. One way to finance continued operations might be for the business to sell the $51,000 in unpaid bills to a business finance company at a price of $46,000. The finance company makes a profit on this arrangement when it collects the total $50,000 in easily collectible debts (for a profit of $4,000) and perhaps some of the $1,000 in debts that the small business may already have written off.

Other finance companies specialize in offering financial services to individuals. **Consumer finance companies** make loans to individuals to enable them to purchase durable goods such as home appliances or furniture or to make improvements to existing homes. **Sales finance companies** make loans to individuals planning to purchase items from specific retailers or manufacturers, such as Sears or Ford Motor Company.

Finance companies finance their operations by issuing debt in the form of commercial paper and bonds and through the sale of equity shares. Many also borrow from commercial banks.

business finance companies
Finance companies that specialize in making loans to small businesses.

consumer finance companies
Finance companies that specialize in making loans to individuals for the purchase of durable goods or for home improvements.

sales finance companies
Finance companies that specialize in making loans to individuals for the purchase of items from specific retailers or manufacturers.

4

What is the special role of finance companies?   Finance companies typically specialize in lending to consumers and firms whose creditworthiness or size sometimes preclude them from qualifying for loans from depository institutions such as commercial banks.

MUTUAL FUNDS

Mutual funds are portfolios of financial instruments managed on behalf of shareholders by investment companies. These investment companies charge fees for managing the funds. Before the 1960s most mutual funds specialized in stock portfolios, but during that decade several broadened their portfolios to include bonds. During the 1970s money market mutual funds also became popular as interest rates on large-denomination financial instruments outstripped regulated rates on deposit accounts at commercial banks and other depository financial institutions. Figure 5.5 depicts the significant growth of stock and bond and money market mutual funds since the mid-1950s.

FIGURE 5.5   Mutual Funds' Share of Financial Institution Assets
The share of total assets of all privately owned financial institutions held by stock and bond and money market mutual funds has risen rapidly since the 1970s. *Source:* Board of Governors of the Federal Reserve System, *Flow-of-Funds Accounts*, various issues.

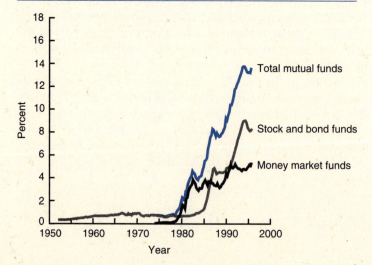

Mutual funds can be categorized along two dimensions. **Load funds** are marketed by brokers, and returns on such funds are reduced by commissions paid to such brokers. Investment companies market **no-load funds** directly to the public. There are no commission charges on such funds, although the investment company charges shareholders a periodic management fee. Both types of funds charge annual management fees.

Some mutual funds are **closed-end funds,** which sell shares in an initial offering. The shares in closed-end funds cannot be redeemed but may be sold to others, much like over-the-counter stocks. The market value of a closed-end fund varies with the market values of the pools of financial instruments held by the fund. In contrast, shares of **open-end funds** are redeemable at any time at prices based on the market values of the mix of financial instruments held by the fund. Because shares of open-end funds are redeemable, they are more liquid than closed-end funds.

load funds   Mutual funds that investment companies market through brokers and that offer returns that reflect commissions paid to these brokers.

no-load funds   Mutual funds that investment companies market directly to the public and that charge management fees instead of brokerage commissions.

closed-end funds   Mutual funds that sell nonredeemable shares whose market values vary with the market values of the underlying mix of financial instruments held by the mutual fund.

open-end funds   Mutual funds whose shares are redeemable at any time at prices based on the market value of the mix of financial instruments held by the fund.

5

How do mutual funds differ?   There are two key ways to categorize mutual funds. One is based on whether they entail paying commission to those who market the funds (load funds) or simply require payment of a management fee (no-load funds). The other is based on whether the shares of the fund are redeemable upon demand (open-end funds) or are nonredeemable shares that can be sold only in secondary markets (closed-end funds).

DEPOSITORY FINANCIAL INSTITUTIONS

As discussed in Chapter 1, financial institutions that have the legal authority to offer traditional checking and savings accounts are called depository financial institutions. Commercial banks, savings banks and savings and loan associations, and credit unions fall into this category.

Commercial Banks

As noted in Chapter 2, commercial banks differ from many other financial institutions in two ways. First, they are depository institutions and hence have the power to offer checking and savings deposits, which are included in monetary aggregates such as M1 and M2. Second, unlike other depository institutions they specialize in lending to business firms. Although commercial banks make many different kinds of loans, commercial and industrial loans and business real estate loans compose a significant fraction of their total lending.

Since the 1930s the Federal Reserve has regarded the commercial banks as "special" financial institutions because they play a key role in facilitating monetary policy. Commercial banks account for the largest bulk of the checking and savings deposits the Fed counts as part of its monetary aggregates. For this reason, the Fed considers policies that can influence the behavior of commercial banks to be crucial aspects of its ability to influence flows of income and spending in the American economy. Commercial bank deposits also are insured by the government.

Because commercial banks traditionally have been regarded as a key link between monetary policy and the economy, we shall devote considerable attention to them in subsequent chapters. As we discuss below, however, many of the distinctions between commercial banks and other depository and nondepository institutions have gradually eroded since the 1970s.

Thrift Institutions

Savings banks, savings and loan associations, and credit unions traditionally have been lumped into a separate category of depository institutions known as *thrift institutions,* or thrifts. These institutions have always offered savings account instruments, but only since the 1970s have they offered checking accounts.

Traditionally savings banks and savings and loan associations have specialized in housing finance. Substantial portions of their portfolios of assets continue to be devoted to mortgage loans and holdings of mortgage-backed securities. Nevertheless, the distinction between these institutions and commercial banks had blurred sufficiently by the end of the 1980s that, in 1989, Congress placed these institutions under the same regulatory umbrella as commercial banks. Congress also restructured the federal deposit insurance system so that savings banks and savings and loan associations are insured under the same system as commercial banks.

Credit unions offer checking and savings instruments and make loans to their members. Traditionally they have specialized in consumer lending, though recently many have branched out into the mortgage lending business. Federal regulation of credit unions is separate from that of other depository institutions, as is the deposit insurance system for credit unions.

Because they offer checking accounts, thrift institutions also are central to the process by which the Federal Reserve influences the quantity of money in the economy. They occupied center stage in recent actions and debates concerning the scope of deposit insurance and federal financial regulation. For these reasons we give considerable attention to these institutions in several of the chapters that follow.

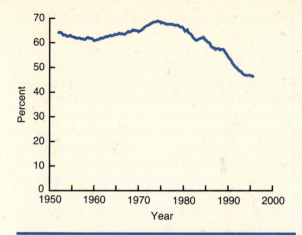

FIGURE 5.6   Depository Institutions' Share of Financial Institution Assets

The share of total assets of all privately owned financial institutions held by depository institutions (commercial banks, savings institutions, and credit unions) has declined steadily since the late 1970s. *Source:* Board of Governors of the Federal Reserve System, *Flow-of-Funds Accounts*, various issues.

Figure 5.6 shows that, measured in terms of shares of assets held at financial intermediaries, depository financial institutions have lost ground since the 1960s. The Fed and other observers have expressed much concern in recent years about this apparent loss of standing of depository institutions. We shall return to this issue in the next chapter.

THE TREND TOWARD OVERLAPPING FUNCTIONS OF FINANCIAL INSTITUTIONS

The blurring of distinctions among depository financial institutions reflects analogous breakdowns in the barriers that traditionally have separated the functions of both depository and nondepository financial institutions. We conclude this chapter by reviewing some of the ways in which financial institutions have become less specialized, resulting in considerable overlap in of their functions.

Competition Among Financial Institutions of Different Stripes

The key reason why some financial institutions are beginning to look more and more alike is that they find themselves competing in the same markets. The best way to see this is to consider recent examples of this phenomenon. This also helps us to speculate about what the future may hold for financial institutions.

Commercial Banks Versus Securities Market Institutions   The *Glass-Steagall Banking Act of 1933* prohibited commercial banks from underwriting most securities and from acting as brokers or dealers in the stock exchanges. But ever since Congress enacted this legislation, commercial banks have sought to have the Glass-Steagall restrictions repealed. Several U.S. presidents have tended to agree. Despite other obvious political differences between Republican Presidents Reagan and Bush on the one hand and Democratic President Clinton on the other, all three administrations proposed eliminating the legal separation between commercial banking and securities intermediation. So far Congress has not cooperated with such proposals, though very recently there has been discussion of relaxing many Glass-Steagall restrictions. As you will learn in Chapter 8, many of the laws governing financial institutions have been in a state of flux for the past twenty years.

Commercial banks have not waited for Congressional action, however. In the 1980s, even as they worked in Congress for direct exemptions, a number of commercial banks began testing the legal limits of the 1933 legislation by offering securities services that pushed the boundaries of legality. For instance, Bankers Trust, J. P. Morgan, and other large banks set up *securities affiliates,* which were companies separate from their basic banking operations that acted as investment banks. The main customers of these affiliate companies were the banks' regular loan customers. Although in 1991 Congress limited the extent to which the commercial banks and their investment banking affiliates could be related, the banks nonetheless won a major victory when they were able to continue operating these companies. By 1995, J. P. Morgan's securities affiliate was the underwriter for about 4 percent of all stocks and bonds, ranking it with the top investment banking firms.

Other commercial banks have tried to get around the Glass-Steagall restrictions through an if-you-can't-beat-them, join-them approach. In 1992 for example, Nationsbank, a large southeastern regional banking firm, joined with Dean Witter, a major brokerage firm, to market securities at about 600 Nationsbank branch offices. Dean Witter viewed the arrangement as a chance to expand its marketing base, and Nationsbank considered it an opportunity to learn about the securities business while getting a share of the commissions and fees that Dean Witter would generate.

Because of problems in coordinating the sharing of profits, the two companies gave up on this arrangement in late 1994. Yet it established an important precedent by proving that securities legally may be marketed from commercial banking offices. The venture raised enough concerns about competition from banks that, in 1995, the NASD considered adopting rules excluding members from setting up similar arrangements with commercial banks.

The competition between banks and securities firms goes both ways. While the Glass-Steagall Act has sharply restricted the securities operations of commercial banks, securities firms have not faced the same restrictions on their ability to compete with commercial banks. While most securities institutions have been content to rely on investment banking and securities brokering and dealing for their livelihoods, a few have made inroads into the traditional provinces of commercial banks.

For instance, consider Merrill Lynch, the nation's largest brokerage firm, with over 12,000 brokers and over 6 million client accounts. Merrill Lynch also is the second-largest mutual fund company and the largest investment banking underwriter. And, to the dismay of some commercial banks, it has become a significant force in the commercial lending business. Beginning in the 1980s, Merrill Lynch jumped into small-business lending, which was a growing loan market that many large banks had ignored and that smaller banks lacked the resources to exploit to its fullest potential. Between 1982 and 1991, the company lent about $2 billion to about 80 small businesses. Not all this lending ultimately paid off for Merrill Lynch, however. By 1996 it had been forced to write off some of these loans. But it now has established a reputation as a major competitor in this market, which previously was the domain of commercial banks.

Banking Inroads into the Insurance Business   Federal law also prohibits banks from selling most types of insurance. In 1916, however, Congress passed an otherwise obscure law that allowed banks to sell insurance in towns with 5,000 or fewer residents. Until 1986 courts generally interpreted the law as applying only to small rural communities where insurance otherwise was not available from traditional insurance companies. But in that year a key regulator of nationally chartered banks, the Office of the Comptroller of the Currency, ruled that under this law national banks could locate a branch office in towns with fewer than 5,000 residents and use that base to market insurance *nationwide!*

Insurance companies and agents fought this action in the courts and in Congress. Following an initial legal challenge, a federal district court ruled in favor of the Comptroller's interpretation of the law. But then in 1992 a federal appeals court reached the opposite conclusion, ruling that in 1918 Congress had passed a law intended to repeal the bank insurance feature of the 1916 legislation. Insurers celebrated for a year, but in 1993 the U.S. Supreme Court ruled unanimously that Congress had, in fact, left the 1916 law intact. A battle over the Comptroller's decision continued in the courts until 1996. Ultimately, the Supreme Court upheld banks' rights to sell insurance in the smallest towns in America.

As discussed earlier, insurance companies traditionally have specialized in selling annuities. This is a big business for insurers, who in

1995 sold over $70 billion in annuities. But banks also have succeeded in getting a chunk of this business, selling over $14 billion worth of annuities in 1995. That year the Supreme Court ruled unanimously that banks have the authority to sell annuities. A U.S. district court judge also ruled that banks can offer "retirement CDs," which are a very close substitute for traditional annuities. And so it appears that competition among banks and insurers in the annuities market likely will continue.

Bank Deposits Versus Mutual Fund Shares   Mutual fund shares differ from bank deposits in two ways. One difference is that a mutual fund share is more like common stock in that the return from holding a share varies with the return earned by the mutual fund. In contrast, the return on a deposit at a commercial bank does not depend on the bank's profitability but is instead predetermined. The other difference is that mutual fund shares are not federally insured, but bank deposits are.

Nevertheless, many people have switched from holding funds in bank deposits to holding them in mutual funds. As Figure 5.7 shows, the share of financial intruments held as bank deposits and currency has fallen from nearly 50 percent in the mid-1970s to just over 20 percent at

---

FIGURE 5.7   Bank Deposits and Currency vs. Mutual Fund Shares

As a fraction of dollars held in financial instruments, holdings of bank deposits and currency have declined during the past two decades. Holdings of mutual fund shares have risen considerably in relation to the dollar amount of all financial instruments during the same interval. *Source:* Board of Governors of the Federal Reserve System, *Flow-of-Funds Accounts,* various issues.

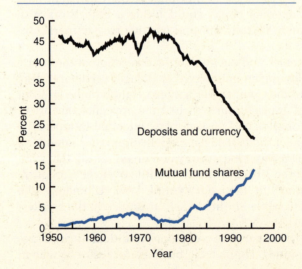

present. During the same interval, the portion of financial instruments held as mutual fund shares rose from under 3 percent to over 13 percent. Apparently, many individuals are willing to sacrifice the certainty of returns on bank deposits and the federal insurance that these deposits provide in return for the higher average returns on mutual fund shares.

Banks have not been oblivious to these trends. Here again the attitude has become, if-you-can't-beat-them, join-them. During the 1980s a number of banks began to offer mutual funds. In the early 1990s the entry of banks into mutual funds accelerated. In 1993 alone the number of bank-sold mutual funds increased by nearly 50 percent. Now banks account for over a third of all new sales of money market mutual funds and about a fifth of new sales of long-term mutual bond funds. Here again, the traditional distinctions between financial institutions continue to erode.

6

In what ways are financial institutions becoming more alike?   Financial institutions have a natural tendency to specialize, but many of the reasons for today's separation of institutions arise from legal restrictions. To the extent that these restrictions have eroded over the years, we have observed institutions competing in markets for financial instruments. This has led them to issue and to hold many of the same instruments, or instruments that are very close substitutes.

Is Financial Institution Consolidation the Wave of the Future?

In light of the increasing overlap in the activities of financial institutions, some observers and policymakers have questioned the need for artificial barriers such as the Glass-Steagall Act. Indeed, the chances appear to be high that Congress may remove many if not all Glass-Steagall restrictions on commercial banks by early in the next century.

What would happen in the absence of legal restrictions that have helped to distinguish financial institutions? Would all financial institutions become alike, or would some continue to specialize in specific kinds of business? Given current banking interests in the securities business and insurance, it seems likely that banks would become more like securities firms and insurance companies. And, certainly, investment banks, broker-dealers, and some insurance companies likely would begin to look more like today's banks.

Yet it also seems likely that some specialization would continue even in the absence of governmental barriers. The business of insurance,

POLICY NOTEBOOK

Is There Any Reason to Distinguish Between Financial Services Companies and Industrial and Service Corporations?

In the mid-1990s, *Fortune* magazine decided to merge its list of the top 500 industrial companies with its list of the top 500 service companies. *Fortune*'s editors also suggested that the distinction between industrial and service corporations and companies that offered financial services was no longer meaningful. In support of their argument, they offered the following table, which they called The Great Convergence.

If you want FDIC-insured savings, you can get it either from a normal bank, American Express, or Merrill Lynch. If you want to buy shares in a mutual fund, American Airlines or John Hancock Insurance will help you. Today, banks and insurance companies make nearly a quarter of new mutual fund sales. Microsoft, the giant software computer company, is trying to get into the home banking business.

For Critical Analysis: *What are the advantages and disadvantages of one-stop shopping for financial services?*

The Great Convergence

	FDIC Insured Depository	Consumer Loans	Credit/ Debit Cards	Mortgage Banking	Commercial Lending	Mutual Funds	Securities	Insurance
American Express	✓	✓	✓			✓	✓	✓
Ford		✓	✓	✓	✓			✓
General Electric	✓	✓	✓	✓	✓	✓		✓
General Motors		✓	✓	✓	✓			✓
Merrill Lynch	✓		✓	✓	✓	✓	✓	✓
Prudential	✓	✓	✓	✓	✓	✓	✓	✓

Source: Fortune, May 15, 1995, p. 178.

for instance, has its own specific information asymmetry problems. So does the business of lending to individuals or companies. And so, what we might expect is that while, in general, financial institutions might engage in several different kinds of business, individual institutions most likely will emphasize one kind of business as a "specialty."

Before we can discuss regulatory issues further, however, you must develop a solid understanding of depository financial institutions.

Because these institutions are so important to the process by which the Federal Reserve conducts monetary policy, we devote the next unit entirely to them. Nevertheless, you should keep in mind that the distinctions between all financial institutions are narrowing. We will confront this issue again and again in the coming chapters.

SUMMARY

1. **Securities Market Institutions:** These are investment banks, brokers, and dealers. Investment banks help to guarantee securities offerings of firms by underwriting the securities, meaning that they buy or have options to buy the securities. Brokers make securities market trades for their customers, and dealers seek to profit from buying financial instruments at low prices and selling them at higher prices. Most of the largest brokerage firms also are dealers. The main government agency that regulates these institutions is the Securities and Exchange Commission, which requires that institutions register with the government, disclose information about their activities, and follow prescribed trading rules.

2. **Insurance Companies:** These financial institutions intermediate significant asymmetric information problems by providing financial guarantees against possible future contingencies. These companies tend to specialize either in life insurance or in property-casualty insurance. States are the chief regulators of insurance company activities.

3. **Pension Funds:** These institutions manage the retirement savings of many employed and retired Americans. The accumulations in non-contributory pension funds come only from employers, but in contributory pension funds employees also can add to their pension savings. Terminally funded pensions have sufficient savings accumulated to fully pay benefits to employees when they reach retirement, whereas pay-as-you-go pension funds depend on current earnings of employers to fund benefit payments to current retirees. As the baby boom generation has matured, pension funds have grown dramatically. Also contributing to this growth has been the growing flexibility of pension plans and the tax-deferred status of current allocations.

4. **Finance Companies:** These are financial institutions that have found their niche in lending to borrowers who either are too small or too uncreditworthy to qualify to issue their own debt instruments, or to borrow from other financial institutions such as commercial banks.

5. **Mutual Funds:** These institutions, which pool savings of shareholders to purchase a mix of financial instruments, can be classified in

several ways. Load funds require commission payments, which reduce shareholders' returns, whereas shareholders in no-load funds simply pay a fixed management fee. Closed-end funds do not permit shareholders to redeem shares at current market values; open-end funds permit such redemptions.

6. **Overlapping Functions of Financial Institutions:** Financial institutions are becoming more alike as they have branched out into areas that previously were the domains of other institutions. Commercial banks and securities market institutions have invaded each other's markets. Commercial banks have begun to offer insurance and annuities previously offered only by insurance companies. In addition, commercial banks recently have begun to market mutual funds as alternatives to traditional deposits.

QUESTIONS AND PROBLEMS

1. Explain why best-effort deals in investment banking now apply primarily for firms whose creditworthiness has not yet been proven, whereas firm-commitment underwriting is common for firms with proven track records. In light of your explanation, can you also hypothesize why best-effort deals are much less common today than they were in the past?

2. What is the difference between a broker and a dealer? Why do you suppose it is so usual for firms to do both kinds of business?

3. What would a broker-dealer give up to be a specialist? What would such a firm gain? In light of your answers, can you surmise why firms that trade large volumes of securities each day are especially likely to be specialists?

4. Many insurance companies will not extend life insurance to individuals who have received treatment for depression. Why do you suppose that companies have this restriction in their life insurance policies?

5. Contrast the pros and cons, from a consumer's standpoint, of term versus whole life insurance.

6. As we discussed, the Pension Benefit Guaranty Corporation (PBGC) insures all pensions with tax-deferred contributions. Some critics believe that the creation of the PBGC helped encourage the growth of pensions and, more specifically, growth in the share of pay-as-you-go pensions. Does this argument make sense to you? Explain your reasoning.

PART

000

Depository Financial Institutions

Depository Financial Institutions

KEY QUESTIONS

1. What are the historical origins of modern banking institutions?

2. How did today's segmented groupings of depository institutions arise?

3. What are the key assets of commercial banks?

4. What are the key liabilities of commercial banks?

5. How do savings institutions differ from commercial banks?

6. How do credit unions raise and allocate their funds?

*I*f you are a customer of a major German bank and you want to buy insurance, you can go to that bank. If you are a business that wants to raise more capital, you can go to that same bank for help in underwriting the issuance of new stock for your company. If you want to buy and sell stocks or bonds, you can go to that same bank. If you examine the financial records of that German bank, you will also see that it owns stock in other companies. Employees of that bank may be elected members of the boards of directors of the companies whose shares of stock the bank owns. The situation with German banks is becoming typical of banks across Europe as economic unification allows them to operate in all European Union (EU) countries similarly to the way they operate domestically. But what about the United States? So far, under current law the United States is served by specialized banking. Banks may not underwrite insurance. Banks generally cannot own shares of stock in nonfinancial companies. Without the use of separate subsidiaries, banks cannot act as agents in buying and selling shares of stocks. A good question, of course, is why all the restrictions on U.S. banks? In this chapter and in Chapter 8 you will find the answers.

THE ORIGINS AND DEVELOPMENT OF DEPOSITORY INSTITUTIONS

Depository financial institutions have existed since the earliest days of human civilization. Consequently, their evolution has spanned the time that organized societies have inhabited the earth.

Goldsmith Bankers

As discussed in Chapter 1, the inconveniences associated with barter ultimately led people to use commodities as money. Among the wide range of commodity monies, gold and silver ultimately predominated. Both metals were relatively scarce and highly valued. Both were easy to divide into units of various sizes so that people could make change.

Bullion and Asymmetric Information   In the earliest times, people used uncoined gold and silver, known as **bullion,** to make transactions. But by using bullion, people exposed themselves to *asymmetric information problems*. Recall from Chapter 2 that such problems arise when one party to a transaction possesses information that the other party does not have. On the one hand, there was an *adverse selection problem* associated with using gold and silver bullion as money. The

bullion   Uncoined gold or silver used as money.

reason was that those individuals with the greatest incentive to offer bullion in exchange for goods and services were those who possessed bullion containing the smallest amounts of pure gold and silver. On the other hand, a *moral hazard problem* also existed when people used bullion as money. Once two parties to an exchange had reached an agreement on how much bullion would be paid for a good or service, there was an incentive for the trader offering the bullion to reduce the level of purity of the gold or silver *before* the exchange took place.

Goldsmiths specialized in reducing the extent of these asymmetric information problems. Parties to a transaction would pay goldsmiths to weigh bullion and to assess its purity. Many goldsmiths issued certificates to the holders of bullion. These certificates attested to the bullion's weight and gold or silver content. Other goldsmiths went a step further. To provide the holder of bullion with ready proof of the bullion's weight and purity, they produced standardized weights of gold or silver imprinted with a seal of authenticity. These standardized units were the earliest *coins.*

Bullion Deposits and Fractional-Reserve Banking   Eventually, some goldsmiths simplified the process further by issuing paper notes indicating that the bearers held gold or silver of given weights and purities on deposit with the goldsmiths. Then, the bearers of these notes could transfer the notes to others in exchange for goods and services. These notes were the first *paper money.* The gold and silver held on deposit with goldsmiths were the first *bank deposits.* Indeed, by providing depository services, these goldsmiths became the first bankers.

Once goldsmiths became depository institutions, it was only a matter of time before they took the final step toward modern banking by becoming lenders. Goldsmiths began to notice that withdrawals of bullion relative to new bullion deposits were fairly predictable. Therefore, as long as the goldsmiths held *reserves* of gold and silver to cover expected bullion withdrawals, they could lend paper notes in excess of the amounts of bullion they actually kept on hand. They could charge interest on the loans by requiring repayment in bullion in excess of the value of the notes they issued.

This was the earliest form of **fractional-reserve banking,** in which goldsmith-bankers would lend funds in excess of the value of reserves of money (gold and silver bullion) they actually possessed. As long as economic conditions were stable and the goldsmiths managed their accounts wisely, those who held the goldsmiths' notes were satisfied with this arrangement. But in bad times or in cases in which a few goldsmiths were overextended, many noteholders might show up at the same time demanding the gold or silver bullion. These were the earliest "bank runs," and if too many noteholders demanded bullion at the same time, the businesses of such goldsmith-bankers failed. Bearers of their notes would discover the notes to be nearly worthless pieces of paper.

fractional-reserve banking
A system in which banks hold reserves that are less than the amount of total deposits.

The Roots of Modern Banking

The first goldsmith-bankers cannot be traced with certainty to any specific time or place. There is evidence that such activities took place in Mesopotamia sometime during the first millennium B.C. In ancient Greece, goldsmith operations existed in Delphi, Didyma, and Olympia at least as early as the seventh century B.C. By the sixth century B.C. banking was a well-developed feature of the economy of Athens.

Banking also arose elsewhere in the Mediterranean world, in locations such as Jerusalem and Persia. Banking facilitated trade, because merchants who shipped goods to faraway locations typically needed loans to fund their operations. After receiving payment from the purchasers of their goods, the merchants then repaid those who had provided loan financing. These lenders then became known as *merchant bankers*. Merchant banking became a permanent fixture that ultimately was a linchpin of the trade linking the principalities of the Roman Empire.

The Italian Merchant Bankers   The modern term *bank* derives from the merchant's bench, or *banco*, on which money changed hands in the marketplaces of medieval Italy. The term *bankruptcy* refers to the *breaking of the bench*, which was what occurred when an overextended Italian merchant banker experienced a run on his notes and failed. Most Italian merchant bankers avoided this fate, however. Indeed, during the medieval period in the twelfth and thirteenth centuries A.D., the merchant bankers flourished throughout Italy.

By the time of the Italian Renaissance in the fifteenth and sixteenth centuries, merchant bankers such as the Medici family of Florence had accumulated enormous wealth and political power. Although these Italian merchant bankers directed some of their wealth to financing the fabulous art of masters such as Michelangelo and Leonardo da Vinci, ultimately they squandered much of it by building private armies and fighting wars over their riches, lands, and religions.

The Advent of Modern Banking   While most of the Italian merchant bankers quarreled, those who originally came from the Lombardy region of Italy worked to maintain their merchant banking operations in other European locales such as London and Berlin. In London, the Italian merchant bankers became such an important fixture that the city's financial dealings were centered around Lombard Street, which remains the financial heart of the city even today. The German central bank, the Deutsche Bundesbank, still calls one interest rate at which it lends funds to private banks the Lombard rate. Even after the Italian city-states fell into political disarray, Italian merchant bankers hailing from Genoa financed the activities of the rising Hapsburg Empire of seventeenth-century and eighteenth-century Europe.

The banking practices of the Italian merchant bankers eventually were copied by others in Europe, however. The modern business of banking took on three key characteristics. First, as in the days of the earliest goldsmiths, modern banking firms took deposits from their customers and maintained accounts on behalf of those customers. Second, the banking firms managed payments on behalf of their customers by collecting and paying checks, notes, and other types of banking currency. Finally, like the merchant banks of old these modern banks provided advances to customers in the form of loans. The interest on the loans and the fees that banks charged for accounting and deposit services were the banks' sources of revenues and, ultimately, profits.

1

What are the historical origins of modern banking institutions? Banks originated in the earliest civilizations as depositories for gold and silver. They evolved into merchant banking firms in medieval Italy. These firms, like modern banks, maintained deposit accounts for, processed payments on behalf of, and made loans to their customers.

Early American Banking

Before the American Revolution (1775–83), British banking firms financed most trading between the American colonies and England. This left the former colonies in a financial bind when the rebellion against British rule cut the ties to British banking firms. While there were a few finance companies operated by Americans when the Revolution began in 1775, there were no independent banking firms on American soil. This complicated financing the Revolution, and the Continental Congress was forced to borrow from governments and bankers in France, Holland, and Spain, and to issue paper currency in the form of Continental dollars, or "Continentals." By the time the Revolution ended in 1783, the Continental Congress had printed so many Continentals that each was worth one five-hundredth (1/500th) of its face value.

The Bank of North America   In 1781 Robert Morris, a Philadelphia financier, spearheaded the establishment of the Bank of North America. This bank was chartered by the Continental Congress and was the first nationally chartered bank on the North American continent. After 1783, however, the Philadelphia-based bank operated under a Pennsylvania charter, though for a time other states, including New York and Massachusetts, granted it charters as well.

The Bank of North America was a privately funded bank, but Morris also served as Superintendent of Finance for the Continental Congress. In this capacity he was able to arrange a series of short-term loans to the Continental Treasury that helped fund Congressional operations during the Revolution. Nevertheless, in most respects the Bank of North America was a conservatively operated private bank. Its significance lies in the fact that it established an important precedent for national government involvement in banking.

Private Versus Public Banking in the New Republic   The national government's role in banking continued after the individual states formally joined the United States of America. Alexander Hamilton, the first Secretary of the Treasury of the new federal republic, looked to the Bank of North America as an example of how to establish a federally chartered bank. Hamilton's ambitions extended beyond simple private banking, however. In Hamilton's view, the United States needed a public bank modeled after the Bank of England. From the time of its charter in 1694, the Bank of England played a key financial role for the British government, and Hamilton believed that such a bank could perform the same duties for the government of the United States. Consequently, he proposed the formation of a national bank—the First Bank of the United States, whose shares would, in part, be owned by the U.S. Treasury Department.

Powerful enemies of Hamilton disagreed. Among these enemies were Thomas Jefferson and James Madison, both of whom opposed the establishment of any federally chartered banking institution. Both of these presidents-to-be challenged the establishment of the First Bank of the United States on constitutional grounds. Madison's role in this argument carried significant weight with President George Washington because Madison had been one of the key figures in the writing the U.S. Constitution. Yet Hamilton had joined Madison and John Jay in writing the *Federalist Papers*, which explained the workings of the Constitution. Hence, Washington also paid close attention to Hamilton's views on the subject. In the end Washington sided with his Treasury Secretary and permitted the legislation authorizing a 20-year charter for the First Bank to become law. Washington's action set the precedent for a **dual banking system** in which American banks could receive either federal or state charters.

Even as the U.S. Congress was getting the federal government involved in banking, the individual states permitted the establishment of growing numbers of banks. As shown in Figure 6.1 (page 144), the number of banks grew from just over 50 in 1803 to more than 300 by 1820.

In 1811 the charter of the First Bank of the United States expired. By this time Albert Gallatin, Treasury Secretary under both President Thomas Jefferson and President James Madison, had convinced Madison that Hamilton's national bank was not such a bad idea after all.

dual banking system   A regulatory structure in which both the states and the federal government grant charters to banks.

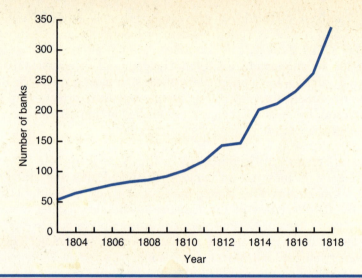

FIGURE 6.1   Growth of Banking in the Early United States

The number of banks in the United States increased at a rapid pace during the early years of the nineteenth century. *Source:* J. Van Fenstermake, "The Statistics of American Commercial Banking: 1782–1818," *Journal of Economic History* (1965).

Nonetheless, Congress did not renew the First Bank's charter. This arguably was not a good decision. Congress declared war on Britain in the following year and found itself without a ready means of financing a war effort. In light of this experience, Congress permitted the establishment of a 20-year federal charter for the Second Bank of the United States in 1816.

A dual banking system with one large national bank and many smaller state banks continued through 1836. But in 1819 many people in frontier states such as Kentucky and Tennessee blamed the Second Bank for a financial panic that ruined many farmers and landholders. Among those who developed a deep distrust of the Second Bank was Andrew Jackson, who successfully vetoed an 1832 bill reauthorizing the charter of the Second Bank. After winning reelection in that year, Jackson removed all federal government deposits from the Second Bank and placed them with state banks. The Second Bank ceased to exist four years later. This suspended for a 26-year interval the federal government's direct involvement in banking.

The Free-Banking Period

From 1837 until 1863, there were two types of banks. One group consisted of banks operated by or on behalf of the state governments. Comprising the other group were private banks incorporated under

POLICY NOTEBOOK

Andrew Jackson and the Second Bank of the United States

Populist president Andrew Jackson wanted the Second Bank of the United States to fold. He attacked it as unconstitutional, but a committee that was formed in the House of Representatives affirmed the constitutionality of the bank. By 1830 the Second Bank of the United States had developed a sort of national currency because it had a large number of branches, and U.S. bank notes were in circulation everywhere. The rate of exchange between U.S. bank notes and all other currencies was the same throughout the nation.

Jackson developed another strategy. He forced the bank to become a noncredit-creating institution. What he wanted was a 100 percent reserve bank. That is, no credit or bank notes could be issued that were not backed by a sound deposit within the Second Bank itself. The Bank, then, would become just a transfer institution. When the president of the Second Bank, Nicholas Biddle, applied for another charter four years before the end of the Bank's original charter, the act was passed by Congress but successfully vetoed by Jackson. By 1836 the Second Bank of the United States was no more.

For Critical Analysis: *If the Second Bank were required, in essence, to have 100 percent reserves, what function could it serve?*

---

free-banking laws enacted in a number of states, such as New York, Michigan, Wisconsin, and Alabama. Before the Civil War, 18 of 33 states experimented with free-banking legislation, and so historians and economists call this the *free-banking era* of American history.

According to today's museum exhibits, such as the one at the Smithsonian Institution in Washington, D.C., the free-banking period was one of considerable instability. Such exhibits reflect the traditional historical accounts of "wildcat banks," fly-by-night operations that printed notes and coins they never intended to redeem. The notes of such banks ultimately became worthless. In addition, counterfeiting was widespread in some locales; by the end of the 1860s there were more than 5,000 separate types of counterfeit notes in circulation in the United States.

Since the late 1970s, however, many historians and economists have reexamined the free-banking period in light of hard evidence unearthed from the accounting ledgers of free banks and state examiners. The evidence indicates that in many of the states with unstable banking systems, a key factor contributing to such instability was state involvement. That is, in many states "free banks" were not very free. Several states required banks to hold risky bonds that the states themselves issued. They also imposed laws prohibiting banks from branching out within a state or across state lines.

Among the states that subjected free banks to fewer restrictions of this type, instability was less pronounced. Some states, notably New York, subjected free banks to state audits to ensure depositors that the banks were soundly managed. In such states the notes of free banks were quite safe, and very few depositors experienced losses. Furthermore, failures and closings of banks in other states with less soundly structured arrangements typically did not cause difficulties for free banks in states with better-designed free-banking laws.

Consequently, the mainstream view among today's economic historians is that free banking ultimately might have been a more successful experiment if events had followed a different course. But the Civil War permanently altered the course of American banking, much as it forever changed the political landscape.

The Two-Tiered Banking System

In 1863 Congress passed the National Banking Act, which granted federal charters to a number of banks (all within the Union states) and, as amended in 1865, placed a federal tax on all notes issued by state banks (mostly based in Confederate states). This Act imposed reserve requirements on the deposits of banks. Banks were required to hold a portion of the funds their customers had deposited as vault cash or as deposits in designated *reserve-city banks* in New York, Chicago, and St. Louis. In turn, these reserve-city banks had to hold their required reserves as vault cash. Furthermore, the National Banking Act prohibited **branch banking,** or the operation of more than one depository institution office in alternative geographic locations, by state-chartered banks. It also required national banks to back their notes by posting government bonds with the Comptroller of the Currency, an official of the U.S. Treasury Department who was designated the chief supervisor of national banks.

branch banking   A depository institution organizational structure in which institutions operate offices at a number of geographic locations.

Congress clearly intended the 1863 legislation to bind the banks of the Union more tightly together while damaging the interests of the banks in the Confederate states. But the National Banking Act had far-reaching consequences for American banking. First, it ended the free-banking experiment. Second, for the first time in the nation's history it involved the federal government directly in the affairs of most of the banks in the nation. Third, it laid the groundwork for today's *two-tiered* system consisting of both state and nationally chartered banks. Dual banking became a permanent feature of the American scene.

The Rise of Thrift Institutions

In the fifth century B.C., Xenophon, a Spartan soldier and historian, proposed the formation of a publicly owned goldsmith institution for the Greek city-state of Athens. He envisioned the mutual sharing of interest returns by all citizens of the city. Xenophon's dream was not realized, but it foreshadowed the development of **mutual ownership** of savings institutions, or the ownership of such institutions by all depositors. In an echo of Xenophon's idea, in 1697 Daniel Defoe, the author of *Robinson Crusoe,* proposed the formation of mutually owned institutions to promote savings among working-class and poor individuals in Britain. A number of years later, in 1765, the first institution of this type was established in England. By the early 1800s such institutions had spread to Scotland and the United States, where they became known as *savings banks.* These were the first of the so-called *thrift institutions.* As we discussed in Chapter 2, thrift institutions today include savings banks and credit unions.

A related type of savings institution also arose in England. This was the *building society,* in which individuals pooled their savings to make loans to society members, who then used the funds to finance the construction of new homes. In 1831 a Philadelphia group formed the first American building society, which was called a *savings and loan association.* Within a couple of decades most savings and loan associations were accepting deposits from the general public, and the number of such associations expanded dramatically throughout the remainder of the nineteenth century. By the 1930s both savings banks and savings and loan associations had become the mainstay lenders in the market for residential mortgages. Today we refer to savings and loan associations and savings banks, collectively, as savings institutions.

Credit unions began in Germany and Italy in the mid-nineteenth century. They were cooperative institutions serving closed memberships of individuals with common interests. Some credit unions were associated with churches, while others had memberships drawn from fraternal orders. Most, however, drew their members from employees of specific firms. Credit unions first appeared in Canada at the beginning of the twentieth century, and the first U.S. credit union was established in 1909.

Until the late 1980s it was common to group savings institutions and credit unions together in the broad category of thrift institutions. As we shall discuss in Chapter 7, however, by the early 1990s many savings institutions in the United States had failed, while most credit unions remained solvent. Because of the differing performances of and prospects for these two groups of institutions, the collective term thrift institutions is not as widely used today as in the past.

Segmented Banking in the Twentieth Century

The Great Depression of the 1930s was, like the Civil War, a defining period for American depository institutions. Congress responded to the events of the Great Depression by involving the federal government even more directly in the affairs of commercial banks, savings institutions, and credit unions.

mutual ownership Depository institution organizational structure in which depositors own the institution.

bank run An unexpected series of cash withdrawals at a depository institution that can cause it to fail.

One key event associated with the Great Depression was a series of bank failures and **bank runs,** or panic-induced deposit withdrawals at banks that often caused the banks to fail, throughout much of the United States. Congress responded to this event with legislation intended to restrict sharply the ability of banks to undertake risky activities. As discussed in Chapter 5, in 1933 Congress passed the Glass-Steagall Act, which separated commercial and investment banking. This legislation also prohibited commercial banks from paying interest on checking deposits, authorized the regulation of interest on bank savings deposits, and enacted an elaborate system of federal insurance of bank deposits under the administration of the Federal Deposit Insurance Corporation.

Another event of the Great Depression was a sharp decline in real estate values as many people lost their jobs and failed to make mortgage payments. This led to widespread foreclosures on mortgage loans by savings institutions and of consumer loans by credit unions. But such foreclosures left thrift institutions in possession of properties whose values had plummeted, causing many savings institutions to declare bankruptcy. Congress responded with a series of laws intended to shore up the shaky thrift industry. In 1932 it passed the Federal Home Loan Bank Act, establishing a system of government-operated financial institutions that could provide emergency funding to savings institutions. In 1933 Congress enacted the Home Owner's Loan Act, which established a federal charter for savings institutions, and in 1934 it passed the National Housing Act, which created a system of deposit insurance for savings institutions under the administration of the Federal Savings and Loan Insurance Corporation. In 1934 Congress also enacted the Federal Credit Union Act, which authorized federal charters for credit unions.

Consequently, within a very short time span in the 1930s, the United States government became closely involved in the business practices of all American depository financial institutions. The U.S. government regulated interest rates, restricted banking practices, and insured bank and thrift institution deposits. Federal laws also formally segmented depository institutions into the categories that existed in the 1930s: commercial banks, savings institutions, and credit unions. Essentially the structure that existed in the 1930s was frozen in place by legislation intended to limit potential risks that might have arisen if depository institutions were left free of governmental controls. As we shall discuss in Chapters 8 and 9, this governmental involvement has had a number of important consequences for the evolution of the entire American financial system. But from the perspective of our current discussion, the main point is that these Congressional actions solidified the separate categories of depository institutions that remain with us today.

2

How did today's segmented groupings of depository institutions arise? The dual, or combined state and federal, structure of American banking has its roots in decisions that the first Congress and President Washington made in the early years of the United States. After later experiments with free banking at the state level, Congress reinstituted dual banking during the Civil War. Savings institutions and credit unions always have occupied specialized niches, but Congress solidified the distinctions among commercial banks, savings institutions, and credit unions in a series of laws passed in the 1930s.

COMMERCIAL BANKS

There presently are over 9,000 commercial banks in the United States, and they are the predominant depository financial institution in the country. Before we discuss them any further, however, let's tackle a tough question: What exactly is a commercial bank? This has become an increasingly more difficult question as savings institutions, credit unions, and even nondepository institutions, such as the investment banks and mutual funds we discussed in Chapter 5, have begun to look more like banks.

In a way it is easier to begin by talking about what is *not* a commercial bank. For instance, institutions that face a variety of legal constraints on their powers to lend to businesses are not commercial banks. This permits us to exclude savings institutions and credit unions, because various laws continue to restrict their abilities to make commercial loans. It also permits us to exclude nondepository institutions such as mutual funds, which do not make loans to businesses.

In addition, institutions that by law cannot issue checking deposits are not commercial banks. Many nondepository institutions now offer mutual fund accounts with very limited checking privileges. However, under current law such nondepository institutions cannot offer *unrestricted* deposit accounts that permit holders to write an *unlimited* number of checks.

So by a process of elimination we can define a commercial bank in the following way. A commercial bank is *a depository institution that faces few legal restrictions on its powers to lend to businesses and that can legally issue checking deposits from which holders may write unlimited numbers of checks.*

Commercial Bank Assets

For any individual or firm, including a banking firm, an **asset** is the value of any item legally owned by that person or business. For instance,

asset Anything owned by a person or business that has a value.

when a commercial bank makes a loan to a business, that loan represents a legal obligation of the business to repay the loan principal and interest within a specified period. Consequently, the loan is an asset of the bank.

Table 6.1 lists the *combined* total assets of *all* domestically chartered commercial banks in the United States. There are three important classifications of assets listed in Table 6.1. We consider each in turn.

Loans   A key reason for the existence of banks is that they specialize in handling problems of asymmetric information in lending markets. Banks carefully assess the characteristics of potential business or consumer borrowers before lending to them. This reduces the extent of the adverse selection problem of the least creditworthy borrowers being among the most likely to want to borrow. Banks also monitor the performances of those to whom they lend. This helps to alleviate the moral hazard problem that arises when a borrower has an incentive to misuse funds obtained from a loan. Because lending is the bread-and-butter business of commercial banks, loans compose the major category of assets held by commercial banks. There are four important loan categories:

Commercial and Industrial Loans   Loans that commercial banks and other depository institutions make to businesses are **commercial and industrial,** or **C&I, loans.** Businesses use funding from C&I loans to meet day-to-day cash needs or to finance the purchase of plant and equipment. Businesses typically must secure C&I loans with **collateral** or assets that a borrower pledges as security in the event of failure to perform its obligation to repay the principal and interest on a loan. A lending bank may seize the collateral, or a portion of it, in the event of nonpayment. Though many C&I loans require collateral, it is not uncommon for some C&I loans to very creditworthy borrowers to be uncollateralized.

commercial and industrial (C&I) loans   Loans made by commercial banks and other depository institutions to businesses.

collateral   Assets that a borrower pledges as security in the event the borrower fails to repay the loan principal or interest.

TABLE 6.1   Commercial Bank Assets ($ billions), March 1996

Commercial and industrial loans	$ 731.3	17.3%
Consumer loans	500.1	11.8%
Real estate loans	1,087.3	25.8%
Interbank loans	203.6	4.8%
Other loans	240.2	5.7%
Total Loans	$ 2,762.5	65.4%
U.S. government securities	709.5	16.8%
Other securities	272.4	6.5%
Total Securities	$ 981.9	23.3%
Cash Assets	$ 208.0	4.9%
Other Assets	$ 269.4	6.4%
Total Assets	$ 4,221.8	100.0%

Source: Board of Governors of the Federal Reserve System, H.8(510) *Statistical Release,* 1996.

Is the Commercial Banking Industry in Decline?

If you look at Figure 6.2, you see that the largest number of commercial banks existed in this country in the 1920s. To be exact, the peak was in 1921 when there were 30,456 commercial banks. Note that this was a time when the population was just over 110 million, as compared with over 260 million today. This means that there was roughly one bank for every 3,500 people in 1921, whereas today there is about one bank for every 26,000 people.

Several other aspects of the commercial banking industry seem to indicate that it is declining. Whereas commercial banks held over 65 percent of all U.S. financial assets in 1974, today that ratio has been cut in half. Further, the commercial bank share of all short-term debt held by financial institutions has dropped during the same period from 82 percent to around 58 percent. The decline in the commercial banking industry is not necessarily due to commercial bank failures. From World War II through the 1970s, there were no more than ten bank failures a year and those were usually small. The number of failures did rise in the 1980s, reaching 206 in 1989. But since then there have been an average of 71 failures per year.

In opposition to the above data that seems to indicate a decline in the commercial banking industry, there are two statistics that stand out. One is that total commercial bank assets relative to the growth in domestic product have increased. Another is that bank profitability has risen in recent years, which is hardly an indication that banking is a dying industry.

For Critical Analysis: *If, indeed, the commercial banking industry is shrinking, this may simply reflect a reallocation of resources towards more efficient uses. Does that necessarily mean the decline is not an important policy issue? Why or why not?*

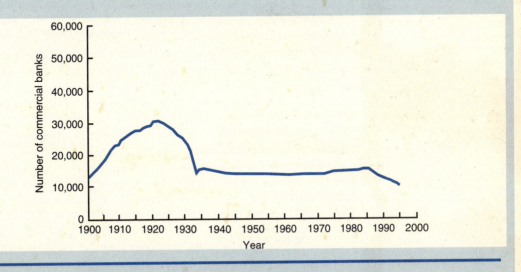

FIGURE 6.2 Commercial Banks During the Twentieth Century

The number of commercial banks in the United States peaked at over 30,000 in 1921 and then declined dramatically until the mid-1930s. From then until the late 1980s, the number of banks remained level. During recent years there has been a steady decline in the number of commercial banks. *Source:* FDIC, *Historical Statistics on Banking*, various issues.

One long-standing type of C & I loan, which dates back to the beginnings of merchant banking, is the *banker's acceptance,* that you were first introduced to in Chapter 2. When companies ship goods across long distances, typically as exports to other nations, they must fund those shipments. They often do this, in part, by issuing banker's acceptances. These are certificates that are marked as "accepted" by a bank. By accepting the certificate the bank agrees to pay the face value if the issuing company fails to honor its obligations. This makes it easier for the exporting company to make the shipment without payment being made up front, because the other party in the transaction knows that the bank will honor any promised payment if the shipper fails to do so.

Banker's acceptances typically have maturities ranging between 30 and 180 days, with payments due at maturity. The stated maturities normally correspond closely with the intended date of delivery of the goods. While most banker's acceptances are used for export shipments, some are issued by firms that ship goods long distances within the United States.

Banks typically purchase banker's acceptances only from companies they judge to be very creditworthy. For this reason, there is an active secondary market for these instruments. One common way for a bank to increase its liquidity is to purchase banker's acceptances near their maturity dates.

All told, C & I loans account for about 17 percent of total bank assets. Such loans have varying degrees of default risk and liquidity. In recent years banks have worked hard to increase the liquidity of their C & I loan holdings, as we shall discuss in greater detail in Chapter 9.

Consumer Loans   Commercial banks also extend credit to individuals. These are *consumer loans.* About a third of such loans typically finance purchases of automobiles. Many individuals also obtain consumer loans for the purchase of mobile homes, durable consumer goods such as household appliances, or materials for home improvements.

installment credit   Loans to individual consumers requiring the borrower to make periodic repayments of principal and interest.

Banks typically issue consumer loans for the purchase of autos or mobile homes in the form of **installment credit.** Under an installment credit agreement, individual borrowers agree to repay principal and interest in equal periodic payments. Payment schedules for consumer loans typically span one to five years. Interest rates usually are fixed and set initially relative to the prime rate or an index of capital market rates, such as an index of Treasury security rates. Some consumer loans, however, have adjustable interest rates.

revolving credit   Loans to individuals that permit them to borrow automatically up to specified limits and to repay the balance of the loan at any time.

Included among consumer loans is **revolving credit,** which refers to bank lending to individuals up to some preset limit, or ceiling. Under a revolving credit agreement, consumer have automatic approval to borrow as long as they do not exceed their specified credit ceilings. They also may pay off their loan balance at any time. Credit cards are the most widely used form of consumer revolving credit.

Real Estate Loans   A third major type of bank lending is classified as *real estate loans.* These are loans that banks make to finance purchases of real property, buildings, and fixtures by businesses and individuals. Banks make the bulk of their real estate loans to businesses. In the 1980s and 1990s, real estate lending became a relatively more important business for commercial banks. The share of total commercial bank assets held as real estate loans rose from around 17 percent in 1985 to the 26 percent figure in Table 6.1. Much of the growth in real estate lending has been fueled by increases in *home equity loans,* which are loans to property owners secured by the owners' shares of title to real estate.

Interbank (Federal Funds) Loans   As discussed earlier, banks extend interbank loans in the federal funds market. Most federal funds loans have one-day maturities, though some, called **term federal funds,** have maturities exceeding one day. Banks typically lend these funds in large-denomination units, ranging from $200,000 to well over $1,000,000 per loan. Although large banks both lend and borrow federal funds, smaller banks predominantly are federal funds lenders.

term federal funds   Interbank loans with maturities exceeding one day.

Nearly all federal funds loans are *nonsecured,* which means that there is no *collateral* placed by a borrowing bank. Because no collateral is pledged by federal funds borrowers, federal funds loans are slightly riskier than repurchase agreements with the same maturities. For this reason, it is not uncommon for the federal funds market rate to exceed the yield on repurchase agreements by some small amount.

Sometimes smaller banks insist on security collateralization of federal funds loans. When federal funds loans are *secured,* they are little different from repurchase agreements. Secured federal funds loans account for a very small share of total federal funds lending by commercial banks.

Securities   Under the constraints specified in the Glass-Steagall Act of 1933, commercial banks have not been permitted to hold most kinds of corporate stocks and bonds. Consequently, banks since that time have limited their securities holdings to low-risk government securities, including Treasury bills, notes, and bonds. Although the yields on these securities are lower than those on loans, such securities typically are much more liquid financial instruments. Commercial bank holdings of U.S. government securities account for about 17 percent of all assets.

Another group of securities held by commercial banks is *state and municipal bonds.* These make up the bulk of the Other Securities category in Table 6.1, or about 6.5 percent of bank assets.

Cash Assets   The most liquid of the assets that banks hold are **cash assets,** which function as media of exchange. One component of cash assets is **vault cash,** which is currency that commercial banks hold at their offices to meet depositors' cash needs for withdrawals on a day-to-day basis. Vault cash typically accounts for around 1 percent of total bank assets.

cash assets   Depository institution assets that function as a medium of exchange.

vault cash   Currency that a depository institution holds on location to honor cash withdrawals by depositors.

Recall from Chapter 1 that such vault cash is not included as part of monetary aggregates because it is held out of circulation from payments for goods and services. Since 1959 commercial banks have been able to include vault cash among the assets that are eligible to count toward meeting the *legal reserve requirements* established by the Federal Reserve. We shall discuss reserve requirements in Chapter 10.

reserve deposits   Deposit accounts that depository institutions maintain at Federal Reserve banks.

A second type of cash asset is **reserve deposits** at Federal Reserve banks. These are checking accounts that commercial banks hold with the Federal Reserve bank in their geographic district. They usually account for about 1 percent of total bank assets. Banks write checks out of or wire-transfer funds from these reserve deposit accounts when they make federal funds loans, purchase repurchase agreements, or buy securities. Funds held as reserve deposits also count toward meeting the Federal Reserve's legal reserve requirements.

correspondent balances   Deposit accounts that banks hold with other banks.

A third form of cash asset, which normally accounts for another 1 percent of bank assets is **correspondent balances.** These are funds that banks hold on deposit with other private commercial banks usually called *correspondents*. A large number of banks in rural areas or small towns hold such accounts with banks in larger cities. For instance, a bank in the farming community of Rushville, Indiana, might hold a correspondent balance with a correspondent bank in Indianapolis. If so, it would have a *correspondent relationship* with the Indianapolis bank. This would mean that the Indianapolis bank might provide computer and check-clearing services for the Rushville bank. The Indianapolis bank also might assist the Rushville bank make securities and federal funds transactions. The Indianapolis bank almost certainly would charge fees for such services, but the Rushville bank probably would receive a discount in return for holding a correspondent balance with the Indianapolis bank.

cash items in process of collection   Checks deposited with a bank for immediate credit but not yet cleared for final payment to the bank; usually referred to simply as "cash items."

The final type of cash asset is **cash items in process of collection** or, more simply, *cash items.* These are checks or other cash drafts that the bank lists as deposited for immediate credit but that the bank may need to cancel if payment on the items is not received. Any time that you deposit or cash a personal or payroll check at a bank, the bank lists that check as a cash item until it "clears" and the bank has received payment on the check from the issuer's financial institution. Cash items in process of collection usually amount to about 2 percent of total commercial bank assets.

3

What are the key assets of commercial banks?   Bank assets fall into three main categories: loans, securities, and cash. Loans include commercial and industrial loans, real estate loans, consumer loans, and very short-term loans that banks make in the federal funds market or through repurchase agreements. Securities include U.S. government securities and municipal and state bonds. Cash assets include vault cash, reserve deposits at Federal Reserve banks, correspondent balances, and cash items in the process of collection.

Trends in Bank Asset Allocations   Figure 6.3 plots the shares of bank assets allocated to cash assets, securities, and all other assets (loans and miscellaneous other assets) at various intervals since 1961. As the figure indicates, there has been a general downward trend in relative holdings of cash assets.

A similar downward trend also existed for bank security holdings until the latter 1980s. The portion of bank assets held as securities drifted upward beginning in 1986 and then rose sharply in the early 1991. The reason was that between 1990 and 1992 banks curtailed lending fairly dramatically. As you can see in Figure 6.3, Other Assets, nearly all of which were loans, declined during this period as the portion of assets allocated to securities increased. Many economists have classified this period as a *credit crunch*, in which banks restrict loans only to the most creditworthy customers. During the early 1990s some observers worried that bank lending had fallen so dramatically that the traditional financial intermediation role of commercial banks as lenders was in jeopardy. But by 1994 banks were making many more loans. Indeed, by 1995 the Federal Reserve was criticizing banks for

---

FIGURE 6.3   Commercial Bank Asset Allocation

During the past three decades there has been a general downward trend in commercial banks' holdings of cash assets relative to total assets and a general upward trend in proportionate holdings of loans and other assets. The portion of assets held as securities trended downward until the early 1990s, when banks noticeably reduced lending in favor of security holdings. *Sources:* Board of Governors of the Federal Reserve System, *Federal Reserve Bulletin,* various issues, and H.8(510) *Statistical Release,* 1996.

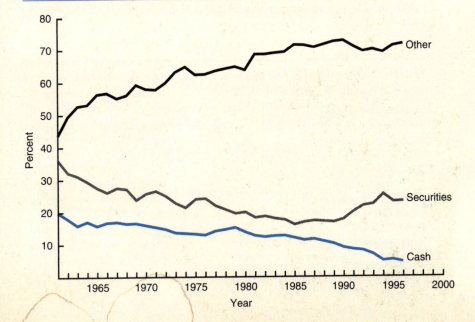

making *too many* loans. In any event, bank lending as a share of total bank assets presently is at a level consistent with past experience.

Commercial Bank Liabilities and Equity Capital

liability   A legally enforceable claim on the assets of a business or individual.

A **liability** is the dollar value of a legal claim on the assets of an individual or business at a given point in time. In the case of a bank loan to a business, the business legally owes funds to the bank, and so the loan is a liability of the business. But banks have liabilities as well. For instance, if you have a checking or savings deposit at a bank, then the bank owes you the funds in the account. While you regard the deposit as an asset, the bank views it as a liability.

If you were to add up estimates of your own assets and liabilities and were to subtract liabilities from assets, you would come up with an estimate of your **net worth.** This is the net amount of total funds that you owe to no one. A synonym for net worth is **equity capital.** A commercial bank's equity capital is its net worth, or the amount by which its assets exceed its liabilities.

net worth   The excess of assets over liabilities, or equity capital.

equity capital   The excess of assets over liabilities, or net worth.

Table 6.2 lists the *combined* total liabilities and equity capital of *all* domestically chartered commercial banks in the United States. Note that the dollar amount of total liabilities and equity capital in Table 6.2 is exactly equal to the dollar amount of total assets in Table 6.1. This illustrates an important accounting definition: Total bank assets always must equal the sum of total liabilities and equity capital.

noncontrollable liabilities   Liabilities whose dollar amounts are largely determined by bank customers once banks have issued the liabilities.

Noncontrollable Liabilities   Bankers typically classify their liabilities into two categories. The first of these they call **noncontrollable liabilities.** This is something of a misnomer, given that a bank certainly could decide not to issue any particular liability. The idea behind this

TABLE 6.2   Commercial Bank Liabilities and Equity Capital ($ billions), March 1996

Transactions deposits	$ 751.7	17.8%
Small time and savings deposits	1,503.8	35.6 %
Large time deposits	429.6	10.2%
Total Deposits	$ 2,685.1	63.6%
Borrowings from banks	$ 203.0	4.8%
Other borrowings	475.6	11.3%
Total Borrowings	$ 678.6	16.1%
Other Liabilities	$ 528.8	12.5%
Equity Capital*	$ 329.3	7.8%*
Total Assets	$ 4,221.8	100.0%

*Authors' estimate

Source: Board of Governors of the Federal Reserve System, H.8(510) *Statistical Release,* 1996.

term, however, is that once a bank issues one of these liabilities to a customer, the *customer*, and not the bank, has considerable discretion concerning how large the customer's deposit holdings will be. It is in this sense that a bank regards such a liability as "noncontrollable."

There are four key types of noncontrollable liabilities. *Transactions deposits*, as discussed in Chapter 1, include demand deposits and other checkable deposits such as NOW (negotiable-order-of-withdrawal) accounts. Demand deposits are noninterest-bearing accounts, but banks pay market interest rates on other checkable deposits. Transactions deposits account for about 18 percent of total bank liabilities and equity capital.

Two other noncontrollable liabilities are *savings deposits* and *small-denomination time deposits*. These deposits account for about 36 percent of total bank liabilities and equity capital. Included among savings deposits are the passbook and statement savings accounts typically held by small savers and money market deposit accounts usually held in somewhat larger denominations. Savings deposits have no set maturities. In contrast, small-denomination time deposits have fixed maturities. They have denominations under $100,000.

The last noncontrollable liability is *deferred availability cash items*. These represent payments by banks to other parties that the banks have not yet made but have promised or that the banks have made but which have not yet cleared. Deferred availability cash items are included among the Other Liabilities in Table 6.2.

Controllable Liabilities and Equity Capital

Bankers refer to the remaining liabilities they issue as **controllable liabilities.** These are liabilities whose amounts the bankers themselves can more readily determine on a monthly, weekly, or even daily basis.

> **controllable liabilities**
> Liabilities whose dollar amounts banks can directly manage.

Banks raise a significant amount of funds by issuing *large-denomination time deposits*. Many of these are *large-denomination certificates of deposit*. These CDs have denominations above $100,000 and typically fund a significant amount of banks' short-term lending operations. Large-denomination CDs pay market interest rates, and many are negotiable. Banks and other depository institutions issue large-denomination CDs in a variety of maturities, but most such CDs have 6-month terms and trade actively in the money markets. Banks issue CDs when they feel the timing is best, and banks also determine the denominations of the CDs. All told, CDs and other large-denomination time deposits account for about 10 percent of bank liabilities and equity capital.

Bankers often refer to another set of controllable liabilities as **purchased funds.** These are very short-term borrowings in the money market. The most important type of puchased funds is *interbank (federal funds) borrowing*. These are borrowings by commercial banks from other banks in the federal funds market, and they account for nearly 5 percent of total liabilities and equity capital of commercial banks.

> **purchased funds**   Very short-term bank borrowings in the money market.

Three other kinds of purchased funds are included within the Other Borrowings category in Table 6.2. These are *sales of repurchase agreements, borrowings from the Federal Reserve*, and *Eurodollar liabilities*. When a bank sells securities under an agreement to repurchase the securities at a later time and to pay interest on the transaction, it borrows for the length of the agreement. Consequently, sales of repurchase agreements are liabilities.

All federally insured commercial banks have the privilege of applying for loans from the Federal Reserve bank in their geographic district. The Federal Reserve permits banks to borrow to meet seasonal fluctuations resulting from agricultural or construction cycles, and it lends to banks during times of acute financial distress in which the banks are illiquid but not bankrupt. Under some circumstances the Federal Reserve can assist banks that are experiencing more chronic liquidity problems. As we shall discuss in Chapter 12, however, Congress recently limited the Federal Reserve's discretion about such longer-term loans.

Many large-denomination CDs and repurchase agreement sales are dollar-denominated liabilities that banks issue outside American borders. Consequently, these are Eurodollar liabilities of banks, which we discussed in Chapter 2. Eurodollar liabilities also are included in the Other Borrowings category in Table 6.2.

The final kind of controllable liabilities that banks can issue are **subordinated notes and debentures.** These are capital market instruments with maturities in excess of one year. Many of these are similar to corporate bonds. But a bank issues subordinated notes and debentures with the understanding that those who hold them have *subordinated claims* in the event of the bank's failure. This means that in the event of bankruptcy, holders of a bank's subordinated notes and debentures would receive no payments until all depositors at the bank have received the funds from their accounts. These commercial bank liabilities are a portion of the Other Liabilities category in Table 6.2.

The equity capital of a bank is the excess of total assets over total liabilities. For the banking system as a whole, we estimate that equity capital amounted to just under 8 percent of all bank liabilities and capital in 1996. The Federal Reserve reports equity capital infrequently, and so we must rely on estimates for this figure.

subordinated notes and debentures   Capital market instruments with maturities in excess of one year that banks issue with the provision that depositors have primary claim to bank assets in the event of failure.

4

What are the Key Liabilities of Commercial Banks?   Noncontrollable bank liabilities are demand deposits, other checkable deposits, savings deposits, and small-denomination time deposits. Controllable bank liabilities are large-denomination time deposits, such as large CDs; purchased funds, including sales of repurchase agreements; federal funds borrowings, or borrowings from the Federal Reserve; and subordinated notes and debentures. The excess of assets over liabilities is a bank's equity capital, or net worth.

Trends in Bank Liabilities and Equity Capital   Figure 6.4 depicts the share of total bank liabilities and equity capital accounted for by total deposits, other liabilities, and equity capital at various dates since 1961. Other Liabilities includes both purchased funds and subordinated notes and debentures.

The figure makes it clear that the general trend has been toward reduced dependence by banks on deposit sources of funding. It also shows a slight downward trend, until recently, in banks' issuance of equity capital. The use of purchased funds and subordinated notes and debentures increased through the 1960s, 1970s, and early 1980s, leveled off in the late 1980s, and since then has increased considerably.

There are several explanations for these observations. A key reason for the shift from deposits to purchased funds was that, as discussed in Chapter 5, for some years banks have faced stiff competition for deposit funds. Savers could earn higher yields by holding other financial instruments, such as government securities. In particular, the growth of mutual funds attracted funds that people previously would have held in deposit accounts at banks. Consequently, banks had to borrow from other sources to fund some of their lending operations.

FIGURE 6.4   Commercial Bank Liabilities and Equity Capital

Since the 1960s there has been a general decline in reliance on deposit funds by commercial banks. During the 1990s banks have increasingly funded their operations with puchased funds and other liabilities, and they also gradually have increased their equity positions. *Sources:* Board of Governors of the Federal Reserve System, *Federal Reserve Bulletin,* various issues, and H.8(510) *Statistical Release,* 1996.

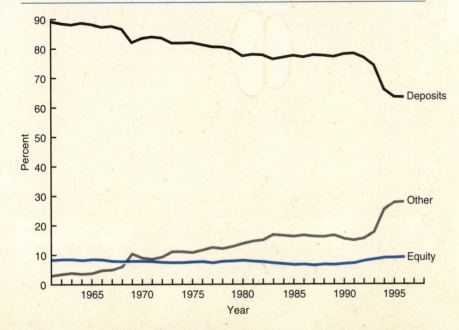

Raising equity funds in the stock market is a fairly expensive operation and can dilute the value of existing shares. Until recently, therefore, banks tried to avoid issuing more stock. The main impetus for the recent change of heart concerning equity capital arose from regulatory pressures that we shall discuss in much more detail in Chapter 9.

SAVINGS INSTITUTIONS

In recent years savings institutions have experienced serious problems. Between 1986 and 1991 savings institutions as a whole failed to earn a net profit. The scope of the problems of the savings institution industry is displayed in Figure 6.5, which plots the total deposits at these institutions since early 1988. Total deposits at savings institutions declined from nearly $1 trillion in the spring of 1988 to today's level of just over $500 billion. Furthermore, even though the general savings institution collapse had ended by the beginning of 1993, these institutions have continued to lose deposits at an average rate of nearly $3 billion each month since that time. If this pace were to continue, savings institutions would cease to exist by the second decade of the twenty-first century.

What happened? There is no single answer to this question. Some savings institutions failed because of fraudulent business practices.

FIGURE 6.5   Deposits at Federally Insured Savings Institutions

Since the end of the 1980s, deposits at savings institutions have fallen by over 40 percent. *Sources:* Board of Governors of the Federal Reserve System, *Federal Reserve Bulletin,* and the Office of Thrift Supervision, *Quarterly Financial Results and Conditions of the Thrift Industry,* various issues.

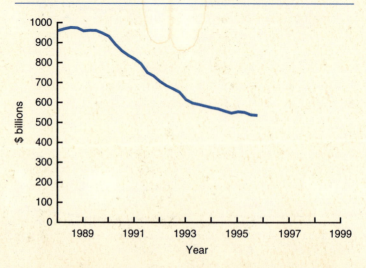

Some failed simply because of economic circumstances beyond their control. Nevertheless, as we shall discuss in Chapter 8, most economists concur that the main reason why so many savings institutions disappeared was that federal regulations and deposit insurance combined to produce a significant moral hazard problem. Their exposure to interest rate risk had already made the savings institutions very fragile by the end of the 1970s. Then, regulatory changes in the 1980s encouraged savings institution managers to undertake riskier activities. Their customers' deposits were federally insured, but the insurance premiums that the savings institutions were paying on their deposits were unrelated to the risks they were incurring. The result was a crisis that engulfed a very large number of savings banks and savings and loan associations. In the end, federal regulators seized and sold over $400 billion in savings institution assets. The ultimate loss to taxpayers for funding insured deposits lost by these institutions amounted to over $200 billion, or enough to fund much of the federal government's deficit for any year in the 1990s.

As we shall discuss in Chapter 9, Congress responded to this experience by requiring the Federal Deposit Insurance Corporation to charge risk-based premiums on deposit insurance. The FDIC's 1994 adoption of such risk-based premiums may reduce the possibility that commercial banks will repeat the experience of savings institutions in the late 1980s and early 1990s. But the savings institution industry remains a shadow of its former self. In 1985 there were over 3,000 savings institutions. Today there are less than half that number.

Assets and Liabilities of Savings Institutions

Table 6.3 lists the *combined* assets and liabilities of *all* 1,400 federally insured savings institutions. Comparing these institutions' assets and liabilities with those of commercial banks listed in Tables 6.1 and 6.2 shows some small similarities. Both types of institution issue deposits and depend on deposit funds in similar proportion to finance their activities.

TABLE 6.3   Combined Assets and Liabilities of Savings Institutions, March 1996

Cash and securities	$104.9	13.8%	Total deposits	$527.6	69.2%
Mortgage loans	447.5	58.7%	Government borrowings	85.9	11.3%
Mortgage-backed securities	119.6	15.7%	Other borrowings	71.7	9.4%
Commercial loans	8.1	1.1%	Other liabilities	16.1	2.1%
Consumer loans	37.5	4.9%	Equity capital	61.6	8.0%
Other assets	45.3	5.8%			
Total Assets	$762.9	100.0%	Total Equity and Liabilities	$762.9	100.0%

Source: Office of Thrift Supervision, *Quarterly Financial Results and Conditions of the Thrift Industry*, 1996, $ billions.

From Table 6.2, about 64 percent of commercial banks' liabilities and net worth is in deposit liabilities; Table 6.3 shows a roughly comparable 69 percent figure for savings institutions. Both kinds of institutions also make loans and hold securities and cash assets. There are dramatic differences, however, in how the institutions *allocate* their assets.

Mortgage Loans   From Table 6.3 we can see that the clearly dominant asset category for savings institutions is mortgage lending, which accounts for about 59 percent of total savings institution assets.

A mortgage loan finances purchase of real estate such as a tract of land or a structure such as a house. The borrower of a mortgage loan has the right to use the property while the mortgage is in effect. In return, the borrower must make regular payments of principal and interest.

Most mortgage loans have maturities ranging from 15 to 30 years. Until the 1970s mortgage loan interest rates typically were fixed over the term to maturity. Such mortgages are **fixed-rate mortgages.**

fixed-rate mortgages
Mortgages with constant interest rates over their terms to maturity.

adjustable-rate mortgages (ARMs)   Mortgages whose interest rates vary with other interest rates or indexes of interest rates.

Since the early 1980s depository institutions nationwide have offered **adjustable-rate mortgages (ARMs)** as well. Interest rates on ARMs adjust periodically—typically every six months, one year, three years, or five years—to changes in other market interest rates. Typically ARM rates are based on a specific interest rate, such as the 6-month or 1-year Treasury bill rate, or on an index of interest rates, such as an index of yields on Treasury securities. Some ARM rates are tied to measures of depository institutions' costs of funds. Examples are averages of yields on bank certificates of deposit or indexes of mortgage lenders' funding costs computed by the Federal Home Loan Bank of San Francisco. Figure 6.6 shows that ARMs now represent a major portion of total mortgages.

Savings banks and savings and loan associations have always specialized in mortgage lending. Traditionally, this specialty has been their strength as well as their great weakness. It has been a strength because savings institutions have developed techniques for dealing with adverse selection and moral hazard problems that are endemic to mortgage lending. Consequently, these institutions have a managerial advantage over other potential competitors in this business.

The mortgage lending specialty of savings institutions has been a weakness because of the *interest rate risk* inherent in mortgage lending. As we said, home mortgage loans typically have terms to maturity ranging from 15 to 30 years. This means that when a savings institution grants a 30-year mortgage loan at a fixed rate of 8 percent, it takes a chance that the rates it must pay on its deposits and other liabilities will stay sufficiently below 8 percent to permit a long-term profit on the mortgage. Many savings institutions made exactly this bet in the early 1970s before ARMs became common. Then, in the late 1970s they watched as market interest rates on deposits rose above rates they were earning on fixed-rate mortgage loans!

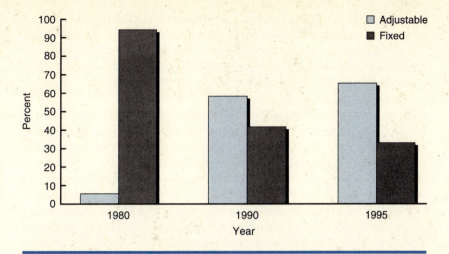

FIGURE 6.6   Adjustable- and Fixed-Rate Mortgages

At the beginning of the 1980s, fewer than 6 percent of single-family mortgage loans issued by savings institutions had adjustable interest rates. By 1990 over half were adjustable-rate mortgage loans, and by 1995 this portion had risen to about two-thirds. *Source:* Office of Thrift Supervision, *Quarterly Financial Results and Conditions of the Thrift Industry,* various issues.

Mortgage-Backed Securities   As discussed in Chapter 2, a mortgage-backed security is a title to a share in the principal and interest earnings from a group of mortgages with similar characteristics, such as nearly identical default risk and the same term to maturity. Many mortgage-backed securities are issued by governmental or government-sponsored agencies. These include the Government National Mortgage Association (GNMA) or the Federal National Mortgage Association (FNMA).

An institution such as FNMA usually purchases mortgage loans from the savings institutions that initiate the loans. Typically, it pays the initiating institution a fee in exchange for continuing to collect principal and interest payments on its behalf. It *pools,* or segregates, the mortgage loans it owns into groups with like characteristics. It then sells mortgage-backed securities whose yields are based on the principal and interest payments derived from the underlying pools of mortgage loans.

Because each mortgage pool has similar risk- and term-structure characteristics, potential buyers can readily assess the risk and liquidity features of each mortgage-backed security. Hence, there usually are many potential buyers in the secondary market for mortgage-backed securities. This makes these securities relatively liquid financial instruments. The liquidity of mortgage-backed securities helps to make the underlying mortgage loans more liquid instruments than they would be otherwise.

Savings institutions themselves usually buy large numbers of mortgage-backed securities. As Table 6.3 shows, savings institutions' holdings of mortgage-backed securities amount to 16 percent of their total assets. Consequently, these institutions allocate a total of 74 percent of their assets to mortgage-related activities.

Other Loans and Assets   Legislation passed by Congress in the early 1980s gave savings institutions the legal power to make commercial and consumer loans within specified limits. Most savings institutions have not reached those limits, however. Together, commercial and consumer loans amounted to under 6 percent of their assets in 1996.

Like commercial banks, savings institutions hold cash assets. They also hold U.S. government securities and state and municipal bonds. Together these assets amount to about 14 percent of the total assets of savings institutions.

5

How do savings institutions differ from commercial banks?   The fundamental difference between savings institutions and commercial banks is that savings institutions are much more specialized in mortgage-related lending, and a much larger portion of their security holdings is devoted to mortgage-backed securities.

The Future of Savings Institutions

Most observers agree that the worst times are past for most savings institutions that survived the crisis years of the late 1980s and early 1990s. Nevertheless, these institutions have not put their problems fully behind them. Their profit rates continue to lag behind those of commercial banks. In addition, their primary federal regulator, the Office of Thrift Supervision, continues to classify about 1.5 percent of their loan assets as "troubled." Recently, some members of Congress have even called for eliminating savings institution charters altogether and converting healthy savings institutions into commercial banks.

Furthermore, the U.S. government responded to the large deposit insurance losses that savings banks and savings and loan associations caused in recent years by raising their deposit insurance premiums significantly. The government uses these higher deposit insurance premiums to pay off the bonds issued to cover the costs of closing failed savings institutions. Currently low-risk savings institutions must pay about six times more for their deposit insurance than do commercial banks that bank regulators judge to have assets with similar risk. Under current projections this premium difference will not decline for several more years.

One predictable response to this situation has been that many savings banks and savings and loan associations that already have stock-ownership structures have sought to receive commercial banking charters. In addition, a large number of mutually owned savings institutions have begun to switch to stock ownership. Some of these institutions undoubtedly hope eventually to seek bank charters. Others have switched to stock-ownership structures in the hope that centralized managerial control will better contain other costs, in light of the higher deposit insurance costs that they face. Consequently, unless Congress actually eliminates savings institution charters, there are two likely trends for savings institutions in the future: There will be even fewer of these institutions, and fewer of those that remain will have mutual ownership.

CREDIT UNIONS

There are nearly 12,000 federally insured credit unions in the United States. Table 6.4 shows the combined assets and liabilities of all federally-insured credit unions.

Credit unions normally are relatively uncomplicated institutions. Share deposits of members account for about 88 percent of the liabilities and net worth of these institutions, and loans to members compose over 62 percent of all credit union assets. What separates credit unions from other depository institutions is that they take in deposits only from members, and they make loans only to members. To qualify for membership in a credit union, an individual must meet criteria specific to that credit union. Typically, an individual must be associated with a particular business or occupation.

Credit unions have faced important risk issues in recent years. Some have run into significant difficulties in recent years because they sought to increase their returns through derivatives speculation. As we shall discuss in Chapter 7, this has caused regulators to contemplate significant changes in the structure of the federal insurance for credit unions.

TABLE 6.4   Assets, and Liabilities and Equity at Federally Insured Credit Unions ($ billions, January 1, 1996)

Loans	$192.1	62.7%	Share deposits	$270.1	88.1%
Securities	100.6	32.8%	Other Liabilities		
Cash assets	7.1	2.3%	and Equity	36.5	11.9%
Other assets	6.8	2.2%			
Total Assets	$ 306.6	100.0%	Total Liabilities		
			and Equity	$306.6	100.0%

Source: National Credit Union Administration, *Statistics for Federally Insured Credit Unions,* 1996. (Special thanks to John Zimmerman of the NCUA.)

6

How do credit unions raise and allocate their funds?   Nearly all the funds raised by credit unions come from share deposits issued to members. They allocate the majority of their funds to loans and the remainder to securities and cash.

SUMMARY

1. **The Historical Origins of Modern Banking Institutions:** Deposit-taking lending institutions have existed since the earliest human civilizations. Modern versions of these institutions originated with the merchant bankers of medieval Italy. Since that time depository institutions have specialized in maintaining deposit accounts for, processing payments on behalf of, and making loans to their customers.

2. **Why Depository Institutions Are Segmented:** Commercial banks, savings institutions, and credit unions have always specialized. In the 1930s, however, Congress enacted legislation that strengthened the distinctions among these institutions.

3. **The Key Assets of Commercial Banks:** These include commercial and industrial loans, real estate loans, and consumer loans; securities, such as U.S. government bonds; and cash assets, such as vault cash and reserve deposits held at the Federal Reserve.

4. **The Key Liabilities of Commercial Banks:** These include noncontrollable liabilities, such as checking, savings, and small-denomination time deposits, and controllable liabilities, such as certificates of deposit and federal funds borrowings.

5. **How Savings Institutions Differ from Commercial Banks:** The key difference is that savings institutions have specialized much more narrowly in mortgage-related activities such as mortgage lending and holding mortgage-backed securities.

6. **How Credit Unions Raise and Allocate Their Funds:** Almost all credit union funds come from share deposits of members. Credit unions lend the majority of these funds to members.

QUESTIONS AND PROBLEMS

1. Explain in your own words why it was so natural in early times for goldsmiths to become bankers.

2. Of today's bank assets which would you expect might be similar to those on the balance sheets of Italian merchant bankers? What kinds might truly be "new"? Explain your reasoning.

3. In your own words, explain the difference between an asset and a liability.

4. Based on the data in Tables 6.1 and 6.2, on average would you expect that bank assets or bank liabilities have longer maturities? Support your answer. Do you think that this could pose problems for bank managers? Explain.

5. Derivative instruments (covered in Chapter 4) do not appear anywhere in the balance sheets discussed in this chapter. Yet depository institutions are active derivatives traders. Explain why derivatives are absent from depository institution balance sheets.

7

The Economics of Depository Institutions

KEY QUESTIONS

1. What are the key sources of depository institution revenues?

2. What are the key sources of depository institution costs?

3. What are common measures of depository institution profitability?

4. What is the main determinant of a depository institution's profitability?

5. How has the philosophy of depository institution management evolved?

6. How have depository institutions performed in recent years?

I t is called the roller coaster and it goes up and down. That seems to describe what has happened to the banking industry in the 1990s. By 1992 major banks were flush with cash and securities and stood ready to get back into their basic lending businesses again. Bankers renewed acquaintances with old corporate and foreign customers in anticipation of opening up a new period of "relationship banking." But then a maverick institution, Bankers Trust, entered the picture in a big way by doing derivative trading on its own account and derivatives management on behalf of some big clients. By 1994 Bankers Trust was managing over $150 billion in assets worldwide.

The challenge was on. Chemical Bank (later to merge with Chase Manhattan Bank) jumped into derivatives trading. So, too, did J. P. Morgan. The future looked bright. But by the end of 1994 the picture changed. Bankers Trust had lost millions for Proctor and Gamble and other major corporations. The bank was being sued and investigated at the same time. Also, a huge derivatives loss in Orange County, California, as well as the failure of the Barings Bank for the same reason put an end to the glow that derivatives added to the banking business. By 1995, J. P. Morgan decided on a 10 percent staff cut. Citibank started cutting back, too. As bank managers looked to the next century, they were not sure what lay ahead.

Only a quarter-century ago, American bankers would never have dreamed that such boom-and-bust cycles would be so common to their business. Banking was a "3-6-3 business": Bankers borrowed at 3 percent, lent at 6 percent, and left to play golf at three o'clock.

Now banking has become a whirlwind of activity compared with such bygone days. In many ways, of course, banking remains a stable business. Nevertheless, sweeping changes have occurred. These have affected how banks earn their profits and how they compete for those profits. The goals of this chapter are to explain the sources of bank profitability, to discuss the factors that influence depository institution profit performance, and to examine the recent performances of depository institutions.

DEPOSITORY INSTITUTION REVENUES, COSTS, AND PROFITS

As we discussed in Chapter 6, banks, savings institutions, and credit unions specialize in various ways. Nevertheless, the fundamental economics of these depository institutions is very similar. All depository institutions incur the same basic kinds of expenses, and all derive earnings from similar, if not always identical, types of operations. The profits they earn, of course, are the excess of revenues over costs. We begin our discussion of the economics of depository institutions by discussing how these institutions generate revenues, how they incur costs, and how they and their owners judge their performance in the marketplace.

Sources of Depository Institution Revenues

In Chapter 6 we reviewed the consolidated balance sheets of commercial banks, savings institutions, and credit unions, and you learned about the various assets held by these institutions. The three main groups of assets are loans, securities, and cash assets. Banks tabulate these assets at a point in time.

In contrast, banks measure their *revenues*, or incomes, as *flows* over time. Because income is a flow, depository institutions can tabulate it for given intervals. For instance, a depository institution can track its interest income from loans and securities over a month, a quarter, or a year. Most depository institutions report quarterly and annual income flows.

interest income Interest revenues that depository institutions derive from their holdings of loans and securities.

Interest Income   The earnings that depository institutions derive from their loans and securities are their **interest income.** To see how interest income is a *flow* of earnings over time, consider an example in which a bank makes a $15,000 loan to an individual to help finance the purchase of a new car. The loan is a $15,000 asset for the bank at the moment it is made. If the auto loan is a typical installment loan, then the borrower will make monthly payments of principal and interest. The loan principal payment is not income, because it is a repayment of funds that already belong to the bank. The interest portion of the payment, however, represents income to the bank. Such interest income is part of the bank's total revenues.

As Figure 7.1 shows, interest income accounts for just over three-fourths of the revenues of commercial banks. It also represents the largest portion of income for savings institutions and credit unions.

noninterest income Revenues that depository institutions earn from sources other than interest income, such as trading profits or fees they charge for services they provide to customers.

Noninterest Income   As Figure 7.1 indicates, commercial banks earn almost a fourth of their revenues as **noninterest income** from sources other than interest income such as fees that they charge for services to depositors. A portion of this noninterest income arises mainly from two interrelated sources: loan sales and loan management fees.

As we discuss in more detail later in this chapter, many depository institutions sell some of the loans (which are assets) that they have made to other financial institutions. Often, they earn revenues by selling loans for somewhat more than the original loan amounts. In addition, such loan sales commonly include an arrangement by which the

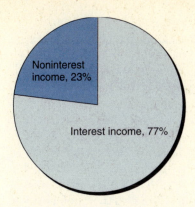

Noninterest income, 23%

Interest income, 77%

FIGURE 7.1   Sources of Commercial Bank Revenues

Although noninterest income has become a more important source of bank revenues in recent years, the bulk of bank revenues continues to flow from interest earnings. *Source:* William English and Brian Reid, "Profits and Balance Sheet Developments at Commercial Banks," *Federal Reserve Bulletin*, June 1995, 545–569.

depository institutions selling the loan continue to maintain the loan account on behalf of the purchaser. That is, they continue to manage and process payments and expenses relating to the loans even though the loans are off their books. In return for such services, the depository institutions charge fees to the loan purchasers. These loan management fees are another source of noninterest income.

Depository institutions also generate noninterest income from trading in derivative instruments such as futures, options, or swaps. As discussed in Chapter 4, derivatives trading often is intended to *hedge* against risks. Such trading typically generates few revenues, because depository institutions design hedges to avoid capital losses, thereby eliminating profit opportunities as well. When depository institutions engage in speculative derivatives trading, however, such trading can generate income for these institutions.

Deposit fee income, the income that depository institutions earn by charging fees for their depository services, has been a growing source of revenues. Many depository institutions now charge many of their customers fees for printing checks, for clearing checks, for making cash withdrawals above a certain number per month, and for making transfers between accounts. Nearly half of all commercial banks now charge a fee to use automated teller machines, whereas in 1989 only a fifth of banks charged such a fee.

GLOBAL NOTEBOOK

Islamic Banking: How to Lend Without Charging Interest

According to at least one interpretation of the Koran, the paying or receiving of interest is a violation of Islamic law. Thus, groups of bankers and Muslim scholars have had to work hard to create an interest-free banking system that nevertheless allows Muslims to borrow, for example, to purchase a house.

In Malaysia, the central bank recently launched a separate check-clearing pool for institutions offering Islamic financial services. Banks following the Koran operate on the basis of profit sharing and commissions or deferred payments. Consider how such a loan can be made for the purchase of a house. The buyer provides a 20 percent down payment. A partnership agreement with the bank is set up in which the bank provides the rest of the funds and leases its prorated portion of the house to the buyer. The buyer, thus, pays rent based on the portion of the home owned by the bank plus a small amount each month to increase equity ownership in the home. If the resident owner defaults on the house and the bank has to sell it, the owner does not lose the equity share. In essence then, no "loan" is made, but a lease is provided by the bank.

Those who put money into an Islamic savings instrument are not paid interest. Rather they are considered shareholders and receive dividends when the bank turns a profit.

For Critical Analysis: *What additional risks do Islamic banks incur that Western banks do not?*

Some banks even charge customers who have small accounts fees to do business with human tellers at their branches. In May 1995, First Chicago Bank began charging a $3 teller fee to account holders with checking balances under $2,500 or a combined checking/saving balance under $15,000. As justification, the bank pointed out that in a given year, a $500 checking account usually would yield $25 in interest income and $100 in fee income. But if the account holder were to make eight automated-teller-machine transactions and four teller transactions per month, maintaining the account would cost the bank $216. Hence, the bank claimed it would lose $91 per year on such an account. For a checking account with a balance of over $5,000, the bank found that it would earn a net profit of $314.

Naturally, account holders do not like deposit fees, and they generate consumer complaints and get a lot of media attention. But in the big picture of depository institution revenues, deposit fees are small potatoes. Such fees account for only about 5 percent of the total revenues of commercial banks. Nevertheless, this amounts to one-fourth of total noninterest income. The total estimated deposit fee income earned by commercial banks in 1996 was over $15 billion, which was over twice the amount of fee income that banks earned in 1985. Deposit fees promise to continue to rise as a share of the noninterest income that banks and other depository institutions earn.

1

What are the key sources of depository institution revenues? The predominant source of revenue for a typical depository institution is interest income. A secondary source is noninterest income, of which a growing portion is deposit fee income.

Costs of Depository Institution Operations

Recall from your basic economics principles course that any business firm requires factors of production to produce a good or service. In turn, expenses that business firms incur in purchasing such factors of production represent the costs of such firms. This is true for depository institutions as well. But because they are financial firms, depository institutions also depend on financial resources.

Interest Expenses Operating a depository institution requires two major kinds of factors of production: dollar funds and real resources. The depository institution's managers use the dollar funds to make loans, hold government and municipal securities, and maintain the liquidity of the institution by holding cash assets.

　　To raise the dollars they allocate to such asset holdings, which in turn generate revenues, depository institutions issue liabilities such as deposits. To attract funds, they must pay interest on these liabilities. Hence, **interest expense** is a major component of depository institution costs. As shown in Figure 7.2 (page 174), interest expense amounts to over 40 percent of the total costs incurred by commercial banks. Typically this ratio is approximately the same for savings institutions and credit unions as well.

interest expense The portion of depository institution costs incurred through payments of interest to holders of the institutions' liabilities.

Expenses for Loan Loss Provisions Banking is a risky business, because from time to time borrowers default on their loans. Depository institutions recognize that some portion of the loans they make will not be repaid, and so they earmark part of their cash assets as **loan loss reserves.** This portion of their cash assets is held in readily available liquid form. The banks will recognize depletion of this liquid cash asset in the event that a loan default actually occurs.

　　On an ongoing basis, depository institutions add to their loan loss reserves as defaults reduce the reserves. Such additions during a year are **loan loss provisions,** and they are an expense for depository institutions.

loan loss reserves An amount of cash assets that depository institutions hold in every liquid assets which they expect will be depleted as a result of loan defaults.

loan loss provisions An expense that depository institutions incur when they allocate funds to loan loss reserves.

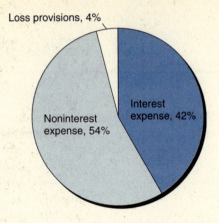

Loss provisions, 4%

Interest expense, 42%

Noninterest expense, 54%

FIGURE 7.2   Commercial Bank Expenses

Over half the expenses of commercial banks are noninterest expenses on real resources such as labor and capital goods. Interest expenses on deposit funds and purchased funds account for nearly all remaining expenses, although expenses for loan loss provisions also account for a small portion. *Source:* William English and Brian Reid, "Profits and Balance Sheet Developments at Commercial Banks," *Federal Reserve Bulletin,* June 1995, 545–569.

That is, the funds that depository institutions must spend to make up for loan defaults are an unavoidable part of their lending operations. Figure 7.2 shows that loan loss provisions account for about 4 percent of commercial bank expenses.

Real-Resource Expenses   Like any other firm, however, a depository institution also uses traditional factors of production—labor, capital, and land—in its operations. It must pay wages and salaries to its employees, purchase or lease capital goods such as bank branch buildings and computer equipment, and pay rental fees for the use of land on which its offices and branches are situated. Such costs are the **real-resource expenses** that depository institutions incur.

Figure 7.2 indicates that expenses for real resources amount to over half of total costs for commercial banks. Clearly, real-resource expenditures are not a trivial portion of total depository institution costs. In recent years many depository institutions have sought to cut these expenses, often by reducing their employment of human resources.

real-resource expenses
Depository institution expenditures on wages and salaries for employees, purchases or leases of capital goods, and rental payments for the use of land.

MANAGEMENT NOTEBOOK

The Rise in On-Line Banking

One way for commercial banks to cut down on human resource costs is to get customers to use on-line banking. After all, banking may be vital to a growing economy, but *physical* banks and personnel are not. Not surprisingly, there has been a spate of deals among banks, on-line services, software companies, and telephone companies.

Recently, Citibank dropped all fees charged for electronic banking in an attempt to encourage more people to use it. First Chicago did the same thing. On-line banking is not just limited to commercial banks. Security First, a savings bank, can now be found on the Internet (at http://www.sfnb.com). One of the reasons why on-line banking is possible today—and was not ten years ago—is that today there

are almost 40 million personal computers in U.S. homes, with millions more on the way. As many banks use the Internet to offer on-line banking services, banking size may not matter much. Security First, for example, has less than $100 million in assets. But through your personal computer, Security First is indistinguishable from, say, Wells Fargo which has $53 *billion* in assets.

In any event, the projected number of homes that will be using on-line technology for banking transactions in 1997 is almost 10 million.

For Critical Analysis: *What costs do banks incur to go on-line?*

2

What are the key sources of depository institution costs?   The two main types of costs that depository institutions incur are interest expense and real-resource expenses. A third key cost is expense arising from provisions for loan loss reserves.

Measuring Depository Institution Profitability

A depository institution's **profit** is the dollar amount by which its combined interest and noninterest income exceeds its total costs. Knowing the absolute profit of a depository institution is the key to judging its success in the marketplace. Nevertheless, the dollar amount of profit by itself does not always tell us much. To see this, suppose that you were told that an unnamed bank had earned $10 million in profit last year. This seems like a lot of money. And it would be if the bank had only $100 million in assets, because then the bank would be earning an average *rate* of profit of 10 percent relative to its

profit   The amount by which revenue exceeds cost.

base of assets. But if the bank had *$10 billion* in assets, a dollar profit of $10 million would be minuscule; its rate of profit relative to its assets would be only 0.1 percent.

Consequently, to make better judgments about how to rate a depository institution's profitability, we need to compare its absolute profit with some measure of the depository institution's size. This can give us a better idea about how the depository institution has done given its base of funds. Then, we can compare the performance of a bank with $100 million in assets to the performance of a bank with $1 billion in assets.

Return on Assets   There are two key measures of depository institution profitability that permit such comparisons. One is **return on assets.** This profitability measure is absolute dollar profit as a percentage of the dollar value of the depository institution's assets. We can compute return on assets using the following formula:

return on assets   A depository institution's profit as a percentage of its total assets.

$$\text{Percentage return on assets} = \frac{\text{Absolute profit}}{\text{Total assets}} \times 100$$

In the case of a bank with $1 billion ($1,000 million) in assets and earning an annual profit of $10 million, the return on assets would be equal to the ratio $10 million/$1,000 million multiplied by a factor of 100, or 1 percent. For the bank with assets of $10 billion ($10,000 million) and an annual profit of $10 million, the return on assets would be equal to the ratio $10 million/$10,000 million multiplied by 100, or 0.1 percent. Using the return on assets measure of profitability, therefore, makes it clear that in this example the smaller bank is much more profitable than the larger bank.

Return on Equity   Another common measure of depository institution profitability is **return on equity.** This is the absolute profit of a depository institution as a percentage of the depository institution's equity capital. To compute return on equity, we use the formula,

return on equity   A depository institution's profit as a percentage of its equity capital.

$$\text{Percentage Return on equity} = \frac{\text{Absolute profit}}{\text{Equity capital}} \times 100$$

Suppose that a small bank has $70 million in equity capital and earns a profit of $10 million during a given year. Then its return on equity for the year is equal to the ratio $10 million/$70 million multiplied by 100, or about 14.3 percent. During the same year, a larger bank with $800 million in equity capital earns a profit of $130 million, and so its return on equity is equal to the ratio $130 million/$800 million multiplied by 100, or 16.3 percent. In this instance, we could conclude that, based on this return on equity measure, the larger bank has outperformed the smaller bank.

Figure 7.3 shows how commercial banks have performed since 1990 based both on their average return on assets and on their average return on equity. As you can see, banks' return on equity nearly doubled during the early 1990s before falling off slightly. The average return on assets at commercial banks generally trended upward over this period.

Net Interest Margin   Return on assets and return on equity are *retrospective* measures of profitability, meaning that we calculate them after the fact. Once we know a depository institution's profit for a given interval and the amount of its assets or equity capital as of a date during that interval, we can compute either profitability measure. Then we can try to judge how well the institution performed in the recent past.

But suppose that we are trying to gauge a depository institution's *current* or likely *future* profitability performance. While recent figures on returns on assets and returns on equity might give us some basis for estimating the institution's present or future profitability, it would be nice to have a more *prospective*, or forward-looking indicator of profitability. This would be especially true for a bank stockholder

FIGURE 7.3   Commercial Banks' Average Returns on Assets and on Equity
According to both measures, bank profitability rose during the 1990s. *Source:* Federal Deposit Insurance Corporation, *Statistics on Banking,* various issues.

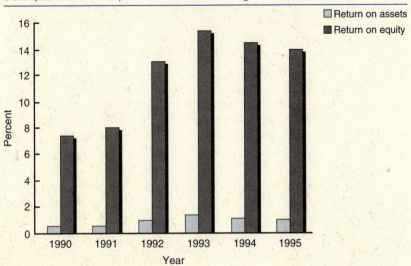

who is trying to assess the current performance of the bank's managers.

The most common prospective indicator of a depository institution's profitability is called the **net interest margin.** This is the difference between a depository institution's interest income and interest expenses as a percentage of total assets. We can calculate net interest margin as follows:

net interest margin   The difference between a depository institution's interest income and interest expenses as a percentage of total assets.

$$\text{Net interest margin} = \frac{\text{Interest income} - \text{Interest expense}}{\text{Total assets}} \times 100$$

Because interest income is such a large portion of depository institution revenues while interest expense represents a significant portion of costs, net interest margin is commonly used as a quick and easy indicator of current and future performance. A depository institution's exact net interest margin can be computed retrospectively by looking at past interest income, interest expense, and assets. But the future net interest margin for a depository institution also can be approximated very easily using current data.

To see how this may be done, consider an example. During the year just past, a bank's net interest margin, calculated by computing the difference between interest income and expenses as a percentage of the banks total assets, was 3.3 percent. During the most recent quarter, however, the depository institution's average interest earnings on loans and securities has been 11.2 percent, while the average interest rate that it paid to borrow funds, issue deposit liabilities, and raise equity funds was 8.4 percent. Assuming that the bank can maintain this most recent level of performance across all assets and liabilities, then the *prospective* net interest margin is simply the difference between 11.2 percent and 8.4 percent, or 3.8 percent. This would indicate that, relative to last year, this bank's performance is improving. While we have to wait until the year ends to know exactly how well it actually will end up doing, using the net interest margin as an indicator can help us judge its performance as the current year progresses.

To see how the net interest margin often proves to be a useful indicator of depository institution profitability in the near future, consider the following figures for the 1990s. The average net interest margin at commercial banks increased from 3.94 in 1990 to 4.41 in 1992 before falling off very slightly to 4.40 in 1993. This rise of nearly one-half percent in the net interest margin preceded the sharp increase in return on equity that Figure 7.3 shows occurred between 1991 and 1994. By 1996 the net interest margin had fallen below 4.30. Following this gradual decline in the net interest margin, there was a slight drop-off in return on equity, as shown in Figure 7.3.

3

What are common measures of depository institution profitability?   One typical profitability measure is return on assets, which is profit as a percentage of total assets. Another is return on equity, or profit as a percentage of equity capital. A profitability measure that people often use to assess the current and future prospects of a depository institution is the net interest margin, which is the difference between a depository institution's interest income and interest expenses as a percentage of total assets.

COMPETITION VERSUS MONOPOLY IN BANKING

A number of factors ultimately determine the profitability of banks and other depository institutions. Among these are changes in factors that affect the two components of bank revenues, interest income and non-interest income, and variations in factors that influence the three elements that comprise bank costs, namely interest expense, loan loss provisions, and real resource expenses.

   As noted, interest income represents the bulk of depository institution revenues. Hence, if interest rates on loans rise, then the interest income that depository institutions earn on given amounts of lending and securities holdings tends to increase. Likewise, interest expense is nearly half of depository institution costs. Therefore, if interest rates on deposits decline, then the total interest expense on any given volume of funding tends to fall. Either type of interest rate movement—a rise in loan rates or a fall in deposit rates—would raise the net interest margin, leading to greater profitability.

Depository Institution Market Structure

How are market interest rates determined for bank loans and deposits? The answer to this question depends very much on depository institution **market structure,** which refers to the organization of the markets in which depository institutions interact. A traditional issue has been how and why the degree of **market concentration**—the extent to which the few largest depository institutions dominate loan and deposit markets—affects the behavior of depository institutions.

   Although there are a number of possible ways to measure market concentration, the most straightforward is simply to look at the market shares of the few largest depository institutions. Typically if the three or four largest institutions together have a large fraction of total loans or deposits, say 70 percent or more, then the market is said

market structure The organization of the loan and deposit markets in which depository institutions interact.

market concentration The degree to which the few largest depository institutions dominate loan and deposit markets.

to be relatively concentrated. But if the three or four largest institutions have a combined market share that is much smaller, then the degree of rivalry, or competition, is likely much greater.

Competition   One possible type of depository institution market structure is **pure competition.** Under pure competition no single depository institution can influence loan or deposit interest rates. Unrestricted rivalry among depository institutions drives loan and deposit rates to levels that just cover the costs the institutions incur in making loans and issuing and servicing deposits.

Economists typically regard pure competition as the optimal market structure. The reason is that if rivalry among depository institutions pushes loan and deposit rates closely in line with the costs of providing loans and issuing deposits, consumers pay interest rates just sufficient to cover those costs. As a result, they are not in any way forced to pay loan rates that are "too high" or to earn deposit rates that are "too low," given the actual costs that depository institutions incur in providing financial intermediation services.

In fact, under pure competition depository institutions earn no more than a **normal profit.** This is a level of profit just sufficient to compensate depository institution owners for holding equity shares in depository institutions instead of directing their funds to other enterprises.

Monopoly   At the opposite extreme from pure competition is a depository institution market structure called **pure monopoly**. This is the dominance of a loan or deposit market by a single depository institution or by a *cartel*, a small group of institutions that effectively coordinate their actions so they jointly maximize their profits.

Although there certainly have been cases in which loan and deposit markets in local areas have been close to pure monopoly situations, pure monopoly has not been a very common type of depository institution market structure in the United States. Nevertheless, there is evidence that in some locations and during some periods, depository institutions have possessed **monopoly power.** This refers to the ability of one or a few depository institutions to dominate loan and deposit markets sufficiently to set loan rates higher than they would under pure competition in lending, or to set deposit rates lower than they would under pure competition in issuing and servicing deposits. The result of higher loan rates would be reduced lending as compared with pure competition, and lower deposit rates would cause reduced holdings of deposits. Depository institution customers would pay more interest for fewer loans and receive less interest for fewer deposits.

If depository institutions have monopoly power, then their ability to set loan rates "too high" or deposit rates "too low" relative to purely competitive levels means that they can earn **supranormal profits.** These are levels of profit that are above the normal profits necessary to

pure competition   A market structure in which no single depository institution can influence loan or deposit interest rates, so that rivalry among institutions yields market loan and deposit interest rates that just cover the costs the institutions incur in making loans and issuing and servicing deposits.

normal profit   A profit level just sufficient to compensate depository institution owners for holding equity shares in depository institutions instead of purchasing ownership shares of other enterprises.

pure monopoly   The dominance of a loan or deposit market by a single depository institution or by a small group of institutions that work together to maximize their profits.

monopoly power   The ability of one or a cartel of depository institutions to dominate loan and deposit markets sufficiently so to set higher loan rates and lower deposit rates compared with purely competitive market interest rates.

supranormal profits   Levels of profit above those required to induce depository institution owners to hold shares of ownership in those institutions instead of in other businesses.

induce depository institution owners to direct their funds to the banking business rather than to some other endeavor. If depository institution owners earn supranormal profits because monopoly power exists, then they effectively have "gouged" consumers who use the services of these institutions by charging higher prices for fewer services.

Depository Institution Monopolies: Relics of the Past?

In the past many people claimed that banks were protected so completely from competition that a bank charter was a license to steal. The reason why these views prevailed was that until the latter part of this century, regulations protected depository institutions from competition. Indeed, many of the restrictions on banking that Congress enacted in the 1930s were intended to reduce competition among depository institutions. As we discussed in Chapters 5 and 6, legislation in the 1930s artificially separated the lines of business of various financial institutions. The result was that depository institutions competed in separate local, regional, and national markets for loans and deposits. This reduced the extent of rivalry in those markets and raised the degree of monopoly power that depository institutions possessed.

In 1982 Stephen Rhoades, an economist at the Federal Reserve Board in Washington, attempted to measure the effects of monopoly power among commercial banks in loan markets in 1978. He found that monopoly power caused total bank lending to be 14 percent lower than it otherwise would have been under pure competition. Rhoades also estimated that banks earned supranormal profits. He concluded that bank profit levels in 1978 were over $1 billion, or about 13 percent, more than they otherwise would have been in purely competitive banking markets.

A lot has changed since 1978. For one thing, Congress has loosened many of the regulations that restricted competition among depository institutions. Furthermore, technological change, particularly in information processing, has blurred the distinctions among local, regional, and national loan and deposit markets. For example, a credit union in Pine Bluff, Arkansas, can use wire transfer facilities to make an overnight loan to a bank in New York. The New York bank then may make a loan to a company based in California. Although such financial market linkages existed in the 1970s, they were much less prevalent than they are today.

Does Market Concentration Matter?

Indeed, we shall discuss in Chapters 8 and 9 how many of the barriers to greater rivalry in depository institution markets have fallen. Yet some economists argue that unrestricted rivalry among depository institutions ultimately can lead to too much market concentration.

Such concentration, they contend, feeds on itself and leads to anti-competitive behavior by commercial banks and other financial institutions. According to this view, there is a natural tendency for unrestricted rivalry among banks to lead to more, rather than less, monopoly power.

structure-conduct-performance (SCP) model
A theory of depository institution market structure in which the structure of loan and deposit markets influences the behavior of depository institutions in those markets, and thereby affects their performance.

The Structure-Conduct-Performance Model Those who subscribe to this view base their evaluation on the **structure-conduct-performance (SCP) model** of depository institution market structure. Figure 7.4 illustrates the basic reasoning of this theory. According to the SCP model, the *structure* of a financial market influences the *conduct* of the institutions in the market. Their conduct, in turn, determines the *performance* of those institutions.

The basic prediction of the SCP theory is that more-concentrated loan and deposit markets lead to monopoly power, which yields higher loan rates, lower deposit rates, and supranormal depository institution profits. This prediction causes proponents of the SCP model to prescribe an active role for governmental oversight of depository institution markets. According to SCP proponents, government regulators need to ensure that greater rivalry in banking markets does not lead to the gobbling up of small competitors by larger institutions.

efficient-structure theory A theory of depository institution market structure in which greater market concentration and higher depository institution profits arise from the fact that when there are few depository institutions, they can operate more efficiently in loan and deposit markets than if there are a large number of institutions.

The Efficient-Structure Theory On the other side are economists who promote the **efficient-structure theory** of depository institution market structure. Figure 7.5 depicts the line of reasoning of adherents of this theory of depository institution market structure. According to this view, greater market concentration arises from the fact that a few depository institutions can operate more efficiently as compared with a large number of institutions, in loan and deposit markets. They can do

---

FIGURE 7.4 The Structure-Conduct Performance Model

According to the structure-conduct-performance model, bank market structure can be measured by the concentration of banking markets (for instance, the combined market share of the few largest banks in a market). Bank market structure, in turn, determines whether banks conduct themselves competitively or monopolistically. Bank market conduct, then, determines the performance of banks, as measured by the amount of lending, by loan and deposit rates, and by profitability.

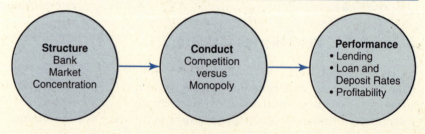

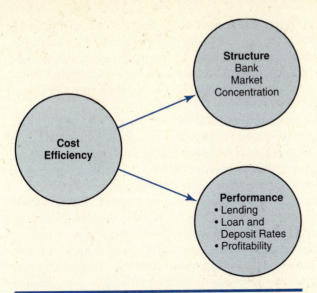

FIGURE 7.5   The Efficient-Structure Theory

According to the efficient-structure theory, any banking organization grows only as long as it remains cost-efficient. Banks that can provide their services at lower cost naturally gain market share, and as a result, are more profitable. Consequently, the structure of banking markets and the performance of banks in those markets depends on cost efficiencies that banks can achieve.

so because they can spread their costs over large computer, branching, and managerial networks.

In the past this argument was based, in part, on the idea of *economies of scale*. As discussed in Chapter 2, economies of scale refer to the ability to reduce average costs by pooling together financial resources. By gaining access to ever-larger amounts of resources, efficient-structure theorists argue, larger institutions can provide services at lower costs than their competitors. The result is lower lending rates and higher deposit rates, so that consumers are better off. And the reward to the more efficient institutions is *higher* profits. Consequently, the efficient-structure theory, like the SCP model, predicts that greater concentration should yield greater profitability. But according to some who promote the efficient-structure view, these higher profits stem from the greater efficiency of the larger firms that dominate financial markets.

The Credit Card Market   To illustrate how these opposing views lead to very different perspectives about the effects of financial market structure, consider the market for consumer credit card lending. The amount of credit card loans exceeds the amount of lending for all auto purchases in the United States. By the year 2000, the dollar amount of such lending is likely to exceed $1.2 trillion. Thousands of financial institutions, including banks, savings institutions, credit unions, and broker-dealers, extend credit card loans. Nonfinancial firms such as General Motors, Ford, and AT&T also are involved in issuing general credit cards.

The dominant credit card group in this market is VISA, which is a collection of over 6,000 member institutions that issue VISA cards, extend revolving credit accounts, collect payments, and charge interest on credit card loans. Over 3 million retailers accepts VISA cards, and more than 220 million cards are in billfolds and handbags across the world.

Clearly, the credit card lending market is extensive and involves a large number of lenders and borrowers. Yet in some respects it also is a relatively *concentrated* market. Although the VISA group of issuers faces competition from MasterCard, American Express, Discover Card, and others, VISA has over half of the credit card business by volume. And about half of this business volume is at the ten largest bank issuers of VISA cards. Several of these banks also are among the largest issuers of the competing MasterCard. Consequently, ten of the nation's largest banks account for well over a third of all credit card lending.

To a proponent of the SCP model, this is bad news for millions of credit card holders. They point to the fact that the top ten banks issuing VISA cards charge sizable annual fees and charge average annual interest rates near 20 percent. In contrast, smaller issuers often charge smaller, or even no, annual fees and offer their cards at significantly lower interest rates. Some SCP proponents have viewed this as evidence that Congress should enact laws to place caps on credit card interest rates, and in recent years members of Congress have offered bills proposing such caps. So far none of these has passed.

Efficient-structure theorists look at the credit card market very differently. They view the dominance of a portion of the credit card market by a few large banks as evidence that those banks have found the most efficient ways to market the cards and to manage credit card accounts. Efficient-structure proponents view the higher average credit card interest rates that these banks charge as the result of their ability to offer cards to so many people, including those who are the greatest credit risks. Smaller banks, they point out, normally restrict their cards to only the better credit risks, and so these banks can charge lower rates. After accounting for risk differences, argue the efficient-structure theorists, large-bank credit card rates, on average, may well be lower than the interest rates that smaller banks charge their more creditworthy customers.

Those who favor the efficient-structure theory also point out that most efforts to restrict competition in the credit card industry arise in legal challenges to new competition. For instance, in 1991 the VISA board of directors passed a specific rule intended to stop Sears from issuing a Prime Option VISA card through a Utah savings and loan association. When Sears persisted, VISA filed a lawsuit claiming that Sears had violated federal law. Ultimately Sears won a jury verdict in a U.S. district court in Salt Lake City. Likewise, in 1991 Dean Witter attempted to offer a VISA card through a bank that it owned, but VISA again filed suit. It again lost its case, but in 1995 an appeals court overturned the jury verdict, and the Supreme Court refused to hear any further appeal.

Recent Evidence on the Market Structure Debate

So who is correct about the effects of unrestricted rivalry on depository institution market structure and performance? So far there has been no final resolution of the controversy concerning the credit card market. But recent work looking at the relationship between commercial bank market concentration and profitability has cast a little more light on the broader debate between SCP proponents and efficient-structure theorists.

In a 1995 study, Allen Berger of the Federal Reserve Board's economic staff analyzed extensive data on 4,800 commercial banks for each year of the 1980s. Berger defined local loan and deposit markets based on Metropolitan Statistical Areas (MSAs) defined by the U.S. Census Bureau and on non-MSA counties. He used batteries of statistical tests to determine how market concentration related to bank profits and used a variety of tests to try to determine which theory received the most support from the data.

Berger reached the conclusion that there is little evidence that the SCP model fits the real world, except perhaps in a much more limited form. According to his study, there is some evidence that large commercial banks earn higher profits because they are successful in gaining sufficient market shares to differentiate themselves from rivals. This, he concludes, gives them some monopoly power. They are able to use this monopoly power to earn some supranormal profits.

The efficient-structure theory's emphasis on economies of scale also did not hold up to the statistical tests that Berger conducted. What Berger found was that a somewhat altered version of the efficient-structure theory seemed to explain banks' performances through the end of the 1980s. According to this variation on the efficient-structure hypothesis, what really counts is the efficiency of the management of commercial banks, irrespective of the bank's absolute size or their market shares. Well-run banks earn higher profits. Banks whose managers do not do a good job of controlling costs can sometimes become large banks, but these banks tend to earn lower profits. In general, however, more efficiently operated banks capture larger market shares. As the efficient-structure theory predicts, this is because they are better at what they do.

Surely this conclusion should not surprise too many depository institution managers. These people must confront the real world of business decisions about lending operations and the provision of deposit services that economic theorists do not see. At this point, however, there seems to be a consensus emerging among *both* economists *and* bankers: What really matters most for the performance of depository institutions, from the perspectives of their owners, managers, *and* customers, is how well they are operated.

4

What is the main determinant of a depository institution's profitability?   Any factor that affects a depository institutions revenues or costs influences the institution's profitability. Although there is limited evidence that loan and deposit-market concentration influence depository institution profitability by affecting the degree of competition and monopoly power, recent evidence indicates that the overriding factor determining profitability is the capability of a depository institution's managers.

BASIC ISSUES IN DEPOSITORY INSTITUTION MANAGEMENT

Certainly, the state of the economy, the stability of financial markets and interest rates, and other factors affecting depository institution costs and revenues can have significant effects on depository institution profitability. Over the long haul, however, it appears that the quality of any given depository institution's management may be the most crucial factor influencing an institution's performance. Consequently, in recent years economists, government regulators, and depository institutions themselves have given much more attention to the proper management of depository institutions.

The Evolution of Depository Institution Management Philosophy

There is no single "right" way to operate a commercial bank or other depository financial institution. Indeed, there are several competing theories of depository institution management.

The Real-Bills Doctrine   The Italian merchant bankers discussed in Chapter 6 discovered that one of the basic problems they faced was a tradeoff between earnings and liquidity. If the merchant banks made loans to Mediterranean traders who repaid the loans very quickly, then the banks felt secure that they could maintain a ready stock of cash assets. Making such loans not only made the banks more liquid but also reduced the riskiness of the bank's portfolio of loans. The problem was that high-liquidity, low-risk loans also yielded low returns to the banks.

The Italian merchant bankers tried to balance liquidity, risk, and return by making short-term loans to traders who needed to finance the transportation of goods to another location for sale. There were risks of damage or loss in Mediterranean storms, but if traders could offer proof of insurance and of ready buyers at the ultimate destinations for the goods, the bankers could feel fairly confident of repayment.

These short-term bank loans, which were the first banker's acceptances (see Chapter 2), had a high probability of repayment. Banks also began to make loans to finance the production of goods, knowing that they would receive payment when production was completed and the goods were sold. Loans to finance the transportation or production of goods came to be called *self-liquidating loans,* because the certainty of repayment was so great that the banks could regard them as highly liquid. Later, as other banks across Europe adopted this approach to lending, the term *real bills* came to be used, because the loans were regarded as bills of credit that were claims on the physical resources whose transit the loans were financing. As a result, the bank management philosophy of restricting most loans to those used by borrowers to finance production or shipping of goods came to be known as the **real-bills doctrine.**

There are two difficulties with the real-bills doctrine. The first is that if banks restrict themselves only to the shortest term, most highly liquid loans, then they also must accept lower returns because more-liquid loans normally carry lower risk and therefore pay lower rates. The second difficulty arises if all banks follow the real-bills doctrine simultaneously and an economic downturn occurs. If producers and traders who otherwise would seek to borrow find that demand for their goods has fallen, then they would be unable to convince banks to lend to them. After all, such loans would not appear to banks to be self-liquidating. But if banks follow the real-bills doctrine and choose not to lend, their borrowers' businesses most likely would fail. This would reinforce the economic downturn. In the end this would be a self-defeating strategy for the banks.

One way to try to salvage the real-bills doctrine would be to create a *central bank* that would stand ready to lend to banks when economic downturns reduce the liquidity of the loans that the banks make to producers and traders. Such a central bank would act as a *lender of last resort* during bad times. It would ensure liquidity of the banking system as a whole and thereby permit banks to follow the real bills doctrine. Although we shall see in Chapter 11 that many economists today question this motivation for modern central banking, it was firmly in the minds of those who designed the Federal Reserve System in the early 1900s.

The Shiftability Theory   In light of the problems that the real-bills doctrine posed for earnings and for liquidity during economic downturns, many banks chose to adopt a compromise position. While they

real-bills doctrine   A bank management philosophy that calls for lending primarily to borrowers who will use the funds to finance production or shipping of physical goods, thereby ensuring speedy repayment of the loans.

continued to make self-liquidating loans when such opportunities arose, they also began to make longer-term loans with higher default risk. To balance the liquidity loss and greater risk associated with such lending, banks used some of their available funds to acquire low-risk securities, such as government securities and commercial paper. Banks regarded these securities as **secondary reserves** that could be converted easily into cash if some borrowers defaulted at the same time that depositors sought to withdraw some of their funds. These secondary reserves of securities supplemented the traditional **primary reserves** of cash assets that the banks held.

This approach to shifting bank asset allocations to attain a different balance among earnings, liquidity, and risk became known as the **shiftability theory** of bank management. It was the original justification for the modern management strategy in which depository institutions hold a mix of long-term loans, short-term loans, and liquid securities.

Many American depository institutions had adopted the shiftability theory by the end of the 1920s. But the stock market crash of 1929 and the subsequent years of the Great Depression exposed a fundamental difficulty with this theory of depository institution management. The difficulty was that even high-liquidity securities with low default risk were subject to significant interest rate risks. Stock and securities prices plummeted at the outset of the Great Depression, and so securities did not turn out to be such an effective counterbalance to longer-term, higher-risk lending after all. A number of banks (over one-third of those then in existence) failed during the Depression years.

The Anticipated-Income Approach   After World War II depository institution managers developed a way to make their loans more liquid. They adopted the **anticipated-income approach** to depository institution management, under which a larger number of their loans were installment loans. As we discussed in Chapter 6, borrowers repay the principal and interest for such loans in a series of installments.

This approach to loan management automatically made the loan portfolios of depository institutions more liquid. Because depository institutions receive continuous streams of payments from borrowers, the anticipated-income approach effectively made loans self-liquidating in a manner that the Italian merchant bankers of old could not have imagined. Even long-term loans now could generate month-to-month cash liquidity for a depository institution.

The Conversion-of-Funds Approach   The anticipated-income approach was a breakthrough in depository institution management and remains a widely used principle of loan management today. But in the 1960s and 1970s depository institutions sought to find ways to better

secondary reserves Securities that depository institutions can easily convert into cash in the event such a need arises.

primary reserves Cash assets.

shiftability theory A management approach in which depository institutions hold a mix of illiquid loans and more-liquid securities that act as a secondary reserve held as a contingency against potential liquidity problems.

anticipated-income approach A depository institution management philosophy that calls for depository institutions to make their loans more liquid by issuing them in the form of installment loans that generate income in the form of periodic payments of interest and principal.

MANAGEMENT NOTEBOOK
Using Computer Models for Small-Business Lending

For many of the nation's banks, gone are the days when the personal relationship between loan officers and businesspersons was important. Human judgment is making way for computer models. This computerized loan-approval method is called *credit scoring*. It is used today by Banc One Corporation, Chemical Bank, Wells Fargo and Company, and Hibernia National Bank, to name a few. It's all a matter of scoring points on a loan application, which is usually completed over the phone. More points are scored for the following: (1) having a high balance in the business' checking account, (2) being a corporation rather than a sole proprietorship, and (3) being a business that is current in payments to its suppliers. Points are deducted for previous late payments or defaults, for an owner who is maxed out on personal credit cards, and for certain high-risk categories such as restaurants. In effect, the business owner's personal credit history is more important than the business' financial statement. The turnaround for the loan application can be done in a matter of hours.

For Critical Analysis: *What is the role of the bank manager in the above bank lending operation?*

---

manage all the items on their balance sheets. This led to the **conversion-of-funds approach** to management, in which depository institution managers sought to fund assets of given maturities with sources of funds with maturities of similar length.

For example, a commercial bank manager contemplating an expansion of short-term business lending would, under the conversion-of-funds approach, fund such loans by issuing short-term deposits. The manager might, for instance, sell a number of short-term money market certificates of deposit. This would ensure that the bank's net interest margin would be fixed over the short end of the maturity spectrum, thereby helping to protect the profitability of its short-term loan portfolio from interest rate risk.

The conversion-of-funds approach to depository institution management was the lastest step to modern management in which depository institution managers actively try to manage both the asset and liability sides of their institutions' balance sheets. They try to mix and match maturities while simultaneously choosing which assets to hold and which liabilities to issue in light of the interest rate risks they face. Today this **asset-liability management approach** is the predominant approach used by depository institution managers. This management approach, simply stated, is the coordination of all balance sheet items so as to maximize the profitability of the depository institution.

conversion-of-funds approach
A depository institution management philosophy under which managers try to fund assets of specific maturities by issuing liabilities with like maturities.

asset-liability management approach   A depository institution management philosophy that emphasizes the simultaneous coordination of both the asset and liability sides of the institution's balance sheet.

Modern Asset-Liability Management

The problem with using an active asset-liability management approach is figuring out how to coordinate asset-liability choices. How should a depository institution decide which short-term or long-term loans to make, which securities to hold and at what maturities, how much cash to keep on hand, how many certificates of deposit to issue and at what maturities, how much borrowing of overnight or term federal funds to do, and so on?

gap management   A technique of depository institution asset-liability management that focuses on the difference (the gap) between the quantity of assets subject to significant interest rate risk and the amount of liabilities subject to such risk.

Gap Management   One technique that many depository institution managers have developed to help them address this question is **gap management.** This is an asset-liability management technique that focuses on the difference, or *gap,* between the amount of assets subject to significant interest rate risk (rate-sensitive assets such as federal funds loans and money market securities) and the quantity of liabilities subject to such risk (rate-sensitive liabilities such as sales of repurchase agreements or short-maturity CDs). If the gap is positive, then rate-sensitive assets exceed rate-sensitive liabilities. Then a rise in market interest rates will tend to raise the depository institution's net interest margin, because earnings from its rate-sensitive asset holdings will rise by more than its expenses on a smaller quantity of rate-sensitive liabilities. In contrast, a negative gap would yield the opposite effect on the institution's net interest margin if interest rates were to rise. Then the depository institution's interest expenses on its rate-sensitive liabilities would rise by a larger amount than would its interest income from a smaller amount of rate-sensitive assets.

It follows that a depository institution manager who expects market interest rates to rise would prefer to maintain a positive gap. In contrast, a manager who anticipates a decline in interest rates would want the gap between rate-sensitive assets and rate-sensitive liabilities to be negative. Alternatively, either manager could attempt to insulate the institution's income from the effects of market interest rate changes by maintaining a zero gap—that is, by matching the institution's amount of rate-sensitive assets by an equal quantity of rate-sensitive liabilities. This led managers to pay closer attention to managing liabilities as well as assets. Many depository institutions began to rely to a greater extent on nondeposit sources of funds, such as large certificates of deposit and federal funds.

Many depository institution managers today do not look just at the overall gap for their institution. They also compute gaps at various maturities. For instance, depository institutions typically have negative gaps at short maturities of 3 months or less. The reason is that because they issue checking and other deposits, to which customers have immediate access, but they use those liabilities to fund longer-term assets. At maturities longer than 3 months most depository institutions have positive gaps between rate-sensitive assets and liabilities. By monitoring gaps at different maturities, managers can better gauge their institutions' exposures to interest rate risk across the term structure of the institutions' assets and liabilities.

Risk Management with Derivatives   The traditional way for a depository institution to try to eliminate a gap at longer maturities would be for it to purchase long-term, fixed-yield government bonds. But a number of depository institution managers realized in the 1980s that they could accomplish the same thing using derivative instruments. As discussed in Chapter 4, financial derivatives, or instruments whose returns are derived from the returns on other instruments, represent a possible means by which financial institutions can hedge against interest rate risk. For instance, instead of buying more long-term government bonds with fixed interest rates, a depository institution manager could instead enter into a *swap* contract, in which the institution would pay a floating interest rate, perhaps tied to the London Interbank Offer Rate (see Chapter 3), in exchange for a stream of payments tied to a long-term Treasury security.

Initially some institutions mainly used interest-rate forward contracts (discussed in Chapter 4) to hedge against risks. Ultimately, however, such swap arrangements and other derivative contracts, such as interest rate futures and options, became more widely used as hedging instruments. The reason, as discussed in Chapter 4, is that these latter derivative contracts are more standardized instruments.

The use of derivatives at commercial banks has increased dramatically since the 1980s. In 1985 the value of swaps traded by commercial banks with more than $100 million in assets amounted to about $186 billion, but if recent growth of such trading continues, then by 1997 this trading volume should be well over $4,000 billion ($4 trillion). The value of futures and forward contracts that these commercial banks traded in 1985 was just over $97 billion, but under current projections the 1997 volume of such trading also should exceed $4,000 billion.

Other things equal, depository institution owners prefer high profits to low profits. Hedging is not the highest-profit activity. To be sure, by hedging against risks a depository institution manager protects the institution from losses. But hedging can also cause an institution to miss out on potentially profitable interest rate movements. For this reason, in the late 1980s and early 1990s several depository institution management teams adopted a more aggressive approach to derivatives trading. As noted in the opening to this chapter, Bankers Trust and J. P. Morgan were prominent examples. These and other institutions sought to earn trading profits on derivatives contracts. In addition, they worked to develop groups of clients who would entrust their funds to the banks for derivatives trading that would yield trading profits for the clients and commissions and fee income for the banks. As discussed in the introduction, these depository institutions have experienced mixed degrees of success in such activities. When managers can predict interest rate movements and make appropriate bets with derivatives, they and their clients can profit. But, as we discussed in Chapter 4, if the managers bet wrong, they—and their customers—can lose. For Bankers Trust and several of its clients, derivatives losses in the mid-1990s were sizable.

Asset Securitization   One of the key banking issues that any depository institution manager must confront when determining what assets to hold is the trade-off between liquidity and earnings. According to the real-bills doctrine, managers should attempt to make only the most liquid loans. In a modern spin-off of the real-bills doctrine, a number of depository institution managers have sought to make the doctrine obsolete by getting many loans off their institutions' balance sheets entirely!

securitization   The process of pooling loans with similar risk characteristics and then selling the loan pool in the form of a tradable financial instrument.

They accomplish this through **securitization.** This is the process of pooling loans with similar risk characteristics and selling the loan pool as a tradable financial instrument. The first use of securitization was by savings institutions, which began selling mortgage loans to the Government National Mortgage Association (GNMA) in the early 1970s. GNMA sold, and continues to sell, mortgage-backed securities to buyers who receive *prorata* shares of the returns derived from the underlying pool of mortgage loans. Although GNMA owns the mortgages, savings institutions typically service them by processing payments and dealing with delinquent borrowers. GNMA pays the institutions fees for these services.

Today depository institutions have extended the securitization concept to several other types of loans. Examples include credit card loans, auto loans, and commercial loans. Although securitization of mortgage loans predominates—well over $1,000 billion in mortgage loans are securitized—since 1993 the extent of securitization of other types of loans has nearly doubled to around $150 billion. Of this amount, $100 billion is composed of securitized credit card loans, which presently represent the fastest-growing type of loan-backed securities.

5

How has the philosophy of depository institution management evolved?   The fundamental trade-off that depository institutions face is between earnings and liquidity. The real-bills doctrine sought to achieve both higher earnings and higher liquidity by lending only for projects that would yield quick and sure returns. Because relatively few such lending opportunities are available, over the years depository institution managers have developed a number of competing approaches to the earnings-liquidity trade-off. The approach that has risen to predominance in recent years is the asset-liability management approach, which uses gap-management techniques, derivatives trading, and securitization as ways to address interest rate risk while striving for high earnings and liquidity.

RECENT PERFORMANCE OF DEPOSITORY INSTITUTIONS

In light of the growth of securitization and the mushrooming use of derivative instruments at depository institutions, many observers in recent years have speculated that the fundamental business of banks and other depository institutions may have changed. Some have even argued that depository institutions are becoming obsolete.

We conclude this chapter by evaluating the recent performance of depository institutions. While it is difficult to make predictions about the long-term future of any industry, our own conclusion is that the basic business of banking really has not changed. Depository institutions will continue to provide the same basic intermediation services that the Italian merchant bankers provided to Mediterranean traders centuries ago. Nevertheless, derivatives and securitization undeniably have fundamentally altered how depository institutions manage their affairs. Depository institution management likely will never again be a "3-6-3" business.

Recent Performance of Commercial Banks

The major changes that depository institution managers have been required to face are most evident in considering developments at commercial banks. These changes also have fostered substantial debate about the likely future of the commercial banking industry.

Banking: A Declining Industry?
During the late 1980s many observers contended that banking was an outmoded means of financial intermediation. Mutual funds, broker-dealers, and insurance companies ultimately would take over the intermediation processes that previously had been the exclusive domain of banks. Furthermore, commentators argued, such innovations as securitization were making some aspects of banking obsolete. For instance, instead of holding mortgages on their balance sheets and taking on interest rate risk as they had in the past, banks were selling them in mortgage pools and allowing other institutions to intermediate such risks.

To back up claims that banking was on the way out, commentators typically referred to a chart such as that in Figure 7.6 on page 194. As the figure indicates, the share of financial instruments intermediated by banks has declined considerably since the middle 1970s.

Or Are Rumors of Banking's Demise Greatly Exaggerated?
Nothing spurs pessimism like low profitability, and bank profits were low by historical standards as the banking industry entered the early 1990s. As discussed earlier in this chapter (see Figure 7.3), however, bank profitability increased considerably in the middle 1990s. These

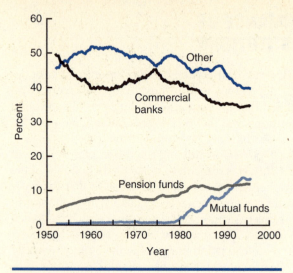

FIGURE 7.6   Shares of U.S. Financial Intermediation

Commercial banks have lost a large portion of their share of private financial intermediation since the 1970s, with pension funds and mutual funds gaining considerable shares at their expense. *Source:* Board of Governors of the Federal Reserve System, *Flow-of-Funds Accounts,* various dates.

near-term developments did much to offset the negative views of some commentators, although a few have continued to argue that banking ultimately is doomed.

Nevertheless, there are several pieces of evidence indicating that the long-run outlook for commercial banks also does not look so bad. Figure 7.7 shows two pieces of evidence along these lines. Panel (a) of the figure plots the ratio of commercial bank assets to U.S. gross domestic product (GDP), a measure of overall economic activity that we shall discuss in more detail in Chapter 14. Although there was a drop-off in this ratio in the early 1990s, the overall trend has been upward. As a percentage of gross domestic product, bank assets rose on net from 50 percent in 1960 to nearly 60 percent in 1995.

Another growth business for commercial banks has been **off-balance-sheet banking.** This term refers to bank involvement in such activities as securitization, derivatives trading, and various financial services that do not show up as assets or liabilities on bank balance sheets. As we noted earlier, these kinds of activities generate noninterest income for banks. Panel (b) of Figure 7.7 displays the long-run trends in commercial banks' noninterest income in relation to total bank income and total bank assets. According to either measure, noninterest income has expanded considerably at commercial banks.

off-balance-sheet banking
Bank activities that earn income without expanding the assets and liabilities reported on their balance sheets.

FIGURE 7.7 Positive Trends in Commercial Banking

Relative to gross domestic product, a key measure of overall economic activity, commercial bank assets have increased since 1960, as shown in panel (a). In addition, in recent years banks have expanded into lines of business that provide them with more noninterest income. Panel (b) displays the ratio of noninterest income to total income and to total bank assets. Both ratios have increased significantly since 1980. *Sources:* Federal Deposit Insurance Corporation, *Statistics on Banking,* and Council of Economic Advisors, *Economic Indicators.*

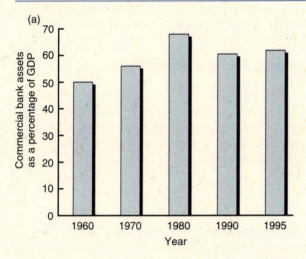

(a)

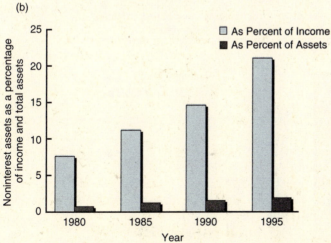

(b)

Another positive development for commercial banks has been the significant decline in institutions that bank regulators classify as troubled, or in some danger of future insolvency. Figure 7.8 shows that the number of such institutions has declined considerably during the 1990s. The figure also indicates a key reason for this development: The number of institutions classified by regulators as unprofitable also fell by a large margin during these years.

Positive performance figures of the 1990s, of course, could be just as misleading as the negative figures of the 1980s. Nevertheless, it certainly is not apparent today that the business of banking is in danger of fading away. Most commercial banks today are healthy institutions. A key reason for this is that they have adapted to circumstances. Off-balance-sheet banking has been a key aspect of that adaptation process.

Recent Performance of Savings Institutions

Broadly speaking, saving institutions have had a very tough time during the past decade. For a while it appeared that this entire class of depository institutions might cease to exist. Lately their fortunes have improved, but their long-run prospects continue to be watched closely by economists, regulators, and Congress.

FIGURE 7.8   Troubled and Unprofitable Banks in the 1990s

A very positive development in commercial banking has been the sharp drop in the number of banks that regulators classify either as troubled or as unprofitable. *Source:* Federal Deposit Insurance Corporation, *Statistics on Banking,* various issues.

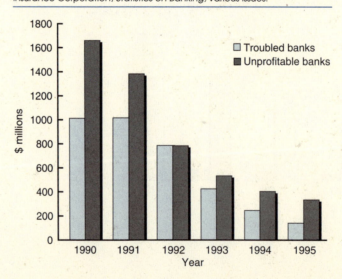

The Great Savings Institution Debacle   As we shall discuss in more detail in Chapter 8, the savings institution industry broadly collapsed in the late 1980s. Between the mid-1980s and 1990, over one-half of all savings institutions failed outright or were closed by savings institution regulators.

In the 1980s many observers forecast that savings institutions would begin to look more like commercial banks and therefore would be able to compete more effectively. As you learned in Chapter 6, however, savings institutions have continued to specialize in mortgage-related lending. They still issue very few commercial and consumer loans.

Figure 7.9 displays total savings institution assets as a percent of commercial bank assets. As you can see, the optimistic forecasts of the 1980s were wrong. During the past decade, savings institutions have lost all the ground they had gained relative to commercial banks between 1950 and 1986. Now, in the 1990s, many are forecasting the ultimate demise of savings institutions.

An Industry Back on Its Feet?   The future for savings institutions probably is not this dire, however. The key to the future of these

---

FIGURE 7.9   Savings Institution Assets as a Percent of Commercial Bank Assets

Between the early 1950s and mid-1970s, savings institutions nearly doubled their size relative to commercial banks. But, since 1986, savings institutions have lost all these gains. *Source:* Board of Governors of the Federal Reserve System, *Flow-of-Funds Acounts*, various issues.

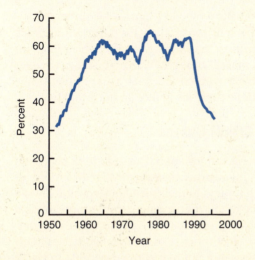

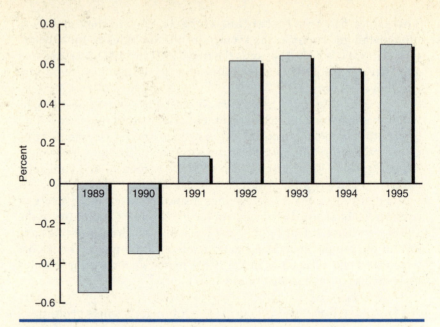

FIGURE 7.10   Average Return on Assets at Savings Institutions

The 1990s have been years of recovery for the savings institutions that survived the collapse of the 1980s. These remaining institutions have returned to profitability. *Source:* Office of Thrift Supervision, *Quarterly Financial Results and Conditions of the Thrift Industry,* various issues.

institutions will be their ability to maintain steady profitability. As Figure 7.10 indicates, since 1990 the average return on assets for savings institutions has been positive. Today savings institutions once again are profitable businesses.

Nevertheless, the annual return-on-asset figures for savings institutions have been 10 to 15 percent lower than the returns on assets earned at commercial banks during the 1990s. Even though savings institutions have returned to profitability, they still have a distance to cover if they are to compete effectively with commercial banks. Unless they close this gap, savings institutions continue to face an uncertain future.

Recent Performance of Credit Unions

As discussed in Chapter 6, credit unions specialize in issuing share deposits and extending credit to members. Consequently, credit unions simultaneously aim to offer high returns to their member depositors while at the same time minimizing members' borrowing costs. This means that performance measures that we use to evaluate the performances of commercial banks and most savings institutions—return on equity, net interest margin, and return on assets—are not as clearly-applicable to credit unions. For instance, because credit unions are owned by their members, return on equity is not a viable measure of credit union performance. In addition, a commercial bank aims to widen its net interest margin, because this increases its interest income while reducing its expense, thereby improving its profitability. But a credit union typically tries to maintain a relatively narrow net interest margin for the benefit of both members borrowers and member depositors (which credit unions call shareholders). This leads to very low return on asset figures for credit unions. In 1995, for example, the aggregate return on assets for all federally insured credit unions was only about 1 percent.

Consequently, when evaluating the performance of credit unions, it is important to recognize that their net interest margins and return on asset figures typically are somewhat smaller than those for other depository institutions. When credit union regulators evaluate the performance of these institutions, they become concerned only when these measures drop to low levels by traditional *credit union* standards. They also look closely at the riskiness of credit union loans and securities.

Most credit unions follow very conservative practices in their lending and securities purchases. This does not mean, however, that credit unions never take on some risks. Because credit unions hold significant portions of their assets as securities, they can face considerable interest rate risk. In addition, in recent years a number of credit unions have made greater use of derivatives. For some, this has further reduced overall risk of loss, but for a few the result has been overspeculation and failure. This has raised some concerns for federal regulators.

6

How have depository institutions performed in recent years?   Overall, depository institution performance during the 1990s has been mixed. Although profitability has been much stronger than in previous years, such institutions continue to account for smaller shares of intermediated U.S. financial instruments. Commercial banks have displayed the greatest willingness to adapt to changing conditions by increasing noninterest income through an expansion of off-balance-sheet activities. Credit unions also have branched into such areas. The outlook for savings institutions is much better than it was in the 1980s, but a gradual decline in savings institution deposits continues to occur, and profitability rates at these institutions still lags behind those of commercial banks.

SUMMARY

1. **Key sources of depository institution revenues:** The main source of revenues for depository institutions is income derived from interest they earn on loans and securities. The other revenue source is noninterest income, which includes fee income and trading profits.

2. **Key sources of depository institution costs:** The two main costs incurred by depository institutions are interest expense on liabilities they issue and real-resource expenses for the use of productive factors such as labor, capital, and land. A third expenditure is provision for loan loss reserves.

3. **Common measures of depository institution profitability:** Two commonly used measures are return on assets, or profit as a percentage of total assets, and return on equity, which is profit as a percentage of equity capital. Another measure that analysts often use to assess the near-term and future profitability of a depository institution is its net interest margin, which is the difference between interest income and interest expense as a percentage of total assets.

4. **The main determinant of a depository institution's profitability:** At present, there is broad agreement that although short-term factors such as changes in the overall economic climate can have large effects on profitability, the key factor determining a given institution's profit performance is the quality of its management. The competence of management also appears to be more important for profitability than the degree of rivalry among depository institutions in their loan and deposit markets and the extent to which economies of scale give large institutions cost advantages over smaller institutions.

5. **The Evolution of the Philosophy of Depository Institution Management:** Under the real-bills doctrine that was popular until the end of the nineteenth century, depository institutions tried to make only the most liquid loans. The shiftability theory sought more liquidity by holding securities, thus offsetting the risk in making less-liquid loans. The anticipated-income approach led to the growth of installment loans as a way to generate liquidity via periodic payments of principal and interest. Under the conversion-of-funds approach, depository institution managers sought to fund assets with liabilities of similar maturity. The modern asset-liability approach, in contrast, typically permits gaps to develop between asset and liability positions at different maturities, though such gaps may be eliminated through hedging against interest rate risk. Alternatively, managers hedge against risk or try to profit from risk by using derivative instruments, and they avoid taking on some risks by securitization of some mortgage, credit card, auto, and commercial loans.

6. **Recent Performance of Depository Institutions:** Managerial adaptations by commercial banks, such as expansion of off-balance-sheet banking, have increased noninterest income as a source of earnings. This has helped fuel greater profitability at commercial banks in the 1990s. Credit unions also generally have had favorable experience during recent years. Savings institutions have stabilized following

the crisis of the late 1980s, but they continue to lose deposits precipitously, and their profit rates lag behind those of commercial banks.

QUESTIONS AND PROBLEMS

1. In the mid 1990s, the aggregate return on assets for all commercial banks in the United States was just over 1 percent, and the return on equity was 14 percent. Explain why the return on equity typically is so much greater than the return on assets.

2. In recent years noninterest income has become a more important source of revenues for depository institutions. Discuss how this may affect the usefulness of net interest margin as an indicator of depository institution profitability.

3. Profitability sometimes is greater at larger institutions for specific loan and deposit markets. Discuss the alternative ways that structure-conduct-performance model proponents and efficient-structure theorists probably would explain such observations.

4. Some have argued that if depository institutions had not given up on strict adherence to the real-bills doctrine, they ultimately would have ceased to exist. Evaluate this argument.

5. Suppose that a commercial bank has a negative gap at maturities of 12 months or less but a positive gap at maturities exceeding 12 months. If the yield curve *rotates* in such a way that short-term interest rates rise while longer-term interest rates fall, what is likely to happen to the bank's profitability? Explain your reasoning.

6. How does the rise of off-balance-sheet banking via derivatives trading and loan commitments complicate evaluating the overall performance of, and prospects for, depository institutions?

Foundations of Depository Institution Regulation

KEY QUESTIONS

1. What are the goals of depository institution regulation?

2. Why does the provision of federal deposit insurance help to justify federal regulation of depository institutions?

3. What accounts for the existence of bank holding companies?

4. How did interest rate ceilings on deposits ultimately help to spur financial innovation and depository institution deregulation in the 1970s and 1980s?

5. How do bank regulators impose capital requirements?

6. Why did so many savings institutions fail in the 1980s and 1990s?

7. How does the FDIC currently charge depository institutions for the insurance it provides?

American citizens had reelected a popular president by a large plu-
rality. The national economy was booming and the Communist
threat was collapsing. Citizens were already anticipating the peace dividend, or tax reduction, they would enjoy because of the diminished
need to maintain a worldwide military presence. The outlook in 1984
was bright. Rarely had national prosperity seemed so assured.

In 1985, however, an unexpected threat emerged within the nation's
borders. Though it had disproportionate effects in the Southwest, and especially in Texas, it left few regions unaffected. It wiped out a multibillion-
dollar government trust fund within months. It ruined careers, fractured
dreams, and soaked up much of the anticipated peace dividend.

Across the land, savings and loan associations and savings banks
were collapsing. Within the first year of the crisis, 135 institutions had
failed. After two more years, another 600 were bankrupt. Eventually
the toll would mount to almost 1,500 closures of institutions that had
been the depository of the life savings of working people across the land.
Managers went to jail, regulators resigned in disgrace, and political
leaders were tainted by the scandal and forced from office.

As we shall discuss in this chapter, this was not supposed to happen.
American depository institutions are among the most carefully moni-
tored and strictly regulated private businesses in the nation. By the end
of this chapter, you will understand the nature of depository institution
regulations today and the historical roots of these regulations. You also
will learn why even these regulations failed to prevent the collapse of
half of the savings institution industry.

THE RATIONALE FOR REGULATION

American depository financial institutions have always faced considerable regulation by state and federal governments. Indeed, since earliest
recorded times governments have sought to restrain or direct the activities of financial firms such as banks and other depository institutions.
Governments typically have singled out depository institutions for
especially detailed regulatory scrutiny.

Goals of Depository Institution Regulation

Why do governments, including state and federal governments in
the United States, regulate depository institutions? The traditional

justification has been that if such institutions were left alone, socially bad outcomes might result. There might be banking panics, widespread losses of life savings, and so on. Certainly, in the broad sweep of world history many such events have occurred. Indeed, in the United States, regional and even national banking panics seemed to occur in nearly regular cycles of 15- to 20-year intervals between the 1830s and 1930s. There were significant panics in 1837, 1857, 1873, 1893, 1907, and 1929. As discussed below, the severity of the last of these panics motivated much of the federal regulation of depository institutions that exists today.

Limiting Depository Institution Insolvencies and Failures

An overriding goal of depository institution regulation is to reduce the likelihood of widespread failure of such institutions. Any business, including a depository institution, fails and declares bankruptcy when it reaches a point of *insolvency*. Insolvency occurs when a business is unable to pay debts as they mature. Although an insolvent business may have positive net worth, it is insolvent if it cannot meet its financial obligations. Because many depository institution assets are financial instruments, which are more liquid than most assets of nonfinancial businesses, bankruptcy and insolvency are used synonymously in relation to depository institutions. Consequently, a depository institution generally is considered to have reached a point of **insolvency** if the value of its assets falls below the value of its liabilities, so that its equity or net worth is negative.

insolvency A situation in which the value of a depository institution's assets is less than the value of its liabilities.

Ultimately an insolvent depository institution cannot continue to operate as an on-going enterprise. The reason is that holders of an insolvent institution's liabilities normally force the institution to liquidate its assets. How soon liability holders force such liquidation depends on their collective view of the institution's long-run viability. But an institution with a negative net worth already has lost all the funds that shareholders placed in the institution, which usually does not engender much optimism in those who hold the institution's liabilities.

A key aspect of depository institution regulation typically is the periodic *examination* of institutions' accounting ledgers to verify that the institutions are solvent. Another aspect normally is the *supervision* of the institutions via the publication and enforcement of rules and standards with which the institutions must comply. A purpose of regulatory supervision is to make insolvency and failure a rare occurrence.

Maintaining Depository Institution Liquidity

As we discussed in Chapter 6, a large portion of the liabilities of depository institutions are checking accounts and other types of deposit liabilities to which customers of the institutions have the legal right of access almost immediately. A depository institution that finds itself without sufficient cash on hand to meet the needs of its depositors suffers from **illiquidity.** Such

illiquidity A situation in which a depository institution lacks the cash assets required to meet requests for depositor withdrawals.

illiquidity inconveniences the institution's customers. But if a large number of depository institutions simultaneously are illiquid, then the result can be serious disruptions in the nation's flow of payments for goods and services, with potentially broader negative effects on the economy.

Another goal of depository institution regulation is to limit instances in which institutions become sufficiently illiquid to induce such ripple effects through the national economy. Again, governmental regulators typically use examination and supervision as tools to ensure sufficient liquidity of depository institutions.

A problem that regulators often face is distinguishing illiquidity from insolvency. It is possible for a depository institution to be illiquid temporarily yet to be solvent otherwise, just as it is possible for an otherwise wealthy individual to experience temporary cash flow difficulties. Depository institution regulators, and particularly a central bank such as the Federal Reserve, can assist institutions suffering from such short-term liquidity problems by extending them credit. The difficulty is that frequently illiquidity is a symptom of pending insolvency. Hence, extending such loans could keep otherwise insolvent institutions operating when they really ought to close. This is another justification for close examination of a depository institution's accounts.

Promoting a Low-Cost Financial System   The third key objective of regulation is to produce an environment in which depository institutions can provide their services at the lowest possible cost. Regulators also would prefer that customers of such institutions pay interest rates and fees that yield no more than *normal profits* to the institutions. As discussed in Chapter 7, this means that depository institution owners would receive profits no greater than necessary to compensate them for owning shares in those institutions instead of some alternative business.

A fundamental difficulty that depository institution regulators face is that it is very difficult to achieve all three goals at the same time. Typically, achieving one objective may entail sacrificing another. For instance, one of the best ways for depository institutions to avoid liquidity and insolvency difficulties is to earn consistently high profits. Consequently, there is a temptation for regulators to find ways to protect depository institutions from competition so that their profits are above normal levels. In contrast, one way to ensure that depository institutions operate as efficiently as possible is to expose them to considerable rivalry from other financial institutions. This would encourage depository institutions to operate as efficiently as possible. But it also would keep their profit margins so low that unexpected shocks to the economy or the financial system could cause them to operate at significant losses, thereby threatening their liquidity and solvency levels. A key issue in depository institution regulation is determining how best to trade off progress toward one goal without sacrificing progress toward another.

1

What are the goals of depository institution regulation?   One goal is to prevent depository institutions from becoming insolvent, or from having negative net worth. Another is to keep them from becoming illiquid and thus lacking sufficient cash assets to meet the needs of their depositors. At the same time, however, a third objective of regulation is to ensure that depository institutions operate at low cost and earn normal levels of profit.

Deposit Insurance and Moral Hazard

In the United States there is a further complication for depository institution regulators. This is that a large proportion of the deposits of nearly all depository institutions are insured by the federal government. We discuss the mechanics of this insurance system in more detail below. But until recently a key feature of the U.S. deposit insurance system was that depository institutions paid flat amounts for federal deposit insurance irrespective of their risks. In addition, all depository institutions are eligible for such insurance as long as they meet certain minimal standards.

The Moral Hazard Problem of Deposit Insurance   Recall from Chapter 5 that private insurance companies use a number of techniques to protect themselves from the fundamental *moral hazard* problems inherent to the insurance business. The difficulty is that once insurance coverage is granted to an individual or business, there is a temptation for the covered person or firm to behave more recklessly. After all, once one is insured, any personal cost that might be expected to arise from losses resulting from reckless behavior will be lower.

The existence of federal deposit insurance likewise can lead depository institution managers to make riskier choices than they might otherwise. This means that federal deposit insurance can expose the entire depository institution industry to significant moral hazard problems.

Regulation as a Partial Solution   The potential solution to the moral hazard problem that arises from federal deposit insurance is depository institution regulation. By conducting periodic examinations of insured institutions and by supervising the insured institutions through the issuance and enforcement of rules for prudential management, depository institution regulators can reduce the likelihood of widespread moral hazard difficulties.

As we discuss below, deposits at American depository institutions have not always been federally insured. However, once the U.S. government extended such insurance, the extent of federal regulation of depository institutions increased markedly.

2

Why does the provision of federal deposit insurance help to justify federal regulation of depository institutions? Providing deposit insurance exposes the federal government to the moral hazard problem that managers of depository institutions will make riskier decisions. One way to try to prevent more-reckless behavior by depository institution managers is to subject them to regulatory examination and supervision.

AMERICAN REGULATION OF DEPOSITORY INSTITUTIONS

As noted in Chapter 6, the federal government's involvement in banking dates to the earliest days of the United States. Nevertheless, the federal government's role was relatively limited until the twentieth century. In response to the economic hardships of the Great Depression, Congress initiated a series of measures in the 1930s that dramatically increased the federal government's involvement in the affairs of depository financial institutions. The McFadden Act of 1927, which restricted the ability of nationally chartered banks to establish branches only as accorded by state laws, already had done much to limit the scope for competition among banks. Nevertheless, many in Congress blamed the large number of bank failures of the early 1930s—about 2,000 per year between 1929 and 1933—on "destructive competition" in banking. Congress therefore set out to reduce the scope for competition and to make the federal government a "traffic cop," overseeing the nation's channels of financial commerce.

Federal Regulation: 1933–1970

The Banking Act of 1933, otherwise known as the Glass-Steagall Act, created the Federal Deposit Insurance Corporation (FDIC), which supervises the nation's taxpayer-guaranteed deposit insurance system for commercial banks and savings institutions. The legislation also separated commercial and investment banking and placed interest rate ceilings on checking deposits in commercial banks. In short, it made the federal government the key regulator of most depository institutions.

Federal Deposit Insurance Under the terms of the Glass-Steagall Act, the FDIC initially supervised a Temporary Deposit Insurance Fund. Both the FDIC and its fund became permanent fixtures of the nation's banking system in early 1935.

deposit insurance premium
The price that depository institutions pay to the FDIC's insurance fund in exchange for a guarantee of federal insurance of covered deposits that they issue.

The FDIC's first act was to study bank failures between 1864 and 1934. It found that the average cost of such failures per dollar of deposits (up to a limit of $5,000) was almost one-fourth of 1 percent. These figures indicated that the FDIC should charge an annual **deposit insurance premium,** or annual charge to banks for deposit insurance, of one-fourth of 1 percent for each dollar of deposits. Then the first head of the FDIC, Leo Crowley, convinced Congress that this premium was too high to make bankers enthusiastic about the new federal system. He also pointed out that the new federal banking regulations imposed as part of the 1933 legislation would reduce bank failure rates relative to historical levels. Consequently, Congress specified an initial deposit insurance premium of 0.083 percent, or one-twelfth of 1 percent. Another 54 years would pass before the FDIC would increase this premium rate, despite gradual increases in coverage from a $5,000 limit per insured deposit to today's current limit of $100,000.

Congress also set up federal deposit insurance for savings institutions as part of the National Housing Act of 1934. It placed this separate federal system under the supervision of the Federal Savings and Loan Insurance Corporation (FSLIC). In turn, the FSLIC was part of a Federal Home Loan Bank System that Congress created in the Federal Home Loan Bank Act of 1932. The Federal Home Loan Bank Board (FHLBB) governed the Federal Home Loan Bank System and, consequently, had jurisdiction over the FSLIC.

Credit unions also have federal deposit insurance. The National Credit Union Administration (NCUA), which Congress established in 1970, supervises this deposit insurance system. Instead of paying annual premiums to the NCUA's National Credit Union Share Insurance Fund, credit unions deposit 1 percent of their deposits with the NCUA fund.

The Separation of Commercial and Investment Banking   Some commercial banks that failed at the outset of the Depression also were heavily involved in securities underwriting. To many observers at that time, it appeared that such activities had entailed significant risk for those banks and had contributed to highly visible failures that had reduced the public's confidence in the banking system. This lack of confidence, many argued, helped to fuel the banking panics that followed.

Consequently, a key provision of the 1933 Glass-Steagall Act was the prohibition of securities underwriting by commercial banks or any other depository institution. Subsequent acts of Congress and court decisions have relaxed some aspects of this prohibition. Nevertheless, today's depository institutions remain unable to engage in most activities of investment banking.

Branching Restrictions   The Glass-Steagall Act also amended the 1927 McFadden Act in ways that further discouraged nationally chartered banks from attempting to open branch offices in states other than those in which their home offices were located. This made nationwide or even regional branching impossible without the explicit permission of both the state of a bank's origin and the state in which the bank wished to branch. For a number of years very few states were willing to grant such arrangements. Consequently, **interstate branching,** or the opening of banking offices in more than one state, effectively was illegal.

Indeed, until the 1970s many states made branching a difficult proposition even *within* their boundaries. These states restricted even **intrastate branching,** permitting banks to open branch offices only within their home counties, or perhaps in adjacent counties. Some *unit banking* states went even further, disallowing banks from operating any branch offices whatsoever. Twelve states continue to restrict branching within their boundaries. The remaining 38 states permit almost unlimited branching within their borders.

In spite of the various state regulations of branching, banks have expanded their branch networks considerably over the years. Figure 8.1 shows that the number of bank branches in the United States grew considerably during past decades, even as the number of banks remained steady and, in recent years, began to decline.

Regulation of Bank Holding Companies   From a depository institution's perspective, there are two reasons why it might like to open

interstate branching   The operation of banking offices in more than one state.

intrastate branching   The operation of banking offices anywhere within a state.

FIGURE 8.1   Numbers of Banks and Branches in the United States

Even though the total number of banks has stayed level or even declined in recent years, the number of bank branches has continued to increase. *Source:* Federal Deposit Insurance Corporation, *Statistics on Banking,* various issues.

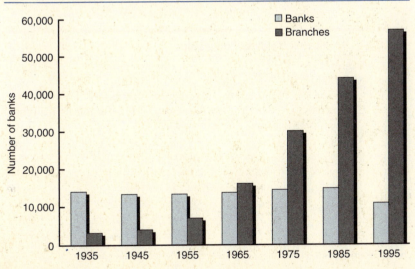

branch offices in other counties within its state or even in another state. One, naturally, is that the institution might see profitable opportunities for issuing deposits and for lending in locations separate from its home office. The other is that spreading its business into other geographical areas can help reduce risk. For instance, a bank in Des Moines, Iowa, might specialize in lending to farmers and companies whose businesses are related to agriculture. If there were a drought that adversely affected agriculture in the Des Moines region alone, then the bank's fortunes would decline along with those of its customers. For this reason, owners of the Des Moines bank might want to be able to open a branch office in Lincoln, Nebraska, where their bank could issue deposits and make loans to farmers and agricultural companies whose fortunes might not be tied to agricultural conditions in Des Moines.

But Iowa and Nebraska are among the twelve states that continue to limit branching even within their boundaries. While it might seem that this would make the Des Moines bank's goal infeasible, there is a legal alternative to branching into Lincoln. This would be to set up a **multibank holding company,** which is a corporation that owns more than one legally separate bank or other depository institution. Then the holding company could purchase a bank in Lincoln. Although the Des Moines and Lincoln banks would remain individually distinct enterprises, the holding company arrangement, which both Iowa and Nebraska permit on an interstate basis, would permit the original owners of the Des Moines bank to spread their risks across a larger geographical area. In a sense, such a multibank holding company arrangement effectively could enable the Des Moines bank to "branch" after all.

In fact, in the face of intra- and interstate branching restrictions, many banking organizations have followed such an approach. As Table 8.1 indicates, during the past 35 years the number of branches and

multibank holding company
A corporation that owns more than one commercial bank or other depository institution.

TABLE 8.1   Multibank Holding Companies

Year	Number of Multibank Holding Companies	Number of Banks	Number of Branches	Assets ($ billions)	Deposits ($ billions)
1960	47	426	1,037	20	18
1965	53	468	1,486	31	28
1970	121	895	3,260	93	78
1975	289	2,264	9,896	371	297
1981	407	2,607	14,121	678	480
1986	1,314	4,431	28,046	1,827	1,315
1991	910	3,706	32,462	2,605	1,683
1995	973	2,835	37,577	3,072	2,045

Source: Board of Governors of the Federal Reserve System. Domestic data.

the dollar amount of assets and deposits of multibank holding companies have increased steadily. Note, however, that mergers and consolidations have reduced the number of holding companies and banks.

Congress first authorized the formation of bank holding companies through passage of the Bank Holding Company Act of 1956. This legislation contained a significant legal loophole that banks used to their advantage in later years. The 1956 act did not explicitly rule out the ability of bank holding companies to engage in a number of potential commercial activities that were unrelated to the narrow business of banking. Furthermore, it did not prohibit holding companies from using nondeposit funds, raised perhaps through the issuance of commercial paper, to fund activities of the banks they owned. Consequently, a number of banks constructed **one-bank holding companies.** These were holding companies that owned a single banking operation, but which also owned other companies that engaged in activities such as data processing, securities brokerage, and insurance. Table 8.2 (page 212) shows the number of one-bank holding companies and growth of the branches, assets, and deposits.

one-bank holding company
A corporation that owns a single banking firm, together with other companies that engage in nonbanking lines of business.

Congress passed the Bank Holding Company Act of 1970 to rein in some of the activities of one-bank holding companies. This legislation also designated the Federal Reserve as the primary regulator of bank holding companies. It charged the Federal Reserve with auditing such companies to ensure that they did not undertake illegal or excessively risky activities.

3

What accounts for the existence of bank holding companies?   A key reason for the existence of multibank holding companies is that this legal structure allows banks to seek greater profits and diversify their business by opening offices across state lines in the face of continuing restrictions on interstate and intrastate branching. The main reason for the existence of one-bank holding companies is that such an organizational structure permits owners of banks to operate nonbanking businesses.

Interest Rate Regulation   The Glass-Steagall Act of 1933 also forbade the payment of interest on demand deposits at commercial banks, which until the 1970s were the only form of checking deposits in the United States. The rationale for this provision of the law was that if banks had to pay market interest rates on demand deposits when economic times were good, then they would be forced to search for high-interest assets that also possessed significant risks. Following an economic downturn, such risky assets would lose their market values. Then banks would lose liquidity and be unable to honor depositors'

TABLE 8.2   One-Bank Holding Companies

Year	Number of One-Bank Holding Companies	Number of Branches	Assets ($ billions)	Deposits ($ billions)
1973	1,282	7,861	262	207
1977	1,607	10,241	496	403
1981	3,093	14,329	756	587
1986	5,162	11,670	517	442
1991	4,843	11,860	679	534
1995	5,124	18,816	968	767

Note: Includes foreign data after 1973.

Source: Board of Governors of the Federal Reserve System.

requests for funds. The result would be banking panics, such as those the country had experienced between 1929 and 1933. Those who framed the 1933 legislation sought to eliminate interest on checking deposits as a means of inhibiting "destructive competition."

In addition, the Glass-Steagall Act authorized the Federal Reserve to place interest rate ceilings on bank savings and time deposits. The Federal Reserve enacted such ceilings through the imposition of a rule called Regulation Q. The ceilings thereafter became known as Reg Q ceilings.

Until the 1960s such interest rate ceilings applied only to commercial bank deposits. But under the terms of the Interest Rate Adjustment Act of 1966, similar ceilings constrained interest rates on savings and time deposits at savings institutions. The result of the imposition of these ceilings was the "credit crunch of 1966." When market interest rates rose well above the deposit rate ceilings at banks and savings institutions, depositors removed many of their funds from these institutions and used those funds to purchase alternative financial instruments, such as Treasury bills. This left depository institutions with fewer funds to lend. They responded by cutting back on loans, making it difficult for otherwise creditworthy individuals and businesses to obtain loans. Congress responded by raising the minimum T-bill denomination from $1,000 to $10,000, thereby inhibiting the ability of small savers to shift funds in this manner.

The Experiment with Partial Deregulation: 1971–1989

disintermediation A situation in which customers of depository institutions withdraw funds from their deposit accounts and use them to purchase financial instruments directly.

By the end of the 1960s it had become apparent that interest rate regulations were likely to cause periodic **disintermediation.** These were intervals in which market interest rates rose sufficiently to induce savers to withdraw funds from depository institutions and other financial intermediaries and use them to purchase financial instruments with higher, unregulated yields. The problem that depository institutions faced was that even when other market interest rates fell back to previous levels, former customers did not necessarily redeposit their funds. Rather than continuing to allow depository institutions to intermediate the saving-investment process, these former customers purchased financial instruments directly, hence the term *disintermediation.*

Financial Innovation as Regulatory Avoidance   A related difficulty for depository institutions was that technological advances in information processing had made it easier for other institutions to offer depository services. Investment companies began promoting money market mutual funds, which customers could establish via postal and telephone arrangements. As discussed in Chapter 5, these companies pool the funds of many savers and use those pools to purchase a variety of money market instruments—including, for instance, $10,000-denomination Treasury bills that individual savers otherwise might not be able to purchase. By the end of the 1970s, money market mutual funds had accumulated almost $200 billion in assets. This amount was equal to about 15 percent of the combined assets of all commercial banks in the United States.

To improve the ability of depository institutions to compete for funds, the Federal Reserve removed interest rate ceilings on certificates of deposit with denominations above $100,000. But savings institutions, which relied more heavily on funds obtained from small depositors, were little helped by this regulatory change. In May 1972 a Massachusetts state court authorized savings banks chartered in that state to offer negotiable-order-of-withdrawal (NOW) accounts, which essentially were interest-bearing checking deposits. In September of that year, the New Hampshire state banking commissioner authorized NOW accounts in that state as well. In response to the outcry by non-state-chartered savings institutions in those two states, in 1974 the U.S. Congress authorized federally chartered savings banks in those states to offer NOW accounts as well. Then in 1976 Congress extended the list of authorized states for NOW accounts to include Connecticut, Maine, Rhode Island, and Vermont. By 1979 New York and New Jersey savings institutions also could offer NOW accounts.

Clearly, these two financial innovations—the development of money market mutual funds and NOW accounts—were responses to the interest rate restrictions that Congress had enacted decades earlier. Those restrictions had been fairly innocuous until the 1960s, because market interest rates had remained close to the deposit rate ceilings established by the Federal Reserve under the provisions of the Glass-Steagall Act. But by the late 1970s, market interest rates were approaching levels that were nearly double those of the 1930s. Even those in Congress who otherwise favored heavy governmental regulation of depository institutions could see that this situation was unsustainable. Either Congress would have to contemplate some deregulation of depository institutions, or those institutions eventually would wither away as a result of disintermediation.

The Depository Institutions Deregulation and Monetary Control Act of 1980   In 1980 Congress made the decision to reduce some of the regulatory constraints on banks, savings institutions, and credit unions. It passed the Depository Institutions Deregulation and Monetary Control Act (DIDMCA). The act contained three provisions that greatly improved the competitive position of all depository institutions. First, it set up a six-year phase-out of all interest rate ceilings that these institutions faced. Second, it permitted all depository institutions nationwide to offer NOW accounts beginning in 1981. Third, the DIDMCA increased federal deposit insurance coverage from $40,000 per deposit account to $100,000. Notably, *Congress raised this limit without increasing the insurance premiums that depository institutions had to pay to the FDIC.* For thrift institutions—savings institutions and credit unions—the DIDMCA had some special benefits. The legislation permitted savings institutions to make consumer loans and to purchase commercial paper up to a limit of 20 percent of total assets. It also enabled savings institutions to issue credit cards. The act authorized credit unions to make residential and real estate loans. These changes permitted more direct competition among savings institutions, credit unions, and commercial banks.

POLICY NOTEBOOK

It's More Than $100,000 of Deposit Insurance

While the DIDMCA of 1980 increased deposit insurance to $100,000, this does not mean that you can be insured only up to $100,000. Rather, Congress and the regulators have written the rules such that you can have deposits insured for much more than $100,000. Consider the following: The $100,000 protection applies to the total number of accounts a single depositor has under his or her name within a *single* bank. Thus, if you have a $56,000 savings account in one bank, plus $50,000 in a checkable account in the same bank, you would be insured up to $100,000, not $106,000. Even if you have one account in the main office and one in another branch of the same bank, the accounts are added together to determine your insurance.

But there is a way to get around this $100,000 maximum. It involves splitting your funds among banks and accounts. For example, if you are married, you can have an account, your spouse can have an account, and together you can have a joint account. Thus, your maximum insurability as a unit is increased to $300,000. If you have children, you can set up guardian or trustee accounts that are insured separately.

In principle, if you have $100,000 accounts, say in certificates of deposit all over the country, you could have federal government insured deposits in the millions.

For Critical Analysis: *What might be the result of a change in the law that limited the $100,000 deposit insurance to one individual for all accounts in all banks in the United States?*

The DIDMCA of 1980 was a complicated piece of legislation. Although in some respects it deregulated depository institutions, in other ways it increased the federal regulatory burdens. For instance, it required all federally insured depository institutions to meet reserve requirements on transactions deposits (demand and NOW account deposits) established and maintained by the Federal Reserve. It also required depository institutions to pay the Federal Reserve for check-clearing and wire-transfer services that they use. Before the DIDMCA, only commercial banks that were members of the Federal Reserve System had to hold reserves with Federal Reserve banks, and these institutions had received Fed services without charge. The advantage of the DIDMCA for Fed member banks was that it effectively reduced their reserve requirements. For institutions that had not been required previously to hold reserves with the Fed, the advantages were access to Fed services (albeit at a cost) and the authorization to apply to Federal Reserve banks for loans when they faced liquidity difficulties.

On net, therefore, the DIDMCA did two things. Without doubt, it significantly deregulated depository institutions. Nevertheless, by placing all these institutions under the regulatory umbrella of the Federal Reserve System, a quasi-agency of the U.S. government, and dramatically raising federal deposit insurance coverage, the DIDMCA effectively *increased* the federal government's stake in these institutions. Consequently, the DIDMCA only *partially* deregulated depository institutions. In several ways it enlarged the federal government's role in the industry.

The Garn-St Germain Act of 1982   In 1982 Congress passed another important piece of legislation, the *Garn-St Germain Act*. Like the DIDMCA, it contained provisions that affected all depository institutions. The most important of these was the authorization of *money market deposit accounts*. As noted in Chapter 1, these are savings deposits that offer market interest rates and a limited number of transfers each year. Within two years after their mid-1982 introduction, these accounts had accumulated to almost $400 billion at all depository institutions. Undoubtedly, depository institutions won back some of their previous depositors, because money market mutual fund shares declined by nearly $50 billion during the same period. But most of the funds were deposited by individuals who already had savings accounts at depository institutions. These individuals simply moved their funds to money market deposit accounts to earn higher yields. As a result, many depository institutions found themselves incurring significantly greater interest expenses for only slightly larger volumes of deposits.

The other key elements of the Garn-St Germain Act attempted to address a festering problem. Since the 1970s the combined net worth of all savings institutions had declined precipitously. Some economists, such as Edward Kane (then at Ohio State University, now at Boston

College) used market value measures to show that the industry in fact was technically bankrupt by the early part of the 1970s. Even without taking into account the market values of their assets, by the middle of 1980 one-third of all savings institutions, with over one-third of the total assets of such institutions, were operating at losses.

To try to help savings institutions compete more effectively with other depository institutions, the Garn-St Germain Act contained three provisions specific to savings institutions. One was an increase bringing the DIDMCA limit on consumer loans and commercial paper holdings to 30 percent of assets. The second provision was the authorization to make commercial real estate loans up to a limit of 40 percent of assets. Finally, the legislation permitted savings institutions to make secured or unsecured loans up to a limit of 11 percent of their assets. Among the unsecured loans the act permitted were purchases of low-rated, junk bonds, as discussed in Chapter 4.

Furthermore, to assist the FDIC and FSLIC in closing troubled banks and savings institutions, the Garn-St Germain Act gave both agencies broad powers to permit institutions to merge with healthier partners, even across state lines. In retrospect, this provision of the legislation may have been the most successful. Many blame the Garn-St Germain Act for spurring the savings institution crisis that mushroomed a few years later. Nevertheless, the FDIC and FSLIC (until its demise in 1987) found themselves putting their expanded powers to much greater use than Congress could have imagined when it passed the 1982 law.

Finally, Congress planted a further seed that would blossom into the savings institution crisis a few years later: As a provision of the Garn-St Germain Act, Congress permitted the FHLBB to issue FSLIC promissory notes (promises of government payments) to savings institutions in exchange for "net worth certificates." Under this arrangement, a savings institution could count the FSLIC note as an asset and the net worth certificate as part of its net worth. Essentially, the FHLBB handed savings institutions promises for taxpayers to pay up if the institutions failed. Many of us might like such an arrangement for our own finances!

4

How did deposit interest rate ceilings on deposits ultimately help to spur financial innovation and depository institution deregulation in the 1970s and 1980s?   Legal interest rate ceilings on deposits placed depository institutions at a competitive disadvantage whenever other market interest rates rose well above the ceilings, thus inducing depositors to withdraw funds in search of higher yields. This so soured the fortunes of banks and savings institutions that Congress felt obliged to reduce the regulatory burdens they faced with laws passed in 1980 and 1982.

Too Big to Fail?   Savings institutions were not the only depository institutions that were faltering as the 1980s began. In 1982 a large bank named Penn Square failed because declining energy prices had caused the market values of the bank's energy-related loans to fall dramatically. Penn Square had close financial dealings with a number of other institutions, including Continental Illinois Bank, which was based in Chicago and at the time was the nation's seventh largest commercial bank. Continental Illinois had purchased over \$1 billion of Penn Square's energy loans and soon found itself on the same slippery slope toward bankruptcy.

It is difficult for a large bank to keep such problems secret. When word of Continental Illinois' problems began to spread, it became the victim of an electronic bank run. Depositors whose account balances exceeded the \$100,000 limit for deposit insurance coverage made wire transfers out of their accounts, causing it to lose over \$10 billion in deposits within a two-month period in the spring of 1984. The bank offered above-market interest rates in an effort to induce individuals and firms to purchase its certificates of deposit, and it sold billions of dollars of its assets, but to little avail. By May of 1984 the FDIC had decided to bail out Continental Illinois by purchasing over \$2 billion of its subordinated notes. In addition, the Federal Reserve Bank of Chicago extended long-term credit to the bank.

These actions by the FDIC and the Federal Reserve were unprecedented efforts to keep a bank from failing. They were taken to protect uninsured depositors of the bank as well as those whose funds were covered by federal guarantees. In September of 1984 the comptroller of the currency, the chief regulator of national banks, announced to Congress that he and his staff had decided that the largest eleven national banks in the United States were "too big to fail." This **too-big-to-fail policy** had its intended effect of shoring up public confidence in the nation's banking system. This ultimately led to the implicit adoption of the same policy by the other federal banking regulators, the Federal Reserve and the FDIC.

Another byproduct of the too-big-to-fail policy, however, was that it effectively gave federal government guarantees to *all* the deposits of the nation's largest banks, insured or uninsured. Smaller banks, naturally, felt that this gave the largest banks an unfair advantage in the marketplace. In fact, a study by Maureen O'Hara and Wayne Shaw of Cornell University demonstrated that the comptroller's announcement of the too-big-to-fail policy led to a significant increase in the stock prices of the largest banks in the nation. Stock prices also increased for the four largest state banks in the country at that time—Bankers Trust, Chemical Bank, Manufacturers Hanover, and J. P. Morgan—that were not even on the comptroller's list, although they had been mentioned in an article in *The Wall Street Journal* the day after the comptroller's announcement.

too-big-to-fail policy   A regulatory policy that protects the largest depository institutions from failure solely because regulators believe that such failure could undermine the public's confidence in the financial system.

Capital Requirements   A bank's equity capital represents a cushion against losses for depositors, who have the first crack at getting back their funds should a depository institution fail. In contrast, holders of equity shares are the last in line for funds in such an event. For this reason, depository institution regulators—and in particular the FDIC as the supervisor of federal deposit insurance—regard capital as the first line of defense against depositor losses in the event of a failure. In recent years this has led regulators to impose **capital requirements,** or enforced minimum standards for depository institution equity capital.

Although various requirements for depository institution equity capital positions had existed prior to the 1980s, it was not until Congress passed the International Lending Supervision Act of 1983 that regulators began to impose relatively uniform standards for depository institutions. A provision of this legislation authorized the Federal Reserve, the Office of the Comptroller of the Currency (OCC), and the FDIC to establish and supervise capital requirements for commercial banks. In 1985 these three regulators set up a system of capital requirements using two measures of capital. The narrower measure included most equity shares and loan loss reserves (see Chapter 7), and the broader measure added the remaining equity shares and subordinated debt. The regulators then required banks to meet a two-tiered requirement involving ratios of the capital measures to assets.

The imposition of this set of capital standards helped end a gradual decline in bank capitalization that had begun in the 1960s (see Figure 6.1). Nevertheless, a commonly recognized problem in using simple ratios of capital to assets is that they treat any two banks with the same dollar-denominated capital and asset positions as identical. In fact, however, one bank may have made huge loans to a developing country on the verge of default, while the other has maintained a well-diversified portfolio of high-quality loans and safe securities. Consequently, simple ratios fail to account for risk differences among depository institutions.

In 1989 the three regulators of American banks joined regulators of banks in most of the advanced, market-based economies at a meeting in Basel, Switzerland, to announce a system of **risk-based capital requirements** intended to factor risk characteristics into the computation of required capital standards. Under this system, which applies to most banks in the developed world, institutions compute ratios of capital in relation to **risk-adjusted assets.** This is a weighted average of all the bank's assets, with the weights accounting for risk differences across types of assets. The safest assets, which regulators perceive to be cash, U.S. Treasury securities, and fully government-guaranteed, mortgage-backed GNMA securities, receive a zero weight and hence do not count at all in the computation of risk-adjusted assets. Assets that regulators view as having a slight possibility of default, such as interbank deposits, municipal bonds, and FNMA partially government-guaranteed, mortgage-backed securities, receive a

capital requirements
Minimum equity capital standards that regulators impose upon depository institutions.

risk-based capital requirements   Regulatory capital standards that account for risk factors that distinguish different depository institutions.

risk-adjusted assets   A weighted average of bank assets that regulators compute to account for risk differences across types of assets.

weight of 20 percent. More risky assets such as first-home mortgages receive a weight of 50 percent. All other loans and securities receive a 100 percent weight. In addition, regulators compute *credit-exposure dollar equivalents* for off-balance-sheet banking activities (see Chapter 7) such as derivatives trading. Typically these also receive a 10 percent weight. Then regulators add up all the weighted dollar amounts to get the bank's total, risk-adjusted asset figure. This amount is the denominator of the capital ratios that banks must compute.

Banks must calculate two ratios of capital relative to risk-adjusted assets, based on two tiers of bank capital. *Tier 1 capital,* or **core capital,** consists of common shareholders' equity plus retained earnings (income not paid out to shareholders). Regulators define a bank's **total capital** to be core capital plus *Tier 2 capital,* or **supplementary capital.** This latter measure includes some types of preferred stock and most types of subordinated debt.

The regulations apply both to banks and bank holding companies. They require that the ratio of core capital to risk-adjusted assets must exceed 4 percent, and that the ratio of total capital to risk-adjusted assets must be in excess of 8 percent. In addition, bank holding companies must meet a simple ratio standard in which the ratio of total capital to *unadjusted total assets* must exceed 4 percent.

Consider a very simple example of two banks. One has $1 million in cash, $2 million in U.S. Treasury securities, and $10 million in commercial loans, and so its total assets equal $13 million. It has $0.5 million in common stockholders' equity and retained earnings and $0.5 million in subordinated debt. Hence, its core capital is $0.5 million, and its total capital is $1 million. The $3 million in cash and Treasury securities do not count toward its risk-adjusted assets. Its $10 million in commercial loans count 100 percent, and so its total risk-adjusted assets equal $10 million. Consequently, its ratio of core capital to risk-adjusted assets is equal to $0.5 million/$10 million, or 5 percent. Its ratio of total capital to risk-adjusted assets is equal to $1 million/$10 million, or 10 percent. Its unadjusted capital ratio would be $1 million/$13 million, or about 7.6 percent. This bank would meet all required capital standards.

Now consider a bank with $0.5 million in cash, $0.5 million in securities, and $12 million in commercial loans. Like the first bank, this one has $13 million in assets on its balance sheet. In contrast, however, it has sufficient off-balance-sheet activities to merit a credit-exposure dollar equivalent rating of $3 million. The bank also has $0.5 million in core capital and $0.5 million in total capital, like the first bank. Consequently, its unadjusted capital ratio is, like that of the first bank, equal to 7.6 percent. Yet the second bank clearly has a riskier portfolio because it has more loans and undertakes off-balance-sheet activities. This shows up in the current capital requirement calculations. For the second bank, the $1 million in cash and securities would not count toward its risk-adjusted assets, but the $12 million in commercial loans

core capital   Defined by current capital requirements as shareholders' equity plus retained earnings.

total capital   Under currently imposed bank capital requirements, this is the sum of core capital and supplementary capital.

supplementary capital   A measure that regulators presently use to calculate required capital; it includes certain preferred stock and most subordinated debt.

and $3 million in credit-exposure dollar equivalents from its off-balance-sheet activities would count fully, giving it a risk-adjusted asset total of $15 million. This bank's ratio of core capital to risk-adjusted assets, then, would be $0.5 million/$15 million, or 3.3 percent. Its ratio of total capital to risk-adjusted assets would be $1 million/$15 million, or 6.7 percent. This second bank, even though it has the same dollar assets and capital as the first bank, would fail both the 4 percent and 8 percent capital standards that apply, respectively, to core capital and total capital.

When banking regulators announced the new capital standards, they phased them in gradually through the end of 1992. A number of banks and bank holding companies failed to meet the three ratio requirements. In particular, bank holding companies often failed the 4 percent simple-ratio requirement, even if the banks they owned met the risk-adjusted ratio standards. According to a 1994 study by Elizabeth Laderman, an economist at the Federal Reserve Bank of San Francisco, this had an important effect on how bank holding companies chose to adjust to the requirements. Bank holding company stock prices tend to decline sharply whenever they announce plans to issue new shares. This tendency may have discouraged many bank holding companies from issuing new stock. Instead, they may have been induced to cut back on issuing new loans. By chance, there also was an economic downturn in 1990 and 1991 that depressed the demand for loans. These two factors together—reduced issuance of loans in response to higher capital standards for bank holding companies and decreased loan demand—may have caused the significant cutback in bank lending between 1990 and 1992.

As Figure 8.2 indicates, however, the adoption of the risk-based capital standards had the effect on aggregate equity positions of U.S. commercial banks that regulators had hoped to achieve. For the first time in almost 50 years, beginning in 1990 the ratio of equity to assets rose. Figure 8.2 shows that the adoption of the new capital standards may have ended a 150-year downward trend in the overall equity ratio of commercial banks.

5

How do bank regulators impose capital requirements?   Regulators have developed narrow and broad measures of bank capital. In addition, they have created a measure of assets that adjusts for differences in risk across groups of assets. The regulators have set minimum requirements for the ratios of two capital measures relative to the measure of risk-adjusted assets. Banks must meet these capital standards or face greater supervision or perhaps even closure.

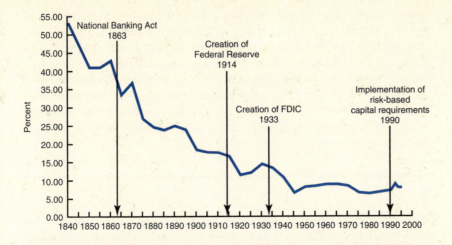

FIGURE 8.2   Equity as a Percentage of Commercial Bank Assets, 1840–1995

Bank equity ratios fell considerably between the mid-nineteenth and mid-twentieth centuries. Recently they have risen slightly. *Sources:* Allen N. Berger, Richard J. Herring, and Giorgio P. Szego, "The Role of Capital in Financial Institutions," *Journal of Banking and Finance* (1995); Federal Deposit Insurance Corporation, *Statistics on Banking*, 1995.

The Savings Institution Crisis   Banking regulators sought to shore up the position of commercial banks in the late 1980s and early 1990s for two reasons. First, bank capital ratios had sunk to low levels. A second reason, however, was that regulators wanted to avoid a commercial banking collapse analogous to the one that had recently engulfed many American savings institutions. The latter collapse, described in the introduction to this chapter, was staggering in its own right. A similar collapse of the commercial banking industry, however, would have been a real catastrophe.

What caused the savings institution crisis? Certainly, the cumulative effects of high and variable interest rates during the 1970s had driven up interest expenses at savings institutions even as their interest incomes remained relatively fixed. By the end of the 1970s this exposure to interest rate risk had pushed many savings institutions to the brink of insolvency. In addition, increased competition stemming from deregulation in the early 1980s compressed the profit margins at many institutions that already were trying to compensate for lack of managerial experience in the new lines of business permitted under the Garn-St Germain Act. Furthermore, a major decline in oil prices slashed real estate prices and mortgage values in the southwestern United States, where livelihoods depended heavily on energy-related industries. Finally, there was outright fraud at some institutions.

Most economists agree, however, that two related factors really caused the crisis: *moral hazard* and *regulatory failure*. By insuring the deposits of savings institutions, the government gave the managers of these institutions an incentive to undertake riskier activities. The deregulation provisions of the 1980 DIDMCA and 1982 Garn-St Germain Act added to these incentives. As discussed earlier in this chapter, a key rationale for regulation is to minimize the moral hazard problem. In the case of savings institutions in the 1980s, regulation failed to perform this function. Indeed, the otherwise well-meaning actions of Congress and the FHLBB largely induced the great savings institution debacle of the 1980s and 1990s.

6

Why did so many savings institutions fail in the 1980s and 1990s? The three factors that played the largest roles in causing these failures were the significant interest rate risk arising from specialization in mortgage lending, the moral hazard problem inherent in deposit insurance, and the failure of federal regulators to adequately address the moral hazard problem.

Reregulation Versus Deregulation: The 1990s and Beyond

By early 1987 the FSLIC technically was insolvent. Yet it was not until 1989 that Congress passed legislation to deal with the savings institu-

GLOBAL NOTEBOOK

Will the Japanese Bail Out Their Banks?

Japan is facing a banking crisis that makes what happened in America look like child's play. The policy question is: How is the Japanese government going to bail out the banking system there? As of the middle of the 1990s, Japanese banks held problem loans equal to about $1 trillion, or 25 percent of Japan's GDP. Japanese authorities continued to allow banks to lend to problem debtors enough money to cover unpaid interest. If the Japanese government chooses to bail out its banking system the way the U.S. Congress did in 1989, the estimated cost will be close to $400 billion. Alternatively, the Japanese government could simply let the weakest banks go bankrupt. Some observers believe that a third way will eventually occur. The Japanese government will pour in enough reserves to shore up the banking system, and in exchange that nation's banks will agree to use all of their profits for the foreseeable future to write off bad debts.

For Critical Analysis: *Who pays for the Japanese banking bailout if the third way is chosen?*

tion crisis. Although many had hoped that Congress would use the new law to reform depository institution regulation and deposit insurance, it chose instead to focus its attention to mopping up the savings institution mess. It did not pass further legislation aimed at deeper reforms for another two years. Even then, as we shall discuss, it was unclear whether Congress had succeeded in addressing the issues that depository institutions will face through the remainder of the 1990s and into the coming century.

The Financial Institutions Reform, Recovery, and Enforcement Act of 1989

The 1989 legislation abolished a couple of federal agencies but on net created more than it abolished. To Congress, apparently, this spelled "reform." The new law also laid out a structure for attempting to salvage, or recover, assets of failed savings institutions so that taxpayer losses could be minimized. Finally, the 1989 act also specified means for enforcement of broad governmental mandates to accomplish the recovery objective. Consequently, Congress called the legislation the Financial Institutions Reform, Recovery, and Enforcement Act (FIRREA).

Although FIRREA left the Federal Home Loan Bank System largely intact, it dismantled the FHLBB. It also abolished the insolvent FSLIC. As a new regulator for savings institutions, FIRREA created the Office of Thrift Supervision (OTS), which it made a unit of the Treasury Department. The legislation also created a Federal Housing Finance Board to supervise the operations of the Federal Home Loan Bank System but gave this board meager regulatory responsibilities. FIRREA reassigned the supervision of the savings institution deposit fund to the FDIC. It continued the traditional separation of bank and savings institution deposit funds, however. One FDIC fund, the **Bank Insurance Fund (BIF),** covers commercial banks; another, the **Savings Association Insurance Fund (SAIF),** replaced the insolvent FSLIC fund. FIRREA increased bank and savings institution premium payments into these insurance funds from the old 1933 premium rate of 0.083 percent to a much higher rate of 0.23 percent—an increase of almost a factor of three times the old premium rate. Ironically, this is very close to the 0.24 percent rate that the first head of the FDIC found to be appropriate back in 1933.

To shore up the SAIF, FIRREA gave the FDIC broadened authority to try to recover assets from insolvent savings institutions, and it authorized tax-financed funding of savings institution "resolutions," which Congress found to be a nicer word than "closings." FIRREA specified that funding for such resolutions was to be handled through the Treasury Department and another new agency, the Resolution Finance Corporation (RFC). Yet another agency, the Resolution Trust Corporation (RTC), handled the day-to-day aspects of closing down

Bank Insurance Fund (BIF)
The FDIC's fund that covers insured deposits of commercial banks.

Savings Association Insurance Fund (SAIF)
The FDIC's fund that covers insured deposits of savings institutions.

insolvent savings institutions. FIRREA set 1992 as the target date for completion of the duties of the RFC and RTC, but these agencies did not go out of business until 1994.

Another set of provisions in FIRREA reversed the deregulation thrust of the DIDMCA and the Garn-St Germain Act. FIRREA prohibited savings institutions from holding junk bonds (high-interest, high-risk bonds), and it toughened the limitation on commercial real estate lending by these institutions. Now, instead of being able to allocate up to 40 percent of their assets to such lending, savings institutions can make loans up to a limit of only four times their equity capital. The 1989 legislation also tightened capital requirements for savings institutions.

The FDIC Improvement Act of 1991   FIRREA basically was a stopgap effort to deal with old problems. In contrast, the FDIC Improvement Act of 1991 (FDICIA) represented a forward-looking effort. By passing this legislation, Congress sought to reform various aspects of depository institution regulation and to revamp specific elements of federal deposit insurance. FDICIA did a number of things:

1. FDICIA forbade commercial bank regulators from loosening the capital standards they had structured in 1989. Indeed, the legislation mandated that regulators be tough on banks that failed to meet the capital standards.
2. FDICIA established a regulatory system of **structured early intervention and resolution (SEIR).** Under SEIR, the FDIC has authority to intervene much more quickly in the affairs of a depository institution that it believes is acting in a manner that might generate losses for either the BIF or the SAIF. The act also requires the FDIC to follow prespecified and clearly structured procedures in such interventions, so that all depository institutions receive more nearly equal treatment. In a feature that attracted much criticism, however, FDICIA gives the FDIC fairly broad discretion to determine these procedures.
3. FDICIA required the FDIC to set up a clear set of rules for determining when a depository institution's net worth reaches a sufficiently low level that it must be closed. The intent of this provision was to keep otherwise bankrupt depository institutions from continuing to operate and to generate further losses that taxpayers ultimately would have to fund.
4. The 1991 legislation authorized the FDIC to shore up both BIF and SAIF. Both of these insurance funds had declined to low levels following the failure and closure of about 1,400 commercial banks and 1,100 savings institutions between 1980 and 1991. FDICIA gave the FDIC authority to set deposit insurance premiums high enough to increase both insurance funds considerably.

structured early intervention and resolution (SEIR)   A regulatory system established by the FDIC Improvement Act of 1991, which authorizes the FDIC to intervene quickly in the management of a depository institution likely to cause losses for the federal deposit insurance funds.

5. The act restricted the extent to which the Federal Reserve can lend to undercapitalized depository institutions. If the Federal Reserve lends to such an institution for more than 60 days within any given 120-day period, then the Federal Reserve incurs a liability to the FDIC for any losses that deposit insurance funds might experience because the troubled institution continued to operate instead of closing its doors.

6. The legislation ended the too-big-to-fail policy that bank regulators had explicitly or implicitly followed since the Continental Illinois bailout in 1984. Under the provisions of FDICIA, regulators are supposed to treat troubled large banks under the same timetables and procedures they apply to small banks that are failing.

7. FDICIA mandated that the FDIC design and implement a system of **risk-based deposit insurance premiums.** Under this system, the premiums that depository institutions pay the FDIC to fund the BIF and the SAIF depend on the institutions' degrees of capitalization. These, in turn, are based on the capital definitions established in 1989.

risk-based deposit insurance premiums   Premium rates that depository institutions pay the FDIC based on the varying degrees to which they are capitalized and on the differing risk factors they exhibit.

Table 8.3 shows how this system works. The FDIC has established three broad categories for both BIF- and SAIF-insured depository institutions that it permits to remain open. It bases these categories on the institutions' capital ratios and defines them as *well capitalized, adequately capitalized,* and *under-capitalized.* Within each of these categories there are three additional classifications, labeled A, B, and C, that the FDIC determines based on aspects of the institutions' risk positions unrelated to their levels of capitalization. Well-capitalized depository institutions that fall into classification A are those that the FDIC views as least risky.

TABLE 8.3   The FDIC Risk-Based Deposit Insurance Premiums

(A) RISK CLASSIFICATIONS FOR BIF-INSURED INSTITUTIONS			
	A	B	C
Well-capitalized	0.00	0.03	0.17
Adequately capitalized	0.03	0.10	0.24
Undercapitalized	0.10	0.24	0.27

(B) RISK CLASSIFICATIONS FOR SAIF-INSURED INSTITUTIONS			
	A	B	C
Well-capitalized	0.23	0.26	0.29
Adequately capitalized	0.26	0.29	0.30
Undercapitalized	0.29	0.30	0.31

Note: All premiums are percentages of insured deposits.

Source: Federal Deposit Insurance Corporation.

In 1996 the FDIC decided that the BIF was sufficiently capitalized so that class A banks would no longer have to pay explicit premiums for deposit insurance. All banks, however, must pay a flat fee of $2,000.

Consequently, as shown in panel (a) of Table 8.3, the FDIC charges commercial banks that fall within group A a premium rate of zero. Almost 95 percent of all commercial banks fall into this category. Under-capitalized depository institutions that fall into classification C are those the FDIC perceives to be the worst credit risks for the BIF and the SAIF. Therefore, the FDIC charges these institutions the highest deposit insurance premium rate of 0.27 percent (27 cents for each $100 of insured deposits). In 1996 there were only 23 commercial banks in risk classification C that paid this higher premium rate.

Panel (b) of Table 8.3 shows that the FDIC uses the same risk-classification system for savings institutions covered under the SAIF. These institutions, however, must pay considerably higher deposit insurance premiums as compared with those paid by commercial banks. The FDIC has kept SAIF deposit insurance premium rates above those charged to commercial banks in an effort to build up the SAIF to the $8 billion funding level specified in FDICIA. In 1996 the SAIF contained only just over $2 billion. A key reason for the shortfall was that many savings institutions either had failed or had switched to commercial bank charters, leaving fewer institutions to pay SAIF premiums. The remaining savings institutions have protested the higher premiums that they must pay to remain covered by the SAIF, but so far to no avail.

7

How does the FDIC currently charge depository institutions for the insurance it provides?   Currently the FDIC charges higher deposit insurance premiums to institutions that maintain lower ratios of capital to risk-adjusted assets. The FDIC also charges higher premiums to institutions that display greater riskiness along other dimensions of their operations.

THE CURRENT REGULATORY STRUCTURE

After all this Congressional and regulatory effort, where do things stand in the 1990s? In fact, surprisingly little has changed in depository regulation since the early 1980s. Since that time, only four true regulatory reforms have taken place: (1) the regulators' 1989 adoption of explicit and well-defined risk-based capital requirements, (2) FDICIA's 1991 requirement that the FDIC follow clear rules in closing weak institutions, (3) FDICIA's restraint on the Federal Reserve's ability to keep weak institutions open by throwing good money after bad, and (4) risk-based deposit insurance premiums mandated by FDICIA.

Certainly, these represent substantial regulatory changes. Nevertheless, in many respects the regulatory structure that depository institutions face today is nearly identical to the one that they faced 20—or even 60—years ago. Only a couple of the names have changed here and there. To see this, let's consider the regulatory environment that each type of depository institution faces in the 1990s.

Regulation and Supervision of Commercial Banks

The present regulatory structure for commercial banks stems in part from the dual banking system that emerged following the Civil War. The Office of the Comptroller of the Currency (OCC) has always been the primary regulator of national (federally chartered) banks, and the OCC continues in this capacity today. The Banking Act of 1935, which you will learn in Chapter 11 significantly restructured the Federal Reserve, required that by 1937 all federally insured state banks either had to join the Federal Reserve System and be regulated and supervised by the Fed, or had to subject themselves to regulatory supervision from the FDIC. This produced a trilateral federal regulatory structure. The OCC regulates national banks, the Federal Reserve regulates state banks that are members of the Federal Reserve System, and the FDIC regulates state banks that do not opt to be members of the Federal Reserve System.

The Status Quo   This commercial bank regulatory structure, therefore, has existed for about 60 years. The only "wrinkle" was the establishment of the Federal Reserve as the chief regulator of bank holding companies, some of which own national banks or state banks that are not Federal Reserve member banks. But the three regulatory bodies have worked out lines of authority that apply to such situations.

Each of the three commercial bank regulators retains staff accountants, statisticians, and economists. These individuals examine and audit the books of the banks they regulate, collect and analyze data from specific institutions and for all institutions combined, and evaluate the effectiveness of current or proposed regulatory policies. Of the roughly 9,500 commercial banks, about 2,500 are national banks that the OCC regulates. Of the 7,000 or so state-chartered banks, about 1,000 are Federal Reserve members and thereby fall under the Fed's regulatory umbrella. The FDIC presently has oversight responsibilities for just over 6,000 commercial banks.

Proposals for Regulatory Streamlining   The administrations of both President Bush and President Clinton agreed with the view that this regulatory structure is too complicated and outmoded. In fact, both administrations made proposals to streamline the structure. A proposal by the Clinton administration called for eliminating the FDIC's day-to-day supervisory responsibilities and transferring most of them to the OCC. According to the plan, this would permit the FDIC to concentrate on maintaining the federal deposit insurance system and closing banks that happened to fail. The Clinton administration also briefly discussed reducing the Federal Reserve's regulatory role. This reflected a view that a number of academic economists have held for years: The Federal Reserve can conduct monetary policy without simultaneously regulating banks.

Nevertheless, a sufficient consensus apparently has not yet emerged in the Congress to alter the current structure. In addition, the regulators themselves typically fight proposed changes. Cynics usually charge the regulators with bureaucratic self-interest, claiming that they oppose reforms simply to protect their own turf—and the jobs of members of their staffs. Yet the regulators offer reasonable arguments countering proposals

POLICY NOTEBOOK
Will Digital Banking Reduce the Effectiveness of Regulation?

Two British banks, National Westminster and Midland, started a plastic and silicone cash substitute called Mondex. They are like ATM cards but carry a computer chip inside. This is *data money.* Bank customers can get data money into their cards over the phone if they have a smart phone in their house. Mondex is the beginning of the true cashless society, but banks still play a large roll.

Now there is E-money, too. Companies other than banks have already started their own forms of electronic money, called E-cash. E-cash moves about completely outside the network of banks, checks, and paper currency. Some of the companies in the E-cash game are well known, such as Microsoft and Xerox; others are less well known, such as CyberCash and DigiCash. Perhaps E-cash's biggest play will be on the Internet, where electronic commerce is growing daily. People will be able to download money to their PC or to palm-sized electronic wallets. People will be able to zap money to Internet merchants.

With the growth of E-cash, the traditional definition of money will certainly no longer hold. The Federal Reserve will have even less ability to control the money supply. Furthermore, E-cash may create problems if it is stored in computer systems. What if the systems crash? Additionally, electronic counterfeiting may be a serious problem. Computer hackers who break into an E-cash system might be able to steal money from thousands or even hundreds of thousands of individuals all at once. Finally, E-cash may allow for an increased amount of tax evasion and money laundering.

For Critical Analysis: *What is the disadvantage of having a Mondex money card instead of cash?*

for streamlining bank regulation. For instance, the FDIC responded to the Clinton plan by pointing out that it would be difficult for the agency to realize that banks were struggling if they did not consistently observe at least a large subset of banks. Likewise, the Federal Reserve reacted to the Clinton administration's ideas about reducing the Fed's regulatory role by arguing that conducting effective monetary policy requires having the opportunity to follow the daily pulse of the banking system.

Our review of the history of depository institution regulation indicates that Congress rarely acts to change the status quo unless there is some evidence of a crisis, or at least a crisis in the offing. Hence, it appears likely that Congress will maintain the current commercial bank regulatory structure until some future event convinces Congress that change is needed.

Regulation and Supervision of Savings Institutions

Under a provisions of the 1989 Financial Institutions Reform, Recovery, and Enforcement Act, the main federal regulator of savings institutions is the Office of Thrift Supervision (OTS). The OTS has the status of a bureau within the Department of the Treasury, and its relationship to nationally chartered savings institutions mirrors in many respects the OCC's relationship to nationally chartered commercial banks.

Nevertheless, in some ways the OTS faces limitations on its authority. Feeling somewhat burned by the regulatory breakdowns that occurred during the savings institution crisis of the 1980s, Congress gave the FDIC the power to overrule the OTS in some instances. For instance, the FDIC can close OTS-regulated institutions or withdraw federal deposit insurance from such institutions even in the face of OTS objections. At the same time, Congress reduced the likelihood of such squabbles developing between the FDIC and this unit of the Treasury Department when it also made the heads of the OCC and OTS members of the five-person board of directors of the FDIC.

State authorities regulate state-chartered savings institutions. Nevertheless, nearly all such institutions are federally insured. Although the OTS does not have supervisory authority over these institutions, the institutions must meet standards established by the FDIC. Consequently, state-chartered savings institutions ultimately must meet federally mandated standards and effectively must satisfy FDIC regulations.

Regulation and Supervision of Credit Unions

The key federal regulator of credit unions is the National Credit Union Administration (NCUA). A board of three individuals governs this government agency, which has sole responsibility for chartering, insuring, supervising, and examining federally chartered credit unions. NCUA administers the National Credit Union Share Insurance Fund, and most state-chartered credit unions contribute to and are covered by this insurance fund. Although state regulatory bodies have immediate supervisory responsibilities for such state-chartered institutions, those covered by the NCUA's insurance program must meet the standards it sets for coverage. Because the NCUA's fund covers all federally insured credit unions, the FDIC plays no role in the supervision or regulation of credit unions.

Indeed, those who have advocated streamlining the regulatory environment faced by commercial banks often point to the NCUA as a possible model for such a simplified bank regulatory structure. Those who favor the status quo for commercial bank regulation respond that even though there are more credit unions than commercial banks, the amount of dollars involved in the two industries differs dramatically. After all, the assets of all credit unions combined amount to less than 10 percent of the assets of commercial banks, and the latter institutions have played a more dominant and varied set of roles in the nation's financial system. This, goes the counterargument, helps to justify the more complex web of regulators and regulations that commercial banks face. We should note, however, that this counterargument may lose some of its force in the future, because the NCUA currently is contemplating the imposition of capital requirements, as well as other bank-type regulations, on the credit unions that it regulates.

SUMMARY

1. **The Goals of Depository Institution Regulation:** These are to prevent or reduce the incidence of insolvency, to maintain depository institutions' liquidity, and to promote the low-cost functioning of these institutions. Achieving reduced costs may require permitting considerable rivalry, which can cause some depository institutions to fail or to operate at low levels of liquidity. Thus, typically there are trade-offs among these goals.

2. **Deposit Insurance as a Justification for Federal Regulation:** Because a large portion of the deposits at depository institutions receive federal insurance guarantees, depository institution managers may be inclined to make riskier asset and liability choices. Hence, federal deposit insurance exposes the government (taxpayers) to a significant moral hazard problem. Monitoring insured institutions via periodic examinations and providing enforceable supervisory rules that managers must follow are the means by which government regulators can reduce the magnitude of the moral hazard problem.

3. **The Reasons Why Bank Holding Companies Exist:** Restrictions on inter- and intrastate branching give depository institutions an incentive to establish multibank holding companies. In contrast, depository institutions usually form one-bank holding companies as a

way to expand into lines of business that normally lie outside their legal range of operations.

4. **How Interest Rate Ceilings on Deposits Spurred Innovation and Deregulation:** During periods when other market interest rates rose well above the legal ceiling rates on deposits, disintermediation resulted. Depository institution customers switched to holding government bonds and other instruments directly, or to holding their funds as shares in money market mutual funds. This induced depository institutions to develop NOW accounts to try to compete. Nevertheless, the threat that disintermediation posed to depository institutions ultimately led Congress to pass laws that significantly deregulated depository institutions.

5. **Current Bank Capital Requirements:** The three commercial bank regulators—the FDIC, the Federal Reserve, and the OCC—currently define two measures of bank capital. Then they look at ratios of these measures relative to a risk-adjusted measure of a bank's assets. Failure of a bank to maintain ratios that regulators deem sufficient results in more regulatory supervision or possibly even closure of the bank.

6. **The Causes of Massive Savings Institution Failures of the 1980s and 1990s:** Although a number of factors contributed to the large number of savings institution failures, three elements were critical. The first was the institutions' exposure to interest rate risk as a result of their reliance on mortgage-related activities. The second was the moral hazard problem arising from federal deposit insurance guarantees to the savings institutions that were deregulated in the early 1980s. A final, closely related factor that induced the crisis was the failure of federal regulators to rein in the moral hazard problem by careful examinations and prudent supervision of savings institutions.

7. **How the FDIC Decides How Much to Charge for Deposit Insurance:** At present, the FDIC uses a system of risk-based deposit insurance premiums. A key measure of depository institution risk is its capitalization, as defined by current capital standards. In addition, the FDIC factors in other information that it gleans from examinations of the institutions. Institutions that the FDIC classifies as higher risks to the deposit insurance system pay higher premiums for their insurance coverage.

QUESTIONS AND PROBLEMS

1. Many economists believe that markets should be as free and unregulated as possible. Yet a number of these same economists have been critical of federal depository institution regulations they perceive to

have been too lax in past years. What might account for these apparently contradictory positions?

2. Periods of disintermediation commonly have corresponded to intervals during which many individuals and firms, who in the past had been able to get bank loans, found that banks no longer were willing to lend. Explain why this makes sense.

3. Suppose that a depository institution has $20 million in cash assets and U.S. Treasury securities. It also has $5 million in GNMA mortgage-backed securities and $10 million in FNMA mortgage-backed securities. It has $48 million in consumer loans outstanding. It is not involved in any off-balance-sheet activities. If its core capital is $2 million and its total capital is $3 million, would this depository institution meet current capital requirements? Show your work and explain.

4. Economists have found that banks that were judged too big to fail in the late 1980s sometimes could pay lower interest rates on their large-denomination certificates of deposit. Explain why this might have happened.

5. Most economists agree that the adoption of risk-based deposit insurance premiums has helped to reduce the moral hazard problem somewhat. In light of the current structure of those premiums, can you suggest any types of general changes that could still be implemented to further reduce the problem? (*Hint:* Economists who had long argued for a premium structure such as that shown in Table 8.3 objected to what they felt were overly narrow differences among premiums for different risk classifications.)

Issues in Depository Institution Regulation

KEY QUESTIONS

1. Has interstate banking become a reality?

2. What are the likely effects of interstate banking?

3. What is universal banking?

4. What are the pros and cons of universal banking?

5. How has off-balance-sheet banking complicated the task of regulating depository institutions?

6. What are the benefits and costs of depository institution consumer protection laws?

*I*n 1989 depository institution regulators from the United States, Western Europe, and Japan gathered in Basel, Switzerland, to announce the mutual adoption of risk-based capital requirements. They recognized that many depository institutions barely met the new standards and that a few large institutions would fail the new requirements. To reach the standards, banks would have to issue new equity shares, cut back on loan growth, or both.

Beginning in late 1990, after depository institution managers had assessed the effects of the new requirements, loan growth declined substantially. By February 1991 over a third of all U.S. commercial banks reported they had tightened lending standards and cut lending by about 1 percent. In Japan, major banks were reducing their lending by as much as 5 percent. Small businesses in both nations began to feel a pinch as credit became difficult to come by. Soon the economy was in a downturn, and the decline in bank lending was reinforced by a fall in the demand for loans. So many businesses had failed or cut back on expansion that they did not want to borrow any more.

While increased capital requirements alone did not cause the nation's business recession, they certainly contributed to the decline. Another unintended effect was a change in the way in which many banks make large loans. Banks began to join together in loan syndicates, or group loans. Banks that found themselves with capital ratios below or close to regulatory minimums could not expand their assets by making large loans alone, and so they had to find partners.

Although the economy ultimately recovered by 1992, loan syndications have remained a major part of big-business banking. The average size of a syndicated loan today is $500 million, and some banks now specialize in managing syndicated loans. Such banks recruit partners in loan syndicates, and take the lead in negotiating contract details and preparing the paperwork. Loan syndication also has fueled the development of a secondary market in bank loans, because syndicate members can sell their shares in the loans to other depository institutions. Largely because of capital requirements, a few banks have a new business niche, and the secondary loan market has matured.

These effects of the adoption of risk-based capital requirements illustrate an important fact: Depository institution regulations can have unintended effects. Some of these effects may be short-term, but others can change the business of banking in unexpected ways. In this chapter we focus on regulatory issues that have been of particular concern in recent years. In each case, the economic effects of the new regulations or reforms have been or are likely to be significant.

INTERSTATE BANKING

As we discussed in Chapter 8, depository institutions effectively have branched across state lines by forming multibank holding companies and acquiring banks located in different states. For some time, most economists have argued that this is a highly inefficient way for banks to branch. Traditionally, small community bankers, who feared out-of-state competition, have sought to block efforts to deregulate interstate banking. In recent years the tide of events has turned against these opponents. As we discuss below, interstate banking is becoming a reality.

The Current Status of Interstate Banking

There are more than 50,000 branches operated in the United States by FDIC-insured depository financial institutions. Prior to 1996 only about 50 of these were interstate branches, and they existed only as a result of specific historical exceptions to the general prohibitions on interstate banking discussed in Chapter 8. A few had existed before the passage of laws restricting interstate branching arrangements. Others serve military installations and receive special exemptions as a result. Regulators permitted several interstate branches to simplify the merger of failing depository institutions with other, healthier institutions located in different states.

Presidents have sought since the 1970s to convince Congress to alter this situation. The Carter, Reagan, Bush, and Clinton administrations successively pushed Congress to give depository institutions greater flexibility to branch across state lines. It finally appears that their efforts may yield significant changes in the late 1990s.

The Forces of Change   There are several reasons why Congress has felt pressure to permit interstate banking. Some states have sought to allow interstate banking in the belief that it would lead to capital inflows for their states. In addition, people who live in metropolitan areas that straddle two or more states have argued that they would benefit from the greater flexibility that interstate branching would allow.

Furthermore, past opposition by many bankers has given way in recent years to a general recognition that many depository institutions could gain from the removal of restrictions on interstate branching. As discussed in Chapter 8, there are two key reasons why depository institutions might desire to open branches across state lines. One is that such branches might permit depository institutions to expand into markets that are at least as attractive as those within the states in which they are based. Another is that depository institutions might be able to reduce risks through geographic diversification.

In recent years supporting arguments have favored interstate branching. Many depository institutions in cities adjacent to state lines found that a number of their customers were moving to suburban areas located in the adjoining state, and so restrictions on interstate banking effectively caused them to lose business. Likewise, as the baby boom generation born in the decade or so after World War II begins to retire and move to new locations, a number of depository institutions envision losing even more customers of long-standing to institutions in other states. Furthermore, many depository institution owners recognized that the market value of their ownership shares likely would increase if depository institutions from other states seeking to purchase their institutions for conversion into branch offices could compete with in-state bids.

But perhaps the most telling argument in favor of having Congress change the rules of the game is that technological change is making the old restrictions on interstate banking increasingly obsolete. Throughout the 1980s and 1990s there has been a proliferation in the number of loan production offices that marketed loans in one state but "officially" granted the loans from another. Large banks and nonbank corporations successfully have marketed credit cards and automated teller machine networks nationwide. Likewise, mutual funds succeeded in collecting funds from customers all across the country. In the face of such sweeping changes, depository institutions whose deposit and lending businesses otherwise were tied to a single state began to look like nonadaptable dinosaurs. And many of their owners and managers began to fear that they might eventually go the way of the dinosaurs.

Legal Considerations   Standing in the way of interstate banking are two pieces of legislation left over from the early part of the twentieth century. The 1927 McFadden Act left it to the states to determine whether national banks could branch across state lines. The 1933 Glass-Steagall Act further toughened this restriction, effectively making interstate branching illegal unless states voluntarily opened themselves to branching by banks based in other states. This meant that all fifty states would have to coordinate legislation to make full interstate banking feasible throughout the nation.

It took several decades, but by the 1990s the states had made significant progress. All states except Hawaii did this largely by permitting multibank holding company mergers across state lines. (Hawaii is the only state that never enacted bank holding company legislation.) Initially, many states required *reciprocity* from other states. For instance, Missouri agreed to let a bank based in Illinois to acquire a Missouri-based bank only if Illinois would allow Missouri banks to acquire Illinois banks. By the mid-1990s roughly half of the states had worked out such reciprocity arrangements with other states. Several of the remaining states permitted multibank holding company acquisitions under an open invitation for reciprocity from any other state. A number have no reciprocity requirement. Consequently, as the nation entered the final decade of the twentieth century, interstate banking arrangements displayed a crazy-quilt design that stemmed from laws enacted several decades before.

Passage of the *Interstate Banking Act of 1994* promises to initiate a change in this situation after the middle of 1997. Under this legislation, a bank holding company will be able to own a depository institution anywhere in the United States. Furthermore, the legislation will allow holding companies to consolidate into a single, multistate bank, thereby saving the holding companies the expense of setting up legally distinct institutions with separate boards of directors and officers. Although Congress undoubtedly will revisit the 1994 legislation in future years, the law essentially has legalized interstate banking as the year 2000 approaches.

1

Has interstate banking become a reality?   In many respects widespread interstate acquisitions by multibank holding companies under state laws has already made interstate banking a reality. Nevertheless, legislation that goes into effect in 1997 will make interstate branching much easier, paving the way toward full interstate banking arrangements.

Consolidation of Depository Institutions

Many commentators have hailed the 1994 legislation as a precursor to truly sweeping changes in the structure of American banking arrangements. Several observers have predicted that within a few years the number of commercial banks would fall from about 9,500 today to fewer than 4,000 or 5,000. They also have predicted that large depository institutions would become even larger as they swallowed up smaller banking organizations around the country, thereby consolidating existing banking operations among fewer institutions.

There is some evidence to support these predictions. Among states that have opened their borders to interstate acquisitions of banking offices, the shares of deposits held by out-of-state depository institutions have increased considerably in recent years. By the mid-1990s, citizens of the "average" state who owned deposits at commercial banks held one-fourth of their deposits in depository institutions based in states outside their own. In extreme cases, such as Arizona, Washington, and Nevada, residents with commercial bank deposits held over 80 percent of their deposits with banks whose headquarters were in other states.

MANAGEMENT NOTEBOOK
Does It Pay to Open More Branches?

The banking industry is indeed in transition. The management of each financial institution faces the question of whether to open more branches to increase its visibility in any particular community. When there is a choice between one large centralized office versus a small central office and numerous branches, the financial institution must ask itself whether there are economies of scale.

Researchers have studied this question in the savings and loan industry. At the end of the 1980s, they discovered that economies of scale seemed to occur when a branch grew to around $50 million in deposits. Cost savings of between 10 and 25 percent could be realized compared with two branches with about $25 million each in deposits. Above $50 million, further economies of scale cease to exist.

In the 1990s banks have been seeking to eliminate smaller branches whenever possible because ATMs and phone banking are making branches extremely cost *in*effective. Consequently, a number of financial institutions have closed thousands of branches since 1990.

For example, in the three-year period from 1990 to the beginning of 1993, over 4,000 existing bank and thrift branches were closed. When Bank of America acquired Security Pacific Corporation, it trimmed almost 575 branches and planned to close more. Although the net number of bank branches increased steadily until the early 1990s because some banks opened new branches in previously unserved locations, one industry study predicted that by the end of this decade, previously existing branches will be gone.

Today, the optimal branch has at least $40 million in deposits. Nonetheless, there is a new phenomenon called *mini branches*, particularly in retirement communities. These are designed to serve senior citizens who prefer "going to the bank," rather than using an ATM or phone services. Mini branches offer a secure environment for senior citizens.

For Critical Analysis: *What effect will interactive cable-phone banking have on the number of financial institution branches?*

Furthermore, the largest banks really have been getting bigger. Before 1960, the largest 50 banks in the United States issued fewer than 40 percent of all bank deposits, and the largest 100 banks issued less than half of all deposits. Today, the largest *50 banks* issue more than half of all deposits. The largest 100 banks now account for two-thirds of all deposits at commercial banks.

Nevertheless, there are good reasons to question just how dramatic banking consolidation will be as interstate banking restrictions wither away. One point that is easy to overlook is just how effectively depository institutions already have sidestepped the McFadden Act and Glass-Steagall Act by using bank-holding-company arrangements. Furthermore, as discussed in Chapter 7, banks will get bigger and bigger only if there are unlimited economies of scale, with larger banks experiencing lower average operating expenses. Yet most studies have indicated that economies of scale are not particularly significant in banking. Certainly, the absolute number of depository institutions will decline dramatically in the coming years. Much of this decline, however, will occur simply because multibank holding companies will be able to consolidate all the separate institutions they have been required by law to incorporate. How much further these holding companies will expand acquisition of existing depository institutions remains to be seen.

Evaluating the Effects of Interstate Banking

The advent of unbridled interstate branching raises a number of questions. For instance, will interstate banking make depository institutions more cost efficient? To the extent that depository institutions consolidate their operations, how might market rivalry and performance be affected? How will the consumers of depository institution services fare under interstate banking arrangements? Let's attempt to answer each of these questions.

Cost Efficiencies from Interstate Mergers
Recall from Chapter 7 that one perspective on depository institution market structure and its implications is offered by *efficient-structure theory*. This theory indicates that the consolidation of banking resources that may result from interstate banking could generate more cost efficiency. If true, this might be a significant benefit from interstate banking arrangements.

As discussed in Chapter 7 and as we noted above, however, the efficient-structure theory's reliance on economies of scale as the source of cost savings from mergers is not supported by real-world data. In recent years most proponents of the efficient-structure theory—and, indeed, depository institution owners and managers themselves—have contended that the main cost savings from mergers are from greater managerial efficiency. According to this argument, interstate consolidations of depository institutions cut the size of administrative bureaucracies by eliminating duplicative layers of management.

Recent studies by Aruna Srinivasan of the Federal Reserve Bank of Atlanta, both alone and with Larry Wall of the same bank, cast doubt on how big such cost savings are likely to be. In their joint work, Srinivasan and Wall looked at data from bank mergers between 1982 and 1986. They found little evidence that such mergers significantly reduced expenses. In her separate study, Srinivasan found some evidence that the larger banks created by mergers were able to reduce total staff salaries by eliminating redundant management and staff positions, as predicted by efficient-structure theorists. But she also found that these savings typically were offset by increased expenses for other aspects of the banks' operations, such as information systems and marketing.

Such studies, of course, emphasize aggregate data for a number of banks. As Srinivasan and Wall emphasize, some mergers among depository institutions can yield significant savings. Their point, which has been mirrored in other studies, is simply that, on average, the efficiency gains from mergers may not be very large.

Of course, to get around interstate banking restrictions, multi-bank holding companies have had to incur significant expenses to set up organizational structures that meet the requirements of various state laws. Under interstate banking many of these artificial structures will not be needed. This means that a movement toward interstate banking must save on some expenses. What is unclear at present is exactly how great such savings will be.

Concentration and Performance   Issues that directly concern the customers of depository institutions are the prices they pay for services, the interest rates they pay on loans, and the yields they receive on deposits. As we discussed in Chapter 7, a theory that competes with the efficient-structure theory is the traditional *structure-conduct-performance (SCP) model* of depository institution markets. This model predicts that more heavily concentrated market structures lead to higher loan interest rates and lower deposit rates. The SCP model also indicates that customers of depository institutions in heavily concentrated markets usually pay higher fees for the services provided by these institutions.

As you also learned in Chapter 7, recent studies have provided very limited real-world support for the SCP model's prediction that greater loan and deposit market concentration lead to higher depository institution profits. Research during the past decade by Allen Berger and Timothy Hannan, also of the Federal Reserve Board staff, has indicated that the SCP model's prediction about the effects of concentration on interest rates and fees may be more relevant. The reduced rivalry among institutions caused by increased concentration of institutions in loan and deposit markets apparently does give those institutions greater monopoly power, leading to higher loan rates and fees and lower deposit rates.

As discussed above, the largest depository institutions have become larger, and the advent of interstate banking promises to increase the trend toward more consolidation of banking resources. Does this mean that consumers will have to pay more for loans and services while receiving less on deposits because of interstate banking?

Defining Depository Institution Markets   To answer this question, the first thing to recognize is that what matters to an individual consumer—such as you—is not whether or not the top 50 or the top 100 banks are getting larger, or even smaller. The SCP model indicates that a key factor affecting the market interest rate that you might have to pay on an auto loan in your location, or perhaps the market interest rate that you might receive on NOW accounts at depository institutions in your area, is the extent of loan and deposit market concentration in your *local market*. Indeed, when depository institution regulators and the federal antitrust authorities review plans for mergers among institutions, they consider the effects that such mergers might have on local rivalry.

Unfortunately, there is no good way to define geographic loan and deposit markets for purposes of measuring the extent of market rivalry. Depository institution regulators define such markets on a case-by-case basis when institutions apply for permission to merge. Most economists approximate local banking markets in towns and cities by using *metropolitan statistical areas*, as defined by the government for census purposes. For rural areas economists typically assume that *non-metropolitan counties* are the relevant geographic markets.

Interestingly, despite the fact that large banks have generally become bigger on a national basis, at these local levels the degree of concentration of banking resources has varied extremely little during the past 20 years. For instance, in 1976 in a typical U.S. metropolitan statistical area, a little over 68 percent of deposits were issued by the three largest banking organizations. At present just under 67 percent of deposits are issued by the three largest depository institutions in a typical metropolitan statistical area. In nonmetropolitan counties the extent of concentration was much higher in 1976, with the three largest depository institutions in a typical nonmetropolitan county issuing about 90 percent of the deposits. At present this figure hovers around 89 percent.

It is not apparent from these figures that changes in interstate—or intrastate—competition have done much to influence the extent of depository institution rivalry in local banking markets. Most economists interpret this evidence as an indication that interstate banking is likely to have little effect on consumer interest rates and fees. For whatever reason, these and other changes in banking arrangements during past years do not seem to have much effect on local market conditions. It may be that there is some natural level of rivalry that loan and deposit markets can support at local levels.

Customer Service   If such a natural extent of market rivalry exists, surely one reason is that size does not necessarily determine success in certain depository institution markets. For example, consider the market for commercial and industrial (C & I) loans to small businesses by commercial banks. Banks with over $30 billion in assets extend less than 5 percent of such loans. In contrast, nearly 50 percent of small-business C & I loans originate from banks with less than $1 billion in assets. In the market for small-business loans, being smaller seems to pay off.

One commonly expressed concern about the advent of interstate banking is the fear that it may reduce the number of smaller, local depository institutions that stand ready to lend to small businesses and

GLOBAL NOTEBOOK
Megamergers Around the World

There is clearly a global trend toward bank mergers throughout the world. From January 1, 1988 through the beginning of 1996, there were almost 650 cross-border banking mergers, valued at over $35 billion, according to KPMG International in Amsterdam. Of course, many of those were in the United States. They included Chemical Banking's merger with Manufacturer's Hanover, NCNB with C&S/Sovran, and Bank America with Security Pacific. The two largest banks in Japan recently merged to form the largest bank in the world. A few years ago the two largest banks in Denmark, Den Danske and Copenhagen Handelsdank, merged. The two largest banks in Spain merged into one. The Hong Kong & Shanghai Bank merged with Britain's Midland Bank. Crédit Swiss acquired Swiss Volksbank. In other countries such as Italy the large banks are simply acquiring all the small banks.

What is causing this mergermania? Some argue that it is because of excess capacity in the banking industry. Others point out that, at least in Japan, mergers are occurring to avoid bankruptcy for troubled banks.

How far will it go? Consider that in the United States there are 45 commercial banks for every one million citizens, whereas in Britain that figure is nine banks per million and in Germany it is four. In Japan there is one bank for every million citizens. Consequently, at least in the United States, mergermania may continue for quite some time.

For Critical Analysis: *What are the costs and benefits of eliminating more and more banking institutions via merger?*

households. In 1980 there were over 9,500 independent community banks that specialized in providing financial services to these clienteles. Today there are just over 2,500. Future interstate banking consolidation promises to reduce this number further. Does this mean the end of the personal touch in lending to small businesses and individual consumers?

It depends. If there are economies of scale, then medium-sized regional banks could have a slight efficiency advantage over smaller community banks in processing small-business loans. As a result, larger regional banks may be able to charge slightly lower loan rates and slightly smaller loan fees. But if small-business borrowers are willing to pay slight premiums for more personalized services, then smaller local banks will still have a competitive niche.

Furthermore, many smaller banks are keeping up with technology and developing new approaches to controlling costs. Those small banks that can maintain efficiency levels almost certainly will remain viable competitors to larger institutions. At the same time, larger regional banks have found that if they do not provide high-quality, personalized services to small businesses, they usually lose customers to the smaller banks that will provide such services. At present, there appears to be room for depository institutions of many sizes, and institutions of all sizes stand ready to provide high-quality services as long as customers are willing to pay for them.

2

What are the likely effects of interstate banking?   Interstate banking likely will lead to a fairly sharp reduction in the number of depository institutions in the United States as multibank holdings companies streamline their operations and as large regional banks acquire more small banks. This may enable some banks to become more cost efficient, although cost savings may not be dramatic. Some local markets may become more concentrated, but others may become less so than they are today. Customer service may become less personalized as regional banks become more dominant, but providing a personal touch may be a feature that helps small community banks compete for customers.

BANKING AND OTHER LINES OF COMMERCE

The American separation of banking from investment banking, insurance, and other lines of commerce stems from its original ties to Britain. In 1694 the British Parliament established the Bank of England, and a key provision of the act was a prohibition on the Bank's ability to sell merchandise. Members of Parliament feared that the Bank of England would use its financial resources to compete with other businesses.

As we discuss below, similar concerns underlie the traditional separation of banking and other forms of commerce in the United States. Nevertheless, during the latter part of this century there has been a steady lowering of the walls separating banking from commerce.

The Pros and Cons of Universal Banking

As we discussed in Chapter 8, a key provision of the 1933 Glass-Steagall Act outlawed commercial banks from underwriting corporate stock. Until recent Congressional and court decisions relaxed this provision somewhat, commercial banking was separate from investment banking. The act also kept American depository institutions from holding ownership shares in corporations.

In countries such as Germany, the Netherlands, and the United Kingdom, however, banks presently face no such restrictions. These and other European nations permit **universal banking,** under which there are few if any limits on the ability of banks to offer a full range of financial services and to own equity shares in corporations. In Japan banks face greater restrictions on their activities, but many Japanese banks have the authority to underwrite stocks and bonds.

universal banking Banking environment under which depository institutions face few if any restrictions on their authority to offer full ranges of financial services and to own equity shares in corporations.

Why has the United States chosen to prohibit universal banking, even though other nations have experienced success with limited or unlimited universal banking arrangements? What might be gained by eliminating existing restrictions on American depository institutions? These are exactly the questions that have occupied the United States Congress in recent years as it has reconsidered the provisions of the Glass-Steagall Act.

3

What is universal banking?   Universal banking is the ability of depository institutions to offer a virtually unlimited set of financial services.

The Arguments Against Universal Banking   As we discussed in Chapter 8, a key rationale for prohibiting universal banking is that equity shares tend to be riskier financial instruments than U.S. government securities and municipal bonds. By taking on greater risk, commercial banks and other depository institutions could increase their likelihood of failure. This also would threaten federal deposit insurance with potential losses.

Another argument against permitting universal banking is the possibility of conflicts of interest. Suppose that a bank were granted universal banking powers and responded by purchasing a significant equity stake in a new microcomputer company. It would be in the bank's best interest for that company's share price to remain high, which could give the bank an incentive to induce its other customers to purchase the company's shares. The bank also might purchase shares in the company for inclusion in portfolios it manages on behalf of clients. Because the bank would have a stake in the microcomputer company's success, it might engage in these activities even if they were not in its customers' best interests. It also might be less willing to grant a loan to a competitive microcomputer manufacturer, even if it were a highly creditworthy company.

A final justification commonly offered for prohibiting universal banking has been a concern about too much centralization of financial resources. Critics of universal banking raise the specter of a few large banks owning significant shares of common stock in American corporations. This would give those banks voting rights in those companies. As a result, individuals controlling the resources of the large banks would be making decisions about the priorities of nonfinancial firms as well. This might concentrate considerable power in the hands of a few people.

Arguments Favoring Universal Banking   Some who favor universal banking contend that even though equity shares typically are riskier financial instruments than government and municipal securities, it is possible that holding equity shares could bring about overall risk *reductions* at depository institutions. How can this be possible? The answer is that it can be easier to diversify—to avoid holding too many eggs in one basket—if depository institution managers can hold a broader mix of financial instruments. Even if the yields on equity shares are more volatile, if some equity yields rise during periods in which many bond yields or returns on loans are declining, then a depository institution's overall risk of failure could be reduced by holding equity shares.

Another possible advantage of allowing depository institutions to hold ownership shares in companies is that this would entitle them to receive **insider information.** This is information known by inside directors and officers of the companies but not generally available to the general public or, under current arrangements, to depository institutions that lend to the companies. Having access to such information would make it easier to monitor these businesses, thereby reducing the institutions' operating costs. In addition, having more information about companies' prospects could make it less likely that depository institutions would seek to force them into bankruptcy if the companies experienced short-term liquidity problems. Because this would reduce market expectations of corporate bankruptcies, corporations could end up paying lower risk premiums on their debt instruments.

insider information   Information that is available to inside directors and officers of a corporation but that generally is unavailable to the general public or to depository institutions that lend to the corporation.

4

What are the pros and cons of universal banking?   Key arguments favoring universal banking are that permitting depository institutions to underwrite or hold business equity shares would allow them to diversify risk, to better evaluate the creditworthiness of businesses in which they own shares, and to be less likely to close such businesses when they face liquidity problems. Arguments against universal banking emphasize the greater volatility of equity share values and the risks that this volatility poses, the potential for conflicts of interest, and the possibility of excessive concentration of financial resources.

Current Prospects for Universal Banking   Throughout the 1980s and much of the 1990s, Congressional committees would approve measures aimed at ending or at least relaxing many of the Glass-Steagall restrictions prohibiting universal banking. Yet when such measures came before the full Congress, they typically were tabled or voted down.

While there is certainly a possibility that this pattern may continue, there have been strong indications that Congressional views on universal banking may have shifted in the 1990s. This does not necessarily mean that approval of full universal banking is around the corner. For instance, efforts to permit banks to sell insurance were met with massive lobbying efforts by independent insurance salespeople. Congress dropped that idea like a hot potato in 1995. Nevertheless, Congress increasingly seems willing to pass provisions relaxing Glass-Steagall restrictions on commercial banks' investment banking activities, thereby permitting commercial banks to underwrite and deal in corporate bonds and equities.

A key issue that Congress must address is how to implement such a change. One approach calls for banks to set up separate investment banking units that would operate independently of the banks themselves, thereby segmenting the balance sheets of the commercial banking and investment banking portions of the company. The idea behind this approach is that the commercial banking component of the company would be better insulated from any excess risks arising from equity holdings. The alternative approach would be to allow commercial banks to operate as investment banks with no artificial separations of their balance sheets.

Should Nonfinancial Businesses Own Depository Institutions?

If Congress were to permit depository institutions to own shares in other companies, fairness would seem to dictate reciprocity. That is, why shouldn't nonfinancial businesses be permitted to own depository institutions? This is yet another issue that relaxing the Glass-Steagall provisions raises for Congress to consider.

The Potential Problems
The most obvious potential problem with businesses owning depository institutions is that some businesses might pressure the banks they own to extend credit to them. If the businesses need the additional credit because they are taking on too many risks, then this would increase the possibility of insolvency of the depository institutions they own. Depositors and other creditors of the depository institutions then would suffer. So would taxpayers, given the existence of federal deposit insurance.

A related problem is that the ownership of depository institutions by commercial firms could further expose depository institutions to the ill effects of economic downturns. Consider, for instance, what could happen if auto manufacturers owned large banks and a sharp recession hit. Such a recession usually causes immediate reductions in sales of new cars. It also is not uncommon for the share prices of automakers to plummet and for their debt issues to be downgraded. If automakers also owned banks, then a particularly sharp recession could cause the public to lose confidence in those banks when the fortunes of their owners sour. The result could be runs on the banks. At a minimum, they would experience liquidity problems.

Finally, the lines of authority of banking regulators and the Federal Reserve System potentially would be broadened by bank ownership by commercial firms. If a nonfinancial company owns a bank, then it would be a bank holding company subject to Federal Reserve oversight. This could lead to the Federal Reserve examining the books of companies such as General Motors or IBM.

The Possible Gains One reason why some have proposed permitting commercial firms to own depository institutions is that this would enable the institutions to more easily raise equity funds. One result of the risk-based capital requirements that regulators imposed in the late 1980s was that many banks were strapped for capital in the 1990s. If nonfinancial firms got into the banking business, they could help recapitalize the depository institution industry.

A related justification for letting companies own depository institutions is that the injection of additional resources into depository institutions might help make American banking more competitive on the international scene. Today the ten largest banks in the world are based in Japan and Europe, as can be seen in Table 9.1.

Finally, it is possible that depository institution customers would gain if commercial firms were allowed to own banks. For instance, if companies such as Wal-Mart or Sears owned banks, then their customers could do one-stop shopping for clothing, hardware, and bank loans.

It will be difficult for Congress to authorize full universal banking without permitting commercial firms to get into the banking business. Consequently, these arguments for and against letting businesses own banks are likely to receive considerable attention as Congress debates the merits of removing the traditional separation between banking and commerce in the United States.

TABLE 9.1 The World's Largest Banks

Bank	Country	Assets ($ billions)
Tokyo Mitsubishi Bank	Japan	819
Sanwa Bank	Japan	582
Dai-Ichi Kangyo Bank	Japan	582
Fuji Bank	Japan	571
Sumitomo Bank	Japan	566
Sakura Bank	Japan	560
Deutsche Bank	Germany	503
Industrial Bank of Japan	Japan	433
Norinchukin Bank	Japan	429
Long-Term Credit Bank	Japan	372

Source: The Economist, April 27–May 3, 1996.

REGULATING OFF-BALANCE-SHEET BANKING

One of the most important modern developments at depository institutions has been their growing reliance on off-balance-sheet activities as a source of income or as a means of reducing risk. As we discussed in Chapter 7, the considerable growth in these activities has complicated assessment of depository institution performance. It also has prompted regulators to reconsider many of the long-standing approaches they previously had taken toward examining and supervising depository institutions.

Securitization and Loan Commitments

Two of the key off-balance-sheet activities of depository institutions are *securitization* and *loan commitments*. As we discussed in Chapter 7, securitization is the pooling of loans into groups that share similar risk characteristics and maturities. These pooled loans are repackaged and sold as asset-backed securities. A **loan commitment** is a depository institution's promise to make a loan up to some specified limit at a contracted interest rate and within a given interval.

loan commitment A lending arrangement in which a depository institution promises to extend credit up to some predetermined limit, at a contracted interest rate, and within a given period of time.

Neither of these activities appears on a depository institution's balance sheet. When an institution securitizes a loan, by definition, it has sold the loan and removed it from its asset portfolio. Likewise, a loan commitment is not a loan until the depository institution must honor the commitment. Nevertheless, these off-balance-sheet activities yield income to depository institutions. They also can complicate the tasks that regulators face. In the case of securitization, there are also some benefits for regulators.

Securitization and "Marking to Market" Securitization has made it feasible for depository institutions to earn fee income for originating, servicing, and insuring loans that are sold to others. Depository institutions issue two basic kinds of asset-backed securities. One type, illustrated in Figure 9.1, is a *pass-through security*. When a depository institution issues this type of asset-backed security, it passes the interest and principal payments it receives from borrowers through to the holders of the securities on a proportionate basis. For example, holders of a specific asset-backed security collateralized by a depository institution's holdings of credit card debts might receive 80 percent of the interest and principal payments paid by credit card customers to the depository institution. To compensate the depository institution for the service it provides in monitoring the underlying pool of loans and making payments to the holders of the pass-through securities, these holders pay fees to the depository institution.

Another type of asset-backed security that depository institutions issue is called a *pay-through security*. Under this type of securitization

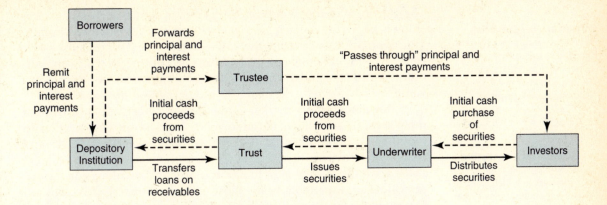

FIGURE 9.1   Asset Securitization via a Pass-Through Arrangement

A depository institution receives interest and principal from borrowers in payment of loans it has originated. It then issues securities backed by these loans, through a trust department and an underwriter, to investors who purchase the securities. The interest and principal payments from the loans are forwarded to a trustee, who passes through to the investors who hold the securities a portion of the payments received from the borrowers as interest payments on the asset-backed securities. *Source:* Thomas Boemio and Gerald Edwards, Jr., "Asset Securitization: A Supervisory Perspective," *Federal Reserve Bulletin* (1989).

arrangement, the interest and principal payments from an underlying pool of loans are held by the depository institution, which reallocates them into two or more separate sets of securities with different payment and maturity structures. The *collateralized mortgage obligation (CMO)* discussed in Chapter 4 is a type of pay-through security. Under the pay-through arrangement for a CMO, principal and interest payments from the underlying pool of loans at the depository institution go first to holders of the CMOs with the earliest maturity dates. Once those payments are "paid through," holders of later-maturing CMOs receive their payments from the depository institution, and so on. Holders of CMOs pay fees to depository institutions for handling the paperwork associated with this arrangement.

Securitization benefits depository institutions by shifting the default risk and interest rate risk of their loans to the holders of the securities. It also generates a stable source of fee income for the institutions. For this reason, depository institution regulators generally have raised few concerns about securitization.

In fact, a key advantage for regulators is that securitization gives them up-to-date information on market values of many types of bank loans. Regulators can determine the market prices of the loans that depository institutions recently have sold in secondary markets. They then can use these prices as indicators of the market values of similar loans that depository institutions do *not* choose to sell in secondary markets.

market value accounting
An accounting procedure in which a depository institution (or its regulator) values its assets in terms of approximate market prices at which those assets would currently sell in secondary markets.

historical value accounting
A traditional accounting procedure in which a depository institution's assets are valued at original values.

The practice of valuing a depository institution's assets at current market value is known as *marking loans to market,* or **market value accounting.** This approach to measuring the value of depository institutions' assets contrasts with traditional **historical value accounting,** in which an institution records the initial value of a loan or security and then carries this value on its books until the loan is repaid or the security is redeemed.

Regulators prefer market value accounting because it provides a more accurate assessment of the solvency of a depository institution. In recent years a number of proposals have suggested that the FDIC and other regulators require depository institutions to switch to market value accounting, or at least to report market values alongside historical values on a periodic basis. Most of these proposals have not advanced in the face of opposition from depository institutions, which argue that market value accounting would be prohibitively expensive to maintain. Typically the institutions also argue that market values fluctuate so much that they provide misleading information about the long-term values of assets. Nevertheless, regulators have continued to use prices of securitized assets as important information for assessing the solvency of the institutions they examine and supervise.

Loan Commitments and Risk   As Figure 9.2 shows, commitment lending has grown significantly since the 1970s. During that decade, loans made under commitment accounted for only about 20 percent of total bank loans. Today over two-thirds of loans that banks extend are commitment loans.

The way a typical loan commitment works is this. A bank and a prospective borrower agree to terms of the commitment, which specify a limit on how much credit the borrower can get from the bank (the borrower's line of credit), what the loan interest rate will be or how it will be determined, and the fee that the borrower must pay for any unused portion of the line of credit. This arrangement yields benefits for both the bank and the borrower. The borrower has a guarantee of credit at a given interest rate whenever it is needed within the specified period. The bank receives interest income on the portion of the credit line that is drawn upon by the borrower, and it received noninterest fee income on the unused portion.

revolving credit commitments   Loan commitments that permit borrowers to borrow and repay as often as they wish within the period for which the commitment is binding on a depository institution.

confirmed credit lines   Depository institution commitments to provide an individual or a business with a fixed amount of credit, upon demand, within some short-term interval.

Under a *fixed-rate loan commitment,* the interest rate on any credit that a depository institution extends is set at a predetermined level. In contrast, a *floating-rate loan commitment* ties the loan rate to another market interest rate, such as the prime loan rate or London Interbank Offer Rate discussed in Chapter 3. Most loan commitments of either type are **revolving credit commitments.** These allow borrowers to borrow and repay as desired, very much like revolving credit agreements for charge cards. Other loan commitments are **confirmed credit lines,** which normally are agreements for a bank to provide a fixed amount of credit upon demand within some short-term interval.

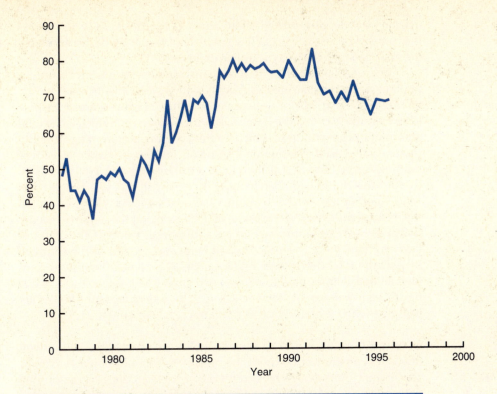

FIGURE 9.2   Growth in the Share of Commitment Lending
This chart shows the portion of total commercial and industrial loans with maturities of less than one year that commercial banks made under commitment. The loan commitment share of bank lending increased considerably during the 1980s but has leveled off in recent years. *Source:* Board of Governors of the Federal Reserve System, *Federal Reserve Bulletin,* various issues.

The growth of loan commitments has raised two concerns for bank regulators. One is that banks might overextend themselves by making too many commitments, thereby creating liquidity problems. A related concern is that banks might extend commitment loans to overly risky borrowers, thereby placing themselves at risk. So far commitment lending does not appear to have caused many difficulties of this type. Nevertheless, the inclusion of loan commitments in the computation of risk-adjusted assets in capital ratio calculations reflects regulators' concerns about such risks.

Derivatives

Recall from Chapter 4 that derivatives are financial instruments whose returns are derived from the yields on other securities. Examples of derivatives include forward, futures, option, and swap contracts. As discussed in Chapter 7, depository institutions have made greater use of derivatives instruments in recent years. A few have tried to establish derivatives trading and management as a major line of business.

Because the values of derivative instruments stem from the values of other assets, measuring the growth of depository institutions' participation in the markets for derivatives is a difficult proposition. One possible measure is called the *notional value* of derivatives, which is the total amount of principal upon which interest payments stemming from derivatives are based. The notional value of commercial bank derivatives holdings grew from $1.4 trillion to $8.6 trillion between 1986 and 1992. By 1996 this figure had risen to more than $15 trillion.

Another measure of bank involvement with derivatives is called the *replacement-cost credit exposure,* which is the cost that a party to a derivatives contract would face at current market prices if the counterparty to the contract were to default before settlement of the contract. In 1992 the total derivatives replacement-cost credit exposure of commercial banks amounted to about 5 percent of their assets. By 1996 this figure had risen to 14 percent. Clearly, by either measure banks are heavily involved in derivatives operations.

Credit Risks of Derivatives   By holding and trading derivatives, depository institutions expose themselves to three basic types of risk. The first includes **derivatives credit risks.** These are the risks associated with potential default by a contract counterparty, or of an unexpected change in credit exposure resulting from changes in the market prices of the underlying instruments on which derivative yields depend.

Part of the business of banking is identifying default risks, and so this aspect of derivatives is not especially new to bankers. What *is* different about derivatives for bankers, however, is the task of evaluating credit risk exposures that can arise simply because the values of derivatives fluctuate with changing asset prices.

Market Risks of Derivatives   Holding or trading derivatives also exposes depository institutions to **derivatives market risks,** which are the risks of potential losses resulting from market liquidity reductions, of payments-system breakdowns or unusual price changes at the time of settlement, or of spillover effects across markets. Sometimes, the total amount of liquidity available to derivatives traders can become squeezed because of events such as a sharp stock market decline or unexpected exchange rate changes. This can make it difficult for depository institutions to adjust their derivatives positions quickly, thereby exposing them to risk of loss.

Sometimes payments-system failures can slow derivatives settlement. For instance, if a bank decides to execute an option at a favorable price, it may try to do so but find that a critical computer link is temporarily "down." This can cost the bank money. Likewise, the price of

---

derivatives credit risks
Risks arising from the potential default by a counterparty in a derivative contract, or from unexpected changes in credit exposure because of changes in yields of instruments on which derivative yields depend.

derivatives market risks
Risks arising from variations in aggregate derivatives market liquidity, payments-system breakdowns, abnormal price changes at the time of settlement, or of spillovers across markets.

an underlying asset in a derivatives transaction can fluctuate unexpectedly at the last moment before settlement.

Market spillovers can arise if problems in one market affect derivative values adversely. For instance, stock index futures trading can be affected by breakdowns in trading mechanisms in the stock market. Indeed, this occurred during the 1987 stock market crash. As stock prices plummeted, so many traders tried simultaneously to sell off shares that market trading systems became overloaded. This delayed settlement on many stock index futures contracts and severely affected the liquidity positions of many stock index traders.

Operating Risks of Derivatives   Depository institutions face **derivatives operating risks,** or risks of unwise management of derivatives, because these instruments still are so new to many depository institution managers. There have been instances in which managers incorrectly valued derivatives and were horrified to learn of their errors only at settlement. Institutions such as Barings Bank, which failed in 1995, and Bankers Trust, which faced several lawsuits, ran into problems because of inadequate internal controls on employees who traded derivatives on behalf of the institutions or their customers. Employees made poor decisions that were not overseen properly by higher management.

Depository institutions continue to face legal risks in their derivatives operations. Because derivatives are fairly new to judges and juries, many of the details of legal responsibilities of parties to derivatives transactions still have not been worked out. Consequently, there is always a danger that institutions may find out after the fact that they have assumed greater risks under the law than they had expected.

Regulatory Responses to Derivatives   Regulators have viewed the growth of derivatives trading by depository institutions as a positive development in some respects, but as a real area of concern in other respects. On the one hand, derivatives permit depository institutions to hedge against a variety of interest rate and currency risks. In this regard, regulators have even promoted the use of derivatives by depository institutions.

On the other hand, a number of depository institutions have faltered in maintaining adequate internal controls over their derivatives operations and in developing appropriate techniques for valuing derivatives contracts. This, in turn, has complicated the task of examining and supervising depository institutions. Regulators now must be well-versed in valuation methods for derivatives, and they must double-check the adequacy of the management methods institutions adopt for their derivatives operations. Derivatives are fairly new to many bank examiners just as they are relatively new to bankers, and so regulators themselves have had a lot to learn.

derivatives operating risks
Risks arising from lack of adequate management controls or from managerial unfamiliarity with derivative instruments.

5

How has off-balance-sheet banking complicated the task of regulating depository institutions?   Although securitization generally exposes depository institutions to reduced risks and helps regulators evaluate market values of loans, more commitment lending has the potential to expose institutions to greater liquidity and solvency risks. Derivatives trading has its own unique risks, of which perhaps the most important is the risk of inadequate internal management controls.

CONSUMER PROTECTION REGULATIONS

Throughout history many leading Americans have mistrusted banks. Thomas Jefferson said that they were more dangerous than standing armies. After Andrew Jackson lost considerable personal wealth when banks foreclosed on loans after he suffered big losses on land speculation, he made bank-bashing a favorite political pastime. More recently, members of Congress have heeded the calls of constituents by passing legislation intended to protect them from possible misbehavior by managers of banks and other depository financial institutions.

There are bad people in all walks of life, just as there is a bad apple in every barrel. Surely there have been unscrupulous depository institution managers in the past, and some probably are sitting behind desks around the country as you read these words. Should the government attempt to protect us from such individuals? Can it?

Of these two questions, the first calls for an opinion. Whether or not the government *should* try to protect us from depository institutions, the fact is that political leaders presumably have acted upon the desires of many citizens by attempting to do so. The question of whether the government *can* protect citizens has the potential, at least, to be answered based on factual evidence. Certainly, if the government expends sufficient resources to enforce efforts to stop unsavory bankers from gouging consumers, such gouging ultimately will be greatly reduced.

Basic Consumer Protection Regulations

Congress has enacted several consumer protection laws that apply to depository institutions and that various governmental agencies seek to enforce. Before we discuss these, however, let's contemplate why such laws exist.

The Rationale for Protecting Consumers   Why can't people just protect themselves? After all, rarely has a lender forced a borrower to sign a loan contract. One key rationale for consumer protection laws and regulations relies on the problem of asymmetric information. Just

as a lender has trouble identifying a creditworthy and trustworthy borrower, a prospective borrower can struggle to find a dependable and honest lender. Indeed, a borrower faces both adverse selection and moral hazard problems. An adverse selection problem arises because unscrupulous lenders have the greatest incentive to disguise their credit terms to make them look more attractive compared with the honest terms quoted by more trustworthy lenders. A moral hazard problem arises because, after a lender grants credit, there is always the chance that the lender may attempt to reinterpret terms of the loan contract in ways that differ from interpretations offered by the lender before the borrower entered into the contract.

The Scope of Consumer Protection via Regulation   The *Consumer Credit Protection Act (CCPA) of 1968* is the foundation for much of the government's effort to protect consumers from costs they might otherwise incur because of problems of asymmetric information. This legislation requires that institutions provide every applicant for consumer credit with the specific dollar amount of finance charges and with annual percentage interest rates computed on the unpaid amount of the total quantity of a loan. Under the law, all institutions must make this information available so that consumers can make direct comparisons across institutions as they shop for credit. This provision of the CCPA attempts to reduce the extent of the adverse selection problem that consumers face in evaluating credit terms. The act also contains provisions that bind lenders to the terms they give consumers, thereby addressing the moral hazard problem.

A difficulty with the CCPA was that it did not anticipate the complications that would arise when adjustable-rate mortgages become popular in the 1970s. A provision of the Depository Institutions Deregulation and Monetary Control Act of 1980 amended the CCPA to account for variable-rate loans. It requires potential lenders to construct hypothetical fixed- and variable-rate examples to enable prospective borrowers to compare the amounts they would pay depending upon which type of loan they choose.

The CCPA applies to all financial institutions that extend credit. It also covers all loan applicants irrespective of race, ethnicity, or gender. In recent years, however, much interest in the consumer protection area has been placed on these applicant characteristics.

Banking Regulation and Race, Ethnicity, and Gender

Many anthropologists today question the meaning of the concept of race. Recent studies have indicated that there is more genetic variability among members of identifiable racial groups than exists across groups. This means that a white individual of Dutch ancestry easily could have more in common "under the skin" with a black individual from Zambia than with another white person of Dutch extraction. Of course, this means that past rationales offered by persons of certain skin colors for dominating or even enslaving individuals of other skin colors have never had any validity. It also means, however, that the issue of race is extremely complicated.

Whether or not scientists can agree on how to classify individuals by race, it remains the case that historically people have done this based upon subjective assessments of "looks." And there certainly is abundant evidence that such subjective assessments have led individuals of one racial group to treat persons of another group differently simply because of their assignment to that group. Likewise, there are documented historical examples of differing treatment of males and females, or of members of different ethnic or religious groups.

A major policy issue in recent years has been the extent to which such differential treatment may occur in the business activities of depository institutions. Congress has enacted laws addressing this issue. Furthermore, Congress has charged depository institution regulators with monitoring and enforcing these laws.

Redlining   One way that depository institutions allegedly have discriminated against specific groups is by refusing to provide loans to individuals or businesses located in specific geographic areas. Such a practice is **redlining,** which refers figuratively to situations in which depository institution managers might have outlined with red ink certain areas on maps as being ineligible for loans. Managers allegedly would instruct lending officers to deny loans to anyone located in such locales, or to applicants for mortgage or real estate loans intending to purchase property there.

redlining   A practice under which some depository institution managers allegedly have refused to lend to individuals or businesses located in particular geographic areas.

Note that redlining is not necessarily a form of racial, ethnic, or gender discrimination. It might be used to discriminate if redlined areas are predominantly occupied, say, by African American or Hispanic households or by female-owned businesses. Nevertheless, the basic allegation is that redlining, if it occurs, discriminates against individuals simply because of where they live or operate their businesses. In the case of mortgage redlining, the depository institutions that redline would discriminate against the owners of property within redlined regions, although those outside the area who wish to purchase property within the redlined area also would feel victimized by discrimination.

Discrimination Based on Race or Gender   For years a number of women and members of identifiable minority groups have contended that depository institutions have denied them loans based on factors unrelated to their creditworthiness. Although such accusations have arisen for some time, a flurry of concern arose in the early and mid-1990s when depository institution data indicated potentially rampant discrimination against African Americans and Hispanics. For instance, in the autumn of 1991 North Carolina National Bank (then NCNB, now renamed NationsBank), which was applying to the Federal Reserve for permission to acquire C&S/Sovran Corporation, released required information about its lending practices. Among the data that NCNB released were statistics on loan applications and denials. These data indicated that in 1990 NCNB had denied 41 percent of loan applications of African Americans and 37 percent of loan applications by those of Hispanic descent. Yet NCNB had denied only 18 percent of applications by those identified as white.

Later in 1991 the Federal Reserve released a study indicating that in recent years banks had rejected minorities for home mortgages two to four times more often than whites who had similar incomes. In the spring of 1992 the Office of the Comptroller of the Currency began to study the lending records of 266 banks it regulated because of large disparities between minority and white credit approvals. The Department of Housing and Urban Development began sending undercover agents to banks to test their willingness to lend to members of minority groups.

Antidiscrimination Laws   The uproar over the 1991–1992 lending data stemmed largely from the surprise that standing laws had not produced greater convergence in lending across groups. Depository institutions must meet requirements established by three key antidiscrimination laws. The first of these is the *Equal Credit Opportunity Act (ECOA) of 1975*. This legislation broadened some of the CCPA's provisions by outlawing retaliation by a lender against a borrower who insists upon rights granted by CCPA, by applying CCPA provisions to many business and commercial transactions, and by extending consumer lending protections in a variety of ways. But the novel feature of ECOA was its prohibition of lending discrimination on the basis of an applicant's race, color, religion, national origin, gender, age, or marital status.

Because of widespread allegations of mortgage redlining by some depository institutions, Congress also passed the *Home Mortgage Disclosure Act (HMDA)* in 1975. This legislation requires depository institutions to retain and report information about mortgage loan applications and lending decisions that they make. It also requires depository institution regulators to collect and analyze this information.

Then, in 1977, Congress passed the now-controversial *Community Reinvestment Act (CRA)*. CRA added considerably to the reporting requirements that HMDA had imposed on depository institutions. Among the basic paperwork that CRA created for each depository institution in the United States is the following:

1. A statement listing the types of loans the institution is willing to make.
2. Acceptable evidence that the institution's board of directors reviews this statement at least once each year.

POLICY NOTEBOOK

The Unintended Consequences of the Community Reinvestment Act

In an effort to build up the inner cities, Congress passed the Community Reinvestment Act of 1977. According to the terms of this act, federal agencies were to encourage banks and savings institutions to make extra efforts to solicit loans in older neighborhoods and to locate branches so that all sections of a city could be served effectively. It wasn't until the 1990s, though, that both Congress and several banking regulatory agencies (the Office of the Comptroller of the Currency and the Federal Reserve) started to really put pressure on our nation's banks to "do something" about lending in the inner cities.

For example, in 1992 Congress amended the 1977 act to provide that if any bank or savings institution donated, sold on unfavorable terms, or made available on a rent-free basis any branch of such institution in a predominately minority neighborhood to any minority or women's institution, the amount of such contribution or loss would be a factor in determining whether the institution was meeting the credit needs of the institution's community. Then, in 1994 several banking regulatory agencies published proposals to strengthen the Community Reinvestment Act. These proposals require banks to produce data on the race, sex, and marital status of the owners of businesses that request loans. Presumably the information is to be used by regulators to make sure the individual banks are making their quotas of loans to minority groups.

The unintended consequences of this legislation, and the increased regulation of banks in order to increase minority lending, has been that there are now fewer banks willing to undergo the scrutiny of bank regulators of banks daring to do business in low-income areas. Consider that the inner-city section called South Central Los Angeles has about as many residents as Washington, D.C. At most times there are fewer than 20 banks in the area. But there are more banks than that in a one-half mile stretch of downtown Washington, D.C.

For Critical Analysis: *What should the correct policy be to encourage equal opportunity banking?*

3. A map displaying boundaries of the communities in which the institution lends.
4. A visible notice to customers advising them of CRA.
5. A CRA file open for review by any member of the public who would like to read it.
6. Implementation of a "CRA planning process," supported by a full analysis of the geographic distributions of their major lines of business.
7. Collection of complete data concerning lending applications, acceptances, and denials.

8. Analysis of how these data relate to the characteristics of the populations within the areas that they lend.

Under CRA, depository institution regulators aim to achieve twelve separate objectives relating to redlining and other forms of lending discrimination. For instance, regulators are supposed to use the data that institutions report to evaluate each institution's record in lending to various groups within the populations that it serves. Furthermore, CRA requires that regulators examine institutions and provide them with ratings of their performances in meeting the credit needs of all groups. All the major regulators have attempted to coordinate their CRA rating schemes so that all institutions receive roughly similar CRA examinations.

Benefits and Drawbacks of Consumer Protection Regulations

Presumably, the consumer protection laws Congress has put in place would not exist if many citizens believed they were not beneficial. Nevertheless, any law can produce unexpected complications. Therefore, it is not surprising that consumer protection laws that apply to depository institutions have both benefits and costs for society.

Benefits of Consumer Protection Regulations
The most obvious benefit of consumer protection regulations is that they reduce the extent of potential adverse selection and the moral hazard problems faced by depository institution customers. By requiring institutions to make comparable quotes for loan terms, these laws confound the ability of unsavory managers to mislead loan applicants. The laws also make it more difficult for depository institutions to alter interpretations of loan terms after customers are bound to agreements.

Consumer protection laws also give customers of depository institutions legal recourse if they receive unjust treatment by lenders. In addition, they follow in the tradition of many civil rights laws by attempting to assure equal treatment of all loan applicants, irrespective of race, gender, ethnicity, or other characteristics.

Costs of Consumer Protection Laws
There are several costs associated with consumer protection regulations in banking. The most glaring are the explicit costs of meeting the reporting requirements associated with the various laws that Congress has passed. A study by the Independent Bankers Association of America found that complying with the various laws generates a total expense for depository institutions of at least $3 billion per year. Of this total, the study estimated that complying with CRA alone costs institutions about $1 billion each year. Some of this expense undoubtedly leads to higher loan interest rates and greater fees for consumers.

Enforcing consumer protection laws such as CRA also is a costly undertaking. Considerable regulatory resources, most of which are taxpayer financed, go into monitoring, analyzing, and investigating possible instances of anticonsumer or discriminatory behavior by depository institutions.

Problems in Measuring Compliance   In addition, efforts to enforce CRA and other legislation requires that regulators develop objective measures of noncompliance. Finding reliable measures can be tricky, however. For example, in 1992 economists at the Federal Reserve Bank of Boston studied the 1990 HMDA lending records of 3,300 white applicants and 1,200 black and Hispanic applicants at 131 institutions in the Boston metropolitan area. They found significantly higher loan rejection rates for blacks and Hispanics after controlling for many other factors. Using the Boston study as a basis, in 1994, the U.S. Justice Department began to use differences in ratios of denials to acceptances by race as an objective indicator of CRA compliance by individual banks. That year, and again in 1995, the Justice Department used these ratios as a basis for launching investigations of large depository institutions. It filed charges against two institutions for using racially biased lending practices. One settled the charges against it by opening a branch in a predominantly African American community, hiring more African American loan officers, and advertising in African-American-owned newspapers and radio stations. The other also settled by opening a branch office in a predominantly African American community and committing to making more loans to individuals in low-income neighborhoods.

In 1995 a study by Harold Black, M. Cary Collins, and Ken B. Cyree of the University of Tennessee challenged an implicit presumption of the Justice Department. This was that HMDA data showing disparities in loan applicant denials by race indicated possible discrimination by white-owned banks against African American and Hispanic applicants. Black, Collins, and Cyree analyzed HMDA data reported by 49 banks with a majority of white owners, which they termed white-owned banks, and 32 banks with a majority of black owners, which they called black-owned banks. They tried to match the two groups so that they were similar in every respect except for the main race of the owners. They also looked at the banks' lending decisions for white versus black applicants for loans. The authors found that in applications for home mortgage loans, the white-owned banks rejected just over 12 percent of white applicants but nearly 20 percent of black applicants. These were similar to the findings of the Federal Reserve Bank of Boston and of the Justice Department. When Black, Collins, and Cyree looked at black-owned banks, however, they found that while these banks rejected only about 7 percent of white applicants, they rejected *37 percent of black applicants*. If one were to interpret this evidence as in the Boston study or in the Justice Department cases, the conclusion would be that black-owned banks discriminated against black applicants in favor of white applicants. Indeed, the extent of lending discrimination against black applicants by black-owned banks appeared to exceed the degree of discrimination against black applicants by white-owned banks. Black-owned banks also appeared to give greater favoritism to white applicants than did white-owned banks.

Certainly, it is possible that black-owned banks really do discriminate against black loan applicants and in favor of white applicants. Another possibility, however, is that using acceptance and denial statistics as objective measures for enforcement of laws such as CRA is fraught with difficulties. In addition, it could be that regulators' presumptions that only white-owned banks discriminate against minorities has led them to induce more lending to minorities at white-owned banks than at minority-owned banks.

Consumer protection laws also can have unintended negative consequences for some groups. For instance, these laws prohibit depository institutions from separating loan applicants into groups based on race, gender, and so on. Yet some economists have determined that if banks were allowed to make credit decisions differently for different racial groups, they actually might extend more credit to more people in each racial category. The reason is that depository institutions today rely to a large extent on **credit-scoring models,** which are statistical mechanisms for evaluating the various characteristics of applicants that influence their overall creditworthiness. Requiring depository institutions to treat all groups the same forces them to lump all applicants together for statistical analysis. The effect of this aggregation can be that more applicants are judged inferior relative to the average applicant. But if separate groupings were analyzed, the average degree of creditworthiness would differ by group, and fewer applicants within each group would be judged to be inferior credit risks.

credit-scoring models Statistical procedures for assessing the characteristics of loan applicants to evaluate their overall creditworthiness.

6

What are the benefits and costs of depository institution consumer protection laws?   Consumer protection laws benefit depository institution customers by reducing the extent to which they face adverse selection and moral hazard problems when they apply for and agree to loans. They also help ensure that depository institutions treat individuals equally, irrespective of their gender, ethnicity, race, or other characteristics. These laws can, however, be costly to administer and enforce. They also can generate large paperwork expenses for regulated institutions. Furthermore, developing reliable regulatory monitoring approaches can be difficult, and some regulations actually cause unintended harm to those they are meant to benefit.

SUMMARY

1. **The Arrival of Interstate Banking:** State laws permitting interstate acquisitions of depository institutions by multibank holding companies already have broken down many of the barriers to interstate branching. The Interstate Banking Act of 1994 removed many of the remaining barriers.

2. **The Likely Effects of Interstate Banking:** Permitting depository institutions to branch across state lines almost certainly will produce a significant decline in the number of depository institutions in the United States. Overall concentration of financial resources among the largest depository institutions is likely to accelerate in coming years, although concentration levels in local markets may not be much affected. Small community banks likely will have to adjust to greater competition from cost-cutting regional banks, but they may be able to compete effectively by continuing to offer more personalized banking services.

3. **Universal Banking:** Throughout much of Europe and in Japan, commercial banks face many fewer restrictions on their ability to hold corporate equities and to offer other financial services. Under the universal banking arrangements in these countries, commercial banks effectively are full-service financial centers. In contrast, in the United States commercial banks and other depository institutions traditionally have faced significant barriers to their ability to offer such services.

4. **The Pros and Cons of Universal Banking:** A key potential advantage of universal banking is that it would give depository institutions more inside information about the prospects of companies in which they hold ownership shares. This would increase the ability of depository institutions to evaluate the creditworthiness of the companies as potential borrowers, and the liquidity and solvency of such companies if they are existing borrowers. In addition, holding equity shares might assist a depository institution in diversifying asset risks. At the same time, the greater variability of equity prices could pose new risks for depository institutions. These institutions also might face conflict-of-interest problems. Finally, some critics of universal banking fear that permitting depository institutions to offer full ranges of financial services might concentrate too much power in these institutions.

5. **Regulatory Complications Arising from Off-Balance-Sheet Banking:** Securitization simplifies the task of regulators by removing risky loans from depository institutions' balance sheets. In contrast, loan commitments expose institutions to greater liquidity risks and to potential default risks. In recent years the rapid growth

of derivatives trading by depository institutions has exposed them to new types of risks, and regulators have had to adjust their examination and supervision procedures in light of these risks.

6. The Benefits and Costs of Depository Institution Consumer Protection Laws: Such laws help reduce the extent of adverse selection problems that consumers otherwise might face when confronted with loan interest rate calculations that are difficult to compare. The laws also decrease somewhat the moral hazard problem arising from the possibility that a lender might attempt to reinterpret loan contract terms before the consumer has repaid the loan. These laws are costly for depository institutions to abide by because they require so much paperwork. The laws also are costly to enforce, and they can have unintended negative consequences for some consumers.

QUESTIONS AND PROBLEMS

1. Explain in your own words why the recent growth of multibank holding company arrangements means that the effects of the 1994 law deregulating interstate branching may be more muted than might otherwise be expected.

2. Why is it that the number of depository institutions is likely to fall following the legalization of interstate banking, even if multibank holding companies do not acquire any more institutions that are based in other states? Explain your reasoning.

3. Is universal banking a good idea or a bad idea? Take a stand, and support your answer.

4. Many observers believe that once depository institution managers become more adept with derivatives operations, most risks associated with the involvement in derivatives will dissipate. Do you agree with this assessment? Why or why not?

5. Some depository institution managers have proposed that the federal government should pay the costs they currently bear in meeting consumer protection laws. Can you see any reasonable economic basis to support such a proposal? Explain.

Central Banking, Monetary Policy, and the Federal Reserve System

10

Depository Institutions and Money

KEY QUESTIONS

1. How are the cash reserves of depository institutions distributed?

2. How does a change in total depository institution reserves cause a multiple-expansion effect on the deposit liabilities of these institutions?

3. What are Federal Reserve open-market operations?

4. What is the money multiplier, and why is it important?

5. What factors influence the money multiplier?

6. What is the credit multiplier?

It started in July 1990 and ended in March 1991. What was it? The *most recent U.S. recession. As could be expected, bank lending activity declined during the 1990–1991 recession. But, in contrast to previous experience, bank lending did not bounce back quickly in 1991. Indeed, by January 1993, almost two years after the official end of that recession, bank lending activity had shown an unprecedented weakness. The total value of outstanding bank loans was actually 7 percent less (uncorrected for inflation) than it had been at the end of 1989. Only by early 1995 was the pace of bank lending returning to historically observed levels. Officials at the Federal Reserve and monetary economists noticed that during this same time period, and extending into today, the M2 measure of the money supply had grown very little, even less than the Fed's targeted growth. Is there a relationship between weak bank lending and the growth in the money supply? Or is it the other way around?*

The first place to start to understand this issue is to see the relationship between reserve requirements and deposit expansion.

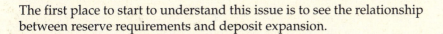

RESERVE REQUIREMENTS AND DEPOSIT EXPANSION

Depository institutions are "special" financial institutions in one key respect: They issue transactions deposits—demand deposits and negotiable-order-of-withdrawal (NOW) accounts. These deposits, as you learned in Chapter 1, are a fundamental component of the most common measures of the quantity of money in our economy. Hence, depository institutions represent the crucial link between governmental policies to influence the quantity of money and the actual effects that these policies have on that quantity.

In this chapter our goal is to explain how depository institutions perform this role.

Required Reserves and Depository Institution Balance Sheets

As we discussed in Chapter 6, the main liabilities of depository institutions are deposit accounts, such as transactions deposit (checking) accounts. Depository institution assets are loans, securities, and cash assets. A significant portion of the cash assets is composed of reserve deposits held at Federal Reserve banks and vault cash. This is true even though neither the reserves at the Fed nor vault cash yield interest to depository institutions.

required reserve ratios
Fractions of transaction deposit balances that the Federal Reserve mandates depository institutions to maintain either as deposits with Federal Reserve banks or as vault cash.

The reason why depository institutions hold so much cash on deposit at the Fed or in their vaults is that they are *required* to do so. Recall from Chapter 8 that the Depository Institutions Deregulation and Monetary Control Act of 1980 gave the Federal Reserve the authority to place reserve requirements on all federally insured depository institutions that offer transactions accounts. The Federal Reserve establishes its reserve requirements using **required reserve ratios,** which are fractions of transactions deposit balances that depository institutions legally must maintain, either as deposits with Federal Reserve banks or as vault cash. At present, the Federal Reserve subjects most transactions deposits to a required reserve ratio of 10 percent. This means that for every $10 of transactions deposits at a depository institution, the institution must hold $1 on deposit with a Federal Reserve bank and/or in its own vault. Ignoring any other complications (and in the real world there are several of these, as we shall discuss in Chapter 12), if the institution issues $1,000 million ($1 billion) in transaction deposits, then the total amount of reserves that it would be obliged to hold would be $100 million. This total amount of legally mandated cash reserve holdings would be its **required reserves.**

required reserves   Legally mandated reserve holdings at depository institutions, which are proportional to the dollar amounts of transaction accounts.

Depository Institution Balance Sheets and T-Accounts   The existence of this reserve requirement implies that a single depository institution can use any new transactions deposit funds to make new loans or buy new securities only to the extent that it has cash reserves above the required level. That is, the depository institution can lend or purchase securities only if it possesses **excess reserves,** or reserves in excess of those it must hold to meet reserve requirements.

excess reserves   Depository institution cash balances at Federal Reserve banks or in their own vaults that exceed the amount that they must hold to meet legal requirements.

Consider a depository institution with $1,000 million in transactions deposit liabilities. To make our example a little more concrete, we'll assume that this depository institution is based in Boston. To simplify, however, we assume that the institution has no other liabilities nor any equity capital. If it were to hold all these funds as cash assets, then it would have total cash reserves of $1,000 million. We use the term **total reserves** for the sake of simplicity. In Figure 10.1 we display the assets and liabilities for this depository institution as a **T-account,** which is just a listing of the assets of the depository institution alongside its liabilities.

total reserves   The total balances that depository institutions hold on deposit with Federal Reserve banks or as vault cash.

T-account   A side-by-side listing of the assets and liabilities of a business such as a depository institution.

FIGURE 10.1   T-Account for the Boston Depository Institution

Assets		Liabilities
Total Reserves	$1,000 million	Transactions Deposits $1,000 million
Required Reserves		
($100 million)		
Excess Reserves		
($900 million)		

You saw the equivalent of T-accounts in Chapter 6 when we discussed the assets and liabilities of commercial banks, savings institutions, and credit unions. As we discussed in Chapter 6, a depository institution's assets must be matched exactly by the sum of its liabilities and equity capital. Consequently, this depository institution's total reserves of $1,000 million exactly balance with its transactions deposit liabilities of $1,000 billion. Because T-accounts display this balance of assets and liabilities, they also often are called *balance sheets*.

As Figure 10.1 indicates, this depository institution's required reserves are $100 million, or 10 percent of its transactions deposits of $1,000 million. This means that its excess reserves are $900 million, or the amount by which its total reserves of $1,000 million exceed the institution's legal reserve requirement of $100 million.

1

How are the cash reserves of depository institutions distributed?   The total reserves of depository institutions are comprised of required reserves, or the cash reserves that the institutions must hold with the Federal Reserve or in their own vaults to meet legal mandates, and excess reserves, which are any additional reserves that the institutions may hold voluntarily.

A "Loaned-Up" Depository Institution   Excess reserves earn no interest income for the depository institution. And so no profit-maximizing depository institution would permit itself to remain in the situation shown in Figure 10.1 for very long. The Boston institution's managers will allocate the institution's $900 million in excess reserves to alternative uses, such as holdings of loans and securities.

Figure 10.2 shows the result of such a managerial reallocation of the depository institution's assets. Once the institution's managers have used all available excess reserves to make loans or to buy securities,

FIGURE 10.2   T-Account for the Boston Depository Institution when It Is Fully Loaned Up

Assets		Liabilities	
Total Reserves	$ 100 million	Transactions Deposits	$1,000 million
Required Reserves			
($100 million)			
Excess Reserves ($0)			
Loans and Securities	$ 900 million		
Total	$1,000 million	Total	$1,000 million

then the institution is said to be fully "loaned up," meaning that it has expanded its loans and other interest-bearing assets as fully as possible in the face of the required reserve ratio that it faces. For a fully loaned-up institution, excess reserves are equal to zero, and total reserves equal required reserves, as in Figure 10.2. Once this depository institution's managers have allocated all excess reserves to loans and securities, the institution's excess reserves fall to zero, and its total reserves decline to the level of its required reserves, or $100 million.

The Deposit Expansion Process

The Boston-based depository institution we have envisioned would be one among thousands of such institutions throughout the United States. To understand how its indirect interactions with other institutions, in the face of transactions by the Federal Reserve, can influence the total quantity of deposits in *all* institutions combined, let's expand our example.

How a Reserve Increase Affects a Single Depository Institution

Suppose that a New York securities dealer has a transactions deposit account at the Boston-based depository institution we considered above. The dealer draws from this account to purchase securities, and funds flow into this account when the dealer sells securities. Let's suppose that the Federal Reserve Bank of New York buys $100 million in U.S. government securities from the securities dealer. Then the dealer would receive $100 million from that Federal Reserve bank, which it would place in its transactions account at the depository institution that we considered above in Figures 10.1 and 10.2.

As shown in Figure 10.2, before the dealer's transaction with the New York Federal Reserve bank, the Boston institution had $1,000 million in transactions deposit liabilities, $100 million in total reserves, and $900 million in loans and securities. Figure 10.3 displays the situation faced by this depository institution after the dealer's transaction. Because $100 million in new funds have flowed into the dealer's transactions deposit account with the institution, the institution now has

---

FIGURE 10.3   Boston Institution's T-Account after New York Securities Dealer's Transaction

Assets		Liabilities	
Total Reserves	$ 200 million	Transactions Deposits	$1,100 million
Required Reserves ($110 million)			
Excess Reserves ($90 million)			
Loans and Securities	$ 900 million		
Total	$1,100 million	Total	$1,100 million

$100 million in new cash reserves, or total reserves of $200 million. But the institution also has $1,100 million in transactions deposit liabilities, and so its required reserves have risen from $100 million to $110 million (10 percent of the $1,100 million in total transactions deposits). Because the institution has $200 million in total reserves but faces a reserve requirement of $110 million, it has $90 million in excess reserves. As a result of its customer's transaction with the New York Federal Reserve bank, the Boston depository institution is no longer fully loaned up.

The managers of this depository institution have an additional $90 million in excess reserves that they either may lend or use to buy securities. Figure 10.4 shows the T-account for the Boston institution once its managers have reallocated its assets so that the institution once again is fully loaned up. When this position is regained, the institution's excess reserves again equal zero, and its total reserves equal its required reserves, which now are $110 million. The amount of loans and securities held by the institution have expanded to $990 million, and so the institution's total assets remain equal to $1,100, which is the same as the amount of its total transactions deposit liabilities.

How a Reserve Increase Spills from One Institution to Others

For the Boston-based depository institution, note in Figure 10.4 that the $100 million transaction between the securities dealer and the Federal Reserve Bank of New York has led to a $10 million expansion of total reserves, from $100 million to $110 million, and a $90 million expansion of loans and securities, from $900 million to $990 million. Yet this cannot be the conclusion of the story for *all* depository institutions. When the Boston institution extends more loans and buys more securities, the recipients of the $90 million in new loans and of the funds used to pay for the securities now have $90 million in funds that *they* can deposit in transactions deposit accounts at their own depository institutions.

To make this point more concrete, let's suppose that the way the Boston-based depository institution expanded its combined loan and security assets was simply by buying $90 million in government securities from a dealer based in Chicago. Furthermore, let's suppose that

---

FIGURE 10.4   Boston Depository Institution's T-Account once It Again Is Fully Loaned Up

Assets		Liabilities	
Total Reserves	$ 110 million	Transactions Deposits	$1,100 million
Required Reserves			
($110 million)			
Excess Reserves ($0)			
Loans and Securities	$ 990 million		
Total	$1,100 million	Total	$1,100 million

the Boston depository institution makes payment by transferring the $90 million directly into the securities dealer's transactions deposit account in a Chicago-based depository institution. Figure 10.5 shows only the changes faced by the Chicago institution after this second transaction occurs. Its transactions deposit liabilities have *increased* by $90 million and its required reserves have *risen* by $9 million (10 percent of the $90 million in new deposits). Hence, the Chicago depository institution now has $81 million in new excess reserves that *its* managers may use to make new loans or to buy new securities.

Suppose that the Chicago-based depository institution makes a loan of $81 million to a Milwaukee-based company. Then, as shown in Figure 10.6, this would mean that the Chicago bank's total reserves would expand by the required amount, or $9 million, and its total assets would rise by $90 million, or the amount of the increase in deposits caused by the security transaction between the Boston-based depository institution and the Chicago securities dealer.

The Ultimate Chain Reaction: Aggregate Deposit Expansion Yet our story *still* is unfinished. When the Milwaukee company spends the $81 million it borrows to purchase a needed piece of equipment, its payment for this equipment will show up in the account that the equipment manufacturer has at some other depository institution, perhaps

FIGURE 10.5   Chicago Depository Institution's T-Account Changes after Second Security Purchase

Assets		Liabilities	
Total Reserves	+$90 million	Transactions Deposits	+$90 million
Required Reserves			
(+$9 million)			
Excess Reserves			
(+$81 million)			
Total	+$90 million	Total	+$90 million

FIGURE 10.6   Chicago Depository Institution's T-Account Changes once It Is Again Fully Loaned Up

Assets		Liabilities	
Total Reserves	+$ 9 million	Transactions Deposits	+$90 million
Required Reserves			
(+$9 million)			
Excess Reserves ($0)			
Loans and Securities	+ 81 million		
Total	+$90 million	Total	+$90 million

in Minneapolis. This would cause the reserve requirement at this new institution to rise by 10 percent of $81 million, or $8.1 million, leaving it with $72.9 million in new excess reserves that it could use to make new loans or to purchase new securities.

Indeed, this process of redepositing followed by further lending and security purchases by depository institutions would continue through a long line of institutions and their deposit customers. Table 10.1 shows how our story would work out if we continued it to its ultimate conclusion. Ultimately, required reserves at *all* depository institutions would rise by $100 million. Loans and securities at *all* institutions would rise by $900 million. Total transaction deposits at *all* institutions would increase by $1,000 million, or $1 billion. (We shall explain shortly how we know that these total changes are correct; for the moment, take our word for these numbers.)

Table 10.1 illustrates how a Federal Reserve Bank of New York transaction with a single securities dealer can cause transactions deposits across all depository institutions to expand by *more* than the amount of the transaction. Here we see that a $100 million reserve injection via the purchase of securities by the New York Federal Reserve bank has resulted in a tenfold increase in total transaction deposits, to $1,000 million.

2

How does a change in total depository institution reserves cause a multiple-expansion effect on the deposit liabilities of these institutions?   An increase in excess reserves induces the institution that receives the reserves to increase its lending or its security holdings. The funds that it lends or uses to purchase securities typically are redeposited at other depository institutions, which in turn can expand their lending and security holdings. The result is a multiple expansion of deposits in the banking system.

TABLE 10.1   The Ultimate Effects Stemming from the Federal Reserve Bank of New York's $100 million Security Transaction

Depository Institution	Increase in Required Reserves	Increase in Loans and Securities	Increase in Transaction Deposits
Boston	$ 10.0 million	$ 90.0 million	$ 100 million
Chicago	$ 9.0 million	$ 81.0 million	$ 90 million
Minneapolis	$ 8.1 million	$ 72.9 million	$ 81 million
All Other	$ 72.9 million	$656.1 million	$ 729 million
All Depository Institutions Combined	$100.0 million	$900.0 million	$1,000 million

The Federal Reserve's Role in Deposit Expansion   The key to the multiple expansion of deposits that occurred in our example was the Federal Reserve's injection of $100 million in *new* reserves. What would have happened if some other securities dealer had instead bought securities already held by the dealer who had the account at the Boston-based depository institution? Then, that other dealer would have transferred funds out of an account at its own depository institution. Deposits would still rise at the Boston depository institution, as in our example above. But deposits would fall by an equal amount at the other institution, which would then have to *reduce* its holdings of loans and securities. As a result, the initial $100 million increase in reserves at the Boston depository institution would be matched by a $100 million reduction in reserves at the other depository institution. There would simply have been a *transfer* of funds *within* the banking system, with no multiple expansion of deposits.

THE FEDERAL RESERVE AND DEPOSIT EXPANSION

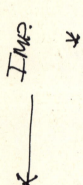

Why does the Federal Reserve's involvement in a transaction make such a difference? The reason is that the Federal Reserve is the single institution empowered to create depository institution reserves. When the Federal Reserve Bank of New York buys a security from a dealer, it produces reserves that previously had not existed in the banking system. This ultimately leads to the expansion of deposits summarized in Table 10.1.

Federal Reserve Open-Market Operations

When the Federal Reserve buys or sells securities in the money or capital markets, it engages in **open-market operations.** In the example above in which the New York Federal Reserve bank purchased $100 million in securities from a New York dealer, we considered the effects of an **open-market purchase.** In contrast, an **open-market sale** entails a situation in which the Federal Reserve Bank of New York sells U.S. government securities.

open-market operations
Federal Reserve purchases or sales of securities.

open-market purchase   A Federal Reserve purchase of a security, which increases total reserves at depository institutions and thereby raises the size of the monetary base.

open-market sale   A Federal Reserve sale of a security, which reduces total reserves of depository institutions and thereby reduces the size of the monetary base.

Open-Market Purchases   To better understand the mechanics of a Federal Reserve open-market purchase, let's consider what would have initiated the first step of our example above. Figure 10.7 displays T-accounts both for the Federal Reserve and for the Boston-based depository institution. When the New York Federal Reserve bank purchases securities from a New York dealer with a transactions deposit account at the Boston institution, one way to make the payment would be for the Federal Reserve bank to write a check for $100 million to the dealer. The dealer would then deposit this check in its account at the Boston institution.

FIGURE 10.7   T-Accounts for a Federal Reserve Open-Market Purchase

FEDERAL RESERVE		BOSTON DEPOSITORY INSTITUTION	
Assets	**Liabilities**	**Assets**	**Liabilities**
Securities +$100 million	Reserve Deposits +$100 million	Reserve Deposits +$100 million	Transactions Deposits +$100 million

Next, the Boston institution would submit the $100 million check to the Federal Reserve for payment. The Federal Reserve would honor its check by crediting the Boston institution's reserve deposit account with the Federal Reserve. Consequently, the Boston-based depository institution would gain $100 million in reserve assets, while the Federal Reserve would increase its reserve deposit liabilities by $100 million. But the Federal Reserve gains a matching $100 million in new assets—the securities it has purchased from the New York dealer.

There is another way for the Federal Reserve to make the purchase. This is to make a wire transfer of funds directly to the Boston institution for deposit into the dealer's account. Indeed, today this would be the most likely way for the Federal Reserve to make an open-market purchase. But the accounting would all be the same as shown in Figure 10.7. Whether the Federal Reserve writes a check or wires the funds, it has created $100 million in depository institution reserves that previously had not existed.

Open-Market Sales   What would happen if the Federal Reserve were to *sell* $100 million in securities to a dealer with a transactions deposit account at the Boston depository institution? As shown in Figure 10.8, such an open-market sale of securities would have exactly the opposite T-account effects. Regardless of whether the dealer pays the Federal Reserve for the securities by writing a check or by transferring funds directly, the dealer's transactions deposits at the Boston institution would decline by $100 million. This would cause the Boston institution's reserve deposits with the Federal Reserve to fall by the same amount.

At the Federal Reserve, the sale of securities would cause its total assets to shrink by $100 million. Balancing this reduction in the Federal

FIGURE 10.8   T-Accounts for a Federal Reserve Open-Market Sale

FEDERAL RESERVE		BOSTON DEPOSITORY INSTITUTION	
Assets	**Liabilities**	**Assets**	**Liabilities**
Securities −$100 million	Reserve Deposits −$100 million	Reserve Deposits −$100 million	Transactions Deposits −$100 million

Reserve's assets would be the decline in reserve deposits of depository institutions. Such an open-market sale, then, effectively *removes* reserves from the banking system.

3

What are Federal Reserve open-market operations?   Open-market operations are purchases or sales of U.S. government securities by the Federal Reserve. Open-market purchases increase the total reserves of depository institutions. Open-market sales reduce the total reserves of depository institutions.

How the Fed Expands and Contracts Total Deposits

We now have developed the key concepts that you need to understand how the Federal Reserve influences the total quantity of deposits in the nation's banking system. Now let's see how to determine the *amounts* by which actions of the Federal Reserve potentially can expand or contract the total quantity of deposits at the country's depository institutions.

Expanding Total Deposits   Consider the example of an open-market purchase of $100 million by the Federal Reserve Bank of New York. The immediate effect of this purchase would be an increase in total reserves in the banking system—specifically, at the Boston depository institution—of $100 million. Let's call a change in total reserves ΔTR, where the Greek letter delta (Δ) indicates a change in a variable. Then the direct effect of the open-market purchase is a reserve increase equal to $\Delta TR = +\$100$ million.

Recall that we assumed throughout our example that the legal required reserve ratio was 10 percent, or 0.10. Let's denote this ratio as $r = 0.10$. In addition, let's denote the change in deposits in the banking system by ΔD. This means that any change in required reserves (RR) in the banking system, ΔRR, would be equal to $r \times \Delta D$, because the level of required reserves would equal $r \times D$, where r is the constant required reserve ratio.

Finally, remember that we assumed that the Boston-based depository institution and all other depository institutions desire to be fully loaned up, meaning that they prefer to hold no excess reserves. That meant that the amount by which required reserves would change would match the change in total reserves, or $\Delta RR = \Delta TR$.

Putting all this together tells us that

$$r \times \Delta D = \Delta TR$$

Now let's divide both sides of this equation by r to get an expression for the change in deposits,

$$\frac{r \times \Delta D}{r} = \frac{\Delta TR}{r}$$

or

$$\Delta D = (1/r) \times \Delta TR$$

This final expression tells us that the change in deposits equals a factor $1/r$ times a change in total reserves. In our example, $r = 0.10$, and so $1/r = 10$. Hence, a change in reserves causes a tenfold increase in deposits. This explains our claim in Table 10.1 that a $100 million increase in total reserves caused by an open-market purchase ultimately causes deposits at all depository institutions to expand by $1,000 million, or ten times the amount of the reserve increase. We determine this amount simply by using the expression just developed:

$$\Delta D = (1/r) \times \Delta TR = (10) \times (+\$100 \text{ million}) = +\$1,000 \text{ million}$$

The factor $1/r$ is called the **deposit expansion multiplier,** because it tells us how much deposits in the banking system can rise or fall as a result of an increase or decrease of reserves by the Federal Reserve. In our example, the value of the deposit expansion multiplier is $1/r = 1/0.10 = 10$.

deposit expansion multiplier
A number that tells how much aggregate transaction deposits at all depository institutions will change in response to a change in total reserves of these institutions.

Contracting Total Deposits   An open-market sale of U.S. government securities by the Fed would have the opposite effect on total deposits, as we can see by using the expression for deposit expansion. A $100 million sale of securities by the Federal Reserve would cause reserves in the banking system to decline, so that $\Delta TR = -\$100$ million in the case of an open-market sale. Then, using our expression for ΔD, we have

$$\Delta D = (1/r) \times \Delta TR = (10) \times (-\$100 \text{ million}) = -\$1,000 \text{ million}$$

Whereas a Federal Reserve open-market purchase induces a multiple expansion of deposits in the banking system, a Federal Reserve open-market sale causes a multiple *contraction* of deposits.

DEPOSIT EXPANSION AND THE MONEY MULTIPLIER

As we discussed in Chapter 1, the amount of transaction deposits in the banking system is a key component of *monetary aggregates*, or measures of the total quantity of money in the economy. This means that we have almost reached a point at which we have explained how the Federal Reserve can influence the nation's money stock.

GLOBAL NOTEBOOK

Oh, Where Have All Those Dollars Gone?

The last time the Federal Reserve analyzed the holdings of U.S. currency, it found that its surveys could not explain what happened to 85 percent of all the dollars the U.S. Mint had printed and that had not been officially removed from circulation. So, today, where are the $300 billion in Federal Reserve notes that cannot be accounted for? The first place to look is the underground economy. University of Wisconsin economist Edgar L. Feige estimates that around $15 billion or more of the missing currency can be accounted for by the underground, or nonreported, economy. He estimates that another 22 percent is being held by individuals and businesses in the United States. The remaining dollars are circulating abroad, particularly in developing countries such as Russia and Latin America. Look at the estimated value of American currency in circulation outside the United States in Figure 10.9. In many developing countries the dollar has become the currency standard. Actually, some researchers believe that there may be more than $300 billion of U.S. currency circulating abroad. Consider how this has benefited the U.S. economy. To get dollar bills abroad, foreigners have had to give up oil, leather handbags and wallets, and everything else they have traded in exchange for dollar bills. As long as those hundreds of billions of dollars remain outside the United States, Americans are, in effect, receiving an interest-free loan from foreigners holding U.S. dollars. After all, all we gave in exchange for the oil, leather handbags, and other goods are pieces of paper that cost almost nothing to print.

For Critical Analysis: *Under what circumstances might a foreigner choose to hold dollars rather than his or her local currency?*

We are not quite all the way there, however. Another key component of any monetary aggregate is the amount of *currency*—the government-produced paper money and coins that we use in simple hand-to-hand transactions. It represents about a third of the M1 measure of money. This is such a large portion that we cannot simply ignore it. Certainly, the Federal Reserve cannot, because it is the institution that supervises the distribution of this currency. If you have any dollar bills handy, take a look at one; you will see "Federal Reserve Note" written prominently on the bill.

Depository Institution Reserves, the Monetary Base, and Money

As we discussed in Chapter 1, the narrowest monetary aggregate is the amount of money produced directly by the government, or the *monetary*

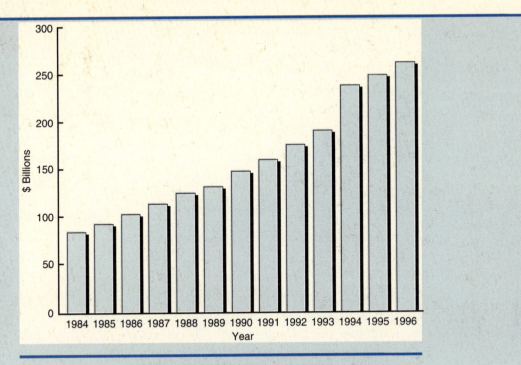

FIGURE 10.9   The Value of American Currency in Circulation Outside the United States

The amount of U.S. dollars circulating beyond American borders has grown steadily in recent years. *Sources:* Board of Governors of the Federal Reserve System; Richard D. Porter and Ruth A. Judson, "The Location of U.S. Currency: How Much Is Abroad?" Board of Governors of the Federal Reserve System, October 18, 1995. Figure for 1996 is authors' estimate.

base. The monetary base, MB, is the amount of currency, C, plus the total quantity of reserves in the banking system, TR, or

$$MB = C + TR$$

We already know that if depository institutions hold no excess reserves, then $TR = RR = r \times D$. Let's also assume that consumers and businesses desire to hold a fraction, c, of transaction deposits as currency. It then would follow that $C = c \times D$, so that the expression for the monetary base, when we make these substitutions, could be written as

$$MB = (c \times D) + (r \times D) = (c + r) \times D$$

Hence, we can express the monetary base as the sum of the desired currency ratio and required reserve ratio multiplied by the amount of transactions deposits in the banking system.

A broader monetary aggregate, and the one upon which we shall focus our attention, is M1. Recall from Chapter 1 that M1 is equal to the sum of currency and transaction deposits, or

$$M1 = C + D$$

Because $C = c \times D$, we can rewrite the expression for M1 as

$$M1 = (c \times D) + D = (c + 1) \times D$$

Now if we divide by MB, we get

$$\frac{M1}{MB} = \frac{(c + 1) \times D}{MB} = \frac{(c + 1) \times D}{(c + r) \times D} = \frac{c + 1}{c + r}$$

If we multiply both sides of this equation by MB, we get

$$M1 = \frac{c + 1}{c + r} \times MB$$

which is an expression for the quantity of money, given the value of the monetary base and the ratios c and r. This expression tells us that once the Federal Reserve determines the size of the monetary base, the amount of the monetary aggregate M1 will depend upon the required reserve ratio, r, and the desired ratio of currency to transactions deposits for consumers and businesses, given by c.

The Money Multiplier

Now let's begin to try to figure out how this algebra relates back to the basic deposit expansion process. First, note that if c and r are constant, then the above expression for the value of the M1 measure of money indicates that a change in the money stock is induced by a change in the monetary base, or

$$\Delta M1 = \frac{c + 1}{c + r} \times \Delta MB$$

Because r is less than 1, the factor multiplied by ΔMB in this new expression is greater than 1. This means that a change in the monetary base has a *multiple* effect on the quantity of money. In fact, if we define a money multiplier, m, to be equal to the factor $(c + 1)/(c + r)$, we can write a final expression relating a change in the monetary base to a resulting change in the quantity of money as follows:

$$\Delta M1 = m \times \Delta MB$$

The **money multiplier,** *m*, is a number that tells us the size of the effect of a change in the monetary base on the quantity of money. To get an idea of roughly how large this multiplier might be, let's suppose that the desired ratio of currency holdings relative to deposits, c, equals 0.25. Then the value of the money multiplier would be $m = (c + 1)/(c + r) = (0.25 + 1)/(0.25 + 0.10) = 1.25/0.35$, which is approximately equal to 3.6. Consequently, an increase in the monetary base would raise the total quantity of money by just over three and one-half times.

Recall that in our earlier example we came up with a deposit expansion multiplier that was equal to 10. Why is our money multiplier almost a third of that size? The reason is that the earlier example ignored the existence of currency. If securities dealers, businesses, and consumers desire to hold some cash in the form of currency, then each time a depository institution purchases new securities from dealers or makes new loans to businesses or consumers some funds leave the banking system in the form of currency holdings. At every step of the deposit expansion process, therefore, fewer funds are redeposited in depository institutions, leaving fewer funds for the institutions to use for security purchases or loans. As a result, the multiplier's value must be smaller when currency accounts for part of the quantity of money.

money multiplier A number that tells how much the quantity of money will change in response to a change in the monetary base.

Federal Reserve Policy Making and the Money Multiplier

Because of the deposit expansion process, the Federal Reserve cannot control monetary aggregates such as M1 directly. What it can do, however, is change the amount of reserves at depository institutions to influence such a monetary aggregate. Because the monetary base, *MB*, is the sum of currency, *C*, and total reserves, *TR*, it follows that the only way the monetary base can change is for the Federal Reserve to change the quantity of currency, the amount of reserves, or both currency and reserves. Typically, the Federal Reserve does not use variations in the stock of currency to influence the total quantity of money. But it can and does conduct open-market purchases to increase total reserves or conduct open-market sales to reduce total reserves. An open-market purchase increases the monetary base and thus causes a multiple increase in the quantity of money. An open-market sale decreases the monetary base and thereby causes a multiple reduction in the quantity of money.

As we shall discuss in Chapter 12, the Federal Reserve does not have to rely on open-market operations to influence the quantity of money through the money multiplier process. The Federal Reserve also can try to change total reserves at depository institutions by inducing depository institutions to borrow more or fewer reserves from the Federal Reserve banks' discount windows. If depository institutions' discount window borrowings increase, then total reserves, the monetary base, and the quantity of money also will increase. If depository institutions' discount window borrowings decline, then total reserves, the monetary base, and the quantity of money also will decline.

The Federal Reserve also could choose to change the quantity of money by altering the required reserve ratio, r. This would change the money multiplier and thereby cause the quantity of money to rise or fall even if total reserves in the banking system were to remain unchanged. As we shall discuss in Chapter 12, however, the Federal Reserve rarely changes reserve requirements. Typically it relies on daily open-market operations, coupled with intermittent changes in its discount window policies.

4

What is the money multiplier, and why is it important?   The money multiplier is a number that determines the size of the effect on the quantity of money caused by a change in the monetary base. The money multiplier is important because the Federal Reserve can influence the quantity of money only by varying the size of the monetary base. Consequently, the money multiplier determines how Federal Reserve policy actions will affect the money stock.

EXTENDED MONEY AND CREDIT MULTIPLIERS

In light of the expressions we have developed so far in this chapter, it might be tempting to think that the Fed can simply compute money multipliers and then determine precisely how to conduct monetary policies. Unfortunately for the Fed, things are not quite so simple.

The Time-Varying Money Multiplier

One problem that the Federal Reserve faces is that the money multiplier is not constant over time. Another is that because M1 is not the only monetary aggregate—recall that the Federal Reserve also defines M2 and M3—there also is more than one money multiplier for the Federal Reserve to worry about.

Figure 10.10 shows estimates of money multipliers for the M1 and M2 aggregates to which the Federal Reserve has paid closest attention in recent years. The M1 multiplier is the ratio of M1 to the monetary base, while the M2 multiplier is the ratio of M2 to the monetary base.

Figure 10.10 shows that the M1 multiplier always is smaller than the M2 multiplier. This is true because the savings and time deposits included in M2 are subject to an expansion process following a change in the monetary base. Note that the overall trend in the M1 multiplier has been downward, but the opposite is true for the M2 multiplier (until the past ten years or so). Yet both multipliers can rise or fall from

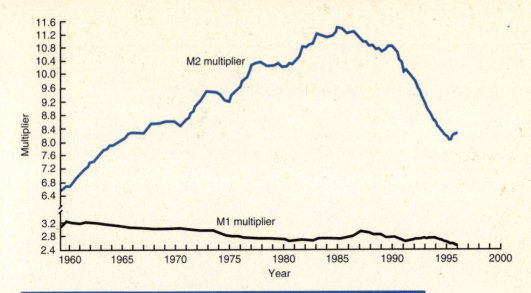

FIGURE 10.10   M1 and M2 Multipliers

Because M2 includes a number of financial assets that are not included in M1, the M2 multiplier is significantly larger than the M1 multiplier. Both money multipliers vary over time. *Source:* Federal Reserve Bank of St. Louis, *Federal Reserve Economic Data,* 1996.

time to time. In addition, the two multipliers do not necessarily change at the same time or in the same direction.

Why do money multipliers vary? One reason is that the desired ratio of currency to deposits, c, is not constant. Instead, this ratio typically changes with the extent to which currency is a favored means of undertaking some types of transactions in the economy. If you look back at the expression for the M1 money multiplier that we computed above, you will see that variations in this ratio will cause the multiplier to vary as well.

Figure 10.10 indicates that normally the M2 multiplier is more volatile than the M1 multiplier. The reason for this is that the inclusion of other kinds of deposits in M2 makes the M2 multiplier much more complicated than the M1 multiplier we calculated above. If we were to calculate an M2 multiplier, we would find that it depends on the ratios of consumers' and businesses' desired holdings of savings and time deposits relative to transaction deposits. Shifts in these ratios thereby cause changes in the M2 multiplier but not in the M1 multiplier.

Excess Reserves and the Money Multiplier

Another important real-world factor that can cause variations in money multipliers is volatility in desired holdings of excess reserves by depository institutions. Up to this point we have assumed that depository

MANAGEMENT NOTEBOOK
Bank Managers Opt for More Mutual Fund Sales

In the past few years the M2 multiplier has been lower than predicted. In other words, increases in the monetary base have not yielded as great a multiple expansion in the M2 money supply as in the past. Economists at the Federal Reserve Bank of Dallas believe that one of the reasons has to do with a shift in bank managers' behavior. Specifically, in order to improve profitability, bank managers have increased their offerings of mutual funds. Recall that a mutual fund is a company that pools the funds of its investors by selling shares to many individuals and then uses the proceeds to buy a portfolio of stocks and/or bonds. The first mutual fund was organized in Boston in 1924. Beginning in 1972 banks and bank holding companies became active in the mutual fund business. Banks are now able to offer mutual funds either by renting lobby space to them or by selling shares through a brokerage firm affil-

iated with the bank. Additionally, banks or their affiliates have served as advisors and administrators of funds underwritten by other entities. Banks market these mutual funds through their brokerage affiliate or a subsidiary. Recently, banks have been extremely aggressive in marketing mutual funds. Commercial banks now account for over one-third of all net sales of mutual fund shares and they hold approximately 12 percent of all mutual fund assets.

Some banking regulators are worried that such aggressive entry into a traditionally nonbank market will further erode the declining role of commercial bank lending in the U.S. financial markets.

For Critical Analysis: *How does bank managers' increased emphasis on selling mutual fund shares influence the M2 multiplier?*

institutions always desire to be fully loaded up. This has simplified explaining the basics of deposit expansion and the money multiplier process, but it is not especially realistic. In fact, depository institutions usually *do* voluntarily hold some excess reserves.

Reasons Why Depository Institutions Hold Excess Reserves

Why do depository institutions hold excess reserves, even though such reserves yield no explicit interest return? They do so because such reserves yield an *implicit* return. To understand this, suppose that you are a depository institution manager. You have just enough reserves at your district Federal Reserve bank to meet your institution's reserve requirement, and it is the last day of the period in which you must meet the requirement. An hour before the close of business, however, you learn that one of your largest business customers plans to withdraw $50,000 from its transactions deposit account. Even though this action will reduce your reserve requirement by $5,000 (10 percent of the deposit reduction), it will cause your reserves to decline by much more.

Where can you get the cash that you now need to meet your institution's reserve requirement? One possibility would be to try to call in some loans that are coming due, but there is not much time for that. Another more likely option would be to sell some securities before the markets close, but you might risk making a bad deal. More than likely you would have to borrow the funds in the federal funds market or even from the Federal Reserve.

Clearly, any of these options would be costly. But if instead you were holding some excess reserves as a *contingency* against such an event, you would not have to face such a situation. Holding such reserves then would yield an implicit return by insuring you against having to bear costs of calling in loans, selling securities, or borrowing funds.

Another possible reason for holding some excess reserves is that doing so permits depository institutions to make speedy loans when good deals arise unexpectedly. If a long-standing customer with a credit line should need funds unexpectedly, it can be useful to have some on hand.

Of course, there is an *opportunity cost* that must be incurred when depository institutions hold excess reserves. This is the interest return that the institutions forgo by holding cash instead of lending or purchasing securities. For this reason, depository institutions try to keep their excess reserve holdings at levels that just cover the kinds of contingencies they usually face in their own special circumstances. Nevertheless, depository institutions do hold positive, albeit small, amounts of excess reserves.

How Excess Reserves Change the Money Multiplier

To see how this affects the money multiplier, let's take a last look at the money multiplier. Recall that the monetary base is $MB = C + TR$. If depository institutions hold excess reserves, then total reserves equal required reserves plus excess reserves, or $TR = RR + ER$, where ER denotes the amount of excess reserve holdings. Suppose that depository institutions desire to hold a fraction, e, of their transactions deposit liabilities as excess reserves. Then $ER = e \times D$, and $MB = C + TR = C + RR + ER$. Using the expressions we already have developed, this means that the monetary base may be expressed as

$$MB = (c \times D) + (r \times D) + (e \times D) = (r + e + c) \times D$$

This states that the monetary base is equal to the sum of the required reserve ratio, desired excess reserve ratio, and desired currency ratio multiplied by total transactions deposits.

Using the definitions for $M1$ and MB, we see that the money multiplier is equal to

$$\frac{M1}{MB} = \frac{C + D}{C + TR}$$

POLICY NOTEBOOK

Changing Reserve Requirements Reduces Implicit Tax on Banks

In 1974 most transaction deposits had a reserve requirement of 18 percent and the requirement for term deposits was 8 percent; by 1992 those requirements were dropped to 10 percent and zero percent, respectively. In effect, the Fed has reduced the implicit tax on banks. After all, reserves do not earn interest. Therefore, the reserves that banks are required to hold over and above what they would in the absence of regulation represent "unproductive" assets. When the Fed reduced reserve requirements on transaction deposits in 1992 from 12 to 10 percent, it estimated that bank profits would increase by between $300 million and $600 million per year, all other things held constant.

Note that the money multipliers developed in this chapter are related to the reciprocal of the reserve ratio. Consequently, a lower reserve ratio leads to a greater maximum money multiplier. Therefore, the lower the reserve requirements, the more the Fed can overshoot its money supply goals when it injects new reserves into the system. A reduced reserve requirement gives banks more flexibility and therefore makes it more difficult for the Fed to anticipate their actions.

In any event, some commentators have argued that the Fed has no reason to tax banks at all by requiring them to hold noninterest-bearing reserves. They believe that the Fed should be required to pay market rates on reserves held in the form of Federal Reserve deposits.

For Critical Analysis: *What would happen to the money supply multiplier if required reserves increased to 100 percent?*

Using the expressions we already have developed, we can substitute for C and TR to rewrite the money multiplier as

$$\frac{M1}{MB} = \frac{(c + 1) \times D}{(r + e + c) \times D}$$

$$= \frac{c + 1}{r + e + c}$$

The value of the multiplier now also depends on the desired ratio of excess reserve holdings to transactions deposits, e.

Note that the desired excess reserve ratio e appears in the denominator of the money multiplier. Consequently, if e increases, meaning that depository institutions desire to hold more excess reserves relative to their transactions deposit liabilities, the money multiplier gets smaller. This makes sense in the context of the deposit-expansion process that underlies the multiplier. If depository institutions hold some excess reserves, then at each stage of the deposit expansion process they will make fewer loans or purchase fewer securities than they would if they did not hold excess reserves. This automatically reduces the extent to which deposits can expand in the banking system following a change in total reserves.

Excess reserve holdings of depository institutions typically are small relative to their total reserve holdings. In a given week excess reserves rarely are much larger than around 1 percent of total depository institution reserve holdings. Yet excess reserve holdings also are highly variable. Figure 10.11 displays total holdings of excess reserves by depository institutions from January 1995 to April 1996. As you can see, there is significant volatility in excess reserves. This contributes to variability in the money multiplier, thereby complicating the Federal Reserve's task in determining how its policies will affect monetary aggregates.

FIGURE 10.11   Excess Reserve Holdings of Depository Institutions

Aggregate excess reserve balances can rise and fall considerably over time. This causes variability in the ratio of excess reserves to transaction deposits, which results in volatility in the money multiplier.
Sources: Board of Governors of the Federal Reserve System, "Federal Reserve Data," *The Wall Street Journal,* various issues.

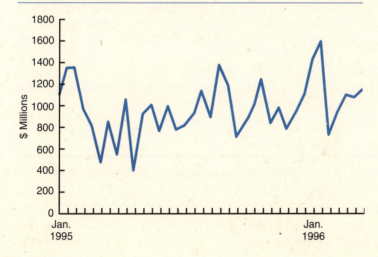

5

What factors influence the money multiplier?   A key determinant of the size of the money multiplier is the amount of currency that consumers and businesses desire to hold relative to transactions deposits. Another important factor is the quantity of excess reserves that depository institutions wish to keep on hand in relation to transactions deposits. Both of these factors influence the amount of deposit expansion following changes in total reserves and, hence, the monetary base. For broader monetary aggregates such as M2, the deposit expansion process also affects savings and time deposits included in such aggregates. Therefore, desired consumer and business holdings of savings and time deposits relative to holdings of transactions deposits also affect the money multipliers for these broader monetary aggregates.

The Credit Multiplier

In recent years the Federal Reserve has not focused its sole attention on monetary aggregates as indicators of the effects of its policies. Federal Reserve officials also look at other financial variables, such as market interest rates, prices of financial instruments, and prices of some commodities such as gold.

Another variable of interest to the Federal Reserve is the total amount of credit that depository institutions extend by lending or purchasing securities. As financial intermediaries, a key function that depository institutions perform is to issue such credit to help finance purchases of goods, services, and financial assets. Because multiple deposit expansion also entails multiple expansion of loans and security holdings at depository institutions, Federal Reserve policies can affect the volume of such purchases, and consequently economic activity, by influencing the aggregate amount of credit that depository institutions extend.

Figure 10.12 displays the conceptual T-account that would apply to all depository institutions that issue transactions deposits to finance lending, securities purchases, and holdings of required and excess reserve balances. The figure indicates that because assets and liabilities

FIGURE 10.12   A Consolidated T-Account for Depository Institutions

Assets	Liabilities
Loans (L)	Transactions Deposits (D)
Securities (S)	
Required Reserves (RR)	
Excess Reserves (ER)	

must balance, the sum of loans, securities, and required and excess reserves must equal the amount of deposits. If we let L denote the dollar amount of loans and S represent the dollar quantity of securities holdings, then this means that $L + S + RR + ER = D$.

Now let's call the combined amount of loans and securities the *total credit* extended by depository institutions, or $L + S = TC$, where TC is the dollar amount of depository institution credit. This tells us that $TC + RR + ER = D$. We can solve for total credit by subtracting RR and ER from both sides. This tells us that

$$TC + RR + ER - RR - ER = D - RR - ER$$

or

$$TC = D - RR - ER$$

Hence, total credit is equal to transactions deposits minus required and excess reserves.

Because our T-account abstracts from reality by ignoring other kinds of deposits and other depository institution assets, let's use our Greek delta notation to look at changes in total credit resulting from changes in deposits or in required or excess reserves:

$$\Delta TC = \Delta D - \Delta RR - \Delta ER$$

We leave it to you in problem 7 at the end of this chapter to show that after a couple of algebraic steps this equation may be rewritten as

$$\Delta TC = \frac{1 - r - e}{c + r + e} \times \Delta MB$$

Consequently, a change in the monetary base is multiplied by the factor $(1 - r - e)/(c + r + e)$ to cause a change in total credit. This factor is the **credit multiplier,** or a number that tells us the multiple expansion effect on total depository institution credit that a change in the monetary base induces. For instance, if $r = 0.10$, $c = 0.25$, and $e = 0.01$, then the value of this multiplier is $(1 - 0.10 - 0.01)/(0.25 + 0.10 + 0.01) = 0.89/0.36$, or approximately 2.47. This would indicate that each \$1 increase in the monetary base would cause the amount of credit extended by depository institutions to rise by about \$2.47.

We can conclude that if the Federal Reserve conducts policies, such as open-market operations, that alter the monetary base, then the result must be a change in the quantities of loans and securities at depository institutions. For instance, an open-market purchase that increased the monetary base would raise the combined amount of lending and security holdings of depository institutions. An open-market

credit multiplier   A number that tells how much total loans and securities at depository institutions will change in response to a change in the monetary base.

sale, in contrast, would reduce total loans and security holdings of these institutions.

Note that the credit multiplier depends on the same basic factors as the money multiplier. These include the required reserve ratio, r, the desired ratio of consumer and business holdings of currency to transactions deposits, c, and the desired ratio of depository institution holdings of excess reserves to transactions deposits, e. Consequently, variations in any of these factors cause changes in the total credit multiplier, just as such variations cause movements in the money multiplier.

Changes in the monetary base exert multiplier effects on both the quantity of money and the total amount of depository institution credit. Which of these variables should the Federal Reserve actually *try* to influence? The answer to this question depends on whether money or credit relates most closely to the volume of economic activity, and we shall consider this issue more fully in Chapter 15. Before we can address this issue, however, you need to learn much more about the Federal Reserve, how it conducts it policies, and how those policies can affect the extent of economic activity.

6

What is the credit multiplier?   The credit multiplier is a number that tells how much the combined amount of loans and security holdings of depository institutions will change as a result of a change in the monetary base. Because credit expansion accompanies deposit expansion at these institutions, the credit multiplier depends on the same basic factors as those that influence the money multiplier.

SUMMARY

1. **The Distribution of the Cash Reserves of Depository Institutions:** The bulk of depository institution cash reserves are required reserves that these institutions hold at Federal Reserve banks or in their own vaults to meet legal requirements. Reserves over and above this amount are excess reserve holdings.

2. **How a Change in Total Depository Institution Reserves Causes a Multiple-Expansion Effect on Their Deposits:** An increase in total reserves at one depository institution induces it to expand its lending and its holdings of securities. The recipients of these funds deposit some or all of the funds in their own transactions accounts at other depository institutions, which enables those institutions as well to increase loans and security holdings. Hence, the initial increase in reserves causes a multiple expansion of transactions deposits throughout the banking system.

3. **Federal Reserve Open-Market Operations:** These are Federal Reserve purchases or sales of securities. An open-market purchase by the Fed increases total reserves of depository institutions. An open-market sale by the Fed reduces total reserves of these institutions.

4. **The Money Multiplier and Its Importance:** The money multiplier is a number that represents the total amount by which the quantity of money will change in response to a change in the monetary base. This number is important because Federal Reserve policies that alter the amount of total reserves in the banking system affect the size of the monetary base. Consequently, to know how much it should change total reserves to induce a given change in the quantity of money, the Federal Reserve needs to know the size of the money multiplier.

5. **Factors That Influence the Money Multiplier:** Any factor that affects the extent of the deposit expansion process influences the size of the money multiplier. One important factor is the amount of currency that consumers and businesses wish to hold in relation to their holdings of transactions deposits. Another is the required reserve ratio for transactions deposits that the Federal Reserve establishes. Finally, changes in banks' desired holdings of excess reserves influences the portion of new reserves that banks lend, thereby affecting the money multiplier.

6. **The Credit Multiplier:** This is a number that tells how much the total amount of credit that depository institutions extend by lending or buying securities will change in response to a change in the monetary base. Because credit expansion occurs alongside deposit expansion, the credit multiplier depends on the same basic factors as those that affect the money multiplier.

QUESTIONS AND PROBLEMS

1. Why is it that you cannot induce any net multiple deposit expansion in the banking system by buying a U.S. government security, yet the Federal Reserve can do so?

2. Suppose that the total liabilities of a depository institution are transactions deposits equal to $2,000 million. It has $1,650 million in loans and securities, and the required reserve ratio is 0.15. Does this institution hold any excess reserves? If so, how much?

3. A depository institution holds $150 million in required reserves and $10 million in excess reserves. Its remaining assets include $440 million in loans and $150 million in securities. If the institution's only liabilities are transactions deposits, what is the required reserve ratio?

4. Consider a world in which there is no currency and depository institutions hold no excess reserves. The value of the money multiplier (for the M1 monetary aggregate) is equal to 4. What is the required reserve ratio? What is the total credit multiplier?

5. Explain in your own words why the money multiplier rises if consumers and businesses desire to hold less currency in relation to their holdings of transactions deposits. Likewise, explain why the money multiplier also becomes larger if depository institutions wish to hold fewer excess reserves relative to transactions deposits that they issue.

6. Suppose that $c = 0.35$, $r = 0.05$, and $e = 0.05$. What is the money multiplier for the M1 monetary aggregate? What is the total credit multiplier?

7. Show that the expression $\Delta TC = \Delta D - \Delta RR - \Delta ER$ can be rearranged into the total credit multiplier expression, $\Delta TC = [(1 - r - e)/(c + r + e)] \times \Delta MB$. [*Hint:* First write $\Delta TC = \Delta D - \Delta RR - \Delta ER = (1 - r - e) \times \Delta D$. Then remember that the monetary base is $MB = C + TR = C + RR + ER = (c + r + e) \times D$, so that a *change* in the monetary base is $\Delta MB = (c + r + e) \times \Delta D$. Now solve this last equation for ΔD and substitute for ΔD in your expression for ΔTC.]

11

Central Banking and the Fed

KEY QUESTIONS

1. What were the first American central banking institutions?

2. Where did responsibility for monetary and banking policies rest in the absence of an American central bank in the nineteenth and early twentieth centuries?

3. What motivated Congress to establish the Federal Reserve System?

4. Why did Congress restructure the Federal Reserve in 1935?

5. Who makes the key policy decisions at the Federal Reserve?

6. How powerful is the chair of the Fed's Board of Governors?

After recovering from a short recession, the American economy faced the renewed potential for a downturn. Inventories of unsold goods were accumulating at businesses and unemployment was beginning to rise. Many wondered if the Federal Reserve might cut interest rates to stimulate the economy. Yet the dollar's value with respect to the Japanese yen and German mark was under major pressure in world currency markets. A cut in American interest rates would reduce the incentive for foreign investors to hold dollar-denominated assets and thereby would increase the potential for further declines in the dollar's international value.

Which way would the Fed go? In the hope of some indication of the Fed's intentions, all ears were attuned to the words of Federal Reserve Board Chairman Alan Greenspan in a speech he gave in Seattle. The day after the speech, a New York Times headline read, "Greenspan Sees Chance of Recession," but The Wall Street Journal headline said, "Fed Chairman Doesn't See Recession on the Horizon." A financial services firm then ran a full-page newspaper ad with both headlines and followed by the comment, "Confused? Who Wouldn't Be?"

Later that same month Greenspan was scheduled to address a black-tie affair at the Economic Club of New York. Newspaper reporters and financial analysts prepared to listen even more carefully to Greenspan's commentary on the current state of the economy and the Fed's plans and objectives. Aware of the attention being given to what he was about to say, Greenspan remarked to his audience, "I spend a substantial amount of my time endeavoring to fend off questions and worry terribly that I might end up being too clear." After the speech, one major newspaper headline read, "Greenspan Hints Fed May Cut Interest Rates." Yet another widely read newspaper said, "Doubts Voiced by Greenspan on a Rate Cut." A third newspaper headline read, "Change Unlikely in Interest Rates." In light of all this confusion generated by Greenspan's unwillingness to be clear on the Fed's intentions, one New York economist speculated about a fitting inscription for Greenspan's future tombstone: "I am guardedly optimistic about the next world, but remain cognizant of the downside risk." In the end, perhaps only one newspaper chose the correct headline to capture the essence of Greenspan's speech: "Greenspan: Uncertainty Abounds."

Because the chair of the Federal Reserve's Board of Governors is the nation's foremost central banking official, financial analysts pick over every word that the chair utters for clues about the Federal Reserve's perceptions and future plans. But it was not always this way. Early in American history many of its leaders never would have dreamed that an individual such as Alan Greenspan would be granted so much widely recognized authority over the nation's financial institutions and markets. The history of how we reached the point at which this has become such a commonly accepted state of affairs is fascinating. But more important, understanding the current role of the Fed chair and other Federal Reserve officials requires an understanding of this history. The Federal Reserve is a unique and complicated institution within the nation's representative democracy.

CENTRAL BANKING IN THE UNITED STATES

Today we take for granted that the Federal Reserve is responsible for managing the nation's monetary affairs. Yet the Federal Reserve has been the U.S. central banking institution for only a little over a third of the nation's history. During nearly half of the American republic's existence there was no formal central bank. Consequently, you must first understand the historical background that led to the creation and development of the Fed.

The Origins of American Central Banking, 1791–1836

Because the thirteen states that formed the United States originated from the British Empire, customs and legal precedents largely reflected those of England. These states, therefore, looked to British practices when developing the banking institutions for the federal government they initiated in 1791. At the center of the British system was the Bank of England, which the British parliament had established in 1694. This central bank was the main depository for the government of England and also served as a key lender to the British government, particularly during times of war. Ultimately, the Bank of England became a central depository for other private banks in the British empire. From this position the Bank in England was able to establish and enforce policies that other banks felt obliged to follow.

The Bank of North America   When Robert Morris lobbied the Continental Congress to approve the 1781 **charter** (official banking license) for the Bank of North America, he and his supporters regarded the Bank of England as an example they should strive to emulate. Morris based many features of the charter of the Bank of North America on the original charter of the Bank of England. He and others who placed their funds in the Bank of North America also had high hopes that it might emerge as a central bank.

charter   A governmental license to open and operate a bank.

GLOBAL NOTEBOOK

The Bank of England—300 Years Old and Still Not Independent

The world's oldest central bank, the Bank of England, celebrated its 300th birthday in 1994. It had been chartered as a joint-stock company in 1694. Until 1946 it was privately owned but not independent of the British government. It had many detractors over time. For example, economist David Ricardo (1772–1823) once observed that "the House of Commons did not withdraw its confidence from the Bank from any doubt of its wealth or integrity, but from a conviction of its total ignorance of political economy."

From the very beginning, the Bank of England was a servant of the government. This became obvious in 1844 when it was divided into two departments—the Issue Department and the Banking Department. The former was strictly regulated by the British Treasury and was given the authority to issue bank notes covered by government securities. The Banking Department is simply the bank for the government and the repository of British monetary reserves. When the government took over actual ownership in 1946, there was no further question about who called the shots. Recently, economist Stanley Fisher of MIT argued that the Bank of England should be released from the control of the British Treasury. He argued that an independent Old Lady of Threadneedle Street would lead to less inflation in England.

For Critical Analysis: *What is the relationship between the U.S. Treasury and the Federal Reserve System?*

Although the Bank of North America generally was a conservatively managed and successful banking institution, it never rose to the stature of a central bank. There were several reasons for this. One was that the American banking and financial systems were very small compared to those of the British Empire. Another was that American financial markets were very decentralized. Finally, while the Continental Congress granted the Bank of North America a charter, it did not give the bank any special powers beyond those held by the few other state-chartered banks of the time.

The First Bank of the United States   As discussed in Chapter 6, Alexander Hamilton, the new nation's first Treasury secretary, reviewed the history of the Bank of North America when contemplating the establishment of the first American central bank. Hamilton's ambition, however, was for the United States to have a central bank that would rival the Bank of England in power and influence. Toward this end, he sought to convince the U.S. Congress to establish a Bank of the United States modeled very much along the lines of the Bank of England.

By the time that Hamilton was contemplating the establishment of the Bank of the United States, however, the Bank of England no longer functioned as a purely private institution. Its affairs and those of the British government had become so interconnected that the fortunes of the British Treasury and the Bank of England were inseparable. Consequently, Hamilton proposed that the newly formed U.S. federal government should own a minority share in the Bank of the United States. This would give the bank an incentive to take the government's interest into account when conducting its affairs. Yet, at the same time, the Bank of the United States would be a private institution.

Although James Madison and Thomas Jefferson opposed the establishment of the Bank of the United States, Congress ultimately adopted the essential features of Hamilton's proposal, and President Washington allowed Congress's action to stand. Congress granted the First Bank of the United States a 20-year federal charter and authorized the U.S. Treasury to purchase a fixed amount of the First Bank's equity shares and to hold deposits at the First Bank. It also authorized the First Bank to open branches throughout the nation and to issue its own currency notes that the federal government would accept as payments for internal taxes, foreign tariffs, and fees for government services.

During its twenty years of existence, the First Bank generally was a stable and profitable institution. But Congress did not renew its charter, largely because of concerns by 1811 that foreigners had accumulated too many of its shares and that the First Bank might accumulate sufficient resources to influence the affairs of state banks. Indeed, by 1810 the directors of the First Bank had begun to recognize that they could reduce the overall volume of credit in the banking system by requesting that state banks redeem their notes with the gold reserves that backed them. In a sense this was the early nineteenth-century equivalent of an open market sale by today's Fed, as discussed in Chapter 10. Although Hamilton had hoped that the First Bank ultimately would develop such financial power, Congress found itself unwilling to let the First Bank develop into a central banking institution capable of exercising authority over the nation's banking and monetary affairs.

The Second Bank of the United States Just as the charter of the First Bank of the United States expired, the nation became embroiled in several disputes with England. During the resulting War of 1812, the U.S. Treasury found itself without an agent to assist it in raising funds to finance its wartime expenditures. The Treasury also lacked a central depository for funds that it was able to raise. Furthermore, a significant period of inflation occurred after the war. These events convinced President James Madison to change his mind about central banking institutions. In 1815 he recommended that Congress grant a federal charter to a Second Bank of the United States. Congress authorized a charter that would span the period 1816–36. It also modeled the Second Bank closely upon the structure of the First Bank. The nation now seemed ready for a central banking institution.

By 1823, when Nicholas Biddle became the Second Bank's president, the bank was well on the way to becoming such an institution. In that year the Second Bank held almost half of all the specie (monetary gold and silver) in the nation. Like the First Bank, it found that it could influence national credit conditions by choosing when and to what extent to redeem state bank notes for the specie that backed them. Under Biddle's direction, the Second Bank liked to think of itself as a benevolent institution, or in Biddle's own words, "the enemy of none, but the common friend of all."

Nevertheless, a severe business downturn from 1818 through 1820 was accompanied by significant deflation and financial panics. Among the biggest losers from these events were politically powerful individuals in newly emerging states such as Kentucky and Tennessee. These individuals, including Andrew Jackson of Tennessee, joined with others from these areas in blaming the policies of the Second Bank of the United States for the negative fortunes of their states. In 1828 Andrew Jackson succeeded John Quincy Adams as President of the United States. Jackson accused the Second Bank of accumulating too much power and violating the terms of its charter. Congress concluded two sets of hearings investigating this charge and then passed a bill authorizing the rechartering of the Second Bank. In 1832, however, Jackson vetoed the bill. The political maneuvering associated with these events now is known as the "bank war" between Jackson and the political forces aligned with the Second Bank. Jackson emerged victorious because he used his veto as a winning issue in his reelection campaign, and Congress failed to override his veto. In 1836 the Second Bank officially closed its doors, and the federal government adopted a policy of accepting only specie in payment for taxes, tariffs, federal fees, and land owned by the federal government.

In 1837 there was a major banking panic and business downturn that now is known as the Panic of 1837. For over a century afterward many historians blamed these events on the failure to recharter the Second Bank of the United States. Such a central banking institution, they argued, might have been able to help stabilize the banking system. Most economic historians today question that argument, however. One reason is that the main cause of the 1837 panic was a significant outflow of specie from the United States to England following a banking panic in that country. Compared with England, the United States at that time was a relatively small country that, at best, could insulate itself only slightly from such events. Another was that during its existence the Second Bank of the United States had shown little interest in trying to offset the effects of national business declines, such as the one that occurred in 1819. Hence, it is doubtful that the closure of the Second Bank "caused" the panic of 1837.

1

What were the first American central banking institutions?   Although neither possessed the extensive monetary policy or bank regulatory powers of today's Federal Reserve, both the First Bank of the United States and the Second Bank of the United States, in various respects, represented the first central banking institutions of the United States. Both institutions had the capability to affect the rest of the American banking system, and the Second Bank of the United States used this power at various times.

Policy and Politics Without a Central Bank, 1837–1912

Following the demise of the Second Bank of the United States, the U.S. Treasury again found itself without a central financial agent. It also was forced to find state-chartered banks in which to deposit its funds. The state banks that it chose became known as "pet banks," because banks the Treasury did not select felt slighted.

The Free-Banking Period   Whether or not they were pets, state banks faced neither federally chartered competition nor federal regulation for over two decades after the closure of the Second Bank. In a number of states, however, the degree of loan and deposit market rivalry among state-chartered banks actually increased with the advent of "free banking." As discussed in Chapter 6, the free-banking period lasted until the Civil War. During this interval, each state had its own banking rules, and many states permitted relatively open competition among banks. This encouraged the establishment of a few fly-by-night, or so-called *wildcat* banking operations, but in general the free-banking system appears to have been relatively stable across most states. In states with greatest banking instability banks often faced the most significant requirements, such as mandates to purchase railroad bonds and bonds sponsored by, or even issued by, state governments.

What did the U.S. Treasury do during this period without a central banking institution? Essentially, the Treasury figured out through trial and error how to get along without a central bank. By 1846 an *Independent Treasury System* was in operation. Under this system, the Treasury Department issued notes that were close substitutes for money, and in 1847 it conducted the first open-market operation in American history when it repurchased outstanding securities it had used to help finance the Mexican War (1846–48). The Treasury made several more repurchases of outstanding securities during the next several years. Although the main justification was to reduce the size of the Treasury's outstanding debt, the Treasury tried to time several of its open-market purchases during the late 1840s and early 1850s so as to stabilize national money and credit conditions.

Nevertheless, in the autumn of 1857 there was a major banking panic. By the standards of the Panic of 1837 and some later financial crises, this episode was muted and short-lived. For the generation of the period, however, it could not have come at a worse time. The nation was already fractured along sectional lines as a result of the Supreme Court's infamous *Dred Scott* decision (1857), in which the Court ruled that a former slave who lived in free states and thus considered himself a free man would have to return to bondage. Arguments over slavery in the Kansas territory had erupted into violence. Antislavery forces in Kansas and throughout the northern part of the nation contended that slavery must give way to free-market capitalism, while primarily southern proponents of slavery argued that such a purely capitalist system was inherently less stable than a slave-oriented agrarian society. Even though the Panic of 1857 was mild by historical standards, it reinforced the position of proslavery forces and thereby had important political repercussions. For its part, the Treasury did little to offset the effects of the 1857 panic and the subsequent economic downturn.

The Civil War, Greenbacks, and National Banking

Most modern historians identify 1857 as the point at which the nation's steady drift toward sectionalism switched to a rushing current pushing toward violent hostility. In December of 1860 South Carolina announced its secession from the United States, and within a few short months it had joined other southern states in forming the Confederacy. By the middle of April 1861, Fort Sumter had fallen and the Civil War had begun. Figure 11.1 displays the components of the $538 million money stock in 1861. Demand deposits accounted for well over half of the quantity of money in that year, and nearly all the remainder of the money stock was bank notes. Only about 4 percent of the quantity of money had been issued by the government.

After the formation of the Confederacy, there were two separate monies: U.S. dollars and Confederate dollars. In spite of its contentions that the U.S. government had become a lawless and corrupt institution, the Confederacy's structure mimicked most features of the original federal government. Consequently, the Confederacy established an independent treasury that mirrored its counterpart in the federal government of the Union states. Both governments' treasury departments were hard-pressed to finance wartime expenditures, and both resorted to issuing paper currency unbacked by specie.

By the end of the Civil War both the Union and the Confederacy were experiencing significant inflation. Confederate inflation was particularly severe and already had rendered the breakaway states' currency all but worthless. The end of the war also left the Union in a quandary about what to do with the paper currency that had become a

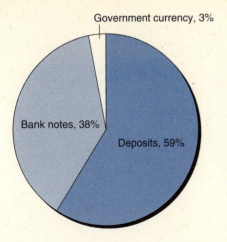

Government currency, 3%

Bank notes, 38%

Deposits, 59%

FIGURE 11.1   The Composition of the Quantity of Money in 1861

At the outset of the Civil War, the quantity of money was composed almost solely of private bank deposits and bank notes. Government currency was a very small portion of the total amount of money in the U.S. economy.
Source: Richard H. Timberlake, *Monetary Policy in the United States: An Intellectual and Institutional History,* Chicago: University of Chicago Press, 1993.

major part of the quantity of money in the United States. This paper currency was known as "greenbacks" (because of its distinctive coloring), and determining how to deal with these greenbacks became an economic and political hot potato for the next several years.

As discussed in Chapter 6, in 1863 Congress enacted the National Banking Act, which encouraged most existing state banks to switch to new federal charters to qualify as depositories of Treasury funds. This legislation also established the first system of national reserve requirements. The 1865 amendment to the law, which added a tax on the notes issued by state-chartered banks, encouraged many state banks to switch to national charters. The amendment also induced a number of banks to offer more demand deposits instead of issuing notes. In these respects the National Banking Act laid the foundation for today's Federal Reserve System and transactions-deposit-based banking system, even though the birth of the Federal Reserve was still a half-century in the future.

Panic and Resumption of the Gold Standard   Refer to Figure 11.2 on page 302, which displays estimates of the components of the

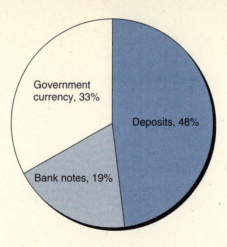

**FIGURE 11.2   The Composition of the Quantity
of Money in 1866**

Following the Civil War, government currency amounted
to a third of the quantity of money in the United States.
Source: Richard H. Timberlake, *Monetary Policy in the United
States: An Intellectual and Institutional History,* Chicago: University
of Chicago Press, 1993.

nation's $1.6 billion money stock in 1866. As the figure indicates, after
the Civil War, government-issued currency—mostly greenbacks—
had replaced bank notes as the second-place type of money held by
the public. Exactly a third of the quantity of money had become government currency.

One further change that occurred was a significant shift from deposits and notes issued by state banks to those issued by national
banks. Figure 11.3 shows that by the end of 1865 the amount of notes
and demand deposits at national banks exceeded the total quantity at
state banks. By 1868, in a dramatic example of how war and a policy
change can combine to alter fortunes, there were over 18 times more
notes and deposits at national banks than at state banks.

In 1873 another and more severe panic struck the nation's banking and financial markets. This event followed a precipitous decline in
the quantities of money and credit that the Treasury made little effort to
offset. The magnitude of the panic was significant. Note and specie reserves of New York national banks collapsed, falling by about two-
thirds during October 1873. Total deposits at those banks declined by
over one-fourth during the same interval.

The effects of the deflation on the rest of the nation also were severe. Western and midwestern farmers suddenly found that the payments they received for their crops were lower than anticipated even

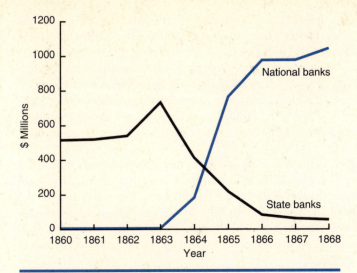

FIGURE 11.3   **Notes and Deposits at State and National Banks, 1860–68**

The state banking system that had existed before the Civil War essentially was replaced by a national banking system by the conclusion of the war. *Source:* Richard H. Timberlake, *Monetary Policy in the United States: An Intellectual and Institutional History,* Chicago: University of Chicago Press, 1993.

though their debts were unchanged. In addition, southern and western states suffered from an additional problem: They lacked national banks. This was a chronic problem throughout the late 1860s and early 1870s. The 1873 banking collapse added to the shortage of money and credit in these regions of the country.

The 1873 panic added fuel to a great national debate about what to do with the greenbacks still in circulation. When Congress authorized the creation of greenbacks during the Civil War, it had promised to remove them from circulation after the war ended. But to citizens of western and southern states, this would mean still a further reduction in the amount of money and credit available. Many citizens of these states began a movement to keep the greenbacks in circulation, and some even argued for increasing their number.

Despite a loss at the polls in 1874, resulting in part from their stand in favor of redeeming the greenbacks and returning to a full gold standard, an outgoing Republican congressional majority passed the *Resumption Act of 1875.* This law committed the federal government to return to a full gold standard by 1879. The 1876 election returned the Republicans to power and the greenback movement splintered.

Populism, Free Silver, and Bimetalism   Although members of the greenback movement had lost the battle, they continued to fight a

free silver   A late-nineteenth century idea for unlimited coinage of silver to meet the monetary needs of a growing U.S. economy.

war to increase the quantity of money in circulation. A new political movement arose. It became known as populism, and ultimately it led to the formation of the Populist Party in 1892. Many adherents of this movement adopted a new monetary proposal: **free silver,** or the unlimited coinage of silver as needed by the expanding American economy. The idea of this new political movement was to allow the quantities of money and credit to grow through *bimetalism.* As discussed in Chapter 1, this is the simultaneous use of gold and silver as commodity standards.

According to the free-silver proponents, Congress had committed the so-called *Crime of 1873* by passing a law that ended the legal coinage of silver dollars. By 1890 the populist and free-silver forces had made enough of an impression on Republican gold-standard adherents that the Republicans gave in and passed the *Sherman Silver Act.* This legislation authorized the Treasury to purchase silver and to issue dollars backed by silver.

This turned out to be bad timing. In 1893 there was another banking panic. Gold's value rose, and the market price of silver fell. Suddenly the Treasury found itself with large stocks of low-priced silver. It was not a good time to issue money backed by silver, and so Congress immediately repealed the Sherman Silver Act.

This set the stage for the final showdown over bimetalism. In a campaign speech in the presidential election of 1896, Democratic candidate William Jennings Bryan accused Republican gold-standard proponent William McKinley of attempting to crush working people under the weight of the gold standard. In the most famous sentence from this speech, Bryan adopted a biblical allusion and declared, "You shall not press down upon the brow of labor this cross of thorns, you shall not crucify mankind upon a cross of gold." Nevertheless, Bryan lost the election—one of his four failed attempts at the presidency.

2

Where did responsibility for monetary and banking policies rest in the absence of an American central bank in the nineteenth and early twentieth centuries? Until the Civil War individual states determined their own banking policies. After the Civil War the federal government established a national banking system and assumed a larger role in determining policies that affected banks. During this period with no central banking institution, the U.S. Treasury functioned as the nation's monetary policy institution.

Prelude to the Federal Reserve   After the Panic of 1893, which in many respects was even worse than the 1873 panic, even those who favored the gold standard began to believe that some type of monetary reform might be in order. This belief was reinforced in 1907 when yet another financial panic occurred. A conglomerate corporation known as the Knickerbocker Trust attempted to corner stock in a company called United Copper. When its effort failed, Knickerbocker's own stock price collapsed. This convinced many stock traders on Wall Street that the stocks of other conglomerates also would plummet. In what economists call a *self-fulfilling* prophesy, the traders' simultaneous efforts to sell off shares in these companies then *caused* the market prices of the stocks to fall. Because so few traders wished to buy stocks, offers to sell were met with successively lower bids to purchase.

Compounding the fears of traders was a speech by President Theodore Roosevelt criticizing Wall Street's "malefactors of great wealth." Traders interpreted these remarks as an indication that the Treasury would be unwilling to help rescue companies whose share prices were taking nosedives. This only added further fuel to their frenzied efforts to sell off more shares.

Ultimately, Secretary of the Treasury George Cortelyou worked out a combined public and private bailout of several Wall Street banks and trusts. Cortelyou entrusted $25 million in public funds to the private use of J. P. Morgan, who made loans to rescue the most financially healthy institutions on Wall Street. Morgan also arranged $25 million in private funding for additional loans to prop up these institutions, and the panic finally ended.

After the Panic of 1907 ended, President Roosevelt and members of Congress agreed that the nation should consider the creation of some type of central bank. The following year Congress passed the *Aldrich-Vreeland Act*, which gave the Treasury secretary emergency powers to issue currency when emerging crises threatened to become more widespread panics. The Aldrich-Vreeland Act also established a National Monetary Commission that was charged with developing a concrete plan for a U.S. central bank. Senator Nelson Aldrich led this commission, and the plan that it developed served as the basis for a bill that was pieced together in 1911 by Senators Carter Glass and Robert Owen. This bill became the *Federal Reserve Act of 1913*.

ORIGINS AND EVOLUTION OF THE FED

The Federal Reserve Act created the *Federal Reserve System* of central banking institutions. It called for this system to be supervised by a *Federal Reserve Board* composed of the Treasury secretary, the comptroller of the currency, and five additional members appointed by the president and confirmed by the Senate to 10-year terms. The Federal Reserve System, which today we often call the *Fed*, was a kind of cooperative arrangement linking consumers, businesses, banks, and the federal government. The central banking institutions that constituted

Federal Reserve banks
Twelve central banking institutions that oversee regional activities of the Federal Reserve System.

Federal Reserve districts
Twelve geographic regions of the Federal Reserve System.

the heart of the system were twelve **Federal Reserve banks,** which were located in major cities in geographic regions called **Federal Reserve districts.** A private bank could opt to join the system by purchasing ownership shares in the Federal Reserve bank in its district. This would entitle it to some say in the selection of the board of directors of the district Federal Reserve bank and to check-clearing and other banking services that the district bank would provide.

To keep the Fed from being simply a "bankers' club," however, Congress required that the majority of each Federal Reserve bank's board of directors be composed of individuals representing interests of consumers and nonfinancial businesses. Furthermore, Congress placed the Federal Reserve Board in Washington, D.C., expressly to supervise the activities of the system of Federal Reserve banks.

Congress charged the Fed with three tasks:

1. To develop and supervise the distribution of a national currency, which the Fed was to stand ready to supply in quantities necessary to help avert budding financial panics.
2. To establish a nationally coordinated system of check-clearing and collection services.
3. To process the federal government's financial accounts and to serve as the central depository for government funds.

3

What motivated Congress to establish the Federal Reserve System?   The key reason why Congress created the Federal Reserve System was to ensure that a central bank would be available to provide monetary resources in sufficient amounts to avert potential banking and financial panics. Another congressional objective was to provide an institution that could centralize the clearing of payments across the nation. Congress also desired the government to have a central depository for its funds.

The Early Fed, 1913–1935

As the Federal Reserve began its operations, it was constrained in two fundamental ways. First, the Federal Reserve Act seemed to be very specific about how the Fed could try to avert panics by lending to endangered institutions. The legislation required the Fed to lend funds through a specific mechanism called *rediscounting.* To borrow from a Federal Reserve bank, a private bank that was a Federal Reserve System member would have to post collateral in the form of discount bonds with low default risk. The Fed then would lend by purchasing these bonds at a further discount, hence "rediscounting" the bonds. The percentage of the additional discount was the Fed's **discount rate,** or the effective interest rate that the Fed would charge for its loan to the bank.

discount rate   The rate of interest that the Federal Reserve charges to lend to a depository institution.

A second constraint stemmed from something important that the Federal Reserve Act *failed* to spell out in detail, namely how powers were to be distributed *within* the Federal Reserve System. Although the legislation gave the Federal Reserve Board supervisory functions within the system, it did not give the Board the power to dictate policies to the individual Federal Reserve banks. At best, the Board could try to muster efforts for systemwide coordination. Such efforts were not always successful, and much of the time the Federal Reserve banks conducted their own regional policies.

The Hesitant Fed   An immediate complication for the Fed was the outbreak of World War I in 1914. The war severely strained international flows of gold and currencies and threatened the stability of American financial markets. Under the emergency provision of the Aldrich-Vreeland Act, Treasury secretary William McAdoo, who also was a Federal Reserve Board member, arranged for the national and state banks to issue currency to help sustain the quantities of money and credit. McAdoo also insisted on Federal Reserve purchases of Treasury securities at very low yields. By the conclusion of hostilities in late 1918 the U.S. money stock had risen by about 70 percent. During the war other Federal Reserve Board members objected to McAdoo's policies, and he responded by threatening to invoke further emergency Treasury powers, including taking full control of all banking reserves. This gave the rest of the Board little choice but to acquiesce.

After the war the center of power within the Federal Reserve System shifted from the Treasury to the Federal Reserve bank presidents. This occurred largely through the efforts of Benjamin Strong, the president of the Federal Reserve Bank of New York. He had numerous political friends and important connections with J. P. Morgan and other financial leaders. Strong initiated the Fed's first open-market operations, which led to conflicts with Board members who objected to this policy innovation. Nevertheless, Strong emerged as the dominant figure in the Federal Reserve System and remained so until he died in 1928. In October of the following year the stock market crashed. In the midst of the continuing power vacuum created by Strong's death, no leading figure appeared at the Fed to coordinate a response to the crisis.

The Great Depression and Reform of the Fed   The Fed's initial response to the panic of late 1929 was to release more reserves into the banking system. As bank failures multiplied, however, Board members hesitated to bail out banks that they viewed as insolvent rather than simply illiquid. In retrospect, it is easy to see today that they missed the point: The entire banking system had become illiquid, and only the Fed could provide the liquidity that was necessary. In the end, the Fed failed in this fundamental task that Congress had given it in 1913.

By 1933 a third of all the commercial banks in the United States had failed. Furthermore, the quantity of money also had declined by about a third. The nation's banking and monetary system shrank, and economic activity shrank as well. The banking crisis reinforced a business downturn, and the economic decline reinforced the financial collapse. The nation had fallen into what we now call the *Great Depression* of the 1930s.

In the area of money and banking arrangements, Congress responded to the Great Depression in two ways. First, it passed the Glass-Steagall Act and other related banking legislation that we discussed in Chapter 8. Second, Congress passed the *Banking Act of 1935*. In many respects this legislation really amounted to a new Federal Reserve Act, because it fundamentally restructured the Federal Reserve System.

A key provision of the Banking Act of 1935 was the centralization of internal Fed authority in Washington, D.C. But Congress no longer trusted the Federal Reserve Board as specified in the original Federal Reserve Act. Instead, Congress replaced that body with a new seven-member **Board of Governors of the Federal Reserve System.** Congress designated the Board of Governors as the key policy-making body within the Fed. To shield the Board from executive branch pressures, Congress excluded the Treasury secretary and the comptroller of the currency from Board governor positions. Instead, Congress required that the president appoint and that the Senate confirm all seven governors. It also specified that no more than four of the seven governors could belong to a single political party. Congress also lengthened the term of each governor to 14 years and established a system of overlapping terms by which the president would have the opportunity to appoint a new governor every two years.

In a further effort to centralize internal Fed policy-making authority, the 1935 legislation created the offices of Chair and Vice-Chair of the Board of Governors. Governors appointed by the president would serve 4-year renewable terms. The new law also gave the Chair, the Vice-Chair, and the remainder of the Board of Governors the authority to determine reserve requirements within ranges established by the law. It also gave the Board of Governors the authority to approve the discount rates set by the Federal Reserve banks.

Finally, the Banking Act of 1935 established the **Federal Open Market Committee (FOMC),** which is composed of the seven governors and five of the twelve Federal Reserve bank presidents. Congress gave the FOMC the authority to determine the strategies and tactics of the Fed's open-market operations. As we discuss later in this chapter, the FOMC is the key day-to-day policy-making authority within today's Federal Reserve System.

Board of Governors of the Federal Reserve System A group of seven individuals appointed by the president and confirmed by the Senate that, under the terms of the Banking Act of 1935, has key policy-making responsibilities within the Federal Reserve System.

Federal Open Market Committee (FOMC) A group composed of the seven governors and five of the twelve Federal Reserve Bank presidents that determines how to conduct the Fed's open-market operations.

4

Why did Congress restructure the Federal Reserve in 1935?   A key defect of the original Federal Reserve Act of 1913 was that it did not spell out the lines of authority for Fed policy-making. This caused internal dissension within the Fed that complicated its ability to respond to crises such as the 1929 stock market crash and the subsequent financial panics. Congress also perceived that having Treasury officials serve on the Federal Reserve Board gave the executive branch of the federal government too much clout, and so it sought to reduce the extent of the Treasury's influence on internal Fed policy-making.

The Evolution of the Modern Fed

In many respects the Banking Act of 1935 created a new institution. It created new offices with clearly defined responsibilities, and it centered the Fed's powers within the Board of Governors and its chair. But the legislation left many points unaddressed, including the proper relationship between the Fed and the Treasury, the full extent of the chair's authority, and the ultimate economic goals that the Fed was to pursue. Much of the Fed's history since 1935 reflects its efforts to deal with these issues.

The Fed's Fight for Independence   The first leader of the new Federal Reserve System was a former Utah banker named Marriner Eccles. President Franklin Roosevelt had appointed Eccles to the original Federal Reserve Board in 1934, and Eccles was instrumental in helping design and promote the reforms that Congress adopted in the Banking Act of 1935. He then served as chair of the Board of Governors until 1948. The original Federal Reserve Board building at 21st and C Streets in Washington, D.C. now bears his name, because later Fed insiders credited Eccles with rescuing the Fed from disgrace following its performance between 1929 and 1933.

During most of Eccles' time as chair, however, the Federal Reserve essentially functioned as an unofficial unit of the Department of the Treasury. This was particularly true during World War II, when the Fed's open-market operations were geared toward maintaining high and stable prices for Treasury securities to assist the government's efforts to raise the funds needed to finance wartime expenditures. The Fed did this by buying and selling securities, as needed, to "peg" Treasury bill yields at relatively low levels.

After World War II, the Treasury pressured the Fed to continue this policy. President Harry Truman replaced Eccles with a new chair, Thomas McCabe, but Eccles remained a Fed governor until his term expired in July 1951. It was in this diminished role that Eccles launched an effort to make the Federal Reserve an independent institution. He helped prompt the Fed to test the Treasury's willingness for Treasury bill yields to rise above their previous levels. The Treasury resisted these efforts, and it became even more hostile to Fed independence following the outbreak of the Korean War in June 1950. In early 1951 President Truman called the entire Federal Open Market Committee to the White House for a "private chat." Afterward, the White House announced that the FOMC had agreed to continue its interest-rate-pegging policy.

Nevertheless, the Fed was convinced that the inflation that had begun to heat up with the outbreak of the Korean conflict would get out of control if it continued pegging Treasury bill yields. Within a few weeks of President Truman's meeting with the FOMC, the Fed again let Treasury bill yields rise somewhat. Behind the scenes, Fed officials successfully negotiated a settlement with the Treasury, which President Truman grudgingly approved. This settlement is now called the **Federal Reserve–Treasury Accord,** or more simply the **Accord.** The Accord was a joint agreement that the Fed could minimize the extent to which it "monetized" the public debt by purchasing securities as needed to keep market yields low.

The initial impact of the Accord was slight: The Fed permitted market interest rates to creep up slightly. By early 1953, however, a new Board chair, William McChesney Martin, adopted a broadened interpretation of the Accord. Interestingly, Martin had been a chief negotiator for the Treasury Department when the Accord was adopted. In his role as Fed chief, Martin chose to view the Accord as a statement of the full independence of the Fed. In 1953 Dwight Eisenhower was the new president, and Eisenhower's administration was willing to accept this broadened interpretation.

Henceforth, the Fed regarded itself as an *independent* institution *within* the government. Later presidents and Congresses would test the Fed's self-interpretation of its proper role "within the government."

"Leaning Against the Wind"

Martin was Board chair until 1970. Shortly after the beginning of his long tenure, Martin announced that the Fed's purpose "is to lean against the winds of deflation or inflation, whichever way they are blowing." Later he offered an alternative analogy to the Fed's job of containing inflationary pressures caused by short-term overexpansion of the economy: The Fed's role, he said, "is to take away the punch bowl just when the party gets going."

During much of Martin's time at the Fed's helm, the Fed sought to stabilize the level of **free reserves,** or the difference between the total amount of excess reserves and the total quantity of reserves borrowed from the Fed's discount window. The idea behind this policy was that if bank holdings of excess reserves were high relative to their borrowings

Federal Reserve–Treasury Accord   A 1951 agreement disassociating the Fed from a previous policy of pegging Treasury bill rates at artificially low levels.

free reserves   Total excess reserves at depository institutions minus the total amount of reserves that depository institutions have borrowed from the Fed.

POLICY NOTEBOOK
The Fed's Lack of Cultural Diversity

While Bill Clinton actively pursued his goal of creating an administration that "looked like America," the Fed continued its reign as one of the most male and least diverse groups in the federal government. For most of its history its seven-member board of governors has been all white and has included very few women. Of the remaining top 30 jobs at the Fed, all are held by white males except for the director of maintenance services, who is an African American. As of the mid-1990s, at the regional Federal Reserve bank all 12 presidents and 98 of the 111 vice presidents were white men.

The chair of the Board of Governors of the Federal Reserve, Alan Greenspan, wrote to House Banking Committee Chairman Henry B. Gonzalez (D., Tex.) that "we are working diligently to improve opportunities for women and minorities throughout the system." But Greenspan's efforts to change the Fed will not happen rapidly. The Fed is an institution that has little turnover and almost all promotions are from within. Those who are high-level staffers have been with the Fed for most of their professional lives. The reason is fairly clear: Working conditions are good and the pay is great—top staff get $162,000 a year plus many perks, which is more than members of Congress or the cabinet earn.

There are some signs of change, though, for at the Fed's Washington headquarters almost 30 percent of second-tier staff jobs are held by women and 14 percent are held by minorities. So far, only one woman—at the Federal Reserve Bank of Boston—has reached the position of Federal Reserve bank president. Currently, two other women are first vice-president at three of the twelve regional banks. They will be next in line to become presidents.

For Critical Analysis: *Is the Fed ruled by the same regulations as U.S. government agencies?*

from the Fed, then it would be easier for them to lend. In contrast, if banks were short on excess reserves relative to reserves they owed the Fed, they would be more constrained in their ability to extend new loans to consumers and businesses. Hence, conducting open-market operations with an aim toward keeping the amount of free reserves relatively stable would ensure that credit conditions would be neither too loose nor too tight.

The growing American involvement in the Vietnam conflict (1964–1973) complicated the Fed's policy-making through the end of the 1960s. When President Lyndon Johnson decided in 1965 to expand the U.S. commitment of ground forces to Vietnam without increasing taxes to pay the expenses, the Fed faced renewed pressures from the president and the Treasury to keep U.S. Treasury bond yields low. At one point President Johnson summoned Martin to his Texas ranch and lectured him on the dangers of raising interest rates.

By 1968 President Johnson had decided that additional taxes would be required to fund the military expenses that the government was incurring. But, by then, the inflation rate had reached 5 percent, which Americans at that time perceived as relatively high. By 1969, when Richard Nixon assumed the presidency, the inflation rate exceeded 6 percent.

The Technocratic Fed   In 1970 President Nixon appointed a new Fed chair, Arthur Burns, a Columbia University economics professor and former advisor to President Eisenhower. Under Burns, the Federal Reserve attempted to take a more scientific approach to policy-making. The Board of Governors assigned a number of staff economists the task of developing reliable measures of monetary aggregates. Then it systematically began to frame its policy-making within the perspective of the likely effects on such aggregates as M1 and M2.

During Martin's term at the Fed, banks had begun to lend reserves in the federal funds market. By the time Burns became the Fed chief, the federal funds rate had become a widely recognized indicator of credit market conditions. A rise in the federal funds rate indicated a tightening of credit market conditions, while a fall in the federal funds rate signaled a loosening. Under Burns, however, the Fed began to use the federal funds rate as more than a policy indicator. Indeed, the Fed began to tailor its open-market operations to move the federal funds rate to levels that it felt were consistent with its goals for magnitudes of monetary aggregates. Although the Fed continued to pay close attention to the effects its policies had on the spectrum of interest rates for other financial instruments, for the first time it began to pay attention to the effects that policies had on the quantity of money.

Early in Burns' tenure at the Fed the link between the dollar and gold was broken. In August 1971 President Nixon formally announced the end of the gold standard that had existed—at least officially—during most years since 1879. Although the United States had suspended its formal adherence to the gold standard during crises such as the Great Depression, this announcement severed entirely the tie between money and gold. Arthur Burns and other Fed officials found themselves truly charged with anchoring the nation's currency system solely to its confidence in the Fed's policy-making. This, to Burns and the Fed, was a key rationale for trying to aim Fed policies at stabilizing monetary aggregates as well as credit market conditions.

Inflation and Monetary Targeting   Despite Burns' effort during his eight-year stint as Board chair to cultivate a reputation as an "inflation fighter," the inflation rate had risen to 8 percent by the time he completed his second term. In addition, there were suspicions that during President Nixon's 1972 reelection campaign, Burns might have conspired explicitly or implicitly to stimulate the economy through loosened Fed policies. This alleged effort to help President Nixon's reelection prospects, critics charged, further added to inflationary pressures caused in large measure by the sharp rises in oil prices that occurred during and after 1973.

In 1978 President Jimmy Carter appointed G. William Miller as the new chair of the Fed's Board of Governors. During Miller's brief 17-month tenure, the inflation rate rose into double digits. In July 1979 Miller resigned his position. President Carter then appointed Paul Volcker, a long-term Fed insider and then president of the Federal Reserve Bank of New York, as the new Fed chief.

Within three months after assuming the top job at the Fed, Volcker had agreed to a new approach to monetary policy. Under the new approach, the Fed would attempt to stabilize the growth of monetary aggregates while deemphasizing interest rate stability. The result, not surprisingly, was that interest rates became much more volatile. What was a surprise was that monetary aggregates actually became more variable as well. Nevertheless, on net, interest rates rose and money growth slowed. Inflation was contained.

In 1982 the Fed discontinued its experiment with trying to stabilize monetary aggregates. Its rationale was that the relationship between such aggregates and economic activity had broken down. Indeed, as we shall discuss in Chapter 15, this did occur. Fed critics, however, charged that the Fed had never really made an honest effort to contain monetary variability. They viewed the abandonment of the new approach as further evidence that the Fed was not serious about controlling monetary aggregates.

Today's Middle-of-the-Road Fed   After 1982 the Fed adopted yet another approach to conducting monetary policy, in which it attempted to stabilize the amount of reserves that banks borrowed from the discount window. As we shall discuss in Chapter 13, this is in many respects an approach similar to the old free-reserves policy of the 1950s and 1960s. It also can resemble a policy of stabilizing the federal funds rate. Indeed, in many respects the policy-making of today's Fed is similar to its approach under Arthur Burns, except that the Fed seems to have been more successful in containing inflation in recent years.

Since 1987 Alan Greenspan has been chair of the Fed's Board of Governors. To date, Greenspan's time in this position has witnessed fewer complications as compared with several of his predecessors. Yet, within the Fed there have been some significant changes in how policies are formulated and implemented. We shall discuss some of these changes in the concluding portion of this chapter.

Currency Boards Impose Discipline on Central Banks

When a country's central bank is basically an arm of its treasury, fiscal profligacy ultimately leads to dramatic increases in the money supply and in inflation. Several countries have found a way out of this dilemma. They have created *currency boards* to impose discipline. Under a currency board system, a central bank can create no money that is not fully backed by foreign exchange reserves. The local currency is pegged at some fixed rate to a key world currency, such as the dollar or the German mark. The local currency is fully convertible into the currency to which it is pegged. The first currency boards were used in Mauritius and New Zealand in 1849 and 1850. More recently, Hong Kong pegged its currency to the U.S. dollar in 1984 and Argentina did the same thing in 1991. Several former Soviet republics have chosen other currencies. In 1992 Estonia pegged its *kroon* to the German mark.

In all cases, when currency boards have been adopted, a country's rate of inflation has stabilized at a very low level.

For Critical Analysis: *Would central bankers be for or against a currency board system? Explain.*

THE STRUCTURE OF THE FED

When Congress created the Federal Reserve in 1913 and revamped its structure in 1935, it was very mindful of traditional American suspicions of the motives of central bankers and distrust of centralized authority. For this reason, Congress sought to construct a decentralized central banking institution that would be responsive to the concerns of American citizens. At the same time, however, Congress recognized that a central bank should be operated by people who possessed essential levels of competence in banking and finance. This meant that Congress needed to find a way to ensure that leaders of the Federal Reserve had banking and monetary policy experience. The somewhat convoluted structure of the Federal Reserve System reflects congressional efforts to trade off these conflicting objectives.

The Board of Governors

The seven Fed governors have several responsibilities. As noted above, the governors must authorize any discount rate change, and they also have the authority to set required reserve ratios within ranges established by law. In addition, the Board has oversight authority over the Federal Reserve district banks.

As noted in Chapter 8, the Fed is a key banking regulator charged with examining and supervising all state-chartered commercial banks that are members of the Federal Reserve System. Under the Bank Holding Company Act of 1956 and its 1970 amendment, the Fed also regulates the activities of bank holding companies. The 1970 amendment to the Bank Holding Company Act also gives the Board of Governors the authority to approve or disapprove proposed depository institution mergers, which invariably entail changes in the structure of a bank holding company.

The various consumer protection laws discussed in Chapter 9 also require enforcement actions by the Board of Governors. Consequently, the Board issues regulations intended to induce depository institutions to comply with the provisions of these laws.

All seven Board governors are automatic members of the twelve-member Federal Open Market Committee. The FOMC sets policy for the Fed's open-market operations, and so the numerical superiority of the Board relative to the other FOMC members gives the Board considerable authority over the day-to-day conduct of monetary policy. The FOMC also oversees Fed trading in foreign exchange markets, and so the Board also has major influence over the Fed's international operations.

Because the Board of Governors has so many responsibilities, the various governors typically specialize in specific areas of policy-making. Normally one governor will have key responsibilities in bank regulation, while another will specialize in foreign exchange operations. The Board also has standing and ad hoc subcommittees in these and other areas of its responsibilities. These subcommittees consider policy issues and then make recommendations to the full Board.

The Federal Reserve Banks

Each of the Federal Reserve banks is a federally chartered corporation that has a sphere of influence largely confined to its own Federal Reserve district. Figure 11.4 shows the locations of the Federal Reserve district banks.

Member banks within each of the 12 districts own the equity shares of the Federal Reserve bank of their district. Ownership of these shares entitles these member banks to elect six of the nine members of the board of directors of their Federal Reserve bank. Three of the six directors elected by member banks must be bankers from small, medium-sized, and large banks. The other three typically represent the interests of business or agriculture. The Board of Governors appoints the remaining three directors of each Federal Reserve bank. This group of directors cannot have banking connections, and the Board designates one member of this Board-appointed group of directors as the chair of the board of directors of the Federal Reserve bank. Each Federal Reserve bank director serves a term of three years, and directors' terms are staggered so that a new director within each of the three categories is elected or appointed each year.

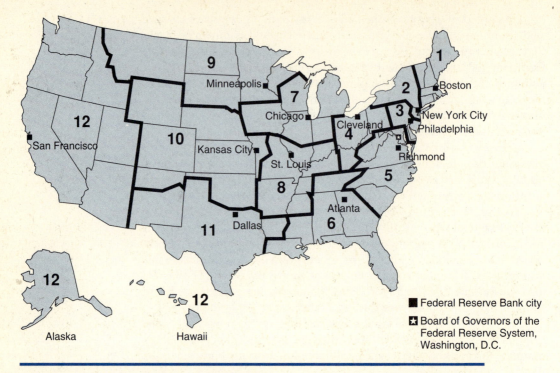

■ Federal Reserve Bank city

⭐ Board of Governors of the Federal Reserve System, Washington, D.C.

FIGURE 11.4   Federal Reserve District Banks

This map shows the twelve Federal Reserve bank districts and the locations of the individual Federal Reserve banks. *Source:* Board of Governors of the Federal Reserve System. *Federal Reserve Bulletin,* all issues.

A key function of each Federal Reserve bank is to process electronic and nonelectronic clearings of payments. Together, then, the Federal Reserve banks truly represent a "system" that routes payments from senders of funds to the ultimate receivers. We discuss the Fed's role in the national and international payments systems in more detail in Chapter 12.

Although we commonly speak of the Fed's discount window, in fact each Federal Reserve bank operates its own lending facility. Furthermore, each has its own rules and regulations for discount window lending, although they are fairly similar across the twelve district banks. Any Federal Reserve bank may apply to the Board of Governors to change its discount rate, but the Board must approve such a change before it can be put into effect. Normally the Board prefers for the discount rate to be the same across all twelve districts, and so typically a coalition of Federal Reserve bank presidents must make a case for a change in the discount rate if the Board itself is not already inclined to change the rate.

Each Federal Reserve bank president is appointed by the bank's board of directors. The presidents are chief operating officers of the district banks. All twelve presidents also have input into deliberations of the FOMC, although only five presidents serve as voting members each year.

The Federal Open Market Committee

As noted earlier, the FOMC is composed of the seven Federal Reserve Board governors and five of the twelve district bank presidents. Because the Federal Reserve Bank of New York implements all the Fed's open-market operations and foreign exchange trading, the president of this district bank is always a voting member in the FOMC. The remaining eleven district bank presidents are separated into four groups, with a member of each group qualifying to vote in the FOMC each year on a rotating basis. The chair of the Board of Governors automatically is FOMC chairman.

Formal meetings of the FOMC take place eight to ten times per year. At these meetings the voting members of the FOMC determine the wording of the **FOMC directive.** This constitutes the formal instructions to the operating officers at the Federal Reserve Bank of New York who supervise open-market operations and foreign exchange trading. The supervisor of open-market operations is called the head of the **Trading Desk** of the New York Federal Reserve bank. The Trading Desk is a figurative term for the office at this district bank that engages in purchases and sales of securities on the Fed's account. The head of the Trading Desk functions as the FOMC's account manager, and this individual communicates daily with designated subcommittees of FOMC members.

FOMC directive   The official written instructions by the FOMC to the head of the Trading Desk at the Federal Reserve Bank of New York.

Trading Desk   The Fed's term for the office at the Federal Reserve Bank of New York that conducts open-market operations on the Fed's behalf.

5

Who makes the key policy decisions at the Federal Reserve?   Two key groups of individuals make the important policy decisions at the Fed. One of these groups is the Fed's Board of Governors, which is composed of seven people appointed by the president and approved by the Senate. The Board of Governors approves discount rate changes, sets reserve requirements, determines regulatory policies for state-chartered commercial banks that are Fed members, and regulates the activities of bank holding companies. The other main policy-making group is the Federal Open Market Committee (FOMC). The FOMC includes the Board of Governors and five of the twelve Federal Reserve bank presidents, and it establishes the Fed's intentions concerning day-to-day conduct of monetary policy through open-market operations.

The Evolving Authority of the Fed Chair

Since the restructuring of the Fed by the Banking Act of 1935, the chair of the Board of Governors has been the most powerful individual within the Fed. This individual does not have dictatorial powers, however. While the chair can use the authority of the position to shape the agendas of the Board of Governors and the FOMC, the chair ultimately has only one vote in meetings of each policy-making body.

Nevertheless, other Board governors and FOMC members typically prefer not to dissent from the chair's inclinations on important policy issues. Likewise, any chair seeks to avoid being in the minority on any vote, because this diminishes the chair's power as perceived by those within and outside the Fed. Consequently, an individual who serves as chair must be able to marshal support for his or her views. This usually requires an ability to communicate, to compromise, and to make the greatest use of the prestige and power of the office.

In 1986, then-chair Paul Volcker found himself in the minority on a key vote concerning the discount rate. This extremely rare event signaled to him and to his successors that it is not impossible for the chair to be outvoted. Volcker's immediate successor, Alan Greenspan faced the implications of this precedent-setting event in 1991. Before that time, if convinced that such an action was appropriate, the chair typically would alter FOMC Trading Desk instructions between FOMC meetings. Protocol required only that the chair inform FOMC members of the decision to do this. But in early 1991 when Greenspan attempted to instruct the Trading Desk to induce a cut in market interest rates, two Federal Reserve bank presidents objected. They requested a ruling from the Fed's legal staff concerning Greenspan's power to continue this long-standing practice. Although the legal staff responded with an ambiguous opinion, Greenspan decided that in the future he would seek more formal FOMC support before changing Trading Desk instructions between FOMC meetings.

Now, FOMC directives are either "symmetric" or "asymmetric." In the past all directives were **asymmetric directives,** meaning that if, at its most recent meeting, the FOMC anticipated that the federal funds rate might need to rise or fall before the time of the next meeting, it would implicitly give the chair the authority to move in whichever direction the FOMC had authorized. Under a **symmetric directive,** however, the FOMC indicates no inclination for the federal funds rate to move either direction. A symmetric directive gives the chair no authorization to instruct the Trading Desk to change course in the interval until the next FOMC meeting. Hence, a symmetric directive ties the hands of the chair.

Since 1994 symmetric directives have been the rule rather than the exception. Indeed, most observers view the Fed as a much more democratic institution than it was before Greenspan became chair in 1987. As a result, decision-making power is much more decentralized. If there is a power center at the Fed, it remains the chair of the Board of Governors. Nevertheless, the Fed today is very much an institution that is run by committee, with the FOMC the main day-to-day authority for monetary policy actions. The advantage of this change is that more Fed officials now have greater input into the policy process. The

asymmetric directive   An FOMC policy directive that gives the chair of the Fed's Board of Governors the power to authorize Trading Desk actions designed to raise or to reduce the federal funds rate.

symmetric directive   An FOMC policy directive that fails to give the chair of the Fed's Board of Governors the power to authorize Trading Desk actions either to raise or to reduce the federal funds rate.

disadvantage is that the Fed may not be as quick to respond to a need for policy changes as in the past. Some members of Congress have expressed concerns about this potential advantage and about the power of Federal Reserve bank presidents within the FOMC. A few, as we shall discuss in Chapter 12, have proposed reducing or even eliminating the policy-making authority of the district bank presidents.

6

How powerful is the chair of the Fed's Board of Governors?   The Fed chair automatically serves as chair of the Federal Open Market Committee (FOMC), and this individual's leadership of the two main policy-making groups at the Fed makes him or her the most powerful person in the Federal Reserve System. In recent years, however, the chair's powers have become more limited, as other members of the FOMC have sought to ensure that the chair does not make important policy decisions without the input of other FOMC members.

SUMMARY

1. **The First American Central Banking Institutions:** The First Bank of the United States and the Second Bank of the United States operated from 1791 to 1811 and from 1816 to 1836, respectively. Although neither developed into full central banking institutions in the modern sense, each had the ability to influence the overall volume of money and credit in the American economy.

2. **Responsibility for Monetary and Banking Policies in the Absence of a Central Bank in the Nineteenth and Early Twentieth Centuries:** From 1837 until the Civil War the individual states established their own banking policies, but from the Civil War onward both state and federal governments formulated policies regarding depository institutions. Between 1837 and the founding of the Federal Reserve in 1913 the responsibility for monetary policy rested with the U.S. Treasury Department.

3. **The Motivation for Congress to Establish the Federal Reserve System:** Historical experiences with banking panics in 1837, 1857, 1873, 1893, and, finally, 1907 convinced national leaders that the United States needed a central banking institution that could help stem such panics by increasing the amounts of money and credit available. Congress also wanted the federal government to have a central depository for its own funds and saw a need for a central banking institution to help coordinate clearing activity for the growing volumes of payments in the nation's large industrial economy.

4. **The Rationale for the 1935 Congressional Restructuring of the Federal Reserve:** The Fed's lack of success in reducing the ill effects of the 1929 stock market crash and subsequent bank failures and financial panics convinced Congress that the Fed needed clearly specified lines of authority and more independence from pressures from the president and the Treasury.

5. **Those Who Make the Key Policy Decisions at the Federal Reserve:** Decisions concerning the discount rate, reserve requirements, and regulation of Fed member banks and bank holding companies fall within the responsibilities of the Federal Reserve's seven-member Board of Governors. Day-to-day monetary policy making via open-market purchases and sales of securities are directed by the Federal Open Market Committee, which is composed of the Board of Governors and five Federal Reserve bank presidents.

6. **The Power of the chair of the Fed's Board of Governors:** Because the Board chair also functions as chair of the Federal Open Market Committee, this individual can spearhead all aspects of Fed policy-making. This undeniably makes the chair the most powerful person at the Fed. Yet recent events have reduced the chair's power somewhat. Now other members of the Federal Open Market Committee, including the district bank presidents, have more authority in the Fed's decision-making process.

QUESTIONS AND PROBLEMS

1. Based on the discussion in this chapter, does it appear to you that the First and Second Banks of the United States actively conducted monetary policies? In what way could they conduct such policies, whether or not they did so on an active basis? Explain.

2. Given that the U.S. Treasury Department functioned without a central bank from 1837 to 1913, do you think that a central bank such as the Fed is really necessary? Support your answer.

3. Before the creation of the Federal Reserve System, monetary issues often were themes of political campaigns. Since the Fed's founding, however, such issues rarely have been discussed during campaigns. Why might this be so?

4. In what fundamental ways did the Banking Act of 1935 truly reform the Fed? In what ways did it leave the institution unchanged?

5. In what respects is the Fed a private bank? In what respects is it a government agency?

6. In your view, should the chair of the Board of Governors have more or less authority? What are the advantages and disadvantages of recent reductions in the extent of the chair's powers?

12

The Fed, the Financial System, and Monetary Policy

KEY QUESTIONS

1. What are the main assets and liabilities of the Fed?

2. In what ways is the Fed the government's bank?

3. What is the rationale for the Fed's role as a bank for private banks?

4. Why does the Fed play a supervisory role in the U.S. payments system?

5. What are daylight overdrafts, and why does the Fed care about them?

6. What are the primary tools through which the Fed conducts monetary policy?

I t is not just another day at the office during every business day of the year for the head of the Federal Reserve Bank of New York's trading desk. This individual's job is to buy and sell government securities in an absolute frenzy for about one hour each morning in order to carry out the Federal Open Market Committee (FOMC) directive that was handed down at the last meeting. Only the seven members of the FOMC and its staff know the contents of that directive, for it is a secret document until it is released to the public six weeks after it is sent to the trading Desk of the New York Fed. Twenty years ago, a Georgetown law student filed suit against the FOMC claiming that the secrecy of its operation violated the Freedom of Information Act. Although a U.S. district court ruled in the student's favor, ultimately the Fed prevailed and its secrecy still continues. Congress has repeatedly questioned Fed chair Alan Greenspan about this secrecy issue. He has argued that the tight-lips policy helps the Fed avoid creating turbulence in the credit market. His critics have pointed out that Germany's central bank, the Bundesbank, announces its monetary decisions at a press conference the day it votes. For the time being, the U.S. central bank gets to keep its policies secret. But actually, Fed watchers can pretty much figure out what the Fed directive is the day after it is issued simply by analyzing the Fed's open-market operations, the subject of this chapter.

THE FED AS A CENTRAL BANK

The Federal Reserve System is a complex public policy institution. It also is a very large bank with twelve district "branches" and a "central office" in Washington, D.C. Before we get too wrapped up in the broader public policy aspects of the Fed, let's begin by considering its banking operations.

The Fed's Balance Sheet

Each of the Federal Reserve banks has its own detailed balance sheet, as does the Board of Governors in Washington, D.C. The best way to gain a concrete understanding of the Fed's activities, however, is to examine the Fed's *consolidated balance sheet*, which is a "T-account" that displays the combined assets, liabilities, and equity capital for all units of the Federal Reserve System.

The Fed's Assets   Table 12.1 displays the Fed's consolidated balance sheet as of March, 1996. The table displays both absolute dollar values and percentages relative to total assets and to total liabilities and net worth.

You should concentrate on the percentages, because dollar amounts change considerably over time, whereas the Fed's proportionate allocations of its assets and its liabilities and equity capital tend to remain stable.

U.S. Treasury securities comprise the most important category of Fed assets. The 89 percent figure in Table 12.1 is a typical proportionate allocation of assets to government securities. About 90 percent of these government securities are Treasury bills and notes (maturities of less than 10 years), and the remainder are Treasury bonds (maturities exceeding 10 years).

In addition to securities issued by the U.S. Treasury, the Fed holds debt issues of other U.S. government agencies. These securities account for a small, and typically stable, fraction of Fed assets.

The Federal Reserve also lends to private depository institutions via the discount window facilities of the Federal Reserve banks. As Table 12.1 indicates, the dollar amount of discount window lending and the percentage of assets allocated to such lending is relatively small. Nevertheless, discount window lending can be an important element of the Fed's procedure for conducting monetary policy, as we discuss later in this chapter.

Gold certificates remain on the Fed's balance sheet as a constant reminder of the nation's former adherence to a gold standard. When the

TABLE 12.1 The Consolidated Balance Sheet of the Federal Reserve System ($ millions, as of March 31, 1996)

ASSETS			LIABILITIES AND EQUITY CAPITAL		
Asset	**Dollar Amount**	**Percent of Total Assets**	**Liability**	**Dollar Amount**	**Percent of Total Liabilities and Equity**
U.S. Treasury securities	$380,952	86.2%	Federal Reserve notes	$392,903	88.9%
Federal agency securities	2,526	0.6%	Reserve deposits	24,740	5.6%
Loans to depository institutions	43	—	U.S. Treasury deposits	7,021	1.6%
Gold certificates	11,053	2.5%	Foreign official deposits	191	—
SDR certificates	10,168	2.3%	Deferred available cash items	4,069	0.9%
Foreign currency assets	19,985	4.5%	Other liabilities	4,610	1.1%
Cash items in process of collection	4,197	1.0%	Total Liabilities	$433,534	98.1%
Other assets	13,062	2.9%	Equity Capital	8,452	1.9%
Total Assets	$441,986	100.0%	Total Liabilities and Equity	$441,986	100.0%

Source: Board of Governors of the Federal Reserve System, *Federal Reserve Bulletin*, June 1996.

gold standard was in operation, the Treasury Department sold gold to the Fed in exchange for money. The Treasury issued gold certificates to the Fed to indicate the Fed's ownership of the gold that the Treasury continued to hold in reserve. Hence, these certificates are Fed assets. As a share of total assets, however, they continue to decline over time as the absolute size of the Fed's assets increases with time.

Another asset, *SDRs*, or *special drawing rights,* are certificates issued by the International Monetary Fund (IMF), which is a financial institution owned and operated by over 150 countries. In the 1970s the IMF issued SDRs as a type of international currency intended to compensate for the declining role of gold as a basis for the world's currency system. The United States government is an IMF member nation, and the Treasury owns shares in the IMF via SDRs. The Treasury financed these SDR shares by issuing a fixed, dollar amount of SDR certificates to the Fed. Consequently, SDR certificates, like gold certificates, constitute a Fed asset category that continues to decline in relative importance.

The Fed maintains a portfolio of assets denominated in the currencies of other nations, or foreign-currency-denominated securities and deposits. A key reason for the Fed holding such securities and deposits is so that it can trade them, if needed, to change the dollar's value in foreign exchange markets. We shall have more to say about this in Chapter 16.

Finally, like any other bank (see Chapter 6), the Federal Reserve receives payments from other parties that it credits to its account but that have not yet cleared the payments system. Because such payments may be subject to cancellation until that time, the Fed lists them as *cash items in the process of collection.*

The Fed's Liabilities and Equity Capital   Over four-fifths of the Federal Reserve's total liabilities and equity capital is composed of *Federal Reserve notes.* This is the currency that the Fed issues and that we use to make purchases of goods and services. As a liability, a Federal Reserve note says that the Fed owes us something in exchange. Before the early 1930s, if you sought to redeem a $1 Federal Reserve note at a Federal Reserve bank, you could have received gold in exchange. Now, however, you would receive a new $1 Federal Reserve note. So in what sense is this note really a liability? The answer is that if Congress were to close down the Federal Reserve System, the Fed would be liable to you for a dollar's worth of goods and services as of the time of its closure.

The second-largest liability of the Fed is reserve deposits of depository institutions. As we discussed in Chapter 10, depository institutions maintain the bulk of these deposits to meet legal requirements established by the Fed. Depository institutions maintain a small portion of these deposits as excess reserves, however. They often lend excess reserves to one another in the federal funds market.

Another deposit liability of the Fed is composed of deposits of the U.S. Treasury. The Treasury draws on these funds to make payments for purchases of goods and services or tax refunds.

Foreign governments or official foreign financial institutions, including central banks such as the Bank of England or the Bank of Japan, hold dollar-denominated deposit accounts with the Fed. These are *foreign official deposits*. Many of these accounts are checking accounts, and foreign governments and central banks draw upon these accounts when they need to make dollar payments.

Deferred availability cash items are payments that the Fed has promised to another party, or that it has made but which have yet to clear.

The Fed's equity capital is composed of the ownership shares of banks that are members of the Federal Reserve System. At 1.9 percent, the Fed's equity capital is very low in relation to its assets.

1

What are the main assets and liabilities of the Fed?   The primary assets of the Fed are U.S. government securities, including Treasury bills, notes, and bonds. The main liabilities are Federal Reserve notes, or currency, and reserve deposits of depository institutions.

The Fed as the Government's Bank

As we noted in Chapter 11, one original rationale for the creation of the Federal Reserve System in 1913 was the government's need for a central bank. As the main banking institution for the U.S. government, the Fed provides depository services to the Treasury. It also performs an important role as the Treasury's *fiscal agent* in financial markets.

Government Depository   The U.S. Treasury holds deposits at each of the 12 Federal Reserve banks. As depositories of the Treasury, the Federal Reserve banks maintain the Treasury's accounts, clear checks drawn on those accounts, accept deposits of federal fees and taxes, and make electronic payments on the Treasury's behalf.

The Treasury also holds deposit accounts at private depository institutions. Many of these are **Treasury tax and loan (TT&L) accounts,** which are special checking accounts that the Treasury maintains with private institutions. Another key function of the Federal Reserve banks is to serve as TT&L account go-betweens on the Treasury's behalf. In this capacity the Federal Reserve banks add to or draw from TT&L accounts at other depository institutions on the Treasury's behalf to assist the Treasury in managing its cash.

Treasury tax and loan (TT&L) accounts   U.S. Treasury checking accounts at private depository institutions.

Most Treasury payments to citizens and businesses flow from Federal Reserve bank deposits. The Fed banks handle payments that the Treasury disburses on a regular basis, such as Social Security disbursements and salary payments to federal employees, by making direct deposits into the accounts of recipients. Since 1991 the number of Fed-processed direct-deposit Treasury payments has exceeded the number of payments that the Treasury makes by check.

Fiscal Agent   The Federal Reserve functions as the key **fiscal agent** of the U.S. Treasury, meaning that it issues, services, and redeems debts on the Treasury's behalf. The Treasury issues debt instruments—bills, notes, and bonds—that the government uses to cover shortfalls between its tax receipts and its expenditures on goods and services. As we discussed in Chapter 5, the Treasury sells these securities at auctions. Although the Treasury announces the terms and conditions of the securities to be sold at such auctions, potential buyers can submit bids for new securities to the Federal Reserve banks as well as to the Treasury's Bureau of the Public Debt. As the Treasury's fiscal agent, the Federal Reserve banks review all bids to ensure that they meet legal requirements and tabulate and summarize all bids. The Federal Reserve banks also issue the Treasury's securities to the purchasers and process the payments that the purchasers provide in exchange.

To facilitate the transfer of securities, the Federal Reserve banks operate two **book-entry security systems.** These are computer systems which the Fed uses to maintain records of Treasury sales, and interest and principal payments on its securities. Financial institutions that purchase large volumes of Treasury securities—and many individuals—do not actually hold paper securities. Instead, they have computerized accounts with the Fed. The Fed provides regular statements to holders of these accounts and automatically transfers interest and principal into their accounts.

When an institution wishes to sell Treasury securities to which it has title, it does not send paper securities to the buyer. Instead, it instructs the Federal Reserve bank that maintains its book-entry security account to transfer title of ownership from its account to the book-entry security account of the purchasing institution. The Fed then makes the transfer electronically. Large institutions can initiate such transfers using direct computer links with Federal Reserve banks. Smaller institutions initiate transfers by telephone, using computer modems and software the Fed has developed for this purpose.

The Federal Reserve also sells and issues *U.S. Savings Bonds* on the Treasury's behalf. These are low-denomination, nonmarketable Treasury securities that are popular instruments for many small savers. The Federal Reserve also credits interest on savings bonds when holders redeem them at authorized depository institutions.

fiscal agent A term describing the Federal Reserve's role as an agent of the U.S. Treasury Department, in which the Fed issues, services, and redeems debts on the Treasury's behalf.

book-entry security systems Computer system used by Federal Reserve to maintain records of sales of Treasury securities and interest and principal payments.

2

In what ways is the Fed the government's bank?   The Fed is the main depository institution for the federal government. It also serves as the government's fiscal agent by operating the systems through which the Treasury sells new securities and makes interest and principal payments on outstanding securities.

The Fed's Income and Expenses   One thorny issue for the Fed has been that the Treasury does not pay in full for the services that the Fed provides. Typically the Treasury reimburses the Federal Reserve banks for only about a third of the costs they incur for providing government depository services or acting as the Treasury's fiscal agent.

Where does the Fed get the funds to cover the unreimbursed expenses that it incurs on the Treasury's behalf? Recall that over three-fourths of the Fed's assets are U.S. government securities. These yield a steady flow of interest to the Fed and constitute its primary source of income. The Fed uses much of this income to fund its operations.

The Fed's other main source of income is fees that depository institutions pay for services the Fed provides. Since 1981 this fee income has increased steadily as the Fed has continued to charge private depository institutions for the services it offers as a bank for bankers.

The Fed as the Banker's Bank

Another justification offered by Congress in creating the Fed was a perceived need for a government-related institution that would centralize, oversee, and regulate the payments systems of the geographically dispersed U.S. economy. Congress also felt that such an institution was needed as a *lender of last resort* to depository institutions suffering temporary liquidity problems that could pose short-term threats to their individual solvency and to the broader stability of the financial system.

Do Banks Need a Central Bank?   This is a question to which Congress answered yes when it authorized the formation of the Fed. A reason often cited for the Fed's role in the banking system is that private depository institutions *need* a central bank. The key rationale for such a need is the perception that financial markets are subject to **externalities,** or situations in which transactions between two parties can spill over to affect others. The classic externality is pollution, such as noise pollution. If you are *not* an enthusiast, say, of country-western or rap music, yet neighbors on either side of your apartment or house enjoy purchasing and playing such music at loud volumes, then you likely suffer a **negative externality.** Even though the companies that produce and sell such music benefit from the sales, and the purchasers and your

externalities   Spillover effects from the actions of one group of individuals on others who are otherwise not involved in the transactions.

negative externality   A reduction in the welfare of one individual caused by a transaction between other parties, even though the individual is not directly involved in the transaction.

neighbors benefit from consuming the music, you find yourself worse off as a result of the transactions between these parties.

Likewise, it is arguable that many financial transactions can generate externalities, many of which could be negative. For instance, suppose that an individual owed you money but could not pay until completing a transaction with another party. If something were to go awry in that other transaction, then you would be worse off even though you were not a direct party to the transaction. You would experience a negative externality effect, because the failure of that transaction to take place would cause you not to get a payment you had counted upon receiving.

A key justification for a central bank, therefore, is that it supervises and regulates the processes and systems by which consumers, businesses, and financial institutions exchange payments. According to this view, financial institutions need a central bank to keep the systems by which payments are exchanged operating smoothly on a day-to-day basis and to repair any breakdowns in these systems should they occur.

Lender of Last Resort   The most dramatic sort of financial breakdown is a bank run, in which large numbers of depositors lose confidence in the ability of depository institutions to retain their asset values and thus seek to liquidate their accounts, thereby driving large numbers of institutions into insolvency. A key justification for the formation of the Federal Reserve System was that the Fed could keep such runs from occurring by serving as the financial system's **lender of last resort.** The Fed is a central banking institution that stands ready to lend to any temporarily illiquid, but otherwise solvent institution, so as to prevent its illiquidity from leading to a general loss of confidence and a run on the bank.

lender of last resort   An institution willing and able to lend to any temporarily illiquid, but otherwise solvent, institution so as to prevent the illiquidity from leading to a general loss of confidence in that institution or in others.

Under the provisions of the original Federal Reserve Act, a key duty of the Fed is to provide lender-of-last-resort assistance when needed. As amended by the Banking Act of 1935, the Federal Reserve Act authorizes the Fed to lend to *anyone,* if it believes doing so is necessary to prevent a financial crisis. In practice, however, the Fed restricts itself to loans to depository financial institutions that find themselves caught in temporary liquidity crunches.

3

What is the rationale for the Fed's role as a bank for private banks?   The key rationale is the possibility of negative externalities, or spillovers, that exist in the financial system. Because financial transactions among depository institutions and others are interconnected, there is a potential for bank runs and other crises. As a supervisory authority and lender of last resort, the Fed potentially can reduce the possibilities that such events might occur.

THE FED AND THE PAYMENTS SYSTEM

When an individual makes a transaction using currency, the transaction is final at the moment the exchange of currency for a good, service, or asset takes place. In contrast, transactions with other means of payment, such as checks or wire transfers, are final only after depository institutions transfer funds from the account of the purchaser to the seller. Using these other means of payment, therefore, requires that parties to a transaction rely upon depository institutions as intermediaries in the nation's **payments system.** This is the institutional structure through which individuals, businesses, governments, and financial institutions make payments.

The Federal Reserve System is a significant part of the payments system of the United States. The Fed also monitors and regulates a significant portion of the payments system that it does not directly supervise and operate. Before we discuss the Fed's roles in the payments system, however, let's consider the current structure of the system.

payments system   A term that broadly refers to the set of mechanisms by which consumers, businesses, governments, and financial institutions exchange payments.

The American Payments System

Today's payments system is a fascinating mix of old and new. As we discussed in Chapter 1, nonelectronic means of payment, such as currency and checks, account for about 98 percent of all transactions in the United States. At the same time, however, electronic payments account for approximately 85 percent of the *dollar value* of all transactions. This means that we continue to use currency and checks for the large number of low-value transactions we make each day, but we have adopted electronic payments as the primary means of transmitting most of our less frequent large-dollar transactions.

Nonelectronic Payments   In terms of number of transactions, the most popular means of payment in the United States are decidedly nonelectronic paper notes and coins. Such currency transactions alone make up over three-fourths of all transactions. Hence, the bulk of transactions in the American economy remain very low-tech. Nevertheless, currency transactions are quite small on average, so small that together they comprise less than 0.5 percent of the total dollar value of all exchanges in the United States. Think of all the times you make minor purchases of such low-ticket items as candy bars or pens or pencils, and you will understand why this is the case.

Checks are the second most popular payment media, accounting for a little under a fifth of all transactions and just below 15 percent of the total dollar value of all exchanges. Depository institutions clear millions of checks each day. This is possible because nearly all checks have magnetic ink encryptions that special machines can read. This permits the machines to sort and distribute checks automatically. They also can process information for crediting and debiting of accounts. This large-scale automation of check sorting, accounting, and distribution has kept the per-check cost of clearing checks very low.

Other nonelectronic means of payment include money orders, traveler's checks, and credit cards. Together these make up less than 1 percent of both the total number of transactions and the dollar value of all transactions.

Consumer-Oriented Electronic Payments Systems   There now are several consumer-oriented electronic payments mechanisms. Most American consumers have experience using **automated-teller-machine (ATM) networks,** which are depository institution computer terminals activated by magnetically encoded bank cards. There are over 90,000 automated teller machines in the United States. On average, consumers perform about 100,000 transactions each year at a typical ATM machine, for an annual total of nearly 9 billion total ATM transactions. Many consumers use ATM networks to make deposits, obtain cash from checking and savings accounts, and transfer funds among accounts. A growing number of consumers also pay some of their bills using ATM networks. A recent innovation in ATM technology is the "Personal Touch" ATM, which offer visual contact with depository institution employees at another location. Using such ATM links, consumer now can apply for loans and mortgages, purchase mutual funds, and obtain information about loan and deposit terms and rates.

Another consumer-oriented electronic payments mechanism is the **automated clearing house (ACH).** This is a computer-based clearing and settlement facility for the interchange of credits and debits via electronic messages instead of checks. ACHs process payments within one or two days after the request for a transfer of funds. Very common ACH transfers are automatic payroll deposits, in which businesses make wage and salary payments directly into employees' deposit accounts. The federal government also makes large use of ACH facilities. The Social Security Administration distributes many payments to Social Security beneficiaries via ACH direct-deposit mechanisms. In addition, the government disperses a growing portion of welfare and food stamp payments using an *electronic benefits transfer (EBT) system.* EBT functions like an ACH system but looks a lot like an ATM network to welfare and food stamp beneficiaries, because beneficiaries receive their welfare funds or food stamps from special cash or food stamp disbursement machines.

Since the 1970s technology has permitted the use of **point-of-sale (POS) networks.** These are systems that permit consumers to pay for purchases on the spot via direct deductions from their accounts at depository institutions. POS networks have not developed as quickly as some observers had expected, given that most large department store chains and other retail outlets use networks of cash register terminals

automated-teller-machine (ATM) networks   Depository institution computer terminals that customers activate with magnetically encoded bank cards.

automated clearing house (ACH)   A computer-based facility for clearing and settlement that replaces check transactions with electronic credits and debits.

point-of-sale (POS) networks   Systems by which consumers pay for retail purchases by direct deductions from their deposit accounts at depository institutions.

that have the capability to process POS payments. The costs of setting up POS systems can be significant, and it has never been clear who would be willing to pay for them. Check-processing costs have remained so low that depository institutions have had little incentive to switch to POS networks, and retailers have had little desire to incur the cost of installing such systems. If POS networks become more widespread in the future, it is likely that it will be because consumers desire to use them—and to pay for them. Recent trends toward more consumer use of on-line banking via the Internet may lead to greater consumer interest in POS networks in future years.

Large-Dollar Electronic Payments Systems   Consumer-oriented electronic payments systems account for a growing portion of both the number of transactions and the dollar value of such transactions. Yet they make up less than 1 percent of both classifications. In contrast, **large-dollar wire transfer systems,** which are systems designed and operated specifically to manage electronic transfers of large sums, transfer nearly 85 percent of the value of all payments initiated by consumers, businesses, governments, and financial institutions. These systems handle less than 1 percent of the total number of transactions, and so they truly specialize in transferring large transactions.

There are two key large-dollar wire transfer systems. One of these is **Fedwire,** which is a wire transfer system that the Federal Reserve System operates. All depository institutions that must hold reserves at Federal Reserve banks have access to Fedwire, although only about 2,000 institutions regularly use the system. Depository institutions pay fees for the wire transfer services that Fedwire provides, and they use Fedwire mainly for two specific kinds of transfers. First, Fedwire is used for book-entry security transactions. As discussed above, the Fed operates book-entry security systems on behalf of the Treasury, and Fedwire is the means by which depository institutions pay for the securities they purchase. The second type of Fedwire transaction is funds transfers among the reserve deposit accounts that depository institutions maintain at Federal Reserve banks. When depository institutions extend or repay federal funds loans to other depository institutions, they send the funds on Fedwire. The average Fedwire transaction is just under $4 million, and the total average daily payment volume on the Fedwire system is nearly $1 trillion ($1,000,000,000,000).

The other major large-dollar wire transfer system in the United States is the **Clearing House Interbank Payments System (CHIPS).** This is a privately owned system, operated by the New York Clearing House Association, which has about 120 depository institution members. These institutions use CHIPS to transfer funds for foreign exchange and Eurodollar transactions, and the average value of a CHIPS transaction is about $7 million. The average daily payment volume on the CHIPS system is now well in excess of $1 trillion.

large-dollar wire transfer systems   Payments systems, such as Fedwire and CHIPS, that permit the electronic transmission of large sums.

Fedwire   A large-dollar wire transfer system operated by the Federal Reserve that is open to all depository institutions that legally must maintain required reserves with the Fed.

Clearing House Interbank Payments System (CHIPS)   A large-dollar wire transfer system linking about 120 depository institutions that enables them to transfer large sums of money, primarily for foreign exchange and Eurodollar transactions.

GLOBAL NOTEBOOK

Trying to Stop Laundered Money from Entering the United States

Illegal drug transactions normally involve large sums of cash, particularly at the wholesale level. Big-time drug dealers need somehow to launder these large sums of money into legitimate businesses and bank accounts. In recent years money launderers have been using wire transfers to move cash into the United States from depository institutions abroad. The U.S. Treasury recently made some changes in its rules in an attempt (possibly futile) to block laundered drug money from entering the U.S. financial system. The Treasury now requires that financial institutions report "suspicious" transactions. In reaction, money launderers have started using currency exchanges, casinos, and brokerage firms.

In any event, because the daily volume of electronic money transfers exceeds several trillion dollars, the probability of filtering out drug laundering transfers is indeed equivalent to looking for a needle in a haystack. The Treasury's Financial Crimes Enforcement Network has therefore tried to impose a new rule called "know your customer." Such a rule might require financial institutions to ask customers for photo I.D.s before accepting money.

For Critical Analysis: *The advent of digital money, or E-money (discussed in Chapter 8) has certain implications for the government's ability to sort out money laundering. What are they?*

Risk in the Payments System

Any financial transaction entails some degree of risk. When you accept a payment in currency, for instance, there is always a small chance that the bills you receive might be counterfeit. Yet, unless you are in the habit of making large cash transactions, your risk of loss in a typical exchange in which currency is the means of payment is fairly small. In the multimillion-dollar transactions on Fedwire and CHIPS, however, the dollar risks are much more significant. It is for this reason that the Federal Reserve is closely involved in monitoring and regulating the CHIPS system, in addition to its own role in operating and supervising Fedwire.

There are three types of risk that arise in any payments system: *liquidity risk, credit risk,* and *systemic risk.* A key function of financial institutions and markets is to intermediate such risks. As we discuss below, however, systemic risk may entail significant externalities for financial institutions and others who use large-dollar payments mechanisms. As we noted earlier, appeal to the existence of such externalities is a key rationale for the involvement of a central bank, such as the Fed, in a nation's payments system.

Liquidity Risk   People do not always make payments on time. The risk of loss if payments are not received when they are due is called **liquidity risk.** Losses arising from late payments may be in the form of opportunity costs, in that some funds not received on time could not be used for other purposes. Sometimes such losses may be more explicit. For instance, late receipt of a payment may complicate one's ability to honor another financial commitment.

The existence of liquidity risk accounts in large measure for the development of large-dollar wire transfer systems such as Fedwire and CHIPS. Before computer technology made such electronic mechanisms possible, depository institutions had to rely on hand delivery by courier or postal services. This sometimes produced delays that generated significant implicit or explicit costs for these institutions. Wire transfers can be initiated within minutes. Once initiated, they are almost instantaneous.

Credit Risk   In many transactions, one party to the transaction makes good on that end of the deal before the other party reciprocates. This means that the first party effectively has extended credit to the second party, thereby exposing herself or himself to **credit risk,** or the possibility that the second party will fail to honor fully the terms of the exchange.

One type of credit risk is *market risk*, which arises when one party to a financial exchange fails to honor the terms of the exchange because of some change in condition that makes this impossible. In such a situation the two parties typically must get together and renegotiate the terms of the exchange, which causes the party that had honored its side of the bargain to incur a loss. Another form of credit risk is *delivery risk*, which is the possibility that one party in a financial transaction fails entirely to honor the terms of the exchange. In such a situation, the other party to the transaction loses the entire value of the transfer.

Large-dollar wire transfer systems have elaborate systems of rules intended to reduce the exposure to both kinds of credit risk by participating institutions. These rules spell out the responsibilities of both parties to a wire transfer and the role of the system in adjudicating disputes concerning failure to settle a transaction in a timely fashion.

Systemic Risk   Participants in large-dollar wire transfer system are interconnected, which can cause payment flows among depository institutions to be interdependent. For instance, a bank in San Francisco anticipating a wire transfer from a New York bank at 12:30 eastern standard time (EST) may agree to wire funds to a bank in Chicago at 12:45 EST. The Chicago bank, in turn, may have committed to wire funds to a Los Angeles bank at 1:00 EST, using the funds that it expects to receive from the San Francisco bank. This means that if the New York bank fails to deliver the funds promised at 12:30 EST to the San Francisco bank, the latter bank may send funds to Chicago at 12:45 EST that it does not

liquidity risk   The risk of loss when a payment is not received when due.

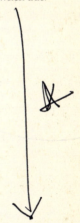

credit risk   The risk of loss when one party to an exchange fails to honor the terms under which the exchange was to take place

systemic risk   The risk that some depository institutions may not be able to meet the terms of their own credit agreements because of failures by other institutions to settle transactions that otherwise are not related.

really have. Furthermore, if the New York bank finds that it is unable to send the funds at all, then the entire chain of payments may occur even though there are insufficient funds to cover the payments.

The risk that the New York bank will fail to settle its transaction with the bank in San Francisco is a liquidity or credit risk for the San Francisco bank. But for the Chicago and Los Angeles banks, it is **systemic risk.** This is the risk that a depository institution, such as the Chicago and Los Angeles banks in our example, may be unable to honor credit agreements because of settlement failures in otherwise unrelated transactions. For institutions, systemic risk is a negative externality that arises from the interdependence of transactions in the payments system. As noted earlier, it is the existence of such negative externalities that the Fed seeks to address via its supervisory role in the payments system.

4

Why does the Fed play a supervisory role in the U.S. payments system?   Although most transactions in the American payments system involve cash or checks, the bulk of the dollar flow is processed through large-dollar wire transfer systems. Because such systems link depository institutions in complex webs of payment flows, there is a potential for large negative externalities, or systemic risk. The Fed supervises these payments systems in an effort to reduce the extent of this risk.

The Fed and the Payments System

Although the Fed helps design the rules for dealing with liquidity and credit risks that institutions face on the Fedwire and CHIPS systems, its key concern in recent years has been the issue of systemic risk. Although it is very rare for depository institutions to fail to settle their obligations on the Fedwire and CHIPS systems, it is not at all uncommon for some institutions to send wire transfer payments even though they do not have the funds on hand to cover those payments.

Daylight Overdrafts on Fedwire and CHIPS   Depository institutions can send wire transfers without having funds on hand because final settlement of Fedwire and CHIPS payments typically does not occur until the end of each business day. As long as institutions can settle their accounts at the end of the day, there is nothing to stop them from sending wire transfer payments even if they do not have funds at that moment to honor the payments.

When depository institutions engage in this practice, they are "overdrawing" their reserve deposit accounts at Federal Reserve banks.

The Fed calls this **daylight overdrafts.** Figure 12.1 displays the typical pattern of daylight overdrafts by a depository institution that engages in such behavior. This institution runs a steady stream of overdrafts beginning at around 10:00 A.M., and so its reserve account balance at a Federal Reserve bank becomes negative shortly after that hour. Just before 2:00 P.M. its overdrafts reach their peak, at which point the reserve balance of the depository institution is at its greatest negative value for the day. As the afternoon progresses, the institution begins to receive funds transfers from other institutions, perhaps as a result of borrowing such funds in the federal funds market. Shortly before 4:00 P.M. its reserve account balance once again becomes positive.

Certainly, many daylight overdrafts are unintentional. Sometimes payment flows do not match up as depository institutions had expected, and the result is that they wire funds before they receive other funds that would cover the payments. But Figure 12.1 would indicate a pattern of intentionally running overdrafts.

daylight overdrafts Depository institution overdraws of their reserve deposit accounts at Federal Reserve banks, which occur when they initiate wire transfers of funds in amounts that exceed their balances in those accounts.

FIGURE 12.1   Daylight Overdrafts at a Depository Institution

This figure shows the typical pattern of daylight overdrafts for a large depository institution. The institution begins to overdraw its reserve account shortly after the beginning of the regular business day. Its overdrafts peak early in the afternoon. During the remainder of the day the institution begins to receive funds from other sources, and by the end of the day, its reserve balance again is positive.
Source: Board of Governors of the Federal Reserve System.

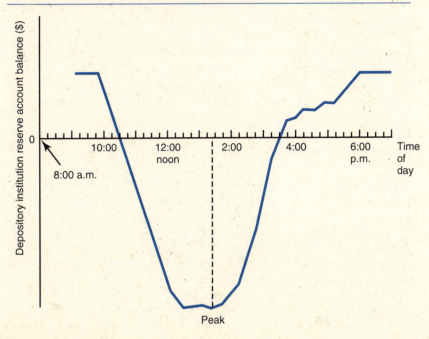

If daylight overdrafts were unintentional, relatively small, and infrequent, the Fed would not be especially concerned about them. In recent years, however, daylight overdrafts often have been intentional, large, and commonplace. The normal daily peak for daylight overdrafts on both Fedwire and CHIPS combined increased from about $125 billion in 1985 to over $200 billion in 1990. This amount was nearly three times the size of the total reserves of all depository institutions. Furthermore, it was not unusual for as many as a thousand depository institutions to overdraw their Fed deposit accounts in a given day.

Fed Policies Concerning Daylight Overdrafts   The Fed has been concerned about daylight overdrafts for two reasons. One is the possibility that if an institution failed to settle on a series of multibillion-dollar overdrafts, other institutions would find themselves unable to settle at the end of a day. Daylight overdrafts thereby represent a major potential source of systemic risk for Fedwire and CHIPS.

A second reason why the Fed is concerned is that it might be left holding the bag in the event that an institution failed to settle its overdrafts. As far as the Fed is concerned, overdrafts of reserve accounts constitute loans from the Fed to the overdrawing institutions. Furthermore, as the operator of Fedwire, the Fed regards itself as the responsible party should there be major settlement failures on that system. Hence, daylight overdrafts also expose the Fed to significant credit risks.

In March 1986 the Fed implemented a policy of *caps*, or limits, on the amounts of daylight overdrafts by depository institutions. It instituted three types of caps. One limited the volume of overdrafts that any one institution could generate through transactions with any other institution on the Fedwire or CHIPS systems. The second limited the total amount of overdrafts that a depository institution could incur on either system. The third limited the quantity of overdrafts that an institution could incur *across* payments networks, say by settling CHIPS overdrafts by overdrawing its reserve account via a Fedwire transfer. These caps reduced the extent to which institutions generated overdrafts in proportion to the volumes of payments. In 1986 Fedwire overdrafts amounted to nearly 20 percent of the total volume of Fedwire transfers; by 1989 this figure had fallen to about 15 percent.

Nevertheless, the total amount of overdrafts continued to grow. And so between 1988 and 1993 the Fed developed a comprehensive system for charging depository institutions fees for daylight overdrafts. In April 1994 the Fed implemented the first stage of this new policy. It calculates every depository institution's average-per-minute daylight overdraft each day. The amount by which this average overdraft exceeds a deductible amount equal to 10 percent of the institution's risk-based capital (see Chapter 8) is subject to a fee. From April 1994 to April 1995, this fee was equal to ten **basis points** on each dollar

basis point   One hundredth of one percent.

of overdrafts above the permitted deductible, which the Fed has established in recognition of the fact that some amount of overdrafts is unavoidable. One basis point equals 0.01 percent, and so this fee amounted to an interest charge of one-tenth of one percent.

Figure 12.2 shows the effect this policy has had on the total amount of overdrafts of Federal Reserve accounts by all depository institutions. As the figure shows, both average and peak overdrafts fell dramatically after the Fed began charging for them. While one-tenth of one percent may sound like a small fee, keep in mind that the rate applies to a single day. Over the course of a year this works out to a hefty interest rate of around 30 percent, if an institution were to continually overdraw its account. Consequently, the new Fed policy gives depository institutions strong incentives to cut their daylight overdrafts on the Fedwire and CHIPS systems. In hopes of reducing daylight overdrafts even further, however, in April 1995 the Fed raised the fee to 15 basis points.

Fees on daylight overdrafts have generated some income for the Fed. A fee of 10 or 15 basis points amounts to significant fee

FIGURE 12.2   Average and Peak Daylight Overdrafts at Federal Reserve Banks (in 1995 dollars)

This figure shows the average and peak amounts of reserve account overdrafts by depository institutions at all 12 Federal Reserve banks. The Federal Reserve's imposition of a fee on such overdrafts in April 1994 induced a sharp reduction in total overdrafts. Nevertheless, depository institutions continue to overdraw their accounts by tens of billions of dollars each day. *Source:* Diana Hancock and James Wilcox, "Intraday Bank Reserve Management: The Effect of Caps and Fees on Daylight Overdrafts," *Journal of Money, Credit, and Banking*, in press.

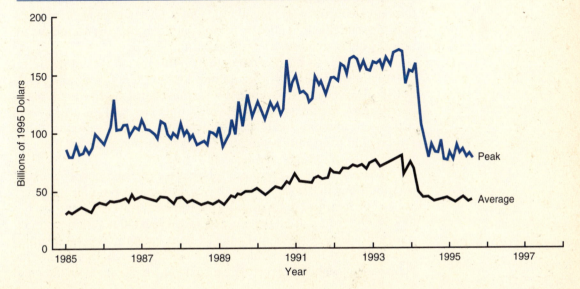

income when it applies to billions of dollars of overdrafts. The Fed earns between $300,000 and $400,000 per week from the fees now charged on daylight overdrafts. It has put some of these funds to work in efforts to extend Fedwire operating hours from 10 hours per day to 18 hours per day by sometime in 1997.

5

What are daylight overdrafts, and why does the Fed care about them?   Daylight overdrafts are depository institution overdraws of their Federal Reserve account balances that occur when institutions wire funds that they do not actually have in their possession at the time the transfer is made. The Fed's concern with daylight overdrafts stems from their large aggregate size and the frequency with which large numbers of institutions incur them. The Fed regards daylight overdrafts as an important source of systemic risk and has adopted cap and pricing policies to discourage the practice.

Potential Complications for Monetary Policy   Charging fees for daylight overdrafts has helped to reduce the aggregate amounts of such overdrafts. The policy has one possible side effect of some concern to the Fed, however. Because the fees on daylight overdrafts amount to a significant interest charge, institutions seek to avoid this charge by making side arrangements with other institutions. For instance, a depository institution may arrange to repay an outstanding *overnight* federal funds loan later in the day to avoid overdrawing its reserve account with the Fed.

Often such an arrangement requires paying additional interest on the extended overnight federal funds loan. Such an extension of a few hours essentially is an *intraday federal funds loan*, and the additional interest really is an *intraday interest payment*.

This suggests the possibility that, in the not-too-distant future, an *intraday federal funds market* could develop. Certainly, continuing technological developments, coupled with the extension of Fedwire hours and the growing linkages among world financial markets, are likely to make such intraday funds markets feasible. The Fed's pricing policy for daylight overdrafts could turn out to be the incentive for more active intraday trading to commence.

Some Federal Reserve officials have expressed concerns about complications that such an intraday market could pose for monetary policy. As discussed in Chapter 11, the Fed's current policy approach is to keep the federal funds rate near a target level. But variations in intraday funds rates could make the 24-hour federal funds rate the Fed seeks to target more variable. How much this might complicate the Fed's task in stabilizing the 24-hour federal funds rate is unknown at

GLOBAL NOTEBOOK
Political Biases at the Fed and the New Zealand Alternative

Is the Fed biased, and if so, is there an alternative? In answer to the first question, there is some evidence offered by economists Thomas Havrilesky (1939–1995) and John Gildea of Wheaten College. They argue that the evidence shows that the administration and Congress systematically signal their desires for changes in monetary policy to the leaders of the Fed. Under certain circumstances, the Fed responds accordingly.

Because the Fed was not created by the U.S. Constitution, Congress could dismantle it if it wanted to. Fed officials know this. Thus, the Fed must pay some attention to statements by Congress and the president that are critical of its behavior. These criticisms are typically called *Fed bashing*, and they signal a desire by Congress or the president for an easing or tightening of monetary policy. Economist Havrilesky found that the Fed seems to be more sensitive to Fed bashing by the president and the executive branch than that done by Congress.

To make sure there is no political bias in how the central bank in New Zealand works, that country's government decided to give its central bank just one job: keep the price level stable. The Reserve Bank Act of 1989 set the desired price stability at inflation rates of zero to 2 percent. If New Zealand's central bank fails to achieve this single goal, its governor can be fired. Variations in GDP, however, have no bearing on the governor's performance evaluation. Consequently, New Zealand's central bank no longer has to concern itself with short-term ups and downs in GDP growth rates. So far, its new independence and explicit mission have seemed to work: In 1989 the CPI increased by 5.7 percent. Today, that increase is running at less than 1.5 percent per year.

For Critical Analysis: *Who would be against an act of the U.S. Congress similar to New Zealand's Reserve Bank Act?*

present. Nevertheless, the potential development of an intraday funds market may lead to policy complications.

MONETARY POLICY AT THE FED

The daylight overdraft issue is a dramatic illustration of how the Fed's central banking role can overlap with its role as monetary policymaker. In this latter role, the Fed can influence the monetary base, monetary aggregates, credit flows, and ultimately, other economic variables such as interest rates, national income, and the rate of inflation. We conclude this chapter by considering how the Fed can affect the quantities of money and credit.

Open-Market Operations

As we discussed in Chapter 10, open-market operations are the means by which the Fed conducts monetary policy on a day-to-day basis. The voting members of the Federal Open Market Committee (FOMC)—the seven Federal Reserve Board governors and five Federal Reserve bank presidents—determine the general strategy of open-market operations at meetings that take place every six to eight weeks. They outline this strategy in the FOMC Directive, which lays out the FOMC's general objectives, establishes short-term federal funds rate objectives, and sets specific target ranges for monetary aggregates. The FOMC leaves it to the Federal Reserve Bank of New York's Trading Desk to implement the Directive from day to day during the weeks between FOMC meetings.

The Mechanics of Open-Market Operations   The Trading Desk's open-market operations typically are confined to a period of around one hour each morning. The New York Federal Reserve Bank's Trading Desk conducts two types of open-market operations. One is called an *outright transaction*. This is an open-market purchase or sale in which the Fed is not obliged to resell or repurchase securities at a later date. The other kind of operation is a *repurchase agreement transaction*. As discussed in Chapters 1 and 2, repurchase agreements are contracts that commit the seller of a security to repurchase the security at a later date. The Trading Desk often buys securities from dealers under agreements for the dealers to repurchase them at a later date. The Trading Desk also commonly uses *reverse repurchase agreements* when conducting open-market sales. These are agreements for the Fed to repurchase the securities from dealers at a later time.

Table 12.2 summarizes the Fed's open-market transactions during 1995. The Trading Desk often uses outright purchases or sales when it wishes to change the aggregate level of depository institution reserves. In contrast, it typically uses repurchase agreements when its main goal is to stabilize the current level of reserves. Nevertheless, the Trading Desk can also use repurchase agreements instead of outright purchases

---

TABLE 12.2   Fed Open-Market Transactions During 1995 ($ millions)

Outright Transactions	
Purchases	$ 20,649
Sales and Redemptions	3,679
Repurchase Agreements and Matched Transactions	
Purchases	2,566,281
Sales	2,567,303
Net Change in Federal Reserve System Open-Market Account	15,948

Source: Board of Governors of the Federal Reserve System, *Federal Reserve Bulletin*, April 1996.

POLICY NOTEBOOK
Does the Fed Really Have to Buy and Sell So Many Securities?

Every business day the Fed's New York Trading Desk engages in a frenzy of buying and selling U.S. government securities to implement the FOMC's Directive. In a typical year the net change in Fed holdings of government securities is a trivial part of total transactions. This process is aptly referred to by its critics as **churning.** Churning has generated a considerable amount of controversy. Some have complained that the only beneficiaries of churning are three dozen or so special securities dealers that earn enormous brokerage fees. (Note that when stockbrokers encourage excessive buying and selling of securities in order to increase their own profits, they are subject to prosecution.)

Federal Reserve officials claim that much of the supposed churning is really not churning at all. They contend that temporary transactions and those arranged on behalf of foreign central banks do not constitute churning. In particular, to provide reserves on a temporary basis, the Fed engages in repurchase agreements with dealers. When there is a "need" to drain reserves temporarily, the Fed arranges reverse repurchase agreements.

For Critical Analysis: *Who benefits from Federal Reserve churning?*

or sales when it wants to change the overall reserve level by making a series of repurchase-agreement transactions on a continuous basis.

churning Excessive buying and selling of securities resulting in little net change in the Fed's holdings.

The Effects of Open-Market Operations on Money and Credit
As you learned in Chapter 10, open-market operations that change the total amount of reserves at depository institutions cause the monetary base to change. A variation in the size of the monetary base, in turn, alters the quantities of money and credit in the economy.

Recall from Chapter 10 that a change in the quantity of money, M, induced by a change in the monetary base, MB, is equal to the money multiplier times the amount of the change in the monetary base, or

$$\Delta M = m \times \Delta MB$$

where m is the money multiplier, whose value we discussed in detail in Chapter 10. Likewise, if m_{TC} denotes the value of the credit multiplier, then the amount by which all depository institutions change total credit, TC, by lending and acquiring securities in response to a change in the monetary base is equal to

$$\Delta TC = m_{TC} \times \Delta MB$$

borrowed reserves   Reserves that the Federal Reserve supplies directly to depository institutions by extending discount window loans to them.

nonborrowed reserves   Reserves that the Federal Reserve supplies to depository institutions through open-market operations rather than discount window loans.

Recall that the monetary base is equal to the sum of currency, C, and total reserves, TR. But we can think of total reserves at depository institutions as arising from one of two sources. One way for depository institutions to obtain reserves from the Fed is to borrow reserves directly from the Fed's discount window. Such reserves are **borrowed reserves,** denoted BR. The primary way for depository institutions to get reserves from the Fed, however, is through open-market operations. These reserves, called **nonborrowed reserves,** denoted NBR, are the amount of total reserves not borrowed from the Fed. This means that total reserves are the sum of borrowed reserves and nonborrowed reserves, or $TR = BR + NBR$.

Hence, open-market operations cause a change in nonborrowed reserves and thereby change total reserves and the monetary base. As a result, changes in nonborrowed reserves caused by open-market operations have direct multiplier effects on the quantities of money and credit. From our relationships above, the amounts of these effects on money and credit could be computed using the following equations:

$$\Delta M = m \times \Delta NBR$$

and

$$\Delta TC = m_{TC} \times \Delta NBR$$

For instance, suppose that the money multiplier is equal to $m = 2.5$, and the credit multiplier is equal to $m_{TC} = 3$. Then a $10 million open-market purchase by the Fed would increase the quantity of money by $25 million and the total amount of loans and securities held by depository institutions by $30 million. This helps us to see why the Fed uses open-market operations as its key means of conducting monetary policy, given that it can conduct such operations any day that it wishes to do so, thereby producing desired changes in the amounts of money and credit.

The Discount Window

As discussed above, borrowed reserves are part of total reserves and the monetary base. This means that another way for the Fed to influence the quantities of money and credit is by inducing changes in depository institution discount window borrowing. The Fed does so through alterations in the terms under which it stands willing to lend to depository institutions.

Discount Window Policy   Earlier in the Fed's history, depository institutions would borrow from the Fed via a process called *discounting.* An institution would post U.S. government securities at a Federal

Reserve bank, which would increase the depository institution's reserve account balance by an amount smaller than the value of the securities. When the discount arrangement expired, the depository institution would repurchase the securities at their fair value. The Federal Reserve bank then would keep the difference as a *discount rate*, or effective interest charge for the loan.

Today most discount window loans actually are *advances*. The Fed simply increases the balance in the borrowing institution's reserve account and has an officer of the institution sign a promissory note. The term discount window borrowing remains with us still, however. And the interest rate that the Fed charges for advances continues to be known as the **discount rate,** even though it really is just a lending rate.

Before 1991 there were three main types of discount window loans: *adjustment credit, seasonal credit*, and *extended credit*. Adjustment credit constituted loans to help depository institutions through times of temporary illiquidity. This is still the primary type of discount window loan. The Fed also continues to extend seasonal credit to depository institutions that face significant outflows of deposits during certain months of the year. Typically these are rural institutions whose key customers are farmers who need loans for planting and harvesting activities at exactly the time that deposits at lending institutions otherwise are at their ebb. Extended credit consists of long-term loans to depository institutions that have chronic liquidity needs. Between 1983 and 1991 extended credit accounted for the bulk of discount window loans. After the savings and loan crisis of the 1980s, Congress included a provision in the FDIC Improvement Act of 1991 that significantly reduced the Fed's powers to offer extended credit. It feared that the Fed was making too many such loans to insolvent, rather than simply illiquid, institutions. Today the Fed makes extremely few discount window loans under extended-credit terms.

Since the 1920s the Fed usually has set the discount rate somewhat below other market interest rates. This means that if the Fed did not restrict access to the Federal Reserve banks' discount windows, there would be an incentive for depository institutions to do all their borrowing from the Fed instead of borrowing in private markets, such as the federal funds market. Hence, the Fed imposes a number of explicit and implicit restrictions on the accessibility of the discount window. It generally restricts depository institutions from borrowing too much or too often.

discount rate   The interest rate that the Federal Reserve charges on the discount window loans it extends to depository institutions.

The Linkage from the Discount Rate to Money and Credit

Inducing a change in the monetary base by altering the discount window policy is much less straightforward than causing the monetary base to change via open-market operations. One way that the Fed might induce more or less borrowing by depository institutions would be to tighten or weaken its restrictions on discount window access. The Fed rarely changes such policies, however, because both the Fed and depository institution managers benefit from consistency regarding accessibility of the discount window. This leaves changing the discount rate as the primary means of inducing depository institutions to vary their borrowing from the Fed.

The main alternative to borrowing new reserves from the Fed is for a depository institution to borrow existing reserves from other depository institutions in the federal funds market. This means that a key determinant of total discount window borrowing is the difference, or *spread*, between the federal funds rate and the discount rate. As the amount by which the federal funds rate exceeds the discount rate rises, discount window borrowing becomes relatively more attractive to depository institutions. Figure 12.3 verifies this relationship. As the figure shows, when the spread between the federal funds rate and the discount rate increases, discount window borrowing typically rises as well. When the spread declines, depository institutions normally cut back on the amount of reserves they borrow from the Fed.

FIGURE 12.3   Discount Window Borrowing and the Spread

This figure shows that when the spread between the federal funds rate and the discount rate increases, the quantity of discount window borrowing by depository institutions also tends to increase. Likewise, a fall in the spread typically leads to a reduction in discount window borrowing. *Source:* Board of Governors of the Federal Reserve System, *Federal Reserve Bulletin*, various issues.

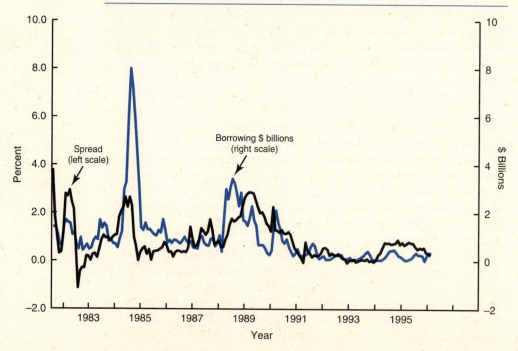

Suppose that the Fed decides to use discount window policy as a means of increasing the quantity of money and credit. This would require increasing the spread between the federal funds rate and the discount rate by cutting the discount rate. The rise in the spread then would cause borrowed reserves to rise by some amount, ΔBR. This would cause a rise in total reserves and in the monetary base, thereby causing a multiplier effect on the quantity of money:

$$\Delta M = m \times \Delta BR$$

That is, the quantity of money would rise by the induced rise in borrowed reserves times the money multiplier. Likewise, the increase in borrowed reserves would cause a multiplier effect on the amount of credit extended by depository institutions:

$$\Delta TC = m_{TC} \times \Delta BR$$

This says that the induced increase in borrowed reserves would be multiplied by the credit multiplier to cause an increase in the total amount of loans and securities at depository institutions.

Note that once the Fed induces a given change in discount window borrowing, the multiplier effects on money and credit are analogous to those caused by open-market operations. Nevertheless, discount window policy is much less direct in its effects, because the Fed must be able to cause the spread between the federal funds rate and the discount rate to change by just the right amount to induce the desired change in borrowing. This requires the Fed to know the relationship between the spread and the desired amount of discount window borrowings by depository institutions. The Fed calls this relationship the *borrowings function*. It has found that the relationship is not always stable. As a result, the Fed does not rely on the discount rate as its main tool of monetary policy.

In fact, the Fed changes the discount rate relatively infrequently, say every few weeks or even every few months. Typically, the Fed changes the discount rate solely to keep the spread from changing when the federal funds market rate rises or falls. And so discount rate changes are not necessarily indicative of active attempts by the Fed to alter the quantities of money and credit via discount window policy. Yet from time to time the Fed has attempted to achieve *announcement effects* from discount rate changes. If the Fed does not wish to use open-market operations to signal its policy intentions to financial markets, it may change the discount rate to make its intentions known. For instance, suppose that market interest rates had recently stabilized after a long decline. If the Fed wanted to signal that it might prefer for market rates to rise somewhat, it might raise the discount rate slightly. Then traders in financial markets would not have to guess whether the Fed might let market rates decline even further.

Reserve Requirements

As we discussed in Chapter 10, the Depository Institutions Deregulation and Monetary Control Act of 1980 empowered the Fed to impose uniform reserve requirements on all federally insured depository institutions. Since that time the Fed has mandated that all such institutions hold reserves as fractions of their transactions deposit balances. This is the final key tool that the Fed has at its disposal to influence monetary and credit aggregates.

The Rationale for and Computation of Reserve Requirements

Why does the Fed require depository institutions to hold certain amounts of reserves in their vaults and at Federal Reserve banks? A traditional argument for such a requirement was that it made institutions "safer," because they would be more liquid in the event of a crisis. Yet banks in some nations, such as the United Kingdom, face effective reserve requirements that are close to zero, yet have experienced few liquidity crises. Furthermore, the federal regulatory umbrella associated with the deposit insurance system is the ultimate means by which the government guards against such events.

The only relevant argument for reserve requirements today must relate to the Fed's ability to influence the quantities of money and credit. To see this, consider a world with a reserve requirement of 100 percent. In such a world, the monetary base would be the total quantity of money, because reserves would equal deposits. Then Fed actions to change the monetary base would exactly translate into changes in the quantity of money. Higher reserve requirements, therefore, give the Fed greater leverage over the amount of money in circulation.

In addition, imposing reserve requirements adds to monetary stability. Recall from Chapter 10 that a key source of instability of the money multiplier are fluctuations in excess reserve holdings by depository institutions. Without reserve requirements, such volatility in excess reserves would translate almost completely into variability of total reserves. Stable reserve requirements thereby add to the stability of total reserves in the banking system, which reduces volatility in the quantity of money.

Today the Fed's reserve requirement is fairly simple. For the first $50 million or so in transactions deposits, any depository institution must hold 3 percent as required reserves. For any amount of deposits in excess of this amount, depository institutions must hold 10 percent as reserves. Because most transaction deposits in the United States are at the largest institutions, this means that the bulk of transaction deposits are subject to the 10 percent requirement.

Before 1984 depository institutions computed their required reserves in the following way. They would average their transaction deposits over a week-long *computation period*, and apply the Fed's required reserve ratios to this average amount of deposits. Two weeks later, during a one-week *maintenance period*, they would maintain average reserve holdings to meet the reserve requirement.

This way of computing and maintaining required reserves was simple for depository institutions, but it complicated Fed efforts to control the quantity of money in the early 1980s. Because required reserves were predetermined, the Fed felt obliged to supply sufficient reserves for institutions to meet the requirement when the maintenance period arrived, even if the Fed might have preferred to reduce the available volume of reserves. Consequently, in 1984 the Fed switched to a system with a 14-day computation period that largely overlaps a 14-day maintenance period. The average reserves held during the maintenance period must meet the required fraction based on average deposits during the computation period. The maintenance period extends two days past the end of the computation period, which gives depository institutions two extra days to adjust their reserves as needed to meet the Fed's requirement. However, as a result of the 12-day overlap, the Fed now has more scope for changing reserves as needed to vary the quantity of money.

How Reserve Requirement Changes Affect Money and Credit

To see how reserve requirements themselves might be changed to influence the amounts of money and credit, recall from Chapter 10 that the final money multiplier we considered was equal to $m = (c + 1)/(r + e + c)$. The credit multiplier was $m_{TC} = (1 - r - e)/(c + r + e)$. A reduction in the required reserve ratio, r, increases the values of both multipliers. This makes sense, because if reserve requirements are lower, then depository institutions can lend more reserves at every stage of the deposit and credit expansion process. In contrast, an increase in the required reserve ratio reduces the multipliers.

This means that reserve requirement changes alter the quantities of money and credit by increasing or reducing the multipliers that link money and credit to the monetary base. In principle, therefore, the Fed could try to influence the amounts of money and credit by varying its required reserve ratios. The Fed, however, rarely does this. Every change in reserve requirements necessitates alterations in planning and management efforts both by the Fed and the depository institutions, and so the Fed changes reserve requirements as rarely as possible. Indeed, the Fed has changed its reserve requirements only three times since 1980, and none of these changes were intended to influence the quantities of money or credit.

6

What are the primary tools with which the fed conducts monetary policy?
The Fed's key tool for conducting monetary policy on a day-to-day basis are open-market operations to change the amount of nonborrowed reserves and thereby affect the monetary base and the quantities of money and credit. A secondary tool is discount window policy. By changing the terms by which it makes discount window loans available, the Fed can influence the amount of reserves that depository institutions borrow, which ultimately affects that amounts of money and credit. A third, but seldom-used, tool is required reserve ratios. Changes in these ratios alter the money and credit multipliers, thereby causing variations in monetary and credit aggregates.

SUMMARY

1. **The Main Assets and Liabilities of the Fed:** Over three-fourths of the Fed's assets are its holdings of government securities. An even larger portion of its liabilities are the total of currency that it issues and reserve deposits of depository institutions, which together compose the monetary base.

2. **Ways in Which the Fed Is the Government's Bank:** The Treasury maintains large deposits with the Federal Reserve banks, which provide a number of depository services to the Treasury. In addition, the Fed issues securities on the Treasury's behalf, and it maintains book-entry security accounts through which the Treasury makes payments of interest and principal to large institutional holders of government securities.

3. **The Rationale for the Fed's Role as a Bank for Private Banks:** Because depository institutions are interconnected, breakdowns in transactions among a few institutions can spill over to create hardships for a large number of institutions. A key role for the Fed, therefore, is to contain the potential for such negative externalities in the financial system.

4. **The Reason Why the Fed Plays a Supervisory Role in the U.S. Payments System:** Most dollar flows in the payments system are large-dollar wire transfers on Fedwire and the Clearing House Interbank Payments System (CHIPS). These two systems connect together thousands of depository institutions. While they increase the efficiency with which depository institutions can make transactions, they also expose the institutions to systemic risk, or the possibility of significant negative externalities spilling over from a few institutions to many.

5. **Daylight Overdrafts, and the Fed's Concerns about Them:** Daylight overdrafts are depository institution overdraws of their deposit accounts at Federal Reserve banks. These occur during the day when institutions wire funds not legally in their possession at the moment of the transfer. Besides creating credit risk for the Fed, such overdrafts have the potential to cause significant risk of systemic failure, particularly because they amount to tens of billions of dollars per day. Consequently, in recent years the Fed has imposed caps and fees on daylight overdrafts in an effort to contain them.

6. **The Primary Tools Through Which the Fed Conducts Monetary Policy:** The most important tool of monetary policy are open-market operations, which the Fed conducts on a daily basis to influence total reserves, the monetary base, and, through the multiplier process, the quantities of money and credit. The Fed's secondary instrument of monetary policy is the terms under which it offers discount window loans. The most important of these is the discount rate, which is the interest rate the Fed charges for advances it makes to depository institutions. A third, but rarely used, policy tool is reserve requirements. Changes in required reserve ratios can alter the values of the money and credit multipliers. Because such changes are costly to implement, both for the Fed and depository institutions, the Fed rarely alters reserve requirements.

QUESTIONS AND PROBLEMS

1. What are the Fed's key roles as a central bank? In your view, what is the single, most important role of a central bank? Could the Fed perform this role without performing its other roles? Explain your reasoning.

2. In your own words, define a negative externality. Explain how such externalities can arise in the financial system.

3. How do daylight overdrafts cause both credit and systemic risks of concern to the Fed? In light of the Fed's concerns, can you rationalize why the Fed does not simply *ban* such overdrafts? Do you think that the Fed could enforce such a policy? Explain.

4. In many nations the terms under which central banks lend to depository institutions—the equivalent to the Fed's discount window policies—constitute the primary means of conducting monetary policy. Often this is true for nations with financial markets that are less developed than those in the United States. Why does this make sense? Could the Fed conduct monetary policy solely via the discount window?

5. Total reserves are equal to the sum of required reserves plus excess reserves. But total reserves also are equal to the sum of borrowed reserves plus nonborrowed reserves. Explain how these two ways of splitting up total reserves make sense from the differing perspectives of the Fed and the depository institutions.

6. Does it make any difference to the Fed whether the required reserve ratio for most transactions deposits is 10 percent or 25 percent? Justify your answer.

Monetary Policy and the Economy

13

Monetary Policy Implementation and Fed Operating Procedures

KEY QUESTIONS

1. What key factors influence the demand for reserves by depository institutions?

2. How do Federal Reserve policies determine the supply of reserves to depository institutions and the federal funds rate?

3. How is the federal funds rate related to other market interest rates?

4. What are the main determinants of the total demand for money by consumers and businesses?

5. How do Federal Reserve policies affect the quantity of money?

6. What are Federal Reserve operating procedures, and what operating procedure has the Federal Reserve used in recent years?

I t is late at night, but the finance committee at Microsoft Corporation in Belleview, Washington, is hard at work. The company's CEO, Bill Gates, thinks he might want to build a major movie studio in the Seattle area. He knows it rains a lot, so he plans to build numerous gigantic indoor shooting sets. The project is going to cost $500 million. The finance committee has decided to issue $250 million in corporate bonds and to pay the rest out of cash reserves. They are just now finishing up all of the legal work prior to the bond sale, which is scheduled for the following week. The phone rings. It is a call from their investment bankers in New York. Word on the street is that the Fed is going to raise interest rates tomorrow in an attempt to cool off the overheated economy. The head of the finance committee calls Gates at his 55,000-square-foot home and finds him at his indoor bowling alley. When Gates hears the news, he decides that it is not worth paying the higher interest rates to borrow money from the public. He cancels the whole project.

While the above scenario is completely hypothetical, it does give you the flavor of how changes in interest rates may affect businesses' desire to invest. Thus, monetary policy and its implementation can be important for an individual company's decision making. You will now read about Fed operating procedures and how it often targets interest rates.

THE DEMAND FOR DEPOSITORY INSTITUTION RESERVES

How does Federal Reserve policy-making influence interest yields, and how do changes in interest rates affect money holdings of consumers and businesses? As you will learn in this chapter, the answer is that the Fed can influence market interest rates through variations in how it uses its tools of monetary policy, such as open-market operations or altering the terms under which it stands ready to lend reserves at the discount window. Such Fed policy actions affect the quantities of reserves demanded by depository institutions and the equilibrium federal funds rate. Therefore, to understand how Fed policies ultimately affect market interest rates and the quantity of money, you must understand the factors that determine the amount of reserves that depository institutions wish to hold.

The Federal Funds Rate and Excess Reserves

Recall from Chapter 10 that, because of the money multiplier process, depository institutions play a key role in determining the quantity of money. From the perspective of depository institutions, the most important interest rate is the federal funds rate. The reason is that this is the day-to-day rate of interest at which these institution can lend or borrow reserves to meet reserve requirements or to fund extensions of credit through lending activities or purchases of securities.

The Opportunity Cost of Holding Excess Reserves

As we discussed in Chapter 10, depository institutions usually maintain some reserve holdings over and above the amounts necessary to meet the Fed's reserve requirements. These reserves are *excess reserves*. Recall that depository institutions normally hold excess reserves as a contingency against a need for cash. Such a need might arise as a result of unanticipated deposit withdrawals or because of unexpected opportunities for profitable loans or security purchases.

Holding reserves as vault cash or as reserve deposits with Federal Reserve banks yields no interest return to depository institutions, however. Instead of holding excess reserves, depository institutions could lend them to other institutions that want to borrow such reserves in the federal funds market. This means that the federal funds rate—the rate of interest at which depository institutions borrow from and lend to one another in the federal funds market—is the best measure of the opportunity cost of holding excess reserves. If the federal funds rate is relatively low, then the opportunity cost that depository institutions incur by holding excess reserves is relatively small, and they will be more likely to hold relatively large amounts of excess reserves. But if the federal funds rate were to rise significantly, then this would increase the opportunity cost of holding excess reserves, and depository institutions would be more likely to lend these reserves to other institutions in the federal funds market.

The Inverse Relationship Between the Federal Funds Rate and Excess Reserves

The above analysis implies that the demand for excess reserves by depository institutions should be *inversely related* to the federal funds rate. If the federal funds rate rises, then the desired amount of excess reserve holdings at depository institutions will decline. In contrast, if the federal funds rate falls, then depository institutions will be more willing to maintain larger balances of excess reserves.

In principle then, the Federal Reserve can influence how much reserves depository institutions desire to hold, even absent reserve requirements. It can do this by enacting policies that alter the federal funds rate. We shall return to this point shortly, when we discuss how the Fed supplies reserves to depository institutions.

Transactions Deposits and Required Reserves

As you learned in Chapter 10, however, required reserves constitute the largest component of depository institution reserve holdings. The Fed assesses two required reserve ratios: a 3 percent ratio for roughly the first $50 million in transactions deposits (the Fed adjusts this threshold upward from time to time) at each depository institution, and a 10 percent ratio for all transactions deposits above this level. The 10 percent ratio applies to the bulk of transactions deposits, and so we can approximate the total amount of reserves that depository institutions desire to hold to meet reserve requirements by

$$RR = r \times D,$$

where RR denotes required reserves, r is the required reserve ratio, and D represents the total amount of transactions deposits at depository institutions.

Suppose that the amount of transactions deposits in the banking system is equal to $700 billion. Then with a required reserve ratio of $r = 0.10$, the amount of reserves that depository institutions would demand equals

$$RR = r \times D = 0.10 \times \$700 \text{ billion} = \$70 \text{ billion}.$$

Depository Institutions' Total Reserve Demand

The amount of total reserves that depository institutions desire to hold is the sum of their desired holdings of excess reserves plus the amount of reserves they require to meet reserve requirements established by the Fed. Because depository institutions must hold sufficient reserves to meet their reserve requirements, the *minimum* amount of reserves they demand is equal to their required reserves. In Figure 13.1 (page 356), this is shown as the $70 billion amount computed above, based on a required reserve ratio of $r = 0.10$ and a level of transactions deposits of $700 billion.

In addition, however, depository institutions usually hold some amount of excess reserves. As we discussed above, how many funds these institutions allocate to excess reserves depends on the opportunity cost, as measured by the federal funds rate, denoted i_f in Figure 13.1. If the federal funds rate is sufficiently high, such as $i_f = 10$ percent, then the opportunity cost may be high enough that depository institutions choose to hold zero excess reserves. In this situation their desired total reserve holdings will be equal to the minimum amount they need to meet reserve requirements, or $70 billion. This is the uppermost point of the reserve demand schedule shown in Figure 13.1, labeled Point A.

But if the federal funds rate were lower, such as $i_f = 7$ percent, then depository institutions would perceive a reduced opportunity cost of holding excess reserves. Consequently, they would be more willing to hold such reserves as a contingency against withdrawals of deposits or the possibility that profitable loan or security opportunities might arise. Figure 13.1 illustrates a situation in which depository institutions are willing to hold an amount of excess reserves equal to $ER = \$5$ billion at this lower federal funds rate. At this rate, therefore, the total reserves

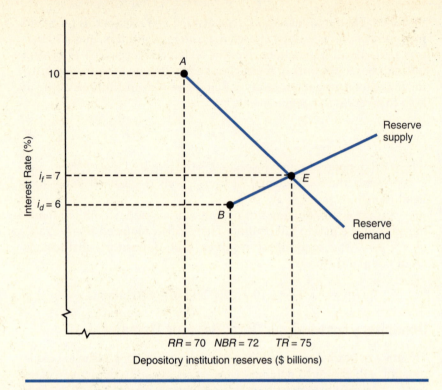

FIGURE 13.1   The Demand for and Supply of Total Depository Institution Reserves

The minimum amount of reserves that depository institutions demand is the amount they must hold to meet their reserve requirements. With a required reserve ratio of 10 percent and total transactions deposits of $700 billion, this amount would be $70 billion. They desire to hold excess reserves only if the federal funds rate falls below 10 percent, and so the total reserve demand schedule for depository institutions slopes downward to the right of point A. If the Fed supplies $72 billion in nonborrowed reserves and sets its discount rate, i_d, equal to 6 percent, then depository institutions desire to borrow additional reserves from the Fed only if the federal funds rate exceeds the discount rate. Hence, the reserve supply schedule slopes upward above point B. The equilibrium federal funds rate is at point E, where the quantity of reserves demanded by depository institutions is equal to the quantity of reserves supplied by the Fed.

demand schedule for reserves A graphical depiction of the inverse relationship between the total amount of reserves demanded by depository institutions and the federal funds rate.

demanded by depository institutions would equal the sum of the $70 billion they must hold to meet their reserve requirements plus the $5 billion in excess reserves they are willing to hold at the federal funds rate of $i_f = 7$ percent, or $TR + RR = ER = \$70$ billion $+$ $\$5$ billion $=$ $\$75$ billion.

This indicates that there is an *inverse relationship* between the total reserves that depository institutions demand and the federal funds rate. The **demand schedule for reserves** in Figure 13.1 depicts this inverse relationship. This schedule shows how the desired total reserve holdings of depository institutions vary with changes in the federal funds rate. Along this schedule, a rise in the federal funds rate causes depository institutions to demand fewer reserves, to as low as the minimum amount needed to meet their reserve requirements. A decline in the federal funds rate, in contrast, induces depository institutions to demand increasing amounts of reserves above the level of the minimum required amount. Hence, the reserve demand schedule slopes downward.

1

What key factors influence the demand for reserves by depository institutions? Depository institutions desire to hold reserves to meet reserve requirements and to ensure against unexpected cash needs. Consequently, the main factors affecting their desired reserve holdings are the required reserve ratio, the quantity of transactions deposits in the banking system, and the opportunity cost of holding reserves in excess of those required. The opportunity cost of holding excess reserves is the federal funds rate that institutions could earn by lending excess reserves in the federal funds market.

THE SUPPLY OF DEPOSITORY INSTITUTION RESERVES

When Congress enacted the Federal Reserve Act of 1913, it gave the Federal Reserve System the authority to lend to depository institutions. Then, in the Banking Act of 1935, it granted the Fed the authority to conduct open-market operations. Hence, these Congressional actions authorized the Fed to supply reserves to the nation's depository institutions. If we want to understand the supply side of the reserves market, we must turn our attention back to the Fed.

The Discount Window and Borrowed Reserves

As we discussed in Chapter 12, one way that the Federal Reserve supplies reserves to depository institutions is through direct discount window loans to individual institutions. The Fed can alter the total volume of such lending to institutions by changing the terms under which it makes reserves available.

The Fed rarely changes the basic rules under which it lends. Hence, the crucial factor affecting the quantity of reserves that depository institutions borrow from the Fed is the *spread* between the federal funds rate and the discount rate that the Fed charges on its loans. Suppose that the amount by which the federal funds rate exceeds the discount rate were to increase. Then depository institutions would respond by borrowing more new reserves directly from the Fed at the discount rate instead of borrowing existing reserves from other depository institutions at the higher federal funds rate. If the federal funds rate were to fall relative to the discount rate, however, narrowing the spread, then depository institutions would borrow fewer reserves directly from the Fed.

Keep in mind, however, that this logic applies only as long as the federal funds rate exceeds the discount rate. If the market-determined federal funds rate were to drop below the discount rate, which infrequently occurs, then there is little incentive for depository institutions to borrow reserves from the Fed at all. This means that the amount of borrowed reserves supplied by the Fed from its discount window depends *positively* on the federal funds rate—provided that the federal funds rate is *above* the discount rate.

Open-Market Operations and Nonborrowed Reserves

As we emphasized in Chapters 10 and 12, the key means by which the Fed supplies new reserves to depository institutions is through open-market purchases of government securities. The reserves that it supplies in this way are *nonborrowed reserves, NBR*.

You will see shortly that the Federal Reserve Bank of New York's Trading Desk can influence interest rates by conducting open-market operations that *change* the amount of nonborrowed reserves in the banking system. In the absence of any open-market purchases or sales, however, the amount of nonborrowed reserves remains constant. This places a *lower bound* on the amount of reserves in the nation's banking system at a given point in time. The reserves can circulate among depository institutions, but the aggregate volume of reserves cannot fall below this level in the absence of open-market operations by the New York Fed's Trading Desk.

The Fed's Supply of Total Depository Institution Reserves

Figure 13.1 on page 356 depicts the supply schedule for total depository institution reserves. As we have discussed, the base level of reserves is the quantity of nonborrowed reserves, *NBR*, that the Fed has supplied through past open-market purchases. Consequently, the total amount of reserves supplied by the Fed cannot fall below this quantity, which in Figure 13.1 is equal to *NBR* = \$72 billion.

Whenever the federal funds rate exceeds the discount rate, however, depository institutions borrow additional reserves from the Fed's discount window. In Figure 13.1, the discount rate is equal to $i_d = 6$ percent. Therefore, if the federal funds rate were equal to or less than 6 percent, depository institutions would have no incentive to borrow

POLICY NOTEBOOK
When Discount Policy Was Important

Discounting was the main instrument of monetary control in Great Britain during the nineteenth century. In the United States, in contrast, this tool was not available until the Federal Reserve System was established in 1913. The Federal Reserve System was created so that the United States would have a central bank that would act as a lender of last resort—lending funds to banks that could not obtain them from conventional private sources. Basically, the Federal Reserve Act of 1913 provided only one monetary control tool—discount policy. Open-market operations were unknown and did not come into use until the late 1920s. Reserve requirements, moreover, were set by Congress; it wasn't until the 1930s that the Fed was empowered to change reserve requirements within congressionally defined limits.

In the 1920s the Fed publicly indicated a preference for setting the discount rate *higher* than the rates on short-term government securities. The implication was that the Fed wanted to impose a penalty on member banks that borrowed from it. In practice, however, the 1921 to 1929 period was characterized by a discount rate set below most interest rates. Thus, it was profitable during these years for member banks to borrow from the Fed. At that time, member bank borrowings were greater than their unborrowed reserve balances. By the 1930s the Fed actively discouraged member bank borrowing in spite of a relatively low discount rate. Open-market operations replaced discount policies as the Fed's most important monetary tool. From 1955 to the early 1980s discount window loans to member banks averaged about 3 percent of member bank reserves. Today these loans have fallen to less than 1 percent of total reserves of depository institutions.

For Critical Analysis: *The Fed still insists that continuous borrowing in a noncrisis situation from its discount window is a "privilege and not a right." Why?*

reserves from the Fed. Under such circumstances the amount of reserves supplied by the Fed would simply equal the amount of nonborrowed reserves, *NBR*. But if the federal funds rate is greater than the discount rate, then depository institutions will borrow additional reserves directly from the Fed. For instance, Figure 13.1 illustrates one possible value for the federal funds rate, $i_f = 7$ percent. At this federal funds rate, there is a 1 percent spread between the federal funds rate and the discount rate, which induces depository institutions to *borrow* $3 billion from the Fed's discount window. Consequently, the amount of borrowed reserves is equal to $BR = \$3$ billion, and the total quantity of reserves supplied by the Fed is equal to the sum of the $72 billion in nonborrowed reserves plus the $3 billion in borrowed reserves, or $TR = NBR + BR = \$72$ billion $+ \$3$ billion $= \$75$ billion.

supply schedule of reserves
A graphical depiction of the
direct relationship between
the total amount of reserves
supplied by the Fed and the
federal funds rate.

The quantity of reserves that depository institutions borrow from the Fed rises as the federal funds rate moves upward above the discount rate. Therefore, the **supply schedule of reserves** in Figure 13.1 slopes upward from the discount rate of $i_d = 6$ percent and above the level of nonborrowed reserves of $NBR = \$72$ billion. This schedule shows how the amount of reserves that the Fed supplies to depository institutions varies with the federal funds rate.

Determining the Federal Funds Rate

Recall from your first course in economics that any market attains an *equilibrium* when the quantity of a good demanded is just equal to the quantity of the good supplied. When this state of balance occurs, there are no pressures for the market price to rise or to fall. The resulting price of the good is the *equilibrium price*.

Likewise, the market for total depository institution reserves attains an equilibrium when the total quantity of reserves that depository institutions demand from the Federal Reserve is just equal to the total quantity of reserves that the Fed has supplied through open-market operations and discount window loans. When this state of balance occurs, there are no pressures for the federal funds rate to rise or to fall. The resulting federal funds rate is the *equilibrium federal funds rate*.

Figure 13.1 on page 356 depicts such an equilibrium situation. The total depository institution reserve demand schedule slopes downward to the right of the minimum amount of reserves that depository institutions desire to hold to meet their reserve requirements, $RR = \$70$ billion. The total reserve supply schedule slopes upward above the discount rate $i_d = 6$ percent and the quantity of nonborrowed reserves $NBR = \$72$ billion. At the point at which the two schedules cross, the quantity of reserves demanded by depository institutions is equal to the quantity of reserves supplied to these institutions by the Fed, at $75 billion.

The equilibrium federal funds rate in Figure 13.1 is equal to $i_f = 7$ percent. At this federal funds rate the total amount of reserves demanded by depository institutions just matches the total quantity of reserves that the Fed has supplied. Consequently, there are no pressures for the federal funds rate to rise or to fall. The reason is that depository institutions are satisfied holding the amount of reserves that the Fed has supplied as long as the federal funds rate is equal to 7 percent.

Figure 13.2 summarizes the factors that determine the quantities of reserves supplied and demanded. The Fed's open-market operations determine the quantity of nonborrowed reserves ($NBR = \$72$ billion in our example), while the spread between the federal funds rate and the discount rate determines the amount of borrowed reserves ($BR = \$3$ billion). Hence, the Fed influences the total quantity of reserves supplied to depository institutions through its open-market operations and its setting of the discount rate.

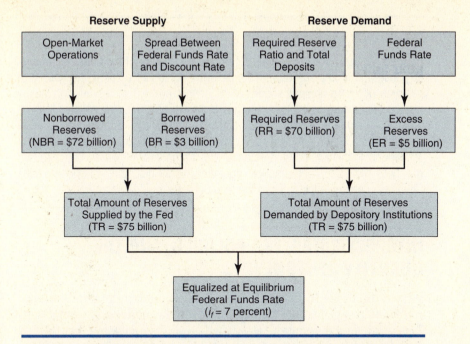

FIGURE 13.2 Factors that Determine the Equilibrium Federal Funds Rate

The Fed supplies nonborrowed reserves via its open-market operations. The amount of reserves that the Fed ultimately supplies depends on the spread between the federal funds rate and the discount rate. In Figure 13.1, these factors together yield $72 billion in nonborrowed reserves and $3 billion in borrowed reserves. Depository institutions hold most of their reserves to meet reserve requirements. Their excess reserve holdings vary with the opportunity cost of excess reserves, which is the federal funds rate. In Figure 13.1, these factors together yield $70 billion required reserves and $5 billion in excess reserves. The federal funds rate adjusts as needed to equalize the quantity of reserves supplied by the Fed and the quantity of reserves demanded by depository institutions. The equilibrium federal funds rate in Figure 13.1 is 7 percent, and the equilibrium total reserves at depository institutions are $75 billion.

The required reserve ratio and total deposits determine the amount of required reserves ($RR = \$70$ billion in our example). The federal funds rate determines the opportunity cost of holding excess reserves and, consequently, the amount of excess reserve holdings of depository institutions ($ER = \$5$ billion). Therefore, reserve requirements, total deposits in the banking system, and the federal funds rate all influence the total amount of reserves demanded by depository institutions.

At the equilibrium federal funds rate, the total amount of reserves supplied by the Fed is equal to the total amount of reserves demanded by depository institutions. That is, the federal funds rate adjusts so that these quantities just balance. In our example, the amounts of reserves demanded and supplied are equal ($TR = \$75$ billion) at an equilibrium federal funds rate of $i_f = 7$ percent.

2

How do federal reserve policies determine the supply of reserves to depository institutions and the federal funds rate?   The Fed controls the supply of reserves by determining the amount of nonborrowed reserves through open-market purchases, or through changes in its discount window policies that influence the amount of reserves that depository institutions borrow. Because the equilibrium federal funds rate occurs when the quantity of reserves demanded by depository institutions is in balance with the quantity of reserves supplied by the Fed, the Fed's open-market operations and discount window policies ultimately determine the value of the federal funds rate.

INTEREST RATES, FED POLICIES, AND THE QUANTITY OF MONEY

As we discussed in Chapter 3, the federal funds rate is only one of many interest yields that are determined in the money and capital markets. And yet it is common to see media reports indicating that the Fed has decided to change the *overall level* of interest rates in the economy. Let's consider how Fed actions that affect the equilibrium federal funds rate can spill over to influence other interest yields.

The Federal Funds Rate and the Treasury Security Yield Curve

Recall from Chapter 3 that interest rates on different financial instruments are related in two respects. One relationship is the *risk structure of interest rates:* Financial instruments with identical terms to maturity will have different market yields as a result of different degrees of risk. The other relationship is the *term structure of interest rates:* Financial instruments with similar risk features will have different market yields if they have different terms to maturity. To understand how the federal funds rate relates to the Treasury bill rate, we must take into account both of these concepts.

Yield Curves for Federal Funds and Treasury Securities   As we discussed in Chapter 3, we can construct a *yield curve* for Treasury securities by plotting yields that correspond to their terms to maturity, such as 3 months, 6 months, 12 months, and so on. Such a yield curve plots a relationship based on maturity only for Treasury securities, because Treasury securities all have the same low risk. The term premium causes the Treasury securities yield curve to slope upward even when traders in financial markets expect no change in interest rates.

We also can construct a yield curve for federal funds loans. As we noted in Chapter 6, most federal funds loans have one-day maturities, but a number of federal funds loans are *term loans* that have maturities of one or more weeks. Typically the yields on such *term loans* increase with the term of the loan. Consequently, the federal funds yield curve also slopes upward.

Federal funds loans, however, are riskier than Treasury securities. The government stands behind the Treasury securities it issues with its full taxing power. This makes defaults on such securities extremely unlikely. In contrast, most federal funds loans are unsecured transactions backed only by the ability of a borrowing depository institution to repay the loan when its one-day or multi-day term ends. Although federal funds loan defaults are fairly rare, they do occur from time to time. In addition, there have been rare situations in which parties to a federal funds transaction have disagreed on how to interpret the terms they negotiated during the transaction, leading to costly delays in final settlements.

Determining the Treasury Bill Rate   Because federal funds loans are riskier financial instruments than Treasury securities, one would expect to find a *risk premium* for federal funds loans whose maturities match those of Treasury securities. This means that the federal funds yield curve would lie *above* the Treasury securities yield curve, as in Figure 13.3 on page 364. At any term to maturity, the vertical distance between the two yield curves represents the risk premium.

Note that the actual terms to maturity on federal funds loans are never as long as the shortest-term Treasury bills, and so portions of both yield curves in Figure 13.3 are dashed lines. Nevertheless, we can *infer* the dashed portions of both yield curves by calculating the federal funds yields that would result from successively renewing federal funds loans from week to week, and by examining the prices of Treasury securities that are within days of final maturity.

Once we have constructed yield curves for federal funds loans and Treasury securities, we can determine the equilibrium interest yield on a 6-month Treasury bill, as depicted in Figure 13.3. Given an equilibrium 1-day term federal funds rate of $i_f = 7$ percent, the 6-month Treasury security rate consistent with the risk and term structures of interest rates must be equal to $i = 6$ percent. Because a 6-month Treasury bill is nearly risk-free, it typically has a lower yield than a 1-day federal funds loan even though the Treasury bill has a much longer (182-day) term to maturity. In the real world, however, the difference between the federal funds rate and the 6-month Treasury bill rate normally is about 0.25 to 0.50 percent, rather than the 1 percent differential we have chosen as a nice round number for our example in Figure 13.3.

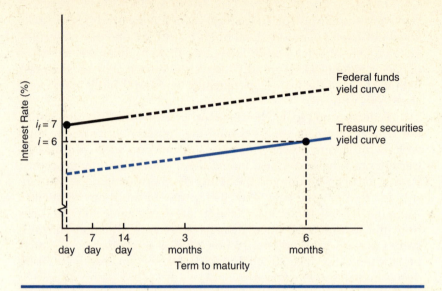

FIGURE 13.3   Determining the Treasury Bill Rate

The Treasury securities yield curve typically slopes upward. Though market yields on very short Treasury maturities do not exist, they can be inferred from the prices of Treasury securities that are within days of maturity, hence the dashed portion of the Treasury securities yield curve. Likewise, the federal funds yield curve also slopes upward over maturities that range from a day to several weeks. Longer term federal funds rates may be extrapolated from actual market rates on short-maturity federal funds loans, hence the dashed portion of the federal funds yield curve. Federal funds are riskier than Treasury securities, and so the federal funds rate typically exceeds the Treasury security rate for a given maturity. Consequently, the Treasury security yield curve lies below the federal funds yield curve. If the equilibrium federal funds rate for a 1-day maturity is 7 percent, then the 6-month Treasury security rate consistent with the term and risk structures of interest rates is 6 percent.

3

How is the federal funds rate related to other market interest rates?   Federal Reserve policies determine the federal funds rate. The risk and term structures of interest rates link the federal funds rate to other market interest rates, including Treasury security rates. Consequently, Fed policies that determine the federal funds rate ultimately influence other interest yields in the money and capital markets.

The Demand For Money

From time to time people like to complain that they "just don't have enough money." Of course, what they really mean is that they wish they earned higher money *incomes*. Theoretically, an easy way to obtain more cash would be to sell assets. Then we would have more money than we do at present. Why do we not do this? The answer is that people allocate only part of their income and wealth to money holdings. The rest is used to purchase goods, services, and assets, such as automobiles, travel services, stocks, bonds, and titles to houses. Furthermore, we hold money because it is useful. Money is a financial asset and a medium of exchange. That is why individuals and business firms demand money just as they demand any other good, service, or asset.

The Demand for Money as a Financial Asset   A key determinant of the amount of money balances that consumers and businesses desire to hold is the interest rate on alternative financial assets. The reason is that significant portions of money balances, including currency and some demand deposits, have no interest yield. NOW accounts earn interest, but the yield on these accounts typically is lower than that on alternative savings instruments such as government securities. Also, at present, depository institutions cannot pay interest on business demand deposits.

The interest yield on bonds such as government securities, therefore, is the *opportunity cost of holding money*. If the bond rate rises, then consumers and businesses incur higher opportunity costs for holding noninterest-bearing currency and demand deposits, or for holding NOW account deposits with relatively low interest yields. Consequently, higher bond rates induce consumers and businesses to reduce their holdings of these essential components of M1 and other monetary aggregates.

As we discussed in Chapter 3, a number of bond yields are determined in financial markets. Which ones are relevant measures of the opportunity cost of holding money? Because consumers and businesses usually plan their financial asset allocations over horizons of three to twelve months, interest rates on financial assets with equivalent terms to maturity are the most appropriate measures of the opportunity cost of holding money. In addition, aside from risk of theft or loss, currency is a relatively risk-free financial instrument, as are federally insured transactions deposits at depository institutions. Consequently, the best measure of the opportunity cost of holding money is the interest rate on a nearly risk-free government security such as the 6-month Treasury bill discussed in Chapter 4.

This means that the aggregate quantity of money demanded by individuals and business firms should be *inversely related* to the interest rate on government securities such as 6-month Treasury bills. A rise in this government security interest rate raises the opportunity cost of holding money and thereby causes a decline in the aggregate amount of desired money holdings. In contrast, a fall in this security rate reduces the opportunity cost of holding money and leads to an increase in the total quantity of money demanded by consumers and businesses.

The Demand for Money as a Medium of Exchange   Given that several components of the quantity of money either have no interest yields or yield interest at lower rates than alternative instruments, why would anyone hold these money assets? The reason, as we discussed in Chapter 1, is that individuals and business firms may use such money assets as mediums of exchange.

Money's medium-of-exchange role gives the various forms of money, such as currency, demand deposits, and NOW accounts, a distinctive and measurable value. This medium-of-exchange value compensates consumers and businesses for the opportunity cost they incur by holding these money assets instead of alternative financial assets such as government securities.

Because people use money assets to buy other goods and services, their demand for such assets as a medium of exchange depends on how many purchases they plan to make. This, of course, depends on their ability to spend, which in turn depends on their income level. As the total income earned by individuals and business firms increases, so does their ability to spend and their desire for money balances for use in making exchanges. Consequently, the aggregate desired holdings of money should be *directly* related to the total income of consumers and businesses. As total income accruing to individuals and business firms increases, the demand for money should increase. In contrast, if total income in the economy declines, then the combined holdings of money by consumers and business should fall.

A simple way to express this idea is through a relationship called the *Cambridge equation*, which is named for economists at Cambridge University in England who developed it a century ago. The Cambridge equation is

$$M^d = k \times Y$$

in which M^d is the total quantity of money demanded for use as a medium of exchange, Y is the total income of consumers and businesses, and k is a fraction that represents the portion of total income that consumers and businesses wish to hold as money.

For instance, suppose that the total income of all individuals and business firms is $7 trillion, which is roughly the size of total income in the United States. Then if the value of k is 0.2, meaning that consumers and businesses desire to hold 20 percent of their income as money, the total quantity of money demanded is equal to $k \times Y = 0.2 \times \$7$ trillion, or $1.4 trillion.

The Total Demand for Money   We conclude that there are two essential factors determining how much money people are willing and able to hold. One is total income. The other is the opportunity cost of holding money, which is the interest yield on a short-term, risk-free asset such as a 6-month Treasury bill.

The Cambridge equation captures only the role of income as a determinant of the quantity of money demanded in the economy. Because it leaves out the interest rate, the Cambridge equation effectively assumes that the opportunity cost of holding money is equal to zero. Consequently, the Cambridge equation is a good approximation only if Treasury bills have very low interest yields. But if the yields on 6-month Treasury bills are significantly above zero, as they usually are, then the Cambridge equation *overestimates* the total amount of money demanded by consumers and business firms.

This means that the Cambridge equation gives an *upper* limit on the total quantity of money demanded in the economy. This upper limit is shown in Figure 13.4 under the assumption that total income is $7 trillion, so that the value of the upper limit on desired money

---

FIGURE 13.4   The Total Demand for Money by Consumers and Businesses

The simplest theory of the demand for money is the Cambridge equation, $M^d = k \times Y$, where k is the fraction of total nominal income that consumers and businesses desire to hold as money and Y is total nominal income. If $k = 0.2$ and $Y = \$7$ trillion, then the Cambridge equation yields $1.4 trillion as the total quantity of money demanded. The Cambridge equation, however, ignores the fact that the interest rate on a relatively short-term, low-risk security such as the 6-month Treasury-bill rate is the opportunity cost of holding money. As this interest rate rises, individuals and businesses hold fewer money balances. In our example, if the 6-month Treasury bill rate is $i = 6$ percent, total desired money holdings amount to $1.2 trillion.

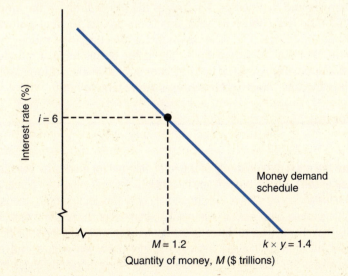

holdings is equal to $k \times Y = \$1.4$ trillion. This would be the amount of money that individuals and business firms would desire to hold if the opportunity cost of holding money, the 6-month Treasury bill rate that we denote as i, were equal to zero.

Suppose, however, that the yield on a 6-month Treasury bill is 6 percent. This would induce consumers and businesses to convert some of their money funds into alternative savings instruments such as T-bills. If they later need these funds for current spending, they can convert them back into currency or transactions deposits. In the meantime, they earn an interest yield on a portion of the funds they otherwise would have allocated to money assets such as currency or transactions deposits. This means that if the 6-month Treasury bill rate is equal to $i = 6$ percent, consumers and businesses will hold a smaller quantity of money, such as the $1.2 trillion figure shown in Figure 13.4.

Of course, if the interest yield on Treasury bills were to rise above this rate, then people would further reduce their money holdings because of the higher opportunity cost of holding money. In contrast, if the Treasury bill yield were to decline from 6 percent, individuals and business firms would raise their money holdings somewhat.

money demand schedule   A graphical illustration of the inverse relationship between the total quantity of money demanded by consumers and businesses and the interest rate on a short-term Treasury security.

Hence, there is an inverse relationship between the total amount of money demanded in the economy and the Treasury bill rate, as depicted by the downward-sloping **money demand schedule** in Figure 13.4. This schedule depicts the total demand for money by consumers and businesses. It indicates that if the 6-month Treasury bill rate is $i = 6$ percent, then the total quantity of money demanded in the economy will be equal to $M = \$1.2$ trillion.

Figure 13.5 sums up the factors that determine the total amount of money that consumers and businesses hold. Because the total income of consumers and businesses determines the upper limit on the amount of money they will choose to hold, this is one key factor that influences their money holdings. The other main factor affecting total money holdings is the Treasury bill interest rate. The value of this interest rate determines the opportunity cost of holding money, which also influences how much money consumers and businesses are willing to hold.

4

What are the main determinants of the total demand for money by consumers and businesses?   There are two key factors that determine the total demand for money in the economy. One is the opportunity cost of holding money, measured by the interest rate on a riskless financial instrument such as a 6-month Treasury bill. The other key factor affecting the demand for money is the total income of consumers and businesses. As income increases, individuals and businesses increase their spending and therefore need more money balances to use as a medium of exchange.

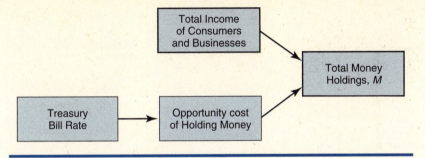

FIGURE 13.5   **The Factors that Determine the Total Demand for Money**

Because people spend more as their income rises, the total income of consumers and businesses is a key factor influencing total money holdings. In addition, the Treasury bill rate determines the opportunity cost of holding money, and so this interest rate also is an important factor in determining the total amount of money that consumers and businesses choose to hold.

The Equilibrium Quantity of Money

We now have evaluated key aspects of how Fed policy making affects the quantity of money. Figure 13.6 on page 370 depicts the linkage from the Fed's main tools of monetary policy to the total money holdings of consumers and businesses using the examples in Figures 13.1, 13.2, and 13.4. In panel (a) of figure 13.6, the Fed's choice of a discount rate of $i_d = 6$ percent and of a level of nonborrowed reserves equal to $NBR = \$72$ billion determines the supply of total reserves to depository institutions. Given the demand for reserves by those institutions, the equilibrium federal funds rate that maintains equilibrium in the reserves market at a level of \$75 billion is equal to $i_f = 7$ percent.

Panel (b) shows the determination of the 6-month Treasury bill rate. The yield on 6-month Treasury bills that is consistent with the risk and term structures of interest rates, as depicted by the federal funds and Treasury security yield curves in panel (b), is equal to $i = 6$ percent. This interest yield is the opportunity cost of holding money. Panel (c) shows the determination of the equilibrium quantity of money. From the money demand schedule for consumers and businesses, we can see that the total amount of desired money holdings at a 6 percent interest yield for 6-month Treasury securities is \$1.2 trillion. This, in our example, is the equilibrium quantity of money.

Of course, this is just an example. Values of the Fed's policy tools, total reserves, the federal funds rate, Treasury security rates, and the quantity of money vary from week to week and even from day to day. But Figure 13.6 shows the essential mechanics by which the Fed's policy choices relate to the final determination of the amount of money in the economy. Understanding the linkages depicted in Figure 13.6 is necessary to understand how the Fed conducted monetary policy in the past and how it conducts monetary policy today.

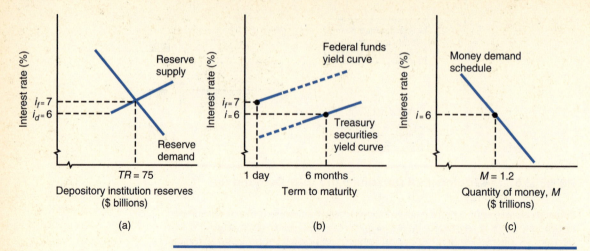

FIGURE 13.6   Determining the Equilibrium Quantity of Money

In the market for reserves, the federal funds rate adjusts to equilibrate the quantity of reserves demanded by depository institutions with the quantity of reserves supplied by the Fed at a level of $75 billion. Given an equilibrium federal funds rate of $i_f = 7$ percent, the term and risk structures of interest rates, as reflected by the positions and shapes of the Treasury security and federal funds yield curves, determine the equilibrium interest rate on a 6-month Treasury bill, $i = 6$ percent. This interest rate is the opportunity cost of holding money. At this rate, and given their current total income, consumers and businesses choose to hold money balances of $1.2 trillion. This is the equilibrium quantity of money.

Figure 13.7 uses solid black arrows to chart the full policy connections that our example illustrates. Through open-market operations and discount window policy, the Fed can control the total supply of reserves to depository institutions. The interaction between the Fed's supply of reserves and depository institution's demand for reserves then determines the federal funds rate. Then, the risk and term structure of interest rates, as reflected by the shapes and positions of the federal funds and Treasury security yield curves, determines the equilibrium Treasury bill rate that measures the opportunity cost of money holdings by consumers and businesses. Given their incomes, individuals and business firms then take into account this opportunity cost and determine the total amount of money they desire to hold. This is the equilibrium quantity of money.

The linkages that the solid black arrows depict in Figure 13.7 imply that the basic connections from the Fed to the quantity of money can be summarized by the *dashed arrows*. Fed policy tools directly influence the federal funds rate, which in turn affects the Treasury bill rate. Then, given the total income of consumers and businesses, the Treasury bill rate influences the total money holdings of individuals and business firms. Consequently, the dashed arrows capture the essential *interest rate channel* through which Fed policy tools affect the quantity of money.

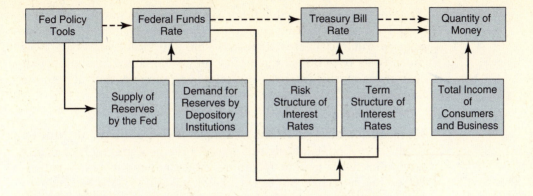

FIGURE 13.7 Linking Fed Policy Tools to the Quantity of Money

This figure summarizes how Fed policy tools relate to the determination of the equilibrium quantity of money. Changes in a Fed policy instrument affect the supply of reserves and influence the equilibrium federal funds rate. Via the term and risk structures of interest rates, this induces a change in the Treasury bill rate, which in turn alters the opportunity cost of holding money and thereby gives consumers and businesses the incentive to change their desired money holdings. The indirect, interest rate channel of monetary policy is indicated by the dashed arrows: Fed policy tools affect the federal funds rate, which influences the Treasury bill rate, which in turn affects the equilibrium quantity of money.

Interest Rates and the Money Multiplier   How does this interest rate channel from reserves to money that we have developed relate back to the money multiplier expression we discussed in Chapter 10 and used to understand basic monetary policy effects in Chapter 12? Recall from Chapter 12 that the money multiplier expression is

$$M = m \times MB$$

where M is the quantity of money, m is the money multiplier, and MB is the monetary base, which is the sum of currency and total depository institution reserves.

Suppose that the quantity of currency is equal to $375 billion. In our example in Figure 13.6, total reserves are equal to $75 billion, and so the monetary base is equal to $450 billion. This tells us that the money multiplier would be equal to $m = M/MB = \$1.2$ trillion/$450 billion = 2.67.

Hence, our basic money multiplier story has not changed. Nevertheless, accounting for the role of interest rates, such as the federal funds rate and the 6-month Treasury bill rate, indicates that the value of the money multiplier normally will depend on interest rates. If changes in circumstances were to cause the equilibrium federal funds rate and Treasury bill rates to change, the result would be changes in the amount of total reserves in the banking system and the total desired money holdings of consumers and businesses. This would cause the money multiplier's value to change. Indeed, we pointed out in Chapter 10 that the money multiplier varies over time. A key reason why the money multiplier is not constant is that changes in market interest rates cause variations in the value of the multiplier.

How Fed Policy Actions Change the Quantity of Money

Recall from Chapter 12 that there are three potential tools of monetary policy: open-market operations, discount window policy, and required reserve ratios. But as we noted in Chapter 12, the Fed changes reserve requirements only infrequently. Hence, the key means by which the Fed makes tactical monetary policy adjustments from day-to-day and from week-to-week are open-market purchases and sales and variations in the terms of its lending to depository institutions. Both of these policy tools exert their effects by changing the total amount of reserves that the Fed supplies to depository institutions. The variations in the supply of total depository institution reserves cause changes in the equilibrium federal funds and Treasury bill rate and alterations in the quantity of money that consumers and businesses desire to hold.

To understand how the Fed can cause such changes to take place, let's think about how an open-market purchase or a discount rate reduction affects interest rates and the quantity of money. As indicated by Figure 13.8, the initial effect of either action would be an increase in the total quantity of reserves supplied at the current equilibrium federal funds rate. Hence, there would be an imbalance in the market for depository institution reserves: The quantity of reserves supplied by the Fed would exceed the quantity of reserves demanded by depository institutions. Depository institutions would increase their excess reserve holdings only if the federal funds rate were to fall, so that the opportunity cost of holding excess reserves would decline. Consequently, the second effect of the open-market purchase would be a reduction in the equilibrium federal funds rate.

The decline in the federal funds rate would lead to an expected decline in the federal funds rate for future periods as well. This means that expected interest rates across the term and risk structure of interest rates would decline. For a 6-month term to maturity, the interest yield on a Treasury security would also fall. The final effect stems from the fact that this reduction in the 6-month Treasury bill rate would cause the opportunity cost of holding money to decline. The result would be that consumers and businesses would increase their money holdings. The open-market purchase thereby causes the quantity of money to increase.

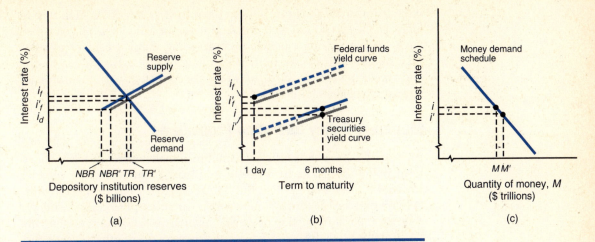

FIGURE 13.8 Inducing an Increase in the Quantity of Money

A Fed open-market purchase would increase the amount of nonborrowed reserves from *NBR* to *NBR'*. This would cause the reserve supply schedule to shift rightward, inducing a rise in the equilibrium quantity of reserves from *TR* to *TR'*, and a decline in the equilibrium federal funds rate from i_f to i_f'. People would expect future federal funds rates to be lower, and so the federal funds yield curve would shift downward. At any term to maturity, the risk premium between a Treasury security and a federal funds loan would remain the same, and so the Treasury security yield curve would shift downward, and the 6-month Treasury bill rate would fall from *i* to *i'*. This reduction in the opportunity cost of holding money would induce consumers and businesses to increase their holdings of money, and so the equilibrium quantity of money would rise from *M* to *M'*.

5

How do Federal Reserve policies affect the quantity of money? Open-market operations and discount rate changes alter the supply of reserves to depository institutions, thereby changing the federal funds rate. Via the risk and term structure of interest rates, such variations in the federal funds rate induce movements in the Treasury bill rate and alter the opportunity cost of holding money. This causes individuals and businesses to change the amount of money they hold.

FEDERAL RESERVE OPERATING PROCEDURES

When military leaders get involved in battles, they are faced with a number of *tactical* decisions. They have to decide how to place and maneuver their land, air, and naval forces in a manner that is consistent with the overall strategic plan they have developed. Likewise, Fed officials must think about how to vary their policy tools each day or week as they try to follow a broad strategy for achieving the goals they have established for a period encompassing many weeks or months. Like military officers, Fed officials must develop *tactics,* or day-to-day and week-to-week policy actions that are consistent with their broader strategy for monetary policy.

Monetary Policy Operating Procedures

As human beings, Fed officials sometimes make mistakes when short-term policy decisions turn out to be inconsistent with their broader strategy for monetary policy. But if the Fed makes a tactical policy mistake on one day or during one week, it can attempt to compensate for its error the following day or week. Nevertheless, ultimately achieving its strategic goals for a period of many weeks or months requires that the Fed follow appropriate daily and weekly tactics in its conduct of monetary policy. Indeed, another way to define a policy strategy is to call it a *set of tactics.* Let's begin by discussing how the Fed can make tactical policy changes using its available policy tools. Once we understand how the Fed conducts policy on a daily or weekly basis, we can then consider how it pursues broader strategies by adopting particular operating procedures for monetary policy.

Sometimes critics contend that the Fed makes too many of its policy decisions by the seat of its pants. Yet the Fed typically follows predetermined *strategies* in its conduct of monetary policy. In military thinking a strategy is the formation of broad plans for achieving an overall objective through an intended set of battlefield movements. Likewise, for the Fed a monetary policy **strategy** is a general plan for achieving some set of economic objectives. The Fed normally tries to implement such a strategy by following an **operating procedure,** which is a self-imposed guideline for conducting monetary policy over a time span stretching across several weeks or months. As we discuss below, the Fed has experimented with a variety of operating procedures during the past 25 years.

strategy   A general plan for achieving a set of economic objectives.

operating procedure   A guideline for conducting monetary policy over several weeks or months.

Alternative Operating Procedures for Monetary Policy

There are two basic types of *strategies* the Fed might adopt over periods of many weeks, months, or even years. One strategy is for the Fed to focus on target levels for depository institutions reserves. The other strategy entails targeting an interest rate.

A Reserve-Targeting Procedure   A possible approach to a reserve-targeting strategy would be for the Fed to establish a target value for total reserves. Then it could conduct open-market operations as needed to keep the level of total reserves at this target level.

To understand the day-to-day tactical approach the Fed would need to follow if it were to pursue a reserve-targeting strategy, consider the following example. Suppose there was a sudden rise in depository institutions' reserve demands, caused perhaps by an increase in desired excess reserve holdings. The amount of reserves demanded by depository institutions would exceed the quantity of reserves supplied by the Fed. Depository institutions then would be satisfied holding the amount of reserves supplied by the Fed only if the equilibrium federal funds rate were to rise. This, in turn, would induce depository institutions to borrow more reserves from the Fed's discount window. In the absence of any Fed response, total reserves would rise above the Fed's target value.

One way for the Fed to keep total reserves from increasing would be to raise the discount rate to discourage further borrowing. Another tactic would be for the Fed to conduct an open-market sale, thereby withdrawing sufficient nonborrowed reserves from the banking system to keep total reserves at the Fed's target level.

Why might the Fed use a reserve-targeting operating procedure? One reason is that if the Fed's objective is to target the quantity of money, and if the money multiplier is relatively insensitive to interest rate changes, then keeping total reserves stable stabilizes the monetary base and the total quantity of money. Furthermore, such an operating procedure automatically keeps interest rate volatility from influencing the amount of reserves at depository institutions, and thus also stabilizes the monetary base.

Note, however, that a Fed operating procedure that stabilizes total reserves tends to make interest rates more variable. For instance, in our example above we observed that the Fed had to let the federal funds rate increase in order to choke off discount window borrowing and keep total reserves stabilized at the target level. As we shall discuss in Chapter 14, however, induced increases in Treasury security yields and other interest rates cause reductions in spending flows in the economy. Consequently, a potentially negative aspect of a reserve-targeting operating procedure is that it can lead to significant interest rate volatility, which translates into more variability in economic activity.

A Federal-Funds-Rate Targeting Procedure   An alternative Fed operating procedure focuses on reducing or eliminating interest rate volatility. To see how the Fed's tactics would work under such a policy strategy, let's again consider a rise in total depository institution reserve demand. In this instance, however, suppose that the Fed's strategy is to maintain the *federal funds rate* at a target level. As we already noted, an increase in reserve demand would tend to cause the equilibrium federal funds rate to rise. To keep this from happening, the Fed would need to *increase* the amount of nonborrowed reserves. This, of course, contrasts with the Fed's appropriate tactical response for targeting total reserves, which we determined would require a *reduction* in nonborrowed reserves. This policy action would, however, stabilize the federal funds rate instead of adding to its volatility in the face of a change in total reserve demand by depository institutions.

Why might the Fed choose to target the federal funds rate? The main reason for doing so is that it eliminates any perceived adverse effects that interest rate variability might have on the economy. As long as the risk and term structures of interest rates are stable, targeting the federal funds rate also keeps Treasury security rates from changing, thereby stabilizing the opportunity cost of holding money. This can contribute to greater stability of the equilibrium quantity of money demanded.

There is, however, a potentially significant drawback to targeting the federal funds rate. Suppose there is variability in the demand for money by consumers and businesses arising from factors other than the opportunity cost of money, such as variations in incomes. Because a federal-funds-rate targeting procedure stabilizes the opportunity cost of holding money, variations in the total demand for money for other reasons translate into the maximum possible changes in the amount of money that consumers and businesses choose to hold. By stabilizing interest rates, the Fed keeps the opportunity cost of money from changing, thereby helping to offset such swings in desired money holdings. This can make the equilibrium quantity of money demanded more volatile than it otherwise would be. If controlling the amount of money is a Fed objective, then this negative aspect of targeting the federal funds rate can make it a less desirable operating procedure. In addition, to the extent that the quantity of money influences aggregate spending—and you will learn in Chapter 14 that it does—such variability in the quantity of money also could lead to greater volatility in economic activity.

Past and Current Federal Reserve Operating Procedures

In light of the trade-offs associated with reserve- or interest-rate-based operating procedures, what strategies has the Fed actually used in past years? How have they worked out? The Fed has been around since 1913, but let's confine ourselves to the last three decades as we consider the answers to these questions.

Targeting the Federal Funds Rate, 1970–1979

As we discussed briefly in Chapter 11, the Fed first began to think more "scientifically" about its policy strategies at the beginning of the 1970s. The approach that it adopted was a procedure to target the federal funds rate. Technically, the Fed established a *target range* for the federal funds rate during the 1970s, but its policy tactics were designed to keep the rate very close to the middle of the range.

POLICY NOTEBOOK
The Difficulty in Targeting Real Interest Rates

When the Fed targets *the* interest rate, it is referring to the nominal rate of interest. Recall that the nominal rate of interest is the real rate of interest plus the expected rate of inflation. But businesses undertake investment decisions based on real, rather than nominal, interest rates. In general, real rates of interest are relatively high when economic growth prospects are buoyant and investment demand is concomitantly strong. During periods of high growth and robust investment, real rates of interest are typically around 3 percent. The average since 1960 has been around 2 percent. According to Harvard economist Robert J. Barro, the Fed does not have much influence over expected real rates of interest even in the short run. He argues that such rates are determined by the world demand and supply of credit, which is a function of the world's willingness to save compared to the world's desire to invest. Barro maintains that the Fed is in fact a "passive observer with respect to movements in real interest rates."

Monetarist economist Milton Freidman is even more direct about this issue than Robert Barro. Freidman states, "I believe that the idea that a central bank can target interest rates is utterly false. Interest rates are partly a real magnitude, partly a nominal magnitude. The Federal Reserve cannot target real interest rates and has done great damage by trying to do so."

The way interest rates are analyzed in the press often fails to make the distinction between real and nominal interest rates. A high nominal interest rate can be evidence that a country's central bank has pursued *loose* rather than tight monetary policy in the past. This would result because, in the long run, consistent increases in the rate of growth of the quantity of money that exceeds the real growth rate of the economy lead to higher rates of inflation. A higher rate of inflation normally leads to expectations of further inflation and therefore higher nominal interest rates. Thus, while many people often associate contractionary monetary policy with high interest rates, the converse may often be true.

For Critical Analysis: *If the Fed cannot control real interest rates, what can it control?*

The Fed adopted targeting of the federal funds rate in an effort to achieve greater stability in the quantity of money and in economic activity. Based on our discussion above, targeting the federal funds rate poses problems in attaining these objectives if the total demand for money becomes more variable. Unfortunately for the Fed, this is exactly what happened after the early 1970s. The Fed began to miss its monetary targets by wide margins, and the nation's income, spending, and inflation rate became more volatile. By 1979 the Fed was searching for a new operating procedure.

Targeting Nonborrowed Reserves, 1979–1982   Fed critics during the 1970s argued that it should switch to a procedure of targeting total reserves and let the marketplace determine the federal funds rate. In the fall of 1979 the Fed decided to experiment with a slightly different type of reserves-based operating procedure. The Fed would try to predict reserve borrowing by depository institutions during the coming months, and then it would determine the amount of nonborrowed reserves necessary to keep total reserves stable in light of its prediction. The Fed considered this level of *nonborrowed reserves* as its policy target.

By setting an objective for nonborrowed reserves, the Fed ended up allowing some variability in total reserves. This offset somewhat the negative aspect of the reserves-based procedure we discussed above: interest rate variability. Nevertheless, interest rates were much more volatile after the Fed switched to targeting nonborrowed reserves in late 1979. Furthermore, by allowing total reserves to vary somewhat, the Fed also ended up permitting the quantity of money to vary from its target level. In the end, targeting nonborrowed reserves led to significant variations in *both* interest rates *and* the quantity of money.

Targeting Borrowed Reserves, 1982–1987   In 1982 the Fed tried an operating procedure that split the difference between targeting reserves and targeting the federal funds rate. It began to target the level of *borrowed reserves*. This really was not such a novel policy, however. Recall from Chapter 11 that during the 1950s and 1960s the Fed tried to stabilize *free reserves*, or the difference between excess reserves and borrowed reserves. By targeting borrowed reserves, the Fed tended to stabilize free reserves, and so this 1980s procedure looked a lot like a return to old-style policy making.

In a sense it also looked like targeting the federal funds rate. As we noted earlier in this chapter, the key determinant of the amount of discount window borrowing by depository institutions is the spread between the federal funds rate and the discount rate. The way the Fed stabilized borrowed reserves was by keeping this spread stable, which in turn required stability of the federal funds rate. And so targeting borrowed reserves also entailed keeping the federal funds rate from being excessively volatile.

Indeed, some critics of the Fed argued that the Fed's borrowed reserves procedure was really a "cover" for a return to targeting the federal funds rate. A few even contended that the Fed never seriously targeted nonborrowed reserves but instead implicitly stabilized the federal funds rate. Nevertheless, in a 1995 study, Thomas Cosimano and Richard Sheehan of the University of Notre Dame found strong evidence that the Fed really did use three separate operating procedures. Their study involved sophisticated statistical analysis, but you can get a hint of why they reached this conclusion by considering Figure 13.9, which is taken from a 1990 study by Carl Walsh of the University of California at Santa Cruz. Panel (a) of the figure shows how the equilibrium federal funds rate moved in response to Fed announcements of

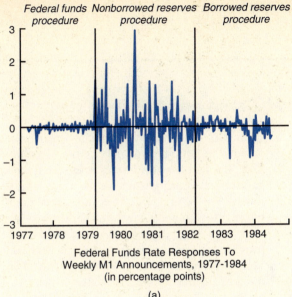

Federal Funds Rate Responses To
Weekly M1 Announcements, 1977-1984
(in percentage points)

(a)

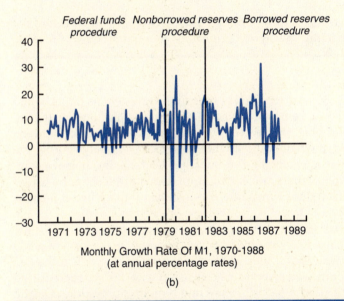

Monthly Growth Rate Of M1, 1970-1988
(at annual percentage rates)

(b)

**FIGURE 13.9   Variability of the Federal Funds Rate and M1 Growth
Under Different Operating Procedures**

As shown in panel (a) federal funds rate variability rose considerably when the
Fed switched from targeting the federal funds rate to targeting nonborrowed re-
serves in 1979, and then fell significantly when the Fed switched to targeting bor-
rowed reserves in 1982. Panel (b) shows that the variability of money growth like-
wise rose after 1979 before declining somewhat after 1982. *Source:* Carl E. Walsh,
"Issues in the Choice of Monetary Policy Operating Procedures," in William Haraf and Phillip
Cagan, eds., *Monetary Policy for a Changing Financial Environment,* Washington, D.C.: AEI
Press, 1990, pp. 8–37.

POLICY NOTEBOOK
The Second Great Stock Market Crash and Fed Targeting

The chair of the Federal Reserve, Alan Greenspan, faced a target choice—the interest rate or the money supply—in a dramatic way during the week starting Monday, October 19, 1987. The Dow Jones Industrial Index (the most commonly referred to stock index) fell by 508 points in one day. Over a one-week period, the value of the Dow Jones dropped by one-third. Would this lead to a general economic panic? There are always many loans outstanding for which shares of stock have been pledged as collateral. Depository institutions might want to call in those loans because the underlying collateral

value had dropped by so much. Greenspan decided to "step up to bat." He basically said that "the Fed is willing to provide whatever amount of liquidity is necessary to avert this crisis." The Fed provided additional funds to the market, thereby lowering short-term interest rates. Greenspan said that the Fed would provide additional funds as long as needed. The next day, stock prices went up. The GDP did not fall that month. A crisis was, in fact, averted.

For Critical Analysis: *How did the Fed's lowering of interest rates avert the crisis?*

the size of M1. Because the Fed kept the funds rate near its target before 1979, such announcements typically had little effect on the federal funds rate. But when the Fed targeted nonborrowed reserves between 1979 and 1982, the federal funds rate varied considerably. During the period after 1982, when the Fed switched to targeting borrowed reserves, the federal funds rate varied more than it did during the period of targeting the federal funds rate, but less than it did when compared with the interval of targeting nonborrowed reserves.

Panel (b) of Figure 13.9 displays the monthly growth rates for M1 between 1970 and 1987. As noted above, variability in the growth of M1 actually *increased* during the 1979–1982 interval during which the Fed targeted nonborrowed reserves, as compared with 1970s period during which the Fed used a federal funds rate targeting procedure. During the period from 1982 to 1987, the variability of M1 growth declined slightly, but still was much greater than it was during the 1970s. Consequently, both panels in Figure 13.9 indicate that the Fed really did use three distinctive operating procedures during the 1970s and 1980s.

Renewed Targeting of the Federal Funds Rate, 1988 to the Present
In October 1987 stock prices plummeted, with many stocks losing over a third of their value within a single day. To help prevent a broader financial crisis, the Fed announced that it stood ready to provide as much liquidity as needed. It also decided to keep interest rates stable to

prevent further volatility in the prices of financial instruments. To do this, it switched to a federal funds rate target once again.

From 1988 until the present the Fed has continued to use the federal funds rate as its strategic variable of monetary policy. Its tactics, however, have differed from its approach in the 1970s. In contrast to the Fed of the 1970s, today's Fed has been much more willing to *adjust* the target value of the federal funds rate when conditions have warranted such action. This increased flexibility has helped offset some of the otherwise undesirable features of this policy procedure. Even former critics of the Fed have given it high marks for its willingness to change its federal funds rate target to stabilize economic activity. Only the future will tell, however, if the Fed will be able to maintain such a flexible approach to this operating procedure.

6

What are Federal Reserve operating procedures, and what operating procedures has the Federal Reserve used in recent years?   Operating procedures are strategies that the Fed adopts to guide its open-market operations and discount window policies over the course of many weeks, months, or even years. The Fed basically can choose between operating procedures that focus on targeting reserves or the federal funds rate. Since the 1970s the Fed has used operating procedures that have targeted the federal funds rate, nonborrowed reserves, and borrowed reserves. Presently the Fed targets the federal funds rate.

SUMMARY

1. **Key Factors that Influence the Demand for Reserves by Depository Institutions:** There are three determinants of depository institutions' demand for reserves. Two of these are the required reserve ratio set by the Fed and the total quantity of transactions deposits in the banking system, which together determine the amount of required reserves. The third factor is the opportunity cost to banks of holding excess reserves, which is the federal funds rate.

2. **How Federal Reserve Policies Determine the Supply of Reserves to Depository Institutions and the Federal Funds Rate:** The Fed's open-market operations determine the amount of nonborrowed reserves in the banking system, and its discount window policies influence the amount of borrowed reserves. Consequently, through open-market purchases and sales or alterations in the terms at which depository institutions may borrow from the discount window, the Fed can change the supply of reserves and affect the equilibrium federal funds rate.

3. **The Linkage Between the Federal Funds Rate and Other Market Interest Rates:** The risk and term structures of interest rates link Treasury security rates and other interest yields to the federal funds rate, which the Fed can influence with its policy tools. Consequently, Fed policy actions that alter the federal funds rate ultimately cause other market interest rates to move in the same direction as the federal funds rate.

4. **The Main Determinants of the Total Demand for Money by Consumers and Businesses:** There are two key factors that determine the demand for money by individuals and business firms. One is the opportunity cost of holding money. This is the interest yield on a riskless security such as a Treasury bill. The other key factor is the incomes of consumers and businesses. As their incomes increase, they increase their spending, which requires more money balances for purchasing goods, services, and assets.

5. **How Federal Reserve Policies Affect the Quantity of Money:** Open-market purchases or sales or discount rate changes cause the federal funds rate to change. Because Treasury security rates are linked to the federal funds rate through the risk and term structure of interest rates, such Fed actions cause Treasury bill rates to change. This alters the opportunity cost of money and thereby induces a change in the aggregate quantity of money demanded.

6. **Types of Federal Reserve Operating Procedures, and Operating Procedures Used by the Federal Reserve in Recent Years:** Operating procedures are the guidelines by which the Fed pursues its broader economic goals. The Fed typically must choose between operating procedures that entail targeting reserves or procedures for stabilizing or targeting the federal funds rate. In recent decades the Fed has experimented with targeting the federal funds rate, targeting nonborrowed reserves, and targeting borrowed reserves. During the 1990s the Fed has targeted the federal funds rate, but has adjusted its rate target more often than it did when it used a similar operating procedure in the 1970s.

QUESTIONS AND PROBLEMS

1. Why does the demand schedule for depository institution reserves slope downward? Why does the supply schedule of reserves slope upward? Explain in your own words.

2. Suppose that the Fed's current operating procedure is to target the federal funds rate. If the Fed finds that it wishes to reduce the discount rate for some reason unrelated to monetary policy needs, then

should it buy or sell securities to keep the federal funds rate at its target level? Explain your reasoning.

3. Why does the federal funds yield curve lie above the Treasury security yield curve?

4. Why does it make sense that the quantity of money demanded by businesses and consumers is inversely related to the 6-month Treasury bill yield? Explain in your own words.

5. Suppose that the total income of individuals and business firms increases while the 6-month Treasury bill rate remains unchanged. Draw a rough diagram to illustrate what would happen to the economy's money demand schedule and to the quantity of money demanded at the unchanged Treasury bill rate.

6. The Fed currently uses an operating procedure in which it targets the federal funds rate, but it changes its target more often than it did in the 1970s, when it used a similar procedure. In light of the drawbacks associated with this procedure, is there any potential gain from the Fed's greater flexibility in setting the federal funds rate target? Explain your reasoning. (*Hint:* Think about how this approach can help split the difference between the gains and losses of interest rate targeting versus reserves targeting.)

Essentials of Monetary Theory

KEY QUESTIONS

1. What is the difference between nominal and real national income?

2. What is the equation of exchange?

3. According to classical monetary theory, how does monetary policy affect prices and real output and employment?

4. How does gradual price adjustment alter classical predictions about the way in which monetary policy actions influence the price level, real output, and employment?

5. What is the difference between adaptive and rational expectations?

6. How do modern monetary theories differ in their assumptions about how monetary policy affects real economic activity?

"The printing presses can't keep up with rising prices." This is not only a real newspaper headline, but one that has appeared dozens of times in the American press over the last three or four decades. This type of headline has been applied to such diverse countries as Argentina, Brazil, Israel, and Russia. In modified form, this notion of printing presses belatedly spewing out currency to keep up with rising prices has been applied to Germany before World War II. All of these situations have been labeled hyperinflation, or extremely rapid rising prices.

Are we making a correlation leading to a false causation? Probably, as you will see in this chapter. In general, the direction of causation between the money printing presses and rising prices is usually the reverse of what the popular press has preached during hyperinflation. You will understand more about this issue when you read about the relationship between the rate of growth in the quantity of money in circulation and the rate of inflation, part of the subject matter of this chapter.

NATIONAL INCOME AND THE EQUATION OF EXCHANGE

At various points in earlier chapters we have referred to the role that economic activity plays in influencing the functioning of financial markets. Up to this point, however, we have not discussed how we measure economic activity. Nor have we considered how monetary policy might influence the volume of economic activity. Now we shall try to get to the heart of these issues.

Real Income, Nominal Income, and Price Deflators

Trying to measure the aggregate volume of all economic activity in the economy is a daunting task. Indeed, even with the best of intentions economists recognize that they really cannot measure all production and trading activities in the economy. After all, economists cannot go to every garage sale to collect data on sales of second-hand goods, nor can they accurately measure the value of services such as those that homemakers provide but for which they receive no explicit monetary payments. Economists also cannot accurately measure illegal transactions that nonetheless constitute a portion of economic activity in the American economy.

In the face of such problems it would be tempting to throw up one's hands and declare that measuring economic activity simply is impossible. But in years past a number of individuals have sought to get around some of these difficulties by developing reliable measures for the bulk of transactions that constitute economic activity in the

United States. Businesses, government agencies, and the Federal Reserve now use these measures as indicators of how well the economy is performing and of how monetary and other governmental policies have affected the nation's economy.

Measuring Economic Activity: National Income and Product

The primary measure of economic activity during a given interval is the total value, computed using current market prices, of the output of *final* goods and services produced by businesses during that period. This is called the economy's **gross domestic product (GDP).** Because it measures only the value of final goods and services, GDP does not include all economic transactions, such as garage sales of second-hand goods, that take place during a given period.

Businesses earn revenues on the output that they sell to consumers, other businesses, and the government. These revenues flow to the individuals who provide the *factors of production* that businesses use to produce the goods and services they sell. Factors of production include labor, land, capital, and entrepreneurship. The earnings of the individuals who supply these factors of production are in the form of wages and salaries, rents, interest and dividends, and profits. If we add together all these receipts for all individuals in the economy, the result is the total income earnings of all individuals, or **national income.**

This means that, ultimately, the total value of output that businesses produce becomes the combined income of all individuals. Consequently, if we ignore some minor accounting details that distinguish the two measures in the income and product accounting procedures that the U.S. government uses, *national income and GDP must be identical.* This means that for all intents and purposes, GDP is also a good measure of the total income receipts of all individuals.

Real Versus Nominal National Income   As shown in Figure 14.1, during the past 50 years national income, as measured by GDP, has risen in the United States. It has done so for two reasons. One is that the economy has grown, meaning that businesses have expanded their resources and found ways to increase production of goods and services.

Another reason, however, is that prices have risen. Such overall price increases, which we call inflation, have increased the *measured value* of income and output in the economy. This means that we cannot necessarily look at Figure 14.1 and conclude that the actual production of goods and services consistently has increased in the United States. Some portion of the general rise in GDP shown in the figure occurred simply because prices rose over time as well. This means that using GDP as a measure of actual productive activity in the economy causes us to overstate the true volume of such activity during inflationary periods.

To see why we need to make this distinction, think about a situation in which an employer doubles the wages you receive for providing

gross domestic product (GDP)   The total value of a nation's output of final goods and services during a given period.

national income   The total earnings of all individuals in the economy, summed across all sources of income, including wages and salaries, rents, interest and dividends, and profits.

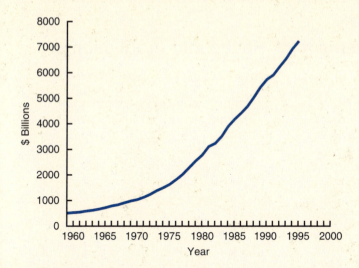

FIGURE 14.1   U.S. Gross Domestic Product

The dollar value of newly produced goods and services has risen each year because actual production has increased and because prices have increased. *Source: Economic Report of the President,* Washington, D.C.: U.S. Government Printing Office, 1996.

---

services. This would increase your measured income. But if the overall prices you have to pay to purchase goods and services also were to double, then you really would be no better off. Likewise, if total national income as measured by GDP were to double simply because prices have increased by a factor of two, then the total volume of economic activity really has not changed.

To avoid this problem, economists use an adjusted measure of GDP, called **real gross domestic product.** This measure of the total production of final output accounts for the effects of price changes and thereby reflects more accurately the economy's true volume of productive activity. Because the flow of final product ultimately makes its way to individuals as a flow of total national income, real GDP also is a measure of *real national income,* or the total amount income that individuals truly receive, net of the artificial increases that result from inflation.

To distinguish real GDP from unadjusted GDP, economists refer to unadjusted GDP as **nominal gross domestic product,** or GDP "in name only," because it has been measured in current dollar terms with no adjustment for the effects of price changes. Likewise, they refer to

real gross domestic product (real GDP)   The total value of a nation's output of goods and services during a given period, adjusted for the effects of price changes.

nominal gross domestic product (nominal GDP)   The total value of a nation's output of goods and services measured in terms of current-year prices unadjusted for effects of price changes.

GLOBAL NOTEBOOK

Correcting GDP Measurement for Household Production in France and Norway

Over ten years ago the Decade for Women World Conference passed a resolution calling for all nations to include in GDP the unpaid contributions of women. A 1995 women's conference held in China renewed this suggestion. At least two countries, France and Norway, have already created "satellite" GDP estimates that do include estimates of unpaid household production. Australia, Canada, and Germany are studying a similar procedure. Of course, any estimate of unremunerated household work has serious problems. Does one add up the market cost of each activity that an unpaid homemaker provides to the family? If so, the number turns out to be quite large, in excess of $30,000 a year. Another problem concerns the *quality* of household work.

Some homemakers serve fabulous gourmet meals while others warm up canned and frozen foods. Should they be valued equally? Yet another problem lies in knowing when to *stop* counting: A person can hire a valet to help him or her get dressed in the morning. Should we therefore count the time spent in getting dressed as part of unpaid household work? Both men and women perform services around the house every day of the year. Should all of these unremunerated services be included in a new measure of GDP?

For Critical Analysis: *As a general statement, which countries would have the smallest amount of unpaid household production? (Hint: Think about labor force participation rates.)*

unadjusted national income as *nominal national income,* or simply nominal income.

The Price Level   Because real income measures the economy's true volume of production of goods and services, then multiplying real income by a measure of the overall price level would yield the value of real income measured in current prices, which is nominal income. That is, if y denotes real income and P is a measure of the overall price level, then total nominal income, denoted Y, is equal to

$$Y = y \times P$$

Because we measure real income using real GDP and nominal income using nominal GDP, the factor P is called the **GDP price deflator,** or simply the GDP deflator. It is called a "deflator" because if we solve our expression for nominal income, $Y = y \times P$, for y, then we get

$$y = Y/P$$

GDP price deflator   A measure of the overall level of prices for a given period; equal to nominal GDP divided by real GDP.

That is, real income y is equal to nominal income Y adjusted by dividing by, or "deflating" by, the factor P. For instance, suppose that nominal GDP measured in current prices, Y, is equal to $7 trillion but that the value of the GDP deflator, P, is equal to 2. Then computing real GDP would entail deflating the $7 trillion figure for nominal GDP by a factor of one-half. To do this, we divide $7 trillion by 2 to get a $3.5 trillion figure for real GDP.

Denoting a Base Year   A value of 2 for P means little, however, unless we define a reference point for interpreting what this value means. Economists do this by defining a **base year** for the GDP deflator, which is a year in which nominal income is equal to real income ($Y = y$), so that the GDP deflator's value is one ($P = 1$). Consequently, if the base year were, say, 1973, and the value of P in 1997 were equal to 2, then this would indicate that between 1973 and 1997 the overall level of prices had doubled.

Currently, in fact, the U.S. government uses 1992 as the base year for the GDP deflator. Panel (a) of Figure 14.2 on page 390 shows the values of the GDP deflator since 1959. As you can see, the overall level of prices increased by almost a factor of 5, from 0.26 to 1.28, between 1959 and 1996. This means that an item that required $1 to purchase in 1959 required nearly $5 to purchase in 1996. Alternatively stated, $5 in 1996 would purchase only the equivalent amount of goods and services that $1 would have purchased in 1959.

Panel (b) of Figure 14.2 plots real and nominal GDP figures since 1959. Note that in 1992 nominal and real GDP are equal because 1992 is the base year in which $P = 1$ so that $Y = y$. Clearly, adjusting for price changes has a significant effect on our interpretation of GDP numbers. This is why it is so important to use the GDP deflator to convert nominal GDP into real GDP. Only the latter measure can really give us information about the actual volume of economic activity.

base year   Year in which nominal GDP and real GDP are equal, so that the value of the GDP deflator is equal to 1 for that year.

1

What is the difference between nominal and real national income?   The measure of national income and product is gross domestic product (GDP). Nominal GDP is the total value of newly produced goods and services, calculated using the prices at which they were sold during the year in which they were produced. In contrast, real GDP is the value of final goods and services after adjusting for the effects of price changes from year to year. To calculate real GDP, we divide nominal GDP by the GDP deflator, which is a measure of the level of prices relative to prices for a base year.

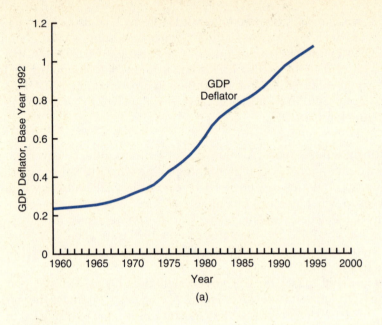

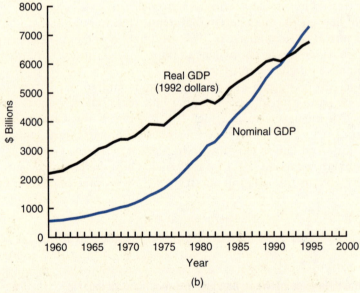

FIGURE 14.2 The GDP Deflator and Real and Nominal GDP

Panel (a) shows annual values of the GDP deflator. Panel (b) shows nominal GDP (the same chart as in Figure 14.1) and real GDP. As you can see, because it accounts for annual changes in the GDP deflator, real GDP displays significantly less growth from year to year. *Source: Economic Report of the President*, Washington, D.C.: U.S. Government Printing Office, 1996.

The Equation of Exchange

How does the quantity of money relate to the nation's income and prices? To answer this question, let's think first about how much people must pay to purchase the total amount of goods and services produced in the economy. This amount must equal the total volume of goods and services actually produced, or real GDP, y, multiplied by the level of prices, or the GDP deflator, P. Consequently, the total amount that people must pay for such newly produced goods and services is equal to $y \times P$. For instance, if real GDP is equal to \$3.5 trillion and P is equal to 2, then the total volume of spending is equal to \$7 trillion, which, of course, is equal to nominal income, Y.

But people use money to purchase goods and services because it is the medium of exchange. Let's use M to denote the nominal quantity of money, such as the M1 measure that includes currency and transactions deposits. Then the total amount of spending on newly produced goods and services must equal M times the average number of times that people spend each unit of money on these goods and services. Economists use the term **income velocity of money**, V, to denote the average number of times that people use each unit of money to purchase newly produced goods and services. Then, total spending on such goods and services must equal M multiplied by V, or $M \times V$. For example, if the total quantity of money in the economy is equal to $M = \$1.4$ trillion and a unit of money is used, on average, five times to purchase new goods and services during the most recent year, so that $V = 5$, then total spending on such goods and services during the year is equal to $M \times V = \$1.4$ trillion $\times 5 = \$7$ trillion.

Whether we measure total spending on newly produced goods and services as $y \times P$ or as $M \times V$, we must get the same answer, which in our example is total spending of \$7 trillion. This indicates that each of these quantities *must always be the same*, or that

$$M \times V \equiv y \times P$$

income velocity of money
Average number of times that a unit of money is used to purchase newly produced goods and services during a particular interval.

This equation is the **equation of exchange.** The three-barred equals sign indicates an equality that is true by definition. Hence, the equation of exchange says the following: The product of the quantity of money multiplied by the average number of times that people use a unit of money to buy goods and services must always equal the amount of real goods and services that they purchase multiplied by the measure of the prices they pay for those goods and services.

Note that the equation of exchange tells us nothing about how the quantity of money is related to real output and the price level. This means that economists must develop theories of how these variables interact in the real world. This issue is at the heart of *monetary theory,*

equation of exchange A definitional relationship in which the quantity of money multiplied by the income velocity of money must equal real GDP multiplied by the GDP price deflator.

which is the body of understanding of how we can conceptualize the interactions between the quantity of money, the total real output of final goods and services, and the level of prices.

2

What is the equation of exchange?   The equation of exchange is a definitional relationship that says that multiplying the quantity of money by the average number of times that a unit of money is used in exchange must equal the total value of newly produced goods and services exchanged, or the price level times real GDP.

THE CLASSICAL THEORY OF MONEY, PRICES, AND OUTPUT

One approach to trying to understand how the quantity of money may influence economic activity and the prices of goods and services is the *classical theory of money and income*. It is so named because it is the original perspective that early economic thinkers used to try to understand the role of money in influencing the economy. The word classical does not imply that the theory is necessarily out of date, however. Many economists today adhere to the basic tenets of the theory.

The Cambridge Equation and the Aggregate Demand for Output

The basis of the classical theory of money and income is the equation of exchange. As we noted above the equation of exchange is an identity, or truism, that must hold no matter what theory we propose for how money, prices, and real income are interrelated. Building a theory of how the quantity of money influences the level of prices and aggregate output in the economy requires that we propose more concrete sources of interaction among these variables.

The Cambridge Equation   In the classical theory the first step in this direction is to consider the demand for money. The classical approach to the demand for money is defined by the *Cambridge equation*, which we discussed in Chapter 13. Recall that this equation states that the quantity of money demanded by consumers and businesses is a fraction of their total income earnings, or

$$M^d = k \times Y$$

where k is the fraction of total nominal income that people wish to hold as money balances.

To see how the Cambridge equation relates to the equation of exchange, let's recall that nominal income is equal to real income times the GDP price deflator, or $Y = y \times P$. Then we can rewrite the Cambridge equation as

$$M^d = k \times y \times P$$

Now, if we divide both sides of this equation by the factor k, we get

$$\frac{M^d}{k} = \frac{k \times y \times P}{k} = y \times P$$

Finally, as long as people hold the amount of money, M, that arises as a result of Federal Reserve policy interactions with depository institutions, then $M^d = M$, and the Cambridge equation indicates that the following relationship must hold:

$$M/k = y \times P$$

The equation of exchange tells us that $y \times P$ must equal $M \times V$, and so M/k must equal $M \times V$. This tells us that the Cambridge equation depends on the assumption that $k = 1/V$, or that $V = 1/k$. But because k is assumed to be a constant fraction, then V, the income velocity of money, must also be constant. For instance, if k were equal to one-fifth, so that people always desired to hold 20 percent of their income as money balances, then the income velocity of money would have to be equal to a constant value of 5.

Recall that the income velocity of money is the average number of times that a unit of money is used to purchase final goods and services during the year. For the Cambridge equation to be a good theory to explain the demand for money, it ought to be the case that the income velocity of money is constant. As you can see in Figure 14.3 on page 394, however, this has not been true for the United States economy. Figure 14.3 shows that the income velocity of M1, which is nominal GDP divided by M1, has changed from year to year. If you think about our discussion in Chapter 13, this should not be a big surprise. After all, variations in interest rates change the opportunity cost of holding money, thereby inducing variations in the amount of money consumers and businesses hold in relation to their total incomes. Consequently, velocity should change from year to year, as it does in Figure 14.3. The figure shows that velocity also has tended to rise over time. The key reason for this is that, as we discussed in Chapter 12, there have been major technological changes in the U.S. payments system. This has simplified the task of making payments, and

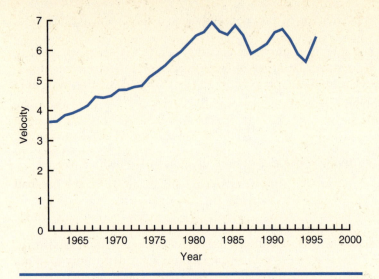

FIGURE 14.3   The Income Velocity of Money (M1)
The income velocity of money rose at a stable pace until the 1980s.
Since then it has been more variable. *Source: Economic Report of the
President,* Washington, D.C.: U.S. Government Printing Office, 1996.

so the average number of times that a unit of money is used to purchase final goods and services has risen.

The economists who proposed the Cambridge equation recognized that interest rate variations would cause short-term variations in
the income velocity of money. They also realized that improvements in
payments technology would induce people to hold smaller money balances. Nevertheless, they argued that, on average, their theory would
work as long as velocity was *stable* and *predictable*. As you can see in
Figure 14.3, aside from a couple of short-term downturns, the general
trend in velocity has been upward. Indeed, if not for the short-duration
falloffs, velocity would have been very predictable. To a classical theorist, such predictability is all that is needed for the Cambridge equation
to be a close enough approximation to reality.

The Aggregate Demand for Real Output   For now, let's go along
with this view and see where it takes us. As we noted above the Cambridge equation tells us that if people are satisfied holding the amount
of money that results from Fed policies, then it must be true that $M/k = y \times P$. Now let's divide both sides of this expression by P to get

$$y^d = (1/k) \times (M/P)$$

where y^d denotes the amount of real output of goods and services that
consumers and businesses desire to hold. This expression tells us that

desired spending on goods and services, y^d, will be a multiple of M/P, or **real money balances** in the economy. The amount of real money balances is the real purchasing power of money, or the nominal quantity of money divided by the GDP deflator.

> **real money balances**   The real purchasing power of the quantity of money; equal to the nominal quantity of money divided by the GDP price deflator.

What this expression says is that if people are satisfied holding the amount of money balances in the economy, then they are also satisfied with the amount they currently are spending on goods and services. And the amount they desire to spend must depend on the real purchasing power of the money they use to make such purchases.

To make this more concrete, consider a simple example. Suppose that the combined price, P, of a hot dog and a soft drink at a baseball game is $4. If you are at the game and have $M = \$8$ in money on hand, then at that price you could consume two hot dogs and two soft drinks. Suppose, however, that during the game the price of a hot dog and soft drink were to double, to $P = \$8$. Suddenly you would discover that the real purchasing power of your $8 had fallen by one-half. For you, the quantity of real money balances, M/P, would be half as large as before, and you now would be able to purchase only a single hot dog–soft drink combination. Your demand for goods would decline as a result of the fall in real money balances caused by the price increase. Economists call this the *real balance effect;* a rise in the price level causes a reduction in the quantity of goods and services that people desire to purchase.

Figure 14.4 illustrates the relationship between the price level, P, and the amount of real output, y, that consumers and businesses desire to purchase. This relationship is the economy's **aggregate demand schedule.** This shows the various combinations of price levels, P, and levels of output, y, that people are willing to purchase given the quantity of money, M. Because the amount of real output demanded declines as the price level rises, the aggregate demand schedule slopes downward.

> **aggregate demand schedule**   Combinations of price levels and amounts of aggregate real output that all individuals are willing to purchase given the total quantity of money in the economy.

Figure 14.4 (page 396) also shows the effect of an increase in the quantity of money in the economy. Such a rise in the amount of money increases real money balances at any given price level, thereby increasing the amount of real output that people desire to purchase. This causes a horizontal shift of the aggregate demand schedule, resulting in the gray schedule shown in Figure 14.4. That is, a rise in the quantity of money causes an *increase* in the aggregate demand for real output of goods and services.

The Aggregate Supply of Output and the Price Level

According to the classical theory, the amount of real output and the price level at which it sells must be represented by a point along the economy's aggregate demand schedule. To determine where this point is, the classical economists had to develop a theory of how much of the output of goods and services businesses desire to produce. That is, they needed a theory of the *aggregate supply of real output.*

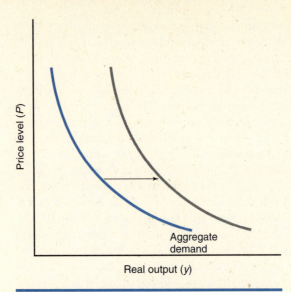

FIGURE 14.4 The Classical Aggregate Demand Schedule

An aggregate demand schedule depicts the levels of real output, y, that all consumers and businesses desire to consume at various possible price levels, P. In the classical theory, the key determinant of the position of the aggregate demand schedule is the quantity of money, M. A rise in the amount of money in circulation causes the aggregate demand schedule shift to the right.

The Aggregate Supply of Real Output   To develop such a theory, the classical economists imagined an environment in which wages and prices are completely flexible, in which the quantities of available factors of production are fixed, and in which the technology for using these factors to produce goods and services is not undergoing rapid changes. In such a setting, if some business firms attempted to expand their production of goods and services by bidding factors of production such as labor away from other firms, then they could do so only by offering higher wages. This would enable these business firms to produce more goods and services, but the remaining firms that had lost some of their labor resources would produce fewer goods and services and would have to pay higher wages to retain many of their workers. Furthermore, because labor costs would increase at all firms, the prices of their outputs would also increase.

The result of this process would be that wages and prices would increase while output of goods and services would rise at some businesses and decline at others. On net, total real output would be unchanged, even though the price level had increased. Figure 14.5

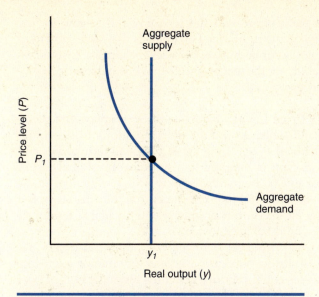

FIGURE 14.5   The Classical Aggregate Supply Schedule and the Equilibrium Price Level

In the classical framework, the aggregate level of output, y_1, depends only on the amounts of available factors of production and the current state of technology. Changes in the price level do not affect the level of output, and so the aggregate supply schedule is vertical. The equilibrium price level, P_1, is determined by the intersection of the aggregate supply schedule with the aggregate demand schedule. At this price level, all consumers and businesses are satisfied producing the level of real output, y_1.

displays the resulting **aggregate supply schedule** for the classical theory of income and prices. This schedule tells us the aggregate levels of real output that all businesses are willing and able to produce, y, at various levels of prices, P. Because the aggregate real output of businesses is assumed not to vary with the price level, the classical aggregate supply schedule is *vertical*. If the amount of real output is equal to some quantity, y_1, then businesses produce this quantity, irrespective of the level of prices.

Just because the aggregate supply schedule is vertical does not mean that classical theorists believed that the economy's real output level is constant. Their contention was simply that the aggregate output that businesses produced does not depend on the level of prices. Certainly, changes in the amounts of available factors of production or in technology would affect the ability of *all* firms to produce goods and services. For instance, population growth would increase the availability of labor resources. As a result, all firms would be able to produce a

aggregate supply schedule
Combinations of price levels and amounts of aggregate real output that all businesses are willing and able to produce given the state of technology and availability of factors of production.

greater volume of real output, and the economy's aggregate supply schedule would *shift* to the right. The key point is that such growth in real output would not occur because of price level changes; it would require greater availability of the real resources that businesses use to produce goods and services.

The Equilibrium Price Level   Figure 14.5 also displays the classical aggregate demand schedule and the determination of the equilibrium price level, denoted P_1. At this level of prices all individuals and businesses are satisfied purchasing the total amount of real final output businesses produce given the available factors of production. If the price level were greater than P_1, then consumers and businesses would be unwilling to buy all the output produced with available resources, and the price level would fall back toward P_1.

In contrast, if the price level were below P_1, then consumers and businesses would desire to purchase a greater volume of aggregate output than businesses could produce given the amounts of factors of production that were available. They would bid against each other to try to purchase desired quantities of goods and services, and the general level of prices would rise toward P_1.

The Classical Theory of Monetary Policy

Now we know how prices and real output are determined according to the classical theory. Let's apply this knowledge to understand the role that the classical theory prescribes for monetary policy-making.

Money and Prices   Figure 14.6 shows the effects of an expansion of the quantity of money. Recall from Chapter 13 that the Federal Reserve can increase the amount of money by purchasing government securities or by reducing the discount rate. This would increase the supply of reserves to depository institutions and lead to a decline in the equilibrium federal funds rate. The reduction in the federal funds rate would, through the term and risk structures of interest rates, induce declines in interest yields on Treasury bills, thereby reducing the opportunity cost of holding money. As a result, the quantity of money held by consumers and businesses would increase. As we discussed in Chapter 12, the amount of the increase in the quantity of money would be a multiple of the increase in depository institution reserves.

Such a rise in the quantity of money would cause an increase in the aggregate demand for real output. Hence, the aggregate demand schedule would shift to the right, as shown in Figure 14.6. At the previous equilibrium price level, P_1, it would now be the case that consumers and businesses would desire more goods and services than businesses together could produce given the available amounts of factors of production. This would cause the price level to increase, to P_2.

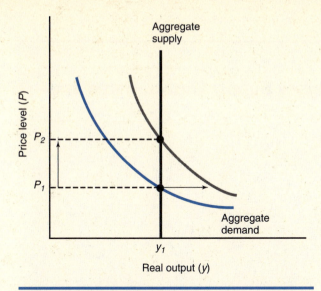

FIGURE 14.6   **The Effects of Monetary Policy in the Classical Theory**

According to the classical framework, if the Fed increases the quantity of money, the aggregate demand for goods and services by consumers and businesses would rise, and the aggregate demand schedule would shift to the right. At the previous equilibrium price level, P_1, consumers and businesses would desire to purchase more output of goods and services than firms could produce. This would place upward pressure on the price level, which would rise to a new equilibrium value of P_2. The equilibrium amount of real output would not change.

Therefore, a key prediction of classical monetary theory is that, if other elements are unchanged, an increase in the quantity of money causes a rise in the price level. That is, if all factors of production in the economy, such as labor resources are unchanged, open-market purchases and discount rate reductions tend to be inflationary policies.

Such policies are not *always* inflationary, though. As the economy expands its resource base, or does so effectively by developing better technologies, real output naturally tends to grow. Consequently, over time the aggregate supply schedule shifts rightward. In the absence of an increase in the quantity of money, prices would fall as such growth occurred. Such growth-induced deflation took place in the United States during the nineteenth century. To keep prices from *falling* as to-day's economy grows, the Fed must gradually expand the quantity of money. Of course, during the latter half of the twentieth century, the United States has experienced *inflation*. To a classical theorist, this is

The Relationship Between Money Supply Growth Rates and Inflation Worldwide

Is there much evidence that the rate of inflation is closely linked to the rate of monetary growth? The answer seems to be that in the long run there is a clear correlation between the two. Look at Figure 14.7. There you see that rate of growth of M1 on the horizontal axis (in ratio form). On the vertical axis is the annual rate of inflation (also on a ratio scale). As you can see, a line drawn through the average of the points slopes upward: Faster monetary growth leads to a higher rate of inflation throughout different countries.

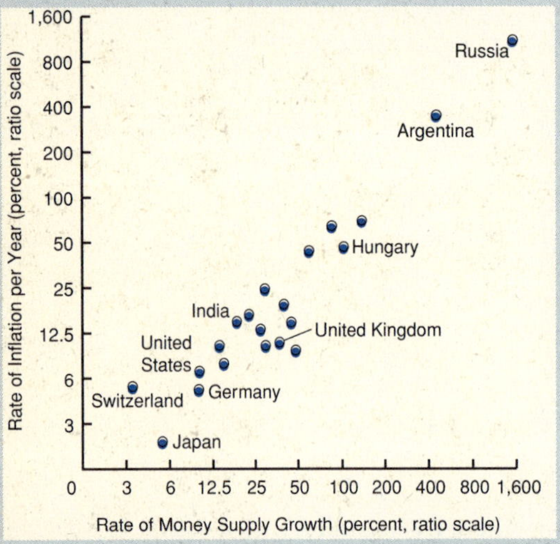

Nowhere is the relationship between the rate of growth in the money supply and the rate of inflation more obvious than in countries that have experienced hyperinflation. Brazil is a good case in point. At times, prices there have changed at a rate of over 1,000 percent a year. Somehow, government authorities in that country have routinely thought that changing the name and denominations of their currency would make a difference. Since the mid 1980s, Brazilians have had to get used to five different currencies. The latest change in the mid-1990s was a new *real* that was swapped for old *reales* at the rate of 1 to 2,750! But even a crude understanding of the classical theory of the relationship between money and prices tells you that changing the name of the currency will not affect the *rate* of inflation. It certainly did not in Brazil recently, when a true effort was made to reduce actual money growth, and the rate of inflation began to come down.

For Critical Analysis: *Do the data in Figure 14.7 "prove" the classical theory of the relationship between money and prices?*

FIGURE 14.7   Money Growth and Inflation
This figure shows a positive correlation between the growth rate of the quantity of money and inflation. Across different nations, faster money growth leads to higher inflation rates. *Source:* International Monetary Fund. Data are for latest available period.

evidence that the Fed caused the quantity of money to expand too fast relative to the natural growth of the economy.

The Neutrality of Money   Figure 14.6 illustrates an important prediction of the classical theory: Changes in the quantity of money induced by Fed policy actions should have *no effect* on the amount of real output of goods and services by businesses. As we noted earlier, according to classical monetary theory changes in aggregate output can occur only as a result of changes in available factors of production or technology. Monetary policy actions can influence only the price level; they have no effect on the aggregate amount of real output.

Classical economists called this the **neutrality of money.** This term means that alterations in the amount of money in the economy should have no measurable effects on the aggregate real amount of final goods and services produced and sold by businesses. That is, monetary policy actions should have no effects on real economic activity.

In light of this conclusion the classical economists have a simple prescription for the conduct of monetary policy. In their view the appropriate course of action for a central bank such as the Federal Reserve is to adjust the quantity of money as needed to assure a stable price level. After all, according to the classical theory that is the one variable the Fed can influence. Because of the neutrality of money there would be little point, according to the classical economists, in the Fed attempting to influence the amount of real output.

Of course, if real output in the economy were at a low level, employment of labor resources also would be low. The Fed might be tempted to try to put more people to work by expanding the quantity of money. But according to the classical theory, such an action would be misguided. It would cause inflation without raising employment. If the government wished to address a perceived problem of low employment, it would have to find another approach to deal with the problem. Monetary policy would not be the answer.

neutrality of money   A situation in which changes in the quantity of money have no effects on aggregate real output or employment.

3

According to classical monetary theory, how does monetary policy affect the price level and real output and employment?   In classical monetary theory all prices adjust quickly, technology is unchanging in the short term, and the amounts of available factors of production are fixed in the short term. As a result, increases in aggregate demand caused by a rise in the quantity of money induce businesses to bid against each other for factors of production, thereby pushing up their costs of producing goods and services. This causes the price level to rise without any effect on real output and employment.

GRADUAL PRICE ADJUSTMENT AND MONETARY POLICY

If monetary policy actions can affect only prices, why do Fed officials often agonize over how their policies may affect economic activity? Likewise, why do members of Congress sometimes criticize the Fed for not doing enough to stimulate the economy? One possibility is that both groups have a political interest in promoting the view that the Fed can influence the real output of goods and services. From the Fed's perspective, its institutional prestige might diminish if people believe that all it can really do is stabilize the level of prices. From the viewpoint of Congress, there might be an advantage to being able to blame the Fed when the economy experiences downturns. We shall have more to say about both of these possibilities in Chapter 15.

But it also may be that Fed policy actions *can* affect real income and employment—at least over the short run. This is the case, it turns out, if the price level adjusts *gradually* to changes in aggregate demand. A key feature of classical monetary theory is the assumption that wages and prices are completely flexible. But if they are not, then it turns out that monetary policy actions may be nonneutral.

Gradual Price Adjustment, or "Sticky" Prices

There is, in fact, considerable evidence that the prices of many goods and services are "sticky." This means that the prices of such goods and services do not change very much or very quickly in response to changes in demand. There are several possible explanations for this.

Wage Inflexibility
On average, wages comprise about three-fourths of the production costs for a typical business. If, for some reason, wages are not very flexible, then a company's costs will not change very much even if the demand for its product changes considerably. For instance, if the demand for a company's product declines, then normally we would expect to see a fall in the price that the company charges. But if the wages paid to employees do not decline in the face of falling sales, then a significant price cut may make the company unprofitable. This may induce the business to reduce its price much less than it would otherwise.

What factors might make wages inflexible? One contributing factor are minimum-wage laws that forbid reducing wages below a specific threshold. Only about one in twenty American workers is a minimum-wage employee, however, and so this factor by itself can account only to a limited extent for wage stickiness in the United States. A more often-cited rationale for wage stickiness is the existence of **explicit contracts,** which are legal contracts between businesses and their employees that bind businesses to specific wages during a given period, such as a year or more. Such contracts are particularly prevalent

explicit contracts Legally binding contracts that specify the wages that businesses must pay workers during a given period, such as a year or more.

in unionized industries. But today less than 15 percent of all workers are union members, and so this rationale for wage stickiness also is limited as an explanation of why *aggregate* wage stickiness might be prevalent.

Today most economists focus on the notion of **implicit contracts,** which are tacit or unspoken understandings that employees' wages will not be reduced even during periods of low demand for the businesses' products. Businesses may be willing to agree to such arrangements if they regard their employees as *investments*. After all, it takes time and money to train new employees, and so businesses may be willing to hold wages constant in the face of lower demand to keep trained employees and avoid the costs of searching for and training replacements at some later date.

implicit contracts Tacit or unspoken understandings between companies and workers that the workers' wages will not be reduced even during periods of low demand for the companies' products.

Imperfect Information   Another rationale for gradual price adjustment is the fact that people do not have perfect information about economic conditions. This means that when they make decisions about how much to work, they must base those decisions on *expectations*.

Consider, for instance, what happens if workers decide how much labor to provide to businesses based on expectations. Because workers generally do not have full knowledge about the prices of all the goods and services they will consume in the coming months, they must decide how much to work at prevailing wages, based on their best estimates of what prices will turn out to be. If the level of prices that businesses actually charge for goods and services were to increase because of a rise in demand, then companies' revenues would tend to rise and they would seek to hire more workers. As businesses bid against each other for labor services, market wages would tend to rise. Not realizing that prices were rising, workers would view themselves as better off because of the higher wages, and they would provide more labor services to businesses. In addition, it would take smaller wage increases, compared to wage gains workers would require if they recognized that prices had increased, to induce workers to provide more labor services. This means that businesses could raise prices less than they would have needed to otherwise to maintain their profitability. Because of the partial wage adjustment, prices would increase gradually.

Aggregate Supply and Monetary Policy with Gradually Adjusting Prices

What are the implications of gradual price adjustment? One is that widespread price stickiness invalidates the classical theory of aggregate supply, which depends on complete price flexibility. Another is that a slowly adjusting price level would give the Fed the ability to influence real output and employment.

Gradual Price Adjustment and Aggregate Supply   As shown in Figure 14.8, the result of gradual price adjustment is that the classical,

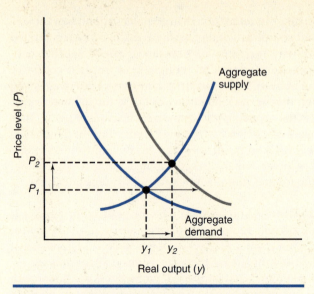

FIGURE 14.8   **Aggregate Supply and Monetary Policy Effects with Gradual Price Adjustment**

If prices adjust gradually because of wage inflexibilities or imperfect information, then the aggregate supply schedule slopes upward. As a result, a rise in the quantity of money that shifts aggregate demand rightward can cause an increase in the equilibrium amount of real output, as well as an increase in the equilibrium price level.

vertical aggregate supply schedule no longer applies. Instead, the aggregate supply schedule is upward-sloping.

The reason why the aggregate supply schedule slopes upward is that if wages are inflexible because of contracts or imperfectly informed expectations, then an unexpected rise in the price level would induce businesses to increase production of final goods and services. Such an increase in the price level would cause business revenues to rise. But if wages are inflexible, then companies' production costs would not rise in proportion to the rise in revenues. Therefore, businesses could increase their profits by hiring more labor services and expanding production. An unexpected rise in the price level would lead to an increase in the total real output of final goods and services in the economy.

Hence, as shown in Figure 14.8, there is a *direct relationship* between the price level and the aggregate amount of real output. The aggregate supply schedule slopes upward.

Gradual Price Adjustment and Monetary Policy   The argument above implies that monetary policy can affect real output when prices adjust gradually to changes in demand conditions. For instance, an increase in the quantity of money causes aggregate demand to increase, as shown in Figure 14.8. This causes a rise in the price level, but it also induces an increase in the aggregate amount of real output.

   Such a policy action also would increase employment. Consequently, under gradual price adjustment, monetary policy would be *non-neutral*. The Fed's policies could influence both real income and labor employment.

4

How does gradual price adjustment alter classical predictions about how monetary policy actions influence the price level, real output, and employment?   If the level of prices adjusts slowly to a rise in aggregate demand induced by an increase in the quantity of money, then businesses respond by increasing their real output of goods and services. To increase production, businesses employ more factors of production, such as labor services. Hence, gradual price adjustment permits monetary policy actions to influence real output and employment.

RATIONAL EXPECTATIONS AND MODERN THEORIES OF MONEY AND INCOME

Many economists have trouble reconciling gradual price adjustment with the assumption that people attempt to maximize satisfaction and businesses attempt to maximize profits. These economists doubt that workers and firms would really tie themselves to binding contracts under which they could be worse off. For instance, if prices were to rise but workers have explicit or implicit contracts that do not permit wages to increase, then the spending power of workers' wages would fall. Workers would be worse off than they would be in the absence of such contracts.

   Particularly bothersome to a number of economists is the idea that imperfect information can lead to slowly adjusting prices and monetary policy nonneutrality. The imperfect-information theory that *in*complete wage changes lead to gradual price adjustment requires that workers suffer from **money illusion.** That is, workers must perceive that a higher wage in current money terms means that their standard of living has increased, without regard to the fact that higher prices have eroded the *real* value of those wages. Under the imperfect-information rationale for gradual price adjustment, that is exactly how workers must behave if the story is to make any sense.

money illusion   The perception that one's standard of living has risen as a result of a wage increase even though the price level simultaneously has risen, thereby reducing the real purchasing power of any such wage increase.

Monetarism and Short-Run Versus Long-Run Price Adjustment

monetarists A group of economists who have emphasized the importance of money as a factor in influencing aggregate demand, and who have developed a theory of the role of expectations in determining short-run versus long-run effects of monetary policy actions.

The first economists to emphasize the imperfect-information concept are known as **monetarists.** They are so named because they strongly emphasized the role that the quantity of money plays in affecting aggregate demand. Yet their real contribution has been the explanation of how crucial expectations are in determining how monetary policy actions ultimately affect prices and real output. Figure 14.9 explains the essential elements of their argument.

The monetarists have been willing to accept the imperfect-information rationale for the upward slope of the aggregate supply schedule. And, as shown in Figure 14.9, they also accept the idea that a rise in aggregate demand caused by an increase in the quantity of money causes a gradual price adjustment (a rise in the price level from P_1 to

---

FIGURE 14.9   Short-Run and Long-Run Effects of Monetary Policy

According to modern theory, any expansion of real output induced by an increase in the quantity of money is likely to be short-lived. While a monetary expansion increases aggregate demand and causes the price level to rise from P_1 to P_2 and real output to rise from y_1 to y_2 in the short run, over the long run workers recognize that higher prices have eroded the purchasing power of their wages. When workers bargain for higher wages, this raises business labor costs and causes the aggregate supply schedule to shift leftward. This causes equilbrium real output to fall back toward its original level of y_1, and it results in a further increase in the price level, to P_3.

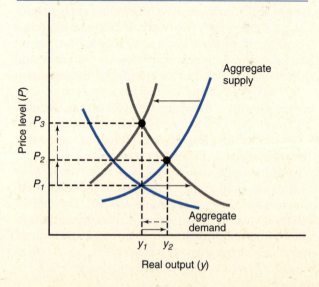

P_2 in the figure) and an increase in real output (from y_1 to y_2). Yet they contend that such output effects of monetary policy, at best, are short-term. The reason, they argue, is that money illusion is a short-run phenomenon. While workers may be imperfectly informed for a few weeks or even a few months, eventually information about price increases become known. Then workers realize that higher prices have eroded the spending power of their wages, and they bargain for further wage increases. In the long run, therefore, business labor costs tend to rise, causing the aggregate supply schedule to shift back to the left, as shown in Figure 14.9. Ultimately prices adjust fully to P_3, while aggregate real output falls back to its original level, y_1.

Hence, the monetarists contend that monetary policy is nonneutral only in the short run. Over periods of weeks or months monetary policy changes influence real output. In the long run, however, monetary policy is neutral in its effects on real economic activity.

Adaptive Versus Rational Expectations

The monetarist perspective on the short-run and long-run effects of monetary policy were widely adopted by economists by the early 1980s. In addition, the monetarist emphasis on the role of expectation adjustment caused many economists to pay closer attention to how people form price expectations.

Adaptive Expectations   Before the monetarists emphasized the importance of expectations, most economists assumed that people formed price expectations *adaptively*. By the term **adaptive expectations,** economists mean that people base expectations only on *past* information. For instance, to forecast the price level for the coming month, they might simply average the GDP price deflators for the preceding six months.

A problem with assuming that people have adaptive expectations is that this does not give people much credit for having common sense. Consider an extreme example in which a person is trying to forecast the price level for the coming month and uses an adaptive approach by averaging GDP price deflators for the past six months. Suppose, however, that the individual learns that the Federal Reserve has started to expand the quantity of money at double the rate of the past six months. This, as you have learned, will probably cause the price level to rise in the coming month. But because the individual is behaving adaptively, the individual's current price expectation ignores this new information.

Rational Expectations   Most economists today do not assume that people base their behavior on adaptive expectations. They do not believe that rational people would consistently ignore information that is important to making good forecasts about future prices. These economists, instead, base their theories of money and income on the **rational expectations hypothesis,** which is a theory that says that people base

adaptive expectations
Forecasts based only on past information.

rational expectations hypothesis   A theory that says that people make economic forecasts based on past and current information and on their understanding of how the economy operates.

their price forecasts on all available past *and* current information *and* on their understanding of how the economy works.

Consider our simple example above, in which a person learns that the Federal Reserve has started to double the rate of money growth. This would indicate to this individual that information about price deflators for the previous six months will be of limited use in forecasting inflation for the next month. Based on an understanding of how such a change in money growth affects prices, the individual would place most weight on the new information when forecasting next month's price level. The forecast will not necessarily be perfect, but it will be much better than it would have been had the individual ignored the new information and behaved adaptively.

5

What is the difference between adaptive and rational expectations?   If individuals forecast expectations adaptively, they use only past information. In contrast, under rational expectations people use all available past and current information, plus their understanding of how the economy works, to make forecasts.

New Classical Theory and the Policy Ineffectiveness Proposition

During the past two decades the rational expectations hypothesis has led to a number of new theories of how monetary policy affects the price level and real economic activity. The first new approach stemming from the rational expectations hypothesis became known as the *new classical theory.*

Anticipated Versus Unanticipated Monetary Policies   According-

ing to the new classical approach to monetary theory, the key factor that determines whether a monetary policy influences real output is how well informed people are about the existence of that policy action. For instance, if people broadly *anticipate* that the Fed will increase the rate of growth of the quantity of money, and if they forecast prices using rational expectations, then the monetarist story as illustrated in Figure 14.8 is sped up significantly. In anticipation of higher prices, stemming from the increase in the growth rate of the quantity of money they know will occur, workers *immediately* would bargain for higher wages. As a result, even as the aggregate demand schedule shifts out with the increase in the quantity of money, the aggregate supply schedule shifts back as business labor costs increase. Because both these events occur virtually simultaneously, real output does not increase, even in the short run. It remains at level y_1 in Figure 14.9 on page 406. Furthermore, the price level very quickly rises to P_3. There is no gradual price adjustment, even in the short run.

Under the new classical theory, monetary policy actions have short-run effects on real output only if they are *unanticipated.* For instance, if workers do not realize that the Fed is about to increase the rate of growth of the quantity of money, then they would not expect a future rise in prices and so would not try to bargain for greater-than-planned wage increases. Consequently, in the short run, if the increase in the rate of growth of the quantity of money were unanticipated by workers, real output *would* increase to y_2 in Figure 14.9. As in the monetarist theory, however, real output falls back to y_1 in the long run, when workers ultimately recognize that the price level has increased.

The Policy Ineffectiveness Proposition According to the new classical theory, monetary policy actions must be widely *un*expected if they are to have even short-run effects on real output and employment. In contrast, policy actions that people fully anticipate will have virtually no effects on real economic activity.

This view forms the basis for the new classical **policy ineffectiveness proposition.** It states that *systematic,* or predictable, monetary policies will not influence real output and employment. Such policies can be anticipated by workers, with the result that there are no effects on real economic activity. Consequently, such policies are ineffective as means of influencing the economy.

policy ineffectiveness proposition A proposition put forward by new classical monetary theory that systematic monetary policies, or policies that people can anticipate, have no effects on real output and employment.

Real Business Cycle Models Since the early 1980s a group of economists has taken the new classical approach one step further. These economists have developed a *real business cycle theory,* which views cyclical movements in real output and employment as the result of changes in real factors, such as the availability of factors of production and the state of technology. Real business cycle theory, in many respects, represents a true return to classical theory because it effectively views the economy's aggregate supply schedule as being vertical. As we discussed earlier, with a vertical aggregate supply schedule, the only way that real output can change is if there are changes in technology or in the availability of resources such as labor or capital.

New Keynesian Theories of Gradual Price Adjustment

The rational expectations hypothesis also has had a major effect on economists who otherwise subscribed to the theory of gradual price adjustment. Initially this group found itself on the defensive, because it was very difficult to justify slowly adjusting prices if people use all the information available to them to make the best possible forecasts. Nevertheless, this group of economists has promoted an approach to monetary theory called the *new Keynesian theory*, in honor of the most famous early proponent of the gradual price adjustment perspective, John Maynard Keynes (1883–1946).

Modern Wage Contracting Theory   One approach that new Keynesians have adopted is to revamp their theory of how wage inflexibility can permit monetary policy actions to affect real output. They have done this by using the rational expectations hypothesis to develop a modern theory of how workers contract their wages.

According to this theory, when workers sign wage contracts, they try to forecast what the levels of prices will be during the interval that the contracts are in force. They do so using rational expectations. But once the contract wage has been set, the basic precept of the old gradual price adjustment approach follows: monetary policy actions influence real output and employment, at least in the short run. Today, arguments among new Keynesians, new classical economists, and real business cycle theorists often focus on how relevant this modern contracting story is for American labor markets and how well its predictions fit real-world experience. At present the evidence is mixed.

Imperfect Competition and Costs of Changing Prices   New Keynesians also argue that wage inflexibility may not be the only reason causing the price level to adjust gradually. Even under rational expectations there may be more direct reasons. One possibility is that *imperfect competition* may prevail. In a number of industries there may be only a few companies because of barriers to entry or exit. If so, then these businesses are insulated from competitive pressures and hence do not have to adjust their prices frequently.

But even businesses that might be pure monopolies would find it in their best interests to cut prices in the face of low demand or to raise prices when demand for their products increases. To understand why businesses might not change their prices when demand varies, economists must consider the possibility that changing prices is costly for many businesses. For instance, companies that change prices have to print new price tags, post new prices in computer data files, print new menus or price lists or catalogs, and so on. While these costs may not seem large, they may be significant enough to offset the small profit gains achieved by raising or reducing prices when product demands vary. This would then lead to slowly adjusting prices at many firms. As a result, the old gradual price adjustment theory, plus most of its predictions that monetary policy can affect real output and employment, is resurrected by this new Keynesian theory.

6

How do modern monetary theories differ in their predictions of how monetary policy affects real economic activity?   All modern monetary theories are similar in their reliance on the rational expectations hypothesis. The hypothesis of new classical theory is that in the absence of other factors that might produce gradual price adjustment, monetary policy actions that are anticipated are ineffective in influencing real output. Real business cycle theories take this idea a step further and predict that monetary policy actions have no short- or long-term effects on real economic activity. New Keynesian theories continue to rely on such factors as wage contracts or the cost of implementing price changes as the reasons for gradual adjustment of prices and the real effects of monetary policy.

SUMMARY

1. **Real Versus Nominal National Income:** Economists measure national income and product using current prices to value newly produced final goods and services. From this data they construct a measure of total income called nominal gross domestic product (nominal GDP). Real GDP is equal to nominal GDP divided by the GDP deflator, which is a measure of the current overall level of prices in relation to prices in a base year.

2. **The Equation of Exchange:** This equation is an identity that defines a relationship between the quantity of money in circulation and total national income. The equation states that multiplying the quantity of money by the income velocity of money, or the average number of times that money is used in an exchange for new goods and services, gives the total value of those goods and services. This, in turn, must equal the GDP deflator multiplied by real GDP.

3. **How Monetary Policy Affects Prices, Real Output, and Employment According to Classical Monetary Theory:** In the classical theory of money and income, wages and prices are very flexible, technology is relatively unchanging, and there are fixed amounts of factors of production. Consequently, if monetary policy actions cause a rise in the quantity of money, that induces an increase in the aggregate demand for goods and services. Hence, businesses compete for the fixed factors of production and thereby bid up the prices of those factors, such as the wages they pay their workers. This raises business costs, and so prices of goods and services rise although the total amount of real output remains unchanged.

4. **How Gradual Price Adjustment Alters Classical Predictions About the Way in Which Monetary Policy Actions Influence the Price Level, Real Output, and Employment:** If prices adjust gradually to a

rise in aggregate demand caused by an increase in the quantity of money, then it is profitable for businesses to increase the amount of real output they produce. Consequently, they employ more workers. And so gradual price adjustment permits monetary policy to influence real economic activity.

5. **The Difference Between Adaptive and Rational Expectations:** Adaptive expectations about future prices are based solely on past information. Rational expectations, in contrast, are based on both past and current information and on people's understanding of how the economy works.

6. **How Modern Monetary Theories Differ in Their Predictions About How Monetary Policy Affects Real Economic Activity:** Today's monetary theories seek to incorporate the hypothesis of rational expectations. New classical and real business cycle theories use this hypothesis to explain how monetary policy works in the absence of gradual price adjustment, and they conclude that, at best, monetary policy can affect real output only when policy actions are not anticipated. New Keynesian theories combine the rational expectations hypothesis with gradual price adjustment to show how monetary policy can have short-term effects on real economic activity.

QUESTIONS AND PROBLEMS

1. Can you think of some economic transactions that would not be included in gross domestic product? How significantly do you think these would affect the reliability of GDP as a measure of economic activity? Explain your reasoning.

2. Suppose that the income velocity of money is equal to 6. Nominal GDP is equal to $9 billion, and the GDP deflator is equal to 3. What is the quantity of money? What is real GDP?

3. Use an aggregate demand–aggregate supply diagram to explain the effects that a classical economist would predict following a *reduction* in the quantity of money induced by Federal Reserve policy actions.

4. Use an aggregate demand–aggregate supply diagram to explain the effects of a reduction in the quantity of money if prices adjust gradually. Then use your diagram to discuss the long-run adjustment that a monetarist economist would predict.

5. Suppose that the rational expectations hypothesis is correct and that wages and prices are flexible. Suppose there is a reduction in the quantity of money that was fully anticipated by workers. Use an aggregate demand–aggregate supply diagram to explain the effects of such a Fed policy action.

15

The Fed and the American Economy

KEY QUESTIONS

1. What are the Fed's ultimate goals for monetary policy?

2. What are monetary policy time lags?

3. Why might the Fed use an intermediate monetary policy target?

4. Why is central bank credibility so important to maintaining low inflation?

5. How might the credibility of central banks such as the Fed be enhanced?

6. Should central banks such as the Fed be more independent public policy institutions?

T he room is filled. At one table are various members of Congress. The table is long and contains a microphone for each member of the committee. In front of that long table is a rather short one that contains only one microphone. The person sitting at that small table is Alan Greenspan, the chair of the Federal Reserve System of the United States. He is appearing before Congress because he is required to by law. He is there to explain to the members of the committee what the Federal Reserve's objectives have been and how well it has fulfilled them. The press follow his every word, attempting to extract some indication of what the Fed will do in the future. The members of the congressional committee, in contrast, are still trying to figure out what happened. More often than not, they are unable to get an exact statement out of Greenspan, for he is a master of obfuscation.

Is there something wrong with this biannual scenario? Some critics of the Fed think so. On the one hand, certain critics think that the Fed should not have to explain anything because it should not engage in any discretionary monetary policy. Rather, it should use a computer to set a steady rate of growth of the money supply. Other critics think that the Fed should be completely independent and not answer to Congress at all.

In any event, under current law the Fed does have to set objectives and targets for its monetary policy, the subject matter of this chapter.

OBJECTIVES AND TARGETS OF MONETARY POLICY

In Chapter 14 you learned that there are a number of competing theories seeking to explain how monetary policy affects the economy. All these theories agree that the quantity of money plays a key role in determining the price level and inflation rate. Theories of gradual price adjustment also claim that monetary policy influences real output and labor employment.

In addition, in Chapter 13 you learned how the Federal Reserve can use policy tools to affect the quantity of money. In light of theories and evidence that changes in the quantity of money can influence prices and perhaps real output and employment, it follows that the Fed should direct its policy instruments toward influencing these economic variables.

The Goals of Monetary Policy

Indeed, the Federal Reserve potentially can pursue *ultimate goals* that involve all three variables. In principle, it can vary its policy instruments with an aim toward achieving objectives relating to prices, real output, and employment.

Inflation Goals and the Costs of Inflation
If there is one economic variable that everyone agrees the Fed can influence, it is the rate of inflation. This also is a variable, most agree, that the Fed should try to influence. High inflation and significant inflation variability impose costs on society, as summarized in Table 15.1.

[handwritten: ✱ most imp. #1 goal.]

In light of the inflation costs listed in Table 15.1, there are strong reasons for the Federal Reserve to keep inflation low. Furthermore, there are good justifications for the Fed's desire to limit year-to-year variability in inflation rates.

Output Goals
As we discussed in Chapter 14, some theories of money and income indicate that there is little the Fed can do to affect real output over the long run. Nonetheless, traditionally the Fed has sought to follow a monetary policy that provides a foundation for significant and stable growth in the production of real output.

[handwritten: ⇒ GDP'S How is the Economy doing.]

Several theories indicate that unexpected changes in the rate of growth of the quantity of money can influence real output over the short run. Consequently, another potential Federal Reserve goal might be to prevent sharp swings in real economic activity. This would maintain a stable business climate, and also would save workers from the temporary displacements that arise from variations in businesses' hiring plans caused by significant output volatility.

TABLE 15.1 The Costs of Inflation and Inflation Variability

Type of Cost	Cause
Resources expended to economize on money holdings (more trips to banks, etc.)	Rising prices associated with inflation
Cost of changing price lists and printing menus and catalogs	Individual product/service price increases associated with inflation
Redistribution of real income from individuals to government	Inflation pushes people into higher, nonindexed, nominal tax brackets
Reductions in investment, capital accumulation, and economic growth	Inflation variability complicates business planning
Slowed pace of introduction of new and better products	Volatile price changes reduce the efficiency of private markets
Redistribution of resources from creditors to debtors	Unexpected inflation reduces the real value of debts

Employment Goals Labor is a key factor of production for both goods and services. Hence, Fed policies aimed at stabilizing output often are consistent with preventing significant variability in worker unemployment rates. Furthermore, promoting greater long-run economic growth also helps to keep average unemployment rates low.

The Fed's ability to pursue employment goals, however, is hampered by a number of factors beyond the Fed's control that affect rates of employment and unemployment. One key determinant of employment levels, for example, is labor productivity, which the Fed cannot affect no matter how much money it creates through policy actions. Nevertheless, keeping unemployment rates as low and as stable as possible often appears on the list of the Fed's ultimate goals. As we shall see below, for good or ill this is also an objective that the Fed is *legally obliged* to pursue.

The Objectives of the Fed

Among the various goals that the Fed might aim to achieve, which are the most important? The answer to this question is hazy. Because the Federal Reserve has considerable independence, it has some autonomy to pursue whichever objectives it finds most compelling in light of the circumstances it faces. At the same time, however, the Fed cannot ignore congressionally mandated goals for American monetary policy.

Legislated Objectives for Monetary Policy There are two key laws that constrain the Fed when it contemplates its ultimate policy objectives. The first of these is the Employment Act of 1946. This law formally commits all agencies of the federal government to the goals of "maximum employment, production, and purchasing power." In other words, the federal government officially seeks the highest possible employment and real output levels, as well as low inflation. Because the Fed technically is a government agency, albeit "independent within government," it technically is covered by this legislation. Consequently, under the law it is supposed to pursue policies that are consistent with "maximum employment, production, and purchasing power."

The 1946 legislation was silent about how federal government agencies were to pursue this broad objective. In 1978 Congress decided to be much more specific by passing the Full Employment and Balanced Growth Act, more popularly known as the Humphrey-Hawkins Act. Some parts of this legislation were nonbinding. For instance, the Act set a goal of 3 percent as the 1983 unemployment rate; the actual unemployment rate in 1983 exceeded 9 percent. The Act also specified an inflation goal of zero percent for 1988, but actual inflation in 1988 was about 5 percent.

Other provisions of the 1978 law have had more lasting effects, however. Under the Humphrey-Hawkins Act, the Federal Reserve's

Board of Governors must review the president's budget and economic report each year and explain to the Congress how its own policies mesh with the objectives of the president. Each year the Fed chair also must give the Congress periodic reports on the Fed's policies and their relationship to the economic goals of the federal government. The chair also must testify before Congress and answer members' questions about these issues.

Evidence on the Fed's Objectives

Have these legal mandates had any effect on the Fed? Which goals receive the most attention by the Fed, and which does it regard as least important? To answer these questions, economists have followed two approaches. One has been to examine how the Fed reacted in the past to changing economic conditions by varying its tools of monetary policy. If certain events caused changes in the price level, real output, and employment, then studying how the Fed responded to such events could, in principle, indicate which policy goals were regarded by the Fed as most important. Most studies of this type have revealed that the Fed has not been very consistent. Over some intervals the Fed has appeared to respond more to movements in the rate of inflation than to variations in rates of unemployment and growth in real output, while during other periods the reverse has been true.

Another approach that economists have taken has been to examine the voting records of Federal Reserve officials. Such studies have revealed that the Fed is not a monolithic institution. Not all Fed officials place the same weights on the three basic goals of monetary policy. Consequently, how the Fed responds to economic events depends also on who is in charge at the time. This helps to explain why the other studies find such mixed evidence about the Fed's responses to reaching ultimate goals.

What all studies indicate, however, is that the Fed does care about all three goals. The Fed tries to contain inflation, promote output growth, and restrain unemployment. It also values stability for all three variables. Even though the Fed's attention to each goal may vary over time, these consistently appear to be the ultimate objectives of Fed policy making.

1

What are the Fed's ultimate goals for monetary policy?   The Fed's ultimate goals are to reach the legislated objectives set out under the employment act of 1946 and the 1978 Humphrey-Hawkins Act. The Fed's formal goals include low and stable inflation rates, high and stable output growth, and a high and stable employment level. Evidence concerning which goals the Fed pursues most aggressively is mixed. It appears that during different periods the Fed emphasizes some goals more than others.

POLICY LAGS AND INTERMEDIATE TARGETS

Once the Fed has determined its ultimate goals, it must figure out how to conduct policies that will achieve those goals. Most Fed officials have broad backgrounds in business or government service, and many have advanced degrees. A number of Fed policymakers are economists. And yet, when it comes time to formulate policies aimed at achieving low and stable inflation rates, high and stable output growth, and high and stable levels of labor employment, the Fed begins to run into some serious real-world problems.

Time Lags in Monetary Policy

A key problem for monetary policymakers at the Fed is the existence of *time lags.* Fed officials are human beings who face limited information and constraints on their ability to recognize and respond effectively to economic events. They also must consider how long it will take for any policy they enact to influence the economy.

The Recognition Lag
A key problem that the Fed faces in pursuit of its ultimate inflation, output, and employment goals is data limitations. Although the Fed can estimate nominal GDP data on a weekly basis, it gets information about real GDP, unemployment rates, and the price level only on a monthly basis. Furthermore, government statisticians commonly revise monthly computations of real output, unemployment, and price data. Consequently, initial figures for these goal variables are not always trustworthy. Although government agencies strive to make their data as reliable as possible, on occasion annualized quarterly GDP growth rates have been corrected by as much as 75 percent!

This informational problem places the Fed in a difficult position. For instance, suppose that inflation was beginning to turn up because of a sudden expansion of aggregate demand. Based on what you learned in Chapters 13 and 14, you know that the appropriate Fed policy response to curtail inflation is to cut back on the supply of reserves and to permit the federal funds rate to rise. This would restrain growth in the quantity of money and reduce the aggregate demand pressure on the price level. Yet data limitations might keep the Fed from realizing that inflation had begun to rise until several weeks after the fact.

The time between the need for a monetary policy action and the recognition of that need is the **recognition lag.** In our example, this lag would be a matter of a few weeks. But other factors can cause the recognition lag to stretch out even longer. For example, even if Fed officials are convinced that inflation has risen, they may disagree about the causes. There might, for instance, be some preliminary information

recognition lag   Interval between the need for a monetary policy action and the Fed's recognition of that need.

[Handwritten margin note: To measure the U.S. Economy which is so large. They might already be affected. If you react late, a this might affect the ongoing period.]

indicating that the inflation is a result of higher business costs that are shifting aggregate supply schedule leftward. Such mixed signals might keep the Fed from acting for several more weeks. As a result, the recognition lag in some instances could stretch into months.

The Response Lag   Once Fed officials decide that a problem requires a policy action, they must determine what the appropriate action should be. The time between recognition of the need for a policy action and its actual implementation is the **response lag** of monetary policy. In principle, the response lag should never be more than six to eight weeks, because that is the normal interval for Federal Open Market Committee (FOMC) meetings. Indeed, because conference calls can link FOMC members, in principle the response lag could be much shorter.

What complicates matters is that, even if FOMC members agree on the need for a policy action, they may not concur about precisely what action the Fed should take. A few members might argue for an aggressive response to the perceived inflation upturn, while others might contend that a strong effort to cut the growth in aggregate demand could cause a recession. Some members might favor using open-market operations, while others might prefer a change in the discount window policy or an alteration of the discount rate. Such internal disagreements can significantly delay Fed policy actions, thereby lengthening the response lag.

The Transmission Lag   Once the Fed has implemented a policy action, it typically takes time for that action to exert its effects on real output, employment, and inflation. Recall from Chapter 13 that the basic *transmission mechanism* for monetary policy begins with a change in a Fed policy tool, such as an open-market purchase or a reduction in the discount rate. Such an action then influences the supply of reserves to depository institutions and alters the equilibrium federal funds rate. Other interest yields in the term and risk structure of interest rates, such as Treasury security yields, respond to the initial policy action. This alters the opportunity cost of holding money, which leads to a change in the quantity of money that businesses and consumers desire to hold. Then, as we discussed in Chapter 14, aggregate demand adjusts to the change in the quantity of money, and prices, real output, and employment respond to the policy action.

These policy effects are not instantaneous. While the federal funds rate and other interest yields typically adjust to an initial Fed policy action within a day or so, individuals and businesses may take weeks to change their desired money holdings. Consequently, it usually takes weeks for aggregate demand to respond to a monetary policy action. Only after this time has elapsed do prices, real output, and employment begin to adjust in any measure to the Fed's policy change. In

response lag   Interval between the Fed's recognition of a need for a policy action and its implementation of such an action.

transmission lag Interval
between the Fed's imple-
mentation of a policy
change and the effects that
this change ultimately has
on the economy.

the end, the **transmission lag** of monetary policy, which is the complete
interval between implementation of a policy action and that action's
eventual effects on the economy, easily could stretch into months. Indeed, economists have estimated that the average length of the transmission lag is just over 12 months. All three lags together, therefore, can
stretch the time between the initial need for a policy action and that action's final effects on the economy to well over a year.

2

What are monetary policy time lags?   The time between the need for a Fed
policy action and the Fed's realization of the need is the recognition lag. The interval between recognition of the need for an action and actual implementation
of a policy change is the Fed's response lag. Finally, the time from implementation of a policy action and the action's ultimate effects on the economy is the
transmission lag. All told, these lags can sum to over a year in duration.

Intermediate Monetary Policy Targets

Policy time lags pose major obstacles to the Fed's efforts to achieve its
ultimate inflation, output, and employment goals. Difficulties in getting current data about these variables can be pronounced, and interpreting the data can be equally difficult. As we discussed in Chapter 14,
there are several theories of how the quantity of money ultimately influences prices, real output, and employment. Some Fed officials might
be swayed by gradual price adjustment theories, while others might
adhere to theories that indicate little scope for monetary policy to influence real output and employment.

intermediate target An
economic variable that the
Fed seeks to control only as
a means of trying to achieve
its ultimate objectives.

In light of informational difficulties, policy lags, and differences in
interpretation, the Fed often has used **intermediate targets** when forming its monetary policy strategies. These are economic variables whose
values the Fed may seek to control because it feels that doing so is consistent with its ultimate goals. As Figure 15.1 indicates, an intermediate

**FIGURE 15.1   The Intermediate Targeting Strategy for
               Monetary Policy**

An intermediate target is an economic variable that the Federal Reserve seeks to influence as a stand-in for its ultimate goals, which are
more difficult to observe or to influence in the near term.

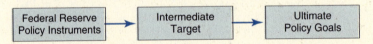

Federal Reserve Policy Instruments → Intermediate Target → Ultimate Policy Goals

target serves as a near-term stand-in for the Fed's ultimate goals. Under an intermediate targeting strategy, the Fed uses its policy instruments to influence the intermediate target in ways that it feels are consistent with its ultimate objectives.

Characteristics of Intermediate Targets   A useful intermediate target should have four key characteristics. First, it should be consistent with the Fed's ultimate goals. If the Fed were to achieve a particular objective for an intermediate target only to find that in doing so it has widely missed objectives for inflation, output, and employment, then its policy strategy is counterproductive.

Second, an intermediate target should be an economic variable that the Fed can observe on a timely basis. As we noted earlier, fairly reliable data on prices and real GDP are available to the Fed at monthly intervals. Hence, an intermediate target that could be observed only at a frequency exceeding one month would not be as useful as one that can be measured from week to week or, better yet, from day to day.

Third, there should be no difficulty in defining and measuring the variable used as the intermediate target. If technological or regulatory changes make a potential intermediate target hard to define, then such a variable will prove difficult to control.

Fourth, an intermediate target needs to be a variable whose value the Fed can control. An intermediate target that the Fed cannot influence is of little use.

Actual and Proposed Intermediate Targets   Over the years the Fed has contemplated using or has actually used a number of intermediate target variables. Indeed, there is no shortage of candidates for the role of intermediate monetary policy target.

Monetary Aggregates   As we noted in Chapter 11, in the 1970s the Fed began to use *monetary aggregates* such as M1 and M2 as intermediate targets. The rationale for this strategy, as we discussed in Chapter 14, was that the quantity of money affects aggregate demand, which in turn influences the price level and real output and employment. Consequently, the Fed believed there ought to be a clear relationship between monetary aggregates and its inflation, output, and employment objectives. In addition, data on monetary aggregates are available on a weekly basis, and so monetary aggregates are observable. Finally, as we discussed in Chapter 13, the Fed can influence the quantity of money using policy instruments such as open-market operations and changes in the discount rate.

The Fed has experienced two problems with using monetary aggregates as intermediate targets, however. The first was that the Fed felt obliged to redefine its monetary aggregates every few years as new financial assets, such as NOW accounts and money market mutual funds, emerged. As we noted in Chapter 1, the growing use of bond and equity accounts for transactions-related purposes has led some economists to argue that further redefinitions of monetary aggregates may be necessary in the near future. Another difficulty, which was particularly pronounced in the 1980s and early 1990s, has been that the relationship between the basic M1 and M2 aggregates and national income and product has not held steady. In fact, since the early 1980s there have been periods in which hardly any consistent relationship between monetary aggregates and economic activity was apparent.

Credit Aggregates   The difficulties noted above have caused the Fed to consider a number of alternative intermediate targets. Some observers have suggested that the Fed should target *credit aggregates* instead of monetary aggregates. One possibility would be for the Fed to target *total credit*, which is the total amount of lending in the economy. Another would be for the Fed to use *bank credit*, or total lending of depository institutions, as a narrower intermediate target. As we discussed in Chapter 10, the Fed can influence bank credit through a multiplier process that links depository institution reserves to the total amount of lending by those institutions. In addition, credit can be easily and frequently measured.

There is a drawback with credit aggregates, however. This is that the relationship between credit aggregates and economic activity generally has been as tenuous as the relationship between monetary aggregates and economic activity. This has led some economists to argue for a two-pronged intermediate targeting approach in which *both* monetary and credit aggregates would be intermediate targets.

Interest Rates   Another credit market variable that a number of observers have promoted as an intermediate target in place of the amount of credit is the *price of credit*. This, of course, is the interest rate. The Fed receives reliable data on most interest rates on a daily and even hourly basis. It even tracks some interest rates by the minute. In addition, as we discussed in Chapter 13, the Fed definitely can influence interest rates by varying in its policy tools.

As in the case of monetary and credit aggregates, however, the difficulty is that interest rates and economic activity are not always closely related. Certainly, lower interest rates encourage people and businesses to undertake investment in durable goods and capital goods and thereby stimulate economic activity. But expansion in economic activity also raises the demand for credit, which places upward pressure on interest rates. And so, the relationship between interest rates and national income and product is not always clear-cut. Nor is there a *single* interest rate that stands out as the best one for the Fed to target. Also unclear is whether it would be better for the Fed to target short- or long-term rates.

In recent years some economists have contended that the difference, or *spread*, between long- and short-term interest rates would be a

POLICY NOTEBOOK
Does the Credit View of Monetary Policy Make Sense?

There have been many studies purporting to show that monetary policy affects the economy through credit channels. This has been called the credit view of monetary policy. Economist Daniel L. Thornton of the Federal Reserve Bank of St. Louis examined these studies and also carried out numerous tests to determine the validity of the credit view. He tried to see whether monetary policy actions had a direct effect on bank lending. If the credit view is correct, then monetary policy actions should not be examined solely on the basis of how they change interest rates. But Thornton notes that financial innovation has dramatically reduced the special nature of bank credit. Financial innovation and deregulation have widened the financing options available to small- and medium-sized firms, reducing their dependency on banks. Consequently, banks have provided a decreasing portion of credit—since the 1970s this figure has declined by 25 percentage points and now accounts for only 45 percent of total credit. Empirically, Thornton found a very small, positive, and statistically significant relationship between Federal Reserve actions and bank loans and bank deposits only prior to the early 1980s. Since then, there appears to be no statistical relationship.

For Critical Analysis: *What are the alternative sources of loans for businesses?*

good intermediate target of monetary policy. As we discussed in Chapter 3, the expectations hypothesis for the term structure of interest rates indicates that a key reason for the difference between long- and short-term interest yields is expectations about future short-term yields. By targeting the spread, therefore, the Fed essentially would keep future interest rate expectations stable. Robert Laurent, an economist at the Federal Reserve Bank of Chicago, has shown that over some periods this makes the spread between long- and short-term rates a strong indicator of the course of economic activity. It remains to be seen, however, if the spread performs well enough in this role to induce the Fed to adopt it as an intermediate target. So far it has not done so, although some Fed officials have said that they keep an eye on the spread as one indicator of economic activity.

Commodity Prices   A few Fed officials, and in particular past board governor Wayne Angell, have advocated using *commodity price indexes,* or the weighted average of prices of specific commodities such as gold or silver as intermediate targets. They contend that changes in economic activity often follow closely after movements in such commodity prices. In addition, commodity price indexes often are good indicators of changes in the overall price level for goods and services.

POLICY NOTEBOOK

Targeting the Price of Gold and the Gold Standard

Gold has always held a special place in the minds of some politicians and economists. Indeed, Fed chair Alan Greenspan once went before Congress and argued that the Fed should target the price of gold directly rather than targeting the federal funds rate. If this were to happen, the Fed would instruct the Trading Desk at the New York Fed to sell bonds, draining reserves from the banking system, until the gold price fell to some specified number, such as $350 per ounce. Presumably, a stable gold price indicates that few people believe that the price level will rise in the future.

One further step is argued by those who support a gold standard in the United States. Actually, the United States operated under a gold standard from 1879 to 1971. During that time span, there were two specific periods defined by two types of gold standards. From 1879 to 1933 the dollar was defined as 32.22 grains of gold, yielding a gold price of $20.671835 an ounce. During that time span, general prices more than doubled during World War I, there was a major recession in 1920–21, and of course the Great Depression began. The second gold standard of sorts prevailed from 1933 to 1971, when the price of gold was pegged at $35 an ounce. A dollar was defined as 13.714286 grains of gold. During that time span, general prices quadrupled.

Clearly, going back to a gold standard guarantees neither stable prices nor economic stability.

For Critical Analysis: *If the chair of the Fed's Board of Governors wants to target the price of gold, why can't the chair simply do so?*

Although commodity price indexes have useful properties as indicators, a key problem is that the linkage between Fed policy tools, such as open-market operations, and commodity price indexes is not straightforward. In addition, although these indexes may be good indicators, they would not necessarily make good intermediate targets. And so, the Fed's interest in commodity price indexes has waned in recent years.

Nominal GDP   Because all the above variables either have not panned out well for the Fed or have never quite been accepted by the Fed as intermediate targets, a large number of economists recently suggested that the Fed use *nominal gross domestic product (GDP)* as an intermediate target. This may seem surprising, given that nominal GDP data are not available any more often than its information on real GDP and the GDP price deflator.

Nevertheless, there is a commonsense argument for targeting nominal GDP. We know that nominal GDP, by definition, is equal to real GDP times the GDP price deflator. Although you learned in Chapter 14 of a number of competing theories on how monetary policy affects real output and prices, targeting nominal GDP would not require favoring any one theory. After all, if the Fed wishes to stabilize real output and prices, then stabilizing nominal output would prevent excessive volatility in either of these variables. Although the Fed has not formally committed itself to using nominal GDP as an intermediate target, some observers believe that the Fed has been doing so informally in recent years.

3

Why might the Fed use an intermediate monetary policy target?   Because there is limited availability of data on ultimate objectives, and because there are time lags and differences in interpreting how Fed policy instruments affect ultimate objectives, the Fed sometimes adopts an intermediate target. A target variable should be measurable at more frequent intervals than ultimate goal variables, easy to measure, able to be influenced by Fed policy actions, and closely related to the Fed's ultimate policy objectives.

RULES VERSUS DISCRETION IN MONETARY POLICY

Fed policy strategies that truly intended to attain target values for monetary or credit aggregates, interest rates, commodity prices, or nominal GDP all would have one thing in common. Each would represent a Fed *commitment* to a particular approach to conducting monetary policy. Suppose, for instance, that the Fed were to adhere to a strategy to keep M1 growing at a constant annual rate of 2 percent, no matter what else might happen in the economy. Under such a circumstance, the Fed would be committing itself to a specific **monetary policy rule,** which is a commitment to a particular strategy irrespective of other economic events.

The Fed and other central banks rarely commit to hard-and-fast policy rules, however. Typically, they respond to changes in economic conditions as they occur. The Fed may do this by varying the value of its intermediate policy target, or even by intentionally missing its intermediate objective in the hope of achieving its ultimate goals. When the Fed departs from a preannounced monetary policy strategy because of certain changes in economic conditions, it engages in **monetary policy discretion.** That is, Fed officials use their own best judgment to alter monetary policy instruments in light of altered economic circumstances, instead of sticking with a fixed policy strategy.

The Drawbacks of Monetary Policy Discretion

There is a very simple reason why the Fed and other central banks typically conduct monetary policy in a discretionary manner. They are

Example: of this pg. 430.

monetary policy rule   A Fed precommitment to a specific policy strategy, irrespective of any specific economic events.

monetary policy discretion The conduct of Fed policy in reaction to economic events as they occur, without precommitment to a monetary policy rule.

very naturally trying to save consumers, workers, and businesses from experiencing economic hardship when real output and employment fall or when inflation increases significantly. When confronted with the likelihood that such events are about to occur, central bankers at the Fed and elsewhere in the world naturally try to minimize the effects on the economy.

Many economists, however, believe that there are substantial losses in social well-being as a whole that result from discretionary monetary policy. The first problem, these economists contend, is that because of policy time lags, discretionary monetary policy actions intended to stabilize economic activity instead often end up *destabilizing* the economy. Another possible social cost of discretionary monetary policy is that it may result in persistent inflation. Indeed, a number of economists now believe that the main reason for worldwide inflation over the past 50 years is the discretionary policymaking of the Fed and other central banks around the globe.

Policy Time Lags and Procyclical Monetary Policy

As noted above, a key justification for discretionary monetary policy is that it minimizes the effects of otherwise destabilizing economic events. For example, a fall in aggregate demand for goods and services might be triggered by an unexpected decline in consumer spending. Seemingly, a straightforward Fed response would be to conduct open-market operations to increase the quantity of money, thereby raising consumers' real money balances and inducing them to increase spending. By so doing, the Fed would be conducting a **countercyclical monetary policy,** meaning that it would be offsetting the tendency for prices, and perhaps output and employment to decline as a result of the fall in aggregate demand. That is, the Fed would be reducing the extent to which prices, real output, and employment would *cycle* over time in response to events such as variations in consumer spending.

As we discussed earlier, however, the Fed would not be able respond in this manner until it recognized that consumer spending had declined. This might take several weeks. Fed officials also would have to agree on the appropriate policy response, which also could take up to several weeks. Then, once the Fed had implemented a policy action, a few more weeks or months might pass. By that time, consumer spending might have begun to return to its previous level. Yet it is at this point that the Fed's actions would begin to stimulate greater consumer spending. Consequently, by the time its policies take full effect, the Fed may be adding to a net *increase* in aggregate demand, rather than stabilizing aggregate demand at its previous level. Thus, a well-intentioned Fed effort to conduct countercyclical policy actually *reinforces* a cyclical upturn in economic activity. The Fed's policy actions then would constitute a

countercyclical monetary policy   Fed actions that reduce the extent of up-and-down movements in economic activity.

procyclical monetary policy; they would *add* to natural cycles in economic activity instead of reducing them.

Critics of discretionary monetary policy contend that policy time lags make such procyclical policy outcomes at least as likely as the countercylical policy results the Fed might be aiming to achieve. For this reason, they claim, discretionary policy actions by the Fed are unlikely to be particularly beneficial for society. In fact, some economists argue that we might all be better off replacing the Fed with a computer. Programmers could tell the computer to keep the quantity of money growing at a constant rate (which, as noted in Chapter 14, would prevent gradual deflation as real output grows). Then monetary policy could not accidentally reinforce existing cycles in economic activity.

The Inflationary Bias of Discretionary Monetary Policy Recently economists have identified another problem with discretionary monetary policy. This is that failure to abide by a monetary policy rule can lead to a bias toward continual inflation.

Figure 15.2 on page 428 illustrates the essential elements of this argument. Suppose that the economy currently is at point A, with a price level given by P_1 and real output equal to y_1. The Fed can conduct discretionary monetary policy, and it has two objectives. First, it would like to contain inflation. In addition, however, it would like to increase real output to a target level of y_T. Clearly, the Fed cannot achieve both these objectives, because increases in the quantity of money to raise aggregate demand also raise real output at the expense of higher prices. Depending on how much weight it places on each of its policy goals, the Fed therefore is likely to split the difference by increasing the quantity of money sufficiently to raise output *toward* its goal level of y_T, but at the sacrifice of some inflation. In the short run such a policy action might push the economy to point B in the figure.

Consider, however, how workers are likely to behave if they recognize the Fed's policy goals. They realize that the Fed will be tempted to increase real output at the risk of greater inflation, which would reduce the real spending power of their wages. Hence, workers will seek wage increases *in anticipation* of an increase in aggregate demand triggered by the Fed's actions. This raises business costs and causes the aggregate supply schedule to shift to the left, as shown in the figure. The net outcome is equilibrium at point D, where inflation has increased with little or no net increase in real output. By pursuing output and inflation goals in a discretionary manner, rather than holding firm at point A, the Fed would cause inflation to occur.

What would happen if the Fed promised not to try to raise aggregate demand? That is, what would be the result if the Fed committed itself to keeping the economy at point A? One possibility is

procyclical monetary policy
Fed policy actions that end up exacerbating up-and-down movements in economic activity.

that workers would not believe that the Fed would honor such a commitment. If that were the case, then workers would seek wage increases that would raise business costs and cause aggregate supply to shift leftward, but aggregate demand would not budge because the Fed stood by its promise. The economy would end up at point C in Figure 15.2. Inflation would occur and real output would decline. Because workers realize that the Fed certainly does not want this to happen, it is even harder for them to believe a Fed promise not to increase aggregate demand through an expansionary monetary policy action. Indeed, the Fed would face intense pressure to keep the shift to point C from occurring. This would give the Fed added incentive

---

FIGURE 15.2   The Inflationary Bias of Discretionary Monetary Policy

If the current equilibrium for the economy is point *A*, and if the Fed's goals are to raise output toward a target of y_T but to keep inflation low, then the Fed is tempted to split the difference between these conflicting objectives by inducing a rise in aggregate demand, to point *B*. But if workers realize that the Fed has an incentive to permit prices to rise, they will bargain for higher wages, thereby raising labor costs for businesses and shifting the aggregate supply schedule leftward. If the Fed ignores the temptation to induce a rise in aggregate demand, the result is higher prices and lower real output at point *C*. To avoid this, the Fed would feel pressure to raise aggregate demand as workers expect. The final equilibrium, therefore, is at point *D*, with unchanged real output but a higher price level.

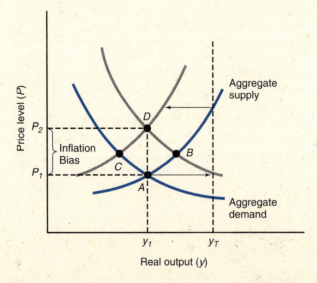

to raise aggregate demand, which would make point D the likely result under discretionary policymaking, despite the lack of a noticeable gain in real output.

The other possibility would be that the Fed's promise to keep the economy at point A is *credible*, or believable. If so, then workers would not seek higher wages and the economy actually would remain at point A. Under such a committed policy rule, there would be no tendency for inflation to occur.

In the absence of a credible Fed promise to stick to a policy rule, point D would be the new equilibrium. The general price level would rise from P_1 to P_2, with little or no change in real output. There would be an *inflationary bias* in monetary policy because this process would continue into the future as the Fed and workers faced the same situation over and over again. Discretionary monetary policy would *perpetuate* inflation.

As Figure 15.3 indicates, there does indeed seem to be an inflationary bias in the United States. Although the average inflation rate has been lower in the 1980s and 1990s as compared with the period from late 1960s through the 1970s, the Fed failed to attain zero inflation in any year, despite its stated intention to control inflation.

FIGURE 15.3   Annual Inflation Rates in the United States, 1960–96

This figure plots annual rates of change in the consumer price index. Although average inflation rates fell in the 1980s and 1990s, as compared with the span from the late 1960s through the 1970s, inflation nonetheless has occurred in every single year. *Source: Economic Report of the President*, Washington, D.C.: U.S. Government Printing Office, 1996.

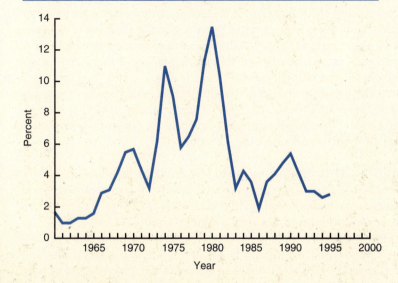

4

Why is central bank credibility so important to maintaining low inflation?   If workers know that a central bank has an incentive to increase aggregate demand to try to raise real output, then they are unlikely to believe the bank's claim that it will control inflation, because that would reduce the purchasing power of workers' wages. Consequently, workers would bargain for wage increases that would push up business costs and, in the absence of higher aggregate demand, cause output to fall. This causes pressure on the central bank to raise aggregate demand, thereby creating an inflationary bias in the economy. The only way for a central bank to prevent such an inflation bias is to make its commitment to low inflation credible to workers.

Making Monetary Policy Rules Credible

In light of the twin dangers that monetary policy can be both procyclical and have an inflationary bias, what can be done to induce the Fed to adopt a fixed rule for its policymaking? In addition, what can be done to make a Fed commitment to such a rule credible?

Constitutional Limitations on Monetary Policy   One possibility would be to change the U.S. Constitution. In its current form courts have interpreted the Constitution as giving Congress wide powers over the nation's monetary affairs. Congress, in turn, has authorized the Fed to use these powers to conduct monetary policy.

A number of economists, such as Milton Friedman of the Hoover Institution at Stanford University, have advocated amending the Constitution and placing clear limits on the discretion of monetary policymakers. Friedman and others have proposed an amendment that would require a constant annual growth rate for the quantity of money. Some critics of governmental involvement in the nation's banking and monetary system would go even further. They would make it illegal for the government to have anything to do with money creation, leaving such matters to private markets. Essentially, these critics of the *status quo* believe that governments will always conduct discretionary policies unless their monetary powers are sharply contained, if not eliminated.

Credibility Through Reputation   So far Constitutional limitations on monetary policy have not advanced beyond the proposal stage. In the absence of such radical institutional changes, how could the Fed make its commitment to low inflation more credible?

One possibility is for the Fed to establish and maintain a reputation as a tough inflation fighter. To understand how it could do this, refer to Figure 15.2. Recall that if the Fed sticks to a promise not to raise

[handwritten margin note: FED should be committed to grow the money sup at an X%.]

aggregate demand in pursuit of short-term output gains, but workers nevertheless seek higher wages that raise business costs, then the result is higher inflation and reduced output. In Figure 15.2 this is shown by the movement from point *A* to point *C*. If the Fed cares only about the present, it would never want a move to point *C* to occur. But if the Fed wants to establish a reputation as an inflation fighter, then it would have to be willing let the economy experience both lower output and inflation at point *C* in Figure 15.2. Thereafter, its promises not to increase aggregate demand might be credible.

A number of observers believe that this was what the Fed did in 1979 after inflation had increased significantly, as shown in Figure 15.3. In 1979 and 1980 the Fed held firm to a commitment to keep aggregate demand from increasing. At first workers did not believe that the Fed would stick to its promise. The result was a sharp recession in 1980 and 1981, as workers' steady escalation in wage demands pushed up business costs that resulted in a reduction in real output—just as depicted by the movement from point *A* to point *C* in Figure 15.2. After that the Fed's commitment to lower inflation was credible and actual inflation rates fell, as Figure 15.3 indicates.

The "Conservative" Central Banker
It is difficult to get a reputation for being a tough inflation fighter unless there is some toughness on the inside as well as on the outside. For instance, one reason why the Fed's anti-inflation policies in the early 1980s may have worked as well as they did was that in 1979, Paul Volcker, whose dislike for inflation was well known, became the chair of the Fed's Board of Governors.

The discretionary theory of inflation outlined above and illustrated in Figure 15.2 indicates that one key factor influencing the Fed's inflationary bias is how much it dislikes inflation relative to how much it wishes to expand real GDP. Nothing the Fed can do actually increases real GDP in the long run, and so society would be better off with a central banker, such as Volcker, who would be less willing to try to increase aggregate demand. Consequently, appointing a **conservative central banker,** an individual who dislikes inflation more than the average member of society, is one way to reduce the extent of the Fed's inflation bias.

conservative central banker
An individual appointed as a central banking official who dislikes inflation more than an average citizen.

Contracts for Central Bankers?
During the past few years another idea for addressing the inflation bias has emerged. This is to enforce explicit **central banker contracts,** which would be legally binding agreements between government and central banking officials. Research by Carl Walsh, of the University of California at Santa Cruz, has shown that such contracts could nearly eliminate the inflationary bias of discretionary monetary policy.

A number of potential contracts that would reduce the incentive for central bankers to inflate have been suggested. One possibility, an approach adopted in New Zealand's 1989 Reserve Bank Act, holds central

central banker contract   A legally binding agreement between a government and a central banking official that holds the official responsible for a nation's inflation performance.

bank officials directly responsible for any failure to achieve price stability. As discussed in Chapter 12, if New Zealand's top central banking official fails to meet clearly specified inflation targets, then under the terms of the contract this individual is subject to immediate dismissal. In principle, a contract also should contain a carrot as well as a stick. For example, one way to induce a central banking official to keep inflation low would be to reward the individual with a higher salary in exchange for better inflation performance. It might seem that this would be paying the person a bonus for doing the job he or she is supposed to be doing. Nevertheless, proponents of such payment schemes point out that salary bonuses could compensate central bankers for fighting political pressures favoring inflationary monetary policies.

5

How might the credibility of central banks such as the Fed be enhanced?
One possible approach would be to make it unlawful for central banks to permit inflation above a certain rate. Alternatively, central bank officials might be required to sign contracts that base continuation in their positions or of their salaries on their inflation performance. To help ensure that central banks would be less likely to create inflationary policies, governments could appoint conservative central banking officials who are known to dislike inflation. Finally, central bankers can gain credibility by permitting output to fall in the near term as a way to convince workers of their commitment to low future inflation.

THE POLITICS OF MONETARY POLICY

To what extent do political pressures affect monetary policy decisions of the Federal Reserve? Are they so significant that the structure of the Fed should be altered to reduce political influences? In recent years these questions have occupied a number of economists.

Political Pressures and the Fed

Under the terms of the Federal Reserve Act of 1913, as amended by the Banking Act of 1935, the president of the United States appoints the seven governors of the Federal Reserve System. Each of these appointments must be confirmed by the U.S. Senate. Then, in theory, the Board of Governors has a free hand to conduct its business without congressional interference in its budgetary or internal policy operations.

In fact, however, the Board Governors and other Fed officials are not nearly so unconstrained. For one thing, they all know that the Fed exists only at the pleasure of the U.S. Congress. During any session of

Congress, votes by the House of Representatives and the Senate could be cast to eliminate the Federal Reserve System. After all, the Constitution gives Congress the ultimate authority "to coin money."

Sources of Political Pressures   Thomas Havrilesky (1939–95) conducted a number of studies, alone and with various coauthors, of the outside pressures that have buffeted the Fed over the years. Havrilesky found evidence of considerable pressures, both by presidential administrations and Congress. These political entities can coerce the Fed directly, in meetings, or in correspondence. Or, as we noted in Chapter 12, administration and congressional officials can send the Fed less direct messages through comments they make in the media.

External pressures on the Fed do not arise only in the executive or legislative branches of government. The Federal Reserve Act established a type of oversight board called the Federal Advisory Council, which is composed of twelve individuals, most of whom are prominent bankers. The Council meets with the Fed's Board of Governors every three months and offers advice on all aspects of Fed policymaking and regulatory responsibilities. Although the Council has no explicit powers under the law, Havrilesky has documented that the Council's recommendations have influenced Trading Desk Directives of the Federal Open Market Committee.

Do Political Pressures Matter?   The possibility that the Fed may cave in to external coercion from time to time matters only if there are negative consequences for monetary policy and, hence, for the economy at large. If occasional Fed acquiescence to such pressures has no bearing on inflation, real output, and employment, then there is little cause for concern.

Willingness by the Fed to comply with outside pressures, however, can have negative effects on the Fed's effectiveness in containing inflation. Recall that a key factor affecting the degree of inflationary bias in monetary policy is the credibility of the Fed's commitment to maintaining low inflation. Whenever individuals and businesses perceive that the Fed has given in to outside pressures for greater ease in monetary policy, its credibility is damaged. Although there are very few documented instances in which the Fed has buckled under completely to external pressures, Havrilesky and others provide strong evidence that the Fed has given in to such pressures inch by inch over the years. Havrilesky refers to the "modern" period, dating from the 1960s, as an interval of "increasing politicization of monetary policy."

Central Bank Credibility and Independence

What, if anything, might be done to improve the ability of the Fed to maintain its credibility? Most economists are in broad agreement that the key to achieving central bank credibility is maintaining independence from external pressures. Hence, many economists in recent years

POLICY NOTEBOOOK

The Fed and the Political Business Cycle

There appear to be two important variables whose values weigh heavily on who will be elected president—the rate of economic growth and the unemployment rate. The relationship between these two variables and presidential election outcomes has been labeled the *political business cycle*. Some economists argue that because of this relationship, the Fed has a built-in bias toward creating more inflation.

The evidence for a political business cycle does not guarantee its validity. Nonetheless, the presidential elections of 1956, 1964, 1972, and 1984 all had the basic pattern of low unemployment and low inflation predicted by the political business cycle, and the incumbents—Eisenhower, Johnson, Nixon, and Reagan, respectively—won by landslides. The elections of 1960, 1968, 1976, and 1980 did not have the political business cycle pattern and, as predicted, the White House changed political party in each of those years. The election in 1988 resulted in a major victory by Republican candidate George Bush, who benefited from the low unemployment, slowing but still healthy economic growth, and moderate inflation inherited from the Reagan years.

Bush's loss in the 1992 election appears to contradict the political business cycle. Although the economy had been in a recession that started in 1990, the rate of growth of real GDP had risen for several quarters and the unemployment level had been falling slightly

for four months prior to the election. Clinton was nonetheless effectively able to campaign on Bush's "dismal" economic record. It was only after the election that government statistics were released showing improvement in the rate of growth of real GDP.

If the above theory is correct, the Fed has to be part of the picture by increasing the rate of growth of the money supply about a year and a half before each presidential election. There is, in fact, some evidence that certain Fed chairs, such as Arthur Burns under Richard Nixon, had actually pursued such politically motivated policies. To the extent that Fed policymaking is motivated by political considerations, there is a built-in bias toward more rather than less inflation. There is a real political incentive to increase the rate of growth of the money supply for short-run economic gains, but there is no political payback for reducing the rate of growth in the money supply *after* presidential elections. Presidents and heads of the Fed simply permit the economy to revert to its natural level of employment and rate of economic growth. Thus, we see changing rates of inflation, but almost never deflation in the United States (and, in fact, in most of Europe).

For Critical Analysis: *If the public had perfect information about the political business cycle, could expansionary and monetary policy have any short-run effects on real output and employment? Explain your answer.*

have promoted *central bank independence* as a weapon in the fight against inflation in the United States and elsewhere.

The Dimensions of Central Bank Independence   Central banks such as the Federal Reserve are independent in some respects but not in others. For example, a central bank might be *politically independent*, meaning that the government and other outside individuals or groups have no direct influence on the central bank's decision-making processes. Yet such a politically independent central bank could still lack *economic independence*, or the ability to control its own budget or to resist efforts by the government to force it to lend to the government or otherwise to support government policies. Likewise, a central bank could be economically independent but not be politically independent. A truly independent central bank would be independent both politically and economically.

Giving central bankers more independence would not necessarily preclude making them *accountable* for their performances as public policymakers. In principle, governments could grant considerable independence to central bankers to conduct monetary policy as they see fit, while continuing to hold them responsible if inflation gets out of hand.

The Gains from Central Bank Independence   Do societies gain from granting central banks greater independence? In a study that has been influential in the 1990s, Harvard University economists Alberto Alesina and Lawrence Summers looked at data across countries to determine the relationships between central bank independence and the level and variability of inflation. Their striking results are shown in panels (a) and (b) of Figure 15.4 on page 456.

In both panels (a) and (b) of Figure 15.4, an index of central bank independence is measured along the horizontal axis. As the value of this index increases, nations' central banks are more independent, politically and/or economically. In panel (a) average annual inflation rates between the middle 1950s and the late 1980s are measured along the vertical axis. The relationship shown in panel (a) clearly is *negative;* there is an inverse relationship between central bank independence and average inflation. Nations with more-independent central banks experience lower average inflation. The two countries with the most-independent central banks, Germany and Switzerland, had average inflation rates of around 3 percent. In contrast, the two nations with the least-independent central banks from the 1950s through the 1980s, New Zealand (before its change in status) and Spain, experienced average inflation rates exceeding 7 and 8 percent.

Panel (b) of Figure 15.4 measures the statistical variance of inflation along the vertical axis. Again there is an inverse relationship: Nations with more-independent central banking institutions tend to experience less volatile inflation rates. Apparently, increased central bank independence yields more price stability, as well as generally lower inflation rates.

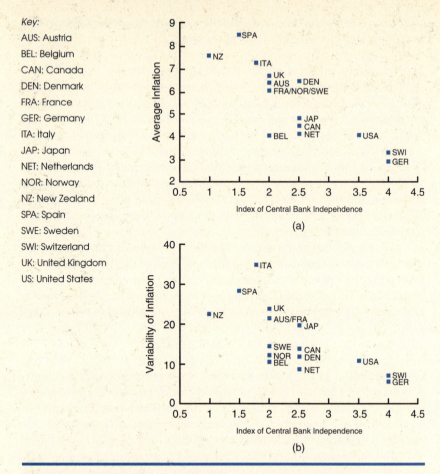

Key:

AUS: Austria
BEL: Belgium
CAN: Canada
DEN: Denmark
FRA: France
GER: Germany
ITA: Italy
JAP: Japan
NET: Netherlands
NOR: Norway
NZ: New Zealand
SPA: Spain
SWE: Sweden
SWI: Switzerland
UK: United Kingdom
US: United States

FIGURE 15.4   Central Bank Independence, Average Inflation, and Inflation Variability

As shown in panel (a), nations with more-independent central banks, such as Germany, Switzerland, and the United States, have lower average inflation rates compared with countries with less-independent central banks. Panel (b) shows that nations with more-independent central banks also have rates of inflation that are less variable. *Source:* Alberto Alesina and Lawrence Summers, "Central Bank Independence and Macroeconomic Performance," *Journal of Money, Credit, and Banking,* May 1993, pp. 151–162.

Should the Fed Be More Independent?   Evidence such as that displayed in Figure 15.4 induced a number of countries, such as Mexico, France, and Pakistan, to grant greater independence to their central banks during the 1990s. In the United States it has led a number of economists to argue for further increasing the independence of the Federal Reserve System.

As you can see in Figure 15.4, the United States already has made the Fed one of the world's most independent central banks. Nevertheless, in light of the potential gains in the form of reduced and less-volatile inflation rates, many observers believe that granting the Fed even more policy independence would be a good move. A 1995 study of the Fed by Henry Chappell of the University of South Carolina, Rob Roy McGregor of the University of North Carolina at Charlotte, and Thomas Havrilesky backs up such a view. These researchers compared data on Federal Open Market Committee (FOMC) votes by Federal Reserve Board Governors, who are subject to a political appointment process, and Federal Reserve district bank presidents, who are not. They found that the more politically independent district bank presidents tended to vote for anti-inflationary policies. Board governors, in contrast, favored policy actions that would cause slightly more inflation. Indeed, the authors of the study concluded that if the FOMC had been composed only of politically appointed governors, the annual inflation rate would have been *4 percent higher.*

Such evidence indicates that one way to increase the Fed's independence and thereby cut U.S. inflation rates might be to reduce the number of politically appointed individuals who play a role in Fed monetary policy. Interestingly, the authors conducted detailed examinations of the backgrounds of Fed governors and district bank presidents and found that another possible way to reduce inflation somewhat might be to bar people with government or Fed experience from serving on the Board of Governors. Adopting such a restriction, the authors found, might reduce the average annual inflation rate by nearly 2 percent per year. Apparently government or Fed experience makes a typical person more willing to vote for more inflationary policies!

One commonly hears criticisms of economists, who seem never to be able to forecast economic activity any more reliably than weather forecasters can predict beyond a two- or three-day horizon the likelihood of sunny skies. Yet in the area of central banking, economists have made notable progress in efforts to understand and predict the consequences of institutional changes. It remains to be seen if such advances will lead to practical, inflation-reducing reforms at the Fed and other central banks around the world.

6

Should central banks such as the Fed be more independent public policy institutions?   While most economists believe that central bankers should be accountable for monetary policies, they also believe that society gains more price stability by giving central bankers more autonomy to conduct their policies. Evidence indicates that nations with more-independent central banks experience lower and less-volatile inflation rates. Although the Fed is a relatively independent institution, compared with many other central banks around the world, some economists believe that reforms that would give the Fed greater autonomy would reduce U.S. inflation rates.

SUMMARY

1. **The Fed's Ultimate Goals of Monetary Policy:** Under 1946 and 1978 legislation, the Fed is supposed to conduct its policies to attain maximum output and employment at the lowest possible inflation rate. The Fed also seeks to achieve stable output, employment, and inflation. Studies indicate that the Fed does not always place equal weight on these ultimate policy goals, and that the relative weights it assigns to the goals vary over time.

2. **Monetary Policy Time Lags:** The recognition lag in monetary policy is the time that passes between the need for a Fed policy action and the Fed's recognition of the need. The response lag is the period between the Fed's realization that it needs to act and its formulation and implementation of a specific policy change. The transmission lag is the interval that passes before a policy action has its fullest effects on the economy.

3. **Why the Fed Might Use an Intermediate Monetary Policy Target:** The Fed gets infrequent information about its ultimate goal variables. In addition, policy time lags complicate efforts to aim policy changes directly at ultimate policy objectives. Differences in interpretation of data and conflicting theories further complicate efforts to pursue ultimate objectives directly. An intermediate target variable can be a useful stand-in for the Fed's ultimate goals if it is related to those goals, is readily measurable, can be observed frequently, and is controllable.

4. **Why Central Bank Credibility Is Important for Maintaining Low Inflation:** The reason why an inflationary bias may exist is that if workers know that central banks have incentives to raise aggregate demand in an effort to expand real output, workers will seek higher wages. This would raise costs for businesses and reduce output. But increases in aggregate demand coupled with higher business costs generate inflation. The only way for central banks to prevent such an inflation bias from occurring is by following through on believable commitments not to raise aggregate demand.

5. **How the Credibility of Central Banks Such as the Fed Might Be Enhanced:** Most central banks try to establish credibility by developing a reputation for a commitment to low inflation. Such a reputation can be bolstered if governments appoint central bankers who are known to dislike inflation. Another possible approach would be to establish contracts with central bankers, punishing them for bad inflation performance and rewarding them for achieving low inflation. Finally, a way to try to constrain inflation directly would be to amend national constitutions to make inflation illegal above certain levels.

6. **The Independence of Central Banks Such as the Fed:** There is strong evidence that the countries with the most independent central banks also experience the lowest average inflation rates. They also have less variable inflation rates. This has led many economists to propose increasing the autonomy of central bankers without necessarily sacrificing their accountability for performance. Some U.S. economists believe that the Fed might usefully be reformed in ways that would increase its autonomy while preserving, or even enhancing, its accountability for its actions.

QUESTIONS AND PROBLEMS

1. Suppose that an economist were to demonstrate conclusively that all the theories of gradual price adjustment discussed in Chapter 14 fail to explain real-world behavior. If this were the case, what ultimate goal(s) would you argue that the Fed should pursue? What ultimate goal(s) do you believe it should abandon in this situation? Justify your choices.

2. Which monetary policy time lag do you believe would typically be the most lengthy? Which do you think would normally be of the shortest duration? Explain your reasoning.

3. Explain how the existence of policy time lags helps to justify the use of an intermediate monetary policy target.

4. Use an aggregate demand–aggregate supply diagram to trace through the theory of the inflationary bias of discretionary monetary policy. Explain why appointing a conservative central banker might reduce the size of such a bias.

5. Based on what you have learned in this chapter, do you believe that central banking arrangements could ever be developed to make monetary policy *completely* credible? Take a stand and support your answer.

6. So far there is little evidence that making central banks more independent has any effect on the levels of real GDP in most nations. Nor does greater central bank independence seem to affect the variability of real output. Do you feel that this helps weaken or strengthen the case for making central banks more independent? Explain.

16

The Fed and the World Economy

KEY QUESTIONS

1. Why do individuals and businesses hold financial instruments issued in other nations?

2. In what ways have world financial markets become more interconnected?

3. How do economists measure international transactions?

4. How are exchange rates determined?

5. Should exchange rates be fixed or flexible?

6. What role does the Fed play in foreign exchange markets?

*T*he hotel security staff was doubled three days ago. Members of the Secret Service have already arrived, as have members of six other countries' secret services, too. The press is kept at bay and not told anything. One by one central bankers or heads of treasury departments from seven nations—Canada, France, Germany, Italy, Japan, the United Kingdom, and the United States—go to their assigned rooms. The next morning, the conference room is filled with a small delegation from each nation in the so-called G-7, or Group of Seven. The first order of business is the weak dollar and the strong yen. How should the Group of Seven handle the overvalued yen? Japan is facing deflation and a fifth year of recession. Can the economic leaders of the assembled nations make a difference? The discussions are intense. The head of the American delegation is upset. He threatens not to participate in the next round of coordinated efforts to prop up the dollar. He points out that all such attempts in the past have failed. The head of the German delegation calms him down, telling him that it is worth another try. Discussions on what to do and how to coordinate monetary policies continue late into the evening.

No one knows how close to the truth our representation of the closed-door meetings of the Group of Seven is. No reporters are present. Each participant is implicitly sworn to secrecy. The group is informal and unofficial. Its members are not elected. Its activities are not scrutinized by any government body anywhere in the world. There are those who say that it does not matter what is decided in these closed-door meetings, because the world monetary system is so vast, moves so rapidly, and is so complicated that even when governments work together they cannot affect it.

INTERNATIONAL BANKING AND FINANCE

During the past two decades many nations of the world gradually have moved toward more fully **open economies.** This means that consumers and businesses in these nations can undertake substantial amounts of transactions in goods, services, and financial assets with residents of other countries. The United States also has become a more open economy. For instance, the amount of goods sold abroad by U.S. companies increased from just over 5 percent of U.S. gross domestic product in 1986 to nearly 8 percent in 1996. In dollar terms, this represented an increase from just over $200 billion in foreign sales to well over $500 billion.

open economies   National economies in which significant portions of economic activity entail international transactions in goods, services, and financial assets.

closed economies   National economies in which insignificant portions of economic activity entail international transactions in goods, services, and financial assets.

Compared with some other nations, however, the United States looks more like a **closed economy,** in which the bulk of transactions take place internally. In many European countries, for instance, international transactions account for more than 25 percent of GDP. And so the United States has a long way to go before it can be called a fully open economy.

Nevertheless, the increasing volumes of world trade and payments are having significant effects on the U.S. economy and financial system. Indeed, it is the financial markets where international relationships have grown more pronounced during recent years. Financial institutions and markets around the world are increasingly interconnected—and interdependent.

International Financial Markets

In Chapters 3 and 4 we discussed the important role that financial markets play in channeling funds from saving to investment. Financial markets perform these roles not only within nations but also between nations.

International Asset Diversification   Nowadays it is common for U.S. money market, bond, and equity funds to offer shares in portfolios that include foreign short- and long-term financial instruments. Likewise, many U.S. pension funds now include foreign-issued securities among their holdings of stocks and bonds.

Why would an American resident, such as yourself or members of your family, wish to hold German government bonds or stocks in Italian auto companies? After all, U.S. Treasury bonds and General Motors stock are much closer to home, and they are denominated in the dollars that you and your family members use to buy goods and services here in the United States.

international financial arbitrage   The act of buying a financial instrument at its market price within one country and selling the instrument or its equivalent at a higher price in another nation.

One possible answer you might propose is that the German government bond yield is higher or the return on the Italian auto company's stock is greater than those of their American counterparts. Certainly, this is one possible reason for holding financial instruments issued in other nations. We would not anticipate today that such differences in bond yields or stock returns can persist in the face of **international financial arbitrage.** This is the act of purchasing a financial instrument at its market price in one nation and then selling the instrument or its equivalent at a higher price in another country's financial market. If enough people engage in arbitrage, then the prices of financial assets equalize across nations. Hence, as we discussed in Chapter 3, interest parity should hold for financial instruments of identical maturities and risks:

> **Exchange-rate-adjusted yields on the financial instruments of different nations with equivalent risk and maturities, on average, should be equal.**

In today's world where we have the option of holding money, bonds, equities, or pension fund shares in portfolios of financial instruments, arbitrage is a very powerful mechanism for producing interest yield parity.

This means that trying to make a killing by holding German bonds and Italian stocks usually is not the main rationale for American citizens purchasing foreign-issued securities. Instead, the key reason for holding foreign financial instruments is that including such instruments in one's portfolio provides protection against risk. That is, there are gains from **international financial diversification,** or holding both American-issued *and* foreign-issued financial instruments.

To see how this might protect an American from risk, consider a possible situation in which political change occurs following the election of a new president and bringing a new party to power in Congress. As a result of these alterations in the political landscape, the prices of American securities decline in financial markets. At the same time, political and economic stability prevail in Germany and Italy, so that the prices of German bonds and Italian stocks remain firm. Indeed, the prices of these securities might even rise as people sell off American securities and place their funds in German and Italian markets. By holding the German bonds and Italian stocks, an American could at least partially offset losses on U.S. security holdings with gains on foreign securities. Consequently, international asset diversification reduces the overall risk of loss on the American's security portfolio.

In today's sophisticated financial markets, international asset diversification has become a science. Managers of money, bond, equity, and pension funds, for instance, now offer **world index funds.** These are carefully designed groupings of financial instruments from around the world yielding returns that historically have tended to move in offsetting directions. By holding a world index fund, an individual can earn the average yield on securities issued in a number of nations while minimizing risk of loss.

international financial diversification   The act of holding financial instruments issued in more than one country.

world index funds   Portfolios of financial instruments issued in various nations whose yields generally move in offsetting directions, thereby reducing overall risk of losses on the portfolios.

1

Why do individuals and businesses hold financial instruments issued in other nations?   International financial arbitrage normally equalizes exchange-rate-adjusted yields on financial instruments with identical risks and maturities. Consequently, the main reason for holding financial instruments issued in other countries is to diversify one's overall portfolio.

International Banking and the Eurocurrency Markets   American-based corporations also have good reason to hold financial instruments issued in other nations. Many of these companies have business interests abroad, and so they commonly hold foreign currencies as well as bank deposits and securities denominated in foreign currencies. As we discussed in Chapter 4, international dealings expose U.S. companies to various foreign exchange risks, which they seek to reduce through trading in derivative instruments such as forward contracts, futures, options, and swaps.

Depository institutions often play a central role both in international asset diversification and foreign exchange risk reduction. Depository institutions permit individuals and corporations to maintain deposit accounts in multiple currencies and obtain loans denominated in foreign currencies. They also manage foreign exchange derivatives on behalf of their customers.

In effect, the depository institutions that provide such financial services are *global financial intermediaries.* They channel savings denominated in one nation's currency to an ultimate use as capital investment in another nation. This activity helps to ensure that funds make their way to nations where returns on investment are the highest.

Depository institutions compete in *Eurocurrency markets* for the deposit funds they use to make loans that span national borders. *Eurocurrency deposits* are depository institution accounts denominated in a particular nation's currency but which are maintained *outside* that country's borders. Analogously, *Eurocurrency loans* are foreign-currency-denominated loans made by a depository institution based outside the country of issue to an individual or a corporation.

An example of a Eurocurrency deposit would be a deposit denominated in French francs that a U.S. corporation maintains at a London bank. If that bank advances a franc-denominated loan to the U.S. company, the loan would be a Eurocurrency loan.

The Globalization of Financial Markets

vehicle currency   The currency that individuals and businesses use most often to conduct international transactions.

After World War II, the American dollar was the world's **vehicle currency,** or the primary currency that individuals and businesses used for international transactions. Just as one might need an automobile as a vehicle of transportation to a remote location, during the decades immediately following World War II one typically found that dollars were the main vehicle for completing international transactions. Consequently, today's Eurocurrency markets originated in the Eurodollar market. The Eurodollar market was a market for dollar-denominated deposits and loans by depository institutions with offices in European nations.

Since the late 1970s the Japanese yen and the German deutsche mark have challenged the dollar's preeminent role as a vehicle currency. For instance, a study by Stanley Black of the University of North Carolina found that before 1980 virtually all New York interbank transactions involved dollar exchanges. By the early 1990s, however, nearly one out of every twenty-five New York interbank transactions involved a foreign currency. Black found that a general increase in the use of non-dollar currencies occurred in all manner of transactions, including merchandise trade and capital transactions. This gradual shift toward greater use of multiple currencies has had a significant influence on the evolution of world financial markets. As individuals and companies in various nations increased their holdings of deposits and loans denominated in yen and marks, the old Eurodollar market gave way to today's more broadly based Eurocurrency markets. This development, in turn, provided the foundation for unprecedented linkages among financial markets around the globe.

The Integration of World Financial Markets   The Eurocurrency markets have become a central connection for national financial markets. Depository institutions can use the Eurocurrency markets to redirect deposit funds to activities in nations beyond the original country of origin. As a result, the Eurocurrency markets are now the focus of world arbitrage.

To see how this arbitrage occurs, envision a situation in which the interest yields on dollar-denominated assets held in the United States decline. This induces many of the individual and corporate holders of such assets to shift them to Eurodollar deposits in London, Paris, and other locations outside North America. It also encourages a number of traders to convert dollar-denominated assets to assets denominated in other nations' currencies. As a result, interest yields on assets denominated in nondollar currencies ultimately have to adjust. The result, as discussed in Chapter 3, is international interest parity. Arbitrage in the interconnected Eurocurrency markets is the crucial mechanism by which such interest parity is maintained.

The continuing process of increasing interrelationship of national financial markets through the arbitrage mechanism of the Eurocurrency markets is known as **international financial integration.** Fully integrated financial markets effectively function as a single market. Certainly, complete integration has not yet occurred. Nevertheless, the growth of the Eurocurrency market, together with rapid developments in communications and computing technology, are speeding the process toward integration. National financial markets do not yet behave as one, but increasingly they react to the same events.

To see why this is true, consider an individual who uses a computer-assisted trading system such as Globex. This is a trading system that is owned and operated by the Chicago Mercantile Exchange. An American trader with a Globex account can enter the system on a personal computer and read bid and offer prices and trading volumes for financial instruments in any major financial market in the world. If it happens to be 10:00 P.M. eastern daylight time in the United States, then

international financial integration   The process by which international financial arbitrage spurs increased interrelationships among national financial markets.

futures markets in the United States are closed, but markets in the Far East are open. If the trader sees an acceptable bid for a Hong Kong futures contract, then a sell order can be placed via the Globex system, which automatically verifies that the order satisfies current exchange terms for Hong Kong futures contracts. The system then places the trader's order next in line, and when that order's turn arrives, the system automatically executes the trade.

As you can see, in today's world few major financial markets are "national." As systems such as Globex become more commonplace, financial markets around the world increasingly will be open to trading initiated from far-flung locales.

International Dimensions of Banking Policies and Markets

The increasing globalization of financial markets has significant implications for American banking policies. One special area of concern for U.S. banking regulators has been the potential for banks to engage in **regulatory arbitrage.** This is the process by which banks can try to escape the effects of regulations imposed by authorities in their home nations by shifting operations and funds to offices in locales where there are fewer regulatory constraints.

To avoid the potential for regulatory arbitrage by U.S. banks, banking regulators have sought to coordinate their policies with those of banking regulators in other developed nations. For instance, in 1988 the Federal Reserve, the FDIC, and the Office of the Comptroller of the Currency joined with banking regulators of most major nations to develop and implement the risk-based bank capital requirements we discussed in Chapter 8. Because all banks in nations such as Germany, Japan, the United Kingdom, and the United States now must meet the same basic capital requirements, the banks in these nations face similar constraints. In addition to limiting the scope for regulatory arbitrage, this coordinated action by banking regulators also helped ensure that major banks would not face competitive advantages or disadvantages in international competition for loans and deposits.

It is important to emphasize, however, that numerous regulatory barriers that inhibit international financial competition continue to exist. Cross-border access to banking, insurance, and broker-dealer services continues to be limited both by legal and regulatory restrictions. A World Trade Organization agreement promised to begin opening national markets for these types of financial services in 1996 and 1997. A recent multinational accord was not joined by the United States, however. In fact, the United States has been as slow to open its borders to international financial competition as many other nations. Even in Europe, where cross-border banking restrictions were supposed to have been nearly eliminated after 1992, markets for such financial services have been slow to open to foreign companies. While international integration in markets for stocks, bonds, and Eurocurrency deposits and

regulatory arbitrage The act of trying to avoid regulations imposed by banking authorities in one's home country by moving offices and funds to countries with less stringent regulations.

loans has occurred at a rapid pace, integrating markets for banking and other financial services promises to be a much slower process.

2

In what ways have world financial markets become more interconnected? The Eurocurrency markets link many of the world's money and capital markets, which permits international financial arbitrage to occur in these markets. In addition, technological developments in computers and in communication systems now permit individuals and businesses to trade in foreign markets even at times when their home markets are closed.

THE BALANCE OF PAYMENTS

International exchanges of goods, services, and financial assets generate considerable flows of payments across nations' borders. To keep track of international transactions, economists use an accounting system called the **balance of payments accounts.** For the United States, this is a record of all the transactions between American residents and the rest of the world. The balance of payments includes cross-border transactions for goods and services, of income receipts and payments, and assets of individuals, businesses, and governments.

The balance of payments accounts have three components. The first is the **current account,** which tabulates international trade, transfers of goods and services, and flows of income. Nongovernmental asset transactions are recorded in the **capital account.** Finally, asset transactions involving governmental agencies appear in an account called the **official settlements balance.**

In all three U.S. balance of payments accounts, any transaction that entails a *payment* by an American individual, business, or government agency is a deficit item that enters the accounts *negatively*, because such a transaction generates an outflow of funds from the United States. In contrast, any transaction that entails a *receipt* by a U.S. resident, company, or government agency is a *positive* entry, because a receipt is an inflow of funds into the United States.

Exports, Imports, and the Current Account

The easiest place to start in the balance of payments is the *current account.* This is the portion of the balance of payments accounts that receives the most attention from the media because it tabulates American trade of goods and services. As you may know from never-ending press accounts, in recent years U.S. residents have tended to

balance of payments accounts A tabulation of all transactions between the residents in one nation and the residents of all the other nations in the world.

current account The balance of payments account that tabulates international trade and transfers of goods and services and flows of income.

capital account The balance of payments account that records all nongovernmental international asset transactions.

official settlements balance A balance of payments account that records international asset transactions of agencies of home and foreign governments.

TABLE 16.1   U.S. Merchandise Trade ($ millions)

	1985	1990	1995
Merchandise exports	+215,915	+389,307	+574,879
Merchandise imports	−338,088	−498,337	−749,348
Merchandise trade balance	−122,173	−109,030	−174,469

Sources: Economic Report of the President and *Economic Indicators,* Washington D.C.: U.S. Government Printing Office, 1996.

purchase more goods and services from abroad relative to the amount that they sell.

The Merchandise Trade Balance   Media reports typically focus narrowly on **merchandise trade,** which is cross-border purchases and sales of *physical goods* only. Sales of goods to foreigners by American residents are *merchandise exports,* while the goods that American residents purchase from abroad are *merchandise imports.* Table 16.1 displays dollar values of U.S. exports and imports for recent years. Note that exports generate receipts by Americans and enter positively, whereas imports entail payments abroad by U.S. residents and hence enter negatively.

merchandise trade   International exchanges of physical goods.

The last row in Table 16.1 gives the *merchandise trade balance* for each period. This is a figure that usually receives considerable media attention. When the merchandise trade balance is positive, Americans are exporting more goods than they import. This is a situation of a *trade surplus.* As the table indicates, in all recent periods the United States has been in the reverse situation: imports exceed exports. Consequently, the merchandise trade balance has been negative, that is, we have a *trade deficit.*

The Current Account Balance   Many economists argue that it is misleading for merchandise trade deficits to receive so much attention. During the past two decades, they contend, U.S. service industries have grown relative to industries that produce goods. For instance, travel, transportation, and financial services have become much more important as components of total production in the United States.

As Table 16.2 indicates, net international transactions for services appear along with the merchandise trade balance in the current account of the balance of payments accounts. As you can see, during recent years American residents have sold more services to foreigners than they have received, and so service transactions, on net, have generated receipts for Americans. Consequently, the entries for this category in the second row of Table 16.2 are positive. Adding the first two rows of Table 16.2 yields the *balance on goods and services,* which are the figures in the third row of the table. Because this balance includes both goods *and* services, most economists prefer to look at this balance rather than the merchandise trade balance that gets the bulk of media coverage. Nevertheless, you can see that the balance on goods and services also

TABLE 16.2   The U.S. Current Account ($ millions)

	1985	1990	1995
Merchandise trade balance	−122,173	−109,030	−174,469
Net service transactions	+78	+29,036	+63,052
Balance on goods and services	−122,095	−79,994	−111,417
Net income flow	+19,673	+20,725	−11,402
Unilateral transfers	−22,950	−33,393	−30,095
Current account balance	−125,372	−92,662	−152,914

Sources: *Economic Report of the President* and *Economic Indicators*, Washington, D.C.: U.S. Government Printing Office.

has been in deficit for all recent periods. The net receipts of U.S. service industries have not made up for the net payments that Americans have made on transactions in goods.

Also included in the current account are cross-border flows of income receipts and payments. American residents and companies earn income on foreign assets that they hold, which enter positively in the U.S. current account. Foreign residents and companies earn income on assets that they own in the United States, which enter negatively in the U.S. current account. The fourth line of Table 16.2 shows the net income flow for each period.

Finally, the current account also includes *unilateral transfers,* which essentially are gifts that Americans give to foreigners or that foreigners give to Americans. Transfers from foreigners to Americans are tabulated as receipts by Americans and enter positively; transfers from Americans to foreigners are tabulated as payments by Americans and enter negatively. The fifth line of Table 16.2 displays net transfers. Because the United States has given considerable foreign aid and military transfers to other nations, the net value of transfers has been negative in recent years.

The sixth and last line of Table 16.2 shows the sum of lines 3 through 5. This is the *current account balance,* which is the sum of all net international flows of goods, services, income, and transfers. As you can see, the U.S. current account balance has been negative for all recent intervals. Hence, the United States has had a *current account deficit* during each interval. The U.S. current account balance has not been positive in any year since 1981. This means that since that year, Americans have paid out more to the rest of the world than they have taken in on trade in goods and services, income flows, and transfers.

The Capital Account, the Private Payments Balance, and the Overall Balance of Payments

International financial market transactions are changes in asset holdings by Americans and residents of other nations. Economists record these transactions in separate balance of payments accounts. They also classify such transactions based on their origin. Asset transactions involving private individuals or companies are recorded in the *private capital account*. Asset transactions involving official governmental entities such as the U.S. Treasury or the Federal Reserve are recorded in the *official settlements balance*. Although these two accounts sometimes are combined into a single, overall capital account, we shall keep them separate in our discussion. As you will learn shortly, maintaining this separation of private and official asset transactions is very helpful for understanding the operation of government policies relating to international trade and finance.

The Capital Account and the Private Payments Balance   The capital account tabulates changes in asset holdings by Americans abroad and by foreigners in America. If Americans acquire foreign assets, such as titles of ownership for plants or equipment or for securities such as bonds, then these acquisitions are recorded as positive entries in the U.S. capital account. If foreigners acquire assets within American borders, then negative entries appear in the U.S. capital account.

The *capital account balance* is the sum of all these asset changes for individuals and businesses, exclusive of governmental entities. The second line of Table 16.3 lists the U.S. capital account balance for recent years. During most intervals this balance has been positive, meaning that on net Americans have acquired more foreign assets relative to foreign acquisitions of American assets.

The first line of Table 16.3 carries down the figures for the current account balance from Table 16.2. The sum of the current account balance in the first line of Table 16.3 and the capital account balance in the second line is the *private payments balance*. This measures the net private transactions between individuals and businesses in the United States and the rest of the world. In common parlance it often is called the "balance of payments." This is a misleading term, however, as we shall point out below.

The U.S. private payments balance has been negative since the early 1980s. This indicates that private American individuals and businesses have made more payments to foreigners relative to receipts

TABLE 16.3   The U.S. Private Payments Balance ($ millions)

	1985	1990	1995
Current account balance	−125,372	−92,662	−152,914
Capital account balance	+109,754	+14,122	+45,814
Private payments balance	−15,618	−78,540	−107,100

Sources: Economic Report of the President and *Economic Indicators*, Washington, D.C.: U.S. Government Printing Office, 1996.

from foreigners. Hence, Americans have had *private payments deficits,* which often are called "balance of payments deficits," during recent years. We shall try to understand why this has been true once we have completed our discussion of the balance of payments accounts.

The Official Settlements Balance and the Overall Balance of Payments   Governmental agencies also engage in asset transactions. Acquisitions of foreign assets by the Federal Reserve, the U.S. Treasury, or other agencies of the U.S. government appear as receipts in the balance of payments accounts. Overseas deposits of funds by the Fed or Treasury also appear as receipts. Consequently, such acquisitions by American governmental agencies are positive entries. Acquisition of American assets by foreign central banks or governments appear as outflows, and so they are negative entries.

Central banks and governments maintain deposit accounts in central banks of other nations. If the Federal Reserve or the Treasury add to their deposit accounts at other countries' central banks, this appears as an outflow of funds, or a negative entry, in the balance of payments accounts. If foreign central banks or governments add to their deposit accounts with the Federal Reserve, this appears as an inflow of funds, or a positive entry.

The net amount of all such central bank or governmental asset transactions is the *official settlements balance.* The second line of Table 16.4 gives the U.S. official settlements balance for recent periods. This balance has consistently been positive, mainly because foreign central bank and government deposits have risen, causing total foreign official asset holdings in the United States to increase.

The first line of Table 16.4 carries down the private payments balance figures from Table 16.3. In theory, the sum of the first two lines of Table 16.4 should be the *overall balance of payments,* or the net of all transactions of individuals, businesses, or governmental agencies in the United States with the rest of the world. This rarely works out, however. One reason is that there are errors in the data collected. Another is the number of illegal, cross-border transactions, such as drug trades, that do not get recorded. As a result, there is a significant *statistical discrepancy*

TABLE 16.4   The Overall Balance of Payments for the United States ($ millions)

	1985	1990	1995
Private payments balance	−15,618	−78,540	−107,100
Official settlements balance	−7,797	+34,059	+100,415
Statistical discrepancy	+23,415	+44,481	+6,685
Overall balance of payments	0	0	0

Sources: Economic Report of the President and *Economic Indicators.* Washington, D.C.: U.S. Government Printing Office, 1996.

each period, which is shown on the third line of Table 16.4. The fourth line is the overall balance of payments, which *always must equal zero*. For every transaction between an American resident and a foreign resident, there is both a payment and a receipt. Consequently, overall such payments and receipts must cancel out and the overall balance of payments must equal zero.

As we noted earlier the private payments balance often is called the balance of payments. The reason why this is a misleading term is that the *overall balance of payments always is equal to zero*. The private payments balance, in contrast, may be positive (a private payments surplus) or negative (a private payments deficit). The traditional, albeit misleading, terminology for a private payments surplus is balance of payments surplus. Likewise, the traditional term for a private payments deficit is balance of payments deficit. These are the terms you see most often in media reports; even economists use these terms, simply because everyone else does. Note that:

> **After allowing for the statistical discrepancy, the private payments balance always must be offset by the official settlements balance.**

That is, if there is a private payments deficit, then the official settlements balance must be positive. If you think about this for a moment, it makes considerable sense. If Americans pay more to residents of other nations than they receive, then other nations' central banks and governments ultimately accumulate dollars, on net, that Americans have paid to them. Foreign central banks and governments hold many of these dollars on deposit in the United States, thereby adding to the U.S. official settlements balance and causing it to be positive. The two balances then offset each other, in the absence of statistical discrepancies, so that the overall balance of payments is zero.

3

How do economists measure international transactions?   They use the balance of payments, which is a set of accounts that tracks transactions between Americans and residents of other nations. There are three key accounts. The current account tracks trade of goods and services, transfers, and flows of income. The capital account records private asset transactions, and the official settlements balance accounts for governmental asset transactions.

The American "Twin Deficit" Problem   As indicated in Tables 16.3 and 16.4, the private payments balance for the United States consistently has been negative since the early 1980s. The United States has operated with "balance of payments deficits" during the 1980s and 1990s; hence, American private individuals and companies have paid out more to foreigners than foreign individuals and companies have paid to Americans.

As you probably know, another deficit also expanded during those years: the deficit in the U.S. government's budget. The U.S. government consistently has spent more than it takes in through taxation. This has been true almost every year since World War II, but beginning in 1982 the scale of such government deficits became significantly greater. This can be seen in Figure 16.1, which plots both the private payments balance and the U.S. government budget deficit since the mid-1970s. Until 1982 the government budget deficit ranged between −$40 billion and −$75 billion, but since 1982 it has ranged from about −$120 billion to about −$340 billion.

As Figure 16.1 makes clear, the United States began to operate with significant international private payments deficits, or balance of payments deficits, at about the same time that the U.S. government's budget deficits mushroomed. Most economists believe this is not a co-incidence, and they refer to it as the *twin deficit problem*. Because the U.S. government has run such sizable budget deficits, it has borrowed significant amounts from foreigners. To purchase large amounts of U.S. government debt in the form of Treasury securities, foreigners must

FIGURE 16.1   The Twin Deficits

In general, a rise in the federal government's budget deficit is followed by an increase in the U.S. merchandise trade deficit. *Source: Economic Report of the President, Washington, D.C.: U.S. Government Printing Office, 1996.*

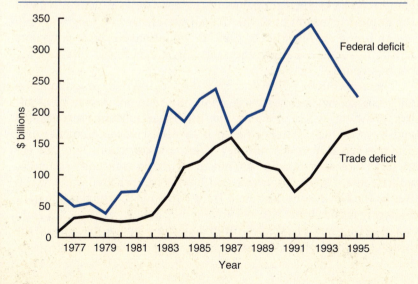

have dollars. Where do they get the dollars? The answer is that they get them from residents of the United States who purchase their products. By operating with significant negative merchandise trade balances that fuel the nation's private payments deficit, the United States effectively provides foreigners with the dollars they use to fund the U.S. government's budget deficit.

Clearly, the two deficits are related. But economists disagree about how to reduce their magnitudes. One perspective focuses on the merchandise trade deficit and taxes. According to this view, the problem is that imports are too high relative to exports and that the government's tax revenues are too low. Hence, one way to attack the twin deficit problem would be to raise import tariffs (taxes on imports) and impose quotas or other import restrictions. This would raise import prices, discouraging Americans from importing goods, and thereby improve the merchandise trade balance and reduce the magnitude of the private payments deficit. In addition, it would raise government tax revenues directly through the higher import taxes. Tax payments also might increase if such a move caused Americans to buy more domestically produced goods, thus raising the total amount of income subject to taxation.

Another perspective focuses on government spending and free trade. Those who promote this view contend that the key to reducing both deficits is for the U.S. government to cut spending and reduce the budget deficit directly. This would lessen the U.S. government's need to borrow from foreigners, thereby reducing the amount of resources that Americans have to transfer to other nations by running private payments deficits. This would reduce the burgeoning private payments deficit. Permitting free trade, with minimal import tariffs, would then let the private payments balance settle at whatever level was appropriate in light of the overall preferences of American and foreign residents. Most likely, the U.S. would have private payments deficits in some years; in others, it would experience private payments surpluses.

Because the two views are so radically different, proponents on both sides do not see eye-to-eye on appropriate policy actions to address the twin deficit problem. The American political process often tends to split the difference on such matters. Hence, in recent years Congress has imposed a number of import restrictions and has enacted tax increases. In addition, however, Congress recently sought to reduce federal spending levels and approved such free-trade initiatives as the North American Free Trade Agreement, which is intended to sharply reduce trade barriers among the United States, Mexico, and Canada. This mix of policies ultimately may reduce the size of the twin deficit problem.

POLICY NOTEBOOK

Should We Worry That America's Continuing Trade Deficit Indicates a Weak Economy?

The current account in the United States has been in deficit most of the time since the late 1970s. This is not something new. During the 1880s the United States had many years of current account deficits. They were matched equally by capital account surpluses, as the rest of the world sent capital to finance the building of the railroads and the development of the trans-Mississippi west. By the early 1900s the United States had accumulated a long string of current account surpluses. By World War I, Americans had repaid all their external debt and had become a net creditor. In 1980 the United States was the world's largest creditor; by 1986 it was the worlds largest debtor nation. But, remember a very important identity: Whenever America has a deficit in its current account, its capital account and official settlements balance together must show a surplus.

Contrary to popular belief, the United States does not have a trade deficit because it has a weak economy and cannot compete in world markets. Rather, the United States appears to be a good place to invest capital because there are strong prospects for growth and earnings opportunities. As long as foreigners wish to invest more in the United States than Americans wish to invest abroad, there will be a deficit in our current account balance. Americans are the beneficiaries of international capital flows. Otherwise stated, the current account deficit is required as long as foreigners want to invest (on net) more in the United States.

For Critical Analysis: *Why are politicians, nonetheless, so worried about the international trade deficit?*

FOREIGN EXCHANGE MARKETS

Another variable that must enter into any discussion of international transactions is the exchange value of the dollar relative to other nations' currencies. Recall from Chapter 3 that an *exchange rate* is the price of the dollar in terms of the currency of another country. There is an exchange rate for the dollar against every other nation in the world, and so there is no single exchange rate. Nevertheless, Figure 16.2 on page 456 displays the behavior of an exchange rate index for the dollar; this index measures the dollar's value in terms of the currencies of major trading partners of the United States. As you can see, the dollar's relative value has fallen in recent years. This means that it takes more dollars than before to buy other nations' currencies. That is, the dollar has *depreciated* in value. The recent performance of the value of the dollar

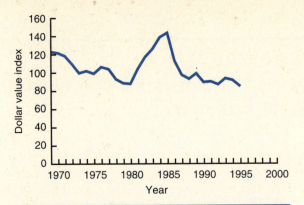

FIGURE 16.2 **The Changing Value of the Dollar**

This figure shows annual values of an index of the dollar's value relative to currencies of America's trading partners. *Source: Economic Report of the President,* Washington, D.C.: U.S. Government Printing Office, 1996.

contrasts with the early 1980s. As indicated in Figure 16.2, in the early 1980s the dollar's relative exchange value increased; the value of the dollar *appreciated* during this period.

How is the dollar's relative value determined? How are the dollar's exchange value and international payments balances related? Let's consider these questions in order.

The exchange rate is a price, and prices are determined in markets. The exchange value of the dollar relative to any other country's currency, therefore, must arise from the interplay of market forces. The markets that determine dollar exchange rate are **foreign exchange markets,** which are the markets in which individuals, businesses, governments, and central banks exchange national currencies.

foreign exchange markets
Markets in which individuals, businesses, governments, and central banks exchange the currencies of various countries.

Foreign Exchange Rates

Before we discuss foreign exchange markets, let's consider how we measure dollar exchange rates. For purposes of discussion, we shall confine our attention to the value of the dollar in terms of Japanese yen. In early 1992, $1 would have purchased about 125 yen. This meant that the exchange rate at that time was 125 yen per dollar, which we can write as 125 yen/$. But this also meant that 125 yen would have purchased $1, or that 1 yen could have purchased $1/125 = $0.008. And so another way to express the 1992 dollar–yen rate of exchange is as 0.008 dollars per yen, or 0.008 $/yen.

Four years later, $1 would purchase only about 90 yen. Consequently, in early 1996 the exchange rate was 90 yen/$. Alternatively, we could state it as $1 per 90 yen, or 0.011 $/yen. The fact that the exchange rate in yen per dollar fell from 125 yen/$ to 90 yen/$ means that it took fewer yen to purchase dollars in 1996 as compared with 1992. Consequently, the yen's value *appreciated* relative to the dollar, and the dollar's value *depreciated* relative to the yen. This is reflected as well by the rise in the exchange rate expressed in dollars per yen, from 0.008 $/yen in 1992 to 0.011 $/yen in 1996. Because the dollar depreciated relative to the yen, it took more dollars to purchase yen in 1996 as compared with 1992.

Note that exchange rates always can be expressed in two ways, because they measure the value of one nation's currency in terms of the currency of another nation. We must be careful to think about which of the two ways of expressing exchange rates we have in mind. Simply saying that the exchange rate "rose" or that the exchange rate "fell" has little meaning by itself unless we know which of the two measures applies. Throughout this chapter we shall look at the dollar–yen exchange rate from an American perspective: We shall express the exchange rate in terms of dollars that must be given up in exchange for yen, such as the 0.008 $/yen exchange rate of 1992 and the 0.011 $/yen exchange rate of 1996.

The Demand for and Supply of Foreign Exchange

As we discussed in Chapter 1, a key reason to hold money is that it is used as a medium of exchange. Hence, an American's primary rationale for wishing to obtain the currency of another nation is a desire to purchase goods, services, or assets produced by or issued in that nation.

Imports and the Demand for Foreign Currency
To think about the factors affecting the amount of a foreign currency, such as the yen, that an American citizen might wish to obtain, consider the following example. Suppose that an American consumer purchased a Japanese-manufactured automobile in 1992. The price at which the Japanese producer transferred the automobile for sale in the United States was 2 million yen. At the 1992 exchange rate of 0.008 $/yen, the dollar price of the automobile therefore was equal to 2 million yen $\times$ 0.008 $/yen, or $16,000.

Now suppose that the same consumer contemplated purchasing the same basic automobile in 1996. Suppose further that the yen price of the automobile had remained unchanged at 2 million yen during the intervening years. The exchange rate, however, rose to about 0.011 $/yen. As a result, the dollar price of the automobile would have increased to 2,000,000 yen $\times$ 0.011 $/yen = $22,000. Hence, in dollar terms the price of the automobile would have risen by $6,000, or a 37.5 percent price increase.

When confronted with such a significant increase in the dollar price of the Japanese-made automobile, the U.S. consumer would be more likely to buy an automobile manufactured in the United States instead. Furthermore, other Americans would tend to reduce their consumption of goods manufactured in Japan, all of which would have experienced similar dollar-price increases. As a result, American import businesses would cut back on their orders for Japanese-manufactured goods, which these importers purchase from Japanese businesses using yen they acquire in the foreign exchange market. Consequently, the quantity of yen demanded in the foreign exchange market would decline as a result of the rise in the increase dollar–yen exchange rate from 0.008 $/yen to 0.011 $/yen. It follows that the *demand schedule* for yen slopes downward, as shown in Figure 16.3.

Though much of the demand for yen in exchange for dollars would arise because U.S. residents needed yen to purchase imports, this is not the only source of the demand for yen. American might wish to obtain yen to purchase Japanese financial assets or to make loans or even transfers to Japanese residents. In addition, residents of any country— including individuals who make a living by trading foreign currencies— may have holdings of dollars that they would like to convert to yen.

FIGURE 16.3   Market for Yen

The equilibrium dollar–yen exchange rate is determined at the point at which the demand and supply schedules for yen cross. Below the equilibrium exchange rate, there is an excess quantity of yen demanded, and so the exchange rate tends to rise. Above the equilibrium exchange rate, there is an excess quantity of yen supplied, and so the exchange rate tends to fall. In equilibrium, the quantity of yen demanded is equal to the quantity of yen supplied.

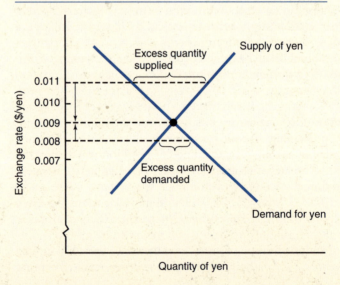

All of these factors contribute to the demand for yen in exchange for dollars.

Exports and the Supply of Foreign Currency   Now let's consider the effect of a change in the dollar–yen exchange rate from the perspective of Japanese residents. Suppose that a Japanese importing firm purchases American-made laptop computers for resale in Japan. Suppose also that a typical computer model has a dollar price of $2,000 and that this base price does not change between 1992 and 1996. At the 1992 exchange rate of 0.008 $/yen, the yen price of the laptop computer during that year is equal to $2,000/0.008 $/yen, or 250,000 yen. But in 1996, at the exchange rate of 0.011 $/yen, the same computer would sell at a yen price of $2,000/0.011 $/yen, or about 181,818 yen. And so, from the perspective of a Japanese consumer, the U.S. laptop computer's price would have fallen by 68,182 yen, or about 27.3 percent.

This sharp decline in the yen price of the American-made laptop computers would tend to induce increased Japanese purchases of these computers. Likewise, similar declines in the prices of other U.S. export goods would cause Japanese consumption of such exports to increase. Japanese importing businesses would raise their orders for U.S. export goods, which they would purchase using dollars they obtain in the foreign exchange market. These Japanese importers would supply more yen in exchange for dollars. Consequently, the rise in the dollar–yen exchange rate from 0.008 $/yen to 0.011 $/yen would increase the quantity of yen supplied in the foreign exchange market. As shown in Figure 16.3, the *supply schedule* for yen generally would slope upward.

Factors other than U.S. exports also affect the supply of yen. Japanese residents may exchange yen for dollars to purchase U.S. financial assets or to lend to or make transfers to American residents. Furthermore, international financial market traders may desire to reduce their holdings of yen and increase their holdings of dollars, perhaps because of speculation about future movements in the dollar–yen exchange rate. All these additional factors also help determine the shape and position of the yen supply schedule.

The Equilibrium Foreign Exchange Rate   Figure 16.2 also depicts the determination of an *equilibrium exchange rate* for the yen and the dollar. This is the rate of exchange of dollars for yen at which the quantity of yen demanded by American and other foreign exchange market traders is equal to the amount of yen supplied by Japanese residents and other traders in the foreign exchange market.

In Figure 16.3, we assume that the equilibrium exchange rate is 0.009 $/yen. Note that if the exchange rate happened to lie below this level, perhaps at the rate of 0.008 $/yen, there would be more yen demanded than supplied. Some U.S. residents or other traders who desired to obtain yen with dollars would be unable to purchase yen at this exchange rate, and so they would be obliged to offer a higher exchange rate. As a result, the market exchange rate would rise toward the equilibrium rate of 0.009 $/yen. In contrast, if the exchange rate rose above the equilibrium level, say to 0.011 $/yen, there would be more yen supplied than demanded, and the exchange rate would tend to fall back toward the equilibrium rate of 0.009 $/yen.

4

How are exchange rates determined?   Rates of exchange for national currencies are determined in foreign exchange markets. A nation's exchange rate adjusts to equate the quantity of a nation's currency demanded by residents of another country with the quantity supplied by its own residents in exchange for the other country's currency.

FIXED VERSUS FLEXIBLE EXCHANGE RATES

A key decision that any national government must make is whether or not to let demand and supply forces in the foreign exchange markets determine the value of its currency. Most governments do not want their currency exchange rates to vary with changes in demand and supply. These governments, alone or in conjunction with their nations' central banks, undertake actions to maintain **fixed exchange rates,** which are exchange rates that governments maintain at artificial levels by buying or selling currencies in foreign exchange markets.

     In contrast, other governments have adopted **floating exchange rates.** This means that the value of their currency adjusts flexibly in the private marketplace. That is, the exchange rates for such currencies "float" to whatever level demand and supply conditions in foreign exchange markets dictate.

fixed exchange rates   Artificial levels of exchange rates that governments maintain by buying or selling currencies in foreign exchange markets.

floating exchange rates
Exchange rate levels that are attained through private markets.

Fixed Exchange Rates

Why might a government wish to peg its currency's exchange rate? The main reason is that the exchange rate influences the country's merchandise trade balance and its private payments balance. For instance, if the dollar–yen exchange rate rises from 0.009 $/yen to 0.012 $/yen, then it takes more dollars to obtain yen, and fewer yen to obtain dollars. This depreciation of the dollar would discourage Americans from importing more Japanese goods or from purchasing additional Japanese financial assets. At the same time, such an exchange rate change would tend to induce Japanese residents to buy more U.S. exports and to acquire additional U.S. financial instruments. Following the passage of time, the result generally would be an improvement in the U.S. merchandise trade balance and private payments balance and a worsening of the Japanese merchandise trade balance and private payments balance.

In a fixed exchange rate system, a nation's government or its central bank seeks to keep the country's exchange rate from becoming "too high" or "too low" relative to a level that the government regards as "just right." A government makes this judgment based on its trade and private payments balance objectives. It seeks to keep the exchange rate at a level it deems appropriate in light of these goals.

Fixing the Exchange Rate   How can a government keep its currency's exchange rate fixed? To answer this question, suppose that the United States wishes to keep the dollar–yen exchange rate at a fixed level of 0.009 $/yen. As shown in Figure 16.4, if the demand and supply schedules happen to intersect at this desired exchange rate, then the Federal Reserve and Treasury would be satisfied. They would not need to conduct any policy actions because private market forces have yielded the desired result.

FIGURE 16.4   Keeping the Exchange Rate Fixed

If the demand for yen were to increase, then the equilibrium exchange rate would tend to rise from 0.009 $/yen to 0.012 $/yen. Suppose, however, that the Fed or the Treasury wishes to keep the exchange rate at 0.009 $/yen. At this exchange rate 45 billion yen are supplied in the private market, but 47 billion yen are demanded. The Fed or the Treasury could satisfy the excess quantity demanded in the market by supplying 2 billion yen, thereby shifting the market supply schedule to the right by exactly this amount.

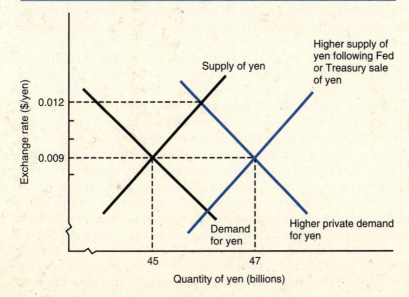

But if the demand for yen increases, then absent any Fed or Treasury actions the exchange rate will tend to increase toward a new equilibrium level of 0.012 $/yen, as shown in Figure 16.3. Otherwise, if the exchange rate remains at 0.009 $/yen, there would be 47 billion yen demanded but only 45 billion yen supplied.

So how could the Fed or Treasury keep the exchange rate from rising? The answer is that either or both institutions could supply the additional 2 billion yen demanded to the foreign exchange market at the fixed exchange rate of 0.009 $/yen. They would draw upon their own reserves of yen to do this. This action would cover the excess amount of yen demanded at the fixed exchange rate and thereby keep the exchange rate from increasing. Note, however, that such a policy can work only as long as the Fed or Treasury has sufficient reserves of yen. A common problem for governments and central banks when they try to keep exchange rates fixed for long intervals is that they run out of reserves of other currencies.

Pros and Cons of Fixed Exchange Rates   The need to have sufficient government and central bank reserves of other nations' currencies is one key problem with a fixed exchange rate system. Imagine what would happen if the demand for yen were to continue to rise in Figure 16.4. The Fed and the Treasury would have to supply more and more yen to keep the exchange rate fixed. This can be a costly activity, and eventually both institutions would find their reserves of yen running low. Once those reserves were depleted neither institution would be able to maintain the fixed exchange rate any longer.

capital controls Legal restrictions that hinder private individuals from obtaining foreign currencies.

This problem induces many nations to supplement a fixed exchange rate system with **capital controls.** These are legal restrictions on the ability of a nation's private residents to obtain foreign currencies. For instance, if the United States desires to keep the dollar–yen exchange rate fixed, one way to avoid losses of Fed and Treasury reserves of yen is to keep the rise in the demand for yen shown in Figure 16.3 from occurring. This might be accomplished by making it illegal for Americans to hold yen. Efforts to enforce such capital controls, however, require expenditure of real resources to police the restrictions. They also restrict the freedom of private individuals. Consequently, this is another drawback of fixed exchange rates.

A fixed exchange rate system does have an important advantage, however. It reduces the extent of *foreign exchange risks* faced by consumers and businesses. Recall from Chapter 4 that such risks arise because unexpected changes in exchange rates can affect the value of one's income or wealth. If exchange rates are fixed, the potential for exchange rate volatility is significantly reduced, thereby reducing risks of such losses.

Experience with Fixed Exchange Rates   Governments around the world have adopted systems of fixed exchange rates throughout history.

From the 1820s until World War I, many countries fixed the rates of exchange of their currencies relative to the British pound, which in turn had a fixed rate of exchange relative to gold. For over two decades following World War II most nations used a similar system, known as the *Bretton Woods System*, with the U.S. dollar replacing the pound as the central currency of the system.

A problem that any system of fixed exchange rates tends to experience is that some nations gain at the expense of others if they change the values of their currencies periodically. An illustration of this is the recent experience of the *European Monetary System*. This is a

GLOBAL NOTEBOOK

Will Europe Ever Have a Single Currency?

Currently, there are 15 members in the European Union (EU), each with its own currency. According to current projections, the EU will use a single currency, perhaps called the *euro* (European currency unit) sometime by the end of this century. There are many observers, however, who doubt that Europe will ever have a single currency. They point out that a single currency is equivalent to a permanent, fixed exchange rate system, similar to what we have within the United States. After all, there is a fixed rate of exchange between dollars in California and dollars in New York. It is one to one. So the *euro* used in Germany will have the same value as *a euro* used in France. This means that the 15 separate countries cannot have 15 separate monetary policies, just as the 50 separate states cannot have 50 separate monetary policies within the United States. There can only be one central bank. Under what circumstances will 15 separate economies with 15 separate political agendas agree to one central bank? Perhaps none.

There is also another serious problem that will have to be faced if a single currency is used through the EU. Currently, Belgium,

Italy, and Sweden have public debts and government-provided pension plan liabilities that are many times one year's GDP. That means that the risk of default in Sweden, Italy, and Belgium on government debt is much higher than, say, in Germany. Nonetheless, despite the default risk, residents of the former countries still buy their own government's bonds if they are worried about the exchange rate risks of investing money in other EU countries. Once exchange rate risks are eliminated through a single currency, it is not clear how many of the residents of Europe's weakest countries will continue to invest in their own government's bonds. At the same interest rate, they will prefer to purchase German government bonds. So, interest rates in the weaker European countries may rise dramatically if a single currency ever comes in to being.

For Critical Analysis: *Initially each country would have to decide on a conversion rate from its own currency to the new single currency. Who should decide what these 15 separate exchange rates should be?*

fixed exchange rate system that many European nations have tried to maintain; the German mark functions as the central currency of the system, but without any link to gold. In the early 1990s the economies of Italy and the United Kingdom were slipping into recession, and both were able to shore up their economies by permitting their currency values to depreciate relative to the mark and other European currencies. These actions increased Italian and British exports while reducing their imports. Of course, the actions were not necessarily in the best interests of their European trading partners, who tended to experience higher imports and reduced exports as a result.

Flexible Exchange Rates

In light of the drawbacks of trying to keep exchange rates fixed, in recent decades a number of nations have given up on the idea of trying to keep their currency values unchanged. They have let exchange rates for their currencies float in the foreign exchange markets.

Pros and Cons of Floating Exchange Rates
There are several advantages of floating exchange rates. Such an approach requires no Treasury or Fed expenses for foreign exchange trading and entails no losses of foreign exchange reserves. It saves the United States and other nations from having to go to the trouble to coordinate efforts to maintain artificial rates of exchange for their currencies. It also eliminates any concern that trading partners may try to gain by intentionally permitting currency values to fall. Many economists feel that another argument in favor of floating exchange rates is that letting private markets determine exchange rates sends very clear signals to central banks about how inflationary their policies can be. For instance, if the value of the dollar were to decline precipitously relative to other nations' currencies, this would indicate that the Fed has created too many dollars and thereby has pursued an overly inflationary monetary policy.

There is one obvious drawback to floating exchange rates: Letting private markets determine currency exchange rates can create volatility in such rates. Such volatility can lead to significant foreign exchange risks for consumers and businesses. As discussed in Chapter 4, to a large extent traders can hedge against such risks by using forward contracts and other derivative instruments. Nevertheless, time and resources must be expended to enter into such contracts.

Experience with Floating Exchange Rates
As Figure 16.2 on page 456 indicated, since the end of the Bretton Woods fixed exchange rate system in 1971, the dollar's exchange value has been quite variable. This has forced Americans to hedge against foreign exchange

risks, which in turn has helped fuel the development of the foreign exchange derivative instruments discussed in Chapter 4.

Note that during the first half of the 1980s the dollar's value in terms of other major currencies appreciated considerably. Since that time, however, the general trend for the dollar's value has been downward. This reflects the large merchandise trade deficits and private payments deficits that have existed since that time. Because Americans tend to purchase more goods and assets from abroad relative to the goods and assets that foreigners purchase in the United States, Americans on net have demanded more of other nations' currencies. This has resulted in a general rise in the values of other nations' currencies relative to that of the dollar. The result has been a relative decline in the dollar's value in terms of the currencies of those nations.

5

Should exchange rates be fixed or flexible?   Under a fixed exchange rate system, a nation's government seeks to maintain the exchange rate of its currency at a level that may or may not be consistent with private market forces. This usually requires that the central bank buy or sell currencies in foreign exchange markets. Problems can arise with a fixed exchange rate system if central banks have insufficient reserves of other currencies to maintain the intended exchange rate levels. In that case the nation may resort to capital controls, which restricts economic freedom. The key advantage of a fixed exchange rate is that it sharply reduces the potential for losses arising from foreign exchange risks, which must be faced under a floating exchange rate.

THE FED AND THE VALUE OF THE DOLLAR

Should the Fed try to influence the dollar's exchange value? This is a question that sharply divides economists. Nevertheless, since the mid-1980s the United States, Japan, and other major nations have tried to influence their exchange rates from time to time. Although these nations do not try to maintain fixed exchange rates, neither do they always allow exchange rates to float freely.

Today's System of Managed Exchange Rates

For over a decade now most nations have informally adopted a system of **managed exchange rates.** Under such a system, national governments and/or central banks permit their exchange rates to float much of the time, but occasionally they buy or sell currencies in foreign exchange markets in an effort to slow or reverse upward or downward trends in exchange rates.

managed exchange rates   A term referring to today's informal system in which governments and central banks generally allow exchange rates to float, although intervening in foreign exchange markets from time to time in efforts to slow or reverse exchange rate movements.

**foreign exchange interven-
tions** Occasional governmental or central bank purchases or sales of foreign
currencies that are intended
to increase or reduce the relative values of their own
currencies.

Fed Foreign Exchange Market Interventions   Such occasional
episodes of central bank or governmental foreign exchange market
trading are **foreign exchange interventions.** In the United States, the
Federal Reserve is the authority responsible for conducting such interventions. It may do so on its own, trading currencies it holds on its own
account. Or it may do so at the direction of the U.S. Treasury, in which
case it trades currencies the Treasury holds on account with the Federal
Reserve Bank of New York.

During the late 1980s the Fed and the Treasury sought to push
the dollar's value down relative to other major currencies following
a steady rise in its value (see Figure 16.2 on page 456). To help raise
the relative values of other currencies such as the Japanese yen and
the German mark, the Fed purchased those currencies with dollars.
By the mid-1990s, however, the Fed directed its efforts toward slowing a swift and steady decline in the dollar's value, and both
agencies sold foreign currencies in their efforts to accomplish this
objective.

Do Interventions Accomplish Much?

In a 1995 study Karen
Lewis of the University of Pennsylvania analyzed data from foreign
exchange market interventions that the Fed conducted on its own or
on behalf of the Treasury in the late 1980s and early 1990s. She found
that such interventions typically were associated with movements in
exchange rates. Fed purchases of other currencies entailed selling
dollars, which in turn increased the U.S. monetary base and the
quantity of money and led to declines in the value of the dollar relative to other currencies. Fed sales of other currencies reduced the
U.S. monetary base and the quantity of money and increased the
value of the dollar.

Less clear, however, is the long-run effectiveness of Fed interventions. Michael Bordo of Rutgers University and Anna Schwartz of the
National Bureau of Economic Research did an earlier study that questioned the significance of the exchange rate effects of such interventions. For instance, they found that during *all* of 1989 the Fed purchased a total of nearly $18 billion in foreign currencies. Yet, during
the single month of April 1989, the average *daily* trading volume of
foreign exchange trading was about $129 billion. The Fed's interven-
tions amounted to barely a drop in the bucket in the foreign exchange
markets.

Can the Fed Go it Alone in Today's World?

In recent years most central banks have found that acting alone to try to
influence exchange rates can be an exercise in futility. For instance, on

POLICY NOTEBOOK
Should the Fed Really Worry About the Weak Dollar?

It took 400 years for Rome's currency to disappear as the world's strongest. Britain saw its currency, the pound sterling, lose its world dominance in 50 years. What about the United States? At first blush, the dollar appears strong. It accounts for over 60 percent of foreign exchange reserves and over 50 percent of global private financial wealth. Additionally, almost 70 percent of world trade is invoiced in dollars, as well as 75 percent of international bank lending. Not bad for a country that accounts for only 20 percent of world output and 14 percent of world exports.

The value of the dollar with respect to the world's two other leading currencies, the Japanese yen and German mark, has fallen rather steadily since 1985. There are several reasons why the yen and the mark have become so strong and the dollar so weak. Both Japan and Germany have had lower rates of inflation than the United States. Also, at least in Germany, investors have found higher rates of return.

To be sure, American tourists going to Germany and Japan are outraged. Americans who buy BMWs, Mercedes, and Toyotas are not as happy as they would be if the dollar were stronger. There is a flip side to this situation, however. Foreigners now find our products cheaper. So employees and shareholders in American companies that export find they are better off. But we still have to ask a larger question: Is the dollar really so weak?

If you look at Figure 16.5, you see the dollar expressed in terms of an index of 45 currencies. The dollar actually became stronger in the first part of 1995, rather than weaker. Weighted against all of the U.S.'s trading partners, the dollar has been relatively stable since 1988. In the last few years it has strengthened considerably against Canada and Mexico.

For Critical Analysis: *Why would a lower rate of inflation in Japan lead to a weaker dollar?*

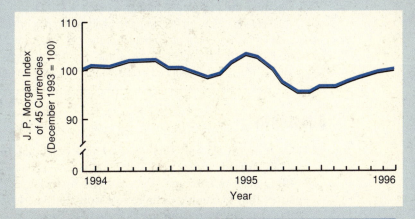

FIGURE 16.5   Recent Movements in the Dollar's Value
This figure shows how the dollar's value, expressed in terms of an index of 45 currencies, recently changed. *Source:* J. P. Morgan company. Federal Reserve Board.

April 3, 1995 the Federal Reserve Bank of New York's trading desk took the unusual step of buying dollars with yen in the Tokyo foreign exchange market, in the hope that such a "dramatic" move would raise the dollar's value. The result was a further decline in the dollar's value that day, which was the opposite of what the Fed and the Treasury had intended.

Even coordinated interventions by major central banks are not always able to influence exchange rates in today's world. For example, two day's after the Fed's unsuccessful April 3, 1995, intervention effort, the German Bundesbank, the Bank of Japan, and the Fed all intervened in foreign exchange markets in an effort to reverse a continuing fall in the dollar's value. Again, the result was a further decline that day. In the end, the three central banks spent over $30 billion of their currency reserves trying to prop up the dollar's value between January and April of 1995 and ultimately incurred a trading loss of $2 billion as a result of the dollar's further decline.

Generally speaking, all that central banks can hope to accomplish with interventions in today's world is to slow the pace of upward or downward movements in exchange rates. Individually, they can only rarely hope to achieve long-lived effects on exchange rates. Coordinated actions are more likely to have longer lasting effects. But as central banks learned in the spring of 1995, even together they have limited ability to influence foreign exchange markets where trading volumes dwarf the currency reserves of the central banks.

6

What role does the Fed play in foreign exchange markets?   The Fed has the ability to intervene in foreign exchange markets by buying or selling foreign currencies on its own account or on behalf of the U.S. Treasury. Although there is evidence that such interventions have some short-term effects on the dollar's value, rarely have most recent Fed interventions had long-run effects.

SUMMARY

1. **Why Individuals and Businesses Hold Financial Instruments Issued in Other Nations:** While some may try to earn higher returns by holding such instruments, international financial arbitrage typically ensures that average exchange rate adjusted yields on instruments with similar maturities and risks are equal. Hence, the main rationale for holding instruments issued in other nations is that doing so can diversify against risks.

2. **Ways in Which World Financial Markets Have Become More Interconnected:** The existence of Eurocurrency markets allows traders to transfer funds from financial instruments denominated one nation's currency into financial instruments denominated in the currency of another nation. This facilitates international financial arbitrage across many nation's money and capital markets. In addition, improvements in computer and communications technology have enabled residents of many nations to trade directly in the financial markets of countries other than those in which they reside.

3. **How Economists Measure International Transactions:** Flows of payments into and out of a nation appear in the nation's balance of payments accounts, which is composed of three key accounts. The current account records income flows and transactions related to international trade and transfers of goods and services. The capital account tracks private asset transactions, and the official settlements balance records governmental asset transactions.

4. **How Exchange Rates Are Determined:** The interacting forces of supply and demand in foreign exchange markets determine exchange rates. In the foreign exchange market for a given nation's currency, the exchange rate adjusts to equate the quantity of the nation's currency demanded by foreigners with the quantity supplied by the nation's residents.

5. **Fixed Versus Flexible Exchange Rates:** The main drawback of flexible exchange rates is that the resulting exchange rate volatility exposes consumers and businesses to foreign exchange risks. They can offset many of these risks by using other financial instruments, such as derivatives contracts, but doing so requires expending time and resources. For this reason a number of nations attempt to maintain fixed exchange rates. They face problems in such efforts, however. Reserves of foreign currencies can become depleted when sales are necessary to maintain desired exchange rates. In such case the nation often must resort to capital controls to limit its citizen's abilities to hold foreign assets.

6. **The Fed's Role in Foreign Exchange Markets:** In today's world of managed exchange rates, the Fed occasionally intervenes in foreign exchange markets, buying or selling foreign currencies on its own account or on behalf of the U.S. Treasury. Such interventions seek to slow or reverse trends in the value of the dollar relative to other currencies. While there is some evidence that Fed interventions do cause short-term changes in the dollar's relative value, in recent years the Fed has found that it can rarely induce long-lived changes in the exchange rates. Interventions that are coordinated with other

central banks often are more effective, but even such coordinated efforts sometimes fall short.

QUESTIONS AND PROBLEMS

1. Markets for financial instruments such as stocks and bonds from around the world have become increasingly integrated. Nevertheless, markets for the services provided by financial intermediaries such as banks, insurance companies, and broker-dealers continue to be localized within nations. Recall from Chapter 2 that financial intermediaries exist to deal with adverse selection and moral hazard problems that arise from asymmetric information. Even in the absence of legal and regulatory barriers to international competition, are there any reasons to suspect that financial intermediaries might tend to specialize in national markets? Explain your reasoning.

2. Why is the U.S. merchandise trade deficit a potentially misleading indicator of U.S. international payments flows?

3. Explain in your own words why, in the absence of any official settlements transactions or statistical discrepancies, the current account balance and capital account balance should sum to zero.

4. Explain why the demand for Belgian francs is negatively related to the dollar price of the Belgian franc. In addition, explain why the supply of Belgian francs is positively related to the dollar price of the Belgian franc.

5. In 1995 the Mexican government found that it was running out of dollar reserves that it could use to try to keep the exchange rate for the Mexican peso fixed relative to the U.S. dollar. It decided to let the value of the peso depreciate considerably. Could the Mexican government have imposed capital controls instead? Why do you suppose that it did not do this?

6. In what ways have recent changes in the world financial environment reduced the Fed's ability to influence interest rates and exchange rates?

Glossary

Accounting risk The possibility that the market value of a foreign-currency-denominated financial instrument may change as a result of variations in exchange rate, even if the interest return on the instrument remains the same.

Actuary An individual who specializes in using mathematical and statistical principles to calculate insurance premiums and to estimate an insurance company's net worth.

Adaptive expectations Forecasts based only on past information.

Adjustable-rate mortgages (ARMs) Mortgages whose interest rates vary with other interest rates or indexes of interest rates.

Adverse selection The likelihood that those who desire to issue financial instruments have in mind using the funds they receive for unworthy, high-risk projects.

Aggregate demand schedule Combinations of price levels and amounts of aggregate real output that all individuals are willing to purchase given the total quantity of money in the economy.

Aggregate supply schedule Combinations of price levels and amounts of aggregate real output that all businesses are willing and able to produce given the state of technology and availability of factors of production.

American option An option in which the holder has the right to exercise the right to buy or sell a security any time before and/or including the date on which the contract expires.

Annuities Financial instruments that guarantee the holder fixed or variable payments at some future date.

Anticipated-income approach A depository institution management philosophy that calls for depository institutions to make their loans more liquid by issuing them in the form of installment loans that generate income in the form of periodic payments of interest and principal.

Appreciation A rise in the value of one currency relative to another.

Asset Anything owned by a person or business that has a value.

Asset-liability management approach A depository institution management philosophy that emphasizes the simultaneous coordination of both the asset and liability sides of the institution's balance sheet.

Asymmetric directive An FOMC policy directive that gives the chair of the Fed's Board of Governors the power to authorize Trading Desk actions designed to raise or to reduce the federal funds rate.

Asymmetric information Possession of information by one party in a financial transaction but not by the other party.

Automated bill payment Direct payment of bills by depository institutions on behalf of their customers.

Automated clearing house (ACH) A computer-based facility for clearing and settlement that replaces check transactions with electronic credits and debits.

Automated-teller-machine (ATM) networks Depository institution computer terminals that customers activate with magnetically encoded bank cards.

Automated-transfer-system (ATS) accounts Combined interest-bearing savings accounts and noninterest-bearing checking accounts in which the former is drawn upon automatically when the latter is overdrawn.

Balance of payments accounts A tabulation of all transactions between the residents in one nation and the residents of all the other nations in the world.

Bank Insurance Fund (BIF) The FDIC's fund that covers insured deposits of commercial banks.

Bank run An unexpected series of cash withdrawals at a depository institution that can cause it to fail.

Banker's acceptance A bank loan typically used by a company to finance storage or shipment of goods.

Barter The direct exchange of one good for another without the use of money.

Base year Year in which nominal GDP and real GDP are equal, so that the value of the GDP deflator is equal to 1 for that year.

Basis point One hundredth of one percent.

Best-efforts deal An investment banking arrangement in which the investment bank has an option to buy a portion of the issuing firm's securities but is not required to do so.

Bimetallic standard A commodity standard in which the value of money depends on the values of two precious metals, such as gold and silver.

Board of Governors of the Federal Reserve System A group of seven individuals appointed by the president and confirmed by the Senate that, under the terms of the Banking Act of 1935, has key policy-making responsibilities within the Federal Reserve System.

Book-entry security systems Computer system used by Federal Reserve to maintain records of sales of treasury securities and interest and principal payments.

Borrowed reserves Reserves that the Federal Reserve supplies directly to depository institutions by extending discount window loans to them.

Branch banking A depository institution organizational structure in which institutions operate offices at a number of geographic locations.

Brokers Institutions that specialize in matching buyers and sellers of financial instruments in secondary markets.

Bullion Uncoined gold or silver used as money.

Business finance companies Finance companies that specialize in making loans to small businesses.

Call option An option contract giving the holder the right to purchase a financial instrument at a specific price.

Capital account The balance of payments account that records all nongovernmental international asset transactions.

Capital controls Legal restrictions that hinder private individuals from obtaining foreign currencies.

Capital gain A rise in the value of a financial instrument as compared with its market value as of the date it was purchased.

Capital goods Goods that may be used to produce other goods or services in the future.

Capital loss A loss in financial wealth resulting from a decline in the market value of a financial instrument.

Capital market Market for a financial instrument with a maturity of one year or more.

Capital requirements Minimum equity capital standards that regulators impose upon depository institutions.

Cash assets Depository institution assets that function as a medium of exchange.

Cash items in process of collection Checks deposited with a bank for immediate credit but not yet cleared for final payment to the bank; usually referred to simply as "cash items."

Central bank contract A legally binding agreement between a government and a central banking official that holds the official responsible for a nation's inflation performance.

Certificates of deposit (CDs) Time deposits issued by banks and other depository institutions, many of which are negotiable instruments traded in secondary markets.

Charter A governmental license to open and operate a bank.

Churning Excessive buying and selling of securities resulting in little net change in the Fed's holdings.

Clearing House Interbank Payments System (CHIPS) A large-dollar wire transfer system linking about 120 depository institutions that enables them to transfer large sums of money, primarily for foreign exchange and Eurodollar transactions.

Closed economies National economies in which insignificant portions of economic activity entail international transactions in goods, services, and financial assets.

Closed-end funds Mutual funds that sell nonredeemable shares whose market values vary with the market values of the underlying mix of financial instruments held by the mutual funds.

Coinsurance An insurance policy feature in which a policyholder pays a fixed percentage of a loss above a deductible.

Collateral Assets that a borrower pledges as security in the event the borrower fails to repay the loan principal or interest.

Collateralized mortgage obligations (CMOs) Mortgage-backed derivatives that split regular principal and interest payments from pools of mortgages into separate payment streams that are paid to CMO holders at varying intervals.

Commercial and industrial (C & I) loans Loans made by commercial banks and other depository institutions to businesses.

Commercial banks Depository financial institutions that offer checking deposits and which specialize in making commercial loans.

Commercial loans Long-term loans made by banks to businesses.

Commercial paper A short-term debt instrument issued by businesses in lieu of borrowing from banks.

Commodity money A good with a nonmonetary value that also is used as money.

Commodity standard A money unit whose value is fully or partially backed by the value of some other physical good such as gold or silver.

Common stock Shares of corporate ownership that entitle the owner to vote on management issues but which offer no guarantees of dividends or of residual value in the event of corporate bankruptcy.

Confirmed credit lines Depository institution commitments to provide an individual or a business with a fixed amount of credit, upon demand, within some short-term interval.

Conservative central banker An individual appointed as a central banking official who dislikes inflation more than an average citizen.

Consumer finance companies Finance companies that specialize in making loans to individuals for the purchase of durable goods or for home improvements.

Consumer loans Loans that banks and other institutions make to individuals.

Contributory pensions Pensions funded by both employer and employee contributions.

Controllable liabilities Liabilities whose dollar amounts banks can directly manage.

Conversion-of-funds approach A depository institution management philosophy under which managers try to fund assets of specific maturities by issuing liabilities with like maturities.

Core capital Defined by current capital requirements as shareholders' equity plus retained earnings.

Corporate bonds Long-term debt instruments of corporations.

Correspondent balances Deposit accounts that banks hold with other banks.

Countercyclical monetary policy Fed actions that reduce the extent of up and down movements in economic activity.

Coupon return A fixed interest return that a bond yields each year.

Coupon yield equivalent An annualized T-bill rate that can be compared with annual yields on other financial instruments.

Covered interest parity If no barriers exist to international financial transactions and a forward exchange market exists, then the interest rate on an American bond should be equal to the interest rate on a foreign bond, plus a forward discount.

Credit multiplier A number that tells how much total loans and securities at depository institutions will change in response to a change in the monetary base.

Credit risk The risk of loss when one party to an exchange fails to honor the terms under which the exchange was to take place

Credit union A type of depository institution that accepts deposits from and makes loans only to a closed group of individuals who are eligible for membership.

Credit-scoring models Statistical procedures used for assessing the characteristics of loan applicants to evaluate their overall credit-worthiness.

Currency Coins and paper money.

Currency risk The possibility that exchange rate movements may affect the underlying returns on financial instruments.

Current account The balance of payments account that tabulates international trade and transfers of goods and services and flows of income.

Current yield The coupon return on a bond divided by the bond's market price.

Daylight overdrafts Depository institution overdraws of their reserve deposit accounts at Federal Reserve banks, which occur when they initiate wire transfers of funds that exceed in amounts their balances in those accounts.

Dealer A financial intermediary that buys and sells stocks and bonds from its own portfolio in pursuit of trading profits.

Deductible A fixed amount of an insured loss that a policyholder must pay before the insurer is obliged to make payments.

Default risk The chance that an individual or a firm that issues a financial instrument may be unable to honor its obligations to repay the principal and/or to make interest payments.

Demand deposits Noninterest-bearing checking accounts.

Demand schedule for reserves A graphical depiction of the inverse relationship between the total amount of reserves demanded by depository institutions and the federal funds rate.

Deposit expansion multiplier A number that tells how much aggregate transactions deposits at all depository institutions will change in response to a change in total reserves of these institutions.

Deposit insurance premium The price that depositor institutions pay to the FDIC's insurance fund in exchange for a guarantee of federal insurance of covered deposits that they issue.

Depository financial institutions Financial institutions that offer checking and savings deposits and that legally must hold reserves on deposit with Federal Reserve banks or in their vaults.

Depreciation A decline in the value of one currency relative to another.

Derivative securities Financial instruments whose returns depend on the returns of other financial instruments.

Derivatives credit risks Risks arising from the potential default by a counterparty in a derivative contract, or from unexpected changes in credit exposure because of changes in yields of instruments on which derivative yields depend.

Derivatives market risks Risks arising from variations in aggregate derivatives market liquidity, payments-system breakdowns, abnormal price changes at the time of settlement, or of spillovers across markets.

Derivatives operating risks Risks arising from lack of adequate management controls or from managerial unfamiliarity with derivative instruments.

Discount broker A broker that specializes only in trading on clients' behalf

Discount rate The rate of interest that the Federal Reserve charges to lend to a depository institution.

Discounted present value The value today of a payment to be received at a future date.

Disintermediation A situation in which customers of depository institutions withdraw funds from their deposit accounts and use them to purchase financial instruments directly.

Dividends Periodic payments to holders of firms' equities.

Divisia aggregates Measures of money that weight individual assets according to the frequency with which they are used to make purchases.

Dual banking system A regulatory structure in which both the states and the federal government grant charters to banks.

Duration A measure of the average time spanning all payments of principal and interest on a financial instrument.

Dutch auction An auction in which the winning bidders all receive a return consistent with the last accepted bid.

Economies of scale The reduction that can be achieved in the average cost of managing funds by pooling savings together and spreading the management costs across many savers.

Efficient-structure theory A theory of depository institution market structure in which greater market concentration and higher depository institution profits arise from the fact that when there are few depository institutions, they can operate more efficiently in loan and deposit markets than if there are a large number of institutions.

Equation of exchange A definitional relationship in which the quantity of money multiplied by the income velocity of money must equal real GDP multiplied by the GDP price deflator.

Equities Shares of ownership, such as corporate stock, issued by business firms.

Equity capital The excess of assets over liabilities, or net worth.

Eurodollars Dollar-denominated deposits located outside the United States.

European option An option in which the holder has the right to exercise the right to buy or sell only on the day that the contract expires.

Excess reserves Depository institution cash balances at Federal Reserve banks or in their own vaults that exceed the amount that they must hold to meet legal requirements.

Exchange rate The value of one currency in terms of another.

Exercise price The price at which the holder of an option has the right to buy or sell a financial instrument; also known as the strike price.

Expectations theory A theory of the term structure of interest rates that views bonds with differing maturities as perfect substitutes, so that their yields differ only because short-term interest rates are expected to rise or fall.

Explicit contracts Legally binding contracts that specify the wages that businesses must pay workers during a given period, such as a year or more.

Externalities Spillover effects that arise from the actions of one group of individuals on others who are otherwise not involved in the transactions.

Federal funds market Money market in which banks borrow from and lend to each other deposits that they hold at Federal Reserve banks.

Federal funds rate A short-term (usually overnight) interest rate on interbank loans in the United States.

Federal Open Market Committee (FOMC) A group composed of the seven governors and five of the twelve of the Federal Reserve bank presidents that determines how to conduct the Fed's open-market operations.

Federal Reserve banks Twelve central banking institutions that oversee regional activities of the Federal Reserve System.

Federal Reserve districts Twelve geographic regions of the Federal Reserve System.

Federal Reserve–Treasury Accord A 1951 agreement disassociating the Fed from a previous policy of pegging Treasury bill rates at artificially low levels.

Fedwire A large-dollar wire transfer system operated by the Federal Reserve that is open to all depository institutions that legally must maintain required reserves with the Fed.

Fiat money A token that has value only because it is accepted as money.

Finance company A financial institution that specializes primarily in making loans to relatively high-risk individuals and businesses.

Financial instruments Claims that those who lend their savings have on the future incomes of the borrowers who use those funds for investment.

Financial intermediation Indirect finance through the services of an institutional middleman who channels funds from savers to those who ultimately make capital investments.

Firm-commitment underwriting An investment banking arrangement in which the investment bank purchases and then resells to dealers and other purchasers all securities offered by a business.

Fiscal agent A term describing the Federal Reserve's role as an agent of the U.S. Treasury Department, in which the Fed issues, services, and redeems debts on the Treasury's behalf.

Fixed annuity A financial instrument, typically issued by an insurance company, that pays regular, constant installments to the owner beginning at a specific future date.

Fixed exchange rates Artificial levels of exchange rates that governments maintain by buying or selling currencies in foreign exchange markets.

Fixed-rate mortgages Mortgages with constant interest rates over their terms to maturity.

Floating exchange rates Exchange rate levels that are attained through private markets.

FOMC directive The official written instructions by the FOMC to the head of the Trading Desk at the Federal Reserve Bank of New York.

Foreign exchange interventions Occasional governmental or central bank purchases or sales of foreign currencies that are intended to increase or reduce the relative values of their own currencies.

Foreign exchange markets Markets in which individuals, businesses, governments, and central banks exchange the currencies of various countries.

Foreign exchange risk The possibility that changes in exchange rates may affect the market value of financial instruments.

Forward currency contract A contract that requires delivery of a foreign-currency-denominated financial instrument at a given price on a specific date.

Forward exchange rate The exchange rate at which a forward currency contract is traded.

Fractional-reserve banking A system in which banks hold reserves that are less than the amount of total deposits.

Free reserves Total excess reserves at depository institutions minus the total amount of reserves that depository institutions have borrowed from the Fed.

Free silver A late-nineteenth century idea for unlimited coinage of silver to meet the monetary needs of a growing U.S. economy.

Full-service broker A broker that offers a range of trading and consulting services.

Futures contract An agreement to deliver to another a specific amount of a standardized commodity or financial instrument at a designated future date.

Futures options Options to buy or sell futures contracts.

Gap management A technique of depository institution asset-liability management that focuses on the difference (the gap) between the quantity of assets subject to significant interest rate risk and the amount of liabilities subject to such risk.

GDP price deflator A measure of the overall level of prices for a given period; equal to nominal GDP divided by real GDP.

Gold standard A monetary system in which the value of money is linked to value of gold.

Gross domestic product (GDP) The total value of a nation's output of final goods and services during a given period.

Hedge A financial strategy that reduces the risk of capital losses arising from interest rate risk.

Historical value accounting A traditional accounting procedure in which a depository institution's assets are valued at original values.

Illiquidity A situation in which a depository institution lacks the cash assets required to meet requests for depositor withdrawals.

Implicit contracts Tacit or unspoken understandings between companies and workers that the the workers' wages will not be reduced even during periods of low demand for the companies' products.

Income velocity of money Average number of times that a unit of money is used to purchase newly produced goods and services during a particular interval.

Insider information Information that is available to inside directors and officers of a corporation but that generally is unavailable to the general public or to depository institutions who lend to the corporation.

Insolvency A situation in which the value of a depository institution's assets is less than the value of its liabilities.

Installment credit Loans to individual consumers requiring the borrower to make periodic repayments of principal and interest.

Insurance companies Financial institutions that specialize in trying to limit adverse selection and moral hazard problems by insuring against future risks of loss.

Interest Payments for the use of the funds of savers.

Interest expense The portion of depository institution costs incurred through payments of interest to holders of the institutions' liabilities.

Interest income Interest revenues that depository institutions derive from their holdings of loans and securities.

Interest rate The percentage return, or percentage yield, that is earned by a financial instrument.

Interest-rate forward contract A financial contract that entails the sale of a financial instrument at a certain interest rate on a specific future date.

Interest rate future Contract to buy or sell a financial instrument at a specified price at a certain date in the future.

Interest rate risk The possibility that the market value of a financial instrument will change as interest rates vary.

Interest rate swaps A contractual exchange of one set of interest payments for another.

Intermediate target An economic variable that the Fed seeks to control only as a means of trying to achieve its ultimate objectives.

Intermediate-term maturity Maturity between one year and ten years.

International financial arbitrage The act of buying a financial instrument at its market price within one country and selling the instrument or its equivalent at a higher price in another nation.

International financial diversification The act of holding financial instruments issued in more than one country.

International financial integration The process by which international financial arbitrage spurs increased interrelationships among national financial markets.

Interstate branching The operation of banking offices in more than one state.

Intrastate branching The operation of banking offices anywhere within a state.

Inverted yield curve A yield curve that slopes downward.

Investment Additions to the stock of capital goods.

Investment banks Institutions that specialize in marketing and underwriting sales of ownership shares in firms.

Investment-grade securities Bonds with relatively low default risk.

Junk bonds Bonds with relatively high default risk.

Large-denomination time deposits Deposits with set maturities and denominations greater than or equal to $100,000.

Large-dollar wire transfer systems Payments systems such as Fedwire and CHIPS that permit the electronic transmission of large sums.

Lender of last resort An institution willing and able to lend to any temporarily illiquid, but otherwise solvent, institution so as to prevent the illiquidity from leading to a general loss of confidence in that institution or in others.

Level-premium policy A whole life insurance policy under which an insurance company charges fixed premium payments throughout the life of the insured individual.

Liability A legally enforceable claim on the assets of a business or individual.

Limit orders Instructions from other stock exchange members to specialists to execute stock trades at specific prices.

Limited-payment policy A whole life insurance policy under which an insured individual pays premiums only for a fixed number of years but is insured during and after the payment period.

Liquidity The ease with which buyer can sell or redeem an asset for a known amount of cash at short notice and at low risk of loss of nominal value.

Liquidity risk The risk of loss that may occur if a payment is not received when due.

Load funds Mutual funds that investment companies market through brokers and that offer returns that reflect commissions paid to these brokers.

Loan commitment A lending arrangement in which a depository institution promises to extend credit up to some predetermined limit, at a contracted interest rate, and within a given period of time.

Loan loss provisions An expense that depository institutions incur when they allocate funds to loan loss reserves.

Loan loss reserves An amount of cash assets that depository institutions hold in very liquid assets that they expect will be depleted as a result of loan defaults.

London Interbank Offer Rate (LIBOR) The interest rate on interbank loans traded among six large London banks.

Long position An obligation to purchase a financial instrument at a given price and at a specific time.

Long-term maturity Maturity more than ten years.

L M3 plus all other liquid assets.

M1 Currency plus transactions deposits.

M2 M1, plus savings and small-denomination time deposits, overnight Eurodollars and repurchase agreements, and balances in individuals' and broker-dealers' money market mutual funds.

M3 M2, plus large-denomination time deposits, term Eurodollars and repurchase agreements, and institution-only money market mutual funds.

Managed exchange rates A term referring to today's informal system in which governments and central banks generally allow exchange rates to float, although intervening in foreign exchange markets from time to time in efforts to slow or reverse exchange rate movements.

Market concentration The degree to which the few largest depository institutions dominate loan and deposit markets.

Market structure The organization of the loan and deposit markets in which depository institutions interact.

Market value accounting An accounting procedure in which a depository institution (or its regulator) values its assets in terms of approximate market prices at which those assets would currently sell in secondary markets.

Maturity Time until final principal and interest payments are due to the holders of a financial instrument.

Medium of exchange An attribute of money that permits it to be used as a means of payment.

Merchandise trade International exchanges of physical goods.

Monetarists A group of economists who have emphasized the importance of money as a factor in influencing aggregate demand, and who have developed a theory of the role of expectations in determining short-run versus long-run effects of monetary policy actions.

Monetary aggregate A grouping of assets that are sufficiently liquid to be defined as a measure of money.

Monetary base The sum of currency in circulation plus reserves of depository institutions.

Monetary policy discretion The conduct of Fed policy in reaction to economic events as they occur, without precommitment to a monetary policy rule.

Monetary policy rule A Fed precommitment to a specific policy strategy, irrespective of any specific economic events.

Money Anything that functions as a medium of exchange, store of value, unit of account, and standard of deferred payment.

Money demand schedule A graphical illustration of the inverse relationship between the total quantity of money demanded by consumers and businesses and the interest-rate on a short-term Treasury security.

Money illusion The perception that one's standard of living has risen as a result of a wage increase even though the price level simultaneously has risen, thereby reducing the real purchasing power of any such wage increase.

Money market Market for a financial instrument with a maturity of less than one year.

Money market deposit accounts Savings accounts with limited checking privileges.

Money market mutual funds Pools of funds from savers that managing firms use to purchase short-term financial assets such as Treasury bills and commercial paper.

Money multiplier A number that tells how much the quantity of money will change in response to a change in the monetary base.

Monopoly power The ability of one or a cartel of depository institutions to dominate loan and deposit markets sufficiently so to set higher loan rates and lower deposit rates compared with purely competitive market interest rates.

Moral hazard The possibility that a borrower might engage in more-risky behavior after a loan has been made.

Mortgage loans Long-term loans to individual homeowners or to businesses for purchases of land and buildings.

Mortgage-backed security Financial instruments whose return is based on underlying returns on mortgage loans.

Multibank holding company A corporation that owns more than one commercial bank or other depository institution.

Multi-employer pensions Pensions whose accumulations and benefit rights may be transferred from one employer to another.

Municipal bonds Long-term debt instruments issued by state and local governments.

Mutual fund A mix of financial instruments managed on behalf of shareholders by investment companies that charge fees for their services.

Mutual ownership Depository institution organizational structure in which depositors own the institution.

NASD automated quotation system (NASDAQ) A national market system of computer and telephone links between over-the-counter broker-dealers.

National Association of Securities Dealers (NASD) A self-regulating group of OTC broker-dealers that determines trading rules for its members.

National income The total earnings of all individuals in the economy, summed across all sources of income, including wages and salaries, rents, interest and dividends, and profits.

Negative externality A reduction in the welfare of one individual that is caused by a transaction between other parties, even though the individual is not directly involved in the transaction.

Negotiable-order-of-withdrawal (NOW) accounts Interest-bearing checking deposits.

Net interest margin The difference between a depository institution's interest income and interest expenses as a percentage of total assets.

Net worth The excess of assets over liabilities, or equity capital.

Neutrality of money A situation in which changes in the quantity of money have no effects on aggregate real output or employment.

No-load funds Mutual funds that investment companies market directly to the public and that charge management fees instead of brokerage commissions.

Nominal gross domestic product (nominal GDP) The total value of a nation's output of final goods and services measured in terms of current-year prices unadjusted for effects of price changes.

Nominal interest rate A rate of return in current dollar terms that does not reflect anticipated inflation.

Nominal yield The coupon return on a bond divided by the bond's face value.

Nonborrowed reserves Reserves that the Federal Reserve supplies to depository institutions through open-market operations rather than discount window loans.

Noncontributory pensions Pensions funded solely by employers.

Noncontrollable liabilities Liabilities whose dollar amounts are largely determined by bank customers once banks have issued the liabilities.

Noninterest income Revenues that depository institutions earn from sources other than interest income, such as trading profits or fees they charge for services they provide to customers.

Normal profit A profit level just sufficient to compensate depository institution owners for holding equity shares in depository institutions instead of purchasing ownership shares of other enterprises.

Off-balance-sheet banking Bank activities that earn income without expanding the assets and liabilities reported on their balance sheets.

Official settlements balance A balance of payments account that records international asset transactions of agencies of home and foreign governments.

One-bank holding company A corporation that owns a single banking firm, together with other companies that engage in nonbanking lines of business.

Open economies National economies in which significant portions of economic activity entail international transactions in goods, services, and financial assets.

Open-end funds Mutual funds whose shares are redeemable at any time at prices based on the market value of the mix of financial instruments held by the fund.

Open-market operations Federal Reserve purchases or sales of securities.

Open-market purchase A Federal Reserve purchase of a security, which increases total reserves at depository institutions and thereby raises the size of the monetary base.

Open-market sale A Federal Reserve sale of a security, which reduces total reserves of depository institutions and thereby reduces the size of the monetary base.

Operating procedure A guideline for conducting monetary policy over several weeks or months.

Option A financial contract giving the owner the right to buy or sell an underlying financial instrument at a certain price within a specific period of time.

Over-the-counter (OTC) broker-dealer A broker-dealer who trades shares of stock that are not listed in organized stock exchanges.

Over-the-counter (OTC) stocks Equity shares offered by companies that do not meet listing requirements for major stock exchanges but are traded instead in decentralized markets.

Pay-as-you-go pensions Pensions that are not fully funded when employees retire.

Payments system A term that broadly refers to the set of mechanisms by which consumers, businesses, governments, and financial institutions exchange payments.

Pension Benefit Guaranty Corporation (PBGC) An agency of the federal government that provides federal insurance for all pensions with tax-deferred benefits.

Pension funds Institutions that specialize in managing funds that individuals save for retirement.

Perpetuity A bond with an infinite term to maturity.

Point-of-sale (POS) networks Systems by which consumers pay for retail purchases by direct deductions from their deposit accounts at depository institutions.

Point-of-sale (POS) transfer Electronic transfer of funds at the time a sale is made from a buyer's account to the account of a firm from which a good or service has been purchased.

Policy ineffectiveness proposition A proposition put forward by new classical monetary theory that systematic monetary policies, or policies that people can anticipate, have no effects on real output and employment.

Portfolio diversification   Holding financial instruments with different characteristics so as to spread risk across the entire set of instruments.

Preferred-habitat theory   A theory of the term structure of interest rates that views bonds as imperfectly substitutable, so that yields on longer-term bonds must be greater than those on shorter-term bonds, even if short-term interest rates are not expected to rise or fall.

Preferred stock   Shares of corporate ownership that entail no voting rights but that entitle the owner to dividends, if any are paid by the corporation, and to any residual value of the corporation after all other creditors have been paid.

Primary market   Market for newly issued financial instruments

Primary reserves   Cash assets.

Prime rate   The interest rate that American banks charge on loans to the most creditworthy business borrowers.

Principal   The amount of credit extended when one makes a loan or purchases a bond.

Procyclical monetary policy   Fed policy actions that end up exacerbating up and down movements in economic activity.

Profit   The amount by which revenue exceeds cost.

Prospectus   A formal written offer to sell securities.

Purchased funds   Very short-term bank borrowings in the money market.

Purchasing power of money   The value of money in terms of the amount of real goods and services it buys.

Pure competition   A market structure in which no single depository institution can influence loan or deposit interest rates, so that rivalry among institutions yields market loan and deposit interest rates that just cover the costs the institutions incur in making loans and issuing and servicing deposits.

Pure monopoly   The dominance of a loan or deposit market by a single depository institution or by a small group of institutions that work together to maximize their profits.

Put option   An option contract giving the owner the right to sell a financial instrument at a specific price.

Rational expectations hypothesis   A theory that says that people make economic forecasts based on past and current information and on their understanding of how the economy operates.

Real-bills doctrine   A bank management philosophy that calls for lending primarily to borrowers who will use the funds to finance production or shipping of physical goods, thereby ensuring speedy repayment of the loans.

Real gross domestic product (real GDP)   The total value of a nation's output of goods and services during a given period, adjusted for the effects of price changes.

Real interest rate   The anticipated rate of return from holding a financial instrument, after taking into account the extent to which inflation is expected to reduce the amount of goods and services this return could be used to buy.

Real money balances   The real purchasing power of the quantity of money; equal to the nominal quantity of money divided by the GDP price deflator.

Real-resource expenses   Depository institution expenditures on wages and salaries for employees, purchases or leases of capital goods, and rental payments for the use of land.

Recognition lag   Interval between the need for a monetary policy action and the Fed's recognition of that need.

Redlining   A practice under which some depository institution managers allegedly have refused to lend to individuals or businesses located in particular geographic areas.

Regulatory arbitrage The act of trying to avoid regulations imposed by banking authorities in one's home country by moving offices and funds to countries with less stringent regulations.

Reinvestment risk The possibility that available yields on short-term financial instruments may decline, making holdings of longer-term instruments preferable.

Repurchase agreement A contract to sell financial assets with a promise to repurchase them at a later time.

Required reserve ratios Fractions of transaction deposit balances that the Federal Reserve mandates depository institutions to maintain either as deposits with Federal Reserve banks or as vault cash.

Required reserves Legally mandated reserve holdings at depository institutions, which are proportional to the dollar amounts of transaction accounts.

Reserve deposits Deposit accounts that depository institutions maintain at Federal Reserve banks.

Reserves Cash held by depository institutions in their vaults or on deposit with the Federal Reserve System.

Response lag Interval between the Fed's recognition of a need for a policy action and its implementation of such an action.

Return on assets A depository institution's profit as a percentage of its total assets.

Return on equity A depository institution's profit as a percentage of its equity capital.

Revolving credit Loans to individuals that permit them to borrow automatically up to specified limits and to repay the balance of the loan at any time.

Revolving credit commitments Loan commitments that permit borrowers to borrow and repay as often as they wish within the period for which the commitment is binding on a depository institution.

Risk-adjusted assets A weighted average of bank assets that regulators compute to account for risk differences across types of assets.

Risk-based capital requirements Regulatory capital standards that account for risk factors that distinguish different depository institutions.

Risk-based deposit insurance premiums Premium rates that depository institutions pay the FDIC based on the varying degrees to which they are capitalized and on the differing risk factors they exhibit.

Risk premium The amount by which one instrument's yield exceeds another's because the latter is riskier and less liquid.

Risk structure of interest rates The relationship among yields on financial intruments that have the same maturity but differ because of variations in default risk, liquidity, and tax rates.

Sales finance companies Finance companies that specialize in making loans to individuals for the purchase of items from specific retailers or manufacturers.

Saving Forgone consumption.

Savings and loan associations A type of depository institution that traditionally has specialized in making mortgage loans.

Savings Association Insurance Fund (SAIF) The FDIC's fund that covers insured deposits of savings institutions.

Savings bank Another type of depository institution that has specialized in mortgage lending.

Savings deposits Interest-bearing savings accounts without set maturities.

Secondary market Market for financial instruments issued at some time in the past.

Secondary reserves Securities that depository institutions can easily convert into cash in the event such a need arises.

Securities Financial instruments.

Securities and Exchange Commission (SEC) A group of five presidentially appointed members whose mandate is to enforce rules governing securities trading.

Securities underwriting A guarantee by an investment bank that a firm that issues a new stock or bond will receive a specified minimum price per share of stock or per bond.

Securitization The process of pooling loans with similar risk characteristics and then selling the loan pool in the form of a tradable financial instrument.

Segmented-markets theory A theory of the term structure of interest rates that views bonds with differing maturities as nonsubstitutable, so that their yields differ because they are determined by separate markets.

Seigniorage The difference between the market value of money and the cost of its production, which accrues to the government that produces and issues money.

Shiftability theory A management approach in which depository institutions hold a mix of illiquid loans and more-liquid securities that act as a secondary reserve held as a contingency against potential liquidity problems.

Short position An obligation to sell a financial instrument at a given price and at a specific time.

Short-term maturity Maturity less than one year.

Single-employer pensions Pensions established by an employer only for its own employees, and nontransferable to other employers.

Sinking fund An account from which a corporation draws funds to make bond interest payments or to redeem bonds upon maturity.

Small-denomination time deposits Deposits with set maturities and denominations of less than $100,000.

Specialists Stock exchange members who are charged with trading on their own accounts to prevent dramatic movements in stock prices.

Spot exchange rate The rate of exchange of two currencies to be traded immediately.

Standard of deferred payment An attribute of money that permits it to be used as a means of valuing future receipts in loan contracts.

Standby-commitment underwriting An investment banking arrangement in which the investment bank earns commissions for helping an issuing firm sell its securities, but with a guarantee that the investment bank will purchase for resale any unsold securities.

Stock exchanges Organized marketplaces for corporate equities and bonds.

Stock index future Promises of future delivery of a portfolio of stocks represented by a stock price index.

Stock options Options to buy or sell firm equity shares.

Store of value An attribute of money that allows it to be held for future use without loss of value in the meantime.

Strategy A general plan for achieving a set of economic objectives.

Structure-conduct-performance (SCP) model A theory of depository institution market structure in which the structure of loan and deposit markets influences the behavior of depository institutions in those markets, and thereby affects their performance.

Structured early intervention and resolution (SEIR) A regulatory system established by the FDIC Improvement Act of 1991, which authorizes the FDIC to intervene quickly in the management of a depository institution likely to cause losses for the federal deposit insurance funds.

Subordinated notes and debentures Capital market instruments with maturities in excess of one year that banks issue with the provision that depositors have primary claim to bank assets in the event of failure.

Supplementary capital A measure that regulators presently use to calculate required capital; it includes certain preferred stock and most subordinated debt.

Supply schedule of reserves A graphical depiction of the direct relationship between the total amount of reserves supplied by the Fed and the federal funds rate.

Supranormal profits Levels of profit above those required to induce depository institution owners to hold shares of ownership in those institutions instead of in other businesses.

Symmetric directive An FOMC policy directive that fails to give the chair of the Fed's Board of Governors the power to authorize Trading Desk actions either to raise or to reduce the federal funds rate.

Systemic risk The risk that some depository institutions may not be able to meet the terms of their own credit agreements because of failures by other institutions to settle transactions that otherwise are not related.

T-account A side-by-side listing of the assets and liabilities of a business such as a depository institution.

Term federal funds Interbank loans with maturities exceeding one day.

Term life policy A life insurance policy under which an individual is insured only for the limited period during which the policy is in effect.

Term premium An amount by which the yield on a long-term bond must exceed the yield on a short-term bond to make individuals willing to hold either bond if they expect short-term bond yields to remain unchanged.

Term structure of interest rates The relationship among yields on financial instruments with identical risk, liquidity, and tax characteristics, but differing terms to maturity.

Terminally funded pensions Pensions that must be fully funded by the date an employee retires.

Too-big-to-fail policy A regulatory policy that protects the largest depository institutions from failure solely because regulators believe that such failure could undermine the public's confidence in the financial system.

Total capital Under currently imposed bank capital requirements, this is the sum of core capital and supplementary capital.

Total reserves The total balances that depository institutions hold on deposit with Federal Reserve banks or as vault cash.

Trading Desk The Fed's term for the office at the Federal Reserve Bank of New York that conducts open-market operations on the Fed's behalf.

Transaction risk The possibility that the market value of a financial instrument used to fund an international transaction may vary because an exchange rate change alters the value of the transaction.

Transactions deposits Checking accounts.

Transmission lag Interval between the Fed's implementation of a policy change and the effects that this change ultimately has on the economy.

Treasury bills Short-term debt obligations of the federal government, issued in maturities of 3, 6, or 12 months.

Treasury bonds Treasury securities with maturities of 10 years or more.

Treasury notes Treasury securities with maturities ranging from 1 to 10 years.

Treasury tax and loan (TT&L) accounts U.S. Treasury checking accounts at private depository institutions.

Uncovered interest parity A condition that applies to bonds denominated in different national currencies but possessing identical risks and maturities, in which the yield on one bond is equal to the yield on the other bond plus the expected rate of depreciation of the currency in which the other bond is denominated.

Unit of account   An attribute of money that permits it to be used as a measure of the value of goods, services, and financial assets.

Universal banking   Banking environment under which depository institutions face few if any restrictions on their authority to offer full ranges of financial services and to own equity shares in corporations.

Variable annuity   A financial instrument, typically issued by an insurance company, beginning on a specific future date, that pays the owner a stream of returns that depends on the value of an underlying portfolio of assets.

Vault cash   Currency that a depository institution holds on location to honor cash withdrawals by depositors.

Vehicle currency   The currency that individuals and businesses use most often to conduct international transactions.

Whole life policy   A life insurance policy whose benefits are payable to a beneficiary on an insured person's death and which also accumulates a cash value that may be redeemed by the policyholder prior to death.

Winner's curse   Situation in which a winning bidder in an auction receives a lower return than at least one participant who submitted a weaker bid.

Wire transfers   Payments made via telephone lines or through fiber optic cables.

World index funds   Portfolios of financial instruments issued in various nations whose yields generally move in offsetting directions, thereby reducing overall risk of losses on the portfolios.

Yield curve   A chart depicting yields on bonds with the same risk characteristics but differing yields to maturity.

Yield to maturity   The rate of return that a bond would yield if held until maturity.

Zero-coupon bonds   Bonds that pay lump-sum amounts at maturity.

Index